The Age of Rossetti, Burne-Jones & Watts

Symbolism in Britain 1860–1910

Edited by Andrew Wilton and Robert Upstone

With contributions by Barbara Bryant, Christopher Newall, MaryAnne Stevens and Simon Wilson

Tate Gallery Publishing

The exhibition at the Tate Gallery is sponsored by Prudential

front cover
Edward Burne-Jones **Night** 1870
(detail, no.27)

back cover
Charles Ricketts
Oedipus and the Sphinx 1891
(no.102)

frontispiece
Simeon Solomon
Love in Autumn 1866
(detail, no.12)

Published by order of the Trustees of the Tate Gallery 1997
on the occasion of the exhibition at
Tate Gallery, London, 16 October 1997 – 4 January 1998
and touring to:
Haus der Kunst, Munich, 30 January – 26 April 1998
Van Gogh Museum, Amsterdam, 15 May – 30 August 1998

ISBN 1 85437 196 7 (cloth)
ISBN 1 85437 230 0 (paper)

A catalogue record for this publication
is available from the British Library

Published by Tate Gallery Publishing Limited,
Millbank, London SW1P 4RG

Designed and typeset by Caroline Johnston
Printed in Great Britain on Parilux silk
by Balding + Mansell, Norwich

The Age of Rossetti, Burne-Jones and Watts

Contents

Sponsor's Foreword

Prudential is delighted to support *The Age of Rossetti, Burne-Jones and Watts: Symbolism in Britain 1860–1910* during the Tate's centenary year. This wonderful exhibition gives a fascinating insight into the background from which modern art emerged.

Prudential has a long-established relationship with the arts through the Prudential Awards for the Arts and support of specific arts events, including our sponsorship of the *Grand Tour* exhibition at the Tate Gallery in 1996.

Prudential is the largest life assurance company in the UK and will be celebrating its one hundred and fiftieth anniversary in 1998. We established our reputation for providing financial services during the second half of the last century, the period covered in this exhibition. We congratulate the Tate on mounting *The Age of Rossetti, Burne-Jones and Watts: Symbolism in Britain 1860–1910* and very much hope you enjoy it.

Sir Peter Davis
Group Chief Executive
Prudential Corporation plc

Foreword

This exhibition was originally conceived as a celebration of the Centenary of the Tate Gallery, which was first opened in 1897. It seemed appropriate in that context to re-examine the work of the artists who dominated British art at that time. The doyen of British painters then was G.F. Watts, who was also a generous contributor to the Gallery's early collections, donating no less than twenty major works. Since then Watts has fallen out of fashion and although in the last thirty years the Victorian period has received a large amount of scholarly attention he has not attracted as much interest as some of his contemporaries. The exhibition attempts a revaluation, not simply of Watts in isolation, but of his period and of the achievements of the British school at a time when Great Britain itself was at the apogee of its international influence.

Despite the popularity Victorian painting currently enjoys, it has rarely been considered as part of the international mainstream of art from which Britain was so effectively severed by the criticism of Roger Fry and Clive Bell in the first decades of this century. Yet an accurate account of the late nineteenth century should acknowledge the international reputations of Rossetti, Burne-Jones, Watts and their associates, and assess them as part of broader currents than the insular ones suggested by the usual labels of Pre-Raphaelite, Aesthetic or Academic. It is possible to do this without distortion of the facts if these categories are set aside and a more inclusive one – Symbolism – is applied instead. Viewed as part of this international late nineteenth-century movement, important areas of British art in the period assume a new significance, and Britain is revealed as having supplied many key literary sources as well as paintings, drawings and sculptures with a wide European influence.

The exhibition does not attempt the all-inclusive panorama created by some recent surveys of Symbolism, notably the impressive *Lost Paradise: Symbolist Europe* mounted at Montreal in 1995. In order to bring out the British contribution as clearly as possible we have felt it preferable to follow the main contours of the subject rather than to explore its multitudinous byways. This is therefore an attempt to define Symbolism in Britain in fairly narrow terms, aiming at clarity rather than comprehensiveness. Examples of the work of continental Symbolists are included for reference and to make specific points about lines of communication and influence, but it is not intended that the international story should be told here in full. We hope that the exhibition will help to bring new light to bear on some familiar artists, and at the same time show a few neglected figures in their proper context. The New Sculpture, so important a feature of late Victorian art, also comes into the account as an essential component of British Symbolism.

The exhibition was conceived by Andrew Wilton, Keeper of the British Collection, and organised by him in conjunction with a group of scholars in the field: Barbara Bryant, Christopher Newall, MaryAnne Stevens and Robert

Upstone. All have also made valuable contributions to the catalogue and we are grateful to them for their enthusiastic involvement.

As always, it is to the lenders, both public and private, to whom we owe the deepest debt. Without their generosity the exhibition could not have been mounted. We are most grateful to them all.

We are delighted that this exhibition will also be seen in Europe, first in the Haus der Kunst, Munich, and subsequently in the Van Gogh Museum, Amsterdam. It has been a pleasure to work with colleagues in both places, with Christoph Vitali in Munich and with John Leighton and Andreas Blühm in Amsterdam.

Finally I should like to thank Prudential who sponsored the *Grand Tour* exhibition at the Tate Gallery in 1996 and decided to return to sponsor this exhibition. We do so much appreciate their continued support.

Nicholas Serota
Director

Acknowledgements

The organisers are indebted to a large number of people for their help in realising this project; first of all, the members of the original consultative committee who were: Judith Bronkhurst, Barbara Bryant, John Christian, Richard Dorment, David Fraser Jenkins, Christopher Newall, Leonée Ormond, MaryAnne Stevens and Simon Wilson.

Secondly, we wish also to thank the following for valuable assistance and encouragement at different stages of the selection process and of preparing the catalogue material: Victor Arwas; Edwin Becker; Anne H. Brand; Christabel Briggs; Peter Brown; Hans Henrik Brummer; Lord and Lady Charteris of Amisfield; Sarah Colegrave; Antony Collieu; Philip Conisbee; Paul Delaney; Patrick Derom; Michel Draguet; Lydia Dufour; Betty Elzea; Eric Falck-Thirkelsen; Solveig Falck-Thirkelsen; Julia Findlater; Veronica Franklin Gould; Chris Green; Véronique Gunner; Julian Hartnoll; Leonie Haywood; Richard Jefferies; Alastair Laing; Emily Lane; Uno Langmann; Rupert Maas; Sheila McGregor; Peter Nahum; Jenny Newall; Gay Norton; Charles Nugent; Godfrey Pilkington; Alison Plumridge; Elizabeth Prettejohn; Siri Refsum; Sydney Resendez; Simon Reynolds; Christine de Schaetzen; William Schupbach; George Shackelford; Peyton Skipwith; Anna Southall; John Sunderland; Virginia Surtees; Tone Wikborg; Stephen Wildman.

Many people in the Tate Gallery itself have earned special thanks, among them in particular John Anderson, Tim Holton, Susan Lawrie, Jacqueline Ridge, Helen Sainsbury and Judith Severne.

Andrew Wilton and Robert Upstone

Symbolism in Britain

Andrew Wilton

In 1881 the Austrian physician Josef Breuer conducted an investigation that was to have a profound influence on the history of psychiatry in the twentieth century. His subject was a young Viennese woman whom he called 'Anna O.', and her case history, which Sigmund Freud studied closely, has become one of the founding legends of Freudian psychoanalysis. Pursuing a theory that Anna O.'s condition could be diagnosed as 'hysteria', Breuer observed and carefully described her behaviour over a long period. At some stages of her illness she was frequently liable to fantastic dreams and hallucinations, which Breuer diligently noted:

> There were extremely rapid changes of mood leading to excessive but quite temporary high spirits, and at other times severe anxiety, stubborn opposition to every therapeutic effort and frightening hallucinations of black snakes, which was how she saw her hair, ribbons and similar things ... her hallucinatory *absences* were filled with terrifying figures, death's heads and skeletons ... She used to hallucinate in the middle of a conversation, run off, start climbing up a tree, etc. ... Her right arm, over the back of the chair, had gone to sleep and had become anaesthetic and paretic; and when she looked at it the fingers turned into little snakes with death's heads (the nails) ... When the snake vanished, in her terror she tried to pray[1]

The imagery of Anna O.'s visions is striking not so much because of its relationship to this twenty-one year old girl's illness (which is now widely regarded as having been completely misunderstood by both Breuer and Freud[2]) but on account of its resonances in late nineteenth-century culture as a whole. The details of hair as snakes, or of skeletons and death's heads, and the image of the young woman in the tree, are recurrent features of the literature, painting, sculpture and even the decorative arts of the late nineteenth century. Breuer and Freud were both to ascribe psychological significance to these fantasies, but they do not seem to have noticed that they were part of the visual currency of the time.[3]

When such images appear in works of art, they can be interpreted either literally or symbolically, as 'metaphors' for aspects of the human condition. A skull represents Death, snakes stand for Evil or Original Sin. Death is often symbolised by the image of Sleep: Freud's subsequent interest in dreams also coincides with the preoccupations of contemporary artists. The picture conjured up of the girl in the tree has comparable echoes: Eve in the Garden of Eden, or Ovidian legends of nymphs transformed into bushes or trees. The dimension of mythological narrative involved in this last example expands the idea of the symbolic image corresponding to a single concept into one encompassing a wealth of images of trees as they figure in national and religious mythologies. At the same date that Breuer and Freud were beginning their work on the hidden causes of 'hysteria', these wider aspects of the mental pictures formed by mankind as a whole were

opposite
detail from D.G. Rossetti, *Paolo and Francesca da Rimini* 1855 (no.30)

being investigated by Sir James Frazer for what was to become *The Golden Bough*.

In this vast work, which appeared between 1890 and 1910, Frazer explored the ramifications of world mythologies, tracing the connections between knowledge and belief in the traditional ceremonials of cultures across the globe, and attempting to bring them into a systematic framework of relations. Like Freud in psychology, Frazer tried to apply strictly scientific and objective principles of description and hypothesis to a subject that had only recently begun to be investigated. He argued that in the early stages of civilisation mankind evolved mythologies as explanations of natural phenomena, that these mythologies, often originating in 'sympathetic magic,' were embodied in customs and rituals that were in due course consolidated as the outward forms of religions. Ultimately, religious accounts of the world had given way to rationalist, scientific ones:

> Yet the history of thought should warn us against concluding that because the scientific theory of the world is the best that has yet been formulated, it is necessarily complete and final. We must remember that at bottom the generalisations of science or, in common parlance, the laws of nature are mere hypotheses devised to explain that ever-shifting phantasmagoria of thought which we dignify with the high-sounding names of the world and the universe.[4]

Frazer's attempt was in some respects a comparable exercise to Darwin's equally wide-ranging investigations into the evolution of species, especially the human species, by natural selection, which since their publication between 1859 and 1871 had radically modified received ideas concerning man's relation to God and his place in the cosmos. If Darwin's subject-matter was complex, Frazer's was perhaps equally so: nothing less than human nature viewed as a whole through the lens of its customs and beliefs. Vast though the topic was, he contrived to reduce his observations to a remarkably simple and coherent hypothesis: that human mythologies embody in narrative form fundamental perceptions of the universe and man's relation to it; and that the traditional ritual and ceremonial surviving in nearly all cultures is the vestigial expression of the beliefs celebrated in those mythologies.

The age of *The Golden Bough*, and of the researches of Breuer and Freud, found a new potency in symbols that had been incorporated into long-established myths, and saw them as connoting something harder to define than simple cultural archetypes: they formed part of a deeper language of fear, aspiration and desire that expressed the obscure instincts and neuroses of the human psyche. This language of the 'unconscious' was being developed by artists and creative writers before Freud or Jung had postulated the existence of such an entity, individual or collective. Tapping a much more ancient tradition of epistemology, the tradition that Frazer was attempting to rationalise, the artists of the post-Romantic generation intuitively formulated their own 'analyses' of aspects of the psyche. These form the subject-matter of a substantial body of the creative art of the late nineteenth century, and the term 'Symbolism' has come to be used to denote that body of work.

As recently as 1984 Michael Gibson could observe that 'art history has bypassed

Symbolism'.[5] Only in the last twenty-five years or so have a series of studies brought together the full range of objects that suggest the diversity and, indeed, the indefinability of this subject. There has been a tendency to regard as 'Symbolist' almost any work of art of the late nineteenth century – even some that are essentially realist or academic – that can be interpreted as having psychological overtones, or considered dream-like or poetic. This has been a useful process, bringing together large anthologies of images, and there are good reasons for arguing that we can apply the term 'Symbolism' to many superficially very different types of work. A comprehensive modern survey is the catalogue of the exhibition *Lost Paradise: Symbolist Europe*, held at the Montreal Museum of Fine Arts in 1995. Although its terms of reference extend from Julia Margaret Cameron to Alfred Hitchcock , its initial claim is that 'the geographical boundaries of Symbolism' are 'well defined'.[6] At the same time, it locates the focus of the movement not in France, as is usually maintained, but in Belgium. Chronologically it is equally precise: Symbolism lasted from 18 September 1886 to 1905.

In the mass of material surveyed by the exhibition, the British contribution was by no means ignored; but the assessment of its position as marginal in European Symbolism is apparent in the selection of works, which broadly follows that of other comparable discussions of the movement. The revaluation attempted here sets out to identify significant aspects of the Symbolist movement as originating specifically in Britain. It will allot to certain British artists and writers leading roles in the movement, while trying to demonstrate that, in Britain at least, Symbolism evolved a distinct tone and technical style which give it a unity more difficult to discern in the European scene as a whole.

On 18 September 1886 an article by Jean Moréas[7] was published in the Parisian paper *Le Figaro*. In it, Moréas gave the name 'Symbolists' to the current French school of poets led by Stéphane Mallarmé and Paul Verlaine. Because the work of these writers characteristically embodied a world-weary, jaded and melancholy sensuality they were viewed as degenerate, and Symbolism was immediately identified with decadence. It was possible to trace the origins of the school back to the 1840s and 1850s, finding roots in the works of Théophile Gautier and Charles Baudelaire – especially Gautier's erotic novel *Mademoiselle de Maupin* (1835) and Baudelaire's notorious series of poems *Les Fleurs du Mal*, published in 1857 with a dedication to Gautier and immediately subjected to partial suppression. The two writers came to be viewed retrospectively as the fathers of Symbolism, and Baudelaire's *'réaliste'* school of poetry as a revolutionary exploration of the depths of the human psyche. With this pedigree it was natural that Symbolism should have been considered a primarily French phenomenon. As the word was in due course applied to other expressions of contemporary culture, notably painting, French art was first in line to receive the new definition.

Another French writer who was quickly identified with the movement was J.-K. Huysmans. In his novel of 1884, *A Rebours*, he described a self-consciously 'decadent' character, des Esseintes, defying the norms and forms of contemporary bourgeois culture by pursuing a life of eccentric gratification through the senses. A second novel, *Là-Bas*, was concerned with further aspects of decadence, including the cult of Satanism. Together, the sybaritic sensuality of *A Rebours* and the Satanism of *Là-Bas* created a material-supernatural dialectic in which Decadence could flourish. In *A Rebours*, Huysmans made use of ideas taken from the art of Gustave Moreau, Odilon Redon and G.F.Watts, thereby co-opting them as Symbolists. Of Watts more later; different as Moreau and Redon are from each other, both artists take their place naturally in the movement, and help to define its salient characteristics. The highly charged, operatic subjects of Moreau, nightmare re-enactments of the historical and mythological scenes of Ingres and Delacroix, perfectly exemplify the descent of Symbolism from Romanticism. The odd, isolated objects that obtrude themselves into our consciousness as we look at Redon's work – often disembodied heads that can metamorphose into Medusas, spiders, or decollated Baptists – prefigure a Surrealist, post-Freudian understanding of the imagery of dreams. That is the historical position of Symbolism: a transition between the Romantic and the Surrealist perception of half-articulated or unexpressed mental phenomena.[8]

With such clear indications of the pre-eminence of France in this historical process, the Montreal claim for Belgium as the geographical centre of the movement is significant. It rests on firm ground: among many Belgians Fernand Khnopff is arguably the archetypal Symbolist artist, and his substantial output is reinforced by a body of Belgian literature – by Maurice Maeterlinck, Emile Verhaeren, Georges Rodenbach and others – that amply challenges the literary genealogy offered by France itself.[9]

It was not until the late 1890s that anyone in Britain made a clear attempt to define Symbolism in terms of current trends. During the years 1895 to 1900 Arthur Symons, a poet and critic who had lived in Paris and had recently joined forces with Aubrey Beardsley on a magazine, the *Savoy*, was preparing a series of studies of recent writing under the working title of *The Decadent Movement in Literature*. His friend W.B. Yeats disapproved of the term 'Decadent' and prevailed on Symons to alter his title to *The Symbolist Movement in Literature*. Under this name the book appeared in March 1900.[10] It was dedicated to Yeats, 'the chief representative of the movement in our country', and defined Symbolism as an 'attempt to spiritualize literature'. Art was to be 'a kind of religion, with all the duties and responsibilities of the sacred ritual'. European luminaries like Mallarmé, Gérard de Nerval and Maeterlinck were treated; so were Britons like Meredith and Carlyle, whose work displayed 'that learned corruption of language by which style ceases to be organic and becomes … deliberately abnormal'.[11]

For Symons as for Moréas Symbolism was essentially a literary phenomenon. By including the poet and novelist George Meredith and the historian and essayist Thomas Carlyle he gave it a very broad frame of reference. Meredith like Carlyle was a 'philosopher and teacher' for his age; both men were called prophets in their day,[12] and were looked to to express the nobler aspirations of their contemporaries. As a contemporary critic said of Meredith, 'Like Zola, Ibsen, or Tolstoi, he goes down into the dark places; but he does not live there always, and he carries his lamp with him.'[13] Yeats's wish to 'raise the tone' of the arts of his day was entirely in tune with the time. His Irish nationalism was one of many positive political impulses, the most powerful of all being the nationalism of the British. By the end of the nineteenth century the nation lay at the heart of a global

fig.1 Gustave Moreau, *Salome Dancing before Herod* ?1876, oil on panel 92 × 61 cm. Musée Gustave Moreau, Paris

empire that was not only militarily and commercially dominant, but aesthetically influential as well. That influence came to a climax in the second half of the 1890s, when Decadence was in the work of many artists transformed into an Idealism that asserted the transcendental qualities of the human spirit rather than its slavery to the passions.

In the early 1890s, however, Decadence was a *fin-de-siècle* fad. In England it was perceived, with a certain *frisson*, as something 'caught' from France. (Even Realism, if it came from France, was suspect: the novels of Zola regularly scandalised British audiences, who considered them depraved and immoral.) By 1895 Decadence was a catchphrase that comprehended more than literature. The drawings that Aubrey Beardsley had made for Oscar Wilde's play *Salomé* – first written in French – gave vivid visual currency to what was seen as a palpable unhealthiness of mind and spirit (nos.89, 92). That unhealthiness was demonstrated with all too glaring clarity when Wilde was convicted of homosexual practices in May 1895 and sent down amid much publicity for two years' hard labour.

Wilde's *Salomé* was produced at the high-water mark of the Parisian fashion for Symbolism, and is also clearly a masterpiece of Decadence. An attraction to the story of Salome had been 'in the air' for some decades. French writers, among them Flaubert and Mallarmé, had been fascinated by it and Moreau had made it the theme of a number of his most important pictures (fig.1). Elsewhere, too, it was adopted by painters, writers, and even photographers. An American, J.C. Heywood, had written a 'Dramatic Poem' on the subject – a romantic verse tragedy *à la* Byron – in 1867; it was republished in London in 1887.[14] When Wilde composed his (prose) version in Paris in 1891, his play quickly assumed a central place in contemporary continental culture, as is testified by Richard Strauss's setting of the text as an opera, first performed in Dresden in 1905. The plot of Wilde's play revolves around the duality of flesh and spirit, and illustrates these polarities in extreme form: the ascetic holy man Jokanaan (John the Baptist), imprisoned by Herod, is loved by Salome, the beautiful daughter of Herod's wife Herodias and her first husband, his brother, whom he has murdered. The prophet rejects her with curses. At her vengeful bidding he is decapitated and she indulges her passion for him by caressing his bleeding head and kissing his dead mouth:

> Ah! thou wouldst not suffer me to kiss thy mouth, Jokanaan. Well! I will kiss it now. I will bite it with my teeth as one bites a ripe fruit ... Thine eyes that were so terrible, so full of rage and scorn, are shut now. Wherefore are they shut? Open thine eyes! Lift up thine eyelids, Jokanaan! Wherefore dost thou not look at me? ... And thy tongue, that was like a red snake darting poison, it moves no more, it says nothing now, Jokanaan, that scarlet viper that spat its venom upon me.

Imagery of blood, the moon, snakes, lilies and roses proliferates throughout the play. *Salomé* is built on themes typical of the Symbolist canon: the beautiful woman who brings about the doom of a man, the fascination with death, and the ambiguous carnal allure of a chastely spiritual being.

These were themes that had surfaced in the Romantic movement, notably in

'Gothick' novels like Matthew Gregory Lewis's shocker *The Monk* of 1795, which explores them with precocious thoroughness.[15] But such books had never been regarded as serious literature and in the course of the nineteenth century had been discarded and overlaid by the morally 'correct' thinking of an increasingly powerful and prosperous middle-class Protestant society. A fascinating intermediary is the American writer Edgar Allan Poe, the author of 'an extra- or superhuman literature', in the opinion of Baudelaire,[16] who translated Poe's *Tales of Mystery and Imagination* into French. But despite his deliberately 'horrific' subject-matter Poe was not shocking in the way that 'Monk' Lewis had been. His horror, in the first place, is rarely erotic. By 1894, when *Salomé* had been translated into English (by Wilde's lover, Lord Alfred Douglas) the genealogy of its emotional content had become alien to British culture. The Lord Chamberlain refused it a licence to be performed. It was foreign, 'decadent'. Beardsley's famous illustrations, executed in 1893 and early 1894, reinforced the message.

Salome was only one of many contemporary manifestations of the idea of the ambiguous and dangerous allure of the feminine. The biblical story took its place with others, from classical or oriental mythology, reworked to express a new awareness, which we have seen emerging in Breuer's analysis of Anna O., of the psychological complexities that lie close beneath the surface of human behaviour. The most immediate symptom of this new awareness was a public debate about the validity of the nude in art – a debate originating in early nineteenth-century, Neo-Classical aesthetic criteria – which acquired a fresh momentum in the 1860s, when the problem of the fine line between art and pornography greatly exercised critics.[17] In practice nudity, with its associated stripping away of material trappings, took its place in the work of the more idealising artists. The received wisdom was articulated by George Du Maurier when he wrote in 1895 that 'Venus herself, as she drops her garments and steps on to the model-throne, leaves behind her on the floor every weapon in her armoury by which she can pierce to the grosser passions of man. The more perfect her unveiled beauty, the more keenly it appeals to his higher instincts.'[18] Degeneracy is associated with dress, with accoutrements rather than with the body itself. Those preoccupied with the darker side of human nature were more inclined to portray the idea of the female enveloped in a nexus of symbols: dressed or half-dressed and dancing like Salome; half-woman half-beast, like the Sphinx or the Chimaera luring the curious traveller to his doom; as Medusa, her head wreathed in snakes, her staring dead eyes ready to turn the rash gazer to stone. These images recur conspicuously in the work of two of the central painters of continental Symbolism, Moreau and Khnopff (figs.1, 2), to say nothing of countless lesser artists.

The failure of the British to recognise Symbolism as a category into which their own art might fall was largely a cultural matter. (It is perhaps significant that the most widely read studies of the world of dreams in late nineteenth-century Britain were Lewis Carroll's two *Alice* books.)[19] Symbolism was identified with Decadence, which was definitely a foreign commodity. Another confusing issue was Aestheticism, which had grown up in England in the 1860s, and became a popular fashion in the 1870s, with the French-trained American James Abbott McNeill Whistler its artistic standard-bearer. The wide dispersal of Aesthetic

fig.2 Fernand Khnopff, *Les Caresses (The Sphinx)* 1896, oil on canvas 50.5 × 150 cm. Musées Royaux des Beaux-Arts de Belgique, Brussels

notions in popular art and culture, and its lampooning by Du Maurier in his *Punch* cartoons and by Gilbert and Sullivan on the stage (*Patience*, 1881) have given it a somewhat frivolous reputation,[20] but it was a serious development which must be assimilated into any full account of Symbolism.

Aestheticism too could trace its lineage to France: its motto, 'Art for Art's Sake,' was purloined from Gautier, who adopted a phrase used by Victor Cousin in a lecture at the Sorbonne in 1818: *'L'art pour l'art'*.[21] As Whistler's painted 'Nocturnes' and 'Harmonies' demonstrated, it laid emphasis on the parallels between music and painting, and the critic Walter Pater's dictum that 'All art constantly aspires towards the condition of music'[22] became a key notion. In this and other salient characteristics it shares common ground with Symbolism, and one might say that Aestheticism literally cleared the way for Symbolism by eliminating the traditional framework of reference of representational painting and asserting the values of paint, form and colour in themselves. Into the *tabula* relatively *rasa* of the Aesthetic canvas, a new symbolic language could be introduced in which old meanings were replaced and even the paint surface could attain associative significance.

Another strand in late nineteenth-century British art which emerged out of Aestheticism is the school of 'Olympians'. This was partly the reflection of a fashion for the Antique, exemplified in the careful reconstructions of scenes from ancient Greek or Roman life for which Lawrence Alma-Tadema became celebrated. A prime reason for the revival was the renewed interest, just mentioned, in the possibilities of the nude as a subject for art. The success of Frederic Leighton, the most prominent of the Olympians, was founded largely on his treatment of the nude, which he presented in a deliberately 'cleansed' atmosphere of clear light and bright, harmonious colour evocative of a pristine dawn of civilisation in which all things were pure. Aestheticism played its part in removing narrative elements that might otherwise have compromised this purity; but in practice the ambivalence of the whole subject remained undeniably in place, and that ambivalence is often crucial in creating the atmosphere in which Symbolism operates. The moral neutrality sought by Aestheticism was an ideal breeding-ground for Symbolism of many kinds.

Decadence, Aestheticism and Olympianism were all fully acknowledged in their time, and can be seen to contribute to the language of Symbolism in Britain. Another, chronologically the first, and the most confusing of these 'movements' was Pre-Raphaelitism – or not so much Pre-Raphaelitism itself as a persistent use of the name to describe artists who had little or nothing to do with the Pre-

Raphaelite Brotherhood or its aims. Pre-Raphaelitism had burst upon the British art world at the mid-century with such force that despite the brevity of its authentic lifespan – Ruskin declared it officially dead in 1857[23] – it continued to exert an almost hypnotic power over all who wrote about art for the next fifty years. The use of the term even today can still be extremely vague.[24]

The reason for the distracting force of Pre-Raphaelitism was the presence among its founding members of Dante Gabriel Rossetti. He, John Everett Millais and William Holman Hunt had instituted their 'Brotherhood' in 1848 in protest against the pretensions of contemporary academic art, determining to return to the directness and simplicity of medieval painting – before Raphael – and to the clarity and truth of work done immediately from nature. In this last respect they were the English equivalents of Gustave Courbet and his Realist school in France, although the results of the two almost exactly contemporary revolutions could not have been more unlike.[25]

Millais and Holman Hunt laid great emphasis on the 'truth to nature' aspect of Pre-Raphaelite theory, adhering with ardour to Ruskin's famous adjuration to artists that they should 'go to nature … rejecting nothing, selecting nothing, scorning nothing'.[26] Rossetti took 'Pre-Raphaelitism' in a quite different, though perhaps more literal sense. For him it was early Italian art and literature that supplied the prime motivation. This enthusiasm sprang from a strong personal intuition fed at least in part by a sense of his Italian ancestry. But even in his youth he did not go out into the woods and fields to paint nature as he found her. He invented medieval romances in his studio, and although a few of the early works that he signed with the Brotherhood's monogram 'PRB' are executed in a more or less strict Pre-Raphaelite technique, he was not committed to it as an ideal, as Holman Hunt was, or even as Millais was for nearly a decade. It was Millais who noted that Rossetti was 'never a Pre-Raphaelite at heart'.[27] When Millais and Hunt turned to scenes from modern life, or from the Bible, Rossetti became more and more committed to his own idiosyncratic vision of the medieval past. Perhaps more importantly, he became obsessed with certain specific moments in that past: the passion of Marguerite for Faust in Goethe's poem; Dante's adoration of Beatrice in the *Divina Commedia* and *Vita Nuova*. These became recurrent images in his work, which was executed, whether in watercolour, gouache or oil, in a manner utterly opposed to the crisp clarity of 'true' Pre-Raphaelitism. On the contrary, Rossetti's style deliberately evoked a blurred, almost dream-like world of the spirit, where profounder and more exalted passions played than were to be found in the practical, if foggy, air of modern London. Taken up by his ardent admirer Edward Burne-Jones, that style seemed to carry 'Pre-Raphaelitism' on into a second generation. Under that title, Burne-Jones's nostalgic and allusive art was to become a principal channel for the dissemination of a distinctive, and highly influential, British Symbolism.

Towards the end of the 1850s the isolation of a particular woman – Marguerite, Beatrice – as the vehicle or object of a desire repeatedly expressed began to focus itself in Rossetti's work into a characteristic image: the head of an individual young woman presented as an object of ambiguous attraction, part temptress, part priestess, both corrupting and innocent. This young woman was increasingly likely to be identifiable as someone with whom the artist himself had a personal relationship of some degree of intensity. The portrait of an individual took on broad significance as a type of human beauty with specific emotive qualities relating not to that individual but to the creator of the image. Rossetti's sirens of the 1860s turn traditional portrait-painting on its head, or rather inside-out, to express the inner world of the artist himself rather than that of the sitter. The interrelationship between autobiography and image takes on a new, revelatory aspect, touching not so much the anecdotal or historical facts of the artist's life as the subtle emotional and psychological springs of his inner being.

A feature of Rossetti's preoccupation with beautiful women who were part of his own life was an instinctive equation of them with the heroines of his favourite mythologies. His wife Elizabeth Siddal is typical. She was first of all an artist's model and had sat to several of the PRB circle, notably to Millais for his *Ophelia* (Tate Gallery). She was therefore not simply her contemporary self: her personality was overlaid with other identities, the identities of past heroines, whose fates formed a palimpsest on her own life and enriched it with borrowed meanings. When Rossetti contemplated Lizzie he contemplated Dante's Beatrice and perhaps Shakespeare's Ophelia as well, and when he painted her he brought to his portrayal the layers of literary and mythological significance that had become identified with her. This process was quite unlike the methods of portraiture used by Hunt and Millais.

fig.3 John Everett Millais, *The Bridesmaid* 1851, oil on wood 27.9 × 20.3 cm. The Syndics of the Fitzwilliam Museum, Cambridge

A comparison of Rossetti's earliest ideal head, *Bocca Baciata* of 1859 (no.2), with a remarkable precursor, Millais's *The Bridesmaid* of 1851 (fig.3), illustrates the extent to which Rossetti was incorporating the allegorical and expressive significance of his subject into a recognisable portrait – in this case a clearly identifiable Fanny Cornforth, who was his mistress. The more literal Millais achieves his remarkably suggestive image without creating a portrait – his model has been identified, but the identification carries no resonance and no associated narratives are brought to mind by it. The artist is telling a story, not celebrating the mystery of his perception of an inamorata. Millais's picture depends for its effect primarily on the vivid presentation of detail. But in its imagery – the long red-gold hair, the girl contemplating an erotic vision, the suggestion that she is reflected in a mirror – it is prophetic of Symbolist ideas. Whereas Millais did not pursue the ideas he adumbrated in *The Bridesmaid*, and was to paint few works that qualify as Symbolist,[28] *Bocca Baciata* marks a turning-point not only for Rossetti but for nineteenth-century art in general. As Virginia Surtees points out, it shows 'a new type of woman … sensual and voluptuous, mystical and inscrutable but always humourless, gazing into the distance with hair outspread and hands resting on a parapet, often with some heavily scented flower completing the design. As the face of the model changed with the years, so the eyes became more wistful, the feeling of distance more remote'.[29]

Whether they lean on a parapet or not, Rossetti's women with their wistful gaze frequently seem, like Millais's bridesmaid, to be at a dressing-table mirror, looking into their own soul. This image may be taken as a paradigm of Symbolist iconography, and it is really where the story of Symbolism in Britain begins. The first stirrings of Symbolist painting in France can be dated to almost exactly the same time: it was in the second half of the 1850s that Gustave Moreau began to transform his art from a perfervidly Romantic historical style, derived from Chassériau and Ingres, into the fully fledged Symbolism of the early 1860s. Rossetti himself had made one of the pioneering statements on the theme of 'the skull in the mirror' with his early pen-drawing *How They Met Themselves* (lost), repeated for George Price Boyce in 1860 (fig.4). Here the mirror-image of the strolling lovers is a pair of *Doppelgänger* whose appearance presages death. The subject presents in narrative form the imagery of 'reflected fate', and while the anecdotal character of the design draws very obviously on a German Romantic idea,[30] Rossetti's interest in the motif is an indication of the direction of his thinking at this critical moment in his development.

fig.4 D.G. Rossetti, *How They Met Themselves* *c.*1850–60, pen and ink 26.7 × 21 cm. The Syndics of the Fitzwilliam Museum, Cambridge

The same preoccupations figure repeatedly in Rossetti's poetry, which he regarded as complementing his pictures, and existing in parallel with them. Characterised as it is by a joining of death with mirror-image, closely linked to the idea of the painted image, as in such poems as 'The Portrait', and an insistence on the identity of the erotic and the deadly, as in Sonnet XXIII, 'Death-in-Love':

> I and this Love are one, and I am Death

it presents a substantial literary basis for British Symbolism which, like Baudelaire's in France, had international resonances. For example, Rossetti's early lyric 'The Blessed Damozel', written in 1848 and published in 1850 in the Pre-Raphaelite magazine *The Germ*, was set to music by Debussy in the 1890s when Symbolism was at its zenith in France (see no.71).

The early date of the poem 'The Blessed Damozel'[31] alerts us not only to Rossetti's precocious use of Symbolist ideas, but also to the fertility, in Symbolist terms, of the English literary environment of the 1840s. The young artist-poet was able to build on the work of several precursors, whose poetry is replete with potentially Symbolist imagery. The first of these is Keats, who with his sensuous lyricism and virtuoso evocations of physical delight has been seen as a forerunner of Aestheticism – which as has been noted was itself an aspect of Symbolism. Many late nineteenth-century artists took up the theme of his early poem 'Lamia' (1819), with its luxuriant description of the eponymous witch-maiden (Lamia means witch):

> She was a gordian shape of dazzling hue,
> Vermilion-spotted, golden, green, and blue;
> Striped like a zebra, freckled like a pard,
> Eyed like a peacock, and all crimson-barr'd;
> ...
> Her head was serpent, but ah, bitter-sweet!
> She had a woman's mouth with all its pearls complete:
> And for her eyes: what could such eyes do there
> But weep and weep, that they were born so fair?
> As Proserpine still weeps for her Sicilian air.
> Her throat was serpent, but the words she spake,
> Came, as through bubbling honey, for love's sake
>
> (Part I, lines 47–65)

fig.5 Fernand Khnopff, *Vivien* 1896, painted plaster 98 cm high. Oesterreichische Galerie, Vienna

The assimilation of Woman into the forms of exotic beasts, the superimposition of pleasure and pain, the emphasis on eyes and throat – all these recur in Rossettian verse. The reference to Proserpine, too, is a foretaste of Rossetti (see no.46) – and, incidentally, of the fertile hinterland of the Persephone myth with its symbolism of rebirth and the cycle of the seasons that was to be so thoroughly explored by Frazer in *The Golden Bough*.[32] Meredith, who shared Rossetti's house in the early 1860s and was later to acknowledge him as 'our Master',[33] brought out these connections in his poem 'The Day of the Daughter of Hades':

> lo, the Great Mother, She!...
> The embrace of the Twain, of whom
> To men are their day, their night,
> Mellow fruits and the shearing tomb:
> Our Lady of the Sheaves
> And the Lily of Hades, the Sweet
> Of Enna: he saw through leaves
> The Mother and Daughter meet.

The development from Keats's use of the Persephone legend as Miltonic simile, to Meredith's many-layered evocation of myth, allegory and religion, illustrates the ways in which Romantic iconography was enriched and transformed into Symbolism.

Rossetti's love of Arthurian legend brought him inevitably close to Tennyson, for whose poems he made illustrations which were to have a considerable influence in Europe.[34] There are Symbolist pre-echoes in several of Tennyson's early poems, notably 'The Lady of Shalott', which was taken up as a popular subject by later nineteenth-century painters just as Keats's 'Lamia' was. The leading motif of 'The Lady of Shalott' – the mirror in which a forbidden world is seen reflected – was full of Symbolist potential, and the Arthurian legends supplied subjects for a wide variety of artists. For instance, 'The Idylls of the King' was to become the inspiration for a sculpture by Fernand Khnopff, his coloured plaster figure of *Vivien* 1896 (fig.5).[35] In George Du Maurier's novel *Trilby* (1895) a British artist trained in Paris in the late 1850s 'was, or thought himself, a passionate realist in those days. He has changed, and now paints nothing but King Arthurs and Guineveres and Lancelots and Elaines, and floating Ladies of Shalott.'[36]

fig.6 Frederick Sandys, *Amor Mundi* 1865, woodcut for the *Shilling Magazine*. Trustees of the British Museum

Dante Gabriel's sister Christina was also a prolific poet whose work made its mark on a number of artists. Frederick Sandys's illustration of her 'Amor Mundi' 1865 (fig.6) is a well-known composition that foreshadows some of the darker imagery of later Symbolist painting. The poem itself is cast in a flowing metre with internal rhyming that recalls Poe and perhaps Swinburne:

> 'Oh what is that glides quickly where velvet flowers grow thickly,
> Their scent comes rich and sickly?'
> 'A scaled and hooded worm.'
> 'Oh what's that in the hollow, so pale I quake to follow?'
> 'Oh, that's a thin dead body which waits the eternal term.'

But it was the intense existentialism of Christina Rossetti's devotional poetry that caught the imagination of the later Symbolists. Her early poem 'The Watchers' of 1850 seems to have played some part in the genesis of one of William Blake Richmond's most Symbolist works, also called *The Watchers*, finished in 1876 and shown in Paris in 1878 (fig.7).[37] And her devotional poem 'Who Shall Deliver Me?' of 1864 was taken up by Khnopff, who paid particular tribute to her in one of his most important pictures, *I Lock My Door Upon Myself* 1891 (fig.8), which takes its title from a line in the poem. It is subtitled with her name: *Christina Georgina Rossetti,* as is another work of that year, *Who Shall Deliver Me?* also derived from her poem (see no.86).

fig.7 William Blake Richmond, *The Watchers* 1873–6 oil on canvas 30.5 × 61 cm. Private Collection

A particular hero of Dante Gabriel's, Robert Browning,[38] was closely involved in literary developments in the Paris of the 1850s, admired by one of the leading apologists of the new French poetry, Joseph Milsand, and counted among the exponents of *le réalisme*. His wife, Elizabeth Barrett, enjoyed hardly less of a reputation, and was the dedicatee (as 'The Noblest of Her Sex') of a work enormously admired in Paris – Poe's 'The Raven', published in 1845.[39] The young Pre-Raphaelite Rossetti chose a passage from one of Browning's poems, 'Pippa Passes', as subject for a small oil painting of 1851. *Hist! – said Kate the Queen* (Eton College) takes a minor incident characterised by the detail of the Queen with a 'maiden, binding her tresses', and in this foreshadows innumerable later works of Rossetti's in which women are shown combing or tending their hair. Long hair, specifically hair that is touched and handled as a surrogate for the woman's body itself, is closely associated with Symbolist images of woman. The idea received definitive expression in Browning's short poem 'Porphyria's Lover' of 1845:

> That moment she was mine, mine, fair,
> Perfectly pure and good: I found
> A thing to do and all her hair
> In one long yellow string I wound
> Three times her little throat around,
> And strangled her.
>
> (lines 16–41)

fig.8 Fernand Khnopff, *I Lock my Door upon Myself* 1891, oil on canvas 72 × 140 cm. Neue Pinakothek, Munich

Browning's technique in the poem is itself prophetic of Symbolist methods: the narrative content is so compactly suggested that it is almost eliminated, while the central incident is given great emphasis so that narrative is subsumed in the description of a state of mind. The moments immediately after Porphyria has been strangled with her own hair are lingered over with a deliberate, morbid eroticism that anticipates Salome's ecstasy over the head of Jokanaan in Wilde's play:

> No pain felt she;
> I am quite sure she felt no pain.
> As a shut bud that holds a bee,
> I warily oped her lids: again
> Laughed the blue eyes without a stain.
> And I untightened next the tress
> About her neck; her cheek once more
> Blushed bright beneath my burning kiss
>
> (lines 41–48)

The episode brings to mind Rossetti's Sonnet 'Lilith' which amplifies his picture of 'Adam's first wife', *Lady Lilith* (see no.6):

> The rose and poppy are her flowers; for where
> Is he not found, O Lilith, whom shed scent
> And soft-shed kisses and soft sleep shall snare?
> Lo! as that youth's eyes burned at thine, so went
> Thy spell through him, and left his straight neck bent,
> And round his heart one strangling golden hair.

The body of Symbolist poetry that the Rossettis were creating was substantially augmented by Algernon Charles Swinburne, who counted himself a follower of both Dante Gabriel and Baudelaire. His writing is characterised by a self-consciousness that, as Huysmans's des Esseintes shows, distinctively stamps Decadence, and indeed all Symbolism:

> Sweet for a little even to fear, and sweet,
> O love, to lay down fear at love's fair feet;
> Shall not some fiery memory of his breath
> Lie sweet on lips that touch the lips of death?[40]

Tellingly, not only Swinburne's poetry but his criticism too is couched in language of an indulgent vagueness that seems, as it were, complicit in a presumption of the ultimately 'Symbolist' character of the work discussed. His account of a Michelangelo drawing showing the bust of a woman exemplifies this process:

> In some inexplicable way all her ornaments seem to partake of her fatal nature, to bear upon them her brand of beauty fresh from hell; and this through no vulgar machinery of symbolism, no serpentine or otherwise bestial emblem: the bracelets and rings are innocent enough in shape and workmanship; but in touching her flesh they have become infected with deadly and malignant meaning.[41]

Swinburne's idea here is of a piece with Pater's famous description of Leonardo's *Mona Lisa*: 'She is older than the rocks among which she sits; like the Vampire, she has been dead many times, and learned the secrets of the grave; and has been a diver in deep seas'.[42] This passage has always been regarded as a touchstone of Aestheticism. But in its evocation of a mysterious and dangerous female presence in an archaic landscape it goes beyond the Aesthetic into a world of myth and dream: it is clearly Symbolist, and illustrates some of the ways in which artists and writers of the period were a part of that movement despite themselves. It was in the *zeitgeist*.

Swinburne's lyrical dilations on the Michelangelo drawing are not so much art criticism as a highly self-indulgent prose poem, a minor work of Decadent art in its own right, like much else in Swinburne's 'critical' writings. We should expect similar utterances to be prompted by Rossetti's paintings of women. They are not lacking. Indeed, those pictures inspire Swinburne to a consistent flow of description that catalogues Symbolist preoccupations with remarkable thoroughness. *Lady Lilith*, for example, gave rise to a description of the woman who

> draws out through a comb the heavy mass of hair like thick spun gold to fullest length: her head leans back half sleepily, superb and satiate with its own beauty ... Outside, as seen in the glimmering mirror, there is full summer ... The sleepy splendour of the picture is a fit raiment for the idea incarnate of faultless fleshly beauty and peril of pleasure unavoidable.[43]

The woman lazily and luxuriously combing, or simply displaying, her 'redundant hair,' as Swinburne calls it, was to become a commonplace of European painting and would re-emerge in many guises. The image was taken up very early in a picture by Gustave Courbet of 1866 which is clearly Rossettian in inspiration: his portrait of his mistress Joanna Hiffernan, known as *La Belle Irlandaise* (no.9). By the last decade of the century, when Symbolism was in its fashionable heyday, the motif recurs conspicuously in the work of such unlikely artists as Degas, who returned again and again to the hair-brushing or combing theme, and in doing so acquired more than a little of the ambivalent erotic patina of Symbolism (fig.9).[44]

fig.9 Edgar Degas, *Woman at her Toilet* c.1894, pastel on tracing paper 95.6 × 119.9 cm. Tate Gallery

Sometimes the overtones are darker. Swinburne described Rossetti's *Beata Beatrix* (no.44), 'An unfinished picture of Beatrice ... a little before death', as

> perhaps the noblest work of Mr Rossetti's many studies after Dante. The work is wholly symbolic and ideal; a strange bird flown earthward from heaven brings her in its beak a full-blown poppy, the funereal flower of sleep. Her beautiful head lies back, sad and sweet, with fast-shut eyes in a death-like trance that is not death; over it the shadow of death seems to impend, making sombre the splendour of her ample hair and tender faultless features[45]

Swinburne couples 'symbolic' here with another term: 'ideal'. The idea of love in Rossetti's vision of the dying Lizzie Siddal is one in which *eros* and *agape* – physical and spiritual love – are fused. The object of desire, transfigured by death, becomes the embodiment of a holy yearning toward the infinite. In this picture Rossetti gives definitive expression to the central duality of Symbolism. We have

fig.10 William Blake, *The Resurrection of Pious Souls* 1806, pencil and watercolour 42.2 × 30.6 cm. Trustees of the British Museum

fig.11 John Roddam Spencer Stanhope, *Love and the Maiden* 1877, oil on canvas 138.5 × 202.5 cm. Private Collection

already encountered it in relation to Symons and Yeats and their dilemma over 'decadent' and 'spiritualized literature'. Perhaps the most remarkable attempt to articulate spiritual values in the earlier part of the century had been that of William Blake (fig.10), and all these men looked back to Blake with an admiration that was unusual for its time.[46] Swinburne described Blake as though he were a Symbolist:

> To him the veil of outer things seemed always to tremble with some breath behind it: seemed at times to be rent in sunder with clamour and sudden lightning. All the void of earth and air seemed to quiver with the passage of sentient wings and palpitate under the pressure of conscious feet. Flowers and weeds, stars and stones, spoke with articulate lips and gazed with living eyes. Hands were stretched towards him from beyond the darkness of material nature, to tempt or to support, to guide or to restrain.[47]

Blake figures regularly in modern literature on Symbolism as a precursor of the movement; yet there are few hints in Blake of the moral and erotic Symbolist ambivalences that we have examined. We might make an exception for 'The Sick Rose',[48] a poem that affirms by contrast that his art as a whole, both literary and pictorial, is not morbid in the later nineteenth-century sense. The Symbolists responded to the vigorous spirituality expressed through his personal mythology, a spirituality placed in firm opposition to the material world, which Blake rejected as Death. Rossetti's own work, curiously, reflects little of Blake's influence, though some of his followers – Burne-Jones, Spencer Stanhope (fig.11), Simeon Solomon, William Blake Richmond – frequently show it. In doing so they evoke a powerful and positive spirituality with connotations quite opposed to those of Decadence. The profoundest secrets of the human spirit may be sublime as well as sordid. Symbolism was always a larger and richer body of ideas than Decadence could aspire to be.

The dual nature of the Symbolist credo in France is exemplified by one of Huysmans's contemporaries, Joséphin Péladan, a writer as eccentric in real life as Huysman's fictional des Esseintes.[49] In the 1880s Péladan was pursuing his own programme of revolution through sensual indulgence. In the year that *A Rebours* appeared, he published a novel setting out this programme, *Le Vice suprême*, which contrasts decadence of the flesh with the ultimate sin – destruction of the soul. The transcendental implications, ambiguous though they seem, reflect Péladan's wider preoccupations.[50] Shortly after this date his penchant for Catholic mysticism inspired him to revive the cult of Rosicrucianism in the form of the Order of the Rose+Croix, composed of writers and artists, and to award himself the obscure but vaguely magical title of 'Sâr'. He echoed Keats in asserting 'Artist, you are a priest: Art is a great mystery and as soon as your effort is rewarded with a masterpiece a divine ray descends as if on an altar'.[51] Under these auspices he founded a new art exhibition, the Salon de la Rose+Croix. His manifesto[52] makes revolutionary gestures which hardly conceal an essentially conservative agenda. It attacks a whole swathe of current schools: realism, history, military, oriental, rustic and marine subjects, still life and sporting painting. At the same time it asserts that 'The Order favours first the Catholic ideal and Mysticism. After Legend, Myth, Allegory, the Dream, the Paraphrase of great poetry and finally all Lyricism, the Order prefers work which has a mural-like character, as being of superior essence.' In this somewhat unlikely context, Idealism emerges as a vital component of continental Symbolism.

Péladan went into considerable detail as to the precise subject-matter of the Order. Among other types he favoured 'Allegory, be it expressive like "Modesty and Vanity", be it decorative like a work by Puvis de Chavannes'; and he specified 'The nude made *sublime*, the nude in the style of Primaticcio, Correggio, or the expressive head in the manner of Leonardo and of Michelangelo.' He invited both Moreau and Puvis to exhibit at his first Salon in 1892, but they did not. Moreau's plethoric canvases represented the sensual, dark side of Symbolism; Puvis, with his blond colour and harmonious compositions of static figures, the reverse – the Idealist calm of a spirit dematerialised, elevated above fleshly desires. In fact Puvis objected strongly to any association with the Rose+Croix. It has been forcibly argued that he should be excluded from the Symbolist movement, except as an admittedly powerful influence on many of its artists.[53] The sense of opposition was not only on Puvis's side. Huysmans was repelled by his work: 'always the same pale colouring, the same fresco-like air; it is always hard and angular; it annoys one, as always, with its pretensions to naivety and affected simplicity'.[54] Puvis's art is indeed so rarefied that its Symbolist qualities are not always apparent; but in his search for a formal expression of subject-matter that was 'not Nature, but parallel to Nature',[55] he reflected many of the preoccupations of the Rose+Croix painters. In the course of that search he evolved a pictorial language well suited to the evocation of the higher realm of abstract values so earnestly desired by Péladan.

In what we may see as a further bid to establish the ancestry of Idealism, Péladan likewise solicited work by Rossetti and Burne-Jones, but had to be content to exhibit photographs. The reputations of these artists in Europe at this date were very high. Their art might be seen as achieving a very British equilibrium between the Decadent outpourings of Moreau and the extreme refinement of Puvis – a poetic resolution, as it were, of the two poles of Symbolism. Both had been seen in Paris exhibitions and Burne-Jones had scored a triumph with *King Cophetua and the Beggar Maid* (no.40) at the 1889 Exposition Universelle.[56] An equally prestigious figure was George Frederic Watts. In an article published in the *Revue des Deux Mondes* in 1886, Robert de la Sizeranne had admired Watts's canvases *Love and Life* (see fig.49 on p.26) and *Love and Death* (no.51), pointing out that they gave visual form to 'the most mysterious of the powers that dominate man': Watts had 'understood what resources, what life, they [those powers] afforded for his abstract creations'.[57] He was a painter who fitted neatly into the Sâr Péladan's catalogue of acceptable art. His highest efforts were poured into expressive allegories, though, as the two examples just mentioned suggest, they tackle subjects considerably more ambitious than Péladan's proposed 'Modesty and Vanity'.

Conversely, the Idealist credo conformed well to the convictions of an English painter with a moral responsibility to the nation. Watts's reputation depended in his own time, and has since suffered as a consequence, on his position as the

fig.12 George Frederic Watts, *Physical Energy* cast 1906, bronze, erected in Kensington Gardens. Watts Gallery, Compton

great visualiser of the ideals of British society at its imperial apogee. He was the sculptor of the Rhodes Memorial in Cape Town, *Physical Energy*, another cast of which is in Kensington Gardens (fig.12).[58] He was acclaimed – and eventually honoured – as the artist, both painter and sculptor, who expressed the enduring truths of Life, in an appropriately grand manner. His conversation too was uplifting and inspiring. His friends expected him to speak authoritatively 'of all that is highest and noblest,'[59] and he contributed *ex cathedra* on 'The Aims of Art' and suchlike topics to *The Magazine of Art* and other journals. His output and opinions were the ultimate statement of Establishment values. His work has been misread as being also an exercise in academic technique. 'You know – you *must* learn to paint like Titian!' Ruskin had advised him while he was working on one of his earliest and most ambitious Symbolist subjects, *The Court of Death*;[60] and it is as a pasticheur of Titian that Watts has often been seen – and dismissed.

The Russian painter Vassily Verestchagin, seeing Watts's work at the Grosvenor Gallery, 'said he had come expecting to find an imitator of the Old Masters, but instead had found the most independent man he knew'.[61] In reality, Watts was far from identifying himself with the Establishment and pursued a high-minded course of his own. His very painting techniques reflected his independence. He paid exceptional attention not only to the tone and colour of his designs but to the surface texture of his paint, in pursuit of a purity and clarity that he conceived as embodying the reality – the true spiritual qualities – of his subject-matter.[62] He would have endorsed the ringing sentiments of Meredith in his 'Hymn to Colour':

> Look now where Colour, the soul's bridegroom, makes
> The house of heaven splendid for the bride.

Indeed, Meredith's symbolism of colour in this poem echoes Watts's own language closely. 'Light, Darkness and Colour answer respectively to Life, Death and Love. Colour is to Light and Darkness, as Love is to Life and Death.'[63] As Mary Watts writes:

> In his desire to preserve this purity of colour, he never allowed himself to put a touch of fresh colour upon his picture until the paint beneath was absolutely dry ... He detested lumps of colour left protruding from the surface, and ... these ... were well rubbed down with a buffalo-horn palette-knife. His method of glazing with oil-colour was, I believe, original ... he ... used stiff colour, and at first applied more than was required. Then with scraps of paper ... he would rub off as much of the colour as it was possible to remove, thus leaving what may be called a mere breath, but all that was wanted.[64]

The result of this process is not the sharp Germanic brilliance of, say, Daniel Maclise, or the early Pre-Raphaelites. He disliked the enamelled finish of Bronzino, describing it as 'bare of mystery'.[65] Watts's technique produced an oddly muted surface, through which his figures are seen as through a slightly frosted glass. This effect is not unlike that of Rossetti's watercolours, and indeed of many of his oil-paintings, notably *Beata Beatrix* (no.44). Burne-Jones and Simeon

Solomon aimed at something similar, Burne-Jones often using tempera, or oil-paint handled in imitation of tempera, Solomon using chalks. Burne-Jones acknowledged a debt not to the painterly Titian but to more linear masters of the Italian quattrocento, Crivelli and Botticelli, insisting on the paramountcy of line, but also on 'finish' as a necessary vehicle for design and 'idea'. That finish, in Burne-Jones, Watts and many other Symbolists, was a picture surface that became a clear yet suggestive membrane through which the world 'parallel to Nature', as Puvis put it, can be perceived as through Alice's looking-glass. It represents perhaps a deliberate reaction to the diamond-sharp immediacy of the modern world of the Pre-Raphaelites. Comparably ambiguous textures can be found in Symbolist work of all countries, very often achieved in pastel, as in the case of Redon and Khnopff (who was heavily influenced by Burne-Jones); and artists as various as the Italian Gaetano Previati and the American Elihu Vedder can be seen aiming at similar effects. Another American Symbolist, Abbot Handerson Thayer, worked at his canvases with as much obsessive perfectionism as Watts, painting and repainting and sometimes using a broom to achieve the balance between clarity and obscurity that he required.[66]

The New Sculpture, which parallels Symbolist painting in Britain, also strives to suppress the immediacy of the carved or moulded form and to achieve a surface through which a world of ideas is revealed by suggestion. Characteristically it is soft, melting, evanescent, the opposite of the crisp marble of the Neo-Classical period. Watts's own sculpture possesses these features. Especially fine are the small figures of wax or clay that he formed, with a mere squeeze of the hand, it seems, to guide him in the construction of his paintings – *Chaos*, for example (nos.49–50). They have an organic fluidity reminiscent of the work of Auguste Rodin, who himself often took up Symbolist themes. Alfred Gilbert, admired by Rodin[67] and now regarded as the leading Symbolist sculptor in Britain, was 'awed' by Watts, and said of him: 'He steals all the best subjects away from the sculptors.'[68] The strange pitted surface of the bronze of Watts's *Physical Energy* can perhaps also be seen as a means of conveying 'subjective and abstract thought – what is called symbolical',[69] imbuing the rocky forms of the work with a subtly different quality from that of everyday realism.

In respect of both subject-matter and technique Watts is, then, in many ways an archetypal Symbolist, absorbed by transcendental ideas. He was viewed by many contemporaries as a priest-like figure, wise and holy. In the opinion of Sir Clifford Albutt, he 'walked hand in hand with the ineffable'.[70] According to Watts himself, his pictures 'represent ideas too far off, taking one outside experience. I want them,' he said, 'to take you as music might, and lead you further even than I myself intended.'[71] His flirtation with spiritualism, his vision of 'poor humanity ... so frail a thing in the midst of what Carlyle calls the Immensities'[72] and his sense of the interconnectedness of painting and music, were entirely in tune with the ideas of Péladan, of Puvis and others. Jean Delville, a Belgian painter (fig.13) who founded a school of 'idealist' painting in Brussels and who was to teach at Glasgow School of Art for six years in the early 1900s, gave utterance to high-minded sentiments that echo the declared intention of many of Watts's pictures:

fig.13 Jacques Delville, *The Love of Souls* 1900, tempera on canvas 238 × 150 cm. Musée d'Ixelles, Brussels

O God of Light in whom all worlds are one,
An atom from that fierce and fiery place
 Wherein men stray, behold before Thy Face
My soul, an eagle mounting to the sun.

...

O God, Who gazing on the perfect whole
Smiles at our loveliness of form or soul
 As gradually the prisoned self escapes,
Beyond all time, division, change, or death,
Thou art the immortal essence of all shapes.[73]

Delville admired both Watts and Burne-Jones, placing them in a modern pantheon with Moreau, Puvis and Wagner.[74] The sublimities of Wagner's music were counted among the highest achievements of art as understood by the Symbolists, and references to him occur frequently in their work. *Tristan und Isolde* was the most overwhelming expression of erotic passion created in any art-form, *Parsifal* the supreme statement of Christian mysticism and renunciation. In his novel *L'Oeuvre* (1886), about the life of artists in Paris in the 1870s, Zola makes one of his characters articulate a general feeling: 'Oh, Wagner! The god, the incarnation of centuries of music! His work, the mighty firmament, where all the arts are blended into one ... What an onslaught on conventions, what wholesale destruction of ineffectual theories it stands for, the revolution, the breaking-down of barriers to infinity! ... The overture to Tannhäuser, what is it but the mighty hallelujah of the new age!'[75] The Aesthetics saw music as providing formal paradigms for the visual artist, the Decadents as an art capable of plumbing the obscure depths of the soul; for the Idealists it was an assertion of the grandeur of human aspirations, and Wagner was the supreme exemplar of that grandeur. We have seen Watts comparing the function of his art with that of music; a German journalist even went so far as to call his gallery of pictures at Compton 'the English Bayreuth'.[76]

If Germans could link Watts's name with Wagner's, it was natural in Britain to link it with that of Carlyle. Mary Watts recorded the opinion of 'a clever and well-connected woman' that 'the earnestness of this age is in great part due to the influence of Mr Watts and of Carlyle;'[77] and there is a constant interplay between the two men's minds and work even though they did not always agree in person – as, for instance, when Watts was attempting to paint Carlyle's portrait.[78] Watts would surely have concurred in Carlyle's dictum that true art is 'Eternity looking through Time: the God-like rendered visible.' When Watts titled one of his pictures *In the Land of Weissnichtwo* 1894 (Watts Gallery), he was alluding to Carlyle's *Sartor Resartus* (1832), the narrative of which is set in a fictitious place of that name (literally 'I know not where'). When he painted his *Mammon* (no.52), he took up an idea canvassed by Carlyle in *Past and Present* (1843), which assaults 'Midas-eared Mammonism' as a pervasive evil of modern life.[79]

The argument of *Past and Present* is built on two fundamental images, one of Mammon, the other the Sphinx 'who sat by the wayside, propounding her riddle to the passengers, which if they could not answer she destroyed them!' Carlyle continues in terms that supply a complete text for the Symbolist interest in the Sphinx:

> Such a Sphinx is this Life of ours, to all men and societies of men. Nature, like the Sphinx, is of womanly celestial loveliness and tenderness; the face and bosom of a goddess, but ending in claws and the body of a lioness. There is in her celestial beauty, – which means celestial order, pliancy to wisdom; but there is also a darkness, a ferocity, fatality, which are infernal. She is a goddess, but one not yet disimprisoned, – the articulate, lovely still encased in the inarticulate, chaotic. How true! And does she not propound her riddles to us?[80]

G.M. Trevelyan's comments on Meredith's 'Hymn to Colour' are relevant here: 'What exactly do the universe and the life of man mean? Perhaps the knowledge cannot be put into words. Perhaps it is too sacred for exact words to signify it. If, then, the dogmatic answer to the Sphinx has nowadays for very shame to be silent, must therefore all voice of faith, hope, reverence, and love fall silent also?'[81] This question might be taken as the Symbolist motto.

Carlyle made use of the same Sphinx image in *Sartor Resartus*: 'The Universe … was as a mighty Sphinx-riddle, which I knew so little of, yet must rede, or be devoured.'[82] Another passage in the same work, on another ancient Egyptian monument, was to make a profound impression on Fernand Khnopff;[83] it refers to the Colossus of Memnon which was supposed to utter a mysterious note each morning at sunrise: 'As from Aeolian harps in the breath of dawn, as from Memnon's statue struck by the rosy finger of Aurora, unearthly music was around him, and lapped him into untried balmy Rest.' *Sartor* was to become a cult book for the Symbolists, especially after it had been translated into French – it appeared in instalments in the *Mercure de France* in 1896. In that year one of the principal Symbolist writers of Belgium, Maurice Maeterlinck, quoted from *Sartor* by way of Introduction to his *Le Trésor des Humbles*: 'Speech is of Time, Silence is of Eternity.'[84]

A very different kind of Symbolist, Paul Gauguin, had already been introduced to *Sartor* by his friend the painter Jacob Meyer de Haan, and included a copy of the book (along with *Paradise Lost*) in one of his portraits of de Haan.[85] We can see how passages such as this would have impressed him:

> Who am I; what is this ME? A Voice, a Motion, an Appearance; some embodied, visualised Idea in the Eternal Mind? *Cogito, ergo sum*. Alas, poor Cogitator, this takes us but a little way. Sure enough, I am; and lately was not; but Whence? How? Whereto? The answer lies all around, written in all colours and motions, uttered in all tones of jubilee and wail, in thousand-figured, thousand-voiced, harmonious Nature[86]

In view of these significant connections, we may agree with a recent suggestion that Carlyle was a writer 'fundamental to the Symbolist'.[87] Certainly *Sartor* is full of ideas prophetic of Symbolism. Book III Chapter iii is a long disquisition specifically on the subject of Symbols.

fig.14 Paul Gauguin, *D'Où venons-nous? Que sommes-nous? Où allons-nous?* 1897, oil on canvas 139.1 × 374.6 cm. Tompkins Collection, courtesy Museum of Fine Arts, Boston.

> In the Symbol proper ... there is ever, more or less distinctly and directly, some embodiment and revelation of the Infinite; the Infinite is made to blend itself with the Finite, to stand visible, and as it were, attainable there ... man ... everywhere finds himself encompassed with Symbols, recognised as such or not recognised: the Universe is but one vast Symbol of God; nay if thou wilt have it, what is man himself but a Symbol of God; is not all that he does symbolical; a revelation to sense of the mystic god-given force that is in him[88]

There are echoes of this passage in Watts's account of his intention in creating *Physical Energy* to 'suggest man as he ought to be – a part of creation, of cosmos in fact, his great limbs to be akin to the rocks and to the roots, and his head to be as the sun'.[89] The founding metaphor of *Sartor*, clothes as symbols of culture and morality, is one that has particular resonance in the context of what has already been said about the significance of clothed and unclothed figures in art:

> Men are properly said to be clothed with Authority, clothed with Beauty, with Curses, and the like. Nay, if you consider it, what is Man himself and his whole terrestrial Life, but an emblem; a Clothing or visible Garment for that divine ME of his, cast hither, like a light-particle, down from Heaven? Thus he is said also to be clothed with a Body.[90]

These ideas were entirely in keeping with the Idealist Symbolism of which we can now see Watts to have been a consistent, and perhaps the leading, exponent. His allegorical subjects of the 1870s and 1880s anticipate the large paintings of Previati and Delville that are so characteristic of the climactic phase of the movement. For his part, Carlyle supplies a Symbolist textbook that antedates the writings of Gautier and Baudelaire by some years. In these two figures alone, hitherto largely ignored in this context, Britain can claim to have made major contributions to the development of Symbolism as an international movement both at its inception and at its apogee.

Another British writer rarely mentioned in discussions of Symbolism is Edward FitzGerald, who had published his translation of the *Rubáiyát of Omar Khayyám* anonymously in 1859. FitzGerald was a friend of Carlyle, Watts and Burne-Jones; though Carlyle was scathing about 'the verses of that old Mahometan Blackguard',[91] Burne-Jones saw Persian poetry like Omar's as 'an excuse for saying daring things about life, and splendid blasphemies'.[92] Swinburne was bowled over by the *Rubáiyát* when he was introduced to it in 1862, and wrote his 'Laus Veneris' as a direct response. The poem inspired a watercolour and later an important picture by Burne-Jones.[93] Elihu Vedder, an American domiciled in Italy with many British contacts, was especially affected by the *Rubáiyát*. He found in its pessimistic yet stoical hedonism a complete personal philosophy which he made the basis for a substantial part of his life's work. The poem was 'a constant companion, a presence that fed his imagination'.[94] It brought him into contemplation of the cosmos, 'grasping many truths by the way, but ever baffled by the master problem of human fate'.

Vedder's visual imagery, while highly personal, is sometimes reminiscent of Burne-Jones, or of Watts; sometimes it is close to the fey, despairing heads found in the chalk drawings of his friend Simeon Solomon – decapitated Perseus, Medusa, St John: an iconography that parallels the more sinister nightmare world of Redon. In Vedder's work there is none of Watts's Theosophical-Christian optimism; but the sense of a complete world-view possessing its own inherent balance and harmony is apparent in the project for illustrating the *Rubáiyát* published in Boston in 1884 (see no.87). The echoes of Blake's prophetic books in the resulting publication, with its panels of text surrounded by illustration, are surely not accidental.

Vedder's work illustrates the ways in which the imagery, even the technical idiosyncrasies, of the British Symbolists were disseminated. Like him they were part of a broadly international professional network, for whom exhibitions in London, Liverpool, Paris, Berlin, Munich and elsewhere provided recurrent opportunities for contact and exposure. The growth of the press and of an informed professional body of art critics fostered ever greater awareness of contemporary events. From 1893 the magazine *The Studio* covered international developments, and was widely read both in Britain and abroad. (Khnopff was its Belgian correspondent.) By the 1890s many of the principal works of Burne-Jones and Watts were known to almost everyone with an interest in the visual arts. When Prince Eugen of Sweden was planning his 1897 International Exposition for Stockholm, works by Watts were a priority for loans, and stole the show.[95] If some people found Burne-Jones disappointingly unshocking, his follower Beardsley was not vulnerable to that accusation. 'You won't find a single picture of Burne-Jones that could not be displayed at Sunday School,' the Norwegian sculptor Gustav Vigeland wrote home from London in 1901, adding: 'It is really interesting to find that England has produced an artist like Beardsley whose works have been publicly acclaimed, although he was not at all a Sunday School boy.'[96]

Beardsley's work was well adapted physically for international consumption. It did not rely on exposure at public exhibitions, or even on the monochrome photogravure reproductions through which Watts, Rossetti and Burne-Jones were known everywhere, but could travel the world through the medium of books and magazines. His idiosyncratic art lies behind the evolution of the equally distinctive manner of the Glasgow architect and designer Charles Rennie Mackintosh: in this late phase of Symbolism the boundaries between the fine and applied arts become ever more indistinct. When in 1900 Mackintosh burst on the

fig.15 Edward Burne-Jones, *Miss Amy Gaskell* 1893, oil on canvas 94 × 50.8 cm. Private Collection

fig.16 Pablo Picasso, *Girl in a Chemise* c.1905, oil on canvas 72.7 × 60 cm. Tate Gallery

fig.17 Pablo Picasso, *The Old Guitarist* 1903, oil on wood 122.9 × 82.6 cm. Art Institute of Chicago, Helen Birch Bartlett Memorial Collection

eighth exhibition of the Vienna Secession,[97] the style acquired a new momentum in the city of Sigmund Freud. In the work of Beardsley and Mackintosh, Burne-Jones's concern for line as a pre-eminent vehicle of expression was adapted and channelled to become a primary source for twentieth-century aesthetic ideas.

Burne-Jones was a prolific designer of ornament for a multitude of objects, from books to tapestries and church furnishings, and these later developments were largely concerned with a language of decoration. But the substantive content of British Symbolist painting was also transported across Europe. Ferdinand Hodler copied Burne-Jones and paraphrased his compositions in his own paintings;[98] Picasso admired his 'white-skinned maidens' (figs.15, 16)[99] and may have unconsciously recollected Watts's *Hope* in his *Old Guitarist* of 1903 (fig.17). In the vampire-women that Edvard Munch was painting in the 1890s, or in the fiery vamps of the great *Beethoven Frieze* that Gustav Klimt executed for the fourteenth Secession exhibition of 1902, we find resurrected, with a new access of mesmeric power, the flaming-haired beauties that had so obsessed Rossetti in the 1860s.

By about 1905 the language of Symbolism had been radically modified. In that year Bernard Shaw's *Man and Superman* reviewed the epoch just passed with wry retrospective humour, epitomising it by reference to a number of celebrities including Watts. Myth and music – the Don Juan legend and Mozart's opera about it – are woven into the backdrop of a fierce comedy of vice and virtue, heaven and hell. The vampire of the last generation becomes the knowing and manipulative New Woman, Nietzsche's Superman the advocate of a 'Life Force' that is to forge a better world.[100] In painting, the inner turbulence of much Symbolist thinking was increasingly to be seen on the surface of pictures which sought no longer to express the transcendental glimpsed through a dream-like mist but to embody directly the emotional life of the artist. Techniques began to be governed by gesture, by instinctive responses: the generation of Munch, Picasso and Hodler evolved ways of painting that in themselves constituted a move away from Symbolism. Yet Symbolist ideas and styles lingered on for decades, and even gained new currency in the apocalyptic events of the First World War. Then, the Symbolist meditation on Death acquired poignant immediacy, and a Europe racked by conflict turned instinctively for consolation to the Idealist celebration of the aspiring and indomitable spirit of man.

Themes of Love and Death in Aesthetic Painting of the 1860s

Christopher Newall

During the 1860s a new understanding of the way in which works of art might operate upon the spectator's imagination came about in the progressive circles of English painting. This was a decade of ferment and confusion, caused in part by a new scientific understanding of man's origins (Charles Darwin's *Origin of Species* was published in 1859) which coincided with and contributed to a general decay in conventional religious faith. Many suffered a sense of intellectual and spiritual void, not knowing which way to turn at this time of new thinking, and for some art presented itself as an object of devotion in place of religion. At the same time, the cult of beauty that was launched in the late 1850s was an escape from the materialism and utilitarianism of the age. Painters in the 1860s were inclined to make experiments in technique and style, as well as to challenge conventions about the purpose and function of art; and thus types of painting which dealt with the very fundamentals of existence, and which utilised sexual attraction and fear of the supernatural to compel the spectator's attention, began to appear. If for the philistine audience works of this type were to be shunned as symptoms of depravity, there was nonetheless a brief florescence of a style of art that was both aesthetically pioneering and potentially subversive in its willingness to treat themes previously (and subsequently) regarded as beyond the bounds of Victorian propriety. W.B. Yeats, writing in 1898, summarised the defining credo of the artistic avant-garde during the previous forty years:

> All Art that is not mere story-telling, or mere portraiture, is symbolic ... A person or a landscape that is a part of a story or a portrait, evokes but so much emotion as the story or the portrait can permit without loosening the bonds that make it a story or a portrait; but if you liberate a person or a landscape from the bonds of motives and their actions, causes and their effects, and from all bonds but the bonds of your love, it will change under your eyes, and become a symbol of an infinite emotion, a perfected emotion, a part of the Divine Essence.[1]

Among the erstwhile Pre-Raphaelites Dante Gabriel Rossetti looked to escape the dictates of narrative from the mid-1850s. In his watercolour *Paolo and Francesca da Rimini* (no.30) different episodes of Dante's story of the adulterous love of a sister and brother-in-law and their fate are placed in compartments, so that the symbolic continuity of their love – in life and in death – is supported by the symmetry of the composition. The forthrightness of the treatment of a theme of fateful sexuality is indicated by John Ruskin's response: 'The common-pretty-timid-mistletoe bough kind of kiss was not what Dante meant. Rossetti has thoroughly understood the passage throughout.'[2]

opposite
detail from Edward Burne-Jones, *The Lament*
1865–6 (no.25)

In the same year, 1855, John Everett Millais embarked on *Autumn Leaves* (fig.18), which was to be described as 'a picture full of beauty and without subject'.[3] The idea for the painting originated in the series of illustrations Millais was then making for Tennyson's poems, but in the finished work all narrative clues are eliminated in favour of an image that is ambiguous and undefinable, and which plays on the poetic imagination of the spectator rather than his ability to read a pictorial text. The wistful feeling which is imparted by the drifting smoke, and the poignant beauty of the evening landscape which will shortly be engulfed in darkness, requires no literal interpretation but puts the spectator in mind of the decay of youth. In reply to F.G. Stephens's published account of the painting Millais wrote: 'I have always felt insulted when people have regarded the picture as a simple little domestic episode, chosen for effect, and colour, as I intended the picture to awaken by its solemnity the deepest religious reflection.'[4] Millais's *Spring* (Lady Lever Art Gallery, Port Sunlight), begun in 1856, again uses the seasons of the year to suggest the cycle of human existence: the young girls shown in the painting are themselves in the springtime of youth and beauty, but, delightful though the scene may be, it is clear that this will not last forever, a point forcefully made by the fearful *memento mori* of a scythe placed menacingly above the figure who lies in the right-hand foreground.

fig.18 John Everett Millais, *Autumn Leaves* 1855–6, oil on canvas 104.1 × 73.6 cm. Manchester City Art Galleries

Thus we see in the mid-1850s paintings in which narrative considerations – clues to the moral significance or didactic intention of the work, or systems of symbols designed to support the internal chronology or sequence of implied events – tend to give way to qualities of mood and poetic sentiment. Painters previously associated with Pre-Raphaelitism sought to express their anxieties and emotions, and looked for ways to address subjects in psychological terms, by treating their subjects obliquely and allusively rather than by representation of received texts or by coded allegory. This movement towards introspection and the unwillingness simply to repeat or translate programmes of thought adapted from another medium was identified in the *Oxford and Cambridge Magazine* as 'the general subjective tendency of modern imagination; i.e., that which directs itself to express the opinions, passions, and perplexities of the writer.'[5]

A further spur to wrest art from a documentary or utilitarian function, to explore instead ways of transmitting sensations of desire or anxiety in noumenal or unspecific terms, occurred in the late 1850s and was led by various artists who had previously lived in Paris. Théophile Gautier in the preface to *Mademoiselle de Maupin* of 1834 had dismissed the idea of a morality of artistic expression, and posited that 'there is nothing really beautiful but that which is useless.'[6] Charles Baudelaire, who called Gautier's novel a 'reverie prolonged with a painter's perseverance, [a] kind of hymn to beauty',[7] demanded that art should be free of all didactic or documentary function. Painters such as Frederic Leighton and James Whistler, each of whom transferred from Paris to London in 1859, adopted abstract and evocative imagery rather than prosaic narrative subjects with moralistic inflection of the kind that the generality of English artists (including the Pre-Raphaelites) had favoured in the 1850s.

On the other hand, pictorial story-telling of a kind which excited and intrigued the spectator remained central to the artistic purpose. Most of the artists with

fig.19 Dante Gabriel Rossetti, *The Maids of Elfen-Mere*, engraved by the Dalziel Brothers 1855, woodcut 12.7 × 7.6 cm. Tate Gallery

whom we are concerned worked as illustrators, and for several this was a vital formative experience. Rossetti, Edward Burne-Jones, Simeon Solomon, Leighton and Frederick Sandys, among others, introduced what Paul Goldman in his discussion of Rossetti's *The Maids of Elfen-Mere* (fig.19), of 1855, has described as a 'heady mixture of sensuality and disquiet'.[8] The illustrators looked to the example of German art, historical and contemporary, with febrile results, and the designs they made were frequently re-worked or interpreted in paintings, their own and by other artists. In the late 1850s and early 1860s illustrators pioneered subject-matter which most painters would have approached with trepidation. Sandys, for example, was capable of truly disturbing images, such as that of *Until her Death* 1862, where a young woman converses with a mob-capped skeleton, or *Amor Mundi* (fig.6 on p.21) done as an illustration to Christina Rossetti's poem on the theme of death. The impact of these designs, which represented a new and powerful pictorial language, is witnessed by Rossetti's tender frontispiece for Christina Rossetti's book of poems *Goblin Market* (1862), *Golden Head by Golden Head* (no.32), having been taken up and adapted by Gustave Courbet in his painting of carnal lesbianism *Sleep* (Musée du Petit Palais, Paris) of 1866.

In 1855 Rossetti had been struck by how different the essentially continental style of Leighton's *Cimabue's Madonna* (Royal Collection) was to that which he and his fellow Pre-Raphaelites practised, as he wrote: 'The choice of subject, though interesting in a certain way, leaves one quite in the dark as to what faculty the man may have for representing incident or passionate emotion.'[9] What Rossetti called 'richness of arrangement' seemed to have obscured the painter's essential purpose of moving his spectator. Even more immaculate in their quality of finish were the paintings of the Roman model Anna Risi (known as Nanna) that Leighton made in 1859, but in these a quality of hermetic containment and emotional ambiguity was introduced which compelled the attention of the quondam Pre-Raphaelites. *Pavonia* (no.1), along with two other representations of Anna Risi, were shown at the Academy summer exhibition, and many were struck by their languorous and voluptuous quality. A woman of evident sexual power gazes unsmilingly upon the spectator. Of the three, F.G. Stephens was moved to write: '[Leighton's] heads of Italian women this year are worthy of a young old master, – so rapt, anything with more feeling, commanding or coldly beautiful, we have not seen for many a day.'[10] However, these paintings were also perplexing to a contemporary audience, because they defied the established classification of picture types. *Pavonia* could not be seen as a portrait, because it conveyed no clues to rank or personality, nor did it contain anecdotal elements to amuse and gratify the spectator. It was the very omission of the usual indicators as to how the painting was intended to be read that gave these works a disturbing psychological power.

It seems that Rossetti saw Leighton's 'La Nanna' series at the 1859 Academy exhibition. Probably with their example in mind, he began work in September 1859 on a painting entitled *Bocca Baciata* (no.2) and which was linked to a line in Boccacio: 'the mouth that has been kissed loses not its freshness.' Rossetti had by this time commenced his affair with Fanny Cornforth (who served as the model for *Bocca Baciata*), and a sexually suggestive quality hangs over this and Rossetti's subsequent paintings of her. In *Bocca Baciata* the model exercises her power of attraction upon the spectator, although she, like Leighton's Anna Risi, remains careless of the emotions she arouses. The background of the composition is filled with a mass of marigolds, while the foreground consists of a shelf or sill upon which the model's hands rest, along with an apple, symbol of sexual temptation.

That this painting was perceived as a celebration of sexual desire is indicated by Algernon Charles Swinburne's response to it. To William Bell Scott, he wrote: 'I daresay you have heard of his head in oils of a stunner with flowers in her hair, and marigolds behind it? She is more stunning than can be decently expressed.'[11] The painting belonged to George Price Boyce, a painter in the Aesthetic circle (fig.20); and the joke went round that he was wearing away the surface of the painting by himself kissing the image of the painted model. Others who saw the painting when it was exhibited at the Hogarth Club in 1861 were less delighted, for example the austere William Holman Hunt who accused Rossetti of 'gross sensuality', going on to explain: 'I would not speak so … of it were it not that I see Rossetti is advocating as a principal the mere gratification of the eye if any passion at all – the animal passions to be the aim of art.'[12]

fig.20 Interior view of West House, home of George Price Boyce; *Bocca Baciata* third from left on lower row

If *Bocca Baciata* is seen as a symbol of desire, its counterpart as an essay on the theme of death is *Beata Beatrix* (no.44), painted some time after Elizabeth Siddal's tragic death in February 1862. Ostensibly a subject from Dante's *Vita Nuova*, the painting is filled with emblematic references to Dante's longing for his departed Beatrice, and thus serves in parallel as Rossetti's memorial to his lost wife. Rossetti was later to explain how the painting was to 'be viewed not as a representation of the incident of the death of Beatrice, but as an ideal of the subject, symbolised by a trance or sudden spiritual transfiguration. Beatrice is rapt visibly into Heaven, seeing as it were through shut lids … "Him who is Blessed throughout all ages".'[13] If in one sense *Bocca Baciata* and *Beata Beatrix* are antitheses, as fleshly and spiritual personifications respectively, they are both utterly remote from actuality in their subject-matter.

In 1868 Swinburne identified polarities of 'sensual beauty and spiritual, the siren and the sibyl'[14] in Rossetti's work. *Lady Lilith* (no.6) represented the former category, its sexual character overtly stated by Swinburne: 'Her head leans back sleepily, superb and satiate with its own beauty; the eyes are languid, without love in them or hate; the sweet luxurious mouth has the patience of pleasure fulfilled and complete, the warm repose of passion sure of its delight.'[15] The second painting, *Sibylla Palmifera* (Lady Lever Art Gallery, Port Sunlight), was intended by contrast as a representation of 'soul's beauty', and was seen by Swinburne as 'a head of serene and spiritual beauty, severe and tender, with full and heavy hair falling straight in grave sweet lines, not like Lilith's, exuberant of curl and coil.'[16]

fig.21 J.A.M. Whistler, *The White Girl (Symphony in White, No.1)* 1862, oil on canvas 214.7 × 108 cm. National Gallery of Art, Washington DC. Harris Whittemore Collection

Whistler's painting of his Irish mistress Jo Hiffernan, *The White Girl* (fig.21), was painted in Paris in the winter of 1861–2. Rejected at the 1862 Royal Academy, it was shown instead at a private gallery in Berners Street. English responses to *The White Girl* reveal how critics instinctively looked for literary pretexts for paintings. F.G. Stephens, for example, was disappointed to find that although 'the face was well done … it is not that of Mr Wilkie Collins's *Woman in White*'.[17] With a tone of assumed outrage, Whistler denied that he had even read the book, but insisted instead that the painting 'simply represents a girl dressed in white standing in front of a white curtain'.[18] Clearly the issue of whether the painting borrowed its theme from a popular novel of the day was a diversion, rebuffed by Whistler for the sake of publicity. However, the stance that he assumed of insisting on the formal qualities of the painting has distracted from its undoubted dependence on the manipulation of mood by symbolical means. When a year later the painting was shown at the Salon des Refusés, French critics read the motifs of the white dress, the menacing wolf mask, and the dropped posy of flowers, in symbolical terms, usually as an oblique reference to first sexual experience, in the words of Jules Antoine Castagnary, 'that troubling moment when the young woman questions herself and is astonished at no longer recognising in herself the virginity of the night before'.[19] Even more telling was the response of fellow painters in Paris, notably Gustave Courbet, who it was reported by Henri Fantin-Latour to Whistler was deriding the picture as 'an apparition, with a spiritual content',[20] thus rejecting its claim as a work of realism.

If contemporaries saw the undressed state of the girl's red hair in *The White Girl* as the record of sexual intimacy, it is hard to imagine that Whistler himself would not have anticipated such a response. The painter was in fact responding to ideas about the power of imagery to spark associations in the mind of the spectator current in London in the early 1860s. It is the very ambiguity of its allusion – the sense which is given of veiled meaning, but the avoidance of conscious allegory, and the way in which the image resists investigation, which makes it a seminal work in the emergence of English symbolism.

Whistler's second painting of Jo (no.15), entitled *The Little White Girl* when he succeeded in having it admitted to the Royal Academy in 1865, and in which the model is seen standing before the fireplace in the house they shared in Lindsey Row, is again more than just a formal figurative subject but one in which there is, in Richard Dorment's words, a 'sense of mystery and ambiguity, the suggestion of a story there to be told'.[21] Swinburne was the first to attempt to read the painting's symbolical sub-text, for his poem 'Before the Mirror' was inspired by it. Whistler received Swinburne's poem with delight, having the verses printed on gold paper which was laid on to the flat of the frame (see fig.22).[22] This exploration into the painting's inner meaning in an autonomous form is the classic example of the type of synaesthesia – the interchangeability and agreement of mood between works with corresponding texts but in different media, which was such a characteristic product of the Aesthetic movement. Because the poem had been endorsed by the artist, we can assume that when Swinburne enquires 'Behind the veil, forbidden, | Shut up from sight, | Love, is there sorrow hidden, | Is there delight?' he is responding as Whistler intended he should. The symbolic tragedy of the painting is summarised in the poem's last verse:

fig.22 Early photograph of J.A.M. Whistler's *Symphony in White, No.2: The Little White Girl* 1864 (no.15). Courtesy Sotheby's

> Face fallen and white throat lifted,
> With sleepless eye
> She sees old loves that drifted,
> She knew not why

As Courbet had perceived *The White Girl* as the representation of something supernatural, Swinburne could write to Whistler of 'the sad and glad mystery in the face languidly contemplative of its own phantom and all other things seen by their phantoms', an idea which he insisted 'was entirely and only suggested to me by the picture'.[23] The girl, who appears young and graceful as she stands before a looking-glass, seems old and haggard in her mirrored reflection.

During the 1860s Burne-Jones painted a series of watercolours, some of them of the subjectless type of which he, along with Rossetti and Leighton, was a pioneer, others treating literary and mythological themes in which he found echoes of his own sexual anxieties and preoccupations. His drawing of *Sidonia von Bork* 1860 (no.20), was inspired by Wilhelm Meinhold's romance, translated as *Sidonia the Sorceress* by Lady Wilde in 1849. The heroine was a woman of such extraordinary beauty that all who encountered her fell in love; and the power that she thus gained she used with the utmost cruelty, destroying those who sought her favours. Rossetti, who had previously introduced the poetic image of 'sweet pain' to his translation of Dante's *La Vita Nuova*, was captivated by the way in which beauty and evil were interwoven in *Sidonia*; while Burne-Jones's intimate friend Swinburne talked and wrote freely about the 'pleasure that is palpable in pain'.[24] G.P. Boyce, in a diary entry for 16 August 1862, described how he 'joined Rossetti at Swinburne's rooms, where they were looking over "Justine," by the Marquis de Sade, recent acquisition of the latter'.[25] Interest in (and in the case of Swinburne the practice of) sado-masochistic sex was intense; and there is clear evidence in Burne-Jones's early paintings that he also was fascinated by female types of menacing and sinister sexual power.

In 1864 Burne-Jones painted a watercolour entitled *Green Summer* (fig.23), which conveys something of the happy life that he and his wife Georgiana lived together, but which is spliced with a darker and more fateful character. A female figure reads aloud to a group of companions who are seen seated on a flower-strewn lawn. The passivity of the figures, whose inactive forms are reduced by the painter to a pattern of line and colour, is an instance of how painters during the classicising phase of the early Aesthetic movement sought to simplify and abstract their compositions. Nonetheless, there is here, as in Millais's *Spring*, a feeling of impending misfortune, and the watercolour has an undefinable but tragic atmosphere. It comes as no surprise to realise that the composition originated in a design for the decoration of a piano, the arrangement described by Georgiana Burne-Jones as 'Death, veiled and crowned, standing outside the gate of a garden where a number of girls, unconscious of his approach, are resting and listening to music'.[26] If in *Green Summer* the figure of Death has been omitted, the spectator is left to wonder what will interrupt the continuum of sight and sound and what the fate of the figures will be.

fig.23 Edward Burne-Jones, *Green Summer* 1864, bodycolour 29 × 48.3 cm. Courtesy of Sotheby's

Burne-Jones's watercolour *The Lament* (no.25) is on one level a purely formal figurative arrangement in an architectural setting, and is as close as the artist comes to the 'subjectless' compositional type characteristic of Aesthetic classicism of the 1860s. However, mood remains the artist's objective, and here we find a scene of outright despair, apparently brought on by the playing of music. Once again, as in Whistler's *The White Girl*, an unspecified loss or bereavement is indicated by flowers cast down on the pavement.

fig.24 Edward Burne-Jones, *The Wine of Circe* 1863–9, watercolour and bodycolour 70 × 101.5 cm. Private Collection

During the course of the 1860s a virulent debate about the suitability of sexual themes as the subject for poetry and painting came about. Advanced opinion held that since art had no function to inculcate a moral code, it followed that the creative artist might refer to any kind of amorous or sexual activity without moral censure. Again, those who wanted to loose themselves from the shackles of Victorian morality looked to French example. When in 1866 Swinburne published *Poems and Ballads* he caused outrage for their perceived immorality and references to necrophilia, lesbianism and hermaphroditism, among other illicit sexual practices. Moxon, the publisher, took fright and withdrew the book from circulation. In due course it was reissued with an accompanying pamphlet entitled 'Notes on Poems and Reviews' in which Swinburne made an impassioned plea – one of the first of its kind in the English language – for the artist's right to treat whatever themes or subject-matter he chooses, and lambasting those who 'demand from one thing the qualities of another – who seek for sermons in sonnets and morality in music'.[27]

Critics were baffled to know how to react to paintings the subjects of which seemed calculated in their attack on the proprieties of contemporary life. In 1869 the French critic Philippe Burty resorted to a literary comparison in his account of Burne-Jones's *The Wine of Circe* (fig.24): 'a painting of the greatest worth: for the mood, which is as disturbing and even more powerful than in certain parts of Baudelaire's *Fleurs du Mal*; and for the treatment, which is masterful. It is in this that one must judge this most gifted artist.'[28] A less favourable response to the watercolour in the *Art Journal* concluded that Burne-Jones's work belonged 'to the realm of dreams, myths, nightmares, and other phantasms of diseased imagination,' while his talent, though 'distinguished', was 'abnormal and perverted'.[29] The ominous and disturbing *Wine of Circe*, which shows the mythological sorceress preparing food and wine for the sailors of Odysseus which when it is consumed will cause them to be transformed into swine, was according to John Christian[30] intended as a commentary on the greed and selfishness of the philistine; for, in the words of Burne-Jones's close friend and mentor John Ruskin, 'the transforming poisons she gives to men are mixed with … pure and right nourishment … it is their own fault if these make swine of them.'[31] Even if few people understood the implication of the theme, the painting was nonetheless a calculated attack on the self-satisfaction and heartlessness of the age.

fig.25 Edward Burne-Jones, *Phyllis and Demophoön* 1870, watercolour and bodycolour 91.5 × 45.8 cm. Birmingham City Museums and Art Gallery

Burne-Jones's mood was becoming darker and more anguished. *Phyllis and Demophoön* (fig.25), which mythological subject he exhibited in 1870, revealed his own emotional and spiritual plight with utter candour. The figure of Phyllis emerges from the trunk of an almond tree to cast her arms around Demophoön, the lover who has announced his desire to be free of her. The watercolour caused outrage or distress, according to the sympathy of the individual for Burne-Jones's cause. In the first place, the nudity of the male figure was offensive to conservative opinion – representations of the male genitalia were simply not considered appropriate for display at the Old Water-Colour Society. Critics were disturbed by an amorous subject in which the female protagonist plays the active role and in which the male shrinks and hesitates, a contrast which may have seemed to question the reliability of male libido. However, it was the recognition by Burne-

Jones's friends of the figure of Phyllis as having been modelled on that of a young girl called Maria Zambaco with whom the painter had fallen in love, and the way in which the chosen mythological subject paralleled his relationship with her, that gave the watercolour a particular significance. For Burne-Jones, a type of art that denied personal associations in its ostensible subject was virtually impossible; instead, he looked to mythology for subject-matter in which he might explore his own emotional predicament and state of mind.

The watercolours that Burne-Jones showed at the Old Water-Colour Society from 1864 until 1870 were especially influential on the younger painters who exhibited at the Dudley Gallery following its inception in 1865. The summer exhibitions of watercolours and drawings, held at the Egyptian Hall in Piccadilly, were open to all comers rather than just to a group of members and associates, and therefore represented an opportunity for a wide circle of younger and professionally disestablished artists. The organisers made no attempt to monitor or regulate the standard or suitability of entries, and therefore artists who were diverging from the conventions of treatment and subject-matter which prevailed in the more prestigious exhibition spaces of the day felt at home. It is perhaps misleading to talk about a Dudley clique because the exhibitions were so large and miscellaneous. However, it is clear from the reminiscences of the artists and from published reviews of the exhibitions that there was a particular painting style that was readily identified with the Dudley. Walter Crane described how the group of painters of which he became part in the second half of the 1860s found in Burne-Jones's watercolours 'a magic world of romance and pictured poetry … a twilight world of dark mysterious woodlands, haunted streams, [and] meads of deep green, starred with burning flowers, veiled in a dim and mystic light'.[32] This quality of detachment from anything mundane or prosaic may be seen as characteristic of the artists of the group. Robert Bateman was regarded as the leader of what was sometimes referred to as the 'poetry without grammar'[33] school, and works by him such as *Three Women Plucking Mandrakes* (no.18) (a bizarre enough subject, showing the elaborate procedure required to harvest the vegetable that grows only where men have been hanged) also have a sinister quality 'removed … from common life and ordinary experience, [and] significant of something beyond the usual course of nature'.[34] Even the characteristic Dudley landscape style (described by the *Art Journal* as 'dreaminess instead of definiteness, and smudginess in place of sentiment'[35]) was remote and other-worldly, and was likely to be the setting for weird events and unnatural practices. Some Dudley artists progressed to membership of the prestigious art institutions of the day, but Bateman, Crane, and particularly Simeon Solomon, were beyond the academic pale.

Simeon Solomon was a regular exhibitor at the Dudley Gallery, and one who, according to the *Art Journal* in 1869, 'stands alone, although signs appear of a new and rising school in which he might shine'.[36] Three years later Solomon sent *Love in Autumn* (no.12) to the Dudley winter exhibition of oil paintings, where it was described as a 'mythological conceit … so enigmatical as to leave us in doubt as to its reading'.[37] Solomon's homosexuality was well known in the Chelsea circle that formed around Rossetti in the 1860s. Swinburne and he were famous for their naked cavorting through Tudor House (although this was not approved of

fig.26 Simeon Solomon, *The Bride, the Bridegroom and Sad Love* 1865, pencil 24.8 × 17.1 cm. Trustees of the Victoria and Albert Museum

by their host Gabriel Rossetti), and for their lewd exchanges. However ambiguous the meaning of *Love in Autumn* – which shows a boy with cupid's wings clutching a drapery to himself in protection from an autumn gust – drawings such as *The Bride, the Bridegroom and Sad Love* (fig.26), in which a naked youth fondles the parts of his erstwhile lover (once again a winged cupid) as his bride draws him to her, were clearly intended for an audience who relished the theme of physical love between boys and men.

In 1871 Swinburne wrote an essay on Solomon's painting and poetry in which their sexual character, even when cloaked in mystery and strangeness, is explicitly stated.[38] Of Solomon's 'mystic and symbolic'[39] paintings Swinburne found 'the latent relations of pain and pleasure, the subtle conspiracies of good with evil, the deep alliances of death and life, of love and hate, of attraction and abhorrence'.[40] Once again comparison is made between the work of an English painter and the poems of Baudelaire, 'most loving of all students of strange beauty and abnormal refinement, of painful pleasures of soul and inverted raptures of sense',[41] but in the 'mixture of utmost delicacy with a fine cruelty in some of the faces of the fair feminine youth' the doctrine of 'a philosopher of the material school' – the Marquis de Sade – is also invoked. Perhaps Swinburne was pressing his audience too far. Solomon acknowledged the 'full beauty of the paper and the great honor that has been done me by the most brilliant of our writers', but sounded a note of caution: 'You know, of course, my dear Algernon, that, by many, my designs and pictures executed during the last three or four years have been looked upon with suspicion.'[42]

The late 1860s and early 1870s saw the flowering of English Aestheticism, of which the principle of 'art for art's sake' was the rallying cry. Rather than seeking to interpret or explain the literal meaning of a work of art, critics attempted to identify abstract qualities which might be applied across the range of artistic creativity. In 1868 Swinburne compared paintings by G.F. Watts and Albert Moore to works of sculpture and music. Watts's *The Wife of Pygmalion* (fig.27) was a '"translation" of a Greek statue into an English picture', allowing the spectator to see how 'a picture may share the gracious grandeur of a statue, [and] a statue may catch something of the subtle bloom of beauty proper to a picture'.[43] Moore's *Azaleas* (no.11) was, according to Swinburne, 'to artists what the verse of Théophile Gautier is to poets; the faultless and secure expression of an exclusive worship of things formally beautiful ... The melody of colour, the symphony of form is complete: one more beautiful thing is achieved, one more delight is born into the world; and its meaning is beauty; and its reason for being is to be'.[44]

fig.27 G.F. Watts, *The Wife of Pygmalion* 1868, oil on canvas 66 × 53.3 cm. Faringdon Collection, Buscot Park

Even so, paintings were often used as vehicles for the artist to express his own desires and anxieties, and mythological themes in particular lent themselves to the recasting of events from the artist's own experience or fantasy. The four paintings of the Pygmalion Series (no.38), which originated in designs for illustrations for William Morris's poem cycle 'The Earthly Paradise' in the mid-1860s, were again deliberate or unconscious commentaries on Burne-Jones's love affair with Maria Zambaco, which lasted until 1871. Burne-Jones is here imagining what it might be to make by his artistry a woman, as Pygmalion created Galatea, who would be the fulfilment of all desires and who would be under the absolute control of her creator. The irony is that Maria was the opposite, making demands upon Burne-Jones that he was unwilling or incapable of fulfilling. Watts was presumably identifying with the Ovidian legend in a like spirit when he painted his *The Wife of Pygmalion*, remembering the unhappy time he had spent with another wilful and spirited woman, the actress Ellen Terry to whom he was married for a brief period in 1864.

The Royal Academy summer exhibition of 1869 contained a number of works which combine classical form with subjects suggestive of sexual attraction and the fear of death. Some took their themes from ancient mythology; others were entirely imaginary. Leighton was on the exhibition hanging committee, and his influence perhaps assisted Sandys in gaining a place for a work which had been accepted but not hung the previous year, presumably because its sinister subject was too much for conservative sensibilities. This *Medea* (no.47) shows the sorceress preparing a poisoned garment to kill the woman who had supplanted her in the affections of Jason. Swinburne had described it in the following terms: 'Pale as from poison, with the blood drawn back from her very lips, agonized in face and limbs with the labour and the fierce contention of old love with new, of a daughter's love with a bride's, the fatal figure of Medea pauses a ittle on the funereal verge of the wood of death ... The picture is grand alike for wealth of symbol and solemnity of beauty.'[45] In 1869 Burty recognised its kinship to the work of Rossetti, finding 'the same bizarre and archaic style, the same singular accumulation of details'.[46] The *Art Journal* was disconcerted by the painting, but conceded that 'as representative of a style which is sufficiently distinctive, it is well that the work should be seen, and thus possibly appreciated by a select few'.[47]

fig.28 Frederic, Lord Leighton, *Helios and Rhodos* c.1869, oil on canvas 166.8 × 108 cm. Tate Gallery

Themes from ancient mythology were treated at the 1869 Academy with a passion and urgency that made them thrilling. Perhaps the most extraordinary and powerful of all was Leighton's weird and supernatural realisation *Helios and Rhodos* (fig.28). The sun deity Helios is seen embracing the nymph Rhodos, who was to be the mother by him of seven sons, the Heliades. The painting was seen in some quarters as sensual, and an anonymous critic in the *Spectator* compared it to 'Mr Swinburne's maddest verses',[48] which as Alison Smith has analysed[49] was a reference to Leighton's representation of female sexual desire, and which was deeply shocking to conservative opinion. At the same exhibition Leighton placed his own *Electra at the Tomb of Agamemnon* (Ferens Art Gallery, Hull), which showed the heroine of Aeschylus' *The Oresteia* vowing to revenge her father's death at the hands of her mother, Clytemnestra, in conjunction with Watts's *Orpheus and Eurydice* (no.37), where Orpheus attempts to save his dying wife as she sinks back into the Underworld. Neither Leighton nor Watts betrays himself on this occasion to the cosmetic blandness or the allegorical vapidity to which they were, respectively, prone.

Works without ostensible subject, but which are nonetheless imbued with an atmosphere of sexual enticement, at the 1869 Academy included George Heming Mason's *Girls Dancing* (fig.29). Burty found Mason 'the landscapist who touched me most deeply. He introduces to his vistas something that is vibrant and impassioned ... He has a feeling for romantic colour, and a quality of light which fills the open spaces and loses itself beneath the leaves like the waves of sound of a

fig.29 George Heming Mason, *Girls Dancing: A Pastoral Symphony* 1869, oil on canvas 68.5 × 180.3 cm. Private Collection

shepherd's song'.[50] Mason's beautiful but elusive painting was one of a group in the exhibition in which the *Art Journal* found 'manifest the idealism and the realism, the romance and the naturalism, which are so strangely blended in certain new phases of the English school; to these characteristics may be added signs of the growing sway of continental styles, together with tendency to intensity of sentiment, and to a sustained rhapsody of colour.'[51] The *Saturday Review* recognised the sophistication of advanced English painting when it pronounced: 'We mark for better and for worse a tendency to exchange naturalism for idealism, to substitute individual forms for generic types, [and] to surrender styles which were illusive to the eye in favour of treatments which appeal to the imagination.'[52] Clearly, by this time a style of art which was remote from mundane experience was coming to the fore.

The turn of the 1870s saw one of the periodic bouts of moralistic retrenchment which mark English public life in the nineteenth century. Emotions connected with physical love and anxieties about death, which in the 1860s had insinuated themselves into painting and poetry, were causing concern among the philistines. Burne-Jones's resignation from the Old Water-Colour Society in response to complaints about his watercolour *Phyllis and Demophoön* is a clear indication of a new determination on the part of the self-appointed guardians of taste to stand against sexually informed works of art in public display; while Simeon Solomon's acknowledgement in his letter to Swinburne that his works were 'looked upon with suspicion' indicates a certain tenseness among artists who sought to experiment with themes of fear and desire, even at a time when superficially the barricades of Victorian morality appeared to be breaking. On all sides there was concern that art and literature had the power to corrupt, as well as providing evidence of corruption. In 1877 Walter Pater suppressed the 'Conclusion' of his *The Renaissance*, which contained the edict of intensity 'To burn always with this hard, gemlike flame, to maintain this ecstasy, is success in life',[53] and he did so on the grounds that 'it might possibly mislead some of those young men into whose hands it might fall'.[54]

Robert Buchanan's article 'The Fleshly School of Poetry' of 1871 amounted to a scurrilous attack on Rossetti's painting and poetry. Buchanan, under an assumed identity which was soon exposed by those in the Aesthetic circle who had previously encountered his mendacity and jealousy, found in Rossetti's work 'the same thinness and transparence of design, the same combination of the simple and grotesque, the same morbid deviation from healthy forms of life, the same sense of weary, wasting, yet exquisite sensuality; nothing virile, nothing tender, nothing completely sane'.[55] The assault, although responded to and effectively rebuffed, served to drive the progressive movement in painting and poetry underground.

The emergence of a radical and risk-taking faction within English art was interrupted, even in a sense aborted, in the 1870s, and forms of art that treated themes of love and death, in which movement we see the emergence of a style which is analogous to that which among European artists has come to be called Symbolism, disappeared from view. Rossetti's paintings had been castigated as coarse and sensual since the time of *Bocca Baciata*, and he hardly ever sent paintings to exhibitions from the time of the demise of the Hogarth Club in 1861. The

Buchanan attack of 1871 shattered any remaining desire for contact with the outside world, so in 1877 he refused to participate in the Grosvenor exhibitions and gradually subsided into drug and alcohol addiction. Simeon Solomon was excluded absolutely from artistic life following his conviction for homosexual offences in 1873; while Frederick Sandys turned to portraiture following a financial crisis in 1868 (commercial prospects for progressive painters had been getting steadily worse since 'Black Friday' on 11 May 1866), and a falling out with Rossetti in 1869. William Blake Richmond likewise cultivated his portrait practice following the cool reception given to his male nude subject, *Bowl Players* (private collection), at the 1871 Royal Academy.[56] It was not just that these artists found the conditions and character of the various exhibition spaces of the day unsympathetic; they also feared critical attack on the grounds of the perceived immorality of their works.

The eventual exception to this pattern of voluntary or enforced exclusion was Burne-Jones. He also had almost entirely withdrawn from public display, just showing a handful of works at the Dudley Gallery in 1873 and otherwise preferring to rely on an inner circle of collectors who appreciated his intentions. However, in 1877 he was catapulted from obscurity to celebrity by the publicity that attached to his display of eight paintings at the first Grosvenor exhibition. Many of his undoubted masterpieces were still to come, but as their scale increased and they became more carefully crafted, something of their intensity was lost.

The issue of how paintings might transmit their themes, either by ostensible or subliminal means, which in the 1860s had caused artists to experiment with works which defied narrative interpretation, or in which they adopted literary and mythological subjects in search of themes which echoed their own anxieties and passions and in which the unstated private dimension gives resonance and individuality to the work, tends to give way in the 1870s to a polarity between 'subjectless' paintings that sank to the level of mere decoration, and prosaic reconstructions of mythological themes. Advanced artists turned to landscape – Whistler, for example, but also various too-little appreciated artists of the rising generation such as Cecil Gordon Lawson – in which sphere they might explore their own subjective responses to their surroundings, and ignore the demands of those who believed that the first duty of art was to be comprehensible.

Welby has written of the decline in creative intensity among poets in the period: 'Victorian Romanticism by, or soon after, 1870 is condemned to death, but with an "indefinite reprieve" which proved to be long.'[57] Likewise, the moment seemed to have passed when artists sought to manipulate the spectator by psychological means, to tantalise his interest in what is being represented by making the subject mysterious or oblique, or by representing figures and their settings as remote and unfamiliar symbols. The instincts towards intrigue and subversiveness that were manifest in the work of various groups of artists in the 1860s, were dissipated as the artists themselves were either defeated by or received into the artistic establishment of the day and as they forgot the sense of excitement and urgency that had imbued the works of their youth. Nonetheless, the burning intensity of artistic experience in the 1860s was not forgotten, and was rekindled in the late century, by the poets, illustrators and painters of the Decadence.

Symbolism – A French Monopoly?

MaryAnne Stevens

> the battle of Symbolism was never fought out in English[1]

In his dedication to W.B. Yeats dated 'June 1899, London' printed at the front of *The Symbolist Movement in Literature*,[2] Arthur Symons admitted that 'France is the country of movements, and it is naturally in France that I have studied the development of a principle [i.e. Symbolism]'.[3] The writer, more fully informed of nineteenth-century French literature than even Walter Pater or Charles Swinburne, then proceeded in his introductory chapter to this study of the Symbolist movement (which ranged from Gérard de Nerval to Stéphane Mallarmé and Maurice Maeterlinck) to identify the central characteristic of this French 'principle'. To do so, he grounded his understanding of the meaning of 'symbol' in a definition given by Thomas Carlyle in *Sartor Resartus*:

> 'In the symbol proper, what we call a symbol, there is, more or less distinctly and directly, some embodiment and revelation of the infinite; the infinite is made to blend with the finite, to stand visible, or as it were, attainable there.' It is in such a sense as this that the word symbolism has been used to describe a movement which, during the last generation, has profoundly influenced the course of French literature.[4]

Symons's focus upon the literary aspect of Symbolism in France is explained in part through his personal affinity with that artistic form. More particularly it reveals his extensive knowledge of French contemporary writing[5] and his understanding of the primacy of literature in defining the movement. Despite myriad attempts to identify the genesis of Symbolism and to craft a workable definition applicable to all art forms – from literature to music and the visual arts[6] – of whatever national origin, it was in Paris on 18 September 1886 that the movement, in its most austere form, was defined. Jean Moréas, the poet of 'Syrtes' and 'Les Cantilènes' and co-author with Paul Adam of 'Thé chez Miranda', had been invited by the newspaper, *Le Figaro*, to 'formulate … for the readers of the *Supplément* [*Le Figaro littéraire*] the fundamental principles of the new manifestation of art.'[7] The 'new manifestation' of art to which the editor referred was defined by Moréas in the ensuing article, 'Le Symbolisme'. After reviewing the cyclical nature of all schools of literature, which thus justified the appearance of a new school in the wake of naturalism,[8] 'to which one can seriously accord a value only as a legitimate but poorly focused movement of protest against the mawkishness of certain fashionable story tellers', Moréas proclaimed the existence of a new school of literature: 'Symbolism'.

The subject-matter of this new literary movement was no longer external nature for its own sake, but rather the 'Idea'. This proposition required Moréas to develop three supplementary points: to define the Idea; to explain its relationship

to the objective, mundane world, and to establish a new formal structure by which the Idea would best be expressed. Symbolism was concerned with the expression of 'primordial ideas'. Negatively, these could not be manifested through 'didactic verse, declamatory prose, false sensibility, objective description'. Rather Symbolism sought, through 'external nature, human actions, concrete phenomena' to give an intimation of the Idea, of profound human emotions, of the workings of the soul. All manifestations of the external world, be they physical or psychological, were mere vehicles for the revelation of the Idea. Thus, while it was imperative that 'symbolist poetry seeks to clothe the idea in tangible form, it must, nonetheless, not have this as an end in itself but merely use it as a means to reveal the idea'. This proposition forced Moréas to caution against establishing too close an analogy between the concrete object in the external world and its metaphysical equivalent, the Idea. Instead, the very existence of the Idea invited myriad, developmental interpretations. It demanded that it reveal itself slowly, elliptically: 'The Idea ... should never make its appearance deprived of the sumptuous trappings of external analogies, for the essential nature of symbolist art is never going straight to the conception of the Idea itself.' In formal terms, the retention of these 'sumptuous trappings of external analogies' was guaranteed by a new literary style which was both 'archetypal and complex'.[9]

Denunciation and advocacy of Moréas's definition of literary Symbolism followed hard on its publication. Anatole France, for example, found Moréas's exposition incomprehensible: 'All that I can distill [from this definition] is that the symbolist poet is allowed neither to describe nor to name [anything]'.[10] To provide enlightenment to Anatole France, and like-minded sceptics, Gustave Kahn published, on the front page of the daily newspaper, *l'Evénement*, his 'Réponse des Symbolistes'. Author, critic, editor of the avant-garde review, *La Revue Indépendante*, and contributor to the review[11] which provided a seedbed for Symbolism in France, *La Revue Wagnérienne*, Kahn laid out far more coherently than Moréas the new movement's form and content. Kahn dismissed the naturalist literature of Zola, the de Goncourt brothers and the early novels of J.-K. Huysmans, declaring that the Symbolists were:

> tired of the quotidien, the near-at-hand, the contemporaneous; we wish to be able to place the development of the symbol in any period, and even in outright dreams (dreams being indistinguishable from life). We want to substitute for the battle of individuals, the battle of feelings and ideas ... the essential aim of our art is to objectify the subjective (the exteriorisation of the Idea) in place of subjectifying the objective (nature seen through the temperament).

Such a revolutionary programme demanded, as Moréas had already demonstrated, a new literary form. Unlike Moréas, however, who qualified his call for an 'archetypal and complex' style with a sequence of definitional phrases strongly coloured by decadent vocabulary,[12] Kahn stated:

opposite
detail from Gustave Moreau *Oedipe Voyageur (L'Egalité devant la mort)* c.1888 (no.54)

> We will give back to the novel the right to use free verse, to accentuate the power of declamation; the tendency is towards a poem in prose which is

very flexible, its line set in differing rhythms according to the pace, the oscillation, the turnings and the simplicity of the Idea.

The year following Gustave Kahn's more transparent articulation of the Symbolist literary programme, its author appointed Edouard Dujardin, author, critic, and co-founder of *La Revue Wagnérienne* in 1884, to the editorship of *La Revue Indépendante*. Dujardin was closely linked to a côterie of young, radical artists, one of whom, Emile Bernard, had declared in the autumn of 1886 that he was rejecting all traditional and contemporary styles of painting in order to create an art in which 'ideas dominate the technique of painting'.[13] Drawing upon the declarations of Moréas and Kahn, Dujardin turned his attention to the visual arts, and provided a definition of pictorial symbolism in a review of the annual exhibition of the Belgian avant-garde group, Les XX, held in Brussels in the spring of 1888: 'Aux XX et aux Indépendents – le Cloisonnisme'.[14] Confronted with the bold outlines, the flat colour fields and the dominant colour cast of three paintings by Bernard's close associate Louis Anquetin, *Morning: The Boat*, *Noon: The Harvest* and *Evening: Boulevard de Clichy* (fig.30), Dujardin declared:

fig.30 Louis Anquetin, *Evening: Boulevard de Clichy* 1887 oil on canvas 69.2 × 53.3 cm. Wadsworth Atheneum, Hartford, Connecticut. The Ella Gallup Sumner and Mary Catlin Sumner Collection Fund

> The point of departure [for these paintings] is a symbolic form of art. In painting, just as much as in literature, the representation of nature is an illusion; ... According to logic, the system of representing nature ends by making a farce of the ultimate objective of art. As opposed to this, the aim of painting, of literature is to express through the specific tools of painting and literature, the *feeling* [author's stress] of things; what ought to be expressed is not the objective image, but the *character* [author's stress] ... One must grasp the essential image, reproduce it – or, better still, produce it.

Dujardin's understanding that, like literary Symbolism, the subject matter of this new art demanded the forging of a new formal pictorial language echoes Téodor de Wyzéwa's call in 1886 for a new form of painting, 'Wagnerian painting',[15] and Paul Gauguin's tentative enunciation the year before of a new, non-naturalist art. In a letter from Copenhagen to his fellow 'Sunday painter', Emile Schuffenecker, Gauguin dismisses the ambition of art slavishly to describe external nature or express literary meaning. Rather, through the most simple means, the artist must search out symbolic line and colour which will express feelings, great emotions:

> Work freely and passionately, that is how you will make progress ... Above all, do not *perspire* [author's stress] over a painting; a great emotion can be translated immediately, dream on it and look for the most simple form in which to clothe it.[16]

Gauguin was to realise this programme fully in the late summer of 1888 when he created the *Vision after the Sermon* (fig.31). Here the artist cast in the role of the priest creates the vision of Jacob wrestling with the Angel for the assembled, praying Breton peasants. In order to remove any reference to overt description of the external world, Gauguin placed the scene upon a flattened, non-naturalist, red background, and described the protagonists of both the wrestling figures and

fig.31 Paul Gauguin, *Vision after the Sermon* 1888, oil on canvas 73 × 92 cm. National Gallery of Scotland

the praying peasants in harsh outline and flattened colour infill, thus denying any reference to realist, three-dimensional space. It was on the basis of an analysis of this painting that the young poet and critic, and friend of Gauguin, Bernard and Auquetin, Albert Aurier, provided a more fully elaborated definition of pictorial Symbolism. Published in the *Mercure de France* in 1891, Aurier's article, *'le Symbolisme en peinture – Paul Gauguin'* (Symbolism in painting – Paul Gauguin), attributed five characteristics to the new art: ideist, symbolist, synthetic, subjective and decorative. Central to an understanding of the significance of this definition was the affinity which Aurier's terminology has with the literary symbolist manifestos of Moréas and Kahn: the use of the symbol as physical manifestation of the new subject-matter of art, the Idea; the subjective apprehension ('the objectification of the subjective'[17]) of the relationship between the external object and the Idea, and the indefinable nature of the Idea. Aurier deliberately used the term *idéiste* as opposed to the more finite *idéaliste*, which implied an absolute definition that the Symbolist programme specifically sought to eschew.[18] Effectively, Aurier laid out a programme which sanctioned the subjective and hence individualistic apprehension of the Idea, and the open-ended vagueness of the Idea as the new subject of art. In both of these respects, Albert Aurier echoed the definitions of Symbolism provided by Jean Moréas, Gustave Kahn and Edouard Dujardin.

For many, the absence of proscriptive means and ends suggested that Symbolism was 'anarchic': 'What gives the strength to the symbolist theory is precisely its anarchy. It demands of the poet not only that he be significant, that is to say, individual, and that he reveal himself in thought and emotion by images as general as possible. Yes, the symbolist is the anarchist of literature.'[19] This vagueness also provided the scope for writers such as Stéphane Mallarmé to explore what was to become, by default, the focus of Symbolism, namely the exploration of the process by which the Idea is revealed. For it was with this process that the creative impulse of the poet or painter was ultimately concerned, and so it was here that the essence of the work of art lay:

> The Parnassians take a thing and describe it completely; in so doing they lack mystery, they deprive the mind of the delicious joy of believing that it too is creating. To *name* [*sic*] an object is to suppress three-quarters of the pleasure of the poem, which consists in the delight of gradual realisation. To *suggest* [author's stress] it, that is the dream. It is the perfect use of this mystery that constitutes the symbol: to evoke an object bit by bit in order to reveal a state of soul; or inversely to choose an object and disengage from it a state of soul by a process of deciphering.[20]

Mallarmé's emphasis upon the process of suggestion implied a new relationship between writer and reader, where the latter was invited to enter into collusion with the former in order to complete the work of art. This position was reflected in both the theoretical writing and the visual art of Odilon Redon where the suggestive role of art as intimator of Truth was manifested in the artist's seemingly hallucinatory juxtaposition of realistically described objects and in the dialogue established between caption and image, most notably in his suites of lithographs created from 1879.[21]

The rejection of naturalism

Jean Moréas had opened his manifesto for Symbolism with the assertion that all art was cyclical. Hence his rejection of the naturalism which currently dominated French literature. To understand more clearly why the Symbolists were bound to reject the productions of Zola and the de Goncourt brothers, it is necessary not only to examine the nature of this dismissal in greater detail but also to review the philosophical and literary sources which were identifed as giving credence to their innovative programme.

The protest of the 1880s had as its leitmotif a rejection of the modern world, of nature as recorded by Courbet, the Realists and the Impressionists, by Zola and the early Huysmans. By the 1860s, industrialisation had swept across Europe, bringing in its wake the benefits and horrors of modern society. Materialism became the dominant social ethos, Positivism the dominant philosophy advocated by Auguste Comte and Hippolyte Taine. It was against this world that the advocates of Symbolism cried out; Aurier cursed it for its science and its positivism which deprived Man of the mysteries of the unknown,[22] and Huysmans, who had drawn upon it to inform his early novels such as *Marthe* (1876), *Les Soeurs Vatard* (1879) and *En Ménage* (1881) lashed out against its most crude manifestations in 1889:

> One began walking ... and saw that horror of modern taste: the street; those boulevards with their vegetating trees, orthopaedically corsetted in metal bands, trussed up by the Highways Department into hoops of cast-iron; those streets shattered by enormous omnibuses and wretched advertising vans; those pavements teeming with a hideous crowd after money, women worn out by childbirth and stupefied by horrible trafficking, men reading vile newspapers or thinking about fraud and fornication as they pass the shops and are spied on by the licensed sharks of business and commerce waiting to fleece their prey[23]

Such disgust could be given political expression through a specific gesture of escapism. Huysmans advocated this for des Esseintes, the hero of his transitional novel, *A Rebours* (1884), who immures himself in a suburban villa surrounded by goldfish tanks, liquour mouth organs and the works of Gustave Moreau and Odilon Redon. Alternatively, the gesture could involve a passing engagement with anarchy, as was demonstrated by Paul Claudel, disciple of Stéphane Mallarmé who converted to hard-line Catholicism:

> Anarchy provided me with an almost instinctive gesture against the congested, suffocating world which surrounded all of us, and in whose direction we made a gesture similar to that of a drowning man who struggles for air, throwing bombs indiscriminately with no forethought or preselected target.[24]

Philosophically this disgust with naturalism called for a rejection of positivism, or the belief that Truth resided in that which could be verified in the objective, or external world. In its place was to be erected a metaphysical system indebted to the German philosopher, Schopenhauer, which held that objects in the external world were apprehended by the senses alone, and were thus merely relative, the indicators or signs of the absolute, unchanging concept, the Idea.[25] Since the Idea possessed no finite form, it was intimated through objects in the external world which established a relationship with the Idea through 'correspondence'. Proposed by the mystic Swedenborg and elaborated by Charles Baudelaire, the perception of the relationship of an object to the Idea was one reserved for the 'seer', that is the artist or poet, the man of genius.

The implications of this programme were twofold. The signalling that an object existed solely as the intimation of an idea required the deliberate rejection of art as naturalist description. Secondly, the assertion that only the 'man of genius' could comprehend the correspondence between an object and the Idea supported the conviction that great art was the domain of the few, the élite. It has already been noted that Moréas and Kahn had dismissed nature as the legimitate subject-matter of Symbolist art. Their conviction had been presaged two years earlier by Huysmans, who had des Esseintes declare that 'Nature has served her purpose; by the disgusting uniformity of her landscapes and her skies, she has definitely worn out the attentive patience of the refined ... There can be no doubt that the sempiternal driveller has by now used up the complacent admiration of true artists'.[26] Huysmans completes his diatribe against nature as the source for 'true artists' by advocating that 'the time has come when [Nature] should be replaced by artificiality as far as possible'.[27] Those who openly professed the Symbolist creed, however, did not seek merely to retreat from the mundane world, but also to realise an art that had the capacity to find within the world the essence, the Idea, the profound emotion, be it through dreams or through evocation. Thus, Charles Morice, in 1889, could call for art to reawaken dreams of happiness: 'Since our life is such a terrible affair ... unable to provide us with the perfect realisation of our dreams of happiness, art will have to deck itself out in widow's weeds of joys which life refuses to give us and which art can still realise in the imagination'.[28] And the Belgian Symbolist Emile Verhaeren demonstrated this relationship between reality and the evocative power of imagination in his description of Paris seen by night:

> A poet sees Paris swarming with night lights, fragmented into an infinite number of lights, gigantic in its shadow and extent. If one gives the direct view, as Zola might have done, that is to say, describing it through its streets, its squares, its monuments ... its nocturnal seas of ink, its feverish movements beneath the immobile stars, a very artistic image will be conjured up, certainly, but nothing could be less symbolist. If, by contrast, what is conjured up for the spirit is the indirect, evocative vision, if what is presented is an immense algebraic formula whose key has been lost, this simple phrase will establish, free from all description and all notation of facts, the luminous, shadowy, resplendent Paris.[29]

Rejection of the modern world, so precisely identified by Huysmans as one dominated by rampant commercialism, engendered a belief that quality in a work of art could only be achieved if it was protected from the popular market.

In 1886 Téodor de Wyzéwa had declared that 'the aesthetic value of a work of art is always in inverse relationship to the number of people who can understand it'.[30] This position was expanded in the following decade by the Belgian Symbolist writer, Georges Rodenbach: 'Art is not for the people. Art is a thing essentially complex, of nuances. The people love only the most direct, the most simple, and the clearest representations of life. That is not a work of art.'[31] And it was fully condoned by Stéphane Mallarmé in his theory of 'le drame', an ideal dramatic work which was to be read by a single poet to an audience ranging from between eight and twenty-four people. In this way, the poet argued, the meaning of the drama would be bastardised neither by a plethora of performers nor by a crowd of spectators.

Britain and continental Symbolism

Thus far, attention has been focused upon an identifiable programme for a new movement in literature and the visual arts, namely Symbolism, which emerged in France around 1886. Leaving aside such issues as the movement's survival into the 1890s, and its position either as a transition between Romanticism and Modernism or as the first manifestation of Modernism, it is necessary to consider whether the articulation of a specific programme, laid forth in manifestos and realised in the works of Mallarmé and Verlaine, Gauguin and the Nabis, had any resonance across the Channel. In addition, despite the undeniable Franco-centric nature of the Symbolist programme, it is worth considering whether the art and literature which was created in Britain under the somewhat looser banner of 'symbolism' (see essay by A. Wilton) did not itself have a significance for new directions in art on the Continent.

Taken at face value, there was no literary equivalent in Britain to the poetry of Mallarmé, no pictorial counterpart to the overt non-naturalism which Gauguin practised after 1888. Nor again was there any move to produce a formal manifesto for Symbolism to embrace writers such as Swinburne, Pater, Symons and Wilde, and artists such as Rossetti, Burne-Jones, Whistler and G.F. Watts. However, while the momentum for change or the search for the new was neither as concentrated nor as coherently articulated in England as it was in France, it can be argued that access to French thought, notably of Merimée, Gautier and Baudelaire, certainly helped to shape the poetry and prose of Swinburne, Meredith and Pater, and hence to have an impact upon pictorial manifestations. As John Conlon has pointed out: 'Pater was there at the beginning of a renaissance of French literature in England of which the critical and poetical works of Swinburne and Arnold are harbingers'.[32]

Indeed, a closer consideration of Walter Pater's aesthetic system reveals two significant elements which appear to prefigure more precise definition within the French Symbolist manifestos. Like his French counterparts, Pater sought from the later 1860s to liberate literature from naturalist description. In so doing he both absolved it from any overt moral responsibility and released it from the need to identify a single Ideal. Instead, he came to comprehend that the perception of beauty was personal, relativist yet also momentarily absolute. Dependent no longer on the appreciation of beauty intrinsic to an object, it was the subjective appreciation of the moment of the experience of the beauty of an object which constituted the knowledge of beauty itself. (The degree to which the rejection of moral responsibility and the pursuit of the beautiful were due more to Pater's renunciation of religious dogma at the age of twenty-one than to his deep knowledge of French literature, both contemporary and of the past, must remain open to question.)

> To define beauty, not in the most abstract terms possible, to find not its universal formula but the formula which expresses most adequately this or that spiritual manifestation of it, is the aim of this student of aesthetics ... Every moment some form grows perfect in hand or face; some tone on the hills or the sea is choicer than the rest; some mood or passion or insight or intellectual excitement is irresistably real and attractive to us – for that moment only.[33]

This significant shift in the appreciation of beauty confronted Pater with the need to craft a new literary style, one which was complex and structurally extended, 'in order to make the sensation of an idea apparent'.[34] As elaborated in the construction of his essays, 'Leonardo' and 'The School of Giorgione', it is possible to draw a parallel with the Symbolists' realisation that the new subject-matter of their art, the Idea, required new literary structures. More particularly, this procedure finds its counterpart, as Lee McKay Johnson has suggested, in Mallarmé's search for a new poetic language:

> To paint, not things, not facts, but the sensation produced by things and facts, involves both Pater and Mallarmé in a search for new verbal structures that go beyond meaning and describing. Mallarmé discovered, like Pater, that he needed the whole structure of a poem or a poetic essay, operating as a unit, to convey the complex aura that surrounds a single experience or idea.[35]

Walter Pater's formulation of his new literary style was most clearly laid out in his collection of essays first published in 1873 under the title *Studies in the History of the Renaissance*. Yet despite sharing with Mallarmé a common source in Baudelaire, he confines his pictorial references to the art of the past, to Botticelli, Leonardo, Michelangelo and Giorgione. No contemporary pictorial manifestation is incorporated into the new aesthetic canon; the closest attempt is in the critical writings of Pater's disciple, Arthur Symons. During the 1890s, Symons initially calls for an art which is more than 'an immediate noting of light, movement, expression ... the instant made eternity. If the instant, however deftly rendered, remains temporary, you may have, perhaps, some of Monet's work, but you will have no more than a shorthand note, which the reporter has not even troubled to copy out.'[36] Instead, if 'the instant, changed not in kind but in degree, takes on that incalculable aspect, as of a thing which has always existed and must always go on existing, you have the equivalence, under new conditions, of those masterpieces of the past which can never be repeated, but which may, in any age, be equalled.'[37] Concerned though Symons was to place G.F. Watts as a painter of 'a thing which always existed and must always go on existing', that is, as revelatory of Moréas's 'primordial idea', it was in the work of James McNeill Whistler and Edouard Manet that he saw its most convincing contemporary manifestation. Likewise, whereas he recognises as haters of reality, dreamers concerned with limitless space, 'poets rather than painters', D.G. Rossetti and G.F. Watts, as well as Chassériau, Moreau, Puvis de Chavannes, Burne-Jones, Simeon Solomon, Rops and Beardsley, these artists ultimately fail in the bid to give to art 'that incalculable aspect'. Unlike their French innovative literary counterparts, they have not accepted the demand of new modes of composition and technique to serve as the primary media for 'the translation of dreams and ideas into visible form'.[38]

Symons derived his knowledge of continental artists, as he had of writers, primarily from direct contact with their work in Paris. The confrontation between British art and the Continent during this period tended however to be more diffuse, involving on the one hand its exhibition primarily in Brussels and Paris, and on the other, its mediation through such advocates as the Belgian artist Fernand Khnopff, who concurrently reinforced knowledge of certain aspects of continental Symbolism.

Following a schism in 1883 within the Brussels avant-garde exhibiting body, l'Essor, a group of twenty Belgian artists formed an alternative exhibiting body, Les XX. This group's founding principle was the promotion of the new in art, where art was understood in Wagnerian terms as encompassing the visual arts, literature and music:

> These are the 'select' amongst the young ... Their works declare that all-conquering audacity guides them, that that which is new and needs to be discovered demands their attention, that tenacity of effort strengthens them, that the Modern Ideal in all its excitement attracts them, that the new programmes which are engaging painting today are their programmes, that the new focus [of art] is their focus. Almost all of them acknowledge the influence of the geniuses of our day, an inevitable influence which casts them within the true milieu of progress. They are in no way imitators, they only work as all non-retrogressive artists work today, breathing the atmosphere of their epoch, outside which it would be madness to wish to seek air.[39]

This broad brief encouraged Les XX from its inception to invite like-minded artists from abroad to exhibit from 1884 at its annual exhibitions, and to hold at each exhibition a series of concerts and lectures. However, whereas the concerts tended to favour works by contemporary composers such as César Franck, Claude Debussy and Gustave Fauré, whose works were seen to complement the predominantly Symbolist character of the lectures delivered on literature, the character of those non-Belgian artists who were invited to exhibit was more catholic, reflecting in some respects the spread of stylistic allegiance which was enshrined in the membership itself. Thus, just as the original members of Les XX ranged from the naturalist painters Willy Finch, Dario de Regoyas, Théo van Rysselberghe and Théodore Verstraete to the proto-symbolists such as Fernand

Khnopff and James Ensor, so too the artists invited from Britain during the ten years of Les XX's existence ranged from Mark Fisher (1885), Walter Sickert (1887) and Wilson Steer (1889, 1891) to Whistler (1884, 1886) and Walter Crane (1891). Burne-Jones received an invitation in 1888 to exhibit with the group in the following year. While he declined it in November 1888 on the grounds that 'many pressing engagements already formed will prevent my having the pleasure of doing this',[40] he and D.G. Rossetti shared an exhibition at the Galerie Dumont in Brussels two years later when photographs of a selection of their work were shown. This interest in the work of two 'symbolist' British artists confirmed, rather than radically changed, the Symbolist direction in the work of such painters as Jean Delville and Fernand Khnopff and of the sculptor Georges Minne. However, by the time that a group of British artists who could have been deemed to be affiliated to the symbolist or decadent persuasion were exhibited in 1895 at Les XX's successor exhibition group, La Libre Esthétique, they were viewed, with the exception of G.F. Watts,[41] more as a robust expression of 'art nouveau' in the applied arts than as a manifestation of a Symbolist or Decadent aesthetic. When Khnopff came to consider the French applied arts shown in La Libre Esthétique of 1896, he declared that the work of Walter Crane, George Frampton, William Morris and Aubrey Beardsley seen the previous year which gave 'evidence of deliberate and careful work, were deeply beautiful and restrained' examples of the applied arts in contrast to the French productions which were 'evidently the outcome of a sudden caprice – a mere fashion, at once startling and disconcerting. It is really painful to see so much knowledge and talent sacrificed to the ridiculous whims of the most deplorably bad taste.'[42]

fig.32 Edward Burne-Jones, *The Beguiling of Merlin* 1874, oil on canvas 186 × 111 cm. Board of Trustees of the National Museums and Galleries on Merseyside (Lady Lever Art Gallery, Port Sunlight)

The possibility of exhibiting in Paris also established a bridge between British symbolist art and the Continent. Despite the critical acclaim earned by Burne-Jones for *The Beguiling of Merlin* (fig.32) when it was shown at the Paris Exposition Universelle of 1878, it was only after the publication in 1885 of Ernest Chesneau's *La Peinture en Angleterre,*[43] a complement to his study of English Literature, that a greater awareness was created in France of the art of D.G. Rossetti, G.F. Watts and Burne-Jones himself. From the early 1890s, Burne-Jones exhibited, together with G.F. Watts, at the newly established, more liberal Salon du Champ de Mars, and Burne-Jones was invited, but declined, to participate in Sâr Péladan's Idealist salon, the Salon de la Rose+Croix. While Chesneau deliberately underscored the potential symbolist element in contemporary English art through his concern to stress its being 'imbued with a deference to reality',[44] other critics did accord this aspect considerable acclaim. *Le Revue Encylopédique*, for example, when summarising the current state of English art for the year 1892–3, praised the fact that it combined 'a passionate love of the Old Masters' with 'the interesting search for modernity and feeling ... a concern for art for art's sake', in contrast to the dominant character of contemporaneous French art which seemed primarily concerned with the cheap pandering to popular taste.[45] However, this acclaim could be frequently tempered by a comparison with French art which encouraged either the conclusion that the native example was ultimately superior or that the foreign manifestation was of no immediate relevance to the native production. The former conclusion was drawn by Léon Bazalgette in his review of Burne-Jones's contribution to the Salon du Champ de Mars of 1893: 'M. Burne-Jones triumphs with all the strength of his subtle, potent art. The *Siren*, *Perseus*, the portrait of a child are of greater value than all the rest of the Salon; less so, it is true, than a Gustave Moreau, but nonetheless how great!'[46] The latter view, combining both admiration and caution, was proffered by Robert de la Sizeranne in a telling article published in *Le Correspondant* for 25 March 1892. Entitled 'Rose+Croix, Pre-Raphaelites and Aesthetes, the Aesthetic Renaissance on Both Sides of the Channel', the article opened with an acceptance of the similarity of intention of the Pre-Raphaelites and Sâr Péladan's Salon de la Rose+Croix, for they both sought 'the soul of the least animated things, the symbol behind the appearance, the eternal idea beneath the form – even those that are complicated or mannered, fleeting and ungraspable.' However, he tellingly concluded that the Salon de la Rose+Croix would never inherit the mantle of the Pre-Raphaelite Brotherhood, since not only did it display no interest (either in Péladan's programme or in its pictorial manifestations) in the search for technical and aesthetic innovation which was central to the Pre-Raphaelites' programme, but also because the literary sources which had informed the art of the latter were now too removed in time from the Rose+Croix: 'The poetry of Rossetti and Swinburne ... of the Decadents and the Symbolists preceded that of the Rose+Croix by a long while ... Our era hardly lends itself, outside the religious domain, to voluntary immolations for an idea.'[47] In other words, the art of the Pre-Raphaelite Brotherhood was no longer relevant to French artistic concerns.

A more personal conduit between continental developments and Britain lay in Fernand Khnopff. Despite his training in Brussels and Paris, his art expressed strong affinities with both the work of Whistler and Burne-Jones. Indeed, sufficient was known in Brussels of the latter's work for this affinity to be viewed by certain critics as a direct borrowing, a position taken by the critic of the *Journal de Charleroi* in respect of *Lawn Tennis (Memories)* (fig.33) shown at Les XX in 1890: 'There is also Fernand Khnopff, subtle and delicate but rather impersonal ... with *Lawn-tennis*, one of the Belgian successes in the Fine Arts Section of the Paris Exposition [Universelle] ... a pillage of Burne-Jones'.[48] Khnopff's anglophilia led him to exhibit in Britain for the first time in 1886 when he showed at the Liverpool Art Club,[49] and then regularly in London from 1890 to 1906.[50] In addition, from October 1895 he became the regular correspondent from Brussels for the *Studio*, a position which he held until 1914 and which permitted him to introduce the British public to the myriad examples of European 'new' painting, sculpture and applied arts presented at La Libre Esthétique.[51] In 1894 he exchanged drawings with Burne-Jones (nos.96, 108) and, on the latter's death in 1898, contributed an article, 'In Memoriam', to the *Magazine of Art*. His awareness of English literature provided him with the inspiration for two works derived from the poetry of Christina Rossetti, *I Lock my Door upon myself (Christina Georgina Rossetti)* 1891 (fig.8 on p.22) and *Who Shall Deliver me? (Christina Georgina Rossetti)* 1891 (no.86). Khnopff also fostered greater understanding of contemporary British art in Brussels, delivering lectures on *'l'Art anglais'* in 1893 at the Maison du Peuple and on Walter Crane at the Cercle Artistique in Brussels the following year.

fig.33 Fernand Khnopff, *Lawn Tennis (Memories)* 1889, pastel on paper pasted on canvas 127 × 200 cm. Musées Royaux des Beaux-Arts, Brussels

Certainly, in many respects, Fernand Khnopff can also be seen as an intermediary between Britain and continental Symbolism, most particularly of the movement's literary manifestations in Belgium and France. From 1882, Khnopff came into contact with the circle of writers around the Brussels avant-garde review, *L'Art Moderne*. This included major Belgian writers such as Emile Verhaeren, Grégoire Le Roy, Georges Rodenbach, Maurice Maeterlinck and Edmond Picard, who were to contribute to the evolution of literary Symbolism and who also gave him access to their French counterparts, notably Stéphane Mallarmé, Jules Laforgue and Téodor de Wyzéwa. As a founding member of Les XX, these affinities with avant-garde literature were strengthened through the regular presentation of lectures on aspects of contemporary, notably Symbolist, literature. Just as English contemporary literature could inspire his artistic production, so too Khnopff responded to the Symbolist texts of his Belgian and French contemporaries. And it was examples of this direct inspiration which Khnopff was to exhibit in London from 1890. At his one-man exhibition held at the Hanover Gallery in that year, he presented two works directly related to Sâr Péladan[52] and a further three which made specific reference to leading Belgian Symbolist writers: *Avec Grégoire Le Roy: Mon coeur pleure d'autrefois* 1889; *Avec Verhaeren. Un Ange* 1889; and *Avec Georges Rodenbach. Une Ville morte* 1890. Three years later, at the Grafton Galleries exhibition of *British and Foreign Artists of the Present Day*, Khnopff presented a *Portrait of Edmond Picard*, Picard being the author of *Le Juré* for which Odilon Redon had created a set of lithographs in 1887. Finally, in 1900, Khnopff showed *La Poésie de Stéphane Mallarmé. La Tendresse: en écoutant des fleurs* (The Poetry of Stéphane Mallarmé. Tenderness: Listening to Flowers) 1892 at the New Gallery's Summer Exhibition.[53]

As was noted earlier, Mallarmé shared with Walter Pater the acceptance of a divorce between art and representation. Both writers had predicated this aesthetic on Théophile Gautier's well-worn formulation of 'l'art pour l'art' ('art for art's sake'). This provided a critical ingredient not only for certain aspects of Khnopff's work (see below) but also in the emergence of Decadence in the 1890s, most especially as expressed by Oscar Wilde and Aubrey Beardsley.[54] The introduction of Decadence in the context of Symbolism suggests a further point of contact between the search in both England and France during the latter part of the nineteenth century for an alternative tradition, an exploration of the psychological and emotional depths of Man and his unconscious, the rejection of naturalist representation in literature and art. Yet even at this juncture, an element of caution must be observed, and an account of a specific event in the formative years of Arthur Symons should be recorded as indicative of the danger of drawing too simplistic a set of conclusions.

In 1889, Arthur Symons, accompanied by Havelock Ellis, visited Paris, ostensibly to marvel at the Exposition Universelle. Their passage through that city took them to the bookshop owned by Léon Vanier, on the Quai St Michel. Here they saw portraits of Verlaine and Villiers de l'Isle Adam, and fingered copies of poems by Mallarmé, Gustave Kahn and Jean Lorrain. In his study of French Symbolist literature, first published in 1900, Symons was to identify all these authors, with the exception of Jean Lorrain, as members of the Symbolist movement who sought:

> an art [which] returns to the one pathway, leading through beautiful things to the eternal beauty ... where form is very carefully elaborated [such that] there is such a thing as perfecting form that form may be annihilated ... [All attempt] to spiritualise literature, to evade the old bondage of rhetoric, the old bondage of exteriority. Description is banished that beautiful things may be evoked, magically; the regular beat of verse is broken in order that words may fly upon subtler wings.[55]

In 1889, however, Symons was to describe these writers as 'most meditative, mysterious, truculent and altogether decadent'.[56] Symons's use in 1889 of the term 'decadent' in respect of French literature was already essentially anachronistic.[57] In the context of British literature, it was possibly before its time.

The Decadent movement in both countries shared common sources which were well delineated in the opening section of George Moore's *Confessions of a Young Man* (1888).[58] The book deals with an autobiographical rite of passage from crude positivist, via the Romanticism of Victor Hugo and Alfred de Musset, to a hermetic Decadence informed by Théophile Gautier and Charles Baudelaire to final redemption in the naturalism of Zola. With Gautier and Baudelaire as his mentors, Moore establishes his decadent phase as one which abjures the modern world, seeking to replace it with an anti-naturalism informed by the celebration of the artificial, the crude and the perverse. While he shared with the earlier Romantics a desire to explore the full range of man's emotional and intellectual potential, he could not accept their belief that the striving for the Ideal was both redemptive and ultimately attainable. Rather, he desired, like Gautier, to plumb the emotions of 'lust, cruelty, slavery',[59] and to acknowledge with Baudelaire that 'all hope is vain'.[60]

When Moore came to list the contemporary French authors whose works he read during his decadent phase, he identified Coppée, Mendès, Léon Dierx, José Maria Hérédia, Richepin, Verlaine, Mallarmé and Villiers de l'Isle Adam. From this list we might conclude that, especially with reference to the latter three, Moore was equally an ardent supporter of the Symbolists. However, revealingly, he declares that he only enjoyed the early, Baudelairean poetry of Mallarmé, and his dismissal of Symbolism as an obtuse, vapid and supine form of literature clearly indicates that he never comprehended the structural innovations of that programme: 'But what is symbolism? Vulgarly speaking, saying the opposite to what you mean. For example, you want to say that music, which is the new art, is replacing the old art, which is poetry. First symbol: a house in which there is a funeral, the pall extends over the furniture. The house is poetry, poetry is dead.'[61]

Moore's perception of an essential difference between Decadence and Symbolism, at least in France, is instructive, and supports the contention that J.-K. Huysmans's novel, *A Rebours*, far from being a manifestation of Symbolism 'avant le manifeste', was in fact an exploration of a decadent theme contained within the full panoply of naturalist description.[62] This absence of stylistic innovation in decadent literature is paralleled in its pictorial manifestations. Artists such as Gustave Moreau resorted to decadent literary sources such as Flaubert's *Salammbô* (1862), Baudelaire's *Les Fleurs du Mal* (1857) and an early poem by Mallarmé, 'Le

fig.34 Gustave Moreau, *The Apparition* 1876, watercolour 105 × 72 cm. Musée Gustave Moreau, Paris

Canticle de Saint Jean' for his *Apparition* (fig.34), and Fernand Khnopff and Odilon Redon to Flaubert's *Tentation de Saint Antoine* for the painting and three suites of lithographs respectively. The desire to escape from the horrors of contemporary life encouraged artists to undertake large decorative schemes,[63] to use temporal and spatial exoticism to express ideals which lay beyond the constraints of contemporary existence, for example, the Orpheus myth, the image of the muse and the sphinx. Equally, the Decadent artists celebrated the perverse, nature *'à l'envers'* (upside down), be it the city, as in the closing sonnet of Baudelaire's *Spleen et Idéal: petites poèmes en prose* (1862) or lesbianism, as in Moreau's *Sapho* (1884) or de Granié's *Le Baiser* (1900). Finally, the Decadents accepted that current society was inherently doomed to destruction, whether through the inevitable degeneration of the human race, or through cataclysmic disaster a view based on the scientific theories of B.A. Morel who, in his *Traité de Dégénérences* (1857) had declared that 'degenerations and deviations from the normal human type are transmissible by heredity and deteriorate progressively towards extinction'. Such was the hold of his theory that Zola applied it to his Rougon-Macquart series of novels, Huysmans has des Esseintes represent the last scion of an old aristocratic family wracked by neuroses, and the self-styled Sâr Péladan incorporated them into his book, *La Décadence Latine* (1884) and his ideas of the final state of man's degeneration being manifested in the Androgyne. Belief in the ultimate destruction of civilisation was derived from Schopenhauer's theory of pessimism, whose much-quoted phrase, 'the world is hell, and men are divided into tortured souls and torturing devils',[64] caused the Decadents to hold that since everything was so dreadful, the end of the world must be nigh. Huysmans expresses this aptly when he causes des Esseintes to declare: 'Could it be that the terrible God of Genesis, and the pale martyr of Golgotha would not prove their existence once and for all, by rekindling the rain of fire that once consumed those accursed towns, the cities of the plain?'[65] It was this destruction that Henri de Groux conveyed in his cycle, *Les Vendanges* (1892–4), which was exhibited accompanied by an extensive text by the reactionary Catholic author, Léon Bloy.[66]

No precise chronological period has been satisfactorily ascribed to the Decadent movement. A.E. Carter saw it as spanning the period 1830 to 1900, and thus running parallel to Symbolism for at least its final decade. Mathew Sturgis favours a far shorter time-scale which is centred on the decade of the 1890s. For those at the end of the nineteenth century, however, the question seems to have been less diffuse. On the one hand, Decadence was seen as the last throes of naturalism, a position adopted by Paul Bourget in his *Essais de psychologie contemporaine* (1881) and reiterated four years later by Paul Bourde in an article in *Le Temps* in which he concluded that decadent poetry represented 'the last period of literary infatuation'.[67] On the other hand, as Jean Moréas pointed out in a riposte to Bourde, decadent poets should be seen as the forerunners of the new literature, namely Symbolism: 'Decadents are neither sick men nor perverts, but innovators who will be accorded their proper due in the future'. In Moréas's view, decadent literature would inevitably give way to a new movement, Symbolism.'[68]

In England, while Arthur Symons held to a view of Decadence derived from both Bourde and Moréas, stating that it was an 'interlude, half a mock-interlude' which 'diverted the attention of the critics while something more serious [i.e. Symbolism] was in preparation',[69] its literary and visual manifestations were generally contained within a broader, looser, far less programmatic understanding of Symbolism. It was therefore quite reasonable for Symons's friend and fellow member of the Rhymers' Club, Lionel Johnson, to consider there to be little fundamental difference between the contemporary French Decadent and Symbolist writers. In his article, 'The Practice and Theory of Verse at the Present Time obtaining in France', published in the *Century Guild Hobby Horse* in April 1891, Johnson declared that both 'schools' were concerned with language. He proceeded to identify as Decadent writers Verlaine, Moréas, Jules Laforgue and Gustave Kahn, and as Symbolist writers Mallarmé, René Ghil, Stuart Merrill, Henri Regnier and Viélé-Griffin. Given that both Moréas and Kahn had publicly declared for Symbolism in the autumn of 1886, and that Symons counted Verlaine and Mallarmé to be exponents of the Symbolist movement in literature, one can only conclude that Johnson, determined to bring these names to a British public, was not much concerned to differentiate between the two movements. Within the English context, there may have been no necessity so to do.

This apparent disregard in Britain for firm definitional distinctions to be drawn between two cultural movements is pertinently demonstrated in pictorial terms in the range of work selected by Fernand Khnopff for his 1890 one-man exhibition at the Hanover Gallery, London. Two pure landscapes,[70] a study of a gamekeeper[71] in a landscape and the *Portrait of Madeleine Lejeune*[72] confirmed Khnopff's deep admiration for Whistler's advocacy of the principle of 'art for art's sake'. Five other works declared an allegiance to Decadence, either through direct reference to Joséphin Péladan[73] or by adopting the specifically Decadent subject of the sphinx.[74] Four works made specific reference to Symbolist authors, namely Emile Verhaeren, Gregoire Le Roy and Georges Rodenbach,[75] or decked out the mundane sport of lawn tennis in the symbolic language of memory and dreams, as was identified by Walter Shaw Sparrow in the *Magazine of Art*: 'The large pastel [*Lawn Tennis*; fig.33 on p.58] ... is a charming group of tennis players. The game is over. The sun has set. After the heat of the day there comes a hush, an hour of dreaminess while the twilight melts into moonlight. And the girls are dreaming in the stillness, busy with their memories.'[76]

This confusion between Decadence and Symbolism is symptomatic of comparable confusions found in other manifestations of what this catalogue defines as English Symbolism. Théophile Gautier's dictum, 'art for art's sake', as we have seen, provided an important ingredient both in the nascent Symbolism of Walter Pater and the effete separation of art from life inherent in the decadent work of Oscar Wilde and Aubrey Beardsley. The formulation also underscored Aestheticism, most clearly enunciated in the canvases of Whistler and Albert Moore, where the formal values of paint, colour and composition gave to traditional representation a merely residual role. Aestheticism thus became one aspect of English Symbolism. Likewise, the concern of such seminal writers as Swinburne, Meredith and Browning to plumb the darker side of man's psyche, the more extreme aspects of human emotion in the search for Truth, finds its roots in the Gothick novel and the Victorian preoccupation with the world of dreams and nightmares, expressed in an obsession with the representation of fairies in literature, music, ballet and the visual arts. It is these associations with cultural preoccupations that range through an extended time-period and across many shades of manifestations of the psychological, the non-narrative and the introspective, which help to explain the 'failure of the British to recognise Symbolism as a category into which their own art might fall'.[77]

Symbolism in Britain could take on many guises: from the serious, high-minded intent of Watts's 'allegories' to the silent, self-obsessive icons of Rossetti, the narrative-free compositions of Burne-Jones and the images of *danses macabres* of Beardsley. While these variants of British Symbolism found their counterpart in the works of continental artists such as Delville, Khnopff, Puvis de Chavannes and Gustave Moreau, a comparison with the more rigorously defined version in France is instructive. The very variety of individual expression encompassed within British Symbolism certainly entitles it to lay claim to be one significant manifestation of the transition from Romanticism to Surrealism. French Symbolism, on the other hand, with its insistent advocacy of new literary forms, of new pictorial language, radically severed the link between art and representation and laid the foundations for a celebration of the individual artist's right to seek out the most effective mode of expressing the new subject-matter, the Idea. Released from the shackles of representation, insistent upon suggestion and the power of the artist as intimator of the Idea, it contained within it the programme for abstraction.[78]

G.F. Watts and the Symbolist Vision

Barbara Bryant

fig.35 G.F. Watts, *Hope* 1886, oil on canvas 142.2 × 111.8 cm. Tate Gallery

George Frederic Watts (1817–1904), an artist whose career and ideals formed during the late 1830s, is not at first glance the most obvious player on the Symbolist stage of the 1880s and 1890s. Yet some of his later paintings, most notably *Hope* (fig.35 and no.76) have entered into the Symbolist canon, appearing in the vast literature and in the many exhibitions devoted to this late nineteenth-century artistic phenomenon. What has never been fully established is how and why Watts belongs to this context. This exhibition provides some answers; this essay examines the path of Watts's contribution to a Symbolist sensibility through the display of his paintings at exhibitions on the Continent together with the attendant critical reactions which shaped the view of his art. The essay will also define those qualities in his art which fed into Symbolism and identify the tangible links and close affinities between his art and that of both Dante Gabriel Rossetti and Fernand Khnopff. It will emerge that Watts's reputation as an artist devoted to 'poems painted on canvas' and 'symbolical' works, inaugurated by the International Exhibition of 1878, gathered strength throughout the 1880s, fuelling developments abroad as Symbolism evolved into a truly international style in the 1890s. Watts's dominant role as a father-figure to the movement will be clear for the first time.

At the Exposition Universelle in Paris in 1878, nine paintings and one sculpture by G.F. Watts could be seen, including his recent masterpiece *Love and Death* (no.51), and *The Three Goddesses* (no.14). This group was large by the standards of other British artists on view. Its impact was such that Watts instantly entered into the European art world as a fully formed artistic personality, specialising in a distinct form of 'symbolical' painting. Watts relied on the term 'symbolical' to describe paintings like *Love and Death*, using it regularly from about 1880.[1] The French authorities bestowed a first-class medal upon him, an honour accorded to only one other artist who lived in England, Lawrence Alma-Tadema (who was, after all, essentially a European). Great names of the day, like John Everett Millais and Hubert von Herkomer, came away with *médailles d'honneur*; Frederic Leighton, Walter William Ouless and Philip Hermogenes Calderon received second-class medals, followed by a spate of third-class award recipients including W.Q. Orchardson, G.D. Leslie and Briton Riviere.[2]

The Exposition Universelle proved to be a significant occasion for British art abroad. Thanks to the inaugural exhibition of the Grosvenor Gallery of 1877, with its telling juxtaposition of British and continental artists, the way was prepared for the importation of British art into Europe.[3] Leading the committee selecting works of art was the President of the Royal Academy, Sir Frederic Leighton; Sir Coutts Lindsay, founder of the Grosvenor Gallery, also played a large role, with the result that many paintings from the first Grosvenor exhibition went on to Paris. These included Watts's *Love and Death* (no.51) and *The Hon. Mrs. Percy*

opposite
detail from G.F. Watts, *Hope* c.1885–6 (no.76)

Wyndham (private collection), Burne-Jones's *The Beguiling of Merlin* (fig.32 on p.57); and Walter Crane's *Renaissance of Venus* (Tate Gallery). Edmond Duranty (1833–1880), realist critic and defender of Impressionism, summed up the English contribution to the Exposition in 1878:

> English art towers above all, original, delicate, intimate and audacious in its honesty, always expressive and significant, full of high intellectual dandyism, full of a refined sensitivity, grace and keen tenderness, keeping a hold on excess, finally an art filled with historical sentiment which relies on the union of the modern with a lofty tone, the strong attraction of the past ... an art of acuteness, elegance and poetry, absolutely entwined with the spirit of the nation; an art in which melancholy joins with brilliance, and singularity with precise reality.[4]

fig.36 J. Benwell Clark after G.F. Watts, *Pallas, Juno and Venus*, etching 31.75 × 26.7 cm (image size), in *L'Art*, vol.22, 1880, repr. opp. p.176. By permission of the British Library

Some of these qualities applied to Watts's work, especially the notion of a poetic art, visually underlined by the drawing of *Love and Death* reproduced in the article.

Not surprisingly it is this quality which Joseph Comyns Carr elaborated upon in his important reviews for *L'Art*. The key role played by Carr in the transmission of new currents in English art to France is now much better understood.[5] As a member of the management at the Grosvenor Gallery and assistant to Sir Coutts Lindsay, Carr aided the implementation of ideas about the primacy of the work of art into the displays there, but as an art critic attuned to post-Pre-Raphaelite trends he is perhaps even more influential. As 'Directeur pour L'Angleterre' for the periodical *L'Art*, and all its associated activities, Carr disseminated information to Paris. His review of the first Grosvenor Gallery exhibition in 1877 for *L'Art* isolated *Love and Death* as a masterpiece: 'next to this group of pallid canvases [by Millais] hangs a richly coloured monumental composition by Mr. Watts. There are few English painters of our time who have so fine an understanding of the principles of poetic designs'.[6] In *Love and Death* Carr admired how the artist 'could dispense with rhetorical gesture and theatrical display' to produce a 'quality of grave simplicity in design ... so rare in modern art'.[7] The enthusiastic reception in French artistic circles marked a turning point in Watts's reputation. The importance of *Love and Death* as a key Symbolist image dates from its first appearance in Paris in 1878.

Watts and Burne-Jones were increasingly linked by admirers for their shared interest in poetic painting. In writing about the first Grosvenor Gallery for *L'Art*, Carr presented Burne-Jones 'as an artist who has done so much for the elevation of English art' and whose work is 'scarcely known at all beyond a limited circle'.[8] *The Beguiling of Merlin* revealed a 'poetic intensity of vision that is new to the English school'. The splendid etching of this work by Lalauze included in the periodical added visual impact to Carr's critical evaluation. Not only were the paintings on view in Paris in 1878 influential, but *L'Art* continued its campaign in favour of advanced artists in London by publishing etchings of works by Watts and Burne-Jones. The large print after Watts's *Three Goddesses*, entitled *Pallas, Juno and Venus* (fig.36), by J. Benwell Clark illustrated Carr's article on the exhibitions in London in *L'Art* in 1880, when he referred to the appearance of the painting at the Exposition of 1878. This work is a key image in Watts's *œuvre*; as a painting of

fig.37 John Watkins after G.F. Watts, *Orpheus and Eurydice*, etching 31.75 × 26.7 cm (image size), in *L'Art*, vol.18, 1879, repr. opp. p.178. By permission of the British Library

the nude it addressed a major theme to which the French readily responded. Carr's text for the article of 1880 foreshadowed the language of the Symbolists in its description of Watts's 'style' – concerning itself not so much with subject, as with the handling and 'spiritualisme raffiné' of the painting.[9]

At the Paris Salon in 1880 Watts showed the main full-length version of *Orpheus and Eurydice* (see no.37), a work filled with the imagery of death and doom. It proved to be another key moment, one extended still further by the etching published in *L'Art* (fig.37). It was unusual for an English artist to be given such prominence at the equivalent of the Royal Academy in Paris: the only exception was the American-born Whistler, a resident in London, whose work appeared regularly at the Salon. No doubt Watts's inclusion followed upon his prize-winning appearance at the Exposition two years before. An even more remarkable occasion, and yet another indication of Watts's growing stature in French eyes, was the important gathering of seven of his works at the exhibition of international art at the Georges Petit Gallery in Paris in 1883. Here the portrait of Algernon Swinburne (National Portrait Gallery) made a highly relevant inclusion given this writer's interest in theories of 'l'art pour l'art'; Watts also sent *Paolo and Francesca* (no.48), *The Denunciation of Cain* (Watts Gallery, Compton),[10] a version of *The Three Goddesses* (see no.14) called simply *Ida*, and three *Eves*, entitled in the catalogue: *Eve (La Création)*, *Eve (Le Repentir)*, *La Création d'Eve*, probably all single figures of Eve. One of these works was almost certainly a version of *'She Shall Be Called Woman'* (see no.124), probably the oil in the Walker Art Gallery.

The exhibition at Georges Petit, following upon Watts's appearance at the Salon in 1880, reinforced knowledge of his actual paintings for an informed French audience. The art critic Joris-Karl Huysmans absorbed the impact of Watts's paintings (including no.48), later assimilating their visionary qualities into *A Rebours*, his novel of 1884. The decadent protagonist des Esseintes, seeing 'more than one Eve', found an almost hallucinatory quality in 'the weirdly coloured pictures by Watts ... a dreamy scholarly Englishman afflicted with a predilection for hideous hues'.[11]

Watts's reputation on the Continent as a poetic painter flourished throughout the 1880s. He was not alone. His younger contemporary Dante Gabriel Rossetti was, like Watts, an artist known for his poetic inclinations and, again like Watts, his career emerged into high relief in the early 1880s (albeit posthumously) feeding the growth of Symbolist attitudes at home and abroad.

Watts and Rossetti had a social and professional friendship, dating back to the salon of Mrs Prinsep at Little Holland House, and continuing into the 1860s when Watts paid regular visits to Rossetti's studio thanks to their shared interest in a Venetian-inspired art (see nos.4 and 8). Watts admired Rossetti's poetry, and it was at the time of the publication of *Poems* in 1870 that Watts sought out his younger friend in order to paint his portrait for the collection of eminent individuals. Although the portrait eventually entered the National Portrait Gallery, Rossetti at one time requested that Watts give it to him (thus forcing Watts to paint a replica),[12] and an exchange took place in which Watts acquired one of Rossetti's large chalk drawings: a study of a woman's head (fig.38) related to the *Roman Widow* (Museo de Arte, Ponce).[13]

fig.38 D.G. Rossetti, *Study for The Roman Window* 1874, black, red and white chalk on grey paper 64.8 × 50.8 cm. Fogg Art Museum, Harvard Univesity, Cambridge, Massachussetts

This softly focused study of a draped woman epitomises how Rossetti developed his drawings as independent works on paper with consequent oddities. In the painting, the Roman widow plays an instrument; but in the drawing her hands, positioned at the lower edge, seemingly disembodied, twist in a strange distorted fashion, giving a distinctly odd feel to the whole image. The drawing belongs so much to a 'Symbolist' sensibility that it is surprising to find it dates from 1874 and that many others partake of the same weird spirit. But it was just this type of work by Rossetti, once revealed to the public, that influenced the emergence of Symbolism.

fig.39 D.G. Rossetti, *A Sea Spell* 1877, oil on canvas 106.7 × 88.9 cm. Fogg Art Museum, Harvard University Art Museums, Cambridge, Massachussetts

Watts probably had no say in the selection of the drawing (Rossetti claimed it was a 'spare' chalk study), but its strange message seems to have found a receptive audience in him. Another work by Rossetti, *A Sea Spell* (fig.39),[14] also reveals an intriguing connection to one of Watts's works. Rossetti painted *A Sea Spell* for Frederick Leyland as a pair to *Veronica Veronese* (no.73); both pictures depict women making music, with the siren in *A Sea Spell* bent and contorted next to her lute; the swirling white drapery twists around her figure as her hands take up the strings. The pose conveys something of the 'wild notes' she plays as 'she sinks into her spell', elaborated in Rossetti's accompanying sonnet. The pose also reflects, in reverse, that of the figure in Watts's *Hope*, also playing a stringed instrument. As images of music-making, both works share an ancestry in the emergent Aestheticism of the 1860s, as reflected in the writings of Walter Pater. But unlike the subdued optimism of Watts's image, Rossetti's painting revolves around a siren luring sailors to their deaths. Watts certainly knew *A Sea Spell* from Leyland's collection; in addition, the work appeared in the Burlington Fine Arts Club exhibition of 1883. *Hope* may well contain an echo of this painting, and it would be entirely in keeping with Watts's opinion of an artist he admired as 'the greatest genius he had ever known'[15] to suggest a recollection of *A Sea Spell* in his own composition.

Watts's reputation grew stronger from the late 1870s onward; Rossetti, however, gained instant fame the moment he died in 1882. For decades after his Pre-Raphaelite phase, his work rarely entered the public arena, with the exception of *Dante's Dream at the Time of the Death of Beatrice* acquired by the Walker Art Gallery in 1881, the year before his death. He was known mainly to fellow artists and a small circle of patrons who bought nearly every oil he produced directly from the studio, even before completion. Were it not for his art-critic friends, like F.G. Stephens and Joseph Comyns Carr, Rossetti would have been even more of an unknown quantity; but his death changed all this. Two major exhibitions, posthumous retrospectives, occurred in 1883, one at the Burlington Fine Arts Club and one, ironically, at the Royal Academy, an institution Rossetti despised. Both were massive accumulations carried out with the full cooperation of his family and friends.

The Burlington Fine Arts Club, founded in 1866 for the study of older art,[16] produced an exhibition of one hundred and fifty-two works which claimed to show Rossetti's art 'here for the first time collected together'.[17] The list of lenders, some of whom were members of the private club, sounded like a roll call of Aesthetic patrons – members of the Ionides family, William Graham, Frederick

Leyland, and Eustace Smith, along with many other artists and friends. Rossetti's early Pre-Raphaelite drawings and watercolours appeared in quantity, but also visible for the first time outside his studio were his later oils and large crayon and chalk drawings. The latter, although often related to known compositions, resulted in independent works of art, with their own haunting qualities of mystery. The impressive scale of these late drawings lent them considerable impact, as in *La Donna della Fiamma* 1870 (Manchester City Art Gallery)[18] and *Ligeia Siren* 1873 (no.72).

The Royal Academy produced its own tribute to the artist who had resolutely refused to have anything to do with it. Frederic Leighton, the President of the Academy and guiding force behind the project,[19] saw to it that Rossetti was claimed in death, if not in life. Watts's portrait of him was displayed upon an easel in the gallery, allowing his spirit to preside over the collection, as Mrs. Watts put it, 'surrounded by all the mystic poetry of Rossetti's imagination'.[20] Indeed this commemoration encapsulated a particularly 'Symbolist' moment, as the dead artist, represented by his portrait, received his posthumous accolades.

The two exhibitions of 1883 thrust Rossetti's art forward for the first time, permitting reverberations on the Continent with reviews in periodicals such as the *Gazette des Beaux Arts*. Theodore Duret's slightly earlier commentary, probably based on a visit to London, defined a Symbolist type:

> The tall women, the sirens, whom he puts on canvas, with their accentuated features, heavy hair, and deep, intense eyes, are vigorous and full of vitality. They are strange and mysterious, and one finds them moving and striking.[21]

Comyns Carr, whose criticism had audiences on both sides of the Channel, wrote his definitive essay on the artist, 'Rossetti's Influence in Art' for the *English Illustrated Magazine*. Like many others, Carr had been captivated by the 'force of his personality', believing that the artist's importance lay in 'the earnest and high purpose with which he sought to enlarge the vision of English painting, and to open to it a nobler inheritance of poetical truth.'[22] He further attributed to Rossetti a shift to thinking about painting as a poet would, and it was just this notion of the poet-painter that represented Rossetti's legacy to contemporary art. Carr expressed reservations about the artist's later works, such as *Astarte Syriaca* (no.45), 'tarnished by the obscurity of tone that shrouds and shadows the work of his later life'.[23] Yet in these very words Carr emphasised qualities which were to come to the fore in the 1880s and 1890s.

fig.40 G.F. Watts, *Eveleen Tennant, later Mrs F.W. H. Myers*, oil on canvas 10.3 × 71.1 cm. Tate Gallery

Some of the most interesting commentary on Rossetti came from writers who were not professional art critics. In early 1883, Frederic Myers wrote a seminal article 'Rossetti and the Religion of Beauty',[24] which effectively defined the artist's role in creating a 'new strain of thought and emotion within the pale of our artistic orthodoxy'. Myers (1843–1901) was a poet and noted classical scholar, whose marriage in 1880 to Eveleen Tennant (fig.40), daughter of collector Sir Charles Tennant and a close friend of Watts,[25] effected his entrée to the art world. Best known as one of the founders of the Society for Psychical Research in 1882, Myers had interests in all matters relating to other-worldly phenomena, perceptions which he brought to bear on his study of the art of Rossetti and also of Watts. His article on Rossetti sought to counteract a tendency to find in the artist's works 'an enigma not worth the pains of solution, and to decry them as obscure, fantastic or even as grossly immortal in tendency'.[26] Myers considered attitudes to female beauty from the 'direct and straightforward outlook on human loveliness' exemplified by Millais (who painted a portrait of Eveleen Tennant in 1874; Tate Gallery), to the views of the French writers Gautier and Baudelaire with the 'cruelty which is the characteristic note of natures in which the sexual instincts have become haunting and dominant'. Rossetti differed completely, as Myers deduced from a study of his translation of Dante's *Vita Nuova*, a work which displayed the mystic union of Love and Beauty. Rossetti personified an artist who 'by the very intensity of his artistic vision, and by some inborn bent towards symbol and mysticism, stands on the side of those who see in material things a spiritual significance'.[27] When applying these ideas to Rossetti's art, Myers found an 'effort to communicate the incommunicable' in the 'remorseful gaze of Pandora, the yearning gaze of Proserpine [no.46]'. Such paintings (including no.46), along with *Lady Lilith* (no.6), 'whose beauty is destruction' and *Astarte Syriaca* (no.45) 'in her sinister splendour', were the 'sacred pictures of a new religion' which reveal that 'mystical worship of Beauty'.[28] Myers dismissed the superficial view of Rossetti as a 'dangerous sensualist', and instead hailed him as a harbinger of the 'reaction of Art against Materialism' in his 'religion of beauty', even though for Rossetti 'we can track his revelation to no source more explicit than the look in a woman's eyes'.[29] Myers's original commentary was just the sort of thinking that finally released Rossetti's art from the shadow of Pre-Raphaelitism, propelling his work into a new realm filled with the 'sense of mystery' and forces beyond mere appearances.

When finally faced with the sum of his late *œuvre*, other writers found similar mysterious and mystical tendencies in Rossetti's art. J. Beavington Atkinson, an astute critic fully attuned to advanced English art of the 1860s onward, made some provocative comments about Rossetti's *Beata Beatrix* (no.44). This painting, like a 'pictorial dream' with the swooning Beatrice, echoed 'the visions of Blake, or the so-called "spirit drawings"'.[30] Given Rossetti's participation in seances,[31] such a link is not unexpected; but just how pervasive were such concerns within the artistic community?

Within a space of two years, the massive Grosvenor Gallery retrospective of Watts's work (1881–2) combined with Rossetti's posthumous exhibitions (1883) brought forth parallels in their art, most especially to critics who knew them personally. Emilie Barrington, artist, writer and Melbury Road matron, wrote 'The Painted Poetry of Watts and Rossetti' for *The Nineteenth Century* in 1883.[32] She conveyed the moment in that year when, as she wrote of Rossetti's exhibition, 'the enthusiasm of a very large majority of the public has been excited by the beauty in it'. She highlighted the chalk drawings, 'fully as interesting as the painted works', but essentially she hailed both Watts and Rossetti for their 'aspiration towards a higher level of thought and feeling', with Watts leaning more to nobility of feeling, while Rossetti evinced 'a strong and weird sense of the *daemon*'. She continued: 'Mr. Rossetti takes us into an atmosphere of enchantment and mystery and we are left trying hopelessly to unravel those mysteries of fate which have always stirred the human brain with the deepest questioning'.[33] The artist focused on the 'beauty in the woman's face which holds in a sphinx-like gaze a secret – the pent up mystery of fate'.[34]

As in Watts's work, the art of Rossetti prompted a seeking out of deeper meanings, challenging the audience in a way that encouraged a resolutely non-naturalistic, anti-materialist stance. This art of the imagination which epitomised the past careers of both painters and the future career of Watts, was fully revealed to the art world by 1883 when the unusual confluence between Watts and Rossetti became clear to the wider circle of the art world.

Shifts in the 1880s: Watts's later subjects

fig.41 G.F. Watts, *Uldra* 1884, oil on canvas 66 × 53.3 cm. Watts Gallery. Acquired with assistance from the National Art Collections Fund

Watts's great monumental 'symbolical' subjects such as *Love and Death* (no.51) and *Time, Death and Judgement* (no.123), although constantly worked on and revised until the 1890s, were conceived in the 1860s, evolving with changes through the 1870s and exhibited in their definitive versions at the Grosvenor Gallery exhibitions, with the latest versions essentially showing refinement, rather than rethinking, of the compositions. By the 1880s one can detect two main redirections in Watts's art: firstly, a stylistic change as experiments in technique led to greater emphasis on an explosion of colour, light and atmospheric effects; and secondly, the introduction of elements of mysticism and reflections on fate, consciousness and the soul.

Watts's technical transformation seems to have come about after some disillusion with the dark appearance of his paintings in the late 1870s. After the Grosvenor Gallery he had largely repainted *Love and Death* to remove the excessive darkness. The French writer, Ernest Chesneau, had commented on the sombreness of a work like *Orpheus and Eurydice* (see no.37),[35] and Watts actively sought to counteract this aspect of his work, as described by Mrs Barrington who became an almost daily visitor to his studio in the early 1880s: 'The love of colour, however, in its fullest chords and most brilliant hues soon reasserted itself. I saw it gradually blending with the more intricate and subtle effects of tone in the years when we first knew him.'[36] The change is evident in a painting like *Uldra* (fig.41) with its riot of colour to create atmospheric effects. Pleased with this quality in his work, Watts sent *Uldra* (not an obviously major effort) to many exhibitions in the 1880s, not least to the Metropolitan Museum of Art in New York and the Exposition Universelle in Paris in 1889.

Love and Life (see fig.49), finished by 1884, also reflects this new interest and is painted in a much lighter key with what Mrs Barrington called a 'sense of atmosphere'. This quality is also evident in some of the landscapes of the 1880s, such as *The Island of Cos* (no.59). Watts at this time renewed his acquaintance with J.M.W. Turner and 'visited the Turner room frequently about that time to drink in the colour' of *Ulysses Deriding Polyphemus*,[37] a painting that depicted celestial creatures, spirits of the sea. Such creatures also entered Watts's *œuvre* with a range of subjects set in the air or up in the clouds, as in *The Judgement of Paris* (fig.42), later named *Olympus on Ida* and *Iris*.[38] Such ethereal visions epitomised Watts's Symbolist style of the 1880s and 1890s.

Watts's visionary subjects relate to an interest in other-worldly matters in the 1880s which shaped works like *The Dweller in the Innermost* (no.75) and *'The All-Pervading'* (no.125). These paintings clearly require some context to illuminate their dense meaning. Indeed there is the contemporary context of the revival of spiritualism in which Watts participated directly, as can now be revealed for the first time. In March 1884, Watts was elected an Honorary Associate Member of the Society for Psychical Research.[39] This investigative group was quite distinct from any of the so-called religious movements of the time. One must resist the temptation to link his work with any one of these movements;[40] Watts was far too much of a doubter to have fallen in completely with any one religion. One must also distinguish between Watts's interests and those of Mary Fraser Tytler, who became his wife in 1886 and who was noted for her indiscriminate pursuit of a succession of alternative religions and cult leaders.[41] Mrs Barrington also warned: 'I think Watts did not feel so definitely the sense of the reality of spiritual life, that inspiration which alone unveils the mystery of the highest psychic experiences, as he did the sense of moral obligations.'[42] Even so he did respond as an artist to some of the currents of the time.

fig.42 G.F. Watts, *The Judgement of Paris (Olympus on Ida)* 1885, oil on canvas 147.5 × 101.5 cm. Private Collection

The first hint of an interest in mystical and other-worldly matters can be identified in Watts's writings from the late 1870s, particularly in his article 'The Present Conditions of Art'.[43] Certain passages, and the vocabulary used, suggest that the artist looked to new areas of inspiration for his works of the early 1880s onward.

In the article, Watts presented his thoughts on the connection he hoped to see between poetry, music and art and in this regard he searched for a meaning in art beyond merely the beautiful, beyond the concerns of the Aestheticism of the 1860s and 1870s. He expressed his distaste for the exhibition rooms where paintings were seen only for the season, undergoing an instant judgement: 'now, consciously or unconsciously, he [the artist] feels that he is working for an immediate and transient effect',[44] and made a plea for 'art that corresponds to the highest literature, both in intention and effect, which must be demanded of our artists, poems painted on canvas, judged and criticized as are the poems written on paper'.[45] He defended the special treatment of subjects which appealed to 'the finest sensibilities and the loftiest emotions'. This treatment

> will often involve, to the purely analytical mind, ludicrous combinations, such as wings growing where they are quite impossible, material drapery upon beings altogether of another element ... but these considerations may be put aside if the result be majestic and beautiful, capable of enlisting the imagination and making a poet of the spectator.[46]

By the time he wrote this article, Watts had already painted *Love and Death* and exhibited it to great acclaim. He himself put wings on his angel in the interests of purely imaginative treatment of his subject.

Watts ranged widely over literature, history, philosophy and the fine art of all eras. In defending an ideal art, and the notion of painting ideas, he resorted to his own strangely Symbolist vocabulary:

> the one thing which is more than ever clearly perceived is the density of the veil that covers the mystery of our being, at all times impenetrable, and to be impenetrable, in spite of which conviction we ever passionately yearn to pierce it. This yearning finds its natural expression in poetry, in art, and in music.[47]

Concluding with an explanation of the thinking behind his own imaginative works, Watts ended suggestively, by pointing to one of his preoccupations, which was to go beyond imagination into more distant, intangible realms:

> Yet as long as humanity is humanity, man will yearn to ascend the heights human footsteps may not tread, and long to lift the veil that shrouds the enigma of being, and he will most prize the echo of this longing in even the incoherent expression of literature, music, and art.[48]

In Watts's work, one can see a metaphorical attempt to 'pierce the veil' and come to grips with the 'mystery of our being' in a painting such as *The Dweller in the Innermost* (no.75).

fig.43 The studio of G.F. Watts, Limnerslease, February 1896. From glass negative in Watts Gallery Archive. Photographer George Andrews

What did Watts mean by using the word 'veil'? For an artist such terminology would also have had a visual meaning. The veil would seem to be related to a distinctly 'visionary' style of painting, much as Watts employed in *'The All-Pervading'* where the image is first seen as a seated figure with clearly readable outlines, to which the artist has added in a hazy atmosphere, until all the firm outlines disappear into a softly focused, and infinitely more ambiguous, image (see fig.43). This suggestive treatment suited particular subjects, as for example in the later version of *Endymion* (Watts Gallery)[49] and quintessentially in Watts's red chalk drawings (see no.106).[50]

The phrase 'lift the veil that shrouds the enigma of being'[51] and other references to the 'density of the veil' suggest a familiarity with spiritualism and some of its popular offshoots. Such interests were widespread in the 1880s and Watts was far from unique in absorbing a pervasive concern of his own social circle,[52] one which should be seen as part of a wider reaction against the values of materialism. Swedenborgianism had had a long-standing appeal to artists, most notably Blake and Flaxman, dating back to the eighteenth century. It enjoyed a revival, with its church in Kensington well situated for artists.[53] The Theosophical Society, founded in 1875, had links with older religions in its search for divine wisdom. Spiritualism and spiritualists abounded at this time, appealing to the upper classes and producing what might almost be considered a form of after-dinner entertainment as the latest spiritualist performed at seances. The publication recording these events was the *Spiritualist*[54] founded by William Henry Harrison. His book *Rifts in the Veil* (1878), drawn from that periodical, comprised a collection of 'inspirational poems and essays given through various forms of mediumship'. This book may well have popularised the notion of the 'veil' as a commonplace when referring to other-worldly matters. Certainly Watts seems to have absorbed the use of this word by 1879.

The Society for Psychical Research was an outgrowth of an earlier group of Cambridge men,[55] including Frederic Myers, who devoted themselves to documenting spiritualist events. When these intellectuals entered into the arena, they lent an authority to the pursuit of the paranormal. It can now be shown that Watts occupied a unique position as the first artist member of this group.[56] By 1887 their subscribers included Tennyson, Gladstone, Ruskin and in 1890 Frederic Leighton.[57] Watts's friendship with Myers represents the closest link thus far (and as yet not fully recognised[58]) between the artist and spiritualism from just the time when new influences can be identified in Watts's work.

Myers wife Eveleen (fig.40) was one of two daughters of Sir Charles Tennant, a noted art collector, whose family spent their holidays in Freshwater on the Isle of Wight, becoming frequent guests at Watts's home, The Briary.[59] Both sisters pursued careers in art. Eveleen (1856–1937) became a professional portrait photographer in the late 1880s; her work has recently been the subject of an exhibition at the National Portrait Gallery.[60] Dorothy (1855–1926), a noted painter who exhibited at the Grosvenor Gallery, had many contacts in the art world, including friendships with artists abroad such as Bastien-Lepage.[61] She knew Watts especially well, encouraging him to write his article 'The Present Conditions of Art' in 1879.[62] Both young women sat to a number of artists, including Watts who painted a series of sympathetic portraits from around 1876 onward.[63]

fig.44 G.F. Watts, *The Messenger* c.1884–5, oil on canvas 274.3 × 150.5 cm. Tate Gallery

After a glittering society wedding in Westminster Abbey, Myers carried on with his literary work, but his greatest energies went into the study of 'forces unknown to science',[64] initially with the Cambridge group and soon after with the Society for Psychical Research. Their attempts at the systematic recording of inexplicable phenomena, encompassing dematerialisations, hallucinations, apparitions, and hypnosis, led to a series of publications. Myers had a particular interest in telepathy, a word he is said to have coined,[65] and his thinking on the use of hypnosis to reveal the 'subliminal self' influenced Freud[66]; his awareness of the multiple levels of consciousness in the human personality was also ahead of his time.

The activities of the Society for Psychical Research intersect tangentially with the art world of the 1880s, but as an individual Myers, through his wife and his career as a poet and critic, forms a more tangible link. In his article 'The Present Conditions of Art', Watts used a distinctly new language; his art reveals even more about concerns related to the spiritual, as, for example, his ongoing preoccupation with death and its consequences in works of the 1880s: the actual moment of death appears in *The Messenger* (fig.44); while *Time, Death and Judgement* (no.123) shows another chapter in the story of death's pervasive power which then culminates with operatic grandeur in *The Court of Death* (fig.45).

Watts was determinedly against any sort of organised religion, but ever open-minded, as an artist, he sought to go beyond mere appearances and suggest ideas on questions of life, death and the cosmos. Myers combined his psychical research with an active interest in the world of art; his writings, particularly in the early 1880s, suggested how much painters and painting of the day formed part of the ongoing speculations of the time. The two artists who attracted Myers were, not surprisingly, Watts and Rossetti. For the latter's posthumous œuvre, Myers identified a 'religion of beauty' replete with mystical elements.

fig.45 G.F. Watts, *The Court of Death* c.1870–1902, oil on canvas 424.2 × 274.3 cm. Tate Gallery

Watts's great retrospective at the Grosvenor Gallery in 1881–2 inspired Myers to write a long poem published first in the *Fortnightly Magazine* in 1882. 'Stanzas on Mr. Watts' Collected Works'[67] reflected Myers's deep classical knowledge which made him open to the resonances of paintings with a cast of characters drawn from ancient mythology. Watts epitomised the continuation of the classical tradition as a living force in his painting. Myers called attention to 'The unrevealing eyes of Death' in the artist's 'symbolical' works. While none of Myers's lines refer directly to aspects of psychic phenomena, there is a sense that Watts's powers as an artist enabled him to reveal the invisible: 'Thereto his soul hath listed long, / When silent voices spake in air'.[68] Watts and Myers knew each other for nearly twenty years, with Myers visiting the artist in his old age. His comments on this occasion were printed as a tribute to Watts in the *Proceedings for the Society of Psychical Research* (and reprinted by Mrs Watts). They reveal that for Myers, Watts was one of the

> saints of a universal religion, who without thought of sect or dogma shall answer to the welcoming Infinite with simplicity and calm. No man, perhaps, has fulfilled this type more perfectly than the great painter who must soon … pass to continue with all readiness his task elsewhere. When last I saw Mr. Watts, in great old age, among the symbolic pictures of his later years, he seemed to me to have become himself a sacred symbol; and I should scarcely have wondered, as I gazed on him, if he had vanished into air.[69]

Watts's paintings of such visionary subjects as *The Genius of Greek Poetry* (no.78) and his series on Death identified him for Myers as the painter *par excellence* among the intellectuals involved in psychical matters in the 1880s. Watts's art spoke to this particular audience, just as it did to continental artists in pursuit of new kinds of imagery.

The paintings Watts executed throughout the 1880s reinforce the view of him as a painter of other-worldly concerns. *Hope*, and *The Dweller in the Innermost* in its first guise as *The Soul's Prism*, both appeared at the Grosvenor Gallery in 1886; Watts worked on *The Messenger* around 1885 and on *'The All-Pervading'* from 1888 onward. Another important example of his writing, 'The Aims of Art' for the *Magazine of Art* in 1888, also serves as a key to understanding some of these later works:

> Profoundly deep in the human mind exists a spiritual yearning dependent on no special creed, questions by nature left without response, yearnings the most perfect knowledge of material things will never stifle. The true prophet, be his language prose or poem, art or music, can transport to regions where earth takes its place among the stars and something beyond of heaven's infinity seems borne upon the air.[70]

fig.46 G.F. Watts, *The Sower of the Systems* c.1902–3, oil on canvas 122.6 × 91.4 cm. Art Gallery of Ontario, Toronto

One detects an artist confident in his search for higher meanings as he writes 'perceptions and emotions are shut up within the human soul, sleeping and unconscious, till the poet or the artist awakens them'.[71] The article paved the way, in its reference to cosmic forces, for the completion of *'The All-Pervading'* and later *The Sower of the Systems* (fig.46 and no.134). It also placed him in the eyes of the public and the artistic community as a painter dedicated to the process of 'awakening' through his art. Such notions lay at the heart of Symbolist literature and art which by the late 1880s were an active force in the art centres of Paris and Brussels.

Watts and international Symbolism

Watts appeared in strength at the Exposition Universelle of 1889 with eight paintings. Among his fellow exhibitors, he stood out with more major oils than anyone else on view[72] and with the type of 'symbolical' painting which by this time he personified. Burne-Jones's sole submission, *King Cophetua and the Beggar Maid* (no.40) created a sensation at the same exhibition. Other British contributions included large, lurid biblical scenes such as John William Waterhouse's *Mariamne* (Forbes Magazine Collection) and Solomon Joseph Solomon's *Samson* (National Museums on Merseyside, Walker Art Gallery) which bore obvious parallels to the work of Jean-Paul Laurens among others. New art from Britain was represented by artists including John Lavery and William Stott; but it was establishment figures like Millais and Leighton, along with Watts and Burne-Jones, who held centre stage.

Among what one critic in 1889 called Watts's 'allégories poétiques',[73] there was *Hope* (fig.35), *Mammon* (no.52) and *Love and Life* (see fig.49 on p.86), the last representing his newer stylistic orientation along with *Uldra* (fig.41) and *The Judgement of Paris* (fig.42). The last three works, airy visions suffused with colour and light, had a direct appeal to contemporary French Post-Impressionism; indeed his work was on occasion linked with 'pointillisme'.[74] Watts's paintings, more than being technical experiments, fuse colour with a spirit of dreamy poetry and capture a mood. This aspect of his work appealed to a very different group of French artists – the Symbolists. Burne-Jones's *King Cophetua and the Beggar Maid* (no.40), also displayed this quality, but without any hint of light-filled, colour-suffused handling. When one French commentator at the Exposition dubbed Watts's works 'fantaisies rêveuses',[75] he isolated the very quality in these paintings that made them so much a part of a Symbolist sensibility.

When Robert de la Sizeranne's series of articles on English art appeared in the *Revue des Deux Mondes*, beginning in 1894 (appearing as a book in France in 1895 and translated into English in 1898),[76] the writer had already visited London some years before and was familiar with the art world here. His original point of departure was the Exposition Universelle in 1889, and this event seems to have prompted him to seek out Watts and other contemporary artists. He referred to Watts as 'the living master who is honoured with a whole room to himself at South Kensington' (now the Victoria and Albert Museum), and he even seems to have visited the artist's own display in the Little Holland House Gallery. Sizeranne's account of his conversion to Watts's distinctive allegories gives a French perspective:

> Some years ago, when I visited the South Kensington Museum for the first time, I took by chance, the staircase leading to the Library, one of the least

> known and least frequented corners of the immense palace. The walls of this staircase are covered with canvases exhibited there for some years ... At that time I held the conviction, common to many, that mythological painting was a false, decadent, commonplace style; that out of such impersonal figures as Death, Justice, Time and Love, nothing more could now-a-days be made than a spiritless decoration for the ceilings of a public building or of a confectioner's shop. I even thought, like many others, that to infuse fresh life-blood, and moving, speaking feeling into these myths ... they must of necessity be metamorphosed into portions of contemporary life ... I still held this opinion when I mounted the first steps of that staircase; by the time I had reached the last step I no longer believed that mythological painting was dead, nor, that in order to enlarge the figure of a fact to the sexless, impersonal universality of an idea, all warmth of feeling and all the drama of life must be extracted from it. What was there between these two opinions? Two pictures by Watts.[77]

These two works, he goes on to explain, were *Love and Death* (no.51) and *Love and Life*. To Watts these paintings were exactly the type of 'symbolical' work he held in highest regard, and had tried to promote abroad. *Love and Life*, along with the other works at the Exposition Universelle, had filtered down to a younger generation, as Sizeranne also confirmed when he famously recorded in the introduction to *English Contemporary Art* (but referring back to a time just after 1889): 'For a long time, at meetings of the symbolists, the names of Watts and Burne-Jones have been heard with reverence, and many adopt and repeat them as magic words, the virtue of which requires no explanation. But some artists have studied their works, they are impregnated with them'.[78]

Burne-Jones's *King Cophetua and the Beggar Maid* exhibited in 1889, and his *The Depths of the Sea* (private collection) seen at the Salon in the same year, had also entered into the Symbolist thinking, to the point where Sizeranne dubbed the great Puvis de Chavannes as 'the French Burne-Jones'. The writer gave full credit to English art when he wrote about 'the newest tendencies which attract young men' that 'it is apparent that they are connected with, or at least that they strangely resemble, contemporary English art'.[79] Some years after, Sizeranne's further comments on the 'silent and beautiful English Art section' in the Exposition of 1889 epitomised the deeply resonant qualities of works such as *King Cophetua* and *Hope* which provided a respite for the eyes and the mind: 'we felt as though everywhere else ... we had seen nothing but matter, and here we had come to the exhibition of the soul'.[80] Watts's work played a key role: 'over all the artists who work in England, it is Watts, the gloomiest of them, who makes a mark on the memory'.[81] This mood of gloom was probably seen as most evident in paintings of deep pathos on the subject of death and in Watts's poetic transcriptions of tales from literature and myth (nos.37 and 48).

Watts's work, visible in France at key moments since 1878, had by the early 1890s fully entered into the French art world, as had a wide range of English art. The importance of English art was soon after reflected in purchases by Léonce Bénédite for the incipient collections of the Luxembourg Museum[82] which included works by Whistler, Sargent and Burne-Jones. Watts, on learning of a proposed purchase, instead presented a large version of *Love and Life* to the French nation in 1893.[83]

In the years around 1890, London emerged as a nexus for the display and cross-fertilisation of Symbolist art with exhibitions at the Grafton Gallery and other smaller exhibiting bodies which attracted a massive influx of continental artists. The medium of pastel with its particular suitability to a suggestive style underwent a revival in the 1880s, first in France at the thriving Société des Pastellistes and then in parallel groups in England where participants included Watts himself. Interestingly, some foreign critics, according to Mrs Barrington, mistook his oil-paintings for pastel;[84] among these perhaps a work like *Hope* (fig.35) when it was seen in 1889. Watts now displayed an interest in pastel, executing works and exhibiting them in the late 1880s. He made a point of belonging to all the major societies for pastel right through to 1900. His real preference was for the closely related medium of red chalk (sanguine) which became a speciality and a major vehicle for the expression of Symbolist ideas (no.106).

This renewed interest in pastel crossed over into England when the enterprising Sir Coutts Lindsay made the Grosvenor Gallery available for the first Pastel Exhibition in 1888. The event prompted a major gathering of international talent with French representatives including Paul Helleu, Paul Besnard and Leon Lhermitte joining Fantin-Latour, another proponent of the medium, and younger artists such as George Clausen, James Shannon and George Frampton, the sculptor; later exhibitions included Jan Toorop (see no.111) who had close ties with England.[85] The pastel exhibition (by this time constituted as the Society of British Pastellists) in 1890 provided the setting for one of Fernand Khnopff's first appearances in England with the large study prosaically entitled *Lawn Tennis* (fig.33 on p.58), a work related to *Memories* (Musées Royaux des Beaux-Arts de Belgique), and the drawing *Silence* (no.107) which opened the eyes of the British art world to one strain of continental Symbolist imagery. It has to be said that for some critics his style in some cases was enigmatic in the extreme: the critic for the *Athenaeum* commented on Khnopff's figures 'looking as if they had lost the way in a fog'.[86] Yet the same writer responded far more positively to *Silence* with its 'poetic suggestiveness'. Khnopff exhibited regularly at the pastel exhibitions when they were transformed into the Society of Pastellists and later into the Pastel Society in 1898. His work was continually available in London at other venues, such as The Society for British Artists, The Society of Portrait Painters and the New Gallery; he also acted as correspondent for *The Studio*.[87] His many friends in London included Burne-Jones (see no.108) and Walter Crane.[88] Khnopff stood as the one omnipresent representative of European Symbolism available to a London audience and he spread the word about English art abroad.

In 1893, the first exhibition at the Grafton Gallery, *Paintings and Sculpture by British and Foreign Artists of the Present Day*, was a landmark event, complete with an artist-designed exhibition catalogue by Violet, Marchioness of Granby. Here in London the art world saw works by Edgar Degas, Khnopff (including *Solitude*, private collection, Switzerland, along with several landscapes, one of his distinctive Symbolist portraits, and a major subject painting, *Samuel and the Witch of*

Endor), Segantini, including *The Punishment of Luxury* (acquired soon after by the Walker Art Gallery, Liverpool), Eugène Carrière, the Anglo-French artist Louis Welden Hawkins (see no.128), and Felicien Rops. Although Symbolism formed but one strain of contemporary continental art, this exhibition at the Grafton Gallery definitively announced its arrival, recognising it as a specific movement.[89]

The large English contingent at the Grafton Gallery was headed by Whistler, Albert Moore, Violet Granby, and Watts whose contributions included small versions of the nudes, *Thetis* and *Daphne* (both now in a private collection).[90] In company with Watts and Whistler, the equally well-established French artist, Degas, also appeared. The idea of Watts's paintings hanging in the same gallery with Degas's *L'Absinthe* 1885–6 (Musée d'Orsay, Paris), is one of the remarkable juxtapositions characteristic of the trend for international exhibitions in the 1890s, for here were two artists whose activities in the 1860s, along, appropriately, with Whistler, helped to formulate later trends in nineteenth-century painting.[91] Watts's *Thetis* and *Daphne* were far from major works, but these ethereal nudes, even more restrained in the small oil versions, restated Watts's position, as described by Comyns Carr in 1880, as a painter of 'spiritualisme raffiné'. What is most remarkable is that an artist of Watts's generation (he was by this time seventy-six), would care to be seen in the company of the much younger group at the Grafton Gallery comprising Frank Brangwyn, George Henry, William Stott, Shannon and Graham Robertson. But, like Whistler, Watts knew the virtues of exhibiting his work as widely as possible, and his constant efforts to do so both at home and abroad continued unabated throughout the 1890s.

In 1893 Watts lent to Munich what was virtually a mini-retrospective when twenty-four paintings and one sculpture travelled for the Jahresausstellung in the Glaspalast, including *Hope*, *The Dweller in the Innermost*, *Death Crowning Innocence* (Tate Gallery), seen in its first major exhibition, and *The Happy Warrior* (no.77). The last work so impressed the German artists and authorities that it was purchased for the Bavarian state, a significant coup for Watts who used to complain in the 1870s that no one bought his paintings. His work became even better known in German-speaking countries, so that when Hugo von Hofmannsthal, writing as Loris in the *Neue Revue*, commented on the international exhibition in Vienna in 1894, he was completely familiar with the œuvre of Watts and Burne-Jones in which he found a 'spiritualization of the corporeal'.[92] He also referred to Rossetti's work, by now well assimilated into the wider art world, especially his 'women with mystic eyes and slender hands' resulting in the 'highest ennobled individual beauty'.[93] One feels that for certain high-minded writers of the 1890s, recent English art provided a purer, more spiritualised vision of beauty, an antidote to some of the more extreme images of French and Belgian Symbolism.

By the early 1890s the Symbolist moment had arrived. Watts's role since the late 1870s can now be seen as crucial. Through works he exhibited abroad during the 1880s and into the 1890s, he was well known to a younger generation on the continent who sought him out as a father-figure of Symbolism. Sâr Péladan in the Manifesto of the Rose+Croix published in *Le Figaro* in September 1891, announced his intention to 'go to London to invite Burne-Jones, Watts and the five other Pre-Raphaelites',[94] although in the event none of these artists did exhibit there. By contrast, the Belgian avant-garde group, La Libre Esthetique (an outgrowth of Les XX), upon holding its first exhibition in 1894 successfully obtained a work by Watts among other British contributors. Again Watts, as an older artist conscious of his international status and supportive of such exhibitions, agreed to lend; but rather than send one of his great 'symbolical' paintings, or even a new work, Watts made an intriguing choice: *Portrait of the Marchioness of Granby* (Violet Lindsay) (fig.47) which in due course went to Brussels. No mere portrait readily available from the Little Holland House Gallery, this painting can be seen as a key Symbolist work itself.

fig.47 G.F. Watts, *Violet Lindsay (Marchioness of Granby)* 1879, oil on canvas 66 × 52 cm. Lord Charteris of Amisfield

Watts painted several versions of Violet Lindsay,[95] turning again and again to a quality of etherealised beauty in her appearance and turning her into a Symbolist muse. Violet Lindsay (1856–1937), aristocrat and artist, first sat to Watts in 1879, several years before her marriage in 1882 to Henry Manners when she became Marchioness of Granby (later Duchess of Rutland). Her sensitive portrait drawings of members of her circle, the 'Souls',[96] reveal their own Symbolist qualities; these were well known and appeared regularly at exhibition, including the Grafton Gallery (for which she also designed the catalogue). Like the Tennant sisters, Violet belonged to an aesthetically aware group so that her friendship with Watts and Burne-Jones followed naturally. Watts painted her for his own pleasure, not for the 'Hall of Fame' portraits but as a way of studying a particular type of beauty. In the prime version (fig.47), she sits against a wierd Leonardesque landscape of rising rocks and mountains,[97] the space extending far into the distance with misty clouds rolling in. Her reddish hair contrasts with the predominantly cool colouring, as tones of blue suffuse the image. The painting went to various exhibitions mainly in the 1890s and was included in the illustrious group of Watts's works at the Munich Jahresausstellung. In 1894 it travelled to Brussels for the first exhibition of La Libre Esthetique,[98] hanging in the same exhibition with a selection of Frampton's sculptures (see no.115). The Symbolist character of Watts's painting was recognised by even such a commentator as Khnopff in his role as art critic. He discussed it in a review for the *Studio* as if it were an icon (and clearly that is the status it held at the exhibition):

> The portrait of the Marchioness of Granby, by G.F. Watts R.A., is the work which dominates the entire exhibition. Placed upon an easel before a bronze-green background, it appears, in its frame of gold, as a superb jewel. The blues of the robe and the blues of the mountains against which is posed the pale head with blond hair form a harmonious *ensemble*, of a richness without parallel.[99]

Watts's ability to create such jewel-like images out of his female sitters attracted Khnopff because he too used female heads in a non-portrait-like way, as their passivity allowed a focus on mood, accentuated by the suggestive handling of chalks. Khnopff's evocation of his experience of seeing Watts's painting almost makes us think that he knew the work from Watts's studio, as perhaps one of the results of his meeting with the older artist. One also wonders if in fact Watts sent this painting because he believed that it would hold considerable appeal for a continental audience. Certainly its status as the portrait of a particlular individual was all but irrelevant; instead its primary appeal was as an icon of mood and colour. An ambiguity of mood, subtle colouring, intense focus on certain elements – here the rocky desolation of the landscape – all combine to give the work of art the suggestive qualities of a poem or piece of music.

Such qualities had their antecedents in the early Aesthetic movement of the 1860s. Watts sought out those qualities in his art for decades. By the 1890s, when Khnopff, an artist from another generation and another country, recognised them, it is evident that these qualities, by this time seen as 'Symbolist', had acquired a relevance beyond the time and place in which they had originated. In Watts's last works, such as *Destiny*, *Progress* (both Watts Gallery) and *The Sower of the Systems* (fig.46), painted in the new century, the artist had engaged in a dialogue not with his own contemporaries, but with posterity.

Symbolism in Three Dimensions

Robert Upstone

In the closing decades of the nineteenth century there was a vigorous revival of British sculpture, and the work that pioneered this revitalisation was explicitly Symbolist. A new generation of sculptors chose to use bronze rather than marble, and took as their points of departure three quite distinct traditions – modern French sculpture, as a direct example and a practical studio training; the bronze sculpture of the Florentine Renaissance, particularly the very detailed work of Cellini; and contemporary British painting by Watts and Burne-Jones. The sculptors' interest in this closest source, the leading artists of the older generation, has sometimes been considered least important. Yet it is a fascinating connection, for it reveals both a pictorial element in the 'New Sculpture', and a sculptural equivalent to Symbolist painting. An avant-garde of sculptors looked to the visual language and innovatory range of subject of the new painting, and translated them into three-dimensional work that was, at its most distinctive, among the purest manifestations of Symbolist art in Britain. The three leading sculptors of this revival were Alfred Gilbert, George Frampton and Harry Bates, and there are remarkable similarities between their sculpture and the paintings of their admired older mentors.

Until the mid-1870s British sculpture remained largely trapped in a stilted version of the neo-Classicism of earlier in the century. Edmund Gosse recalled in 1894 that twenty years before: 'The very thought of English statuary was ridiculous ... sculpture in England was practically dead ... all that survived was a debased and sunken tradition of the Georgian age.'[1] The revival was christened the 'New Sculpture' by Gosse, who regarded the sculptors who had brought it about – Frederic, Lord Leighton, Hamo Thornycroft, Edward Onslow Ford, Henry Armstead, Alfred Gilbert, George Frampton, Harry Bates, William Goscombe John, Thomas Brock and Frederick William Pomeroy – as a homogeneous group with the common ideals of naturalism and vigour of conception. They shared a background of training in the French tradition, received either directly in Paris or from Jules Dalou and his successor Edouard Lanteri at the National Art Training School in South Kensington (later the Royal College of Art). Within the group Gosse surveyed, however, there were significant differences in both the subjects and the treatment of sculpture. While Gilbert and Frampton produced consciously Symbolist works, other sculptors, such as Thornycroft, made sculpture that was ideal or naturalist in concept: male and female nudes, or modern subjects of mothers with children, and rural workers.

The Symbolist New Sculptors produced works which used both explicit symbols and concealed suggestion to express ideas and emotions of an often intangible kind, concerning love, death and the spiritual. Fine modelling and unusual decoration emphasised the Symbolist content, and was frequently more adventurous than French counterparts before Rodin, and the 'meaning' more

opposite
detail from George Frampton, *My Thoughts are my Children* 1894, cast c.1900 (no.116)

intangibly complex. The New Sculptors' revival of bronze 'lost wax' casting allowed the creation of a wonderfully expressive surface, and sometimes in combination with this, they began to use richly diverse materials such as ivory and precious metals and stones. Sculpture flourished in the 1880s and 1890s in Britain and succeeded in captivating the mind as well as the eye, so that by 1901 the critic Marion Spielmann could note 'a radical change has come over British sculpture – a change so revolutionary that it has given a new direction to the aims and ambitions of the artist and raised the British school to a height unhoped for'.[2]

The Symbolist subjects were drawn from, and often transformed, both classical myth and the Arthurian romances of Mallory and Tennyson, while Keats inspired both Frampton's *Lamia* (no.69) and William Reynolds-Stephens's *Happy in Beauty, Life and Love and Everything* 1895–6. Burne-Jones's *Briar Rose* series of paintings was particularly influential, having a pronounced effect on Gilbert and prompting Reynolds-Stephens's relief version of the central panel *Sleeping Beauty* 1897 (Royal Academy).

Although most British sculptors encountered modern French sculpture at first hand in Paris, which became increasingly easy and cheap to visit, it was also glimpsed in London exhibitions in the last two decades of the century. Jean-Léon Gérôme's *Bellona* was shown at the Royal Academy in 1893, an interesting comparison with Frampton's *Mysteriarch* (no.115) standing a short distance away. Rodin had exhibited for the first time in London in 1882, sending *John the Baptist* to the Academy and *Man with the Broken Nose* to the Grosvenor Gallery. His *The Age of Bronze* caused a sensation when shown at the Royal Academy in 1884. W.F. Henley's *Magazine of Art* enthused: 'The modelling throughout is extraordinary for suavity, force, and fidelity, the pose full of nobility … Reserved force and energy are expressed with wonderful skill and reticence',[3] but Gosse warned of 'the danger of M. Rodin's manner', believing it too sketchy.[4] In a display that neatly summarised the different strands of contemporary sculpture, the Academy that year also included Thornycroft's life-size *The Mower*, Onslow Ford's *Linus* (a full-size nude posed surprisingly similarly to *The Age of Bronze*) and *Icarus* (no.117) by Gilbert, whom Rodin considered the finest of British sculptors. In 1888, when Marion Spielmann told him that British critics considered Gilbert equal to Cellini, Rodin replied 'Oh, far beyond that!'[5]

While still a student Alfred Gilbert was widely recognised as the most gifted sculptor of his generation. From the beginning he wanted his work to express ideas and feelings, and to go beyond illustration to convey an implicit content that was often ambivalent or indefinable. Both in youth and later life he spoke with reverence of Watts and Burne-Jones, whose art had suggested to him much that became the basis of his own. Gilbert trained first at the Royal Academy schools in London and then at the École des Beaux-Arts in Paris under Pierre-Jules Cavelier. From 1878 to 1884 he lived in Italy, where he formed the ambition to emulate Renaissance sculpture, particularly the bronzes of Donatello and Cellini. Gilbert appreciated the crucial importance of casting, and produced bronzes with a sensuous surface capable of embodying the emotional expression that came from precise modelling. This is perhaps what Rodin admired most about his work, and indeed, in some of Gilbert's sculpture there is something in

fig.48 Alfred Gilbert, *Study of a Head* 1883, bronze 31.1 cm high. National Museum of Wales, Cardiff

the fluid surface modulation and rejection of neo-Classical crispness that echoes that of the French master. Gilbert's criticised habit of sometimes leaving mould lines visible also recalls Rodin's attitude to 'finish'.

Gilbert's early *Study of a Head* 1883 (fig.48) was a radical innovation in British sculpture. This turbaned head of a young woman with down-turned eyes rejected straightforward portraiture or naturalism in favour of atmosphere and the expression of a complex and ambiguous mood. Gilbert derived the turban – later a commonplace of his and other sculptors' work – from Antonin Mercié's *David with the Head of Goliath* 1878 (Musée d'Orsay, Paris), which he had seen at the 1878 Exposition Universelle in Paris. The model's down-cast eyes have an Italian Renaissance source in Michelangelo's *Dying Slave* in the Louvre, but could also be found in many painted heads by Burne-Jones. Enigmatic, subjectless heads, neither portraits nor ideal, and without any literary subject, became a vogue after Gilbert's *Study* was exhibited, and it was an example too for Frampton's series of imaginative female busts. It is tempting to look for the origin of the ideal of introspective and beautiful women adopted by Gilbert and his imitators in Rossetti's series of female 'portraits' of the 1860s and 1870s (see nos.2–6), which achieve a similar aesthetic and emotional effect.

Gilbert demonstrated his new pre-eminence with a series of nude male figures in bronze. Their subjects, he admitted, were an allegory of his own ambition, and were frankly autobiographical. The first was undertaken after seeing Cellini's *Perseus and Medusa* in Florence. Gilbert represented himself as *Perseus Arming* 1882 (private collection), comparing his own position on the brink of heroic success as a sculptor to that of Cellini's young hero in arms:

> After seeing the wonderful and heroic statue by Cellini, amazed as I was by that work, it still left me somewhat cold insomuch that it failed to touch my human sympathies. As at that time my whole thoughts were of my artistic equipment for the future, I conceived the idea that Perseus before becoming a hero was a mere mortal, and that he had to look to his equipment. That is a presage of my life and work at that time and I think the wing still ill-fits me, the sword is blunt and the armour dull as my own brain.[6]

Adapting archetypal legends for personal expression, creating new meanings for time-honoured imagery, was characteristic of British Symbolist art, and in his nudes Gilbert also added unusual and personal elements.

The brilliant modelling and difficult twisted pose of *Perseus Arming* aroused much admiration, and made Gilbert's reputation when it was shown at the Grosvenor Gallery in 1882. To his surprise it also won an honourable mention at the 1883 Paris Salon, giving him 'encouragement to continue the task I had set myself, that was to go on writing my own history by symbol'.[7] Leighton, President of the Royal Academy, was greatly impressed by *Perseus Arming*, and encouraged Gilbert by commissioning a bronze of a subject left to the sculptor's discretion. The result was *Icarus* 1884 (no.117),[8] in which Gilbert now characterised himself as the doomed youth: 'I was very ambitious: why not "Icarus" with his desire for flight?'[9] Such identification suggests that Gilbert was already conscious of his own recklessness, which was ultimately to lead to his ruin.

The pose and exquisite casting of *Icarus* recalls Donatello's bronze *David*, as does the integration of the base into the composition and the accentuation of the figure's sensuality by contrasting nude flesh with headgear and wings. The overall mood of the piece – sombre anticipation, the inevitability of doom dictated by character – is also reminiscent of Watts's paintings of the preceding years. Watts had painted many characters from classical myth, whom he considered relevant to contemporary life. Gilbert's winged, naked figure finds its visual counterpart perhaps in the angel in Watts's *Love and Life* c.1884–5 (fig.49). The sculpture's rocky base, the figuratively distinct area that holds the symbolic comment of a snake devouring a bird, is an echo of the rocky outcrop in Watts's picture. Such similarities may be coincidental, but exhibited within a year of each other, these works at the least illustrate a common iconography between Gilbert's sculpture and contemporary British painting.

fig.49 G.F. Watts, *Love and Life* c.1884–5, oil on canvas 222.2 × 121.9 cm. Tate Gallery

Gilbert and Watts later formed a warm friendship, albeit based on the much younger sculptor's rapt admiration for the dignified and self-absorbed genius revered by his circle as 'Signor'. Mary Watts asked Gilbert to make a portrait bust of her husband in the summer of 1888, and he was given eighteen sittings over a number of months. Gilbert was able to talk extensively with Watts, and view his work, which he undoubtedly already knew in some depth from the retrospective exhibition held at the Grosvenor Gallery in 1881–2. Even on the first visit, Mary recalled Watts and Gilbert 'talking together earnestly of things deeply interesting to both. They were finding themselves in mutual sympathy'.[10] She remembered Gilbert looking round the gallery one day, where 'shaking his fist at some design, he exclaimed, "He steals all the best subjects away from the sculptors ... Mr Watts tells me things that are of such infinite value, and they are so simple!"'.[11] In a gesture of admiration for Watts, Gilbert refused payment for the bust. Watts reciprocated by painting Gilbert's portrait on the same terms.[12] He clearly much admired Gilbert and judged his huge *Jubilee Memorial to Queen Victoria* in Winchester Castle 'the finest thing since the Colleone',[13] an interesting comparison to Verocchio based presumably on its size, its skill in bronze technique, and its portrayal of power.

Gilbert would have found little disagreement with Watts's well-known statement: 'I paint ideas, not things. I paint primarily because I have something to say ... my intention is not so much to paint pictures which shall please the eye, as to suggest great thoughts that shall speak to the imagination and to the heart and arouse all that is best and noblest in humanity.'[14] These aims could equally apply to Gilbert's art, albeit with the rider that he sought additionally to enrapture the eye.

It is possible that Gilbert inspired Watts in one of the pictures most admired by his contemporaries. In 1882 Gilbert exhibited his marble group *The Kiss of Victory* (fig.50) at the Royal Academy. Victory is traditionally represented as a winged figure, and groups showing Victory holding a dead warrior had been executed earlier by both Antonin Mercié and Gustave Doré. Mercié's sculpture is *Gloria Victis* 1872–5 (Petit Palais, Paris), which Gilbert saw at the 1878 Exposition Universelle; Doré's is *La Gloire* 1878 (Musée des Beaux-Arts, Maubeuge), shown at the Salon in 1887. However, while Doré's Victory inflicts death by stabbing her hero, and

fig.50 Alfred Gilbert, *The Kiss of Victory* 1878–81, marble 147.4 cm high. Minneapolis Institute of Arts

Mercié's is also aggressive, holding the naked youth as an inert corpse, Gilbert's characterisation is entirely different. His Victory holds with a remarkable delicacy the still living warrior, whose figure, caught at the moment of falling backwards, seems to hang in space. An overwhelming tenderness suffuses the whole piece, culminating in the touch of the angel's lips, the feeling of softness accentuated by the sensuousness of the carving. Notions of Victory awarding the kiss of Death, the reciprocal relation of Victory and Death, and of death being the gateway to everlasting life are essentially Wattsian. Watts undoubtedly saw this sculpture at the Academy in 1882, and he borrowed both mood and aspects of the design for his picture *The Happy Warrior* (no.77), exhibited two years later.

Burne-Jones was a further rich source of inspiration for Gilbert. The figures of virtues in his *Monument to Henry Fawcett* 1885–7 (Westminster Abbey) included, for the first time in Gilbert's work, both draped female figures and a knight in armour, much in the manner of Burne-Jones.[15] They apparently first met in 1884, for Burne-Jones wrote that year: 'Gilbert the sculptor is a gain. I go warily, taught by old follies – but I think he will be a comfort on the way down', and in 1885 'As for my sculptor ... there is an artist ... we are such friends that we are shy of meeting ... I hear that he talks about me and I know that I think of him a great deal'.[16] Gilbert himself remembered their first meeting was later, at the Grosvenor Gallery in 1886, when Sir Coutts Lindsay introduced them by saying 'You and this boy must know each other, Ted. You are kindred spirits'.[17] Gilbert was proud of their subsequent 'sincere friendship which lasted to the day of his death, a friendship of which the memory has cheered me in hours of despondency'.[18] These feelings were evidently reciprocated, for Lady Burne-Jones wrote 'Edward's hope was raised ... as it had not been for a long time, by seeing the work and making the acquaintance of Mr Alfred Gilbert'.[19]

Dining with the Burne-Joneses at their Fulham house, Gilbert much admired *King Cophetua and the Beggar Maid* (no.40), which:

> roused feelings of wonder and joy, and I felt such a rush of enthusiasm and sympathy with the artist and his aims, as still recurs when I think about his works ... The *Briar Rose* series, as yet incomplete, was a revelation of the power of human genius to assert itself as a teaching factor over material effort. From that moment I became a humble proselyte[20]

From this time Gilbert's sculpture regularly incorporated ideas from Burne-Jones's pictures. Nude figures were abandoned, and instead he investigated the evocative possibilities of drapery, intricate decoration, and the opportunities for both provided by figures in medieval armour.

The culmination of Gilbert's work of this kind was the *Tomb of the Duke of Clarence* 1892–1928 (Albert Memorial Chapel, Windsor Castle), his fullest development of the ideas underlying the Fawcett Memorial. The tomb is constructed from variously coloured decorative materials – bronze, marble, aluminium, ivory and brass. The central life-size figure of the recumbent duke is surrounded by an intricate grille, with uprights supported by angels with flowing robes and banners; at his head an angel holds over him a crown in the form of a miniature city. The grille is surmounted by a series of saints serving as mourners, highly original in their design and modelling. The aluminium and ivory *St George* seems derived from knights in Burne-Jones's *Perseus* and *Briar Rose* series (see no.113), the armour being of a similar although by this time generic type. The figures of *St Elizabeth of Hungary* and *The Virgin* (no.118) owe something to painted Gothic ecclesiastical sculpture, but Gilbert embellished them with sumptuous ornament. His *Virgin* 1899 is an early example of Art Nouveau, covered with bronze roses painted in soft red and gold, again referring to the floral motifs found in Burne-Jones, but reworked in a startlingly original idiom. The figure of *St Edward the Confessor* is recognisable as a portrait of Watts, which Gilbert admitted was 'an indulgence which I permitted myself as my personal recompense for my labour, by portraying a suggestion of a contemporary existence of the greatest poet-painter of our era. The head is actually a portrait, and I have not thought it impertinent to dress my hero as a King in his art and a Confessor in his modesty of purpose'.[21]

The *Clarence Tomb* is one of the most conspicuous examples of Gilbert's deliberate denial of realism through disparity of scale. While many New Sculptors such as Thornycroft, Pomeroy and Albert Toft aimed at an ever more naturalistic figure style, Gilbert contradicted the realism of his figures with weird but compelling disjunctions of scale, such as the life-size Duke of Clarence with his miniature mourners, the face of Henry Fawcett looming out of a cartouche over smaller full-length figures, or the putti writhing beneath his portrait of Eliza Macloghlin as a face emerges from her left breast (1906–7, Tate Gallery). His work became increasingly richly encrusted, with varied decorations that fight for equal attention, or influence our understanding of the principal subject. The clean, pure modelling and casting of Gilbert's earlier nudes was replaced by an urge to cover every surface with decoration, to the extent of evoking feelings of claustrophobia and satiety. The thread of fantastic strangeness that runs through Gilbert's mature work is disquieting, disturbing the psyche on an unconscious level in a way that is wholly Symbolist.

Like Gilbert, George Frampton was also inspired by Burne-Jones, and especially by his *King Cophetua and the Beggar Maid*. He first saw this in Paris in 1889, when, although still a student, he was already a member of the Art Workers' Guild alongside many of Burne-Jones's circle. Frampton had trained at the Royal Academy schools, and then from 1887 to 1889 in Paris in Mercié's atelier. He later played down this part of his background, stating 'excepting a short period in Paris, after I had left the Royal Academy schools, I had no continental tuition'.[22] In fact Frampton had stronger links with the continent than any sculptor in London, and Spielmann noted in 1901 that he was perhaps even more popular in Germany than in Britain.[23] He exhibited widely, in Paris, in Brussels – including the first Libre Esthétique – at the first Vienna and Munich Secessions, at the Dresden 1897 International Exhibition and elsewhere, winning critical praise. Frampton had absorbed recent developments in French and Belgian sculpture, particularly a taste for polychromy and diversity of materials. Echoes of sculpture by Gérôme, Moreau-Vauthier and Paul Dubois can be recognised in his work, but he elaborated them into something altogether more striking, that subtly provoked and unsettled the imagination.

Frampton chose a Wattsian subject for his first major sculpture, *The Angel of Death* 1888 (destroyed).[24] It won an honourable mention at the 1888 Salon, where he also showed a bust-length portrait entitled *Christabel* (untraced).[25] This has been thought to be a portrait of Christabel Cockerell, his future wife, but their son denied this.[26] It might therefore depict the eponymous virtuous heroine of Coleridge's strange poem 'Christabel', in which she resists the enchantment and evil advances of the witch Geraldine; but perhaps it is both these things, as an allegorical portrait. The most obvious sculptural precedents are the half-length portrait busts of the Renaissance, with which it has similarities of costume, expression, design and modelling. *Christabel* was the first of what became a series of head and shoulder imaginative portraits of women, which became progressively more unsettling.

In 1888 Frampton made a coloured plaster bas-relief titled *Mary* (untraced).[27] The Virgin is depicted in profile, eyes lowered, her turbaned head outlined against the disc of a halo, a motif Frampton later developed in the whole-heartedly pagan *Mysteriarch* 1892 (no.115). Cast in plaster and painted in soft colours, this was a work of startling originality. While it borrowed elements of Moreau-Vauthier's allegorical portrait of a female warrior *Gallia* (Paris International Exhibition 1889), through ambiguity of expression and title Frampton created something piercingly Symbolist. The source for his title is unknown, but the subject of woman as mysterious priestess and goddess may relate to his feelings for Christabel, who posed for it. The flaming disc behind her head is a pagan version of a halo, and may allude to sun worship. If so, it identifies her as the goddess Isis, who in Egyptian art bears the solar disc on her crown. Alternatively, the *Mysteriarch* may be a characterisation of one of the priestesses who officiated over the 'Mysteries' of the secret cults of ancient Greece.

The *Mysteriarch*'s mystic, all-seeing, inward-looking gaze and androgynous features found their counterpart in Fernand Khnopff's pictures of women (no.108), and the Belgian artist took particular interest in this sculpture. Frampton sent it to the inaugural exhibition of La Libre Esthétique in Brussels in 1894, where fellow exhibitors included Pierre Puvis de Chavannes, Odilon Redon, Jan Toorop, Paul Gauguin, Maurice Denis, Eugène Carrière, James Ensor and Aubrey Beardsley. Reviewing the exhibition, the French critic Roger Marx singled out Frampton, writing: 'Beyond our frontiers the movement against materialism accelerates … The fight for spiritual expression was taken up by Watts … and is now continued by another artist from across the Channel, Mr George Frampton, a sculptor-decorator obsessed with dream and mysticism'.[28] Khnopff also reviewed Frampton's contributions, writing 'All of these are full of curious research, cleverly presented, and, above all, modelled in a scholarly and delicate fashion'.[29]

fig.51 Fernand Khnoff, *Sibyl* 1894, wax. Untraced, probably destroyed

Khnopff was clearly struck by the *Mysteriarch*, for in 1894 he exhibited a remarkably similar piece at the Brussels Salon, *Sibyl* (fig.51); this repeated the ambiguous title, polychromy and format, the background disc and androgynous features. The principal differences in Khnopff's version are the lowered eyes and hands framing the face. Khnopff had presumably already seen the *Mysteriarch* earlier in London when it was shown at the Royal Academy in 1893, for from 1891 he visited England every year to see the large exhibitions of new work. The

Mysteriarch brought Frampton recognition from the Royal Academy, for he was elected an Associate the year after it was shown there.

Frampton's next bust-length sculpture was *Mother and Child* 1894–5 (Victoria and Albert Museum, London). This depicts Christabel and their new-born son Meredith, the future painter. It has certain affinities of modelling with Gérôme's *Sarah Bernhardt* 1895 (Musée d'Orsay, Paris), but presumably this is coincidental. The apparent simplicity and charm of the subject is somewhat subverted by the oppressive detail and brightness of the piece. Woman is characterised here as Mother rather than Priestess, but the sculpture has an unexpected ambivalence of feeling: where it should be warm, charming and celebratory, it has instead the frozen aura of a funerary monument.

Frampton's series culminated with *Lamia* 1899–1900 (no.69). Constructed from bronze and ivory, it is decorated with opals, symbols of doom and ill-luck. Their choice may have been inspired by sensational popular obituaries of King Alphonso XII of Spain (d.1885), whose antique opal ring brought premature death to all who wore it, including, finally, the King himself. The bold combination of bronze and ivory is a manifestation of the same approach to polychromy that on the Continent is exemplified by Charles Van der Stappen's silver and ivory *Mysterious Sphinx* 1897, Paul Dubois's *La Liberté*, and to a lesser degree Alfons Mucha's *Nature* 1899 which uses different materials.

Ivory was used increasingly at this time, a phenomenon which Khnopff explained in 1894. He described how Van Estvelde, Secretary of State for the Congo, had invited Belgian sculptors 'to utilise the ivory which came to Antwerp in great quantities'; the results were shown with great success in Brussels, where 'almost all the works were purchased, and many found their way to England'.[30] Khnopff noted how 'the calm, serene quality of the ivory' could be accentuated by combination with a contrasting material.[31] The availability of good quality, modestly priced Congo ivory from the 1890s coincided with an admiration throughout Europe for Belgian carving, and marked a concomitant rise in its use.

In Frampton's *Lamia*, woman is portrayed as temptress and murderess, a recurrent theme in continental Symbolism. The original story comes from Greek mythology. Lamia's children were murdered by a jealous rival, and she took revenge by murdering the children of others. Her cruelty turned her face into a mask, and later she seduced young men and killed them in their sleep by sucking their blood. Keats's poem provides an additional source, and Frampton may illustrate the moment where under Apollonius's gaze 'Lamia, no longer fair, there sat a deadly white'.[32] Susan Beattie noted the sculpture's sexual undercurrents: 'infected by the … sado-masochistic delight in flesh constrained and corseted by metal and gems … *Lamia* is one of the most self-revealing statements ever made by its creator … concerned with the conflict between the nature and fact of female sexuality and the myth of purity; with the relationship between the conscious and unconscious mind'.[33] The choice of a subject who devoured her victims might be seen as part of the widespread *fin de siècle* fear of women, a recurrent theme in Symbolist art often treated using the myth of the Theban Sphinx.[34] Frampton's perception of women was evidently a complex mixture of attraction and fear, and whether unconsciously or not, his sculptural portrayals

fig.52 Harry Bates *The Story of Psyche* 1887, silvered bronze 33 × 24.1 × 74.9 cm. Board of Trustees of the National Museums and Galleries on Merseyside (Walker Art Gallery)

became progressively more disturbing. That Frampton's lasting fame was later secured with his realisation of the eternal boy *Peter Pan* (1910, Kensington Gardens) perhaps adds further insight into the Edwardian collective unconscious.

Lamia was one of the last of Frampton's overtly Symbolist salon sculptures. His life-size full-length monument in bronze and marble *Dame Alice Owen* 1896–7 (Owen's School, Potter's Bar) attracted massive press attention, and he devoted the remainder of his distinguished career to portraits and memorials of a progressively more stylised design, including the exceptional *Edith Cavell Monument* 1920 (St Martin's Place).

Like Frampton, Harry Bates came from a background of architectural carving, and continued to be the leading exponent of the sculptural decoration of buildings throughout the 1880s and '90s. His most notable work was for the Institute of Chartered Accountants. Taught first by Dalou, and then at the Royal Academy schools, in 1883 he won the gold medal for his relief *Socrates Teaching*, and with a travelling studentship of £200 went to Paris. Here he

> broke through the usual custom of joining a crowded atelier, picking up what he could from master and fellow students. He took a studio of his own, worked from models of his own, and engaged no less a person than Rodin to be his mentor … it is to Rodin's honour that as soon as he saw what his pupil could do, and what his ambitions were, he declined all return for his trouble beyond the pleasure of watching its fruition.[35]

Bates was not directly influenced by Rodin, but he greatly admired the energy and vitality of his sculpture, a quality exemplified in his own *Hounds in Leash* 1889 (Tate Gallery). However, Watts and Burne-Jones were also frequent sources of inspiration to him, as is often visible in the figures in his reliefs. In the relief triptych *The Story of Psyche* (fig.52), Zephyrus in the central panel evidently draws upon the figure of Death in Watts's *Love and Death* (no.51). Psyche's pose is virtually identical with that in Burne-Jones's gouache *Cupid finding Psyche* 1865–87 (Manchester City Art Gallery), although here she is naked.[36] Bates's Cupid in the right-hand panel also comes partly from this source, but here crouches rather than bends. The panel of Psyche sitting on a rock is close in pose and mood to Watts's *Hope* (no.76), exhibited the previous year.

Burne-Jones himself was greatly interested in sculpture and held firm views about sculptural quality. As John Christian has noted, there is a strongly sculptural character to many of his draped figures, deriving from passionate admiration of the Elgin Marbles.[37] His designs for the Lanercost Priory reliefs (1879) foreshadow Bates's relief work.[38]

Bates displayed his absorption of Watts's iconography in the startlingly imaginative *Mors Janua Vitae* ('Death the Gateway to Life' 1899; figs.53, 54) in which an Angel of Death raises a young woman away from the world. It is a subject worthy of Watts, and the two principal figures are partly taken from his *Love and Life* c.1884–5 (fig.49), while an additional source for the woman is Watts's *Psyche* 1880 (Tate Gallery). Beneath them the globe recalls the crown held by the angel in Gilbert's *Clarence Tomb*. The procession of women around the base derives from the Dance of Time in Watts's *Chaos* (no.49), although the maidens in Burne-Jones's *The Golden Stairs* (no.68), and *The Wedding of Psyche* 1894–5 (Musée d'Art Moderne, Brussels) may be additional sources. There are also similarities to Leighton's *Daphnephoria* c.1874–6 (Lady Lever Art Gallery, Port Sunlight). The twisting figures emerging from the rocks below are based on the Titans in *Chaos*. Bates worked on *Mors Janua Vitae* while ill, and its gloomy subject turned out to be eerily prophetic for it was his last work, and he died shortly after its completion.

The demise of Symbolist sculpture in Britain coincided with the triumph of Edwardian imperialism in both sculpture and architecture. There was no place here for the introspective and personal, and it was the more confident work of sculptors such as Thornycroft and Bertram Mackennal which took greatest advantage of this brief episode of rich patronage. The great memorial exhibitions of Leighton, Burne-Jones and Watts also marked a watershed. Inspired by French painting and aesthetic theory, subsequent successive waves of the British avant-garde rejected these artists and their followers as irrelevant to the modern age. To the modernists, the Great War seemed to confirm this break between the old world and the new, although others took refuge in the traditional imagery of knights and angels.[39] The advent of the new century largely marked the disappearance of Symbolist sculpture. Bates was dead, and Frampton, a knighted Academician, gradually abandoned his Symbolist work. Gilbert, facing bankruptcy and scandal, fled to Bruges in 1901. His choice of refuge is revealing, for Bruges had been the capital of European Symbolism since the publication of Georges Rodenbach's novel *Bruges-la-Morte* (Paris, 1892). This Symbolist novel's hero, an inconsolable widower, finds echoes of his grief in the atmosphere and architecture of the town. Indeed, Rodenbach's Bruges must have perfectly matched Gilbert's feelings there of exile, bitterness and mortality, before the eventual resurrection of his return to England in 1926.

fig.53 Harry Bates, *Mors Janua Vitae* 1899, bronze, ivory and mother of pearl 94 cm high. Board of Trustees of the National Museums and Galleries on Merseyside (Sudley Art Gallery)

fig.54 Harry Bates, *Mors Janua Vitae* 1899, detail of base

Catalogue Note

Note on authorship

Authorship of catalogue entries is indicated by initials:

AW	Andrew Wilton
BB	Barbara Bryant
CSN	Christopher Newell
MAS	MaryAnne Stevens
RU	Robert Upstone
SW	Simon Wilson

Measurements

Height is given before width, centimetre size before inches (the latter in parentheses); for irregularly shaped exhibits, the maximum extent is cited.

Support

The support is given in each catalogue entry, except where a work is simply 'on paper'.

Provenance (*'Prov'*)

Three full points indicate lacunae in our knowledge of the history of a work.

Exhibition history (*'Exh'*)

Abbreviations are used in the catalogue entries. For full references, see pp.294–6.

Literature (*'Lit'*)

Exhibition catalogues are not cited under *'Lit'* if the exhibitions in question have already been cited under *'Exh'*. Abbreviations are used in the catalogue entries. For full references, see pp.296–9.

General Abbreviations

b.l.	bottom left
b.r.	bottom right
bt	bought
exh. cat.	exhibition catalogue
repr.	reproduced
t.l.	top left
t.r.	top right

Lilith and her Daughters

In the 1850s the British were to an extent cut off from the continent of Europe by a real cultural difference: the high-minded Protestant moralism that developed under the young Victoria ensured that much of what was happening in the arts abroad was deemed unfit for public consumption in Britain. But among artists, links with the France of Napoleon III were strong. Several British painters found a market in Paris, and Pre-Raphaelite pictures were shown at the Salon there in 1855. A number of writers including Robert and Elizabeth Barrett Browning enjoyed close ties with the French in that decade. The young Algernon Charles Swinburne was quick to absorb and identify with the poetry and ideas of Charles Baudelaire, 'one of the most exquisite, most delicate, most perfect poets of the century', and soon became his self-appointed apologist in the circle of Dante Gabriel Rossetti in London.

Baudelaire argued that art should not be used for narrative or moral purposes, but simply to express the artist's state of mind, which in his case was, even in the eyes of the French themselves, often gloomily self-indulgent and perverted. As Swinburne put it, 'Not the luxuries of pleasure in their simple first form, but the sharp and cruel enjoyments of pain, the acrid relish of suffering felt or inflicted, the sides on which nature looks unnatural, go to make up the stuff and substance of this poetry. Very good material they make, too'. Swinburne and Rossetti both found in Baudelaire's affirmation of the value of the aesthetic experience *per se* an authority for their own burgeoning sense that both painting and writing should concern themselves with things other than the functional – the mere telling of stories, the sententious delivering of moral truths. They exemplified a new preoccupation with internal and private mental states that was emerging out of the self-searching of the Romantics in the earlier part of the century. Long before Freud came to the conclusion that a central aspect of our psychology was the part played by sexuality, artists had isolated the subject and explored it in ways that opened up levels of awareness that had previously been submerged. In France, the redeployment of classical myths by Gustave Moreau in the late 1850s transformed the subject-matter of Ingres into the stuff of erotic nightmare. At the same time, in England, Rossetti and a few others, among them Frederick Sandys and Frederic Leighton, were reinventing a genre that had been popular in the romantic period – the idealised female portrait, usually of a literary heroine – to convey more personal and complex emotions.

In Rossetti's *Bocca Baciata* of 1859 (no.2), the painter's mistress, gazing pensively at the viewer – the artist himself – or perhaps at her own reflection in a mirror, embodies the painter's own desire, and simultaneously represents a distant ideal. The implication that the picture surface itself is a mirror through which we may be observing a reflection invests the image with further ambiguity: reality is opposed to reflection, to a dream world, or to an ideal world existing in parallel with our own. These themes were to be developed by Rossetti in many works. One is *Lady Lilith* (no.6), a reference to the Talmudic Mother of Eve who takes on herself the persona of priestess and temptress that so preoccupied the Victorians.

FREDERIC, LORD LEIGHTON 1830–1896

1 Pavonia 1858–9

Oil on canvas 53 × 41.5 (20⅞ × 16⅜)
Prov: Bt from the artist by George Payne; by family descent; Sotheby's, New York, 28 Oct. 1982 (78); Owen Edgar Gallery
Exh: RA 1859 (32); RA 1996 (14)
Lit: *Art Journal*, 1859, p.162; *Athenaeum*, 1859, p.618; Barrington 1906, II, pp.39, 41, 62; Staley 1906, pp.55–6; Ormond 1975, pp.41–2, 49, 152; Dorment 1977, pp.2–11; Newall 1990, pp.6, 28, pl.1

Private Collection

Leighton returned to Rome (where he had previously lived from 1852 to 1855) from Paris in the autumn of 1858. This painting is one of a series of at least four portraits of the Roman model Anna Risi (known as Nanna) that Leighton worked on between November 1858 and the time of his departure for Capri in April 1859, and which have come to be known as the 'La Nanna' series. Three paintings from the series, including *Pavonia*, were included in the Academy summer exhibition of 1859, which coincided with Leighton's decision to settle in London and the commencement of his participation in English artistic life.

In each of the paintings the model wears a white peasant chemise, which sets off the raven darkness of her hair and eyebrows as well as the waxy olive complexion of her face and arms. Pearls appear in the different compositions, either dressed in the girl's hair or at her throat. Anna Risi was known both for her statuesque beauty and her melancholy temperament, traits which Leighton brings forward in his paintings of her. In the version entitled *A Roman Lady (La Nanna)* (Philadelphia Museum of Art) she looks out at the spectator with a haughty awareness of her own beauty and the effect she makes. In *Nanna (Pavonia)* (The Royal Collection) the model's face is seen in profile and in soft shadow, while here she turns her head languorously towards the spectator, but with the sense that our opportunity to look upon her is but momentary. In *Pavonia* and *Nanna (Pavonia)* the girl's head is seen against a spray of peacock feathers, a motif referred to in the titles, which lends luxuriant decorative richness and colour to the compositions. The 'La Nanna' paintings were conceived as a series, each of the images complementing the others. Whatever Leighton's feelings towards the model may have been, in his attempt to abstract a woman's appearance into a single iconic sequence, he was anticipating among the work of British artists Rossetti's series of portraits of Jane Morris and Burne-Jones's equally obsessive drawings and pictures of Maria Zambaco, as well as a further series of paintings of Anna by the German artist Anselm Feuerbach, who was to become her lover.

The way in which the 'La Nanna' paintings convey a consciousness of sexual power was noted by those who saw them in 1859, and the critical response that they prompted indicates the degree to which the works seemed to ignore, even to overturn, the artistic conventions of the mid-century. F.G. Stephens considered the three exhibits 'worthy of a young old master, – so rapt, anything more feeling, commanding or coldly beautiful we have not seen for many a day'. As usual literary and historical prototypes were sought; Anna, in the Philadelphia version, 'might be a Vittoria Corombona [the tragic heroine of Webster's *The White Devil*], so feeling and passionate she looks', while of the present painting Stephens admired the model's 'backward yet proud look … worthy of a Lucrezia Borgia' (*Athenaeum*, 1859, p.618).

CSN

Dante Gabriel Rossetti 1828–1882

2 **Bocca Baciata** 1859

Oil on panel 32.2 × 27.1 (12⅝ × 10⅝)
Inscribed with monogram lower left corner; 'Bocca baciata non perde ventura, anzi [sic] rinnova come fa la luna', 'Boccaccio' (not Rossetti's hand) and 'painted by D G Rossetti 1859' (in Boyce's hand) on reverse

Prov: Commissioned by George Price Boyce (1826–1897) in July 1859; his sale, Christie's, 1 July 1897 (211); owned jointly by Agnew and Charles Fairfax Murray until 1897; sold by Murray to Mrs Edward Brandegee 1906; lent by her to the Boston Museum of Fine Arts intermittently between 1907 and 1925; by descent to Mrs James Lawrence; James Lawrence; given to Boston Museum of Fine Arts 1980

Exh: Hogarth Club 1860 (?7); RA Winter 1883 (309); RA Winter 1906 (126)

Lit: Sharp 1882, pp.167–8, list no.69; Stephens 1894, pp.52–4; Rossetti 1895, I, pp.202–3, II, pp.152–3; Marillier 1899, pp.50, 102, 132, 240 (list no.88), 249; *Masterpieces of Rossetti*, London and Glasgow 1923, p.13; Baum 1940, p.2; Doughty and Wahl 1965–8, I, p.358; Surtees 1971, I, no.114, pp.68–70 (prov. and exh. for both versions combined); II, pl.186 (other version); RA and Birmingham 1973, p.14; pp.125–6; Nicoll 1975, pp.125–6; Elzea 1980, letter nos.7, 48–9, 68, 74–80, 109, 119–21; Cherry 1980, pp.241, 243–4, fig.16; Surtees 1980, pp.27, pp.88–9; Tate Gallery 1984, p.25, fig.iv (other version); Marsh 1985, pp.155–9; Faxon 1989, pp.150–1, 166; pl.159; Tokyo 1990, p.28; Macleod 1996, pp.268–71

Museum of Fine Arts, Boston. Gift of James Lawrence 1980.261

Now seen as a landmark in the emerging Aestheticism of the post-Pre-Raphaelite era, *Bocca Baciata* is a small oil on panel initially begun as a portrait of Fanny Cornforth in 1859. Here Rossetti forged a new interest in decoration and allusive meaning, initiating a series of oils depicting sensual women embellished with rich accessories and flowers, providing an example for contemporary painters of sheer visual delight as an end in itself. In 1894, F.G. Stephens defined its importance as the first of the 'women – amorously, mystically, or moodily lost in dreams or absorbed by thoughts too deep for words'.

The title, which translates as 'the kissed mouth', derives from the lines of a sonnet by the fourteenth-century Italian writer, Giovanni Boccaccio. Inscribed on the back of the panel in Italian, these translate as: 'The mouth that has been kissed loses not its freshness; still it renews itself even as does the moon'. Rossetti's affinity with Dante extended to Boccaccio, his younger Florentine contemporary and biographer, whose collection of stories comprising the *Decameron* had long appealed to to artists in England. Paintings by Watts and others were doubtless familiar to Rossetti. In the same year that he painted *Bocca Baciata*, his young friend Edward Burne-Jones also drew inspiration from Boccaccio in an elaborate drawing of *Buondelmonte's Wedding* (Fitzwilliam Museum, Cambridge), but that dense image is illustrative and narrative, and hence far removed from Rossetti's suggestive use of poetry, linked with a visual image but not describing it.

Rossetti's painting sparked off great interest in 1859 for its innovative qualities, but it also provides a modern variation on the eighteenth-century tradition of fancy pictures; a tradition which extended into early Victorian times in the more diluted form of the 'Keepsake', engraved illustrations of lovely young women, usually enhanced by a single-name title, common in periodicals and gift books. More immediately relevant was the contemporary context. Watts's portraits of women in the last years of the 1850s, certainly familiar to Rossetti, increasingly included decorative elements to enrich the image, and Leighton's paintings of Nanna Risi (see no.1) relate even more closely to Rossetti's new direction.

On one level *Bocca Baciata* is a portrait; indeed the artist referred to it as such. The sitter, Fanny Cornforth, provided a robust contrast to the spiritualised beauty of Rossetti's long-time paramour Elizabeth Siddal, who had hitherto formed an obsessive subject for the artist in a series of watercolours and drawings on Dantesque themes throughout the 1850s. Rossetti married Lizzie in 1860, but Fanny had already entered his circle some time during the previous few years, first modelling for the fallen woman in *Found* (begun 1854; Bancroft Collection, Wilmington, Delaware). *Bocca Baciata*, one of the earliest paintings of Fanny, celebrated her sensual presence and crinkly golden hair by association with the vibrant orange of the marigolds and the emblematic detail of the apple.

What began as an experiment in technique for Rossetti ended up as a commission. In July 1859, his fellow artist and friend George Price Boyce committed himself to buying the painting while it was still in progress. Rossetti told Boyce that it 'has taken after all a rather Venetian aspect.' This is to be seen in Fanny's 'late 16th century costume' (Surtees 1980, p.27) and in the 'rapid flesh painting' which Rossetti adopted to avoid the stippled technique of Pre-Raphaelitism.

It may well be that Boyce sought to possess *Bocca Baciata* as a substitute for the woman herself, who fell more under the spell of the charismatic Rossetti, becoming a fixture in his studio for many years. Arthur Hughes's remark about the painting, which played on the title in suggesting that Boyce 'will kiss the dear thing's lips away' (noted in Nicoll 1975, p.125), seems to imply that Rossetti's friend harboured his own amorous feelings toward Fanny.

Bocca Baciata apparently became the source of some controversy (Surtees 1980, p.vii) and much admiration from Boyce's fellow artists such as Hughes and Spencer Stanhope. It even attracted the attention of the young Swinburne, soon to be an integral member of Rossetti's circle. He considered it 'more stunning than can be decently expressed' (Surtees 1980, p.89). From Rossetti's comments to Boyce after completing the work (see below), it seems he did not want the fact that it was a portrait to be common knowledge, probably for the very reason that the appeal of the work lay distinctly in its status as a beautiful object, devoid of specific associations. In this way *Bocca Baciata* encapsulates the first moment of Aestheticism.

Holman Hunt wrote that while most people 'speak to me of it as a triumph of *our school*', he himself found it 'remarkable for gross sensuality of a revolting kind', abhorring Rossetti's 'mere gratification of the eye' (letter to Combe 12 Feb. 1860; quoted in Cherry 1980, p.241). However, it was just such 'gratification of the eye' that summed up the appeal of *Bocca Baciata*, making this painting such a talisman for the artists of the 1860s.

The importance of *Bocca Baciata* justifies a look at the question of the two versions which it is now possible to clarify. For the first time the main version can be identified. At the time Surtees's catalogue raisonné was published in 1971, it was not known that there were two virtually identical versions of *Bocca Baciata*; hence the provenance given there conflates the two. Further complication ensued because both versions are in the United States. The painting in Boston is, however, certainly the one owned by Boyce and seen in the Royal Academy exhibition in 1906. It still bears a label from this exhibition, providing reliable evidence that it is the prime version. An even older label (now removed) seems likely to have related to the Hogarth Club exhibition.

The sketch at the top of Rossetti's letter to Boyce (dated by Surtees to 5 Sept. 1859; Humanities Research Center, The University of Texas, Austin) clearly shows the design for *Bocca Baciata*, though there are very slight differences, probably indicating the state of the painting before its final completion. Rossetti explains that Boyce's painting was his second attempt at the composition, the first having suffered from 'being painted with a good deal of copal and on panel, a combination which I never before attempted and which I found produced an unpleasant glossiness of surface'. He said he 'threw it aside after making considerable progress with it' and further noted that its design was different in that 'the present one is the same action of the head as in the *Golden Water*' 1858 (Fitzwilliam Museum, Cambridge). Rossetti then painted the Boyce version, i.e. the first finished version of the composition. The second known version would seem to be the copy of Boyce's painting painted by Fairfax Murray while he owned (and tried to sell) Boyce's *Bocca* (Elzea 1980, letter no.79). It may be this painting which is now in a private collection in California, and reproduced in the literature on Rossetti before the Lawrence gift in 1980, and even, in some cases, after that date (as in Tate Gallery 1984).

BB

Dante Gabriel Rossetti 1828–1882

3 **Helen of Troy** 1863

Oil on panel 32.8 × 27.7 (13 × 10⅞)

Prov: W. Blackmore; Herr Amsinck, by whom bequeathed to Kunsthalle, Hamburg 1921

Lit: Rossetti 1889, p.49; Marillier 1899, no.139, pp.129–30; Surtees 1971, no.163, pl.232; Surtees 1980, pp.37, 98 n.3

Hamburger Kunsthalle

Helen was a perfect subject for one of Rossetti's allegorical portraits, for her story demonstrated the weakness of men in the face of sexual attraction and its possible disastrous consequences. Paris abandoned his mistress Oenone and with the help of Aphrodite eloped with the Spartan beauty Helen, wife of Menelaus. This led to the ten-year Trojan War, which ended with the siege and burning of Troy, and Paris's death. Rossetti chose to paint Helen as the ultimate cause of these events, for in a note on the back of the picture he quotes Aeschylus's *Agamemnon*: 'Helen of Troy ... destroyer of ships, destroyer of men, destroyer of cities. Painted by D.G. Rossetti 1863'.

However, this is not just a historical subject, for it had a personal reading for Rossetti. His model was Annie Miller, a woman of humble origins whom Holman Hunt had taken up. She modelled for the courtesan in his *Awakening Conscience* 1853–4 (Tate Gallery). Pygmalion-like, Hunt undertook to educate and turn her into a gentlewoman, with the view of eventually marrying her. While he was away in the Middle East from 1854 to 1856, he left strict instructions with F.G. Stephens as to her continuing tuition, and whom among their circle she might or might not see. Rossetti, who was not on the approved list, took Annie to the kind of entertainments Hunt disapproved of, and finally started an affair with her. Like Paris, he had stolen her away, and also like Paris, Rossetti abandoned his current partner, Lizzie Siddall, albeit temporarily, to do so. Lizzie was distraught, but with Hunt's return in 1856 the affair died out, and Rossetti's affections once again reverted to her. Although they apparently did not quarrel about it directly, Hunt never forgave Rossetti, and their already tenuous friendship was dissolved. In Hunt's absence Annie had also been Lord Ranelagh's mistress, and feeling humiliated, Hunt abandoned his marriage plans. Rossetti seems to have maintained friendly terms with her and she continued to sit for him on occasions. Nevertheless, if the personal connotations of using Annie for Helen are extended, then Rossetti may have equated her impact on his relationship with Lizzie, and upon Hunt, and his friendship with him, to that of the disasters of the Trojan War.

This painting evidently greatly appealed to Swinburne's fantasies about cruel women and punished men. He wrote describing it as: 'The picture of Helen, with Parian face and mouth of ardent blossom, a keen red flower-bud of fire, framed in broad gold of wide-spread locks, the sweet sharp smile of power set fast on her clear curved lips, and far behind her the dull flame of burning and light from reddened heaven on dark sails of lurid ships ...' (*Essays and Studies*, 1875, p.99).

RU

Dante Gabriel Rossetti 1828–1882

4 **Fazio's Mistress (Aurelia)** 1863

Oil on panel 43.2 × 36.8 (17 × 14½)

Prov: W. Blackmore; George Rae; bt by NACF and presented to the Tate Gallery 1916

Exh: Liverpool Academy 1864 (149a); RA 1883 (300); Liverpool 1886 (857); Guildhall 1892 (157); Bournemouth 1951 (19); Tate Gallery 1984 (123, repr.)

Lit: Rossetti 1889, p.49; Rossetti 1895, I, pp.238, 241; Marillier 1899, no.144, pp.103, 132; Surtees 1971, no.164, pl.234

Tate Gallery. Purchased with assistance from Sir Arthur Du Cros Bt and Sir Otto Beit KCMG through the National Art Collections Fund 1916

4

This is one of a group of pictures by Rossetti that began with *Bocca Baciata* (no.2) and feature buxom, sensual, flame-haired women. In an act of narcissism or deep self-contemplation, Fazio's mistress gazes into a mirror, lost in reverie. The subject was taken from the verses of Fazio degli Uberti (1326–1360) to his Lady, Agniola of Verona, which Rossetti had translated and included in his *Early Italian Poets* in 1861. Grieve has noted the poem's suggestion of female beauty being used to ensnare men (Tate Gallery 1984, no.123):

> I look at the crisp golden-threaded hair
> Whereof, to thrall my heart, Love twists a net,
> Using at times a string of pearls for bait,
> And sometimes with a single rose therein
>
> (1–4)

Rossetti's recurrent theme of male weakness in the face of the power of beauty is echoed by Fazio:

> Song, thou canst surely say, without pretence,
> That since the first fair woman ever made,
> Not one can have display'd

More power upon all hearts than this one doth;
Because in her are both
Loveliness and the soul's true excellence
(86–91)

The picture seems to illustrate many of the physical attributes of his mistress that so enchant Fazio:

I look at the amorous beautiful mouth,
The spacious forehead which her locks enclose,
The small white teeth, the straight and shapely nose,
And the clear brows of a sweet pencilling
(18–21)

I look at her white easy neck, so well
From shoulders and from bosom lifted out;
And at her round cleft chin, which beyond doubt
No fancy in the world could have design'd
(35–8)

I look at the large arms, so lithe and round, –
At the hands, which are white and rosy too, –
At the long fingers …
(52–4)

So similar are the subject and style of the poem to Rossetti's that it is possible he might have written it himself (see Rossetti 1911, p.488).

Working on the picture in October 1863, Rossetti wrote to Ellen Heaton 'I am now painting a lady plaiting her golden hair. This is an oil and chiefly a piece of colour' (quoted in Surtees 1971, no.164). The combination of self-consciously rich colour with rich glazes suggests that Rossetti probably had Titian in mind while working on it. He greatly admired the Venetian colourist, and the debt of much of his work in this period to Titian's *Alphonse Ferrare and Laura de Diante* (Musée du Louvre, Paris) has been noted by Grieve (loc. cit.), who also draws comparisons of colour, pose and mood between *Fazio's Mistress* and Whistler's *Little White Girl: Symphony in White No.2* (no.15).

The model for the picture was Rossetti's own mistress, Fanny Cornforth. When in 1873 he retouched the picture for its second owner, George Rae, Rossetti wrote to her: 'I have got an old picture here which I painted many years ago. It is the one where you are seated doing your hair before a glass. Rae, to whom it belongs, has sent it to me as it wants some glazing, but *I am not working at all on the head*, which is exactly like the funny old elephant, as like as any I ever did. Your affectionate R.' (Baum 1940, p.61)

RU

DANTE GABRIEL ROSSETTI 1828–1882

5 The Beloved ('The Bride') 1865–6

Oil on canvas 82.5 × 76.2 (32½ × 30)
Inscribed with Rossetti's monogram and '1865–6' b.l.

Prov: George Rae; bt by NACF and presented to the Tate Gallery 1916

Exh: Arundel Club 21 Feb. 1866; RA Winter 1883 (297); Liverpool 1886 (843); Manchester 1887 (700); RA Winter 1906 (117); RA 1973 (319); Tate Gallery 1984 (133, repr.); Tokyo 1990 (35, repr. in col.); Barbican 1991 (79, repr. in col.); Tate Gallery 1995 (12); Washington 1997 (36, repr. in col.)

Lit: Hueffer 1896, pp.215–17; Marillier 1899, no.177; Bate 1899, p.46, repr. opp. p.41; Rossetti Angeli 1954, p.101; Doughty and Wahl 1965–8, pp.1149, 1150, 1152, 1467; Surtees 1971, no.182, pl.263; Surtees 1980, pp.41–2

Tate Gallery. Purchased with assistance from Sir Arthur Du Cros Bt and Sir Otto Beit KCMG through the National Art Collections Fund 1916

Rossetti's theme is once again the overwhelming beauty of woman, and man's weakness and fascination in the face of it. The subject was inspired by the biblical Song of Solomon. It shows the bride pulling back her veil; looking straight out of the picture, she places the viewer in the role of her lover, gazing at her revealed beauty.

The picture started life as a portrait of Dante's beloved Beatrice for Ellen Heaton. However, Rossetti wrote to her on 2 July 1863:

> I have painted the whole of the face and much to my liking as a piece of painting – it is certainly one of my best things, but the model does not turn out to make a perfect Beatrice, and at the same time I do not like to risk spoiling the colour by altering it from any other model. I have got the model's bright complexion, which was irresistible, and Beatrice was pale, we are told, nor is the face altogether just what it ought to be. In fact, I reckoned on adapting, but the attraction of nature was too much & I have copied instead.
>
> Now if you have no objection, I propose to find another subject to suit the figure – the Bride from Solomon's Song is specially in my head, though I have not yet looked into the matter.
>
> (quoted in Surtees 1971, no.182)

Rossetti subsequently described 'Solomon's Bride' to her as a 'subject I myself delight in and have always had an eye to' (quoted ibid.). His development of the subject raised its price from the one he quoted Ellen Heaton for a Beatrice subject, and she subsequently ceded the picture to George Rae.

The Song of Solomon was certainly a natural subject for Rossetti; its praise of physical attraction and pleasure fitted his own temperament and its sensuous language and rich imagery are similar to that used in much of his own poetry. Inscribed on the frame are lines taken from the Song of Solomon and the 45th Psalm:

> My Beloved is mine and I am his. (Song of Solomon, 2:16). Let him kiss me with the kisses of his mouth: for thy love is better than wine. (Solomon 1:2). She shall be brought unto the King in raiment of needlework: the virgins her companions that follow her shall be brought unto thee. (Psalms 45:14)

Rossetti clothed the Bride in exotic fabrics and trappings to increase her sensuality. Her intricate leather headdress is Peruvian (see Marillier 1899, p.132) while her dress is a Japanese kimono. Rossetti wrote 'I mean the colour of my picture to be like jewels and the jet would be invaluable' (quoted in Rossetti 1894, p.51). Marie Ford, whose beauty Rossetti much admired, sat for the principal figure. The Virgin Bridesmaid in the foreground on the left was Ellen Smith. The one on the right was Frederick Sandys's gypsy mistress Keomi. The black boy was a model Rossetti chose from a chance meeting, 'at the door of an hotel' (Rossetti 1903, p.175). The boy was added to the picture in 1865, replacing a mulatto girl. Rossetti's inspiration for this element may have been seeing *Olympia* 1863 (Musée d'Orsay, Paris) in Manet's studio on his visit to Paris in November 1864 (see Tate Gallery 1984, no.133). Rossetti's inclusion of a black figure in *The Beloved* was intended, along with other items in the composition, to add to its exoticism.

The boy holds up roses, which in Christian imagery indicate someone who is without peer, but in this context they also symbolise love. The Virgins hold lilies, emblems of purity, but their red colour suggests they are intended to represent the sanctity of passion and physical love. They may well be an allusion to the passage in Christ's Sermon on the Mount in which He says 'And why take ye thought for raiment? Consider the lilies of the field, how they grow: they toil not, neither do they spin: And yet I say unto you, That even Solomon in all his glory was not arrayed like one of these' (Matthew 6:28–9).

Grieve has noted how the composition is deliberately arranged so that the Bride's face is at the centre of a sumptuous setting (Tate Gallery 1984, no.133).

RU

Dante Gabriel Rossetti 1828–1882

6 **Lady Lilith** 1864–8

Oil on canvas 95.3 × 81.3 (37½ × 32)

Prov: Bt from the artist by F.R. Leyland; his sale, Christie's 28 May 1892 (56), Samuel Bancroft; gift of the estate of Samuel and Mary R. Bancroft, 1935; the Bancroft Collection in the Delaware Art Museum

Exh: Burlington Fine Arts Club 1883 (47); Philadelphia 1892 (1); Wilmington 1976 (4–7); Tokyo 1990 (41); for further exhibitions see Bancroft 1984

Lit: Rossetti and Swinburne 1868, p.46 (reprinted in Warner and Hough 1983, pp.245–6); Sharp 1882, pp.207–10, list no.131; Stephens 1894, pp.66–9; Marillier 1899, pp.132–4, 154, 245, no.148; Rossetti 1903, pp.407, 483–6; Barrington 1905, pp.1–4; Doughty and Wahl 1965–8, II, p.850 (21 April 1870); Surtees 1971, I, no.205, II, pl.293; Ainsworth 1976, pp.77–9; Fennell 1978, esp. letter nos.1–4, 10, 12, 22, 24, 35, 46; Surtees 1980, p.45 (27 Oct. 1866); p.47 (27 March 1868); Elzea 1984, pp.114–17; Faxon 1989, p.203, pls.220–1; Stephen Wildman, in Tokyo 1990, p.29

Delaware Art Museum. Samuel & Mary R. Bancroft Memorial

Rossetti reputedly began the oil *Lady Lilith* in 1864, before composing his own related poems on it. Real progress does not seem to have occurred until 1866, when he offered it for the first time to his new patron, Frederick Leyland (who originally wanted *Sibylla Palmifera,* Lady Lever Art Gallery) for 450 guineas in April. He characterised it not by a title but with a description as 'a lady combing her hair ... 36 × 31 inches, and will be full of material, – a landscape seen in the background. Its colour chiefly white and silver, with a great mass of golden hair'. Leyland accepted the offer by providing the requested down-payment of 150 guineas; by August 1866, when Leyland paid in full, the artist had dubbed the work *Lady Lilith*.

Rossetti enlarged the canvas two inches each way 'in order to get in all I want in the picture', and carried on with work through 1868 when he mentioned painting a kitten (which does not however appear in the final version). Still later he painted a 'garland of silver flowers' on the lap of the sitter, and repainted the lower area which had been 'so much altered as to be spoilt in execution'. He seems finally to have parted with it to Leyland in 1869, only to have it back for repainting in 1872, when at the request of the patron (and with uneven results), the face of the more elegant Alexa Wilding replaced the original of Fanny Cornforth, deemed 'too sensual and commonplace'. (For the original appearance of the painting see Marillier 1899, repr. opp. p.133). Interestingly, the two known watercolour replicas (both signed and dated 1867), which provide the best way to assess the original, were carried out before Rossetti sent the oil to Leyland, almost as if he retained it for his own use in making replicas.

In *Lady Lilith*, Rossetti returned to a favourite theme of a woman combing her luxuriant hair. As in no.33, the presence of Fanny Cornforth *en déshabille*, as she first modelled for Lilith with her ample proportions and long reddish-gold hair, fostered an overtly erotic reading of the painting, somewhat dissipated by the cooler persona of Alexa Wilding. Lilith gazes dreamily at her image in the hand-held mirror, as she combs through her hair. White is the keynote, and in this respect *Lady Lilith* is descended from Rossetti's earlier *Ecce Ancilla Domini!* (Tate Gallery) which he considered the first of the 'white paintings' that became so prevalent during the 1860s in the work of Whistler (see Staley 1971, no.124) and Albert Moore. The reputation of *Lady Lilith* spread even before it left Rossetti's studio. Visitors included Watts (see p.67) whose admiration for Rossetti's work seems to have influenced his own interpretation of a bust-length study of a female figure in white in *The Wife of Pygmalion* (*c*.1868; see Staley 1978, no.17). The motif of the woman combing her hair and contemplating her own image can also be found in Courbet's portrait of Joanna Hiffernan (see no.9) of 1865–6 (see Staley 1971, no.61).

Rossetti wrote the sonnet 'Lilith' for the painting, along with other sonnets for pictures in the late 1860s; he published it in *Poems* in 1870 (later entitling it 'Body's Beauty' in the edition of his poems published in 1881):

Of Adam's first wife, Lilith, it is told
(The witch he loved before the gift of Eve)
That, ere the snake's, her sweet tongue could deceive,
And her enchanted hair was the first gold.
And still she sits, young while the earth is old,
And, subtly of herself contemplative,
Draws men to watch the bright net she can weave,
Till heart and body and life are in its hold.

The rose and poppy are her flowers; for where
Is he not found, O Lilith, whom shed scent
And soft-shed kisses and soft sleep shall snare?
Lo! as that youth's eyes burned at thine, so went
Thy spell thorough him, and left his straight neck bent,
And round his heart one strangling golden hair.

The sonnet, inspired as it was by the painting, adds further resonance to the image of Lilith, a character from Talmudic and Assyrian legend, here realised as a modern woman. Rossetti's poem 'Eden Bower' also focuses on the apocryphal Lilith, wife of Adam, rather than the Lilith of the painting. *Lady Lilith* is clearly a temptress, using her beauty to ensnare unsuspecting victims. In a letter of 1870, Rossetti described her in the painting and in the sonnet as 'a *Modern Lilith* combing out her abundant golden hair and gazing on herself in the glass with that self-absorption by whose strange fascination such natures draw others within their own circle. The idea ... of the perilous principle in the world being female from the first ... is about the most essential idea of the sonnet'. Rossetti's thoughts on the idea of the eternal feminine found vivid form in the painting of *Lady Lilith*.

After Rossetti's death in 1883, Leyland lent the picture to its first public exhibition at Burlington Fine Arts Club. At this time, along with a range of the artist's work, it took on a new meaning for a new generation. The catalogue information added further layers to the image. An extract from Burton's *Anatomy of Melancholy* of 1624 explained: 'The Thalmudists say that Adam had a wife called Lilis, before hee married Eve, and of her he begat nothing but diuils [devils].' A reference to Gesenius's *Commentary*

6

on Isaiah alluded to the Hebraic tradition of Lileth as 'a female spectre in the shape of a finely dressed woman'.

Swinburne's poetic evocation of *Lady Lilith* (see p.24) arose from the image itself, as a depiction of a woman whose female qualities lent her considerable power and fascination. As a key image, underlined by Swinburne's text and widely known from *c.*1866 onward, the painting allies the Aestheticism of the 1860s as an essentially subjectless art about beauty with much deeper meanings, a combination which set the pattern for the later Symbolist era.

BB

FREDERICK SANDYS 1829–1904

7 Mary Magdalene *c.*1859

Oil on panel 33.6 × 27.9 (13¼ × 11)
Inscribed on the reverse 'Mary Magdalene by F. Sandys' and 'Queen Ele [anor] by Fr. Sandys'

Prov: James Anderson Rose; Christie's 5 May 1891 (156); Charles Fairfax Murray; Agnew's, from whom bt by Samuel Bancroft 1894; given by the family of Samuel Bancroft to the Wilmington Society of Fine Arts 1935

Exh: BI 1860 (467); Wilmington 1899; Wilmington 1917; Wilmington 1934 (36); Brighton and Sheffield 1974 (46), repr.; Wilmington 1976 (3-12), repr.; Washington 1977 (19); Tate Gallery 1984 (101)

Lit: *Art Journal*, 1860, p.80; Elzea 1984, p.136, repr. p.137

Delaware Art Museum. Samuel & Mary R. Bancroft Memorial

This early picture by Frederick Sandys was first exhibited at the British Institution in 1860. Sandys had come to notice in 1857 with his engraving entitled *A Nightmare* – a parody of Millais's painting *Sir Isumbras at the Ford* – which appeared that year at the Royal Academy. This satire was taken in good part by the quondam Pre-Raphaelites, and in the years that followed Sandys was drawn into the circle that formed around Rossetti.

This is the first of two paintings by Sandys of Mary Magdalene, the woman 'out of whom went seven devils' (Luke 8:2). She is seen holding the ointment with which she was to anoint Christ, as described in the Gospel of St Matthew: 'There came unto him a woman having an alabaster box of very precious ointment, and poured it on his head, as he sat at meat' (Matthew 26:7).

The mood of the painting is solemn and devout, as the Magdalene approaches Christ with downcast eyes and tender expression. Nonetheless, it is clear that the picture reflected contemporary preoccupations with female sexual identity, as well as the instinct on the part of a male painter to look for an opportunity to reflect on the person of a young woman whose submissive demeanour might also indicate sexual awareness and accommodation. Its choice of subject, that of the repentant harlot who was regarded as unfit to attend Jesus because of her immoral life, was tinged with sexual connotation. Furthermore, Victorian viewers of the present painting would immediately have seen it as the representation of a prostitute (reformed or not), simply because such people were often spoken of as Magdalenes.

That the picture was intended to suggest sexual intimacy is further demonstrated by the undressed state of the woman's hair, which flows like molten metal across her shoulders and back. Such hair is part of the iconography of the Magdalene, for, having washed Christ's feet with her tears, she then 'did wipe them with the hairs of her head' (Luke 8:38). However, this is more than just a dutiful treatment of a New Testament subject according to tradition. Here, as on other occasions in Victorian art where a woman is represented with her hair undressed (as, for example, in Whistler's *The White Girl*, fig.21 on p.38, where it symbolised the loss of virginity), viewers of the work of art are invited to speculate about that person's sexual persona.

About ten years later Rossetti was to accuse Sandys of plagiarising his own watercolour *Mary Magdalene Leaving the House of Feasting* (Tate Gallery), writing in 1869 'and, as to the Magdalene, the moment taken by me was taken then for the first time in art, and constituted entirely the value of my design' (Doughty and Wahl 1965, II, p.698). It seems likely that it was the present oil that Rossetti had in mind when he made this charge, for the position of the heads and the hand gestures are very alike. Otherwise, however, Sandys's *Mary Magdalene* is to be regarded as among the genre of paintings of artists' models and mistresses treated as symbolical icons of the female persona and closed to narrative interpretation, and in this sense it transcends the story-telling function of Rossetti's 1857 watercolour.

Here the spectator is invited to gaze and to admire, and the physical beauty of the model is more important than the role she plays. Primacy in the invention of this type is hard to allocate; as has been seen, Leighton's *Pavonia* (no.1) was painted in Rome in the spring of 1859, while Rossetti's *Bocca Baciata* (no.2) followed in the latter part of the year. Sandys's *Mary Magdalene* may in fact have been begun before either of these.

CSN

George Frederic Watts 1817–1904

8 A Study with the Peacock's Feathers *c.*1862–5

Oil on panel 66 × 56 (26 × 22)
Inscribed 'G F Watts' lower left

Prov: Probably sold by Watts after its exhibition in 1865; not in his collection in 1886; ...; Jean Louis Miéville, his sale, Christie's 29 April 1899 (10, as *Fair Haired Girl*), bt Gribble; Lt Col. Fairfax Rhodes by 1906, his sale, Sotheby's 11 July 1934 (129, as *The Amber Necklace*); Agnew's in 1954; Sotheby Parke Bernet, N.Y. 25 Jan. 1980 (338); FAS

Exh: French Gallery 1865 (108); RA Winter 1906 (118); Tokyo 1989 (1); Nottingham 1994 (74)

Lit: F.G. Stephens, *Athenaeum*, 4 Nov. 1865, pp.618–19; *Art Journal*, 1865, p.369; Spielmann 1886, p.32; MS. Cat., I, p.115 (incorrect title, no contemporary exh. ref.)

Pre-Raphaelite Inc by courtesy of Julian Hartnoll

A Study with the Peacock's Feathers is an exercise in the painting of the beautiful and as such it belongs to a distinct trend in the art of the 1860s. It also pays homage to the Venetian Renaissance,with its luxuriant colour and gorgeous nudes. The allusion to the art of the past coexists comfortably with modern aestheticising tendencies, and this way of combining past and present can be seen as a preparation for Watts's later, more ambitious endeavour to update allegory for a contemporary audience.

As a half-length female figure in a setting of flowers and decorative accessories, this work might be considered as a direct descendant of Rossetti's *Bocca Baciata* (no.2). For Watts, a tendency toward painting women as objects of beauty already formed a clearly identifiable strain in his art, initially approached through the genre of portraiture, then as head studies even more obviously conceived as independent works of art. Leighton's decorative studies of the model Nanna Risi, seen in London in 1859 (including no.1), also essayed this type, and the motif of peacock feathers in *Pavonia* is a detail that found its way into Watts's work, suggesting perhaps a conscious reference amongst a close-knit group of artists.

According to M.H. Spielmann, a very reliable commentator, Watts painted *A Study with the Peacock's Feathers* in 1862, a date that seems thoroughly plausible, though the painting did not appear at exhibition until 1865. Rather than send it to the Royal Academy, Watts instead chose the French Gallery where he could feel more relaxed about showing a work in a minor, or experimental, mode. This study was essentially a private image, probably destined for the cabinet of a connoisseur (and perhaps even a specific commission). But F.G. Stephens's long, appreciative review in the *Athenaeum* brought the painting into prominence for its new aesthetically oriented audience. His language lingered on the purely painterly values of the picture: 'the tones are most subtly pronounced, and the artist's skills triumphantly manifested in the exquisite colour of the work. We rarely see such true Art as this; still more rarely does it present itself so wealthy in beauty and completeness.'

In exhibiting the picture, Watts moved freely into territory associated with Rossetti, and the links between the older and younger artist come into play.

A comparison with *Bocca Baciata* makes Rossetti's painting look positively medievalising; however, closer parallels exist between Watts's *Study* and some of Rossetti's near-contemporary studies of women, especially depictions of the nude, as in his earliest version of *Venus Verticordia* dating from 1863 (Surtees 1971, no.173B) – a large red chalk drawing of a half-length nude – and the various painted versions (see no.43) worked on from 1864 onward. In these nude studies, both artists depict their models in a state of languorous repose, inviting a slow perusal of the beautiful painted surfaces. Rossetti's titles layer meaning upon meaning. By contrast, *A Study with the Peacock's Feathers* is emphatically art about art – the blonde Venus amid pearls and silks evokes Titian's nudes, but the title emphasises that it is a product of the artist's studio, and as a study of the model, it becomes a thoroughly modern exercise. By 1865 the taste for this type of subject had become more widespread among artists, critics and patrons, with Watts as the prime exponent of this genre.

Even though this work highlights a range of concerns preoccupying Watts in the mid-1860s, it should also be remembered that Watts admired Rossetti hugely and this painting, while hardly conceived as a homage, has much in common with Rossetti's output at this period.

BB

GUSTAVE COURBET 1819–1877

9 Jo, the Beautiful Irish Girl (La Belle Irlandaise) 1865–6

Oil on canvas 54 × 65 (21¼ × 25⅝)
Inscribed '..66 Gustave Courbet' b.l.
Prov: See Fernier 1977, II, no.537
Exh: See Fernier 1977, loc. cit.; Hamburg 1978 (244)
Lit: See Fernier 1977, loc. cit.

Nationalmuseum, Stockholm

EXHIBITED IN LONDON ONLY

The sitter for this painting was Jo Hiffernan, the Irish mistress of James McNeill Whistler during the early years of the 1860s. It was started in the summer of 1865, when Courbet was working with Whistler at Dieppe. It has been suggested that Courbet first met Jo a few years earlier when Whistler had been working on his *The White Girl (Symphony in White No.1)* 1862 (fig.21 on p.38). His meeting with her in Dieppe certainly confirmed his favourable response to her. Writing to his friend and patron Alfred Bruyas, he declared: 'Among the two thousand ladies who have come to my studio, I admired more than Princess Karoly and Mlle Abbe the beauty of a superb red head whose portrait I have begun' (quoted in Borel 1951, p.116n). Indeed, he proceeded not only to create four versions of this painting (the other three being in the Metropolitan Museum of Art, New York, the Nelson Atkins Museum, St Louis, and a private collection, Switzerland), but he also made a small portrait study (private collection, New York) and used Jo as one of the two models in his major commissioned painting of 1866, *The Sleepers*, or *Sleep* (Musée du Petit Palais, Paris).

Unlike the small study of Jo's head, which retains all the directness of observation normally associated with Courbet's realist approach to his subjects from the later 1840s, the creation of *Jo* employs certain procedures of pose, dress and general composition which seemingly distance it from a strictly 'Realist' treatment. His model is dressed in a rich garment with copious sleeves and a square-cut neckline, worn over a white, tightly drawn undershirt finished with a puckered edge. It hints at a costume of the sixteenth century. The background of the painting is neutrally flat, forcing the figure to the front of the picture plane to create an enclosed, claustrophobic space. Within this enclosure, Jo does not adopt a conventional portrait pose, looking out at the spectator in order to permit immediate identity. Rather, she turns to one side, absorbed in looking at herself in a mirror as she settles her flowing tresses of Titian-red hair. It is this isolation of the female subject, framed by her undulating hair and wholly absorbed in self-

regard, which links the work with Rossetti's iconic women of the same decade. Its dependence on an image such as *Fazio's Mistress* (no.4) is evident. See also no.32.

As is also the case with Fantin-Latour (see nos. 83–5), the conventional designation of Courbet as the prime exponent of Realism is problematic. Indeed, the monumental 'programme' paintings of 1849–55 are framed by a sequence of 'costume' pieces created in his early career whose historicising intent finds an echo in the exotic costume of *Jo*, and by a series of subject paintings which expound a truth to a personal vision, not necessarily a truth to an objective reading of external reality. In this latter context it should be noted that, contemporaneous to *Jo*, Courbet was working beside Whistler at Dieppe to create a sequence of seascapes in which depth is no longer indicated by the diagonal recessional line of the sea, but is consciously eliminated through a rigorous horizontal banding of beach, sea and sky up the surface of the canvas. It is significant that Courbet gave these marines such suggestively abstract titles as *L'Immensité* and *L'Eternité*.

Of the four versions which Courbet made of the subject of Jo, it is assumed that the one shown here was probably the first. It was the version which figured in Courbet's estate sale of 1881, confirmation of the fact that Courbet declared that he had kept a portrait of Jo with him to the last year of his life (1877).

MAS

The Suppression of Meaning

Bringing image and symbol together in order to present a psychological state independent of any narrative element was an important change of direction in nineteenth-century painting. Historical subjects and scenes from modern life had held sway all through the century; now painters sought to purge their canvases of such precise significance and to create images whose simplicity and clarity of design were meaning enough. The opening up of Japan to Western trade, and, from the early 1860s, the appearance in large quantities of the colour woodblock prints of Hokusai, Kunisada and others supplied a new and exotic stimulus to the search for refined design and colour, while the writers of the Aesthetic movement, notably Swinburne and Walter Pater, provided a literary, theoretical and philosophical context in which these experiments could take place.

The American James McNeill Whistler, who had come to London in 1862 having spent the years since 1855 in France with frequent visits to England, became a leading exponent of the new principles, painting pictures that created harmonies which he thought of as abstract in the way that music is abstract. Whistler took to naming his pictures after types of musical composition, favouring especially such titles as 'Harmony' and 'Nocturne' which evoke ideas of contemplation and of sleep. Music was to become an obsession with the Symbolists, with its power to express profound spiritual states independently of specific meanings. The link with poetry was, however, equally strong. The equivalence between poetry and music explicitly acknowledged in the theoretical writing of the period, especially in France, was seen as holding true for painting too. A 'symbolism of all the senses' was celebrated by Baudelaire in his poem 'Correspondances' which gives economical expression to these ideas: 'La Nature est un temple où de vivants piliers / Laissent parfois sortir de confuses paroles; / L'homme y passe à travers des forêts de symboles / Qui l'observent avec des regards familiers. / Comme de longs échos qui de loin se confondent / Dans une ténébreuse et profonde unité, / Vaste comme la nuit et comme la clarté, / Les parfums, les couleurs et les sons se répondent.' By the middle of the 1860s an unexpected community of purpose had been arrived at among a diverse group of young painters, who were all seeking to create a language of pure 'mood', of atmosphere and feeling achieved entirely by means of colour and form.

These developments had considerable importance for the way artists treated the nude. The naked human body had by hallowed tradition been the vehicle for the grandest statements about passion, virtue and heroism, but as Neo-classicissm became an increasingly weak impulse in the mid-nineteenth century the conviction and intensity of that convention disappeared. In the 1860s the nude too was emptied of associative meaning and became itself a means of purely aesthetic pictorial suggestion rather than the embodiment of specific ideas or qualities. A pioneer of this new approach to the nude was George Frederic Watts (no.14), who was to develop it into one of the principal conduits of Symbolist imagery in the ensuing decades.

The divorce of the nude from its connotations of sexual, as opposed to abstract, beauty was of course a precarious separation at best, and the delicate ambiguities that resulted from the attempt were to have their part to play in the next phases of the story.

Frederic, Lord Leighton 1830–1896

10 Lieder ohne Wörte *c.*1860–1

Oil on canvas 101.7 × 63 (40 × 24¾)

Prov: James Stewart Hodgson; his sale, Christie's, 3 June 1893 (26); bt Sir Charles Cavendish Clifford, 4th Bt; his sister Augusta Cavendish Clifford; her cousin Mme Ernest Mallet, Paris, *c.*1930; by descent; Christie's, 29 Feb. 1980, (208); bt by the Tate Gallery 1980

Exh: RA 1861 (550); Brighton 1884 (124); RA 1996 (21)

Lit: *Art Journal*, 1861, p.172; *Athenaeum*, 1861, pp.600–1, 698; *Saturday Review*, 1861, p.531; *Macmillan's Magazine*, 1861, pp.206–7; Barrington 1906, II, pp.17, 57–63, 65, 76, 367; Staley 1906, p.60; Ormond 1975, pp.49, 60, 153, no.64; Tate Gallery, *Illustrated Catalogue of Acquisitions 1978–80*, pp.31–5; Newall 1990, pp.19, 32–3, 35

Tate Gallery. Purchased 1980

Lieder ohne Wörte was the first significant painting that Leighton undertook following his establishment in London in the latter part of 1859. He worked on it in 1860, and exhibited it at the Royal Academy in 1861. Torn as he was between a desire to establish his reputation in the wider art world (1861 was the year when he first sought election as an associate of the Royal Academy) and an allegiance to the more rarefied circle of ex-Pre-Raphaelites and painters who had trained abroad that gathered at the Hogarth Club, *Lieder ohne Wörte* may be seen as a declaration towards the progressive movement in painting.

Leighton announced his intention of pursuing the noumenal and hermetically enclosed character of the 'La Nanna' series (see no.1) in a letter to his father: '*Before* I began to paint "Lieder ohne Wörte" ... I intended to make it *realistic*, but from the first moment I began I felt the mistake, and made it professedly and pointedly the reverse' (Barrington 1906, II, p.62). The tangible, quantifiable and comprehensible character of a painting implied by the word 'realistic' was what painters who understood the precepts of French Aestheticism or 'art for art's sake' in the early 1860s were seeking to overturn in favour of images that were perplexing or even disturbing in their ambiguous and undefined nature.

In a letter written in the spring of 1861 to his erstwhile master Edward von Steinle, Leighton explained his intention in the work: 'It represents a girl, who is resting by a fountain, and listening to the ripple of the water and the song of a bird. The subject is, of course, quite incomplete without colour, as I have endeavoured, both by colour and by flowing delicate forms, to translate to the eye of the spectator something of the pleasure which the child receives through her ears. This idea lies at the base of the whole thing, and is managed to the best of my ability in every detail' (ibid., p.63). A few days earlier, when Leighton had invited friends to his Orme Square studio to see the works intended for the Royal Academy, *Lieder ohne Wörte* had attracted the most admiration. It was on this occasion that its German title – 'Songs without Words' – had been suggested.

Although the work was badly hung at Trafalgar Square, it met with some enthusiastic reviews, such as that which appeared in *Macmillan's Magazine* (perhaps echoing the words that Leighton himself had used to describe the painting): 'There is nothing to tell that the fair young girl who sits before us, lost in a dream, is of Roman, Egyptian, Grecian, or Medieval time or country. As her fancies are proper to girlhood, so her costume, her beauty, and the architecture with which she is surrounded are indefinite and only beautiful' (1861, pp.206–7). Conversely, the *Art Journal*, while conceding that the painting had 'caused considerable talk in artistic and literary circles', condemned it as of the 'lower forms of mere decorative ornamentation' (1861, p.172).

CSN

11

ALBERT JOSEPH MOORE 1841–1893

11 Azaleas *exh.*1868

Oil on canvas 198.1 × 100.3 (78 × 39½)
Signed with Greek anthemion motif, lower right

Prov: Hugh Lane, by whom given to the Hugh Lane Municipal Gallery, Dublin; on loan to the National Gallery of Ireland, Dublin

Exh: RA 1868 (621); Newcastle-upon-Tyne 1972 (20); Sydney 1975 (20); Manchester 1978 (72); Tokyo 1985 (51); Barbican and Tokyo 1991 (84)

Lit: *Art Journal*, 1868, p.106; Rossetti and Swinburne 1868, pp.23, 32; Colvin 1870, p.5; Baldry 1894, pp.35, 102; Staley 1967, pp.80–7, repr.

The Hugh Lane Municipal Gallery of Modern Art, Dublin

Azaleas shows a young woman, wearing a flowing toga-like drapery, standing within a loosely defined interior space. On the floor is a mat, and behind her and to the left is a flowering azalea, growing in a pot of oriental design. With her right hand the girl picks the blossom, which she is about to place in a china basin that she holds in her left arm. No further indication is given as to her purpose or her circumstances, and in this sense the painting is without ostensible subject.

Moore had been moving towards a type of art which was unshackled from the dictates of narrative subject at least from the middle of the decade. His painting *The Marble Seat* (untraced), exhibited at the Royal Academy in 1865, showed three draped females being waited on by a nude boy, and clearly owed much to the study of antique sculpture. *Pomegranates* (Guildhall Art Gallery), of 1866, shows three figures searching the contents of an Oriental cabinet, while *A Musician* (Yale Center for British Art, New Haven), of 1867, shows a man and two girls engaged in music-making. *Azaleas* represents the logical next step in this line of progression, for where the three previous paintings represent a shared activity, the solitary figure of the present painting is by definition alone in her thoughts. Here the viewer is given no clue to the inner preoccupation or mood of the figure; nor indeed is it clear whether the painter intends to allow speculation about the figure he has represented, or whether the picture is to be regarded purely as a decorative ensemble the abstract mood of which is determined by its tenor of colour and rich pattern.

When *Azaleas* appeared at the Royal Academy in 1868 Swinburne used the picture as a pretext for a discussion of the cult of beauty. The painting shared with Watts's *Wife of Pygmalion* (fig.27 on p.43) 'the loftiest quality of beauty pure and simple. Indeed, of all the few great or many good painters now at work among us, no one has so keen and clear a sense of this absolute beauty as Mr Albert Moore. His painting is to artists what the verse of Théophile Gautier is to poets; the faultless and secure expression of an exclusive worship of things formally beautiful' (Rossetti and Swinburne 1868, pp.31–2).

CSN

SIMEON SOLOMON 1840–1905

12 Love in Autumn 1866

Oil on canvas 84 × 64 (33 × 25¼)
Inscribed with monogram 'SS', dated '1866' and inscribed 'Florence' lower left

Prov: Mrs William Coltart, of Birkenhead; by descent; Parke-Bernet, New York 28 Oct. 1982 (76)

Exh: Dudley Gallery 1872 (812, as *Autumn Love*); Liverpool 1886 (812); Manchester 1887 (114 as *Love in Winter*); Guildhall 1894 (140); Glasgow 1901 (361); RA Winter 1906 (108); White City 1908 (83); Auckland 1962 (59); Geffrye Museum 1985 (53, repr. in col.); Barbican 1989 (20, repr. in col. p.13)

Lit: Bate 1899, p.64, repr. opp.; Reynolds 1984, pp.19, 24, repr. in col. pl.1

Private Collection

EXHIBITED IN LONDON AND MUNICH ONLY

The figure of a cupid, naked except for a red drapery with which he attempts to shield himself, is buffeted by the cold winds of autumn. The sky is lit by the setting sun. Night, as well as winter, is approaching and the discomfort of the boy is apparent. Solomon, encouraged by Swinburne and the members of a circle of homosexuals with which he had become involved in the later 1860s, treated themes of sadism and the physical suffering of boys. *Love in Autumn* was much admired among this group, and Solomon presumably had it in mind when a year or two later he wrote to his friend Oscar Browning, a master at Eton, encouraging him to treat with particular cruelty a boy, Gerald Balfour, whom they both especially admired: 'Balfour should be beaten, he should be scourged with rods of iron, pray, my dear Oscar, beat him till the wings, which are latent in his shoulder blades, sprout' (quoted in Reynolds 1984, p.16). That the subliminal theme of the painting is one of flagellation is indicated by the straining trunks of an olive

12

tree and a grove of cypresses in the background and by a menacing branch of twigs and leaves that seems to whip the boy as it is blown in the wind. Flurries of leaves fly past like flecks of blood.

The intended allegory of the painting – the transience implied by the passing of the seasons, which is also seen in the case of Sandys's *Gentle Spring* (no.13) was a contemporary preoccupation – is conflated with the more sinister theme of the confrontation of an individual by forces within himself. In Solomon's prose poem 'A Vision of Love Revealed in Sleep' (1871) the narrator is conducted by his soul through a dream landscape in which a tragic and abandoned figure is found:

> Then, as we went along, while the shallow wave drew back from the grey beach, my spirit took upon itself a great sadness; and lifting my eyes I beheld one, whom I then knew not, seeking shelter in the cleft of a rock. The shame

that had been done him had made dim those
thrones of Charity – his eyes; and as the wings
of a dove, beaten against a wall, fall weak and
frayed, so his wings fell about his perfect body;
his locks, matted with the sharp moisture of
the sea, hung upon his brow, and the fair
garland on his head was broken, and its leaves
and blossoms fluttered to the earth in the chill
air. He held about him a sombre mantle, in
whose folds the fallen autumn leaves had
rested.

(p.5)

Love in Autumn was painted in Florence, to which city Solomon had travelled for the first time in 1866 to study the work of painters such as Botticelli, Luini and Sodoma. The experience of historical schools encouraged Solomon towards a more Classical treatment of figure subjects, and of this type the present painting is his most ambitious. Sidney Colvin believed that 'among the class of rising artists whose aim it is to paint beautiful things beautifully, Mr Simeon Solomon is certainly entitled to a place', explaining that 'his work is to set forth the figures both of certain phases of the historical past, and of his own very fertile and peculiar fancy, in the choicest presentment of line and colour which he can devise for them' (Colvin 1870, p.33).

CSN

13

FREDERICK SANDYS 1829–1904

13 **Gentle Spring** 1863–5

Oil on canvas 121 × 64 (47⅝ × 25³⁄₁₆)

Prov: Ernest Gambart; A.A. Ionides; Christie's, 1 April 1871 (232), bt A.C. Ionides, to his son, A.A. Ionides 1890; Ionides sale, Christie's 15 March 1902 (32), bt Maclean; Mrs A.A. Ionides 1905; Leicester Galleries 1921; Captain R. Langton Douglas, by whom presented to the Ashmolean Museum, Oxford, in memory of his son Lieutenant Archibald Douglas, killed in action 1916

Exh: RA 1865 (359); RA Winter 1905 (268); RA Bicentenary 1968 (349); Brighton and Sheffield 1974 (66)

Lit: Bate 1905, pp.3–17 (repr. p.5); Ashmolean Museum, Report of the Visitors, 1923, p.19

Visitors of the Ashmolean Museum, Oxford

EXHIBITED IN LONDON ONLY

O virgin mother! of gentle days and nights,
Spring of fresh buds and spring of swift delights,
Come, with lips kissed of many an amorous hour,
Come, with hands heavy from the fervent flower,
The fleet first flower that feels the wind and sighs,
The tenderer leaf that draws the sun and dies;
Light butterflies like flowers alive in the air
Circling and crowning thy delicious hair,
And many a fruitful flower and floral fruit
Born of thy breath and fragrant from thy foot.
Thee, mother, all things born desire, and thee
Earth and the fruitless hollows of the sea

Praise, and thy tender winds of ungrown wing
Fill heaven with murmurs of thy sudden spring.
(A.C. Swinburne, *Posthumous Poems*, 1919)

In this abstract evocation of the season of spring, a statuesque draped female figure stands before the viewer in a verdant and flower-strewn landscape. Beneath her feet are a profusion of spring flowers: pansies, narcissi, primulas, gillyflowers, dandelion clocks, with an unfurling fern. Beside her, on her left side, is a beautiful mauve-pink poppy, while in the background are apple trees in blossom. More flowers are found dressed in the woman's hair and in the folds of her dress. Brightly coloured butterflies flutter around her head and alight upon the flowers.

There is in *Gentle Spring* an implicit reference to the decay which is inevitable in the cycle of the seasons. The woman seems to be bringing flowers to the spectator, and these in their profusion cascade to the ground and are so many that she inevitably tramples upon them. This is intended as a *memento mori*, for in their effulgent beauty they are already (like the dandelion) preparing for their own dispersal and death. Furthermore, a sense of foreboding is given by the passage across the distant landscape of clouds heavy with rain, against which a rainbow shines brightly, and one perceives that the woman herself is lit by a momentary beam of sunlight which will be shut off by the oncoming storm. All of these elements speak of the transience of spring weather, and by analogy the uncertainty of happiness and fortune.

Gentle Spring seems to echo the equivocal mood of hope mixed with despondency induced by the beauty of nature found in the poems of another poet in the Rossetti circle, George Meredith (in whose garden in Surrey apparently it was painted). Poems such as 'Ode to the Spirit of Earth in Autumn', part of the collection *Modern Love* (1862), convey the same pantheistic belief in the spirituality of the woods and fields, and the same acknowledgement of the insignificance of man when placed against the cycles of nature.

Swinburne's poem, the verses of which accompanied *Gentle Spring*, was written in response to Sandys's picture. The *Art Journal* applauded the parallel of poem and painting, finding the poem 'of rare loveliness, clothed in that lustrous apparel of metaphor which sparkles in the poems of Keats and Shelley [while] the painting itself is set as with jewels; and it intones impassioned rhapsody' (1865, p.166).

CSN

George Frederic Watts 1817–1904

14 The Three Goddesses *c*.1865–72

Oil on canvas 80 × 65.4 (31½ × 26)

Prov: Sold by the artist to Louis Huth by 1878; sold by him by 1902; Sir Alexander Henderson, Bt (later first Lord Faringdon); his sale, Sotheby's, 13 June 1934 (137), bt by 2nd Earl of Faringdon; by descent

Exh: Deschamps Gallery 1876 (55, as *The Three Graces*); Paris 1878 (235, as *Pallas, Juno and Venus*); Grosvenor Gallery 1881 (17, as *Three Goddesses*); ?Paris 1883 (1, as *Ida*); Glasgow 1888 (368, as *Judgement of Paris*); Wolverhampton 1902 (63, as *Judgement of Paris*); RA Winter 1905 (230, as *Judgement of Paris* 1874); Whitechapel 1974 (27); New Haven, Denver and Newcastle 1996 (61)

Lit: 'Art Notes', *Academy*, 15 March 1872, p.108; [?W.M. Rossetti] 1876, p.482; Comyns Carr 1880, p.176 with engraving by J. Benwell Clark (as *Pallas, Juno and Venus*); Chesneau 1887 (1882), pp.265, 267; Spielmann 1886, p.30; MS. Cat., I, p.83 (without early exh. history); Watts 1912, II, pp.44–5; *The Faringdon Collection: Buscot Park*, 1975, no.87

The Faringdon Collection Trust

EXHIBITED IN LONDON ONLY

The title of this painting underwent several permutations, as its exhibition history shows, eventually ending up, after it left the artist, as *The Judgement of Paris*, although Paris is nowhere to be seen. The three goddesses are named by one of the titles of the painting: Pallas, another name for the Greek goddess of war, Athena; Juno, Roman goddess associated with women (the Greek Hera), and wife of Jupiter (Zeus); lastly, Venus, Roman goddess of love. None bears any traditional attributes, and although the gathering presumes the occasion of Paris's selection of one of the goddesses as most beautiful, the mythological story from Ovid's *Heroides* seems incidental to this study of the nude with drapery.

The Three Goddesses is a key example of Watts's treatment of the nude, a speciality in England almost uniquely associated with him in the late 1860s and 1870s. It entered the collection of Louis Huth, a noted connoisseur with a taste for this particular aspect of Watts's output; in 1872 he also purchased the artist's full-length nude *Daphne* (untraced), a major work exhibited at the Royal Academy in 1870. Antecedents of *The Three Goddesses* could be found in the life class, as each figure takes up a different pose, with opportunities for varying the drapery. At this stage in his career, Watts relied on a particular model, 'Long Mary', who inspired this painting and a number of others begun in the latter half of the 1860s. Her 'noble form' and 'flexibility of movement as well as magnificence of line' impressed the artist (Watts 1912, II, p.44). The numerous large chalk drawings and oil sketches he executed provided him with a repertory of poses and attitudes which formed the basis of his ideal nudes from then on. Before the mid-1870s, Watts depicted mainly single figures. In *The Three Goddesses* he presents a group of three interrelated figures, and further offers a new type of sketchy handling of a limited range of low-toned, almost chalky, colours. Perhaps underlining the experimental nature of the work, Watts sent it in 1876 to Deschamps Gallery (a venue linked to Durand-Ruel's in Paris) where French art could be seen as well as English, a venue also favoured by Whistler. Here Huth, who was also busy buying and commissioning works by Whistler, probably found the painting, which appealed to his own taste, and one can well imagine the potential juxtaposition of this study of ideal nudes in the same gallery setting with Whistler's *Symphony in White No.3* (Barber Institute), which as a celebration of white relies on the same pale tones.

Not surprisingly, given Deschamps's connection with Durand-Ruel and Huth's own taste for French art, *The Three Goddesses* formed part of the group of nine paintings (and the only one lent by a private collector) which travelled to the Exposition Universelle in Paris in 1878 where it was much admired by French writers. Chesneau based his whole discussion on Watts's ability to portray the nude, using *The Three Goddesses* as his chief reference:

> He is the only painter of the English school who has treated the female nude simply from the point of view of style, and with no other object than to realise its purely plastic beauty. His mythological works, entitled 'The Three Goddesses,' only aims at showing simultaneously the front, back and profile of a woman.

Joseph Comyns Carr had commented on just the same feature of Watts's work in general, and *The Three Goddesses* in particular, when he wrote in *L'Art* in 1880 of 'the abstract simplicity of style' and 'the conception of form, the elevated sentiment and the poetry'. Although this modestly sized and conceived painting is by no means a major statement, it did represent an aspect of Watts's output which only became known and admired in the 1870s, and which had particular resonance abroad. It enjoyed an extended reputation in France thanks to the etching published in *L'Art* in 1880. Benwell Clark executed this graphic translation of the painting under the supervision of Alphonse Legros (fig.36 on p.66).

In the 1880s Watts reworked the composition resulting in a new work, *The Judgement of Paris* (fig.42 on p.66), first exhibited at the Grosvenor Gallery in 1887, and again triumphantly in Paris in 1889. This reworking is more overtly Symbolist in its ethereal figures in a cloud-like setting, filled with opalescent colouring characteristic of the mid-1880s.

BB

JAMES ABBOTT MCNEILL WHISTLER
1834–1903

15 The Little White Girl: Symphony in White No.2 1864

Oil on canvas 76.5 × 51.1 (30⅛ × 20⅛)
Inscribed 'Whistler' and originally dated '1864' upper right

Prov: Bt at the RA by Gerald Potter 1865; Arthur Studd 1893; by whom bequeathed to the National Gallery 1919; transferred to the Tate Gallery 1951

Exh: RA 1865 (530); International Exhibition, London 1872 (260); Goupil Gallery 1892 (33); Munich 1892 (1950a); Glasgow 1893; Antwerp 1894 (2369); Venice 1895 (363); Paris 1900 (76 in American section); Edinburgh 1902 (240); Boston 1904 (28); Paris 1905 (5); Tate Gallery 1994 (15)

Lit: Pennell and Pennell 1908, I, pp.127–30, 144, 147, 178, II, pp.251, 261–2, 280; revised ed. 1911, repr. opp. p.124 in its original frame; Sutton 1966, p.185, repr. as frontis.; Young et al. 1980, I, no.52, pp.28–9, II, pls.31, 371 (with further bibliography); Anderson and Koval 1994, pp.149–59, 353, 374, 390, 443

Tate Gallery. Bequeathed by Arthur Studd 1919

EXHIBITED IN LONDON ONLY

Whistler's painting *The Little White Girl*, as it was known when first exhibited at the Royal Academy in 1865, shows the artist's mistress Jo Hiffernan standing beside a fireplace in the house in Lindsey Row, Chelsea, that they shared. Dressed in white, and holding a Japanese fan, she gazes with unseeing eyes, apparently lost in thought. The reflected image of her head and face is seen in the looking-glass. The circumstances of her life are not specified (although she wears a wedding ring on the third finger of her left hand), and the spectator is left to imagine what events have caused her sad mood, or what her eventual fate might be.

Swinburne's poem 'Before the Mirror' was inspired by *The Little White Girl*, and its verses, written on sheets of gold paper, were attached to the flats of the original frame (sadly now not extant, but see fig.22 on p.39). The poem concludes:

> Deep in the gleaming glass
> She sees all past things pass,
> And all sweet life that was lie down and lie.
>
> There glowing ghosts of flowers
> Draw down, draw nigh;
> And wings of swift spent hours
> Take flight and fly;
> She sees by formless gleams,
> She hears across cold streams,
> Dead mouths of many dreams that sing and sigh.
>
> Face fallen and white throat lifted,
> With sleepless eye
> She sees old loves that drifted,
> She knew not why,
> Old loves and faded fears
> Float down a stream that hears
> The flowing of all men's tears beneath the sky.

In 1865 the *Times* critic found Swinburne's 'very beautiful but not very lucid verses' unhelpful as to the painting's meaning. 'Nevertheless', he concluded, 'the picture is one … that means more than it says, though not so much perhaps as the poet has said for it. Thought and passion are under the surface of the plain features, giving them an undefinable attraction' (quoted in Young et al. 1980, I, p.29). The idea of a person being confronted by a past existence, or a sad premonition of what is to come – for while the girl standing before us is young and graceful, her mirrored image seems stooped and worn – appealed to a generation who looked for evidence of the spirit world in their daily surroundings and who sought the means of translation into the spheres of other worlds. In passing, one wonders whether Charles Dodgson ('Lewis Carroll') saw Whistler's painting at Trafalgar Square in 1865, and whether perhaps he may have had it in mind when writing *Through the Looking-Glass and What Alice Found There* in 1871.

The detached way in which the spectator is invited to inspect the figure of a woman who faces away from the viewer and who seems to avoid psychological engagement, but the expression of whose face – as seen in the image of her reflection – may be studied quite independently, is surely owed to Whistler's memory of Velázquez's *Rokeby Venus* (National Gallery, London), which he must have seen at the Manchester Art Treasures Exhibition of 1857. In that painting, as in *The Little White Girl*, the careworn appearance of the woman as transmitted to the viewer through her reflection seems at odds with the idealised beauty of her actual presence.

Swinburne may perhaps have suggested to Whistler the notion of individuals coming upon themselves by supernatural agency and of the anxiety induced by such premonition of one's fate. In 1864, the year of *The Little White Girl*, Swinburne had visited Florence to study Renaissance paintings, and the essay that he subsequently wrote describing what he had seen explores this theme, in for example his account of paintings by Leonardo, whose works he found to be 'full of … indefinable grace and grave mystery': 'Fair strange faces of women full of dim doubt and faint scorn; touched by the shadow of an obscure fate; eager and weary as it seems at once, pale and fervent with patience or passion; allure and perplex the eyes and thoughts of men. There is a study here of Youth and Age meeting; it may be, of a young man coming suddenly upon the ghostly figure of himself as he will one day be; the brilliant life in his face is struck into sudden pallor and silence, the clear eyes startled, the happy lips confused' (*Fortnightly Review*, vol.4 (NS), 1868, pp.16–40).

CSN

James Abbott McNeill Whistler
1834–1903

16 Three Figures: Pink and Grey
1868–78

Oil on canvas 139.7 × 185.4 (55 × 73)

Prov: Frederick Leyland (ownership disputed by Whistler); Alfred Chapman, Liverpool *c.*1886; Agnew's 1905; Princess Edmond de Polignac; sale Christie's 28 July 1950 (140), bt Agnew's; bt by the Tate Gallery 1950

Exh: London 1905 (399); Berlin 1969 (12, repr.)

Lit: Sutton 1966, p.22, pl.41; Young et al. 1980, no.89, repr. pl.63

Tate Gallery. Purchased with the aid of contributions from the International Society of Sculptors, Painters and Gravers as a Memorial to Whistler, and from Francis Howard 1950

The composition of this canvas was based on a design that Whistler had produced as an oil sketch in 1868 as part of a plan for a frieze commissioned the previous year by his patron F.R. Leyland of Liverpool. These subjects were all scenes with women (in one case a single nude) and flowers, showing the strong influence of Japanese art. Another source has been noted (Dorment and MacDonald 1994, pp.92–4): the frieze of *The Story of St George* that Burne-Jones executed for the house of his fellow artist Myles Birket Foster in 1865–7. Parallels with the work of Albert Moore (no.11), whom we know that Whistler admired, are also obvious. The measured rhythms of Burne-Jones's figures, deployed across the pictorial space in a way that was later to fascinate Ferdinand Hodler (see no.136), and Moore's deliberately subjectless schemes of carefully modulated colour, are translated by Whistler into an altogether more airy, exuberant language. The oil sketches for the scheme, which was later dubbed the 'Six Projects', are all now in the Freer Gallery, Washington, D.C. They are executed with great vigour and freedom, emphasising the bold simplicity of their compositions and concentrating on bright, pale colour. It has been suggested that Whistler derived his colour schemes from the polychrome Tanagra figures that he looked at in the British Museum, opposite his studio in Great Russell Street, and some of the figures themselves, with their rhythmically flowing drapery, seem to come from the same source.

In the event the series of large pictures that Whistler must have intended was never produced; only one was finished – *The White Symphony: Three Girls* 1867 (Young et al. 1980, no.88), which is now lost. The fragment of another version of it (Young et al. 1980, no.90) exists in a private collection. The Tate Gallery's version was for a long time supposed to have been painted in the late 1860s but it is now known that Whistler made it much later, and was not satisfied with it. It was, he wrote, 'a picture in no way representative, and in its actual condition, absolutely worthless'. Despite his strictures, it is in fact full of fresh touches and characteristic handling, and shows a number of pentimenti which suggest that it is not a simple copy of the lost work, though it follows the original sketch in most essentials. In so far as it is relatively finished (though it is clearly not consistently finished throughout) it serves to illustrate the way in which Whistler planned to create substantial finished pictures from extremely economically conceived designs. Whereas Moore was content to leave his harmonious compositions to speak for themselves,

16

Whistler intended to compensate for the absence of literal or narrative meaning in his pictures by explicit references to music in their titles, as the *White Symphony* showed. The idea was apparently to have been reinforced by quotations from actual pieces of music on the frames. The frame of the *White Symphony*, for instance, is known to have been inscribed with some bars from Schubert's F minor *Moment Musical*, Op.94 no.3. This leads Dorment (loc. cit.) to speculate that the frieze was intended for a music room, in which Leyland, an able amateur pianist, could 'accompany' the pictures with appropriate performances.

In blending both the Classical and the medieval styles of the day with the fashion for Japanese woodblock prints, and at the same time invoking music as a natural participant in the meaning of the paintings, the 'Six Projects' scheme put in place all the elements of a new aesthetic – one that seemed at first to be simply 'Aesthetic' but which was in reality the soil out of which a fully formed Symbolism was to grow.

AW

Pierre Puvis de Chavannes
1824–1898

17 **Le Recueillement** 1867

Oil on canvas 106 × 52.5 (41¾ × 20⅔)
Signed and dated 'P. Puvis de Chavannes 67', lower left

Prov: The family of the artist; acquired by present owner

Exh: Montreal 1995 (334, repr p.198, no.267); Takamatsu 1996 (1, repr. p.33)

Lit: Mourey 1895, p.179, repr.; Brown Price 1972, no.111; d'Argencourt and Foucart 1976, p.85

Private Collection

EXHIBITED IN LONDON ONLY

Le Recueillement (Reminiscence) is a variant of one of the four decorative panels commissioned from Puvis de Chavannes by the sculptress, novelist and art critic, Claude Vignon, for the hall of her house built at Passy (a western suburb of Paris) in 1866 (demolished

17

1912). Three of the original panels are owned by the Musée du Louvre, Paris, and are in the Musée d'Orsay, Paris; the fourth, *Imagination*, is in the Ohara Museum of Art, Kurashiki.

Each panel is of the same height and contains a cartouche set into the bottom of the painting upon which its title is inscribed: *l'Histoire* (History); *Le Recueillement* (Reminiscence); *Fantasie* (Imagination), and *La Vigilance* (Vigilance). While *History* and *Imagination* are multi-figure compositions, both *Vigilance* and *Reminiscence* present a single, classically draped woman whose pose and gesture establish a contrast of message and mood. While *Vigilance* is portrayed by a forceful figure who looks purposefully out from the canvas, her right hand holding a lamp high above her head, *Reminiscence* is evoked by a passive, retiring figure whose eyes are closed and whose forehead is touched by the fingers of her right hand, as if totally absorbed in her own thoughts. Taken in the context of the decorational scheme's iconographic programme, the four panels convey the source and process of artistic creation. The subject-matter of a work of art is given by History distilled through *Reminiscence*; it is given formal expression by Imagination which is reined in by Vigilance. The programme represents a personal manifestation of Puvis's own belief in the superior role of the intellect in the creative process.

Compared to the original version of *Reminiscence*, the variant shown here gives greater detail in the foliage in the foreground and applies a slightly more extended tonal range. However, Puvis has divested his figure of any allegorical attribute, relying solely upon the dominant grey-green of the palette, the formal vertical stress given by the pose of the figure and the grove of trees, the absence of movement and the inner absorption of the figure to convey the intellectual idea of the subject, namely silence and reflection. While the challenge to convey the theme of inner thought and memory was explored by many Symbolist artists, for example Moreau, Redon and Khnopff, the realisation that the mood of a subject could be conveyed through colour and compositional structure represents an important contribution by Puvis to the Symbolist aesthetic. Not only did he adopt this vocabulary in this picture, but he also developed it more fully in his later work, most strikingly in *The Poor Fisherman* 1881 (Musée d'Orsay, Paris) where an empty landscape, a high horizon line, a dead, grey sea and a drained grey-pink sky combine to convey the idea personified in the figure of the downcast fisherman – poverty. There are close parallels with Puvis's aesthetic programme in the 1860s to be found in the work of Leighton, Moore and Whistler of the same period; see nos.10, 11, 16.

MAS

Private Thoughts I

The revolution in aesthetic thought and practice that affected many of the most distinguished young artists of 1860s London often found its expression in works of small scale and great intensity of both conception and colour. The painters who showed at the Dudley Gallery's exhibitions of watercolours in the Egyptian Hall, Piccadilly, from 1865, were preoccupied with the development of their medium as a vehicle for the expression of intense states of seeing and being. By that date Edward Burne-Jones, still only thirty-two, had established himself as a leading spirit, and exercised an enormous influence on many of the younger generation, such as the eccentric Robert Bateman (nos.18, 19). Burne-Jones joined those of his colleagues who were abandoning subject-matter for the evocation of states of mind, and in a watercolour like *Green Summer* (fig.23 on p.40) of 1862 transformed the Rossettian Middle Ages into a timeless world, as much modern as medieval, in which the joys of life are overshadowed by the unuttered expectation of death and decay. The theme of *Green Summer* was to be taken up in an idiom close to that of Burne-Jones by Puvis de Chavannes in *Death and the Maidens* of 1872 (no.55). In *The Madness of Sir Tristram* 1862 (no.22) or his design for a Bible illustration, *The Return of the Dove to the Ark* c.1863 (no.24), Burne-Jones's musings take him into the darker regions of the mind, and foreshadow the nightmare imaginings of many Symbolists in the next decades.

The surface textures that emerged from the watercolour experiments of these years were to have a profound effect on Symbolism. Dense yet subdued in colour, imperceptibly obscure rather than sharp in outline and detail, they share none of the biting immediacy of Pre-Raphaelite surfaces, seeking not a vivid and present reality but a dreamlike truth beyond reality. Rossetti had already shown the way, and Burne-Jones, Simeon Solomon and others essayed similar surface textures, not only in watercolour but in other media such as gouache, pastel and tempera. Later even oil paint was to be coaxed into this new mould.

ROBERT BATEMAN 1842–1922

18 **Three Women Plucking Mandrakes** exh. 1870

Bodycolour on paper laid on to canvas
31.2 × 45.8 (12¼ × 18)

Prov: Bt at auction, 2 Oct. 1912, for the Wellcome Historical Medical Museum, Wigmore Street
Exh: Dudley Gallery 1870 (194)
Lit: *Art Journal*, 1870, p.87; Kavanagh 1989, pp.174–9

Wellcome Institute Library, London

A group of women are shown attempting to pull mandrakes from the ground. The mandrake or devil's apple, known to botanists as *Mandragora officinarum*, is a plant of the potato family, the fleshy tubers of which often resemble a human figure. Mandrakes grow in the countries of southern Europe, and since ancient times have been the object of superstition. They are supposed to resist being plucked, and when they are pulled from the ground they are reputed to give a scream that will frighten the hearer to death. For this reason, those who attempt to harvest mandrakes (and they have been valued as a putative cure for barrenness and as a means of inducing abortion) resort to elaborate systems of lines and pulleys, as seen in the present watercolour. According to the traditions of folk magic, the mandrake grows at a place where a criminal, or one whose mother had committed crimes while he was in her womb, or conversely one who had been unjustly condemned, has been hanged. The plant is supposed to germinate from semen or urine voided by the dying man, or, according to other sources, from decomposing flesh.

The strangeness of the subject was picked up by the reviewer of the *Art Journal* on the occasion of the watercolour's first appearance, at the Dudley Gallery in 1870: '"Plucking Mandrakes" recalls descriptions in the works of Sir Thomas Browne, which recount how the mandrake shrieks when drawn from its roots. There is evidently much mystery in the process as depicted by Mr Bateman, and this picture in its forms, action, colour, removed as they are from common life and ordinary experience, are significant of something beyond the usual course of nature.' Robert Bateman was an erudite man whose private income allowed him to devote himself to the investigation of the natural sciences and philosophical matters, as well as botany and horticulture. It is likely that he would have known Thomas Browne's writings, and it is in the Second Book of *Pseudodoxia Epidemica* (known as *Vulgar Errors*), originally published in 1646, that Browne weighs fact and popular superstition in connection with the mandrake.

That conservative opinion continued to regard the progressive artists of the Dudley Gallery as overtaken by the baleful influence of Burne-Jones is testified by the *Art Journal*'s comment in 1870 (in connection with the notorious *Phyllis and Demophoön*; fig.25 on p.41) that 'to judge how degenerate this style may become in the hands of disciples, it is needful to walk to the Dudley Gallery' (*Art Journal*, 1970, p.173).

CSN

19

ROBERT BATEMAN 1842–1922

19 **The Dead Knight** *c.*1870

Watercolour 28 × 39 (11 × 15⅜)
Exh: Barbican 1989 (25, repr. in col.); Munich and Madrid 1993 (73, repr. in col.)
Lit: Newall 1987, pp.103–6; Kavanagh 1989, pp.174–9

Robin de Beaumont

This strange but beautiful watercolour is not dated; nor has it been identified as one of Robert Bateman's Dudley Gallery exhibits. It was perhaps inspired by Book I of Edmund Spenser's *The Faerie Queene*, which tells the story of the Redcrosse Knight of Holiness. A figure in armour, apparently lifeless and stretched out on the grass, is guarded by a faithful hound. Close to the body appears what may be a broken lance, and to the left is seen a water cistern. A half-light is cast upon the scene, and an evening sky is glimpsed through the dense screen of trees. A point of light reflects in the surface of the water, and the glade in which the figure lies is starred with cow parsley.

Robert Bateman was one (and possibly the unofficial leader) of a group of artists that gathered at the Dudley Gallery in Piccadilly (where summer exhibitions of watercolours were held from 1865 onwards). Among others who exhibited there were H. Ellis Wooldridge, T. Blake Wirgman, Edward Clifford, Edward Henry Fahey, Alfred Sacheverell Coke and Walter Crane. Each of these painters was deeply impressed by the drawings that Edward Burne-Jones showed at the Old Water-Colour Society between 1864 and 1870; and Crane's characterisation of the archetypal Burne-Jones subject, as adopted by the Dudley artists, as 'a twilight world of dark mysterious woodlands, haunted streams, meads of deep green starred with burning flowers, veiled in a dim and mystic light' (Crane 1907, p.84) might serve to describe works by Burne-Jones such as *Green Summer* (fig.23 on p.40) or the present example by Bateman.

CSN

EDWARD BURNE-JONES 1833–1898

20 **Sidonia von Bork 1560** 1860–1

Watercolour and bodycolour 33 × 17 (13 × 6¾)
Inscribed '1860 E. Burne Jones. fecit', lower left, and 'Sidonia von Bork 1560' on the original oak boards
Prov: James Leathart; Goupil Gallery 1896; William Graham Robertson; by whom given to the Tate Gallery 1948
Exh: New Gallery 1892 (8, 11); Goupil Gallery 1896 (10, 12); New Gallery 1898 (24); Bradford 1904 (118, 126); Rome 1911 (400, 401); Tate Gallery 1933 (33); RA 1934 (841–2); Newcastle 1968 (26–7); Hayward Gallery 1975 (24); Tate Gallery 1984 (230); Tate Gallery 1993 (2); Nottingham 1994 (4)
Lit: *Athenaeum*, 1873, p.343; Bell 1892, pp.30–1; G.B.-J. 1904, I, p.215; de Lisle 1904, pp.48–9, 179; Harrison and Waters 1973, p.70; Christian 1973b, pp.100–9; Fitzgerald 1975, pp.73–4

Tate Gallery. Bequeathed by W. Graham Robertson 1948

20

This watercolour, with its pair, *Clara von Bork*, was inspired by Johannes Wilhelm Meinhold's *Sidonia von Bork, die Klosterhexe*, translated by Speranza Wilde as *Sidonia the Sorceress* (1849). Penelope Fitzgerald has called the two watercolours 'his two real apprentice pieces, which mark the beginning of an individual style' (1975, p.73). Burne-Jones's choice of subject reflects the intense interest the book held for the circle of late Pre-Raphaelite artists: Rossetti had first discussed it in a letter to William Allingham in September 1854 (comparing it to *Wuthering Heights*) and was said to have 'a positive passion' for the book (Ruskin, *Works*, xxxvi, p.457, n.2). Ruskin was concerned that Ellen Heaton might be shocked: 'You seem mightily scandalised about Sidonia – I have never read the book. Edward [Burne-Jones] told me she was only a witch ... as it was, I saw no more harm in it than in his drawings of Medea and Circe, or any other of his pet witches and mine' (ibid., p.457).

According to Meinhold's story, Sidonia was a woman of great beauty who used her powers of sorcery to destroy innocent lives, and who was particularly vicious and unforgiving to the men who could not prevent themselves from falling in love with her. It was this mixture of beauty with evil, cruelty in sensuality, and invitation mixed with menace, that Rossetti and his circle found so thrilling, and the one that defined the instinct towards submission to female sexual power that is connected with the cult of the 'Stunner'. Burne-Jones's relish for such a subject, and the psychological skill with which he captures the deviousness and mendacity of the figure (modelled on Rossetti's mistress Fanny Cornforth), is revealed absolutely when the drawing is compared to its pendant, the portrait of Sidonia's cousin-in-law the virtuous Clara von Bork (Tate Gallery) (for whom Georgiana Macdonald, shortly afterwards to be married to Burne-Jones, served as model) whose innocence is symbolised by her loving protectiveness towards a nest of chicks stalked by a vile cat.

Burne-Jones's *Sidonia von Bork* was intensely admired by the artist's friend Algernon Swinburne, who was reminded of it by paintings by Filippino Lippi that he saw in Florence in 1864. When Swinburne wrote up his account of the Florentine school he gave himself the opportunity to praise 'Mr E. Burne Jones's nobler drawing of the young Sidonia wearing a gown whose pattern is of branching and knotted snakes, black upon the golden stuff' (*Fortnightly Review*, 1868, pp.16–40).

CSN

EDWARD BURNE-JONES 1833–1898

21 **Clerk Saunders** 1861

Watercolour 69.9 × 41.8 (27½ × 16½)
Inscribed 'E.B.J. | 1861', b.r.

Prov: Henry Tanworth Wells, RA; Mrs Winifred Hadley, by whom presented to the Tate Gallery 1927

Exh: New Gallery 1898 (1); Tate Gallery 1933 (4); Tate Gallery 1993 (7)

Lit: Bell 1892, p.34; G.B.-J. 1904, I, p.224; de Lisle 1904, pp.58, 179, repr. opp. p.58; Harrison and Waters 1973, pp.45, 75, pl.5, repr. in col.

Tate Gallery. Presented by Mrs Winifred Hadley through the National Art Collections Fund 1927

An intense interest in the folk ballads of the Border country had grown up among the members of the Rossetti circle since about 1856. Walter Scott's collection of ballads *Minstrelsy of the Scottish Border*, gathered together from the surviving oral tradition and published in 1802–3, were much loved. In 1856 Elizabeth Siddal embarked on a watercolour of Clerk Saunders, based on Scott's poem (the drawing was lent to the 1857 Russell Place Pre-Raphaelite exhibition), and from 1858 until 1861 Swinburne (always proud of his Northumberland roots) devoted himself to gathering together a further collection of folk ballads of the Border country (published as *Ballads of the English Border*, 1925), which supplemented that of Scott's *Minstrelsy*. Burne-Jones's drawing *Clerk Saunders* reflects this preoccupation, and may be seen as a gesture of friendship to Swinburne, to whom he was very close in the early 1860s.

According to the catalogue of the New Gallery Burne-Jones memorial exhibition, this watercolour shows the moment when 'Clerk Saunders entreats May Margaret to let him into her house; she faintly repels him.' The rain pours down on the exhausted couple, but she hesitates to allow him into her father's house, knowing how her family will react if they believe that Saunders has seduced her. Swinburne sets the scene in the opening verses of his version of the ballad:

> It was a sad and rainy night
> As ever rained frae town to town,
> Clerk Saunders and his lady gay,
> They were in the fields sae brown.
>
> 'A bed, a bed,' Clerk Saunders cried,
> 'A bed, a bed, let me lie down;
> For I am sae weet, and sae wearie,
> That I canna gae, nor ride frae town.'
> 'A bed, a bed,' his lady cried,
> A bed, a bed, ye'll ne'er get nane.
>
> For I hae seven bauld brethren,
> Bauld are they, and very rude,
> And if they find ye in bower wi' me,
> They winna care to spill your blood.'

The poem has a tragic outcome, for May Margaret does in fact take pity on Saunders and he is discovered in her bed. Six of her brothers spare him, but the seventh kills him. Swinburne's version of the ballad ends with Margaret's father's attempting to comfort his daughter, but being rebuffed, while in Scott's the ghost of Clerk Saunders appears at Margaret's window to take his leave of her. Margaret asks him to kiss her farewell, but he resists: '"My mouth it is full cold, Margaret, / It has the smell, now, of the ground; / And if I kiss your comely mouth, / Thy days of life will not be lang.'

CSN

EDWARD BURNE-JONES 1833–1898

22 **The Madness of Sir Tristram** 1862

Bodycolour 59 × 55 (23¼ × 21⅝)
Inscribed 'EBJ. 1862', lower left

Prov: Mrs Aglaia Coronio 1893; sold Hampton's, 21 Nov. 1906 (502); Sir William Tate; his daughter, Mrs Caroline Robinson; her son, Col. M.R. Robinson DSO, OBE; sold Christie's, 14 Nov. 1967 (134); Leger Galleries; Stone Gallery, Newcastle-upon-Tyne; Mrs B. Clark; acquired by the present owner 1976

Exh: Royal Society of British Artists 1892; New Gallery 1892 (1); New Gallery 1898 (37); Leger Galleries 1968 (44); Sheffield 1971 (16); Hayward Gallery 1975 (76); Tokyo 1989 (27); Tate Gallery 1993 (18)

Lit: Bell 1892, p.35; de Lisle 1904, pp.67, 180; Maas 1969, p.144, repr. p.158; Harrison and Waters 1973, pp.54–6, 75; Christian 1973c, p.68, fig.20

Private Collection

A placard hanging from the central tree is inscribed: 'So would Sir Tristram | come unto his harp And hearken the | melodious sound thereof and Sometime | he would harp himself – Thus he Endured | there a quarter of a year.'

This watercolour takes its subject from Chapter IV of Book IX, 'Tristram's Madness and Exile', of 'The Book of Sir Tristram de Lyones', which forms the fifth part of Thomas Malory's *Le Morte Darthur.* Sir Tristram, misled by false tales of Iseult's love for another, leaves his castle in despair: 'Than uppon a nyght he put hys horse from hym and unlaced hys armour, and so yeode unto the wyldirnes and braste downe the treys and bowis. And othirwhyle, whan he founde the harpe that the lady sente hym, than wolde he harpe and play thereuppon and wepe togydirs.'

Le Morte Darthur had been a compelling inspiration for each member of the group of painters that had formed around Rossetti after the demise of the original Pre-Raphaelite coalition. Burne-Jones had sought out Rossetti in 1856, and the following year they and various others – Arthur Hughes, Valentine Prinsep, John Hungerford Pollen and Spencer Stanhope – joined together to paint murals based on Malory's book on the walls of the new Debating Chamber of the Oxford University Union building. Although this ended in debacle, the continuing popularity of Malory's text is demonstrated by the firm Morris, Marshall, Faulkner & Co.'s having been commissioned in 1862 to produce panels of stained glass on the theme for a house in Yorkshire (these are now in Cartwright Hall Art Gallery, Bradford). Burne-Jones undertook four of the thirteen panels, and subsequently worked up two of them – the present and another entitled *The Marriage of Sir Tristram* (untraced) – as watercolours.

CSN

Edward Burne-Jones 1833–1898

23 **Going into the Ark** *c.*1863

Pen and ink on woodblock
17.5 × 13 (6⅞ × 5⅛)

The Board of Trustees of the Victoria and Albert Museum

This small, strong drawing of Noah and his family boarding the Ark was made in connection with the Dalziel Bible project of the early 1860s. Beautifully adapting to the requirements of simplicity and legibility of images that are to be transferred to the woodblock, Burne-Jones has conveyed the press of mocking people – from which Noah retreats – and who are about to be overtaken by God's punishment.

Burne-Jones was for a period very excited about making illustrations of Bible subjects, although he found that he had little time to devote to them. He wrote to the Dalziel brothers (from 52 Great Russell Street, and therefore before the end of 1864):

> In a few days you will have 'Ezekiel,' and soon after 'The Coming of the Dove to the Ark.' My work has simply overwhelmed me and my walks for the last month. Your private

23

24

commission still delights me with its congenial nature. The three subjects you name explain the 'Noah' subject ... Do you think of having a 'Temptation of Adam and Eve'? It would be famous for engraving, with a horny snake all round the tree, and the naked figures could be sufficiently concealed in the thicket so as not to offend the prurient (for they ought not to offend the modest). I shall thoroughly enjoy all this work.

(*The Brothers Dalziel*, 1901, pp.254–6)

In the event, when the book was finally published in 1880 only the Ezekiel drawing had been used. See also no.24.

CSN

EDWARD BURNE-JONES 1833–1898

24 **The Return of the Dove to the Ark** *c.*1863

Pen and ink on woodblock
17.5 × 13.5 (6⅞ × 5⅜)

Lit: Harrison and Waters 1973, pl.80

The Board of Trustees of the Victoria and Albert Museum

This sinister and unpleasant treatment of the Old Testament story of Noah was made, along with its pair (no.23), as an illustration to Dalziel's Bible Gallery, but for whatever reason was never used nor even cut.

The drawing shows the return of the dove that Noah sent out in search of land. 'And the dove came in to him in the evening; and, lo, in her mouth was an olive leaf, pluckt off: so Noah knew that the waters were abated from the earth' (Genesis 8:11). All around the wooden walls of the Ark, floating in the greasy surface of the ebbing waters and lit by the weird rays of the returning sun, are the cadavers of the men and women whom God had sought to punish, their dead eyes staring blankly in the contorted expressions of death. With them are the corpses of strange creatures, like winged monsters – representing the evil spirits that had lived with man on earth – and weird birds peck at the jumbled mass of carrion.

This is truly an image with power to horrify the spectator, who finds himself witness to holocaust at the moment when hope is reborn.

CSN

EDWARD BURNE-JONES 1833–1898

25 **The Lament** 1864–6

Watercolour and bodycolour on paper laid down on canvas 47.5 × 79.5 (18¾ × 31¼)
Inscribed 'EBJ 1866' lower left

Prov: Bt from the artist by John Hamilton Trist; his sale, Christie's 9 April 1892 (15); Frank Brangwyn, by whom given to the William Morris Gallery, Walthamstow 1941

Exh: Old Water-Colour Society 1869 (43); Hayward Gallery 1975 (93); Riverside Studios 1981 (10); Tate Gallery 1984 (240); Rome 1986 (10)

Lit: Bell 1892, p.34; de Lisle 1904, p.180; Harrison and Waters 1979, p.64, repr. pl.14; Benedetti 1980, pp.70–91, repr. pl.80; Benedetti 1985, pp.85–99

William Morris Gallery (London Borough of Waltham Forest)

EXHIBITED IN LONDON AND MUNICH ONLY

Two draped figures, a girl holding a dulcimer, the other with his head resting on his hands in a gesture of exhaustion or despair, sit on the stone benches of a castle chamber and with a view beyond into a courtyard. The architectural setting seems loosely medieval, but as in Leighton's *Lieder ohne Wörte* (no.10), no specific historical epoch is intended. In this sense *The Lament* anticipates Burne-Jones's *Love among the Ruins* (see no.41), the early bodycolour version of which was painted in 1870.

If the mood of the present work is intriguing and impenetrable, its title must be taken to indicate that the state of mind of the figures is one of grief and despair. Whether this is a response to the plaintive music that the left-hand figure has that moment ceased from playing (her hands rest on the stringed instrument as if in momentary pause, and she herself – although more composed than her companion – seems also transfixed by the emotion induced by playing), or indicative of some larger but unknown tragedy is not stated. In the absence of a given narrative Burne-Jones allows himself the use of symbolic codes, such as the fallen rose and strewn petals beside the right-hand figure – a motif which may here be understood, as in Whistler's *The White Girl* (fig.21 on p.38), to signify loss perhaps specifically the loss of virginity or the end of a love affair.

Burne-Jones was one of a number of English artists who in the mid-1860s sought to introduce a balance and harmony into their compositions which was inspired by study of Classical sculpture. Since 1863 he had been making intensive study of the Antique, and particularly of the Parthenon frieze of the Elgin Marbles at the British Museum, as may be judged from

25

his surviving sketchbooks. This was in part a response to the advice he received from Ruskin that as an artist without academic training he needed to teach himself how to draw well, and by this means be able to control and choreograph the figurative elements of his compositions. However, Burne-Jones's interest in ancient sculpture was more than self-educational. Like Moore and Whistler, who similarly sought qualities of equilibrium and calm in compositions such as *The Marble Seat* by the former (untraced; see Baldry 1894, repr. opp. p.28), and *Symphony in White No.3* by Whistler (Barber Institute, University of Birmingham), both of 1865, Burne-Jones learnt from relief sculpture how to place his figures in a foreground plane and thus to emphasise the abstract decorative patterns of the arrangement.

The Lament was kept back from exhibition until 1869, when it appeared at the Old Water-Colour Society along with *The Wine of Circe* (see fig.24 on p.41). On this occasion the French critic Philippe Burty wrote of Burne-Jones:

> Here is a style of painting of the greatest worth: for the mood, which is as disturbing and even more powerful than in certain parts of Baudelaire's *Fleurs du Mal*; and for the treatment, which is masterful. It is in this that one must judge this most gifted artist.
>
> (*Gazette de Beaux-Arts*, Paris, 1869, pp.44–61)

CSN

26

EDWARD BURNE-JONES 1833–1898

26 **Vesper, or The Evening Star** 1872

Watercolour, bodycolour and gold paint on canvas 79 × 56 (31⅛ × 22$^{1}/_{16}$)
Inscribed 'EBJ' lower left

Prov: Bt from the artist by Frederick Craven; H.W. Henderson; private collection
Exh: ?New Gallery 1892 (53); New Gallery 1898 (80); Tate Gallery 1984 (247); Tokyo 1987 (12)
Lit: Bell 1892, p.48; G.B.-J. 1904, II, p.29;

Private Collection

This watercolour, also known as *Hesperus*, is a version of a subject shown at the Old Water-Colour Society in 1870 alongside *Phyllis and Demophoön* (fig.25 on p.41), the work that caused such outrage by its treatment of the male nude that Burne-Jones withdrew both from the exhibition and the association. The first version, which was more loosely treated, and with the girl's face turning away from the spectator rather than being shown in profile, met with a hostile response when first seen – the figure represented was, according to the *Art Journal*, 'a nondescript being, neither fowl nor fish, and yet scarcely human. The colour, too, is like nothing in heaven above or on the earth beneath' (*Art Journal*, 1870, p.173). F.G. Stephens, generally a friend to the Pre-Raphaelites and their successors, thought it 'grand poetry [but] expressed in bad grammar' (*Athenaeum*, 1870, p.586). Whether or not it was this cool response to the picture that subsequently belonged to George Howard caused Burne-Jones to make the present more carefully drawn and more weirdly lit version, the innovation that both paintings represented – the move towards abstract allegorical figures personifying times of day, seasons, the stars and moon – was an important one for the artist, and represented a further loosening of the ties of pictorial narrative upon him.

CSN

EDWARD BURNE-JONES 1833–1898

27 **Night** 1870

Watercolour and bodycolour on canvas
79 × 56 (31$^{1}/_{16}$ × 22)
Inscribed 'E. BURNE JONES 1870' lower right

Prov: Frederick Craven; his sale, Christie's 18 May 1895 (53), bt Agnew's; I.F. Schwann; H.W. Henderson; Agnew's 1967; present owner
Exh: Hayward Gallery 1975 (103); Tokyo 1987 (11)

Private Collection

As in *The Evening Star* (no.26), a draped female figure floats through an open sky by supernatural power. Her dress billows in the night air, and she extends her hands forward in the gesture of a somnambulist. A distant coastline, and mountains on the far horizon, can be made out, but otherwise the landscape above which the figure of Night flies is wrapped in darkness.

This is much more loosely and expressively treated than either *The Evening Star*, or indeed the paired figures of *Night* and *Day* (Fogg Art Museum, Harvard) which Burne-Jones had painted in 1868, and which are respectively draped and nude figures of a woman and a man, each standing at a doorway with distant views of sea and a harbour. Although the present work entered the collection of Frederick Craven (who also owned the first *Pygmalion* series – private collection; see no.38 – and works by Solomon and Rossetti), it has the feel of something done for the painter's own delectation and pleasure.

CSN

27

EDWARD BURNE-JONES 1833–1898

28 The Wheel of Fortune *c.*1871

Bodycolour 48.3 × 24.1 (19 × 9½)
Prov: G.F. Watts; ...; Carlisle Museum and Art Gallery
Lit: Harrison and Waters 1973, p.105 repr.

Tullie House Museum and Art Gallery, Carlisle

This is an early treatment of a subject Burne-Jones subsequently realised in the large oil painting of the same title exhibited at the Grosvenor Gallery in 1883. The principal differences are in the treatment of the figure of Fortune, who is blindfolded and placed within the wheel, which has more figures attached to it than in the later version and subsequent replicas.

Fortune and her wheel had been a staple subject in European art and literature since medieval times. Burne-Jones appears to have found the image particularly relevant to his own experience, writing to Helen Mary Gaskell 'My Fortune's Wheel is a true image and we take our turn at it, and are broken upon it' (quoted in Fitzgerald 1975, p.245). The subject had first appeared in his designs for the *Troy Triptych* in 1870. Never realised and known only from a design in Birmingham City Museum and Art Gallery (repr. Harrison and Waters 1973, pl.144), this sought to illustrate the history and destruction of Troy. Four allegorical figures of Fortune, Fame, Oblivion and Love flank predella panels relating to the story. Fortune is shown with her wheel as in the 1883 oil. This series of subjects seems to have held particular personal resonance for Burne-Jones. In the wake of his destructive affair with Maria Zambaco, he perhaps identified with the story of Paris, Helen and the burning of Troy (see also Rossetti's use of this myth, no.3). Burne-Jones emphasised the pain that love can bring in another of the predella panels, *Venus Discordia*, which shows Venus, Goddess of Love, presiding over a scene of vicious carnage, watched by the allegorical figures of Anger, Envy, Suspicion and Strife.

Several of the subject groups in the Troy Triptych were developed into independent works, notably *The Wheel of Fortune*. Apart from their personal emotional connotations, they held a particularly important place in Burne-Jones's art because of their debt to Michelangelo, whose genius he considered unsurpassed. In the oil version of *The Wheel of Fortune* the massive, straining torsos of the Slave and King strapped to the wheel clearly derive from Michelangelo's sculptures *The Dying Slave* *c.*1513 (Louvre, Paris) and *The Captives* 1530–4 (Accademia, Florence), which Burne-Jones had sketched on his 1871 trip to Italy. In the sheet exhibited here, the wheel-bound figures are also influenced by these sources, but to a lesser degree, and may be partly more closely inspired by Michelangelo's *Last Judgement* 1537–41 (Sistine Chapel, Rome). The principal figure of Fortune is copied from Michelangelo's *Delphic Sibyl* 1509 in the Sistine Chapel, which in 1871 Burne-Jones had carefully studied with the aid of opera glasses while lying on his back. This similarity is felt to a lesser degree in the oil, where the figure's pose has been adapted.

Most interestingly, this drawing differs from the finished design in that Fortune is blindfolded. In this respect, but also in the theme, pose, drapery and colouring of the figure, it has similarities with *Hope* (no.76) by Watts, who indeed was the drawing's first recorded owner.

RU

WALTER CRANE 1845–1915

29 **The White Knight** 1870

Watercolour 45.7 × 61 (18 × 24)
Inscribed with monogram 'WC' and date '1870' lower right

Prov: ?Somerset Beaumont; ...; present owner
Exh: ?Dudley Gallery 1871 (320); Barbican 1989 (33, repr. p.12)
Lit: Girouard 1981, p.196, pl.XXII

Private Collection

John Christian has suggested (exh. cat., Barbican 1989, p.89) that this romantic evocation of medieval chivalry should perhaps be identified with Walter Crane's 1871 Dudley Gallery exhibit *The Red Cross Knight in Search of Una*, a subject taken from Edmund Spenser's *Faerie Queene*. Although, as Christian points out, Crane's image does not correspond exactly to Spenser's description of the knight, who 'on his brest a bloodie Crosse he bore ... Upon his shield the like was also scor'd' (*The Faerie Queene*, bk I, canto I, verse II), the stream that flows through the landscape may be intended as the enchanted water from which the Redcrosse Knight drinks as he searches for Una, and which causes him to lose his strength and be captured by the giant Orgoglio. Crane described his 1871 Dudley Gallery exhibit, which was bought by Somerset Beaumont is corroborated by Crane's description of it as showing 'the knight [as] a small figure on horseback wandering through a green landscape taken from one of the Derbyshire "cloughs"' (Crane 1907, p.106).

Spenser intended the Redcrosse Knight as a personification of St George, patron of the Anglican Church, while Una, who was taken from him by Archimago ('hypocrisy') and Duessa (the Roman Catholic church), is seen as 'true religion'. All of this would strongly have appealed to Crane's robust sense of patriotism and fondness for allegory. In addition to the 1871 Dudley exhibit, he was later to produce a series of illustrations to Spenser's poem as

30

well as a painting entitled *England's Emblem* (ex Seeger collection, Berlin), which showed a mounted knight (a type of St George or Spenser's Prince Arthur) slaying a monster.

In 1870, in the course of discussing Crane's watercolour *Ormuzd and Ahriman* (Charles Jerdein collection), the critic of the *Art Journal* identified a clique of artists at the Dudley Gallery whose works were both strange and beautiful, progressive and thoroughly remote from mundane reality:

> These Dudley people are proverbially peculiar. Thus it would be hard to find anywhere talent associated with greater eccentricity than in the clever, yet abnormal, creations of Walter Crane, Robert Bateman, and Simeon Solomon ... Such a style may be set down as an anachronism; yet, beset as we are by the meanest naturalism, we hail with delight a manner which, though by many deemed mistaken, carries the mind into the regions of the imagination ... Though not wholly satisfactory, we hail with gladness the advent of an Art which reverts to historic associations, and carries the mind back to olden styles, when painting was twin sister of poetry.
>
> (*Art Journal*, 1870, p.87)

CSN

Dante Gabriel Rossetti 1828–1882

30 **Paolo and Francesca da Rimini** 1855

Watercolour 25.4 × 44.9 (10 × 17¾)
Inscribed 'Quanti dolci pensier Quanto disio' at the lower edge of the left compartment; 'Menò costoro al doloroso passo' at the lower edge of the right compartment; and 'O lasso!' in the upper part of the central compartment

Prov: John Ruskin; William Morris; George Rae; bt by the Tate Gallery 1916

Exh: Burlington Fine Arts Club 1883 (13); Birmingham 1947 (101); Whitechapel 1948 (66); Leicester 1968 (36); Newcastle-upon-Tyne 1971 (50); Paris 1972 (228); Rotterdam 1975 (200); RA 1979 (217); Tate Gallery 1984 (215); Munich and Madrid 1993 (61)

Lit: Sharp 1882, pp.181–2; Marillier 1899, no.41, pp.53, 66, 81; Surtees 1971, I, no.75, pp.36–7

Tate Gallery. Purchased with assistance from Sir Arthur Du Cros Bt and Sir Otto Beit KCMG through the National Art Collections Fund 1916

The story of Paolo and Francesca comes from canto v of Dante's *Inferno*. Of the three parts of Rossetti's composition, that on the left represents Francesca and her brother-in-law Paolo embracing. The centre shows Dante and Virgil wearing crowns of laurel and bay and looking with concern at the right-hand compartment, in which the lovers drift in each other's arms through the fires of hell following their murder by Sigismondo Malatesta, Francesca's husband and Paolo's brother. Quotations from the original text are inscribed around the edge of the composition.

The arrangement, analagous to a strip cartoon, allowed Rossetti to treat the subject with stark simplicity, each part complete in itself, but symbolically linked across the width of the composition. As early as 1849 W.M. Rossetti described how his brother had planned to combine scenes showing the lovers kissing and their 'spirits blowing to and fro' (Rossetti 1900, p.232) The previous year G.F. Watts had shown the first version of his *Paolo and Francesca* (see no.48) at the British Institution, and this may have prompted Rossetti's interest in the subject.

Gabriel Rossetti had five watercolours of biblical and literary subjects in hand in the autumn of 1855, mostly embarked upon at the behest of John Ruskin. *Paolo and Francesca*, however, was done on an impulse, because Rossetti found himself in need of ready money to send to Lizzie and a companion, who were stranded in Paris. Ford Madox Brown described the circumstances: 'Gabriel, who saw that none of the drawings on the easel could be completed before long, began a fresh one, *Francesca da Rimini*, in *three compartments*; worked day and night, finished it in a week, got 35 guineas for it from Ruskin, and started off to relieve them ... This is how Gabriel can work on a pinch' (Rossetti 1899, pp.46–7). Ruskin allowed Ellen Heaton of Leeds, who had previously asked Rossetti for a watercolour, to choose between it and *Rachel and Leah* (Tate Gallery), another Dante subject completed at about the same time. Ruskin described no.30 as 'a most gloomy drawing – very grand – but dreadful – of Dante seeing the soul of Francesca and her lover!' In a second letter to Miss Heaton he expressed concern that she might be shocked by the direct way in which the drawing told its story: 'The common-pretty-timid-mistletoe bough kind of kiss was *not* what Dante meant. Rossetti has thoroughly understood the passage throughout' (quoted in Surtees 1971, I, p.37). In the event Ellen Heaton chose to buy *Rachel and Leah*, which allowed Ruskin to keep *Paolo and Francesca* for himself.

CSN

31

DANTE GABRIEL ROSSETTI 1828–1882

31 **Dantis Amor** 1860

Oil on mahogany panel 74.9 × 81.3 (29½ × 32)
Inscribed 'QVI EST PER OMNIA SAECVLA BENEDICTVS' t.l., in halo

Prov: William Morris, for whom painted; Ernest Gambart 1865; F. Treharne James, by whom presented to the Tate Gallery 1920

Exh: Tate Gallery 1923 (12); London and Birmingham 1973 (102); Rotterdam 1975 (203); Tate Gallery 1984 (104)

Lit: Marillier 1899, no.91; Ironside and Gere 1948, pp.34–7, repr. pl.43; Surtees 1970, no.117; Lucie-Smith 1972, p.42; Lochnan, Shoenherr and Silver 1993, pp.104–7

Tate Gallery. Presented by F. Treharne James 1920

Rossetti designed this panel as one of three to decorate a piece of furniture – a large settle-cum-cupboard – which William Morris had made by Henry Price, a local cabinet-maker, for his London house at 17 Red Lion Square. In the period immediately after Morris's marriage to Jane Burden in April 1859 the settle was removed and dismantled; at this point Rossetti produced two panels for it, *The Salutation of Beatrice on Earth* and *In Eden*, as a wedding present. In 1860 it was installed in the Red House at Bexley Heath and it seems that this third panel was executed there. The timber of the settle was apparently painted a dark 'dragon's blood' red which, as Lochnan, Shoenherr and Silver point out, would have set off Rossetti's designs to great advantage. The decorations were later sold, though the settle remains at the Red House. A substitute for this subject was inserted after the present panel had been removed in about 1863; that and the two *Salutation* panels are now in the National Gallery of Canada, Ottawa. There are pen-and-ink drawings for both versions of *Dantis Amor* in the collection of Birmingham City Art Gallery (Surtees 1970, nos.117A, 117B). The earliest design for the multiple subject dates from 1849 (Fogg Art Museum, Harvard).

Dantis Amor was intended to be mounted in the settle between the earthly and the heavenly Salutations of Beatrice. The likeness of the earthly Beatrice was taken from Morris's new wife Jane, with whom Rossetti was already smitten, and who would later become his mistress; the heavenly Beatrice was a portrait of his own mistress, soon to become his wife, Lizzie Siddal. Rossetti's later obsession with the death of Lizzie, celebrated particularly in *Beata Beatrix* (no.44), is therefore fortuitously prefigured in *Dantis Amor*, with several touches of irony, both conscious and unconscious. The intention of the design is to give a sort of heraldic diagram of the death of Beatrice and her union with Christ. The figure of the angel holds a sundial marking the moment of her death, which the drawing in Birmingham specifies is the ninth hour, 12 June 1290, while she is portrayed on the lower side of a diagonal line of separation in a crescent moon surrounded by stars, looking up towards the haloed head of Christ, on the upper side, which is the centre of a stylised corona of irradiating flames. On the drawing Rossetti inscribed along the dividing diagonal the concluding line of Dante's *Divine Comedy* 'L'AMOR CHE MVOVE IL SOLE E L'ALTRE STELLE' (*Paradiso* xxxiii, l.145), and round Beatrice's head 'QVELLA BEATA BEATRICE CHE MIRA CONTINVAMENTE NELLA FACCIA DI COLVI' from the close of his *Vita Nuova* – as well as the quotation in Christ's halo, which continues the same passage.

The schematic presentation of the Beatrice myth here is a significant development of Rossetti's use of the original legend. He abandons entirely the narrative devices that remain, if only vestigially, in the side panels, reducing his image to a boldly diagrammatic statement of the essential relationships, and of the central meaning of Dante's writings: the all-pervading power of love in life and death throughout Creation. Rossetti's translation of Dante's own words suggests the quasi-geometrical conception: 'Love tells the poet: 'I am in the centre of a circle to which all parts of the circumference bear an equal relation, but with thee it is not so.' Rossetti's gloss on this was: 'all loveable objects, whether in heaven or earth, or any part of the earth's circumference, are equally near to Love; not so to Dante, who will one day lose Beatrice when she dies.' While the angel and the two heads are finely rendered, it has been suggested that the pattern-like background is the work of another hand. This may well be the case; but it is entirely in keeping with the reductive nature of the image that the idea of the firmament, and of the sun and the moon, should be converted into a formula. The device of stars against a solid ground of deep blue had been a prominent element in the decorative vocabulary of A.W.N. Pugin in his ecclesiastical designs of the 1840s; but there are implications in the panel as a whole for the development of a much simplified formal language of design in the later years of the century (one might compare Beardsley's diagonal-line decoration for the cover of Ernest Dowson's *Verses*, 1896; Reade 1967, p.457).

AW

DANTE GABRIEL ROSSETTI 1828–1882

32 **Golden Head by Golden Head** 1861

Pen and black ink with traces of pencil
6.5 × 8.5 (2 9/16 × 3 3/8)
Inscribed '"Golden head by golden head"' lower centre

Prov: Sotheby's, 12 Nov. 1992 (149)
Lit: Surtees 1971, I, no.143; Marsh 1994, pp.277–81; New York 1995, pp.85–6

Jacqueline Loewe Fowler

This is Rossetti's design for the frontispiece of his sister Christina's volume of poetry, *Goblin Market and other Poems*, published by Macmillan in 1862. It was made, along with another design entitled *Buy from us with Golden Curl*, by way of an apology for his slowness in looking at the final draft of the poems intended for the book in the autumn of 1861 and perhaps also as a sweetener to the publisher who was hoping to make 'an exceedingly pretty little volume and to bring it out as a Christmas book' (quoted in Marsh 1994, p.277). In fact further procrastination from Gabriel, and difficulties about getting the blocks made, caused publication to be delayed until April 1862.

The present drawing shows the two sisters, Lizzie and Laura, asleep together following their encounter with the goblin merchants who had offered them magic fruit, which Lizzie resisted but which Laura accepted in exchange for a lock of her golden hair. Sated by the delicious feast, Laura returns to her sister and the couple sleep contentedly:

> Golden head by golden head,
> Like two pigeons in one nest
> Folded in each other's wings,
> They lay down in their curtained bed:
> Like two blossoms on one stem,
> Like two flakes of new fall'n snow,
> Like two wands of ivory
> Tipped with gold for awful kings.
> Moon and stars gazed in at them,
> Wind sang to them lullaby,
> Lumbering owls forebore to fly,
> Not a bat flapped to and fro
> Round their rest:
> Cheek to cheek and breast to breast
> Locked together in one nest.

However, almost immediately the temptation to which Laura had succumbed begins to destroy her. Night after night she returns to the goblins for more of the fruit which she discovers she cannot do without and more of which is always offered. Each day she becomes weaker and more distraught, until she is close to death, when Lizzie intervenes by herself buying fruit from the goblins but then refusing to eat. The goblins are furious, but she escapes with a quantity of the juice with which she can break their magic spell. On her return Lizzie calls to Laura:

> 'Did you miss me?
> Come and kiss me.
> Never mind my bruises,
> Hug me, kiss me, suck my juices
> Squeezed from goblin fruits for you,
> Goblin pulp and goblin dew.
> Eat me, drink me, love me;
> Laura, make much of me:
> For your sake I have braved the glen
> And had to do with goblin merchant men.'

The book was received with critical enthusiasm, and at least one reviewer (in the *British Quarterly*, July 1862; quoted Doughty and Wahl 1965–8, II, p.449) found space to praise Gabriel's part in it. The two illustrations mesh beautifully with the poem 'Goblin Market', and the book is yet another instance of the way in which writers and artists of the 1860s believed that different media could be used in combination to interpret and magnify the creative gist.

As William Michael Rossetti wrote, 'different minds may be likely to read different messages into [the poem]' (quoted in *The Post-Pre-Raphaelite Print* 1995, p.86). It is in the first place a reminder of the contemporary awareness of the hazards of physical addiction at a time when people were using drugs such as the opium-based laudanum for recreational purposes and health remedies. It is hard to imagine that Christina Rossetti was not thinking of her sister-in-law Lizzie, who was dependent on the drug (and who was to die of an overdose on 11 February 1862) when she wrote it.

A further aspect of both the poem and the present drawing is the apparently erotic character of the relationship between the sisters. Lesbian themes are seldom if ever treated by painters and illustrators of the Aesthetic movement; but that Rossetti's frontispiece was perceived as to do with physical love between women is testified by its having been taken up by Courbet, whose painting of female lovers, *Sleep* (Musée du Petit Palais, Paris) of 1866, appears to owe the placing of the two girls' heads together, one resting on the other's bosom, to the artist's knowledge of Rossetti's work.

This is not as surprising a connection as it might seem. Whistler had become a friend and acolyte of Gabriel Rossetti soon after he settled in London in 1861, and would have known and understood the suggestion of carnality that lay behind Rossetti's illustration. Whistler remained in contact with Courbet in the period, and his mistress Jo Hiffernan acted as model for various of his paintings of the mid-1860s (see no.9), including (it was said) the notorious *Origin of the World* (Musée d'Orsay, Paris) and *Sleep*. It was perhaps during the stay that Whistler and Courbet made together in Trouville in 1865 that the French artist's attention was drawn to the engraving.

CSN

DANTE GABRIEL ROSSETTI 1828–1882

33 **Woman Combing her Hair** 1864

Watercolour 34.3 × 31.1 (13½ × 12¼)
Signed with monogram and dated '1864' lower right

Prov: John Bibby; his sale, Christie's, 3 June 1899 (37); Major C.S. Goldman; by descent to his son, John Monck; Christie's 16 Nov. 1965 (18); present owner

Exh: Newcastle 1971 (58); RA and Birmingham 1973 (314)

Lit: Sharp 1882, no.119 (incorrectly described as replica); Stephens 1884, pp.408–9; Marillier 1899, pp.132, 245, no.147 (as *Lady in White at her Toilet*); Baum 1940, p.21; Surtees 1971, I, no.174; II, pl.252 (for the pencil study, Surtees no.174A)

Private Collection

EXHIBITED IN LONDON ONLY

Woman Combing her Hair is almost certainly not the original title of this watercolour. The first known reference to the work, in Sharp's book, calls it *Fazio's Mistress*, as does Stephens in 1884 (confirmed by the description). A favourite formula with the artist (cf. *Bonifazio's Mistress*, Surtees 1971, no.121) which he used the previous year for no.4, eventually renaming that work *Aurelia*. *Woman Combing her Hair* did not appear in any of the memorial exhibitions, and does not seem to have been included in any other exhibitions in London or elsewhere. Later sources refer to it as *Lady in a White Dress* (sale catalogue 1899) or *Lady in White at her Toilet*. Deprived of its evocative Italianate title, the work loses a context established by Rossetti's translation of Fazio degli Uberti's sonnet (published in *Early Italian Poets* in 1861) glorifying the woman as a beautiful temptress.

It is one of a number of images of women at their toilet, painted by Rossetti when he realised the appeal held by his head studies of women initiated by *Bocca Baciata*. The setting allowed the artist to concentrate on the beauty of his sitter, usually Fanny Cornforth, as she displays her charms amid an array of luxurious accessories and dressing-table accoutrements. In this work, the sitter combs through her hair with one hand while holding an elaborate silver brush with the other; with a turn of her head to allow a self-regarding look, she displays her neck, around which is tied a red cord with tasselled ends. The loose tresses suggest an erotic dimension as personified by the sensual Fanny. A small blue and white vase, reflecting Rossetti's fascination with Japonisme, sit with other objects upon the dressing table. In the background, a mirror reflects a window with its curtain drawn back halfway, suggesting the enclosed setting of the boudoir.

Although the same type of female head study as *Bocca Baciata*, this work reflects the influence of Rossetti's trip to Paris for his honeymoon in May 1860 when he saw and admired paintings by Veronese. It is still relatively small in scale, but there is an increased breadth and lushness in the conception and realisation which remove it from the more restrained, medievalising spirit of *Bocca Baciata*, or other earlier examples of this format: *Regina Cordium* 1860 (Johannesburg Art Gallery); *Fair Rosamund* 1861 (National Museum of Wales, Cardiff) and *Girl at a Lattice* 1862 (Fitzwilliam Museum, Cambridge). These works found ready patrons, including the owner of no.34, John Bibby, a Liverpool magnate and senior partner of Leyland (until bought out by him in 1872, see Fennell 1978, p.xii; see also Macleod 1996, p.393) who began to amass a collection of Rossetti's paintings (for example Surtees 1971, nos.168R, 173A, 198, 201R1, etc.) by 1867 (Doughty and Wahl 1965–8, II, p.622).

Common interests among younger artists in the early 1860s are evident in comparing *Woman Combing her Hair* with works by Whistler, Rossetti's friend and, by this time, neighbour in Chelsea – especially if one considers it as one of the many 'white paintings' of the early Aesthetic era.

BB

Frederick Sandys 1829–1904

34 **Morgan le Fay** *c.*1862–3

Ink and brush, with scratching out
62 × 44 (24⅜ × 17⁵⁄₁₆)

Prov: W.H. Clabburn; Spelman's, Norwich 15 May 1879 (129); …; Sotheby's 10 Nov. 1981 (30), bt by present owner

Exh: Manchester 1984 (115)

Lit: *British Architect*, 31 Oct. 1879 (repr.); 'Frederick Sandys', *Art Journal*, 1884, pp.73–8; Wood 1896, p.31; Bate 1905, pp.3–17; White 1903 (repr. as frontis.)

Victor Arwas, London

Sandys's subject, Morgan le Fay, as seen in the oil painting of 1862–3 (Birmingham City Museum and Art Gallery), was the queen of Avalon, who in Thomas Malory's *Le Morte Darthur* was so jealous of the esteem in which her half-brother King Arthur was held that she attempted to use powers of witchcraft and sorcery to murder him. In Sandys's painting as well as in the present drawing she is seen waving a magic lamp and chanting spells over a garment that she has woven for Arthur which, when he puts it on, she intends will burn him to death.

Clearly the mendacious and predatory character of such mythical females as Cassandra, Medusa and Medea (from Greek mythology), or Vivien and the present Morgan le Fay (from Arthurian legend), had a particular hold on Sandys's imagination and appealed to his sexual consciousness. Exotic figures, combining physical beauty with evil and destructive purpose, range from the passive but disdainful individuals represented in drawings such as *Proud Maisie* (Victoria and Albert Museum; other versions elsewhere), to frenzied and maniacal images such as the present. Sandys's fondness for pictorial drama was analysed by Esther Wood: 'A classicist by nature and temperament, yet steeped in the same romantic mysticism that inspired the Pre-Raphaelite Brotherhood, he is stronger than any of them in the presentment of a dramatic crisis … He deals less than they with the subtle intimacies of passion, and more with the typical effects and expressions' (Wood 1896).

Some uncertainty remains concerning the original purpose and date of the present drawing which was commissioned – along with the oil version – by W.H. Clabburn. Percy Bate described it as 'a finished and elaborate study' for the Birmingham oil version, thus implying a date of *c.*1862. (Bate 1905, p.7) More recently Stephen Wildman has suggested that the drawing belongs to the 'type of highly-finished pen and ink drawing executed by the "second generation" Pre-Raphaelite artists in the late 1850s and early 1860s (Manchester 1984, p.170).

CSN

SIMEON SOLOMON 1840–1905

35 Heliogabalus, High Priest of the Sun 1866

Watercolour 46.4 × 29.2 (18¼ × 11½)
Inscribed with monogram 'SS' and dated '1866'

Prov: W.A. Turner; ... Christie's 1 Oct. 1973 (88); J.S. Maas & Co.
Exh: Dudley Gallery 1868; Manchester 1878 (173)
Lit: *Art Journal*, 1868, p.45; Colvin 1870, pp.33–5; Reynolds 1984, fig.42

The Forbes Magazine Collection, New York

Simeon Solomon's watercolour shows Elagabalus, who was emperor of Rome (taking the title Aurelius Antoninus) for four years from AD 218, and who before the uprising that brought him to power had served in his native Syria as the priest to the oracular sun-deity at Emesa. Elagabalus brought with him to Rome the sacred conical black stone worshipped by his followers, and established the cult as the supreme religion of the empire giving the sun-deity precedence even over Jupiter. During his brief reign – Elagabalus and his mother were murdered by soldiers of the Praetorian guard in AD 222 – Rome witnessed scenes of the utmost debauchery linked with the fanatical excesses of the worship of the Baal of Emesa. Government fell into the hands of cronies of the emperor, who were for the most part as depraved and corrupt as he was, and two extravagant temples were built in which midsummer festivals were celebrated 'with a ceremonial no less ludicrous than obscene' (*The Oxford Classical Dictionary*, ed. M. Cary, Oxford 1949, p.310).

The interest that Simeon Solomon shared with Swinburne in all things licentious and bizarrely erotic, combined with the particular fascination that he felt for the elaborate rituals of religion, makes this a telling choice of subject. The emperor-priest is seen leaning in a pose of nonchalant satiety against an altar in a richly decorated chamber. When the drawing was first exhibited, the *Art Journal* considered it to be aberrant and arcane, explaining that 'Solomon is a genius of eccentricity, he can do nothing like other people, and in being exclusively like himself, he becomes unlike to nature. As for choice of subject, most religions of the world have struck by turns the painter's fantastic and splendour-loving fancy.' (*Art Journal*, 1868, p.45). A couple of years later, in his series of articles on progressive English painters, Sidney Colvin focused on the technique of the present drawing as representative of the extraordinary works Solomon had been showing at the Dudley Gallery:

36

'In the management of water-colour Mr Solomon developed a peculiar genius. He produced a richness and splendour of effect in the imitating of lustrous or metallic surfaces, cloths of gold or silver, or gold or silver ornaments, crowns, chains, caskets or chased work, that no other painter has rivalled ... For the last five years the Dudley Gallery exhibition has seldom been without a ceremonial piece, whether of one figure or many, done with this unique splendour and lustre of imitative colour. The Roman decadence, with its emperor Heliogabalus, high-priest of the sun, supplied another occasion for such an achievement.'

(Colvin 1870, p.34)

CSN

SIMEON SOLOMON 1840–1905

36 The Sleepers, and the One that Watcheth 1870

Watercolour 34.7 × 44.7 (13⅝ × 17⅝)
Inscribed with monogram 'SS' and dated '1871' lower right

Prov: Frederick Craven (1887); Cecil French, by whom given to Leamington Spa Art Gallery

Exh: Dudley Gallery 1870 (625); Manchester 1887 (1372 as *The Sleepers and the One that Watcheth*); Guildhall 1894; Tokyo 1989 (43)

Lit: *Art Journal*, 1870, p.87; Reynolds 1984, p.94, col. pl.6

Leamington Spa Art Gallery and Museum

Solomon had previously explored the motif of three heads side by side in his Old Testament subject *Shadrach, Meshach and Abednego* (Reynolds 1985, pl.31)

of 1863. In that drawing, as in the present, he seems to have been interested in showing a range of states of consciousness from alertness, through degrees of somnolence, to complete unconsciousness. In *The Sleepers, and the One that Watcheth* the two right-hand figures are lost in sleep, while the woman on the left, although awake, seems to stare with unseeing eyes into space.

The drawing has no ostensible subject, and represents the move that Solomon made in the late 1860s towards abstract, noumenal subjects, which play upon the spectator's emotional responses rather than his ability to interpret narrative clues. The *Art Journal* analysed this direction in connection with the present drawing: 'The pictures of Mr Simeon Solomon present … interesting problems, which whether problems in poetry, philosophy, or Art, remain, it must be confessed, after these attempted solutions or pictorial elucidations, painfully enigmatical and perplexed.' (*Art Journal*, 1870, p.87)

It is possible that the arrangement of *The Sleepers, and the One that Watcheth* is intended as an allegory of sharing and exclusion, rather in the same spirit as the earlier pencil drawing *The Bride, The Bridegroom and Sad Love* (fig.26 on p.43). The two sleeping figures, locked in an embrace and with hands clasped together, are seen to have entered a shared dream world, their loving bond symbolised by the jasmine flowers they each hold and which they wear around their necks (and which in their bright star-shapes echo the night sky). The third figure, who watches over the other two, is felt to be barred from this elysium, and may be seen as a type of the artist himself who was – on account of his jewishness and homosexuality – the victim of exclusion; and who just a year or two after the present drawing was made was to be driven out of the circle of artists and writers in Chelsea of which briefly he had been such a notable member as, in the words of his erstwhile friend Swinburne, 'a thing unmentionable alike by men and women, as equally abhorrent to either – nay, to the very beasts' (Gosse and Wise 1918, p.46).

CSN

GEORGE FREDERIC WATTS 1817–1904

37 **Orpheus and Eurydice** 1872–7

Oil on canvas 65 × 38 (25⅝ × 15)

Prov: Sold by the artist to Charles Rickards 1877; his sale, Christie's 2 April 1887 (40); …; Cecil French, by whom bequeathed to the Watts Gallery, Compton 1954

Exh: Manchester 1880 (49); Grosvenor Gallery 1881 (36, as *Orpheus and Eurydice: Design for the larger picture*); Rome 1996 (9)

Lit: *Academy*, 21 Oct. 1876, p.416; Spielmann 1887, pp.3, 24; MS. Cat., I, p.112

Trustees of the Watts Gallery

The Greek legend tells of Orpheus, musician and singer, married to Eurydice. Her death by the bite of a snake and passage to Hades prompt Orpheus's descent to the underworld. By the music of his lyre, Orpheus charms the king and queen, Neptune and Persephone, who released Eurydice on condition that Orpheus should not look back at her. Unable to resist, Orpheus glances backward, and Eurydice dies yet again, collapsing as she falls into the gloom of Hades.

In celebrating the musical hero, the myth of Orpheus had a long-standing appeal to artists, not least Watts, who returned to it again and again from the 1860s onward. The continual fascination for him centred on the moment of loss which he painted in several versions in varying formats (see Staley 1978, no.19), culminating in the grand full-length (Salar Jung Museum, India) seen at the Grosvenor Gallery in 1879.

This work can be definitely identified for the first time as the 'design' for the eventual large painting of 1879. Watts's method of working involved a 'design' for the large picture, always in his mind as the eventual outcome of the smaller works (see Bryant 1990, pp.54–7). The small works, used for experimenting with composition, colour and tonal values, were more than studies and usually ended up as finished pictures which Watts exhibited and/or sold once he no longer required them. They were, of course, particularly suitable as cabinet pictures for connoisseurs, whereas Watts invariably intended the large versions for public exhibition.

Earlier versions of *Orpheus and Eurydice* show a draped female figure, and the most significant change here is Eurydice's nudity, reflecting a feature of Watts's work which came to the fore in the 1870s. This is also a more visionary treatment of the subject, especially in the extremely pale body of Eurydice, corpse-like in the unreality of the thin, grey light. Orpheus strains to reclaim his wife, but she is already dead. In connecting the idea of death with

37

love and with the nude, the work resonates ominously. This visualisation offers no beautiful, ideal nude, but a disturbing study of eternal loss and bodily death. Fittingly the treatment is subdued, with murky greens and grey light, filling the confined space, with only one virtuoso flourish of orange against which Eurydice's hand is silhouetted, suggestive of Hades and the catastrophe of the story.

The large version, exhibited to much acclaim at the Grosvenor Gallery in 1879, is virtually unknown since it went into a collection in India in the 1920s (Wilcox 1986, pp.29–30, fig.7). It retains the central idea of the design, though the setting is more fully characterised with a bleak rocky landscape, and the artist has worked up a range of telling details, including Orpheus's lyre with all its strings broken but one (a motif which later appears in *Hope*, no.76). Doubtless this painting has all the operatic grandeur one would expect of Watts's large works, but the virtue of the smaller 'design' is its mood, so suggestive of death.

Orpheus and Eurydice did much to extend Watts's reputation in France. The publication of the engraving in 1879 in *L'Art* (fig.37 on p.67) may well have led to the request for Watts to lend it to the Salon in 1880. This appearance of the subject at the primary exhibition venue in France brought him into the sphere of art critics like Théodore Duret and Joris-Karl Huysmans, who each in the early 1880s wrote about Watts's work.

BB

Reinventing Mythologies

By the 1870s Darwin's writings on evolution had transformed the perception of man's place in the universe and many artists sought to reconcile themselves to the new knowledge by reconstructing traditional accounts of the world in terms of their inner emotional life. Conversely, they might incorporate scientific discoveries into their myths. Moreau, for instance, copied the careful drawings of marine life that had been made by Philip Henry Gosse, the marine biologist, father of the novelist Edmund Gosse, presumably with a view to the contribution these forms of life could make to the strange subaqueous ambience in which Moreau's dramas take place.

Rossetti, having been in eclipse for some years, with his large *Astarte Syriaca* of 1875–7 (no.45) brought to a weird climax his series of paintings presenting woman simultaneously as priestess and seductress, bringing into a single identity his own mistress and Astarte, the love goddess of ancient Babylon. If it is the grandest and most extreme of Rossetti's statements on this theme, the most poignant of them is his *Beata Beatrix* c.1864–70 (no.44) which celebrates his wife Lizzie Siddal at the point of her death. A beautiful woman, the object of his desire, is shown at the moment of transformation into a guardian angel. Here we see the meeting of two preoccupations that were shortly to become the central strands of Symbolism: Decadence and Idealism.

A further ambiguity is explored by Burne-Jones in his *Pygmalion* series 1868–78 (no.38), and again in *King Cophetua and the Beggar Maid* 1884 (no.40). These pictures deal with the creative power of physical desire, and, by extension, the shadowy area between art and pornography which had troubled both artists and critics since the 1860s, and which underlies much of the unease inherent in Symbolist art. Such subjects may reflect Burne-Jones's guilty love affair with Maria Zambaco, the Greek-born wife of a doctor who was twenty-five when he met her in 1866 (see Hayward Gallery 1975, p.46, no.114). The relationship was a rite of passage from the concentrated intensity of his early work to the more expansive, 'public' art that he was to practise henceforth as an acknowledged leader of the British school.

In the work of G.F. Watts the Symbolist unease is not local or personal but always emphatically general, even universal. He had painted the first of his cosmic allegories, *Time and Oblivion* (Eastnor Castle), in 1848, and was therefore a very early exponent of what were to become Symbolist ideas.

It was at the end of the 1870s that the modern British painters began to exert some real influence in France. The Grosvenor Gallery opened in London in 1877 with an exhibition including work by French artists as well as by young British painters. In 1878 the Paris Exposition Universelle was to mark 'a decisive turning-point in the history of Pre-Raphaelitism in France' (Laurent 1996, section 4, p.45). With five large rooms of British painting, including work by Millais, Watts, Sandys, Crane and Burne-Jones, it took the influence of the British as far afield as Finland (see Sarjas-Korte 1981, pp.140–4).

After Rossetti's death in 1882 his reputation was resuscitated in Britain with two large London exhibitions which drew the attention of foreign as well as British critics. British art now began to appear frequently in Paris. In Brussels, the Groupe des Vingt (Les XX) established an annual exhibition for art concerned with 'the Modern Ideal'. The first exhibition was held in 1884, and in subsequent years they sought contributions from Whistler, Crane and Burne-Jones. In 1889 photographs of work by Burne-Jones and Rossetti were shown at the Galerie Dumont.

EDWARD BURNE-JONES 1833–1898

38 Pygmalion and the Image (second series) 1868–78

(a) **The Heart Desires** 1875–8
Oil on canvas 99 × 76.3 (38⅜ × 29½)
Inscribed 'E. Burne-Jones inv. 1868. pinxit 1878'
(b) **The Hand Refrains** *c.*1868
Oil on canvas 98.7 × 76.3 (38⅞ × 30)
(c) **The Godhead Fires** 1875–8
Oil on canvas 99.1 × 76.5 (39 × 30⅛)
Inscribed 'EBJ 1878' lower right
(d) **The Soul Attains** 1868–78
Oil on canvas 99.4 × 76.6 (39⅛ × 30⅛)

Prov: Bt from the artist by Frederick Craven; his sale, Christie's 18 May 1895 (60–3), bt Agnew's; Sir John T. Middlemore; whose trustees presented the series to Birmingham City Museum and Art Gallery 1903

Exh: Grosvenor Gallery 1879 (167–70); Manchester 1887 (199–202); New Gallery 1892 (47–50); New Gallery 1898 (126, 128, 132, 134); Manchester 1911 (282–5); Tate Gallery 1911 (47–50); Tate Gallery 1933 (14, as *The Godhead Fires*); Sheffield 1971 (92–5); Hayward Gallery 1975 (137); Rome 1986 (33–6); Seattle 1995 (105–8)

Lit: Bell 1892, pp.52, 57, 63, 95–6; de Lisle 1904, pp.118–20, 181; Jenkyns 1980, pp.141–2; Hartnoll 1988, pp.26–7; Cheney 1995, pp.103–16

Birmingham Museums and Art Gallery

EXHIBITED IN LONDON ONLY

38 A

38 B

In 1867 Burne-Jones made a sequence of drawings which treat the story of Pygmalion, according to the text of William Morris's poem 'Pygmalion and the Image'. They were intended to form part of a projected illustrated edition of his friend Morris's cycle of epic poems, *The Earthly Paradise*. In these twenty-five preparatory drawings (which are now divided between Birmingham City Art Gallery and the William Morris Gallery, Walthamstow) lay both the first ideas for the compositions and the division into four parts of both series of paintings – those made in 1868–70 (private collection), and the present series which were begun in the late 1860s but not completed until 1878.

Morris had followed Ovid in telling the story of 'a man of Cyprus, a sculptor named Pygmalion, [who] made an image of a woman, fairer than any that had yet been seen, and in the end came to love his own handiwork as though it had been alive; wherefore, praying to Venus for help, he obtained his end, for she made the image alive indeed, and a woman, and Pygmalion wedded her.' The differences between the corresponding images from each of the two series have been analysed by Stephen Wildman (in Seattle 1995). The narrative sequence of the four paintings in the present series was described by Malcolm Bell in his book of 1892: 'The first, "The Heart Desires," is the idealization of unsatisfied longing for the unknown ... A sculptured group of the three graces ... typifies the cold beauty of artifice.' 'In the second, "The Hand Refrains," the days of long labour are ended, and the artist's ideal, the cold pure figure of the yet soulless image stands finished'. The subject of the third painting, *The Godhead Fires*, is as follows: 'Into the sculptor's chamber, silent and solitary, while Pygmalion is away in the temple, floats lightly the Queen of Love.' Lastly, in *The Soul Attains*, 'Heart and soul alike are satisfied' (Bell 1892, pp.95–6).

Burne-Jones was a highly sensitive and emotional man, whose works reveal much about his state of mind. In 1868 he had fallen in love with the captivating and beautiful young Greek woman, Maria Zambaco. The affair lasted until 1871, and therefore almost exactly coincided with Burne-Jones's work on the first Pygmalion series (which were in fact painted for Maria's mother Euphrosyne Cassavetti). The paintings are dense with clues to the artist's state of mind during these years of turbulence and crisis. Burne-Jones turned to the legend of Pygmalion to explore the difference between an intellectual concept of beauty, from which the artist might remain detached, and the reality of physical attraction which could take over one's entire existence.

CSN

38C

38D

EDWARD BURNE-JONES 1833–1898

39 Souls on the Banks of the River Styx *c.*1873

Oil on canvas 89.6 × 71 (35¼ × 28)

Prov: Sir Philip Burne-Jones, Bt, his sale, Christie's 5 June 1919 (172)

Exh: The Garden Studio, The Grange, *c.*1900; Peter Nahum Galleries 1993 (7, repr. p.14); Montreal 1996 (35, repr. illus. 224)

Lit: Waters 1993, pp.12–14

Private Collection

The canvas is apparently a preparatory study or unfinished work, and may have been cut off at the right. Burne-Jones made pencil studies of some of the hunched, cowering and huddling figures that he planned to include in the picture (two are repro-

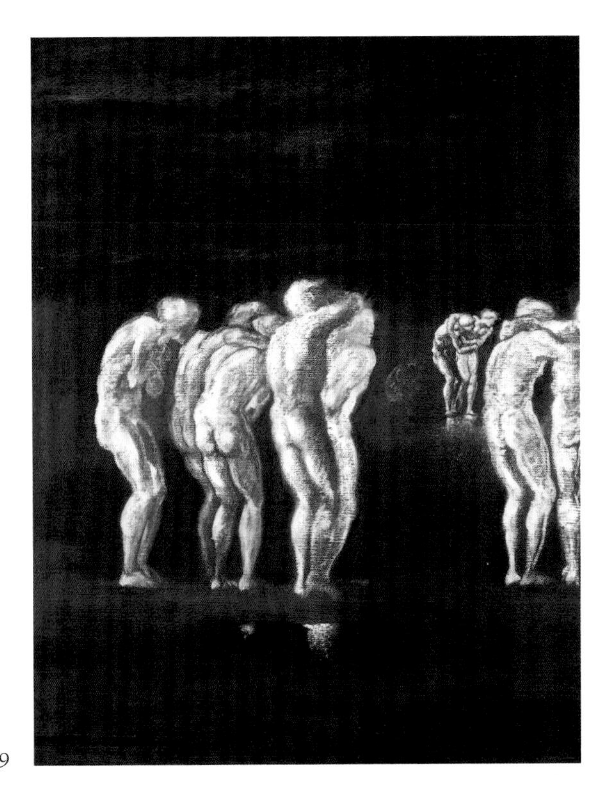

39

Waters suggests that the intensity of this image, along with some others dating from the same moment, reflects the unhappy circumstances surrounding Burne-Jones's affair with Maria Zambaco, which came to an end in 1871 (see no.38). He also points out that the two figures in the right background echo the poses of the protagonists in Watts's *Orpheus and Eurydice* (no.37), an appropriate allusion since theirs too is a story of mortals visiting the Underworld and hovering on the brink of death. The theme echoes that of Dante's *Inferno*, with which once again there are obvious parallels. The motif of two or more figures clutching each other in mutual protection against the forces of fate and death recurs repeatedly in British Symbolist work; compare Leighton's *And the Sea Gave Up the Dead which Were in it* (no.120); and see comments on the Swedenborgian idea of complementary souls, no.70.

AW

duced in Waters 1993) – studies that themselves suggest he had in mind a more elaborate work than this canvas. There is however no known version showing a more complete image, and indeed the bleak emptiness of this sketchlike design and its stark absence of colour are entirely appropriate to the text it illustrates, from Virgil's *Aeneid*, Book VI. Virgil lays stress on the darkness and barrenness of the Underworld landscape through which Aeneas passes on his way to visit his father Anchises in Dis:

> All dim amid the lonely night on through the dust they went.
> On through the empty house of Dis, the land of nought at all.
> E'en as beneath the doubtful moon, when niggard light doth fall,
> Upon some way amid the woods when God hath hidden heaven,
> And black night from the things of earth the colours clear hath given.
> Down thither rushed a mighty crowd, unto the flood-side borne;
> Mothers and men, and bodies there with all the life outworn
> Of great-souled heroes; many a boy and never-wedded maid,
> And youths before their fathers' eyes upon the death-bale laid:
> There stood the first and prayed him hard to waft their bodies o'er,
> With hands stretched out for utter love of that far-lying shore
>
> (trans. William Morris)

EDWARD BURNE-JONES 1833–1898

40 King Cophetua and the Beggar Maid 1884

Oil on canvas 293.4 × 135.9 (115½ × 53½)
Inscribed 'EBJ 18 | 84' b.l.

Prov: Purchased from the artist by the first Earl of Wharncliffe 1884, from whose executors bt by subscription by the Tate Gallery 1900

Exh: Grosvenor Gallery 1884 (69); Paris 1889; New Gallery 1892 (62); New Gallery 1898 (98); Tate Gallery 1933 (59); Hayward Gallery 1975 (146)

Lit: *Art Journal*, 1884, p.189; *Art Journal*, 1894, p.23; *Magazine of Art*, 1898, pp.515, 522; Bell 1903, pp.59, 62; G.B.-J. 1904, I, p.253, II, pp.85, 134–5, 139, 146, 201; de Lisle 1907, pp.1–2, 126–7, 168, 185; Ironside and Gere 1948, p.46; Harrison and Waters 1973, pp.141–5, col. pl.34; Taylor 1973, pp.148–55

Tate Gallery. Presented by subscribers 1900

Cophetua was an ancient African king who disdained women and was immune to love. However, one day he saw a beggar girl, and, falling instantly in love with her, vowed to make her his queen. Burne-Jones drew upon two sources for the subject. Richard Johnson's ballad 'A Song of a Beggar and a King' (1612), reprinted by the Percy Society in 1842, supplied such details as the colour of the maid's dress: 'As he out of his window lay / He saw a beggar all in grey'. Tennyson's poem 'The Beggar Maid' provided the mood of intense admiration:

> Her arms across her breast she laid;
> She was more fair than words can say:
> Barefooted came the beggar maid
> Before the king Cophetua.
> In robe and crown the king stept down,
> To meet and greet her on her way:
> 'It is no wonder,' said the lords,
> 'She is more beautiful than day.'
>
> As shines the moon in clouded skies,
> She in her poor attire was seen:
> One praised her ankles, one her eyes,
> One her dark hair and lovesome mien.
> So sweet a face, such angel grace,
> In all that land had never been:
> Cophetua swore a royal oath:
> 'This beggar maid shall be my queen!'

Burne-Jones's visual inspiration is evidently the Italian quattrocento. Several writers have compared the composition with Mantegna's *Madonna della Vittoria* (Musée du Louvre, Paris) of which Burne-Jones owned a photograph. Carlo Crivelli's *Annunciation*,which entered the London National Gallery in 1864, seems to have provided him with the idea for the elaborate architectural setting and sumptuous decorative details. Gail Weinberg has suggested the source of the beggar maid's garment may be the figure of St John in Mantegna's altarpiece in the National Gallery, and connotations of sanctified poverty appropriate to both St John and the maid add weight to this.

Studies in a sketchbook in use in the mid-1870s indicate that by this date Burne-Jones had already decided upon the high and narrow format and the general disposition of the figures (Fitzwilliam Museum, Cambridge; see Duncan Robinson's letter, *Apollo*, June 1973, p.626). Most of the work on the painting, however, seems to have taken place in 1883 and 1884, Burne-Jones taking great pains over it: 'I work daily at Cophetua and his Maid. I torment myself every day ... But I will kill myself or else Cophetua shall look like a King and the beggar like a Queen, such as Kings and Queens ought to be'. (G.B.-J. 1904, I, p.253). Burne-Jones wrote to Mrs Wyndham on 23 April 1884 that 'This very hour I have ended my work on my picture. I am very tired of it – I can see nothing more in it, I have stared it out of all countenance and it has no word for me. It is like a child that one watches without ceasing till it grows up, and lo! it is a stranger' (G.B.-J. 1904, II, p.139).

The picture was exhibited at the Grosvenor Gallery that spring, where it attracted considerable

40

attention and praise, the *Art Journal* noting 'It is the idea, the inspiration of this picture which makes it so fine, and raises it to the level of the work of the great masters of a bygone age' (1884, p.189). Five years later when it was shown at the Paris Universal Exhibition in 1889, it aroused even greater enthusiasm, and Burne-Jones was rewarded by the French government with the Cross of the Legion of Honour. The theme of the inferiority of riches and power of love, and the rejection of the material for the spiritual held particular relevance for a French generation influenced by Symbolist writers and artists who had promulgated similar ideas. In England the theme can be compared with the rejection of Mammon in pictures by Watts (no.52) and Evelyn De Morgan (no.97). Lady Burne-Jones stressed the importance of this aspect of *King Cophetua* and noted that her husband painted it

> during the divergence of opinion between himself and Morris, on the subject of Socialism, bringing it to an end soon after Morris joined the Democratic Federation. The thought of the King and the Beggar lay deep in both their minds and the reception of 'Cophetua' in Paris by some who saw it there in 1889 proves how strongly it impressed on them a distinct meaning. M. de la Sizeranne writes that it seemed to himself and his friends as though in standing before it they had 'come from the Universal Exhibition of wealth to see the symbolical expression of the Scorn of Wealth'.
>
> (G.B.-J. 1904, II, p.139)

There may also be more personal dimensions to the picture. The beggar maid's face looks very much like Georgiana Burne-Jones, as shown for instance by the similarity to her husband's 1883 portrait of her (private collection; repr. Hayward Gallery 1975, no.236). The picture exhibited here might therefore also represent the artist's feelings for his wife, and the lack of importance of worldly reward in comparison to their affection. However, their marriage had not been untroubled, as Edward's affair with Maria Zambaco and his conflicting loyalties testified. Indeed, Taylor has proposed that the maid can be identified as Frances Graham, on whom Burne-Jones doted, but who to his distress married John Horner in 1883 (see Taylor 1973, pp.148–55). The inclusion of anemones in the picture, symbols of rejected love, may support this, for they do not fit the story of Cophetua. Their significance might equally, however, be a comment on the relationship between the Burne-Jones's.

This picture was particularly admired by Fernand Khnopff, who in his obituary of Burne-Jones in the *Magazine of Art* gave a rhapsodic account of his first encounter with it in at the Universal Exhibition in Paris in 1889:

> there appeared, like a queen, supreme and glorious, the lovely picture by Burne-Jones, 'King Cophetua and the Beggar-Maid,' in the place of honour, the centre of a panel, with its beautiful frame of pale gold pilasters ornamented with scrolls.
>
> Before the pallid beggar-maid, still shivering in her little grey gown, sits the king clad in brilliant black armour, who, having surrendered to her his throne of might, has taken a lower place on the steps of the dais. He holds on his knees the finely modelled crown of dark metal lighted up with the scarlet of rubies and coral, and his face, in clear-cut profile, is raised in silent contemplation. The scene is incredibly sumptuous: costly stuffs glisten and gleam, luxurious pillows of purple brocade shine in front of chased gold panelling, and the polished metal reflects the beggar-maid's exquisite feet, adorable feet – their ivory whiteness enhanced by contrast with the scarlet anemones that lie here and there. Two chorister-boys perched above are singing softly, and in the distance, between the hanging curtains, is seen a dream, so to speak, of an autumn landscape, its tender sky already dusk, expressing all sweet regret, all hope in vain for the things that are no more, the things that can never be. In this exquisite setting the two figures remain motionless, isolated in their absorbed reverie, wrapped in the interior life.
>
> How perfectly delightful were the hours spent in long contemplation of this work of intense beauty! One by one the tender and precious memories were revived, the recondite emotions of past and present life, making one more and more in love with their superb realisation in this marvellous picture. The spectator was enwrapped by this living atmosphere of dream-love and of spiritualised fire, carried away to a happy intoxication of soul, a dizziness that clutched the spirit and bore it high up, far, far away …
>
> (Khnopff 1898, p.522)

RU

EDWARD BURNE-JONES 1833–1898

41 **Love among the Ruins** 1893–4

Oil on canvas 96.5 × 160 (38 × 63)

Prov: Mrs R.H. Benson by 1900; George McCulloch; his sale, Christie's 23, 29–30 May 1913 (118), bt Charles Davis; Lord Bearstead, by whom given to the National Trust as part of the contents of Upton House, Warwickshire 1948; transferred to Wightwick Manor, near Wolverhampton

Exh: New Gallery 1894 (106); New Gallery 1898 (106); Rome 1911 (400); Sheffield 1971 (74)

Lit: Bell 1892, pp.50, 90, 92; G.B.-J. 1904, II, pp.237–8, 243, 341; de Lisle 1904, pp.95–7, 147, 182, 186; Harrison and Waters 1973, pp.173, 180, 185; Hartnoll 1988, pp.48–9

The Bearsted Collection (The National Trust) on indefinite loan to Wightwick Manor

EXHIBITED IN LONDON ONLY

The composition of *Love among the Ruins* was first seen in a gouache version begun in 1870 and exhibited at the Dudley Gallery in 1873. It occurred again as a miniature set within a decorative border designed by William Morris in an illuminated manuscript of *The Rubáiyát of Omar Khayyám*. The gouache version was described by the *Art Journal* in 1873 as 'a very elaborately worked drawing ... whereon a chapter might be written, as it illustrates the beginning, progress, and end of much that is, and has been, done in recent water-colour art' (p.87). It became one of the artist's most admired and best-known works, being exhibited on a number of occasions most notably at the Universal Exhibition in Paris in 1878 – and was therefore the first work which Burne-Jones sent to an exhibition abroad.

In 1893 it was sent to France again, to the Société Nationale des Beaux-Arts, at which time it was also to be reproduced as an engraving. As a result of an injury to the watercolour version at a photographer's studio in Paris, the present oil version was undertaken. Burne-Jones and his old friend Stopford Brooke met by chance one day and discussed the relative merits of the two versions. 'It's better painted', opined Brooke of no.41, 'but the ineffable spirit of youth which was in the other, is not there.' 'O that is true', replied Burne-Jones, 'and it will not come back again' (Pearsall Jacks 1917, II, p.579).

42

Love Among the Ruins struck Burne-Jones's first biographer as 'one of the most impressive of the painter's works, with its vague hint of an untold tragedy which haunts the memory and refuses to be banished' (Bell 1892, p.50). Although the painting borrows its title from Robert Browning's poem of 1855, it is not in any sense an illustration, but rather follows *The Lament* (no.25) in suggesting a wistful mood to the spectator in terms of abstract allegory, and was of the type described by Bell 'which convey a sentiment or an idea but not a story' (ibid., p.90). All around are signs of the decay of worldly power, as brambles invade the precinct of a rich building and column drums are strewn about. The woman looks into the distance with foreboding and 'with heavy eyes that see too plainly still the unspeakable horrors of the past' (ibid., p.50), but clearly she is loved by her companion who has interrupted his playing to comfort her with an embrace.

Even in the oil version the face of Maria Zambaco may be recognised. As the gouache was painted at the time when the love affair between Burne-Jones and Maria was reaching its unhappy climax, and when her impact upon his art was most profound, it and its oil version may be seen among all his paintings of her as a deliberate and conscious declaration of love.

CSN

WILLAM BLAKE RICHMOND 1842–1921

42 Sleep and Death Carrying the Body of Sarpedon into Lycia *c.*1875–6

Oil on canvas 242 × 90.3 (95¼ × 35½)

Prov: The artist; by descent to his son, Rear-Admiral Sir Herbert Richmond 1922

Exh: Grosvenor Gallery 1879 (22); RA Winter 1922 (44)

Lit: Lascelles 1902, pp.16–17 (repr. p.2); Stirling 1926 (repr. opp. p.430); Reynolds 1995, pp.111, 122–3, fig.43

Vancouver Museum

To two swift bearers give him then in charge
To Sleep and Death, twin brothers, in their arms
To bear him safe to Lycia's wide-spread plains:
There shall his brethren and his friends perform
His funeral rites, and mound and column raise,
The fitting tribute to the mighty dead.

Homer, *Iliad* XVI

Sarpedon was the son of Zeus and Laodamia, and was commander of the Lycian army who fought in the Trojan Wars as the allies of King Priam. He was known for his strength and valour in battle, and it was he who killed Tlepolemus, the son of Heracles, in the course of an assault on the Greek defences. Book XVI of the *Iliad* describes how Zeus foretold the killing of Sarpedon by Patroclus, and how he threatened to intercede to save his beloved son. Hera, however, would not allow this, saying to her husband: 'No; if you love and pity Sarpedon, let him fall in mortal combat with Patroclus, and when the breath has left his lips send Death and the sweet god of Sleep to take him up and bring him to the broad realm of Lycia, where his kinsmen and retainers will give him burial, with the barrow and monument that are a dead man's rights.' (*The Iliad*, transl. E.V. Rieu, 1950, p.304). Sarpedon went to his death and Zeus in his grief caused a shower of bloody rain to fall. A terrible battle for the corpse of the fallen warrior ensued, only concluded when Hector and the Trojans were driven from the field of battle. Then Zeus sent Apollo to recover the body, and the twin brothers Death and Sleep (Thanatos and Hypnos) were bidden to carry it home to Lycia for fitting and honourable burial.

Helen Lascelles considered the subject to have been treated 'with intense poetic feeling', and one that 'gives a feeling of limitless space to the spectator, the blue, misty background of sea and sky seeming to recede for miles beyond the central figures' (Lascelles 1902, p.17). The same author compares Richmond's painting with John Flaxman's line engraving of the subject which appeared in the first English edition of the *Iliad*, published in Rome in 1793. Although Richmond has transposed the horizontality of Flaxman's original into his own pronouncedly upright composition, both images are starkly supernatural. Richmond and Flaxman of course were connected through William Blake, who was Richmond's godfather and who had known Flaxman, and who had in fact engraved plates after Flaxman's drawings for the 1805 Homer edition.

This work was shown at the third summer exhibition of the Grosvenor Gallery, in 1879. Richmond, along with many of his contemporaries, had been increasingly dissatisfied with the Royal Academy as a venue, and when in 1877 Coutts Lindsay opened the Grosvenor, Richmond switched his allegiance to the new and fashionable exhibition space.

CSN

Dante Gabriel Rossetti 1828–1882

43 **Venus Verticordia** 1864–8

Oil on canvas 82.5 × 70 (32½ × 27½)
Inscribed with Rossetti's monogram b.l.

Prov: J. Mitchell, Bradford; John Graham; his sale, 30 April 1887 (82), bt Arthur Anderson; Christie's 19 May 1894 (34); H.S. Sanders-Clark, his sale Christie's 30 July 1936 (71); ...; bt by Russell-Cotes Art Gallery and Museum, Bournemouth 1946

Exh: *Special Loan Collection*, Birmingham Museum and Art Gallery 1891 (179); Bournemouth 1951 (9); Commonwealth Institute 1978; RA 1973 (317, repr.); Tate Gallery 1984 (130, repr.); Las Palmas 1990; Rome 1996 (37, repr. col.)

Lit: Marillier 1899, no.149, pp.54 n.1, 134–6; Rossetti 1903, pp. 227, 308, 407; Doughty and Wahl 1965–8, pp.516, 518–19, 570, 822, 836–7; Surtees 1971, no.173, pl.248

The Russell-Cotes Art Gallery and Museum, Bournemouth

The title of this picture derives from an invocation to the Roman goddess of beauty and sensual love to 'turn the hearts' of women to virtue and chastity. Rossetti, however, illustrated it with a complex set of mythological and symbolic allusions on the theme of the compulsion and dangers of sexual attraction. The golden apple is a reference to the first temptation, in the Garden of Eden. But it is also the Apple of Discord which Paris, asked to judge which was most beautiful of Hera, Athena and Aphrodite, awarded to Aphrodite (Venus). As rewards the Graces had offered him respectively power, martial triumph or the most beautiful woman in the world, Helen of Troy. Paris chose the last of these, demonstrating the supremacy of sexual compulsion over all else, even at risk of disaster. His consequent elopement with Helen resulted in the death and disasters of the Trojan War. At the siege of Troy Paris was killed by a poisoned arrow, which Rossetti refers to here with the dart held by Venus. It is also intended to represent Cupid's arrow of love, and Rossetti therefore suggests both the joy and harmful consequences of love's compulsion. Grieve has noted other iconographic and symbolic references in the picture (Tate Gallery 1984, no.130). The roses in the background represent the physical sensuality of love, and honeysuckle also had sexual connotations for Rossetti, as shown in its form and traditional reputation for attracting bees. Rossetti mentioned this in his poems 'The Honeysuckle' and 'Chimes' (see Rossetti 1911, pp.199, 127). The blue bird is an omen of ill luck and represents the fleeting transitoriness of love and life.

43

The butterflies surrounding Venus's halo – which itself symbolises the sanctity of love – may refer to flitting from pleasure to pleasure, in this context perhaps sexual pleasure. Grieve has suggested also that they may represent the souls of dead lovers (ibid.).

Rossetti started painting *Venus Verticordia* in 1864, having been commissioned by J. Mitchell of Bradford in April that year, although an earlier study in red chalk is dated 1863 (Surtees 1971, no.173b, pl.249). It took him four years to paint and underwent various alterations. The original model was a cook for a family in Portland Place, 'almost a giantess' as William Allingham described her in June 1864 (1907, p.100). However, in 1867 Rossetti repainted the body and head, substituting the features of Alexa Wilding. The composition and subject-matter are very close to other works by Rossetti such as *Regina Cordium* 1866 (Glasgow Art Gallery). Grieve noted the possible compositional debt of *Venus Verticordia* to van der Weyden's *Antoine, Grand Bâtard de Bourgogne,* a picture which Rossetti could have seen on the visit he made to Brussels in 1863.

Rossetti's enthusiasm for painting subjects of dominating femmes fatales, Grieve has also suggested, may have been a result of the influence of Swinburne, with whom he shared his house in the early 1860s and whose poetry dealt with similar subject-matter. Writing in 1865 before the painting was adapted, the *Athenaeum* clearly grasped its underlying themes of compulsion and enslavement, describing how Venus 'guards the apple with the threatening dart, while the Psyche, tremulous of wing, traverses its surface. Winner of hearts, she reeks not of the soul; fraught with peril, her ways are inscrutable; there is more evil than good in her; she is victorious and indomitable' (21 Oct. 1865, p.546).

In an apparent objection to the overt sensuality of the picture, and by implication the decadence of Rossetti's Cheyne Walk existence, Ruskin criticised the honeysuckle, writing: 'I purposely used the word "wonderfully" painted about those flowers. They were wonderful to me, in their realism; awful – I can use no other word – in their coarseness: showing enormous power, showing certain conditions of non-sentiment which underlie all that you are doing – now' (Ruskin, *Works*, XXXVI, p.491).

In January 1868 Rossetti completed the sonnet that accompanied the painting:

She hath the apple in her hand for thee,
Yet almost in her heart would hold it back;
She muses, with her eyes upon the track
Of that which in thy spirit they can see.
Haply, 'Behold, he is at peace,' saith she;
'Alas! the apple for his lips, – the dart
That follows its brief sweetness to his heart, –
The wandering of his feet perpetually!'

A little space her glance is still and coy;
But if she give the fruit that works her spell,
Those eyes shall flame as her Phrygian boy.
The shall her bird's strained throat the woe
  foretell,
And her far seas moan as a single shell,
And her grove glow with love-lit fires of Troy.

This had clearly evolved concurrently with the painting for an earlier variant text is included in the drawing dated 1863 mentioned above.

RU

Dante Gabriel Rossetti 1828–1882

44 **Beata Beatrix** *c.*1864–70

Oil on canvas 86.4 × 66 (34 × 26)
Inscribed with Rossetti's monogram b.l.

Prov: Hon. William Cowper, later Lord Mount-Temple; his widow, by whom presented to the National Gallery 1889

Exh: RA Winter 1883 (293); Manchester 1911 (219); Tate Gallery 1911–12 (1279); Tate Gallery 1948 (21); Tate Gallery 1984 (131, repr.)

Lit: Marillier 1899, no.138, pp.126–8; Ironside and Gere 1948, p.37; Surtees 1971, no.168, pl.238; Surtees 1980, pp.44, 103 n.3

Tate Gallery. Presented by Georgiana, Baroness Mount-Temple in memory of her husband, Francis, Baron Mount-Temple 1889

This is a very different type of picture from the 'fleshly' female portraits Rossetti made in the 1860s, for it is a memorial to his wife Lizzie Siddall, who had died on 11 February 1862. In it Rossetti draws parallels between the death of Beatrice and Lizzie, and compares Dante's loss with his own. The title translates as 'Blessed Beatrice' and refers to the *Vita Nuova* ('The New Life') – Dante's account of his unrequited love and mourning for the young Beatrice Portinari. Rossetti began his translation of this text in 1845, and it appeared in 1864 as part of his volume *The Early Italian Poets*. The *Vita Nuova* was a story which had fascinated Rossetti since his youth, but it took on close personal significance with the death of his own beloved. He characterised the picture as a 'poetic work' (Doughty and Wahl 1965–8, II, p.603), and it is filled with symbolic or allegorical references to Beatrice and Lizzie. In the background Dante looks across at the figure of Love, in whose hand a flickering flame around a heart represents the gradual waning of Beatrice's life and temporal love. Dante continues watching until the last moment possible as Beatrice's heart is taken to Purgatory to await judgement. Love is portrayed not as Cupid but as an angel surrounded by an aura, and depicted very much in the manner of Burne-Jones's figures. In the distance, dimly glimpsed as if through a Victorian London fog, is the Ponte Vecchio, a reminder of the setting of the medieval story. The central figure of Beatrice is posed in an attitude of ecstasy. A dove descends to her, an emblem of the Holy Spirit and impending death, but also a reference to one of Rossetti's pet names for Lizzie, 'the Dove'. It is presumably coloured red as the colour of love, as are the robes of the figure of Love in the background. Held in its beak is an opium poppy, a traditional symbol of sleep, dreams and death, but in this context also a reference to the manner of Lizzie's death from an overdose of laudanum. The colours of her dress are significant, for as Rossetti's friend F.G. Stephens pointed out, green and grey are 'the colours of hope and sorrow, as well as of love and life' ('*Beata Beatrix* by Dante Gabriel Rossetti', *Portfolio*, vol.22, 1891, p.46). Rossetti designed the frame himself, and on it are further references to Dante. At the top, now partly erased, is the date of Beatrice's death 'Jun: Die 9: Anno 1290', while at the bottom is the phrase from Lamentations 1:1 that Dante quoted in the *Vita Nuova* – 'Quomodo sedet sola civitas' ('how doth the city sit solitary') – a reference to the mourning of Beatrice's death throughout Florence. The roundels represent the sun, moon, earth and stars, referring to the last lines of Dante's *Divine Comedy*: 'Love which moves the sun and all the stars.'

In a letter to the Hon. Mrs Cowper-Temple in 1871 Rossetti himself gave a detailed account of the picture's subject, and its treatment of Dante:

> It must of course be remembered, in looking at the picture that it is not at all intended to represent Death … but to render it under the resemblance of a trance, in which Beatrice seated at the balcony over-looking the city is suddenly rapt from Earth to Heaven. You will remember how much Dante dwells on the desolation of the city in connection with the incident of her death, & for this reason I have introduced it, as my background, & made the figure of Dante and love passing through the street & gazing ominously at one another, conscious of the event, whilst the bird, a messenger of death, drops a poppy between the hands of Beatrice. She sees through her shut lids, is conscious of a new world, as expressed in the last words of the *Vita Nuova* 'Quella beata Beatrice che gloriosamente mira nella fascia die colui est per omnia soecula benedictus' ['that blessed Beatrice who now gazeth continually on His countenance who is blessed throughout all ages']
>
> (quoted in Surtees 1971, no.168)

Swinburne, one of the few among the Rossetti circle to be close to Lizzie, admired the picture's sensual treatment, and judged it:

> perhaps the noblest work of Mr Rossetti's many studies after Dante. The work is wholly symbolic and ideal; a strange bird flown earthward from heaven brings her in its beak a full-blown poppy, the funereal flower of sleep. Her beautiful head lies back, sad and sweet, with fast-shut eyes in a death-like trance that is not death; over it the shadow of death seems to impend, making sombre the splendour of her ample hair and tender faultless features …
>
> (quoted in Hyder 1972, p.133)

The sundial shows the hour of Beatrice's death, nine o'clock, and Rossetti noted in a letter to Ellen Heaton in 1863:

> You probably remember the singular way in which Dante dwells on the number nine in connection with Beatrice in the Vita Nuova. He meets her at nine years of age, she dies at nine o'clock on the 9th of June, 1290. All of this is said, and he declares her to have been herself 'a nine', that is the perfect number, or symbol of perfection.
>
> (quoted Surtees, loc. cit.)

The mystical connotations with 'perfection' of the number nine arise from its being the sum of three times three, three being the number of the Trinity. However, it additionally held traditional connections with hell. There were said to be nine rivers there, or as Dante himself described in the *Divine Comedy*, hell comprised nine circles. Milton wrote of the gates of hell as being 'thrice three fold' with nine folds, nine plates and nine linings (*Paradise Lost*, II, 645). Rossetti would certainly have known of all these implications, and his inclusion of a reference to nine in *Beata Beatrix* might, in addition to the connections with the *Vita Nuova*, indicate some fear in his mind that Lizzie's sin of suicide might have condemned her to the infernal regions. In Dante's *Inferno* the suicides are leaves on trees which are fed upon by harpies (XIII, 2–108).

The picture has a hazy, unfocused quality, especially around Beatrice's head and in the background, which emphasises its visionary, dream-like, transcendent character, perhaps not unconnected with its references to opium. Wilton (p.28) compares this with Watts's work. Such a surface suggests a membrane through which the parallel, anti-materialist world of the imagination or the ideal can be glimpsed, as if through frosted glass. Grieve has noted similarities with the 'soft focus' photographs Julia Margaret Cameron started making in January 1864, and which Rossetti much admired (Tate Gallery 1984, no.131). However, the photographs of spirit manifestations at seances, whether faked or otherwise, frequently have a similarly diffuse character. During the time Rossetti was working on *Beata Beatrix* he was deeply involved in spiritualism, trying to make contact with Lizzie, and this experience must have been an influence on the picture (see nos.70, 71).

As Rossetti explained in his letter to Georgiana Cowper-Temple, in the picture Beatrice 'sees through her shut lids, is conscious of a new world'. Thus in her ecstatic state she experiences a direct revelation of God and the afterlife. But Beatrice is frankly depicted in a way that resembles sexual ecstasy. Her facial expression, raised head, straining throat and parted lips are overtly sensual, and Rossetti evidently intends to suggest a connection between the sexual and the divine, between orgasm and revelation. This was a concept that had been proposed by Emanuel Swedenborg (1688–1772) in his book *Conjugial Love* (1768), a text which seems to have influenced Rossetti deeply (see nos.70, 71). Swedenborg proposed that sexual union was in itself a religious experience and one which brought people closer to the experience of God's love. Sexual ecstasy and love on earth, he believed, came closest to that divine love and revelation found in Heaven. Sexual congress echoed the union of two souls in Heaven which he suggested were needed to form a single angel.

Rossetti also seems to be making darker, more complex and deeply psychological connections between sex and death. Such feelings about the eroticism of death, and the sexual dimension of grief, were much later to be explored by Freud. The exhuming of Lizzie's body in 1869, and ensuing reports of her state of preservation, including the continued radiance of her golden hair, which in life had so fascinated Rossetti, can only have made such responses more complicated (see Ashmolean 1991, p.7). So too must Rossetti's apparently successful contact with Lizzie's spirit. It appears that after Lizzie's death, in one sense, his passion for her was revitalised, their differences now forgotten. In his grief, his longing for her included sexual yearning. The picture is composed like an altar-piece, and posed with her hands before her and her lips parted, Lizzie looks as if she is about to receive Communion. This suggests that death, and also sex, are a sacrament. The painting therefore functions on several levels – as a symbolic illustration to Dante, and a comparison of Rossetti's life to Dante's, as a *memento mori* to Lizzie, and as a summary of Rossetti's beliefs in the sanctity of sex.

As noted above, *Beata Beatrix* expresses the central duality at the heart of Symbolism between the Decadent and the Ideal (see p.24). Rossetti's representation of the dying Lizzie signifies a fusion of his physical and spiritual love for her, thus proposing that through the transfiguration of death, these two dimensions of earthly human relations will become one. This is an inherently Swedenborgian notion, although in his philosophy true union could only be achieved with the passage through death of both partners, and the pain and longing of the separation until this happened was treated by Rossetti in his poem and painting *The Blessed Damozel*. Here the Damozel longs for the moment of her earth-bound lover's death, and this, combined with his eroticised, ecstatic treatment of the experience of dying in *Beata Beatrix* may indicate a corresponding yearning by Rossetti for his own extinction. This reading is not unlikely, for while staying with William Bell Scott at Penkill Castle in autumn 1869, contemplating Lizzie's impending disinterment, Rossetti spoke daily of suicide and came close to throwing himself from a precipice. It was shortly afterwards that Rossetti believed he was visited by Lizzie's soul in the form of a bird (see no.71; Bell Scott 1892, II, pp.112–13).

Rossetti worked on *Beata Beatrix* over a long period of time. It was actually started in Lizzie's lifetime, but abandoned. Rossetti's assistant Henry Treffry Dunn reported:

> The picture might have met with destruction and passed away into oblivion had it not been for Mr. Howell. It was begun and so far as head and hands went completed from Rossetti's wife, but her untimely death so saddened him that he took no further interest in it and for a considerable time it lay in the studio thoroughly uncared for & subject to all sorts of damages. Howell being once in the house discovered it in a very dirty condition and without saying a word to Rossetti took it away and had it relined, bringing it back to him in a most inviteable state to work upon and with Howell's persuasions and entreaties he took fresh heart of grace & completed it.
>
> (quoted in Surtees 1971, no.168)

Howell's desire for Rossetti to take up the picture may well have been conceived as a way of helping him with his grief. Although in life Lizzie had been a recurrent subject for Rossetti's art, after her death she did not figure again until *Beata Beatrix*. This is partly explained by Rossetti's preference for working from life. After rediscovering the laid-in canvas, in December 1863 Rossetti wrote to Ellen Heaton: 'I remember you once asked me whether it would be possible to do anything of the kind from recollection; and though I then said No I think the beginning and sketches in question might enable me to do so' (quoted ibid.). The sketches, Rossetti mentioned elsewhere in the letter, were 'pencil sketches for it as a half figure comprising the arms & hands'. These presumably included the studies of the figure of Delia for his watercolour *The Return of Tibullus to Delia* *c*.1853 (Birmingham City Museum & Art Gallery; Surtees 1971, no.62, studies nos.62a–f). In these drawings Lizzie has a similar expression to that found in the oil exhibited here.

RU

Dante Gabriel Rossetti 1828–1882

45 **Astarte Syriaca** 1875–7

Oil on canvas 182.8 × 106.5 (72 × 41⅞)
Inscribed 'D. G. Rossetti. 1877' lower left

Prov: Clarence E. Fry; bt Manchester City Art Gallery 1891

Exh: RA 1883 (332); Manchester 1911 (220); RA and Birmingham 1973 (363); Rotterdam 1975 (208); Tate Gallery 1984 (147); Tokyo 1990 (85)

Lit: Stephens 1877, pp.486–7; Sharp 1882, pp.241, 244–5, list no.272; Myers 1883, pp.325–6; Stephens 1892, pp.45–6; Stephens 1894, p.88; Marillier 1899, pp.190–3 and 255 (no.282); Doughty and Wahl 1965–8, III, pp.1344 et seq.; IV, pp.1473, 1475, 1481–2; Surtees 1971, I, no.249; II, pl.371; Fennell 1978, esp. letters 87–9, 105, 106; Surtees 1980, p.62 (5 June 1875); Faxon 1989, pp.191–4, pl.213

Manchester City Art Galleries

EXHIBITED IN LONDON ONLY

From the outset Rossetti conceived *Astarte Syriaca* as belonging to a class of ambitious works, describing it as 'so important an ideal subject' that it could not be sold for less than 2,000 guineas. In July 1875 the design was in hand with Rossetti telling Leyland that he was 'cartooning' the *Astarte* (Fennell 1978, no.87). It depicted, according to the artist's own description on its completion, the 'Syrian Venus with ministering spirits' (letter from Rossetti to his uncle Henry Polidori, 31 Jan. 1877, Doughty and Wahl 1965–8, IV, p.1473). A specially designed frame, in common with Rossetti's usual practice, bore the last six lines of the sonnet composed for the painting which was printed in full in April 1877 in the *Athenaeum*:

> Mystery, lo! betwixt the Sun and Moon
> Astarte of the Syrians: Venus Queen
> Ere Aphrodite was. In silver sheen
> Her twofold girdle clasps the infinite boon
> Of bliss whereof the Heaven and Earth commune:
> And from her neck's inclining flower-stem lean
> Love-freighted lips and absolute eyes that wean
> The pulse of hearts to the spheres' dominant tune.
>
> Torch-bearing, her sweet ministers compel
> All thrones of light, beyond the sky and sea,
> The witnesses of Beauty's face to be:
> That face, of Love's all-penetrative spell,
> Amulet, talisman, and oracle, –
> Betwixt the Sun and Moon a mystery.

At the time that the sonnet appeared, F.G. Stephens wrote a descriptive article allowing Rossetti to take centre stage even though he refused to participate in the first exhibition at the new Grosvenor Gallery.

45

Stephens brought *Astarte Syriaca* to life for the readers of his unillustrated text by focusing on the face 'with glowing, mysterious, and steadfast eyes looking from under the shadow of her ample brows and ascendant masses of bronze-black hair, shadows which add to the mystery and wonder of a face'. Lighting effects also command attention for the 'amorous goddess of the Syrians, standing in the weird contrasted light and darkness, in opposed illumination of the sun and moon, and ruddy glare of torches'. Stephens, elaborating on such arcane details as the eight-pointed star of Venus above Astarte's head, was, of course, Rossetti's mouthpiece in this key article which tellingly conveys the artist's own ideas about the 'majestic passion' of the design.

The working title, *Venus Astarte*, allows identification of the main figure with the powerful ancient Semitic goddess of Syria-Palestine in the pre-Greek era. Astarte was eventually subsumed in the identity of the Greek Aphrodite and Roman Venus. Lemprière's *Classical Dictionary*, tells of Astarte: 'A powerful divinity of Syria' with a temple attended by three hundred priests who paid court to her while the moon shone; 'she was represented in medals with a long habit, and a mantle over it, tucked up on the left arm.' Rossetti's *Astarte* wears such garb, and although her pose differs from the ancient depictions which show one hand stretched forward and the other holding a cross-like staff, there is, in the painting, much play with the hands as they contort into seemingly significant gestures calling attention to Venus's role as a fertility goddess.

This Near Eastern incarnation of Venus, goddess of love, seems an unusual choice for the artist, though Alastair Grieve has suggested the influence of his friend Watts-Dunton, who had an established interest in Eastern mythology. Yet one should also remember Rossetti's own fascination with Venus in her various guises (see no.43). Grieve also points out that the model, Jane Morris, was more Eastern-looking, with her thick black hair and heavy eyes, than Classical (Tate Gallery 1984, no.147). Rossetti anticipated a fascination with the distant East and its deities in later manifestations of Symbolism.

What also seems relevant is the very obscurity of the subject, which lends the painting an air of mystery that is further enhanced by the floating attendant spirits. The background space with the eclipse-like convergence of the setting sun of 'fierce gold' and the rising moon of 'paler lustre' evokes inexplicable cosmic forces, later a feature in the Symbolist canon of non-naturalistic imagery (see no.134). The Michelangelesque proportions of Jane Morris on colossal scale, with her impassive, enigmatic face and expressive hands, project the powerful, even terrifying, persona of *Astarte Syriaca*.

BB

DANTE GABRIEL ROSSETTI 1828–1882

46 **Proserpine** 1877

Oil on canvas 119.5 × 57.8 (47 × 23)
Inscribed 'Dante Gabriele Rossetti ritrasse nel capo d'anno del 1877' on scroll b.l. and Rossetti's sonnet in Italian t.r. (see below)

Prov: Head and hands painted for F.R. Leyland in 1873; relined and part repainted, sold to W.A. Turner 1877; his sale, Christie's 28 April 1888 (116), bt Charles Butler; by descent to his grandson, Charles Butler; his sale, Christie's 20 Nov. 1964 (25), bt Lefevre; L.S. Lowry; private collection; Christie's 27 Nov. 1987 (140), bt by present owner

Exh: Manchester 1878; Royal Institution, Manchester 1882 (250); Burlington Fine Arts Club 1883 (86); Manchester 1887 (699); *Loan Exhibition*, Guildhall 1895 (48); New Gallery 1897 (21); Dublin 1907; RA 1973 (358);

Manchester 1977 (13); Tate Gallery 1984 (131, repr.)

Lit: Marillier 1899, no.260, pp.172–4; Doughty and Wahl 1965–8, pp.1226, 1251; Surtees 1971, no.233, pl.331; Bryson and Troxwell 1976, pp.45, 49, 63, 65

Private Collection, London

Rossetti made a total of eight oil versions of *Proserpine*, one of which he strove to complete in the final days of his life (1882, Birmingham City Museum and Art Gallery). The sitter was Jane Morris, and Rossetti's almost obsessive love for her means that the story of Proserpine held personal significance in his relationship with her. Married to another man she was, like Proserpine, unattainable and trapped. Proserpine divided her time between the Underworld and Earth, where her return brought the Spring, thus perhaps showing how Rossetti felt about the time he spent with Jane Morris. Rossetti related the myth and his treatment of it in a letter to W.A. Turner, the first owner of the picture shown here:

> The figure represents Proserpine as Empress of Hades. After she was conveyed by Pluto to his realm, and became his bride, her mother Ceres importuned Jupiter for her return to earth, and he was prevailed on to consent to this, provided she had not partaken of any of the fruits of Hades. It was found, however, that she had eaten one grain of a pomegranate, and this enchained her to her new empire and destiny. She is represented in a gloomy corridor of her palace, with the fatal fruit in her hand. As she passes, a gleam strikes on the wall behind her from some inlet suddenly opened, and admitting for a moment the light of the upper world; and she glances furtively towards it, immersed in thought. The incense-burner stands beside her as the attribute of a goddess. The ivy branch in the background (a decorative appendage to the sonnet inscribed on the label) may be taken as a symbol of clinging memory.
>
> (quoted in Shone 1882, p.236)

Rossetti composed a sonnet for the picture, which appears in Italian inscribed in the top right corner. On the frame, which features roundels resembling cut pomegranates, an English version is appended:

> Afar away the light that brings cold cheer
> Unto this wall, – one instant and no more
> Admitted at my distant palace-door.
> Afar the flowers of Enna from this drear
> Cold fruit, which, tasted once, must thrall me here.
> Afar those skies from this Tartarean grey
> That chills me: and afar, how far away,
> The nights that shall be from the days that were.
>
> Afar from mine own self I seem, and wing
> Strange ways in thought, and listen for a sign:
> And still some heart unto some soul doth pine,
> (Whose sounds mine inner sense is fain to bring,
> Continually together murmuring,) –
> 'Woe's me for thee, unhappy Proserpine.'

The last six lines could easily describe the frustration of Rossetti's separation from Jane Morris. The strength of his attraction to her is tangible in the painting. Proserpine's full red lips, flowing hair and intense gaze create a mood of heavy sensuality heightened by the form and glistening pink flesh of the cut, ripe pomegranate, and the burning incense. The arrangement of Proserpine's hands suggests that one hand is restraining the other from raising the pomegranate to her lips, or else catching hold of it after having done so. This implies an inner conflict between compulsion and restraint, as found in the story of Eve and the forbidden apple, the subject which Rossetti had originally intended to depict in the picture. In this context the consumption of the pomegranate must represent sexual temptation and consummation, although within the internal logic of the picture's personal references, with William Morris rather than Rossetti. The full extent of Rossetti and Jane's relationship remains inconclusive, but by the summer of 1869 they were on increasingly intimate terms, and in view of Rossetti's past history may well have been lovers. Whatever the dynamics of their relationship, which on Rossetti's part involved a passionate attraction, William Morris appears to have tolerated it. Indeed, the three shared Kelmscott House together from 1871 to 1874. Against this background Rossetti might well have characterised Jane's continuing life with Morris, including perhaps marital relations, as sexual temptation and inconstancy on her part.

Rossetti's *Proserpine* pictures seem to have enjoyed unrivalled ill fate during his lifetime. Several were damaged and either destroyed or cut down. The version exhibited here utilised parts of a picture completed for Frederick Leyland in 1873 but wrecked in transit to him. Rossetti cut out the face and hands and mounted them on a fresh canvas, and the design was completed for Turner, Leyland having been sent another version which is now in the Tate Gallery (see Surtees 1971, no.233).

RU

Frederick Sandys 1829–1904

47 **Medea** 1866–68

Oil on panel 62.2 × 46.3 (24½ × 18¼)

Prov: W.H. Clabburn; by descent to his daughter Mary and son-in-law E. Meredith Crosse 1879; their son E. Mitchell Crosse; Christie's 8 May 1925 (74); Trustees of the Public Picture Gallery, by whom presented to Birmingham Museums and Art Gallery 1925

Exh: RA 1869 (99); Paris 1878 (235); Grafton Gallery 1894 (123); RA Winter 1905 (269); Dublin 1907 (208); Rome 1911 (87); National Gallery, Millbank 1923 (71); Lyons 1966 (115); Barbican and Tokyo 1991 (80); Seattle 1995 (88)

Lit: 'Frederick Sandys', *Art Journal*, 1884, pp.73–8; Wood 1896, p.31; Bate 1899, pp.62–3 and repr. opp. p.59; Bate 1905, pp.3–17; Chamberlain 1925, pp.258–63, repr.; Brighton and Sheffield 1974 (72, not exh.) p.27, repr. no.43

Birmingham Museums and Art Gallery

In ancient mythology Medea was an archetype of barbarian womanhood – scheming, mendacious and vengeful – who used sorcery and witchcraft to achieve her purposes, but one who was both destructive of men and the victim of her own futile love. Both Pindar and Apollonius described how Medea loved Jason, and how he used her in his quest for the golden fleece, persuading her to prepare potions for his protection and to overcome the dragon that guarded the fleece. For a while Jason and Medea lived together happily at Corinth and had children. However, in the story made famous by Euripides's play, Jason fell in love with and married Glauce, daughter of King Creon. Medea's revenge was to make a magic garment – Sandys's painting shows her treating the threads from which it is to be woven with fire – which when Glauce puts it on causes her to be consumed by flame.

The subject, revenge – aided by the power of sorcery – partaken by a woman aggrieved in love, is analagous to that of Sandys's earlier painting *Morgan le Fay* (see no.34). An early commentator compared the two paintings: 'In the "Medea," which was painted while the artist was the guest of Mr D.G. Rossetti, we have again a transcript of female beauty, but, like the "Morgan le Fay," it is beauty distorted by passion and made ghastly by despair' (*Art Journal*, 1884, p.77).

Swinburne, in his 1868 account of the painting, catalogued with utmost relish its sinister elements:

> Pale as from poison, with the blood drawn back from her very lips, agonized in face and limbs with the labour and the fierce contention of old love with new, of a daughter's love with a bride's, the fatal figure of Medea pauses a little on the funereal verge of the wood of death, in act to pour a blood-like liquid into the soft opal-coloured hollow of a shell. The future is hard upon her, as a cup of bitter poison set close to her mouth; the furies of Absyrtus, the furies of her children, rise up against her from the unrisen years; her eyes are hungry and helpless, full of a fierce and raging sorrow. Hard by her, henbane and aconite and nightshade thrive and grow full of fruit and death; before her fair feet the bright-eyed toads engender after their kind. Upon the golden ground is wrought in allegoric decoration the likeness of the ship Argo, with other emblems of the tragic things of her life.

Burne-Jones had likewise been exploring the possibilities of a similarly sinister subject, *The Wine of Circe* (fig.24 on p.41) – in which another mythological figure (and in fact as the daughter of Helios, Medea's aunt) prepared wine and meat poisoned by magic potions to turn the soldiers of Odysseus into swine. Sandys and Burne-Jones – both members of the circle of artists that congregated around Rossetti at Tudor House in Cheyne Walk – would undoubtedly have known, and probably discussed, each other's subject. Clearly, both were excited and attracted by wilful, sexually voracious female types, and there are other works of the 1860s beside *Circe* and *Medea* by each of them that combine themes of lubricity and death.

Both *Circe* and *Medea* were first shown in the summer of 1869, for although Sandys's painting had been accepted for display at the previous year's Royal Academy exhibition (and was thus described in Algernon Swinburne's critique of the 1868 exhibitions) it was withheld from view, presumably on the grounds that its subject was too macabre and threatening to fit easily with the prevailingly bland pattern of exhibits at the Royal Academy. Progressive opinion was outraged at this attempt to suppress a challenging and original painting, and the issue of whether the Academy had the right to act in the capacity of monitor of public taste was aired in the press. It may have been due to the influence of Frederic Leighton (who served on the hanging committee of the 1869 exhibition) that Sandys was admitted on the second occasion and the painting hung on the line in Gallery II at Burlington House.

Critics were learning to hedge their bets as slowly they came to understand that according to the new aesthetic, beautiful images might serve fearsome subjects. Although conservative opinion had condemned Burne-Jones's *Circe*, when it appeared at the Old Water-Colour Society, as 'abnormal and perverted', its compelling power was also conceded, for 'none can come near, at least for any length of time, to the magic circle of this mystic art without falling more or less as a sacrifice to its deadly spell' (*Art Journal*, 1869, p.173). In a like spirit, it was accepted that some deluded (or worse) individuals would respond to Medea, which was described by the same journal as a 'highly elaborate, but somewhat repellent, performance ... [which] will be either vastly admired or supremely detested' (*Art Journal*, 1869, p.164). F.G. Stephens found beauty in an image that was full of terror, being struck by the 'withered, ivory-like look of her skin and the deep, hard anger and woe of her eyes [and] the ruthless, parted lips; – expression that deepens in force with the observer because of the beauty of the features, which are transformed but not debased' (*Athenaeum*, 1869, p.675). A year earlier Swinburne had dismissed 'the "common cry" of academics. For this, beyond all doubt, is as yet his masterpiece ... The picture is grand alike for wealth of symbol and solemnity of beauty.'

CSN

George Frederic Watts 1817–1904

48 **Paolo and Francesca** *c.*1872–84

Oil on canvas 151.5 × 125.5 (59⅝ × 49⅜)

Prov: Collection of the artist

Exh: Grosvenor Gallery 1879 (73); Grosvenor Gallery 1881 (51); Paris 1883 (2); New York 1884 (89); Birmingham 1885 (132); Nottingham 1886 (18); Guildhall 1892 (18); Chicago 1893 (488); New Gallery 1896 (95); Stockholm 1897 (1436); RA 1905 (180); Manchester 1905 (125); Newcastle 1905 (106); Edinburgh 1905 (86); Dublin 1906 (47); Tate Gallery 1954 (59); Whitechapel 1974 (26); Manchester 1978 (28); Munich and Madrid 1993 (70); Washington 1997 (32)

Lit: Spielmann 1886, p.15, cat. p.31; Macmillan 1903, pp.167–70; Barrington 1905, pp.92, 125–6; MS. Cat. I, p.117; Watts 1912, I, p.64; Loshak 1963, pp.484–5; Staley 1978, no.28, pp.86–7; Bryant 1996, pp.121–4

Trustees of the Watts Gallery

This is one of only a handful of Watts's pictures to derive from literary sources. The fifth canto of Dante's *Inferno* tells the tragic story of the lovers Paolo and Francesca, discovered by her husband, the lord of Rimini, and killed. Doomed to the second circle of hell with their fellow carnal sinners, the two lovers are buffeted by the 'warring winds' of hurricanes upon tempestuous seas for eternity. The subject had long fascinated Watts, along with many other nineteenth-century artists, including John Flaxman, Ary Scheffer and Rossetti (see no.30 and Staley 1978, p.86). He painted several versions from as early as the 1840s when he was a young man in Italy. Indeed the years from 1843 to 1847 allowed him to submerge himself in Italian art and culture and here his personal affinity with Dante's epic poem deepened. The remarkable Italian Baroque frame, which the painting probably had from the outset (now removed), bore witness to the creation of the composition in Italy and underlined the homage to Italian culture.

The three earlier oil versions of the subject (see

Loshak 1963) went to contemporary exhibitions and were eventually sold. Watts exhibited this, the definitive version of the picture, at the Grosvenor Gallery in 1879. He had begun it around 1872, working on it for some years. Between 1879 and Watts's retrospective in 1881–2, he continued to work on it until it travelled to New York in 1884 when he considered it one of only two works that were 'finally finished'. It appeared in exhibitions constantly throughout the 1880s and 1890s and formed part of Watts's personal display in the Little Holland House Gallery. In 1883, Watts sent the painting, along with others, to the exhibition of international art at the Georges Petit Gallery where it was seen by Huysmans among others. The appearance of *Paolo and Francesca* in Paris lends it particular significance as a work that encouraged the taste for death-related imagery in French art circles.

BB

George Frederic Watts 1817–1904

49 **Chaos** *c.*1873–82, reworked later

Oil on canvas 106.7 × 304.8 (42 × 120)

Prov: Collection of the artist (on view at the Little Holland House Gallery); given to the Tate Gallery as part of the Watts Gift 1897

Exh: Alpine Club 1894 (50); New Gallery 1896 (148)

Lit: Spielmann 1886, p.4 and list p.30 as 'large picture in the collection of the artist'; Macmillan 1903, pp.193–4; Barrington 1905, pp.93, 131–2; MS. Cat. I, p.25; Watts 1912, I, pp.101–2, 105, 275, 301–3; II, p.105; Staley 1978, no.23 (Watts Gallery version)

Tate Gallery. Presented by the artist 1897

The sprawling composition of *Chaos* shows scenes in which turmoil contrasts with graceful movement and comparative calm. Reading the long horizontal progression from the left, the observer is first plunged into cataclysmic activity. Faceless giants battle with the forces of nature against the background of a raging fire. The contortions of the nude figures echo the upheaval of the land masses and rocky outcrops. This fragmentation of the earth's surface gives way, in the middle of the composition, to a watery setting beyond which are distant mountains bathed in light. A lone figure pushes himself upward from the sea; no longer fighting, he seems to suggest survival. In the third phase of the composition, a chain of female figures fly across the space while above a group of massive giants rest on an elevated plain removed from the realm of action to a more contemplative zone.

The ideas behind *Chaos* date from the years around 1850 when Watts formulated one of his grandest conceptions: to paint a series of murals representing 'the progress of cosmos', which he also considered as a 'history of the world' (on this project, eventually called The House of Life, see Staley 1978, pp.80–1). The first finished composition, *The Titans*, painted during the 1860s, showed just the right portion of *Chaos*; by the early 1870s, Watts had worked on the expanded design which included what we see in the long horizontal format of the small study in the Fitzwilliam Museum, Cambridge, the large unfinished oil in the Watts Gallery, Compton, and this finished version (as well as the later, smaller, finished work in the Walker Art Gallery, Liverpool; see Morris 1996, pp.466–7), all of which are essentially the same in conception. The version in the Watts Gallery he left unfinished on the advice of his friends and fellow artists Burne-Jones and Leighton. Around 1873, he began no.49, which was probably laid in by his young studio assistant, Matthew Ridley Corbet (1850–1902), later a landscape painter. From the mid-1880s onward, finished large versions of *Chaos* appeared at public exhibitions, though it is not clear which version went to New York. It was, however, probably the Tate's painting which Watts sent to the Alpine Club's exhibition in 1894, at a time when he was readying this version for his planned bequest. Interestingly, in this context, the painting was seen as 'an example of the place of mountains in the poetry of art'.

In the long course of the evolution of the composition, Watts used a series of plaster maquettes to study the vigorous poses of the key figures (see no.50). A recent cleaning of *Chaos* has revealed much more of the vivid colour and handling, ranging from passages of great delicacy to broader, eye-catching areas of paint applied with the palette knife.

Although one can deduce much from the action depicted in *Chaos*, a clearer understanding of Watts's intentions is available from his comments on the subject, and those of writers with whom he was in close contact. Watts wrote that *Chaos* was 'intended to be the introductory chapter of a general history of mankind'. In 1884, the catalogue for the exhibition in New York contained an extended description (reprinted in Barrington 1905, pp.131–3 and Staley 1978, p.81) which identifies the upheaval of the earliest moments of 'our planet' passing to a 'vaporous uncertainty of atmosphere, of unborn creatures' until the figure emerging from the 'swollen tides marks the beginning of the strides of time'. The final section shows 'colossal forms ... symbols of mountain ranges' with the chain of flying figures showing the now 'continuous stream' of time. According to Mrs Watts, Watts preferred the title *Chaos Passing to Cosmos*, as more indicative of his real meaning. Here indeed Watts created what might almost be looked upon as a Darwinian landscape, with the stages in pre-history visualised, not by a scientist, but an artist. Indeed, *Chaos* becomes an even more powerful statement when seen as a landscape of evolution, filled with cataclysm and eventual calm.

By the 1890s, when Watts's work could be seen in the new context of Symbolism, he himself seems to have refined his thoughts on *Chaos*. In the catalogue for the retrospective at the New Gallery in 1896, immediately prior to his bequest to the nation, he explained: 'The intention of this picture is to convey in the language of symbol an idea of the passing of our planet from chaos to order'. Observers of the 1890s may well have been more open to the conjunction of the contrasting imagery of the apocalyptic horror of chaos with the heavenly calm of flowing time.

BB

George Frederic Watts 1817–1904

50 Four Maquettes for 'Chaos'
late 1860s–1870s

Plaster casts, height varying from 10–15 (4–5⅞)
Prov: Studio collection of the artist
Exh: FAS 1968 (181, ?182)
Lit: [On Watts's sculpture in general: Gutch 1968, pp.693–9]; Read 1982, p.273

Trustees of the Watts Gallery

These plasters, cast from clay or wax figures, relate directly to *Chaos* (no.49), and were presumably used by Watts as he carried out the composition. He probably modelled the original clay or wax figures as studies for four of the most prominent of the struggling titans: one, Atlas-like, forces his back against a crushing rock; one arches upward echoing the earth's upheaval; and another figure, like a tortured river-god, writhes in anguish. These quickly modelled figures vividly convey the cataclysmic activity denoting the earth's formation. The fourth one, seen in the middle of the composition, is the figure 'in the swollen tides [who] marks the beginning of the strides of time' (described in the New York 1884 catalogue). The full composition and large versions of *Chaos* probably date from *c*.1870 and after. One visitor to the artist's studio in 1870 described a painting with 'recumbent gigantic figures typifying the mountains which arose in the progress of the making of the earth' – a group which can be seen on the right-hand side. It seems it was not until after this

50

time that, as Watts expanded the composition, the area of cataclysm and upheaval took shape. In studying the extreme actions of the 'period of violence' (described in the catalogue of New York 1884), he had recourse to these small models. As a major work on a large scale, *Chaos* had, according to Watts, 'fifty figures in it, perhaps more' and he carried out much careful study of these maquettes which are approximately the same size as the actual figures in the painting.

Such models served a particular purpose in the studio, but Watts obviously kept them on, using them for the several versions of *Chaos* painted in the 1880s, and eventually casting them in plaster. His use of such clay studies certainly dates from the 1860s and probably from as early as the 1850s (see no.78). Early training with a sculptor, close study of the Elgin marbles, and his own work as a sculptor from the 1840s onward led him naturally to seeing his painted compositions in sculptural terms. These models and others from later in his career (see Gutch 1968, illus. 62) reveal the artist's dependence on the physical reality of the human body in action when painting complicated poses within large multi-figure compositions. Such studio survivals indicate that the artist valued them as successful studies of the human form *in extremis*, struggling with forces beyond control.

Watts's maquettes can also be seen as part of the tradition of small-scale, hand-held sculptures, quickly executed and valued for their spontaneity, as in the terracottas of Nollekens or Banks in the late eighteenth century. This tradition carried on and was particularly strong among the Holland Park artistic community. Watts greatly admired Leighton's small sculptural 'sketches' in clay (Barrington 1905, p.198), and particularly deplored the loss (in the course of bronze casting) of the plaster group of sleeping women for Leighton's *Cymon and Iphigenia*, a sinuous study of entwined female forms (Stephen Jones noted that Leighton gave this work to Watts, see RA 1996, no.89, pp.199–200). Watts owned the tiny study for *An Athlete Wrestling with a Python* (Leighton House, London), considering it 'the most beautiful thing he possessed', according to Mrs Barrington (1905, pp.201–2). The energetic figure of the *Athlete* in the full-scale bronze of 1877 (Tate Gallery), worked on at the same time as *Chaos*, can be seen as a near relation of Watts's own vigorous, struggling titans.

The maquettes for *Chaos* are studio survivals of a special order. They illuminate the working process and underline Watts's commitment to the human body as a vehicle for expressing ideas. The sheer energy displayed in the small models gives an indication of Watts's appeal to an emerging generation of sculptors.

BB

GEORGE FREDERIC WATTS 1817–1904

51 **Love and Death** *c.*1874–7; reworked until 1887

Oil on canvas 248.9 × 116.8 (98 × 46)

Prov: Collection of the artist (on view at Little Holland House Gallery); presented by Watts to the Whitworth Art Gallery, Dec. 1887

Exh: Grosvenor Gallery 1877 (23); Paris 1878 (267); Grosvenor Gallery 1881 (135); St Jude's, Whitechapel 1883 (137); New York 1884 (115); Birmingham 1885 (114); Liverpool 1885; St Jude's, Whitechapel 1886 (216); South Kensington Museum *c.*1886–7; Manchester 1887 (253); Munich 1893 (1642); New Gallery 1905 (66); Manchester 1905 (50); Edinburgh 1905 (62); Dublin 1906 (37); Munich 1979 (381)

51

Lit: Colvin 1877, p.824; Carr 1877, p.265 (included in Carr 1878, pp.3–4); Chesneau 1887, pp.265–7; Spielmann 1886, engraving p.3, p.21 (including sonnet by Henry Norman), cat. p.31; Cartwright 1896, p.10; Sizeranne 1898, pp.92–3, 100 et seq. *Manchester Guardian*, 24 Dec. 1887; Barrington 1905, pp.92–3, 102–7, 112–19; Chesterton 1905, pp.140–3; MS. Cat. I, p.88; Watts 1912, I, pp.210–12, 280, 254, 307, 314, 323–4; II, pp.49, 86–7, 105–9; Staley 1978, no.20; Bryant 1996, pp.109–21, pl.60

The Whitworth Art Gallery, University of Manchester

Love and Death, one of Watts's best-known and most original works, evolved throughout the 1870s, resulting in the prime large-scale version exhibited at the landmark opening of the Grosvenor Gallery in 1877. Although the artist had shown two versions before, this painting was the culmination of earlier efforts, and represents a major statement in what Watts considered the 'Symbolical' mode (see Bryant 1987 and p.65).

The draped figure of Death, a ghostly white-grey, advances toward the open doorway of what was eventually identified as the 'House of Life'. The youth, Love, a cupid with massive wings, attempts to resist the monumental figure of Death as she steps upward, trampling the vines of roses which grow around the door. Scattered petals hint at the imminent loss of life. A dove, supposedly the waiting playmate of Cupid, appears for the first time in the lower corner of the scene in this version (and at least one critic felt it was a mistake that was 'not helpful to the dignity of the composition'; Colvin 1877, p.824).

Watts's first substantive comments about *Love and Death* occurred in 1874 while writing to an interested patron upon the exhibition in Manchester of the second version (Bristol City Art Gallery). The artist explained:

> Love is not restraining Death for it could not do so. I wished to suggest the passionate though unavailing struggle to avert the inevitable. You know my great desire to use such talents as I may have and such experience in art as I have been able to acquire, with the object of proving that Art, like Poetry and Music may suggest the noblest and tenderest thoughts, inspiring and awakening, if only for a time, the highest sensibilities of our nature …
>
> (Watts to Charles Rickards, 27 Dec. 1874, Watts 1912, I, pp.283–4).

The triumphant appearance of *Love and Death* at the Grosvenor Gallery, with a star position in the main room, revealed to a select London audience

Watts's confidence in essaying a new category of art, one which he himself characterised a few years later as 'poems painted on canvas' (see Bryant 1996). It attracted many accolades, completely confirming his decision to paint his 'symbolical suggestions' on a large scale. William Michael Rossetti, a critic attuned to Aesthetic trends, hailed the work as 'a majestic one, in which the author's highest powers have been worthily exercised' (*Academy*, 16 June 1877, p.396). Another post-Pre-Raphaelite, F.G. Stephens, placed it 'among the noblest works of our time'. He further commented that while most other paintings in the exhibition, such as Burne-Jones's *Days of Creation* (Fogg Art Museum, Harvard) suffered 'chromatic extinction', Watts's *Love and Death* with its 'strong deep tones and simple pictorial scheme' (*Athenaeum*, 5 May 1877, p.584) could be seen to advantage glowing out from dark crimson damask.

The young Oscar Wilde turned a poet's eye on *Love and Death* in one of his early forays into art criticism. Looking more closely than most reviewers, he read the details for meaning. To Wilde the marble doorway was not just overgrown with vines, but with 'white-starred jasmine and sweet briar-rose'. He noticed the little dove waiting 'for her playmate', but could also convey the terror felt by Love as Death 'Medusa-like ... turns all it looks upon to stone'. It was exactly in such ambiguous details as the face of Death that the artist allowed his observers to contribute their own readings.

On the occasion of the Grosvenor Gallery exhibition in 1881 (see Bryant 1996, pp.126–8), the artist himself provided a key text for *Love and Death*:

> Love stands upon the threshold of the House of Life barring the entry against the fatal advance of Death. The bright wings of the god are already crushed and broken against the lintel of the door, and the petals are falling from the roses that Love has set around the porch. The pale form of Death presses inward with calm resistless tread, and the white uplifted arm passes above the head of Love in token of sovereignty.

Concerned that his paintings should have the impact of poetry, Watts called attention to several aspects of the composition and a range of details. Particularly disturbing (yet easy for the viewer to miss) are the crushed wings of Love, forced against the door and broken, as Death progresses. The fallen rose petals foreshadow Death's advance into the 'House of Life'. But for artists and aesthetes, passages of painting in which drapery is elaborately wrought into folds, falling stream-like over rocks, take on a life of their own. The subtle gradations from white to grey suggest shared concerns with Whistler, the master of tonal values. The sheer monumentality of the life-size figures, sculptural in their solidity, had no equal in contemporary English painting, but related more directly to the conventions of funerary monuments and tomb sculpture (Dorment 1978, pp.47–8). The impact of simplified design and massive figures set the stage for a whole series of paintings on the theme of death in Watts's oeuvre (see no.123). The ambitious ideas he sought to convey were instantly seen as his own high-minded contribution to contemporary painting. Yet the artist also evoked an atmosphere of mystery and of the unknown which were to have greater repercussions on the Continent.

It was not until 1884 that the specific inspiration for *Love and Death* was revealed. For the exhibition in New York, Mrs Barrington assisted Watts in preparing the catalogue. Her text was the result of long discussions with the artist. The entry for *Love and Death* adds a level of meaning to the painting: 'The idea of this picture first came to the artist's mind about fifteen years ago. He was then painting the portrait of a man who, while still young, and showing every promise of becoming one of the most distinguished men of his time, was attacked by a lingering and fatal illness' (New York 1884, p.42). This young man was William Schomberg Kerr, 8th Marquess of Lothian (1832–1870), who had married Lady Constance Talbot in the 1850s. Watts, a close friend of Lady Constance, came to admire Lord Lothian's fortitude in the face of his debilitating disease, from which he eventually died in his late thirties. Watts exhibited the first version of *Love and Death* late in 1870, only a few months after Lothian's long-anticipated death. While not a memorial to the deceased, its association with the loss of a specific person lent its imagery of death an even greater resonance.

Love and Death appeared at exhibition almost continuously for ten years, with Watts never failing to miss any opportunity to put this 'one of the most important things I can do and shall ever do' before an audience. As the key painting by Watts shown in Paris in 1878, its historical importance in launching the artist's reputation in France (see pp.65–6) remains unchallenged. In 1884, F.G. Stephens called it Watts's masterpiece and in many ways this statement is still true.

BB

George Frederic Watts 1817–1904

52 Mammon: Dedicated to his Worshippers 1884–5

Oil on canvas 182.9 × 106 (72 × 41¾)

Prov: As no.49

Exh: Birmingham 1885 (161); South Kensington Museum *c*.1886; ?Melbourne 1888–9 (42); Paris 1889 (164); South Kensington Museum, *c*.1890–1; New Gallery 1896 (141)

Lit: Spielmann 1886, pp.15, 21–2, 31 including a line engraving; Sizeranne 1898, pp.87, 94; Macmillan 1903, pp.194–6; Chesterton 1904, pp.108–13, 115; Watts 1912, II, p.149; Tate Gallery 1954 (65) and Whitechapel 1974 (37)

Tate Gallery. Presented by the artist 1897

Watts painted *Mammon* as an entirely new subject for his own collection. It sums up many of his concerns at this stage in his career. With forthright clarity, its indisputable message cannot be denied and is enhanced by the nearly life-size scale of the work. The word 'Mammon', in origin Aramaic for riches, can be defined as wealth elevated to the position of an idol, amounting to an evil influence. In medieval times, the word was used as the proper name for the demon of covetousness. Throughout Watts's own writings, one finds many of the ideas which fed into *Mammon*. In 1880, Watts wrote in his article 'The Present Conditions of Art' (see p.72) about contemporary life: 'Modern habits of investigation have sapped unquestioning faith, and have not supplied anything more consoling. Material prosperity has become our real god, but we are surprised to find that the worship of this visible deity does not make us happy' (reprinted in Watts 1912, III, p.166). *Mammon* follows a few years after these remarks as a visualisation of Watts's firmly held belief in the evil of accruing money for its own sake.

Mammon is enthroned, like an ancient king, but further consideration reveals his grotesque physical appearance and his heartless cruelty. He crushes a youth under one foot; while a beautiful girl collapses under his massive fist. These figures, clearly emblematic of youth, innocence and beauty, appear lifeless and inert. Mammon, colossal in scale by comparison, sits in full glory with his 'gorgeous but ill-fitting golden draperies, which fall awkwardly about his coarse limbs' (Spielmann 1886, p.21). Moneybags fill his ample lap. In the oil study (Watts Gallery, Compton), Mammon is also characterised by his bandaged, gouty foot, another sign of his indulgence in luxuries, and further transforming him into a malformed monster.

Watts consciously manipulated art-historical conventions to heighten the impact of the picture. The format, with a nearly full-scale figure seated against a curtained background, calls to mind the tradition of the grand manner portrait, chiefly associated with masters of this genre in the late eighteenth century. In the case of *Mammon*, expectations are confounded: instead of an established worthy or famous beauty, the artist instead presents an object of disgust and horror seated on a throne decorated with skulls. The glimpse behind the curtained background reveals not a peaceful landscape garden or estate, but a view of fire and destruction.

Mammon's headgear is a clear reference to the 'Midas-eared Mammonism' excoriated by Carlyle in *Past and Present* (see p.29). It consists of a crown circled with upended gold coins, with ass's ears affixed to each side. It carries several iconographic meanings of its own, usually referring to ignorance and stupidity. Ovid's *Metamorphoses* told the story of King Midas, whose touch turned everything to gold, to whom Apollo gave ass's ears because he did not respond the music of the lyre. A link with Midas underlined Watts's message about the evils of wealth. There was also a saying current in the nineteenth century, 'King Death hath asses' ears', from *Death's Jest Book* of 1850 by Thomas Lovell Beddoes, which also relates to and enhances the meaning of *Mammon*.

The best-known reference to Mammon in literature appeared in Spenser's *Faerie Queene*, book II, canto 7, when Sir Guyon discovers the cave of Mammon, the treasure-house, or 'house of Richesse', of the god of wealth. Watts had frequently turned to Spenser's work, as, for example, in the various versions of *Britomart*. Spenser's lines characterise Mammon as bearing long claw-like nails and as tanned by soot from the blacksmith's forge, a detail one can link with the smoke in the Watts's painting. In his lap, Mammon carried a mass of gold coins and around him were great heaps of gold with which he tried to tempt the good knight.

The subtitle of the painting – *Dedicated to his Worshippers* – suggests other meanings for the work. Mrs Watts recorded that the artist would often preach against Mammon-worship, once saying 'Holy Mammon – Divine Respectability – Sacred Dividend'. He told the artist Briton Rivière, a good friend, that 'he was going to propose to one of our sculptors to make a statue of Mammon, that it might be set up in Hyde Park, where he hoped his worshippers would be at least honest enough to bow the knee publicly to him' (Watts 1912, II, p.149). As a sculptor himself, Watts may well have intended carrying out this idea; indeed the subtitle to the painting is like an inscription on a monument. A public monument would have had the advantage of being seen by an audience even wider than those attending fine art exhibitions.

In 1889, *Mammon* appeared as part of a group of nine works sent to the Universal Exhibition and of all of these works, including *Hope* (see fig.35 on p.65), *The Judgement of Paris* and *Love and Life* (Musée d'Orsay, Paris), *Mammon* presented the most disturbing vision. Recalling that Sizeranne identified the exhibition of 1889 as a defining moment when the Symbolists seized upon the works of Watts and Burne-Jones (see pp.76–7), it must surely have been the imagery of cruelty, destruction and evil in *Mammon* that appealed to the more extreme members of French decadent circles.

BB

Gustav Klimt 1862–1918

53 **Idyll** 1884

Oil on canvas 49.7 × 74 (19⅝ × 29⅛)
Inscribed 'IDYLLE' lower left, and 'G.K.1884.' lower right

Exh: Vienna 1896 (155); Zurich 1992 (G4; repr. p.79)
Lit: Novotny and Dobai 1967, no.19; Waissenberger 1984, p.90, pl.8; Whitford 1990, pp.41, 50, pl.29

Museen der Stadt Wien

EXHIBITED IN LONDON ONLY

This decorative panel was painted in response to a commission from the Viennese publisher Martin Gerlach to contribute to a series of designs issued in three portfolios over the period 1882–1900 illustrating 'Allegories and Emblems'. Klimt had already produced one such painting for it, *Fable*, in 1883, and was to execute another, *Love*, in 1895 (Novotny and Dobai 1967, nos.18, 68). The latter is very much of its moment, with bold gilt borders imposing an appearance of abstract rigour on a central image of mistily suggested lovers. The *Fable* is a work still in the idiom of the mid century, while *Idyll* occupies an interesting transitional position in Klimt's output.

Although this is not a large work it is conceived on a grand scale. Its architectural qualities are explained by Klimt's activities at this date, with his brother Ernst and a colleague from the Vienna Kunstgewerbeschule, Franz Matsch, as a designer of decorations for public buildings in different parts of the Austro-Hungarian Empire. The central roundel showing a happy mother and her two infant children (a scene from the Golden Age, perhaps) is conventional, in an academic late neo-Classical style. The larger-scale supporting figures, free adaptations of

53

Michelangelo's Sistine *ignudi*, belong to the later nineteenth-century world in which the nude was being reinvestigated for its more abstruse expressive value. The inward, meditative expressions of the youths are significant here. Christoph Doswald (Zurich 1992, p.79) points out that the background belongs to yet another aesthetic world, foreshadowing Klimt's *Jugendstil* period. However, the immediate inspiration for the organised tangle of jasmine against which the figures are placed seems to be the decorative work that Burne-Jones was producing for William Morris in the 1870s and 1880s, and the patterned 'frame' is likewise strongly reminiscent of Morris's border designs. Burne-Jones's *Briar Rose* subjects of 1870 and later are also relevant. There is no evidence of any direct influence, but the growing international reputation of Burne-Jones, and indeed of Morris, in the 1880s would make some connection possible if not likely.

AW

54

Gustave Moreau 1826–1898

54 **Oedipe Voyageur (L'Egalité devant la mort)** *c.*1888

Oil on canvas 148 × 117 (58¼ × 46⅛)
Inscribed 'Gustave Moreau' b.l.

Exh: Zurich 1986 (100); Rome 1996 (33, lists further exh.)
Prov: Bt from the artist by Antony Roux 1888
Lit: Mathieu 1976, no.358; Bittler and Mathieu 1983, no.2414

La Cour d'Or-Musées de Metz

The art of Gustave Moreau as it evolved up to 1880 was a major force in the creation of Symbolism in painting. During Moreau's reclusive studio existence, academic training and the legacy of Classical literature gave way to oils and watercolours inspired by his solitary visions, often verging on nightmares, best exemplified in a work like *Salome Dancing before Herod* (fig.1 on p.15). Contemporary writers discovered parallels between Moreau's work and the dreamy images of Burne-Jones. As Claude Phillips pointed out in his key article on Moreau of 1885 (*Magazine of Art*, p.231), in France Burne-Jones was styled 'le Gustave Moreau Anglais' and later Léonce Bénédite devoted an entire book to *Deux Idealistes: Gustave Moreau et E. Burne-Jones* (1899). Yet in his obsession with Death, as in *Young Man and Death* 1865 (Fogg Art Museum, Harvard) in which Death is embodied as a benign angel, in his deep pessimism, and in his self-conscious view of himself as an artist (in creating a studio museum for posterity), Moreau displayed a far more revealing kinship with Watts, another father-figure to the younger Symbolists. When Moreau's art returned to the public domain in the 1880s, with works at the Salon and attendant critical reaction by writers such as Huysmans, a commission for illustrations to the fables of La Fontaine from Antony Roux (his patron and the purchaser of no.54) and their exhibition at Goupil's, the stage was set for the maturity of Symbolism.

In *Oedipe Voyageur* Moreau completely reworked the subject of his early masterpiece *Oedipus and the Sphinx* (Metropolitan Museum of Art, New York), exhibited at the Salon in 1864. He presents an overtly Symbolist version of the subject, with the Sphinx's dead victims scattered across a fantastical cavernous space amid bizarre rock formations haunted by scavenging birds.

The story of Oedipus, son of the king of Thebes, occurs in Greek legends and in the tragedies of Sophocles and Euripides. The oracle predicts that any son of the king will kill his father, so when Oedipus is born his mother, Jocasta, sends him to be exposed on a mountain. He survives, is adopted and lives in Corinth, but, eventually questioning his background, he consults the oracle of Delphi who announces that he will murder his father and marry his mother. Terrified, he resolves not to return to the home he knew, and thus begin his travels, during which he unknowingly meets and slays Laius, his real father. On arriving at Thebes, Oedipus presents himself to the Sphinx. The Sphinx asks riddles of all those who pass and devours those who fail to solve them. In particular it asks 'What walks on four feet, two feet and then three?'

The Sphinx, a horrific composite creature formed from the parts of a woman, a lion, a snake and an eagle, is the dominant motif in Moreau's painting. In contrast to his work of the 1860s, in which the Sphinx accosts the calm and academically studied form of Oedipus, *Oedipe Voyageur* instead dwells on the bloodlust of the Sphinx with Oedipus himself a supplicant at the altar of death. Relegated to the edge of the scene, he droops his head like a weary traveller or pilgrim, appearing no match for the exultant Sphinx. Although the story was familiar enough for observers to know the outcome: that Oedipus solves the riddle (the answer being man, who as a baby crawls on all fours, then walks on two legs, but ends up by leaning on a stick), this solution is hardly touched on by the artist in his vision of carnage, which is as lovingly painted as a bejewelled still-life.

In *Oedipe Voyageur* the artist fulfils the lines of Huysmans who, in *A Rebours* (1884), as the character of des Essientes, speaks of Moreau: 'His sad and scholarly works breathed a strange magic, an incantatory charm which stirred you to the depths of your being ... so that you were left amazed and pensive, disconcerted by this art which crossed the frontiers of painting to borrow from the writer's art its most subtly evocative suggestions, from the enameller's art its most wonderfully brilliant effects, from the lapidary's and etcher's art its most exquisitely delicate touches' (transl. Robert Baldick v, pp.69–70).

Knowledge of Moreau as the quintessential Symbolist filtered through to an English audience initially via his appearance in the first Grosvenor Gallery exhibition (see Bryant 1996, pp.120–1) and even more in the following decade through articles such as that of Phillips in the *Magazine of Art* in 1885 which focused on his 'peculiar melancholy'. Moreau's legacy to the Symbolist canon of subjects with his disturbing studies of fatal women or female monsters reached out to a new generation (see no.102).

BB

Pierre Puvis de Chavannes 1824–1898

55 **Death and the Maidens** 1872

Oil on canvas 146 × 105 (57½ × 41⅜)
Inscribed 'P. Puvis de Chavannes 1872', lower right

Prov: Galerie Durand-Ruel, Paris by 1873; Catholina Lambert by 1894; Scott Fowles, New York; M. Knoedler & Co., New York; bt Robert Sterling Clark 1918, whose collection became a museum in 1955

Exh: New York 1894 (12); New York 1923 (42); Williamstown 1955 (54); Toronto 1975 (17); Paris and Ottawa 1976 (93, repr. p.120)

Lit: Silvestre 1873, p.26; Silvestre 1887, p.3; Riordan 1891, p.34; Jouin 1897, p.48; Alexandre 1905; Phythian 1908, p.224; Michel and Laran 1911, pp.51–2; Mauclair 1928, pp.13, 116

Sterling and Francine Clark Art Institute, Williamstown, Massachusetts

EXHIBITED IN LONDON ONLY

The subject of this painting derives from traditional iconography. The juxtaposition of youth and a bearded old man accompanied by a scythe represents the fragility of man's temporal existence. Variants of the theme include a skull as *memento mori* in a *vanitas* still life or a confrontation between a young man and the shrouded figure of Death, as in paintings by both

Moreau and Watts (see no.51). However, Puvis has introduced certain significant modifications, not least the inclusion of a number of young girls, in place of the one recorded in the Claudius poem which served as the text for a song by Schubert (D531; 1817) 'Der Tod und das Mädchen' (later used in the Quartet D810 [1824]). An immediate model for this *dramatis* personae is Burne-Jones's *Green Summer* (fig.23 on p.40), which itself depends on Millais's *Spring* (*Apple Blossoms*) of 1856–9 (Lady Lever Art Gallery, Port Sunlight).

The group of carefree young girls in the upper left of the composition contrasts significantly with the two more pensive girls in the lower right. Not only does the maiden carrying flowers in her skirt move towards the recumbent figure of the old man but her flowers are echoed in the pile of cut blooms that rest beside the old man's scythe. That the message of the painting is one of imminent tragedy is conveyed not only in the descent of the maiden towards the figure of Death but also in the contrast established between the two maidens and the sombre backdrop of the wood, considered by Puvis as early as 1864 as indicative of a disturbing presence: 'The word, forest, does not only describe a group of trees, young or old, but should also make one shudder' (Paris and Ottawa 1976, p.118). The spring-like meadow, the juxtaposition of Youth and Old Age, and the downward passage of the central girl also make reference to the Persephone myth in which the daughter of Ceres, goddess of summer, is permitted to ascend to Earth from the realm of Pluto, god of the Underworld, but once a year. Her return to the Underworld heralds the end of spring and the arrival of summer.

While this modification to the established iconographic representation of the allegory of the fragility of man's temporal existence sets Puvis's painting within a wider movement in which artists sought to reinvent traditional mythologies, it has also been suggested by Aimee Brown Price that, given the date of the work, its particular treatment of the subject may also be a reference to the heedless disregard by the French nation of the threat posed by Prussia, which eventually led to the ignoble defeat of France in 1871. The search to provide a novel personification of events connected with the Franco-Prussian War was also explored by Puvis in two versions of his painting *Hope* 1872 (Walters Art Gallery, Baltimore, and Musée d'Orsay, Paris). In both works, Hope, represented by either a clothed or nude maiden holding a single olive branch, is seated in a barren landscape punctuated only by ruins and a cemetery. Compositional elements, a limited tonal range and a Classicised figure translate, as in *Death and the Maidens*, traditional allegory into a contemporary context.

MAS

The Symbolist Landscape

Although the figure was the obvious vehicle for the visual expression of ideas about human psychology, artists also turned to the natural world as a responsive context for human emotions. There was nothing new in this. Since the seventeenth century landscape painters had sought to relate their representations of natural phenomena to the dramatic situations of history and mythology. Now, just as the figure shed its traditional narrative associations, so the natural world became for the Symbolists the repository of a vast complex of inexplicit, shifting resonances, echoing emotional states or the workings of the unconscious.

Frederic Leighton's large *Clytie* of *c.*1890–2 (no.56) illustrates the use of myth in conjunction with landscape to investigate the workings of desire, with its contrast between the glowing cloud that fills the sky and the small figure of Clytie, hopelessly in love with the Sun-god. This clearly Symbolist work, with its vivid sense of nature as a personal experience, emerges out of Leighton's lifelong interest in the study of landscape, often by means of the oil sketch. In that preoccupation he was close to several contemporaries, notably, in England, William Blake Richmond, and in Italy, the group of artists in the (very loose and ill-defined) circle of Giovanni Costa (1827–1903) who became known as the Etruscans (see Stoke on Trent 1989). Leighton was an early member of the group, which included other English artists, among them George Heming Mason (1818–1872) and Matthew Ridley Corbet (1850–1902), and the American Elihu Vedder (see nos.64, 65). The Etruscans resist clear identification as a 'school', but they had in common a direct, intimate approach to nature, and a desire to distil an essence of the spiritual, the ineffable and the inspiring from the Italian countryside and the Mediterranean coast – places crowded with the unseen *dramatis personae* of long ages of history and legend. Richmond's *Near Via Reggio, where Shelley's Body Was Found* 1875 (no.58) is an exercise in this vein, ostensibly a simple view, but charged with the significance of a particular place with strong historical associations. Watts too was inspired to paint landscape in Italy, and although he remained aloof from the Etruscans adopted something of their visual language and choice of subject-matter.

Costa maintained close ties with England, and when the English Etruscans returned to their native land they set about creating a new type of landscape, concentrated yet understated, in which the gentler, quieter phenomena of nature are presented with an inward intensity that is belied by the restraint of colour and composition. Mason was one of the chief of these 'Idyllists', and we find, in the early 1870s, the great Millais himself adopting their themes and idioms in pictures like his *Flowing to the River* of 1871 (private collection, on loan to the Tate Gallery). Here too was the germ of a Symbolist landscape, though Idyllism, like the work of the Etruscans, was perhaps too understated to be counted strictly Symbolist itself. However, in the last years of his life Millais, like Leighton, took the step further that enabled him to produce a wholly Symbolist nature study, the extraordinary *Dew-drenched Furze* of 1892 (no.57). This goes beyond any mere careful record of a natural effect: its strange colour and bizarre detail suggest a heightened personal response to nature that is fraught with inner tensions.

FREDERIC, LORD LEIGHTON 1830–1896

56 **Clytie** *c.*1890–2

Oil on canvas 85.1 × 137.8 (33½ × 54¼)

Prov: The artist; the artist's sale, Christie's 11 and 13 July 1896 (114); C. Brinsley Marlay 1912; by whom bequeathed to Fitzwilliam Museum, Cambridge; on loan to Leighton House, London

Exh: RA 1892 (489); Manchester City Art Gallery 1892 (486); *Free Picture Exhibition* 1897; RA Winter 1897 (22); RA 1996 (110)

Lit: Ormond 1975, pp.120, 123, 127, 171; Newall 1990, p.128, pl.90

The Syndics of the Fitzwilliam Museum, Cambridge

EXHIBITED IN LONDON ONLY

Clytie – which is unlike any other painting by Leighton in its reduction of the relative scale of the figure to the overall setting – shows a diminutive figure, at the lower right corner of the composition, kneeling on a stone plinth beside an altar, with her arms outstretched towards the sun, which is setting at the distant horizon among a mass of towering cumulus clouds. The story represented is that given by Ovid in book IV of *Metamorphoses*, where the nymph Clytie was abandoned by her lover, the god Apollo. In her distress Clytie went out into the landscape to watch as Apollo drove the chariot of the sun across the sky each day, and gradually she was transformed into a plant – a heliotrope that turns its face to the sun – her limbs becoming the stems and leaves, and the draperies that spread out around her the roots.

The artist had had the subject in mind for a long period, and it was one that had a special association for him, as he recalled in a letter of 1892: 'I have myself a weakness for this picture, which I brewed for some 15 years' (see *Catalogue of Paintings*, Fitzwilliam Museum, Cambridge 1977, pp.152–3). Clearly Leighton found the Ovidian legend of Clyties's forlorn passion for the god of the sun particularly apposite, and one that allowed him to explore his own philosophical stance in symbolical terms. He was himself without conventional religious faith, but since the late 1860s, in paintings such as *Helios and Rhodos* (fig.28 on p.44), he had expressed his belief in the elemental power of the sun. However, if in his early career he had looked to represent the sun as a bringer of energy and fertility, here, in the last years of the painter's life, the sun is seen to be departing from mankind and thus denying its life-giving force. At the time of Leighton's death in 1896 he was working on a further painting of the present subject, showing the figure of Clytie on a monumental scale (private collection).

CSN

John Everett Millais 1829–1896

57 **Dew-drenched Furze** *c.*1889–90

Oil on canvas 172 × 122 (67¾ × 48)
Inscribed and dated 'JM 1890' in monogram

Prov: Bt by Everett Gray, Millais's brother-in-law; Mrs Sandars, 1898; Christie's, 27 May 1910 (82) (bt Obach); Miss Veronica MacEwen; Christie's; Julian Hartnoll 1978; from whom bt by Sir Ralph R. Millais, 3rd Bt; by descent to the present owner

Exh: New Gallery 1890 (119); RA Winter 1898 (97); Liverpool and RA 1967 (113);Southampton 1996 (237); Washington 1997 (14)

Lit: *Magazine of Art*, 1890, p.308, repr. p.305; *Art Journal*, 1890, p.218; Spielmann 1898, p.113; Millais 1899, II, pp.210–14, repr. p.295

The Geoffroy Richard Everett Millais Collection

Dew-drenched Furze was painted in Scotland in the autumn and winter of 1889–90. Millais's son described how the painter had that year gone up to Birnham Hall, the house on the River Tay that he rented from 1882 to 1891, for the shooting season and with the fixed determination 'not [to] look at his paints'. 'He stuck to his word until one fine day in November the potent voice of the wood spirits compelled him to change his mind. In the early morning the long grass bearded with dew lay at his feet, and all around were firs, bracken, and gorse bushes, festooned with silver webs, that showed a myriad diamonds glittering in the sun' (Millais 1899, pp.210–13). Quite different from the generality of Millais's late landscapes – which are gently descriptive of the familiar setting in which he and his family lived during their Scottish holidays – this painting represents an attempt to transcend the prosaic tendency of his art.

As Anne Helmreich has pointed out (Washington 1997, p.75), the title of the painting comes from Tennyson's 'In Memoriam' (1850). Millais had known Tennyson in the 1850s, and among the first paintings that he undertook after his departure from the principles of Pre-Raphaelitism is *Autumn Leaves* (fig.18 on p.36), a work that originated from his meditations on Tennyson's poetry. The second verse of section XI of 'In Memoriam' runs as follows: 'Calm and deep peace on this high wold, / And on these dews that drench the furze, / And all the silvery gossamers / That twinkle into green and gold'. Something of the poem's mood of equivocation between a rhapsody inspired by the beauty of nature and the perplexity and confusion induced by the enigma of natural creation is felt in Millais's painting. Tennyson despaired of understanding the physical world, but hoped at least for 'a calm despair'; while Millais seems to have attempted 'a scene such as had probably never been painted before, and might possibly prove to be unpaintable' (Millais 1899, p.213) as a refuge from the inevitable actuality of his portrait trade.

The originality and abstraction of the painting was appreciated when it was first exhibited. Spielmann feared that it might be 'well-nigh inexplicable ... but the desired effect is marvellously reproduced, while

58

the yellow-golden haze and russet-brown form a strange harmony, which grows upon the spectator' (*Magazine of Art*, 1890, p.308). The question of how landscape subjects might inspire sentiments of delight or regret was aired in the *Art Journal*, where it was concluded that 'the landscape painter no longer is ... the ardent nature worshipper', but vivifies 'the result of his observation with the sympathetic warmth and transforming power of his own emotion' (1890, p.218).

CSN

WILLAM BLAKE RICHMOND 1842–1921

58 Near Via Reggio, where Shelley's Body Was Found 1875

Oil on canvas 91.5 × 228.5 (36 × 90)
Prov: The artist; given by his sons to Manchester City Art Gallery 1924
Exh: RA 1876 (945); New Gallery 1900 (106) (as *Shore at Spezia, near Via Reggio, where Shelley's Body Was Found*); York 1989 (23, repr. in col.)
Lit: *The Academy*, 1876, p.519; Reynolds 1995, p.112, fig.40

Manchester City Art Galleries

Richmond's awesome canvas *Near Via Reggio* shows the shore and coastline of Tuscany, with the Carrara mountains forming the horizon to the north. As is implied by the title, the painting was intended as a memorial to the English poet Percy Bysshe Shelley, who in the last months of his life had lived an isolated existence at Lérici, and who was drowned in August 1822 when his small boat was wrecked in a storm off the coast as he returned from a visit to Byron and Leigh Hunt at Leghorn. His body was burnt on a pyre on the shore. When the painting was first exhibited, at the Royal Academy in 1876, critics recognised the 'half-naked man bronzed almost to blackness ... advancing upward from the sea-beach, carrying a burden of faggots; intended probably to lead the mind on to the idea of Shelley's funeral-pyre, without, however, strictly representing anything belonging to those events which invest the coast of Via Reggio with so tragic and so sublime an interest' (W.M. Rossetti, *The Academy*, 1876, p.519).

Shelley was revered by all those who loved Italy, as he had done, and who believed in that country's right to be free of foreign domination. His most famous work, the lyrical drama *Prometheus Unbound* (1820), presents a benign Prometheus-Lucifer figure who triumphs over the forces of tyranny on behalf of the oppressed. Also remembered in the Victorian period was Shelley's pantheistic 'The Triumph of Life', unfinished at his death, and the melancholy 'Lines Written in the Bay of Lerici'. Richmond had first turned to the works of Shelley with his painting *Prometheus Bound* (previously Birmingham City Art Gallery; deaccessioned 1960; untraced), of 1874.

That this part of Italy was associated in the Victorian imagination with the Romantic poet is demonstrated by the Revd Stopford Brooke's account of a supernatural event that he witnessed there:

> I went to Viareggio, to see the place where Shelley's body was burned. That too was

romantic enough to satisfy me ... One little cottage was near, and the woman came out and brought me with the most delightful and interested talk to the very spot where the Inglese, as they called Shelley, was burned ... The mountains, which press down too close and too high to the shore, were fortunately half concealed by huge storm-clouds pressing up against their flanks and breaking into white vapour above their peaks. I saw the ghost of Shelley flitting by in a drift of mist, and his eyes were soft and burning. 'I am now,' he cried, 'a creature of the earth and water, and the nursling of the sky.' 'Alas,' I said, 'why? But perhaps that is best.' 'Yes, that is best,' he said, and the thin fleece in which he was melted in the sun.

(Lawrence Pearsall Jacks, *Life and Letters of Stopford Brooke*, 1917, II, pp.521–2)

This idea of the Italian landscape as the setting for alarming and fateful events which had far-reaching if mysterious consequences, was impressed upon Richmond by the Italian painter and patriot Giovanni Costa, with whom Richmond had first made painting expeditions into the Roman Campagna in the later 1860s. A landscape style which allowed the forms of nature to be simplified and abstracted and in which emphasis is given to the volumes of mountains, clouds and vegetation so as to lend pictorial drama to the compositions was adopted by Richmond as one of the leading figures of a small group of Costa's English followers, known to their contemporaries as 'The Etruscans'. Perhaps the painting by Costa which Richmond had in mind when he conceived *Near Via Reggio*, was *Scirocco Day* (private collection, Italy), which Costa finished at about the time Richmond painted *Near Via Reggio*. When the Revd Stopford Brooke bought *Scirocco Day* in 1879 he wrote of it in terms which would apply equally to Richmond's work: 'I like its unity of feeling; I like the way in which Nature herself seems to have been at work in it; and I like even more in it that which is beyond Nature's power to do, and which belongs to the artist alone. I like the old classic sadness in it, and the sadness, closer to us, of the poor man whose life and toil are a part of the nature about him, and with whom the trees sympathise' (Agresti 1904, p.171).

CSN

George Frederic Watts 1817–1904

59 **The Island of Cos** 1883

Oil on canvas 86.5 × 112 (34 × 44)
Inscribed 'G.F. Watts 1883' lower right

Prov: Sold by the artist to James Buchanan Mirrlees by 1888; by descent until 1905; ...; Christie's 11 Nov. 1949 (96); ...; Mr Stephens in 1961; ...; Sotheby's, 9 June 1994 (219); present owner

Exh: Birmingham 1885 (149); Nottingham 1886 (48); Glasgow 1888 (185); Newcastle 1905 (152)

Lit: Spielmann 1886, p.11; MS. Cat., I, p.79

Private Collection

EXHIBITED IN LONDON AND MUNICH ONLY

This version of *The Island of Cos*, dating from the early 1880s, is a reworking of an idea which inspired the artist on his travels around the Greek islands in 1855–6, some twenty-five years before. He first completed a small painting (private collection; Sotheby's, 8 June 1993, no.19, repr in col.) with the same title in the 1860s; its long horizontal composition shows the island appearing above a calm sea in which swim nude figures of nymphs.

In this later version, however, while the artist took the same point of departure – the mirage-like appearance of the island seen through the limpid warm air of the Mediterranean – he instead contrasted it with the ruins of an ancient building. The massive fragment of an Ionic capital, once part of a great temple, looms in the immediate foreground, an antique amputee now merging into the rocky shoreline. Upon it a butterfly has alighted. The meaning seems clear as we see the ruins of a past civilisation lying in heaps while the beauty of nature remains constant through time. The butterfly, a traditional symbol of the human soul, adds a further dimension which Watts himself explained to the eventual purchaser, James Mirrlees, in a letter of 27 December 1883 (Watts Papers):

> In my picture 'the Island of Cos' the unchanging serenity of sky and sea, unchanging and eternally serene as far as human influence extends! is in contrast with the decay of human efforts in the visible destruction of their triumphs. The butterfly hovering over these ruins is the emblem of that undying part of humanity which the religious enthusiast (no matter what creed) and the philosophers alike may accept – However little [?]there may be ... to certify respecting the spiritual side of man's nature and However little I may be satisfied with any explanations of the unknown that have been [?]formed, a base materialism does not recommend itself to me.

Despite such a thought-provoking exegesis Watts entitled it simply *The Island of Cos* as if determined to encourage a reading which rests at least in part on the actual place depicted.

In several of the early exhibitions of the work, a longer title appeared in the catalogues giving more information about its geographical position: *The Isle of Cos (Archipelago) between Greece and Turkey*. Later, in one of the memorial exhibitions, one could read that the island was destroyed by an earthquake during the Peloponnesian War, 431–404 BC. This piece of information did not seem to relate to the fact that the island was (and is) still very much in existence, now spelled Kos. Under the dominion of Turkey for most of the nineteenth century, it is situated not far off the coast of Asia Minor, nearly opposite Bodrum, the site of the ancient city of Halicarnassus which Watts had visited in company with Sir Charles Newton's expedition in 1856. This famous archeological dig, on behalf of the British Museum, unearthed a major group of late Hellenistic sculptures. For Watts this experience was in many ways a defining one, placing him in contact with antique remains, some retaining their original polychromy, in their original settings.

The composition is resolutely untraditional. There is no gentle recession into the picture space, nor any careful creation of a foreground area. Instead the ruins pile up on each side of the composition where the foreground should be, while the island in the background is so far away as to be virtually a vision. The comparatively empty area comprising most of the picture space is a clear invitation to melancholy speculation on the ultimate futility of man's achievements.

The butterfly, of course, is a conventional detail, and if one considers the artist's letter to his potential client, one almost wonders if it found its way into the painting simply to enhance its saleability. This seems possible when we recall that most of Watts's landscapes remained in his own collection. Perhaps it was the search for new patrons that resulted in his sending *The Island of Cos* to exhibition at the large gathering of his work which commemorated the opening of the museum in Birmingham, rather than to a venue in London.

BB

George Frederic Watts 1817–1904

60 After the Deluge: The Forty-First Day *c*.1885–91

Oil on canvas 105 × 179 (41⅜ × 70½)

Prov: Collection of the artist (on view at the Little Holland House Gallery)

Exh: ?St Jude's, Whitechapel 1886 (9, as *The Sun*); New Gallery 1891 (238); New Gallery 1896 (155); Manchester 1905 (70); Edinburgh 1905 (122); Dublin 1906 (22)

Lit: Spielmann 1886, cat. p.30; Spielmann 1891, p.260; Bayes *c*.1906, pp.vii, xi, pl.vi; MS. Cat., i, p.1; Watts 1912, ii, p.192

Trustees of the Watts Gallery

This first appeared at the New Gallery in 1891, though the work dates from *c*.1885 and in 1886 Spielmann referred to it as *Cessation of the Deluge*; later it became known as *After the Deluge*, with the addition of a subtitle, *A Reminiscence*, at the time of the memorial exhibitions. It is probably one of the artist's least-known works.

Watts's remarkably empty seascape is much larger than most of his landscapes. At the retrospective of the artist's works at the New Gallery in 1896, a quotation accompanied the painting: 'A transcendent power of light and heat bursts forth to recreate; darkness is chased away; the waters, obedient to the higher law, already disperse into vapoury mists and pass from the face of the earth.' These lines, not taken from the biblical account in Genesis, seem to be the artist's own version of the subject. Previously attracted by the story of the deluge, with its associations of punishment, divine intervention and salvation, Watts painted several compositions during the 1870s and 1880s (*The Dove that Returned not Again*, *Return of the Dove to the Ark*, and *Mount Ararat*). *After the Deluge* is, however, the most distant from its source, and

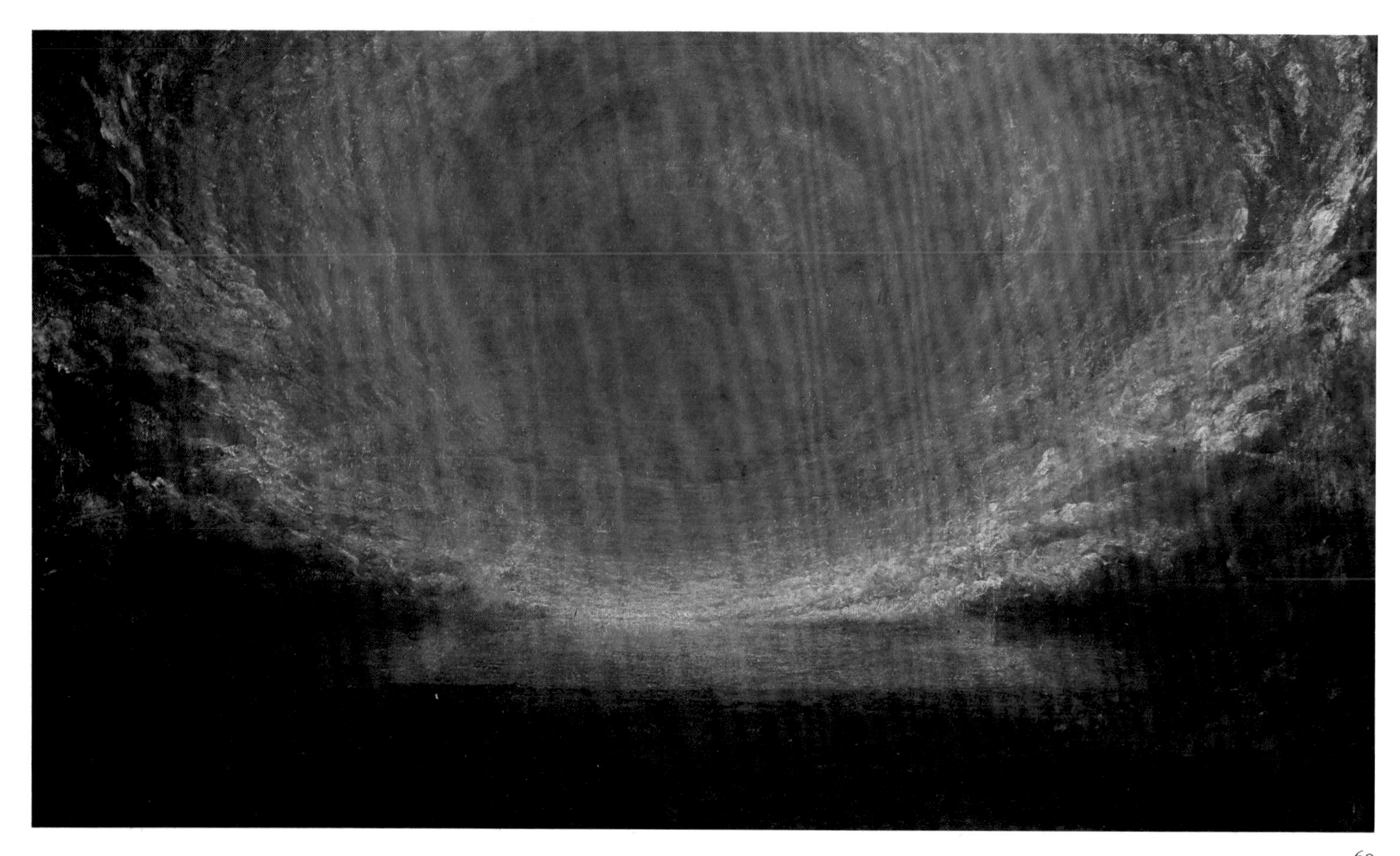

60

without any explanatory details. Instead it is simply an image of the sun setting, an explosion of colour and light. According to Mrs Watts, the artist commented to one observer concerning 'The hand of the Creator moving by light and by heat to recreate. I have not tried to paint a portrait of the sun – such a thing is unpaintable – but I wanted to impress you with the idea of its enormous power'. The all-powerful character of the sun can be translated into spiritual terms; yet the artist's preoccupation also allows the work to be seen as an almost abstract study of light.

In this respect the picture provides an insight into Watts's attitude to nature. As Walter Bayes noted, Watts retained a childlike wonder when observing natural forces, allowing himself to be carried away by moments of great beauty as in *Sunset on the Alps* (no.62). Unlike that painting, however, no.60 did not result from a specific, observed experience; rather the scene came straight from the artist's imagination. The painting is a powerful image linked in Watts's thinking with the biblical event.

In taking the sun as his prime subject, Watts invoked previous masters of such imagery, specifically, J.M.W. Turner. Watts greatly admired Turner, making regular visits to the National Gallery where he saw such works as *Dido Building Carthage*. This painting, and others by Turner and by his own inspiration, Claude Lorrain, were part of Watts's visual repertoire. In *After The Deluge: The Forty-First Day*, Watts exploded the image of the sun onto a far grander scale, with an accompanying glow of colour that marks it as a landscape of the end of the nineteenth century. Close in date to Watts, Vincent van Gogh painted images of the sun, centralised, and radiating lines of light in various compositions showing the Sower (late 1880s). A further comparison with Watts's painting (which was exhibited several times in the 1890s and until 1906) can be made with Edvard Munch's *The Sun*, a massive oil painted as a mural on the walls of the Aula at the University of Oslo (1909–11; see Rosenblum 1975, p.121, ills.168–9). The broadly similar layout of the design, with its radically simplified expanse dominated by the sun, reveals an artist who also found the divine in nature.

When Watts's picture was seen at exhibition in 1891, Marion Spielmann, one of the artist's best interpreters, found a 'sublimity of conception' in the 'all-conquering radiance of the Deity, shown only as a great central sun'. He also commented on the 'opalescent light', an indication of Watts's renewed interest in colour in the mid-1880s. In *After the Deluge*, the strangely anti-naturalistic lighting and colour go beyond an exaggeration of effects to purely imaginative display, rich in meanings and associations of creation and benevolence, all conveyed within the transformed genre of landscape.

BB

George Frederic Watts 1817–1904

61 **Neptune's Horses** 1888–92

Oil on canvas 172.7 × 96.5 (68 × 38)

Prov: George Baillie-Hamilton, Lord Binning and Lady Binning by 1894 (according to MS. Cat.); probably bequeathed by Lord Binning to Major-General Lord Rankborough Jan. 1917, by whom presented to British Red Cross sale, Christie's 24 March 1917 (410); ?bt Lady Binning; bequeathed by Lady Binning to the National Trust as part of the contents of Fenton House, Hampstead in 1952

Exh: New Gallery 1893 (78); New Gallery 1896 (59)

Lit: Macmillan 1903, pp.135–6; von Schleinitz 1904, p.122, pl.105; MS. Cat., I, p.106; Watts 1912, II, p.104; see Morris 1996, p.500 on the oil sketch

Fenton House, Hampstead, The Binning Collection (The National Trust)

EXHIBITED IN LONDON AND MUNICH ONLY

While on his honeymoon in the winter of 1886–7, Watts used the new opportunity of travel to execute a wide range of landscapes, from small directly observed studies of various sites in the Mediterranean (see Whitechapel 1974, nos.67–8) to views in Egypt when he travelled down the Nile (ibid., nos.69–70). However the real value of these travels did not emerge until he returned to London and painted a group of oils which in their transformation of nature attain the level of Symbolist landscapes (ibid., no.62).

Neptune's Horses is just such an example, based on a specific and observed occasion while staying near the sea at Sliema, in Malta, when he witnessed 'a fine sea roll in upon the coast'. Winds from the land hit the waves, throwing back the spray from the crests. Mrs Watts recounted that as they walked by the sea in Malta, and wind blew the white wave crests upward: 'Neptune's horses seemed to be racing towards us'. Seeing this phenomenon, with the white crests of the waves reminding him of horses' manes, Watts spoke of the gift of the horse to the Greeks from the sea-god, Poseidon, known as Neptune in his Latin incarnation. The horse, as the emblem of war and slaughter, suited Neptune's tempestuous personality as the god capable of causing earthquakes.

Walter Crane, a friend of Watts (see no.75) and one of his recent artist-sitters (1891; National Portrait Gallery), painted a large, horizontally shaped oil-painting of virtually the same subject, with the same title, seemingly independently of Watts (see Macmillan 1903 and von Schleinitz 1904). It is worth noting, however, that Crane exhibited sketches for this work at the Royal Water-Colour Society in 1892–3. Also seen at the New Gallery in 1893, Crane's *Neptune's Horses* (Neue Pinakothek, Munich) shows the sea-god himself driving on a team of horses in a more literal interpretation of the subject.

Watts's first version, an oil sketch on board (Walker Art Gallery, Liverpool), was not as severely vertical as the final work – a narrow, upright canvas – that prompted one writer to speculate that the oil might have formed part of a decorative scheme. This format almost seems to contain the thrust of forward motion. Similarly, the final version shows, rather than the turbulent sky of the study, a calm vision, with the overall blue tonality varying from the thinly painted sky to a lower area near the horizon overlaid with a rose-tinged haze. The only hint of energetic paintwork can be seen in the frothy white manes of rushing horses that loom out of the sea as ghostly presences. Their skeletal heads, frenzied expressions, and protruding eyeballs add a sense of the grotesque to the subject. These elements seem quite deliberately introduced by the artist to create a disturbing rather than reassuring presence to contrast with the limpid calm of the sky. Indeed this spectral vision marks *Neptune's Horses* as a Symbolist landscape charged with the preoccupations of the 1890s.

BB

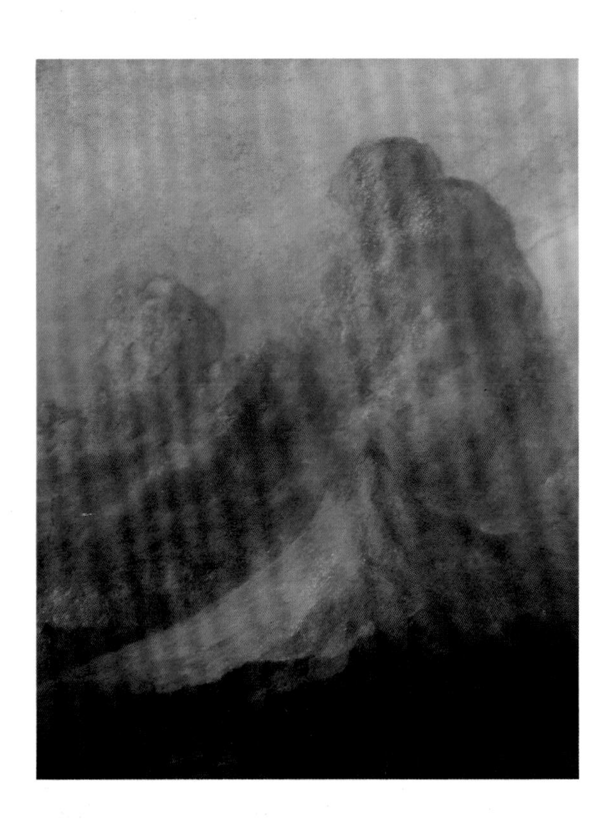

GEORGE FREDERIC WATTS 1817–1904

62 Sunset on the Alps: A Reminiscence 1888–94

Oil on gilded canvas 141 × 110.5 (55½ × 43½)
Prov: As no.60
Exh: The Alpine Club 1894 (114, as *An Alpine Peak*); New Gallery 1896 (149); Manchester 1905 (67); Arts Council 1983 (12)
Lit: Bayes *c*.1906, p.xix, pl.XVIII; MS. Cat., I, p.139; Watts 1912, II, pp.126–7

Trustees of the Watts Gallery

Watts saw this view from a train window when it stopped at the village of La-Roche-sur-Foron, while en route from Aix-les-Bains to Monnetier, near Geneva (Haute-Savoie) in the spring of 1888. Watts and Mary, married late in 1886, had been staying at the Villa Baron, near Mentone, where Watts painted and sketched. They planned to return to England but the artist's health was so bad that on doctor's orders they went in search of 'more bracing air' high up in the mountains. Watts was not familiar with the Swiss Alps, having only passed through some thirty years before. From the medieval town of La-Roche-sur-Foron, often called 'the gateway to the high Alps', one can see a ridge of grey rock towering above the wide river valley of the Arve. As Watts observed the landscape 'steeped in the crimson of the setting sun, suddenly a line of snowy peaks blazed out upon a background of giant cumulus clouds ... a celestial city'.

While abroad in 1888, Watts conceived and began several Alpine landscapes, such as *The Alps, Savoy* (Watts Gallery, Compton) and *Sant'Agnese, Mentone* (FAS in 1991), which reveal the artist's attraction to the high Alps, and in particular the conjunction of mountain peaks and sky. Watts was familiar with Ruskin's exhortations to seek out 'mountain beauty' and cloud effects (in the fourth and fifth volumes of *Modern Painters*) but one feels that it was the 'varying moods of the mountains' (Watts 1912, I, p.115) that commanded Watts's attention.

One directly observed study of Alpine scenery, *Clouds over the Alps* (collection of Sir Brinsley Ford; Whitechapel 1974, no.71), in watercolour and gouache, is close to *Sunset on the Alps*, showing a similarly dominating cloudscape. When Watts returned to London and began the large oil, he dramatised his vision considerably. Massively enlarged, and using a vertical format, *Sunset on the Alps* has a majestic feel, far removed from the immediacy of the small gouache. The mountain with its smooth curve rising to a delicate peak is placed against a background of brilliantly rich orange, and the clouds take on the character of mountains themselves. The gloriously ascending movement results in an image of optimism, even joy, displaying the transforming power of light as one proceeds from the dark areas of foreground through the clear light on the peak, eventually culminating in the near celestial heights beyond. The choice of a gilded canvas (recorded by Mrs Watts and seemingly his only experiment with this unusual ground) lent a powerful glow to the hot colours.

Exhibiting this work in 1894 with the title *An Alpine Peak*, Watts no doubt provided the description which itself dwells on the emotive power of the painting: 'a reminiscence of a vision of one of the peaks of the Mont Blanc chain.' By incorporating the word 'reminiscence' into the title in his retrospective exhibition of 1896, the artist allows the quality of memory to enter into the meaning of the work.

BB

ARNOLD BÖCKLIN 1827–1901

63 **Vision at Sea** 1896

Oil on canvas 41 × 144 (16⅛ × 56¾)
Inscribed 'AB [monogram] 1896' lower left

Prov: Heinrich Tramm, Hanover 1902; Heinrich Tramm, Mülheim-Speldorf 1955

Exh: Hayward Gallery 1994 (ex cat.)

Lit: Schmid 1903, no.396; Andree 1977, pp.516–17, repr.

Private Collection

Böcklin was born in Basel and trained in Düsseldorf, and his art epitomises a decidedly Teutonic Symbolism. His buxom mermaids cavorting with tritons and seals, blending the fantastical with the heavily comic, or his all-too-fleshly nymphs and satyrs, denizens of a Germanic Arcadia, are unlike the work of any other artist. But there are occasional parallels with contemporaries elsewhere, and links with British painting are sometimes striking, even though they are usually attributable to the shared interests of the time rather than to any documented influence in either direction. Böcklin's lyrical landscapes with Classical buildings and figures are in the same genre as the flower-strewn woodland scenes of Walter Crane (see no.29), and his *Flora* of 1875 (Museum der Bildenden Künste, Leipzig) has affinities with Burne-Jones, while his later allegorical subjects, such as *War* of 1896 (Gemälde Galerie Neue Meister, Dresden) are somewhat in Watts's mode. Comparisons of this kind, however, ought not to be pressed too far.

In 1862 Böcklin moved to Rome and thereafter travelled frequently between Switzerland and Italy. In Rome he became a member of the circle of artists that included Anselm Feuerbach and Hans von Marées, both Symbolists whom he influenced, and the collectors Otto and Mathilde Wesendonck, friends of Wagner. He eventually settled in Florence, and in 1894 bought the Villa Belaggio at San Domenico, which the following year, with the help of one of his four painter sons, Carlo, he decorated with 'Pompeian' designs (Andree 1977, nos.450.1–3).

In addition, he painted three overdoors for the villa, of which this is one. Brooding marine fantasies in Böcklin's most Nordic vein, they are in complete contrast to the Classical decoration of the main scheme. One of them, *Ulysses and Polyphemus* (Andree 1977, no.453), it is true, takes a subject from Greek mythology but treats it in a bleak, almost tragic style. It was worked up into a highly finished painting (private collection, Switzerland; Andree 454) which, with the exception of *The Chapel* of 1898 (Andree 1977, no.468) was to be Böcklin's last sea-picture. The other two subjects are more imprecise evocations of northern literary ideas. One, *Breakers* (Andree 1977, no.452), has two mermen in a heavy sea swell at the mouth of a dark cave. The other, this canvas, summons up the world of the Flying Dutchman, with its distant silhouetted ship and suggestions of wraithlike figures round an abandoned and drifting boat, 'almost grey on grey, wonderfully ghostly in its handling', as Böcklin's biographer Schmid remarked. The Wagnerian overtones are obvious enough. There are also similarities with Burne-Jones, especially his large canvas *The Sirens* of 1870–98 (John and Mable Ringling Museum of Art, Sarasota), which presents a crepuscular harbour peopled by sea spirits watching a ship that silently glides past them. Another evocation by Burne-Jones of wandering spirits in semi-darkness is *Souls on the Banks of the River Styx* (no.39), which shares the loosely handled monochrome paint of Böcklin's canvas. Watts was another artist who explored the idea of a Flying Dutchman-like marine apparition in his picture *A Sea Ghost* 1887 (Watts Gallery, Compton), in which the faintest spectre of a sailing ship can just be discerned in an envelope of silvery grey haze.

AW

ELIHU VEDDER 1836–1923

64 Memory 1870

Oil on mahogany panel 52.2 × 37.5 (20½ × 14¾)
Inscribed 'Elihu Vedder' lower right
Prov: ?H. Fargo, Buffalo, sale 30 March 1875
Lit: Soria 1970, pp.79, 303, 310, no.265; Soria et al. 1979, pp.116, 117, repr. pl.139

Los Angeles County Museum of Art. Mr and Mrs William Preston Harrison Collection

EXHIBITED IN LONDON ONLY

For most of his career Vedder lived and worked in Europe, and like Whistler or Sargent he is in many ways as much a European as an American artist. He first visited Italy in 1857, when he was twenty-one, and studied in Florence under Raffaelle Bonaiuti. In 1866 he returned, married, to settle in Rome and remained based in Italy for the rest of his life, with a house on Capri as well as a home in Rome itself. He became a member of the large international circle of artists living and working in Rome, painting historical and religious subjects at first, but developing his own distinctive brand of Symbolist allegory. He was also a prolific landscape painter, working with Giovanni Costa and the 'Etruscans', including William Blake Richmond. From these landscape artists he took a love of low horizontal compositions that appear in his work in other genres. He visited England frequently, was much interested in 'Pre-Raphaelitism' and became a friend of Simeon Solomon, with whose work his own has affinities. On his first visit to London in 1870 he met Watts and admired the work of Rossetti, Alma-Tadema and Leighton. In Rome in 1890 he was among the artists, including several from Britain, involved in the 'In Arte Libertas' group inspired by Gabriele D'Annunzio. Vedder hoped to receive the commission for the decoration of the American Episcopal Church in Rome, where he was a vestryman, but it was given to Burne-Jones. In the 1880s and 1890s he made frequent trips to the United States, and brought out his edition of FitzGerald's *Rubáiyát of Omar Khayyám* there (no.87); after 1901 he remained in Italy, publishing his memoirs, *The Digressions of V*, in 1910.

Vedder had made a chalk drawing of a subject similar to that of *Memory* while he was in France in 1866 (repr. Soria et al. 1979, p.116). This oil painting, which was untraced until recently, is a subtler treatment of the same idea, in which the woman's face that appears in the dark clouds above the empty shore is not the main focus, as in the drawing, but is only perceived at a second glance, its presence impinging on the spectator with an element of shock. The female head appears in several other drawings of the same series, in one instance irradiating streaming hair and sun rays; it is titled 'Weirdness'. The series of chalk designs was evidently inspired by the drawings of Burne-Jones; the motif of the isolated female head floating in space has links with both Rossetti and Redon. *Memory* has an ominous undertone, as though the inexplicable vision were to be read as parallelling the presence of the Sphinx on another seashore in Vedder's painting of 1879–80 (no.65).

AW

ELIHU VEDDER 1836–1923

65 The Sphinx of the Seashore 1879–80

Oil on canvas 40.6 × 70.8 (16 × 27⅞)
Inscribed 'Copyright 1899 by E. Vedder Roma' lower right
Prov: Anita Vedder; Peter Sargent 1912; Mr and Mrs Lawrence A. Fleischman, Kennedy Galleries, New York; Mr and Mrs John D. Rockefeller
Lit: Soria 1970, pp.15–16, 326, no.379; Soria et al. 1979, p.146, repr. pls.117, 180

Fine Arts Museum of San Francisco, gift of Mr and Mrs John D. Rockefeller 3rd

65

Vedder's fascination with Edward FitzGerald's translation of the *Rubáiyát of Omar Khayyám* – 'a poem so much in harmony with my thought' (letter to Joseph B. Millet, 1883; Houghton Library, Harvard) – led him to make a long series of illustrations expounding his interpretation of its gloomily hedonistic philosophy. These were published in a sumptuous edition of the poem in 1884 (see no.87). One of the plates shows the Sphinx lying on a pile of the detritus of human civilisations: bones and parts of machinery are jumbled together in a filthy heap. Vedder explained his meaning in a manuscript note: 'This figure of an all-devouring Sphinx stretched over the remains of Creation typifies the destructive side of Nature, taking all shapes from Máh to Máli'. The last words (glossed by FitzGerald as meaning 'from Fish to Moon') quote from the *Rubáiyát*, stanza LI (57 in Vedder's order), which is one of three on this page of the book:

A Hair perhaps divides the False and True;
Yes; and a single Alif were the clue –
  Could you but find it – to the Treasure-house,
And peradventure to THE MASTER too;

Whose secret Presence, through Creation's veins
Running Quicksilver-like eludes your pains;
  Taking all shapes from Máh to Máli; and
They change and perish all – but he remains;

A moment guess'd – then back behind the Fold
Immerst of Darkness round the Drama roll'd
  Which for the Pastime of Eternity,
He does himself contrive, enact, behold.

Elsewhere Vedder commented: '[Omar] had evidently pondered on the fact of the disappearance of so many forms of life and the certainty that in time even man himself with all his inventions must disappear from the face of the earth. What wonder that he calls the brief moment of existence between two eternities a spangle' (Vedder Papers, American Academy and National Institute of Arts and Letters, New York). The title of the plate is *The Inevitable Fate*. In the painting the crowded heap of detritus is replaced by a spacious, dream-like desert across which the evidences of civilisation are scattered rather as in a Surrealist landscape. Soria (1970, pp.15–16) suggests that the image of the Sphinx by the ocean was derived from the content of a nightmare experienced by Vedder in his boyhood.

Vedder had essayed an earlier Sphinx subject in his picture of 1863, *The Questioner of the Sphinx* (Museum of Fine Arts, Boston). Although this illustrates more literally a colossal sculpture in a plausible Egyptian desert, the picture also achieves a surreal power, presenting as it does a lonely human figure engaged in the apparently futile act of listening intently at the Sphinx's mouth. A second version was painted in 1875 (Worcester Art Museum, Mass.).

AW

Music and Poetry

The Symbolist movement had its roots in literature, especially poetry, and was accompanied in all its phases by works of criticism and appreciation, philosophy and aesthetics, which defined the territory in words as vividly as it was in visual terms. There was a symbiosis between painting or drawing and poetry that was crucial to the movement. Rossetti had made the point at the outset with his paired poems and pictures (fig.55; see Yale 1976) and in the course of the half-century of Symbolism a wide repertory of poetry was put under requisition to supply themes for artists in all media. Whistler's habit of inscribing poems on the frames of his pictures (see no.15) was a further confirmation of the trend.

fig.55 Dante Gabriel Rossetti, *The Blessed Damozel* 1875–8, oil on canvas 212 × 132.4 × 8.9 cm (framed). Fogg Art Museum, Harvard University Art Museums. Bequest of Grenville L. Winthrop

When he also placed musical quotations on his frames (see no.16) Whistler summed up another important argument about the parallelism of art forms. His own pictures were often designated as pieces of music – Symphonies, Nocturnes etc. – and the intention to suggest the non-verbal ambiguity of music is of the greatest significance, opening up the possibility of abstract art, which indeed as it evolved in the early twentieth century was in some important respects the logical development of Symbolism. (One of the pioneers of abstraction, Piet Mondrian, was very much a Symbolist in his thinking, taking as he did a great interest, as Watts had done, in spiritualism and Theosophy and regarding the horizontals and verticals of the gridlike compositions that he evolved in 1910s as having specific, if transcendental, symbolic meaning.) It is therefore natural that one of the great celebrations of music in Symbolist art, Burne-Jones's *The Golden Stairs* 1872–80 (no.68), is itself an essay in a form of abstraction, a pictorial evocation of the rhythms and counterpoint of music. The design emerges directly out of the purely 'aesthetic' canvases of Albert Moore in the 1860s (no.11). Another tribute to music, Watts's *Hope c.*1885–6 (no.76), can also, despite its meaning-laden allegory of the indomitable spirit of mankind, be seen as an aesthetic exercise in which design and colouring recreate in visual terms the effect of music: perhaps it is no accident that Watts adopts in this work a pervasive subtle blue reminiscent of Whistler's Nocturnes.

Piano music was often invoked by Symbolist artists. Aubrey Beardsley celebrated a Chopin Ballade in a drawing of 1894 (private collection; Reade 1967, no.320); in the 1880s and 1890s the German Max Klinger produced series of etchings entitled *Intermezzi* and *Brahmsfantasien*. In 1883 the Belgian Fernand Khnopff painted his *Listening to Schumann* (Musée Royal des Beaux-Arts, Brussels), which was to be echoed in the eulogies of Schumann offered up by the passionate Paris art students of Zola's novel *L'Oeuvre* (1886). But there was nothing of the piano recital, of chamber music, about Watts's inventions. He is orchestral, if not operatic, conceiving his dramas on a scale and with a universal reference that might not unjustly be termed Wagnerian.

Certainly Wagner loomed large over all the arts in the period; his music had a strong visual component which coloured the inspiration of others working in other media. The way Wagner's music-dramas straddle several art-forms, and penetrate the ill-defined territory between them, is one sign that his own work is in the fullest sense Symbolist. He was the priestlike interpreter of national mythologies; his choice of themes from Nordic and medieval legend – the Ring of the Nibelung, Tristram and Iseult – was in complete accord with the preoccupations of Rossetti or Arnold Böcklin. When a French painter, Henri Fantin-Latour, celebrated his admiration for Wagner in paintings and lithographs (nos.83–5), he visualised the content of the operas in a pictorial language close to that of Watts.

AUBREY BEARDSLEY 1872–1898

66 **The Third Tableau of *Das Rheingold*** 1896

Ink over pencil 25.4 × 17.5 (10 × 6⅞)
Prov: …; bt Rhode Island School of Design 1931
Exh: National Gallery, Millbank 1923–4 (46); V&A 1966 (523); Munich 1984 (211)
Lit: Reade 1967, no.430, repr.; Maas, Duncan and Goode 1970, pp.123–4, 170; Chan 1983, p.94 n.49, repr.; Wilson 1983, no.34, repr.; Heyd 1986, p.178; Fletcher 1987, p.149

Museum of Art, Rhode Island School of Design, Providence. Museum Appropriation Fund

Beardsley's enthusiasm for Wagner is widely attested in his letters, in contemporary reminiscences of him and, not least, in his drawings. The most notable recent discussion of his Wagner illustrations and the *fin de siècle* Wagner fever among artists and writers that was the context for them and for Beardsley's own enthusiasm, is by Chan, but Snodgrass (1995, p.312, nn.9, 11) has an extremely useful summary that includes details of the first Wagner performances in German in London in the summer season of 1892–4, many of which Beardsley undoubtedly attended. Heyd devotes an entire chapter to Wagnerian themes in Beardsley. Chan cites the view of Edouard Dujardin, founder (in 1885) of *La Revue Wagnérienne,* that 'Wagner était un des maîtres du symbolisme' (Wagner was one of the masters of Symbolism) and Mallarmé's line 'Le dieu Richard Wagner irradiant un sacre' (The god Richard Wagner irradiating a rite). Snodgrass quotes Beardsley's comment that 'I would do anything and go anywhere – if I could – to hear Wagner's music' and Max Beerbohm's statement that Beardsley rarely missed a Wagner night at Covent Garden. In Beardsley's unfinished novel, itself inspired by Wagner, *The Story of Venus and Tannhäuser*, the hero, widely seen as a self-portrait of the author, retires to bed with a copy of the score of *Das Rheingold*, Wagner's 'brilliant comedy', and an enthusiastic account of the opera follows.

Beardsley's letters make it clear that he intended to write his own version of *Das Rheingold*; it was to be published by Leonard Smithers (the publisher of Wilde and Beardsley after the disgrace of Wilde) with Beardsley's illustrations. In 1896 he made six drawings of subjects from *Das Rheingold*, of which this is one, for publication in the *Savoy* magazine, of which he was art editor. Beardsley's letters also make clear that he intended to make a fresh set of drawings for his own *Rheingold* book, but the project came to nothing.

Beardsley's account of *Das Rheingold* in his *Venus and Tannhäuser* includes the following description of the third tableau (Beardsley's term for scene): 'Alberic's savage activity and metamorphoses, and Loge's rapid, flaming, tongue-like movements, make the tableau the least reposeful, the most troubled and confusing thing in the whole range of opera. How the Abbé rejoiced in the extravagant monstrous poetry, the heated melodrama, and splendid agitation of it all.' It was this scene that Beardsley had chosen as one of the subjects of his *Rheingold* drawings and which he then used as one of the five illustrations of *Venus and Tannhäuser* that accompanied its publication, in bowdlerised form and under the title of *Under the Hill*, in the first two issues of the *Savoy* magazine, which appeared in January and April 1896. In this version the hero's name became the Abbé Fanfreluche ('bauble or penis' – Fletcher 1987). Abbé is a pun on Beardsley's initials pronounced in French, but at one point in the original manuscript (Rosenbach Foundation, Philadelphia) Fanfreluche becomes the Abbé Aubrey, reinforcing the identification of the author with his hero.

The Third Tableau of Das Rheingold precisely evokes in visual form Beardsley's verbal account of the scene. Wotan, king of the gods, and Loge, the wily god of fire, are in the Underworld of the Nibelungen, the Rhine dwarfs, attempting to recover the gold stolen by the dwarf Alberich. The power of the gold, part of it now forged into a ring, has enabled Alberich to enslave his people and to acquire a magic helmet. As a first step towards obtaining the ring for himself, Loge taunts Alberich into demonstrating the power of the helmet, which he does by turning himself into a dragon, at which Loge makes a great pretence of fear. Beardsley illustrates this one of Alberich's 'metamorphoses', and Loge's 'flaming tongue-like movements' are given vivid expression by Beardsley's development of Loge's draperies into extraordinary, baroque, intensely art nouveau, tongue-of-flame-like forms. And these are echoed in the great tongue, or tongue of flame, emerging from the dragon's mouth. For further comment on Loge's draperies, see no.67. In a letter to his publisher, Leonard Smithers, Beardsley described this drawing, either disingenuously or too modestly, as 'an elaborate piece of nonsense'.

SW

AUBREY BEARDSLEY 1872–1898

67 The Fourth Tableau of *Das Rheingold* 1896

Pen and black ink 30.5 × 22.3 (12 × 8¾)
Inscribed in top panel 'pierce' within an oval flourish and with the artist's initials lower left

Prov: …; R.A. Harari by whom bequeathed to the Victoria and Albert Museum 1972

Exh: National Gallery, Millbank 1923 (50); V&A 1966 (524); New York 1967 (207); Munich 1984 (218)

Lit: Reade 1967, no.438, repr.; Maas, Duncan and Goode 1970, pp.160–1, 165, 174; Chan 1983, p.91, repr.; Wilson 1983, no.34, repr.; Heyd 1986, p.179; Fletcher 1987, p.149; Snodgrass 1995, p.33, repr.

The Board of Trustees of the Victoria and Albert Museum

For an account of the background to Beardsley's illustrations to Wagner's *Das Rheingold*, see no.66.

The Fourth Tableau was drawn for the cover of the *Savoy* October 1896 issue and is certainly the drawing described by Beardsley as follows in a letter to Smithers of September 1896:

> The names of the characters in my *Rheingold* picture are
> Loge (the fire god)
> Wotan
> In the depths of the valley below, the Rhine maidens are singing unseen and bewailing the loss of their gold. Loge turns round and speaks to them jeeringly, whilst the gods, with Wotan at their tail, pour into the new palace which they have built with the wealth they have robbed from the daughters of the Rhine.

The originality of Beardsley's conception of Loge, with his extraordinary flame-like garment and even flame-like body hair, has been much remarked; the body hair, says Reade, 'has no precedent in European art'. The correspondence of Beardsley's image of Loge to what has been described as the 'flickering flame' motif that accompanies Loge in the score of the opera supports Chan's view that Beardsley was 'not only the English artist who made the most of Wagner's dramas, but perhaps the only Symbolist in England who seemed able to aspire toward a Wagnerian style of composition in which images served the same purpose as the composer's leitmotif'.

At the time he drew this, autumn 1896, Beardsley's tuberculosis was advancing rapidly and both Heyd and Snodgrass have associated Loge's chest 'consumed with flickering flames' (Heyd) with the burning sensation of tubercular lungs. Snodgrass quotes Beardsley's comment 'I never wear an overcoat. I am always burning' and seductively goes on to relate this to Walter Pater's notorious injunction to the would-be aesthete 'to burn always with [a] hard gem-like flame'.

SW

Edward Burne-Jones 1833–1898

68 The Golden Stairs 1872–80

Oil on canvas 269.2 × 116.8 (106 × 46)
Inscribed 'EBJ 1880', b.l.

Prov: Cyril Flower, Lord Battersea; by whom bequeathed to the Tate Gallery 1907; presented by Lady Battersea 1924

Exh: Grosvenor Gallery 1880 (120); Manchester 1887 (206); New Gallery 1892 (51); New Gallery 1898 (108); White City 1908 (100); Sheffield 1971 (180); Hayward Gallery 1975 (138); Tate Gallery 1984 (154)

Lit: Bell 1892, pp.54, 59; de Lisle 1904, pp.122, 184; G.B.-J. 1904, I, p.297, II, pp.30, 68, 103; Battersea 1922, p.312; Bell 1927, repr. opp. p.106; Harrison and Waters 1973, fig.78; Hartnoll 1988, pp.32–3

Tate Gallery. Bequeathed by Lord Battersea 1924

The Golden Stairs, the composition of which was first devised in 1872 and worked on between 1876 and 1880, represents the consummation of Burne-Jones's interest in subjects that address the spectator in terms of mood rather than narrative, and is therefore in line of succession to works such as *The Lament* (no.25). The fact that various alternative titles for the present painting, including 'The King's Wedding' and 'Music on the Stairs', were contemplated demonstrates to what degree it fulfils a purely decorative purpose, and in this sense – in its abstract and formal character which depends not at all on the spectator's ability to comprehend or interpret – it is remarkably modern. This was occasionally recognised in the artist's lifetime, as for example on the occasion of the second Grosvenor Gallery exhibition when the *Magazine of Art* observed that 'these archaic affectations [Burne-Jones's paintings *Chant d'Amour* (Metropolitan Museum of Art, New York) and *Laus Veneris* (Laing Art Gallery, Newcastle-upon-Tyne)] are more modern, more entirely of the nineteenth century, than is a factory or a Positivist' (1878, p.81). In 1885, in a survey of Burne-Jones's art which dwelt on his debt to the Renaissance traditions, Claude Phillips concluded: 'The spirit which informs his art is essentially and entirely modern, and as far asunder as the poles from that which inspired his great prototypes' (*Magazine of Art*, 1885, p.228).

The Golden Stairs has a strange and compelling dynamic power. The girls seem to form an endless chain, wending their way down the spiral of the staircase which they descend, and the sense of continuum is mesmeric. As F.G. Stephens said of these figures who 'troop past like spirits in an enchanted dream, each moving gracefully, freely, and in unison with her neighbours': 'What is the place they have left, why they pass before us thus, wither they go, who they are, there is nothing to tell' (*Athenaeum*, 1880, p.605). The eighteen girls shown in the painting seem so alike (although it was said that each was drawn from a specific model), and the Fortuny-style dresses that they wear again form echoing patterns in the line of their pleats and folds. Burne-Jones, like Ruskin, was fascinated by patterns that flow in broad repetition but in which discrepancies and differences cause the eye to search for clues to the mentality of the artist in the way he has observed or invented the forms.

This fondness for the infinity of abstract variation allows Burne-Jones – a man who thought of himself as a reactionary in his love of line, and who despised what he saw as the Continental contamination of undisciplined Impressionism – to be regarded as an artist who was unconsciously engaging with issues that would, after his death, galvanise a new generation of progressive artists. We know that Burne-Jones's paintings were admired by Paul Gauguin in Paris in the early 1890s, and by the young Picasso in Barcelona at the turn of the century. Is it possible that Marcel Duchamp had been looking at a copy of Felix Jasinski's etching after *The Golden Stairs* (printed in Paris, published in 1894, and known to have circulated and been admired in France) when in 1912 he conceived his Cubist masterpiece *Nude Descending a Staircase* (fig.60 on p.272)?

CSN

68

George Frampton 1860–1928

69 **Lamia** 1899–1900

Bronze, ivory, opals and glass 62 × 54.5 × 25.4 (24¾ × 21½ × 10)
Inscribed 'George Frampton 1899' on back and 'George Frampton 1900' base right side

Prov: Bt from the artist by William Vivian; bt back 'before the First World War' by Lady and Meredith Frampton, by whom presented to the Royal Academy 1938

Exh: RA 1900 (1970); RA Winter 1933 (602); RA Bicentenary 1968 (888); Whitechapel 1981 (19); Barbican 1989 (193, repr.); Stoke on Trent 1992 (14, repr.); Amsterdam 1996 (91, repr. col.)

Lit: *Studio*, vol.20, 1900, pp.269, 270 (repr.); Spielmann 1901, pp.93–4 (repr.); Maryon 1933, fig.14; Read 1981, p.45; Read 1982, p.315; Beattie 1983, pp.160–2, pl.155, and col. pl.1; Read and Barnes 1991–2, p.100, no.10

Royal Academy of Arts

EXHIBITED IN LONDON ONLY

69

The original story of Lamia comes from Greek mythology. Her children were murdered by a jealous rival, and she took revenge by murdering the children of others. Lamia's cruelty turned her face into a terrifying mask, and later she seduced young men and killed them in their sleep by sucking their blood. Her name derives from 'lamyros', meaning gluttony, and in this context implies female lechery. Lamia was worshipped as a goddess by the Libyans, whose rites involved sacrificing children to her. An additional source is provided by Keats's famous poem, in which Lamia is an evil serpent-woman who takes on the guise of human form to enchant a young man. Frampton's bust may illustrate the moment of climax where under Apollonius's gaze 'Lamia, no longer fair, there sat a deadly white' ('Lamia', II, 276). She is an altogether terrifying figure, whose combination of sex, death and vampirism makes her ideally suited as a subject for Symbolist art.

Whether consciously or unconsciously, much of the content of Symbolist art and literature deals with conflicting male feelings towards women – fear and strong attraction to them. Frampton's choice of subject links into this widespread *fin de siècle* anxiety, for Lamia is both a temptress and murderess. As the young man in Keats's poem discovers, she is a source of sublime sexual pleasure, but also ultimately exposed as a deadly threat. Susan Beattie believed that *Lamia* revealed Frampton's own ambivalent feelings about women, and noted also the sculpture's strong sexual undercurrents of 'sado-masochistic delight in flesh constrained and corseted by metal and gems' (Beattie 1983, p.231).

Frampton's richly varied materials and decoration in *Lamia* owe much to developments in contemporary French and Belgian sculpture, although it is a work of greater originality and depth than anything produced on the other side of the Channel. It is particularly close to Charles Van der Stappens's *Sphynx Mystérieux* 1897 (silver and ivory, Musées Royaux d'Art et d'Histoire, Brussels), and Alfons Mucha's *La Nature* 1899 (silvered and gilded bronze, Badisches Landesmuseum, Karlsruhe). In its overall design Frampton was looking to the Renaissance, as he did for so much of his work, and in particular the bronze, bust-length portraits of Donatello, Laurana and Rossellino. Frampton made a patinated plaster version of *Lamia*, now in Birmingham Museum and Art Gallery (see Read and Barnes 1991–2, no.10), which he presented to 'my old friend Walter Bell', brother of Robert Anning Bell.

Lamia is studded with opals, which are traditional symbols of doom and ill-luck. Frampton may have been inspired to use them by sensational popular obituaries of King Alphonso XII of Spain (d.1885), whose antique opal ring brought premature death to all who wore it, including, finally, the King himself. Hanging from the brooch on Lamia's breast is a tiny sphere of crystal, which implies divination. The ivory of her face is beautifully and sensuously carved, evoking a mood of mystery and anticipation. Sculptors used ivory increasingly around this time, owing to the availability of good quality, modestly priced tusks from the Congo.

RU

Dante Gabriel Rossetti 1828–1882

70 **Sancta Lilias** 1874

Oil on canvas 48.3 × 45.7 (19 × 18)
Inscribed with Rossetti's monogram and '1874' t.l.

Prov: Given by the artist to Hon. William and Mrs Cowper-Temple, Broadlands 1876; by descent to their adopted daughter Mme Deschamps, by whom presented to the Tate Gallery 1909

Exh: Burlington Fine Arts Club 1883 (87); Tate Gallery 1911 (2440)

Lit: Surtees 1971, no.244c, pl.358

Tate Gallery. Presented by Madame Deschamps in memory of Georgiana, Baroness Mount-Temple 1909

This is an abandoned and cut-down first version of one of Rossetti's most important Symbolist pictures,

70

The Blessed Damozel 1875–8 (fig.55 on p.186). Whereas Rossetti's paintings often prompted verses, this is the only one to have derived from a poem of his. Started in 1848, the poem of the same title was first published in February 1850 in *The Germ*, but underwent continuous alteration until the final version of the text appeared in 1881. It tells of the yearning of a dead woman in Heaven for reunification with her still-living lover. In the painting, Rossetti shows the Blessed Damozel looking down upon her beloved, who is depicted below her in a predella. Behind her, pairs of lovers embrace, united once again in Heaven. This situation has a poignant parallel in Rossetti's own life through the death of his own wife Lizzie Siddall (see no.44). The literary sources he drew upon for the theme of separation caused by death are partly Philip James Bailey's *Festus*, first published in 1839, which Rossetti read constantly while writing the poem, and Edgar Allen Poe's *The Raven* (1845). Rossetti told Hall Caine in 1887 'I saw that Poe had done the utmost it was possible to do with the grief of the lover on earth, and so I determined to reverse the conditions and give utterance to the yearning of the loved one in heaven' (Caine 1928, p.284).

However, an evident additional if not pre-eminent source of inspiration is to be found in the writings of the Swedish philosopher, theologian and mystic Emmanuel Swedenborg (1688–1772). In *Conjugial Love* (1768) Swedenborg wrote extensively about how each man and woman has a single, ideal partner – a 'conjugial partner' – and that their conjunction creates an eternal, sanctified love. In Heaven, the union of these two partners creates a single being, an angel, and it is only through this conjunction that they can become whole. In his text Swedenborg also stresses the divine nature of sexual delight.

The background of embracing couples in *The Blessed Damozel* therefore depicts the conjunction of lovers' souls: 'Around her, lovers, newly met / Mid deathless love's acclaims, / Spoke evermore among themselves / Their heart-remembered names' (36–40).

The Damozel looks forward to her own reunion, asking when: '... shall God lift / To endless unity / The soul whose likeness with thy soul / Was but its love for thee?' (99–102).

It might be assumed that Rossetti was thinking of his reunion with Lizzie, but his inner conflicts and complex feelings are displayed in the picture. The women in the background are all apparently modelled on Jane Morris, and it might be that Rossetti was considering whether Lizzie or Jane was his true 'conjugial' partner. In either case, it would only be Heaven where they would be reunited. Rossetti's dilemna had a Swedenborgian basis, for *Conjugial Love* contains dire warnings about the consequences of spending the earthly years with anyone other than one's ideal partner.

There are further Swedenborgian elements as well as symbolic allusions connected to Classical mythology in both painting and poem. The stars in the Damozel's hair 'were seven', a number to which Swedenborg attached great symbolic significance, corresponding to his beliefs about the 'seven stages of the mind', as well as the seven days of Creation. Stars to Swedenborg represented someone's knowledge of good and truth. Among many other things grouped in seven, seven stars are referred to in the Book of Revelations, a key text in Swedenborg's philosophy which he 'decoded' in *The Apocalypse Explained* (1757–9) and *The Apocalypse Revealed* (1766). However, the principal source Rossetti had in mind were the seven stars of the Pleiades. In Classical myth the seven daughters of Atlas and Pleione were transformed into seven stars. However, one of them, Merope, shines invisibly out of shame for her love for a mere mortal, Sisyphus. Alluding to this myth, Rossetti painted only six stars around the Damozel in *The Blessed Damozel* and *Sancta Lilias*. This reference to Merope might perhaps indicate that he perceived the Damozel (Lizzie) as a goddess, and her lover (himself) as Sisyphus. Sisyphus was condemned to roll a giant boulder eternally up a hill, and Rossetti's identification with him may suggest that he viewed his life as a widower-painter as being similarly relentless and unrewarding. What might seem strange in this context is that Rossetti did not use Lizzie's portrait for either *The Blessed Damozel* or *Sancta Lilias*, as he had done in *Beata Beatrix* (no.44). Instead Alexa Wilding modelled for the Damozel, perhaps at the suggestion of his patron William Graham.

The three lilies held by the Damozel may refer both to the Trinity and the Annunciation. In Christian art lilies symbolise purity, chastity and innocence, and in images of the Annunciation Mary is presented with a lily by the Archangel Gabriel. This allusion to the Annunciation may also have personal resonance. Gabriel was of course Rossetti's first name, although he later changed the order so that Dante was first, and Lizzie had been pregnant with his child. In *Sancta Lilias* the Damozel holds three irises, flowers which are members of the lily family. In Classical myth Iris was the goddess of the rainbow, using it as a bridge from heaven to the earth, and in this context may be an allusion by Rossetti to contact between the spiritual and temporal worlds (see no.7). The sensuality of his later drawing *The Spirit of the Rainbow* 1876 (Surtees no.245) is also undoubtedly relevant here.

Rossetti was not unusual in responding to Swedenborg's ideas. Many of his texts were first published in London, and the Swedenborg Society was founded there in 1810 to promote his works. The Church of the New Jerusalem which was founded on his ideas grew throughout the nineteenth century. Rossetti is likely to have known of Blake's interest in Swedenborgian philosophy, but his closest connection with such ideas may have come through his friendship with Robert Browning. Browning and his wife Elizabeth were enthusiastic about Swedenborg and owned a copy of *Conjugial Love*. Some of the poems in Browning's *Men and Women* (1855) praising the pleasures of marriage might well be seen as developing themes taken from Swedenborg. This group of verses was greatly admired by Rossetti, and in his own *House of Love* (1870), some poems, greatly criticised by Buchanan as a product of the 'fleshly school of poetry', extol the virtues of physical love, repeating the philosophy Swedenborg proposed in *Conjugial Love*. In 1855 Rossetti presented a fair copy manuscript to the Brownings, the only one to have survived, an act which may be interpreted as confirming the Swedenborgian links between the two poets.

The publication of 'The Blessed Damozel' in France evoked great interest, as manifested by Debussy's setting of the poem (see no.82). Rossetti's poems had first been known in France in 1871 through the efforts of Emile Blémont, a friend of Fantin-Latour's. However, it was the appearance of the translation by Gabriel Sarrazin in 1885, in his series *Les Poètes Modernes de l'Angleterre*, that sparked widespread knowledge and admiration for Rossetti's poetry. Swedenborg's ideas were already popular there, and Symbolists such as Baudelaire and Mallarmé were familiar with his texts. Indeed, Baudelaire's poem 'Correspondances' in *Les Fleurs du Mal* (1861) can be read in Swedenborgian terms. The continental Symbolists' concept of the correspondence between art, music and literature finds its parallel in Swedenborg's analysis of the correspondence between the temporal and the heavenly, and between the spirit and matter, as for example in *Arcana Caelestia* (1749–56) and *The Apocalypse Explained* (1757–9).

Sancta Lilias was Rossetti's first realisation in oils of *The Blessed Damozel*. Clearly he disliked something about it, and abandoning it, had it cut down to its current form and began the composition anew. The drapery of the dress has been left unfinished. The picture was apparently started in September 1873, as this date was inscribed on an old label on the reverse. A drawing for the predella of *The Blessed Damozel* is no.71. See also Hodler's *Dream* (no.135).

RU

DANTE GABRIEL ROSSETTI 1828–1882

71 The Lover – Study for 'The Blessed Damozel' *c.*1878

Black chalk, pencil and red chalk
35.6 × 83.8 (14 × 33)

Prov: Probably Rossetti sale, Christie's 12 May 1883 (21), bt Agnew's; ...; Christie's 17 June 1969; Earl of Gowrie; Sotheby's Belgravia 19 March 1979; Roy Miles Gallery; present owner

Exh: RA 1973 (354, as *The Blessed Damozel: Study for the Predella*)

Lit: Surtees 1971, App. 10

Nicholas Bagshawe

This is a study for the predella of *The Blessed Damozel* (fig.55 on p.186). It shows the Damozel's poet-lover on earth, looking up towards her in Heaven, and illustrates the lines in the poem where, fleetingly, he imagines her presence: Yet now, and in this place, / Surely she lean'd o'er me – her hair / Fell all about my face ... / Nothing: the autumn-fall of leaves. / The whole year sets apace' (20–4).

Rossetti's theme of lovers separated by death took on a very personal dimension when his wife Lizzie Siddall died in 1862 from a laudanum overdose. This experience underlay Rossetti's conception of the painting, which was commissioned by William Graham in 1871, a project which occupied him for the next seven years. Rossetti had first met Lizzie in 1850, but he did not marry her until ten years later. By then his ardour seems to have cooled slightly, and there

71

are intimations of his feeling guilty in devoting time to the company of his models and circle. When Lizzie died, Rossetti was overcome with self-recrimination and loss.

In a gesture of devotion, remorse and sacrifice he put the only manuscript of his poems in her coffin. Wanting to recover and publish them, however, in 1869 Rossetti had the coffin exhumed. For this he appears to have sought Lizzie's approval in a series of seances, recorded in his brother William's unpublished 'Notes of Spiritual Séances' (see Rossetti Angeli 1949, pp.xvii, 206). Swedenborg, with whose ideas Rossetti seems to have been familiar (see no.70), believed that the Day of Judgement had occurred in 1757 and that the temporal and spiritual worlds therefore coexisted. By the 1860s many Swedenborgians and members of the Church of the New Jerusalem were enthusiastic spiritualists. Table turning, automatic writing and spirit manifestations were cited as evidence to deny the godless rationale of Darwinism and support the existence of an afterlife.

In addition to seances, Rossetti's niece believed he used 'other efforts to get into communication with his wife' (Rossetti Angeli 1949, p.206). These may have been the 'Darker arts that almost struck despair in me' mentioned in the 'Epilogue' of Browning's 'Fifine at the Fair' (1872, III, ii). Rossetti believed Browning's verses to be an attack on him, and although his suspicions were dismissed by his brother William as paranoia, the 'Epilogue' can be read as a description of the conversation between a man and his dead lover. Its theme of separation is very similar to that of Rossetti's 'Blessed Damozel', and Rossetti could have been offended by this alone. However, he seems to read himself into the principal character, and was apparently particularly disturbed by the reference to 'Darker arts'. Browning's dismissive view of spiritualism was well known, as evinced by his poem 'Mr Sludge, the Medium' (1864), and he regretted his wife Elizabeth's enthusiasm for it. Rossetti himself seems to have become increasingly dependent on spiritualism for a justification of his wife's disinterment. Insomniac, chloral-addicted and with several mistresses, by the time of Browning's 'Fifine' Rossetti had become a strikingly decadent contrast to the years of what he saw as his pure love for Lizzie. Whether it was intended to portray Rossetti or not, Browning's poem tells a story of similar disintegration. It was following its publication that Rossetti suffered his breakdown.

Further evidence of Rossetti's belief in the contact of the dead with the living through communication or symbol was related by the spiritualist-sceptic William Bell Scott. When he and Rossetti were walking together at Penkill the autumn before Lizzie was exhumed, a chaffinch settled before them and allowed Rossetti to pick it up. 'I can tell you what it is', Rossetti said, 'it is my wife, the spirit of my wife, the soul of her has taken this shape; something is going to happen to me' (Bell Scott, II, 1892, pp.113–4).

It is interesting to compare this drawing, and the predella in Rossetti's *Blessed Damozel,* with the panel in *The Dream* by Hodler (no.135), who was clearly aware of Rossetti's painting and poem.

RU

Dante Gabriel Rossetti 1828–1882

72 **Ligeia Siren** 1873

Coloured chalks 80 × 55 (31½ × 21⅝)
Inscribed with monogram and dated '1873' lower right; inscribed with title 'Ligeia Siren' upper right

Prov: Given to Charles Augustus Howell for arranging the sale of Rossetti's *Dante's Dream at the Time of the Death of Beatrice* to Leonard Valpy 1873; Constantine Alexander Ionides *c.*1880; William Connal; Christie's, 14 March 1908 (22), bt Sampson; Pickford Waller; Miss Sybil Waller; Christie's, 1 Oct. (83), bt Hartnoll & Eyre on behalf of the present owner

Exh: Burlington 1883 (74); Tokyo 1990 (76); Rome 1996 (39)

Lit: Rossetti 1889, p.85; Marillier 1899, p.172, no.258; T. Watts-Dunton, *Old Familiar Faces*, 1916, p.86; Rossetti Angeli 1954, p.101; Pedrick 1964, p.131; Doughty and Wahl 1965–8, pp.1143, 1145; Surtees 1971, I, no.234, p.134; Fennell 1978; Cline 1978; Macleod 1982, pp.89–102; Benedetti 1984, pl.425; Smith 1996, pp.39–40, pl.6

Private Collection

In 1869 Rossetti drafted a libretto for an opera, *The Doom of the Sirens* (never performed; see Rossetti 1886, I, pp.431–6) in which he describes the journey by sea of a Christian prince. Ignoring the warnings of a hermit, the prince and his party approach the rock where the three Sirens – Thelxiope, Thelxinoë and Ligeia – attempt to lure him to destruction. The prince believes that his faith will protect him from sorcery, and although he resists the temptations of wealth and greatness, the allurements of the Ligeia Siren, who offers love, overcome him and he dies under her spell. The Ligeia Siren, whose name comes from the Greek *ligys* and means melodious and clear toned, is thus a female personification who uses the beauty of her voice and music-making to entrance men and destroy them. What seems like a victory for paganism is mitigated by the curse that the prince's wife, moments before her suicide, places on the Ligeia Siren, that she 'may yet love and be hated and so destroy herself and her sisters' (ibid., p.432). The plot is worked out when twenty-one years later the prince's son, prompted by a dream about his childhood and the death of his parents, and commanded by an Oracle, returns to the Sirens' rock to seek vengeance. Rossetti's libretto describes how the Sirens, in anticipation of the prince's arrival, are 'possessed by a spirit of baneful exaltation, and in their songs alternate from one to the other wild tales of their triumphs in past times and the renowned victims who have succumbed to them. As they reach the name of the Christian Prince and his wife who died by their means, a vessel comes in view.' The denouement comes when 'The Prince tells Ligeia of his parentage and mission, but she still madly craves for his love and holds forth to him such promises of infernal sovereignty as her gods afford, if he will yield to her passion. He meanwhile, though proof against her lures and loathing her in his heart, is physically absorbed into the death-agony of the expiring spell; and when, at his last word of reprobation, the curse seizes her and her sisters, and they dash themselves headlong from the rock, he also succumbs to the doom, calling with his last breath on his Bride to come to him' (ibid., pp.435–6).

Dianne Macleod has analysed Rossetti's knowledge of Wagner's operas and particularly the connection between *Tannhäuser* and 'The Doom of the Sirens', and the way in which Rossetti interweaves and counterbalances Christian and pagan forces. This duality is seen to be characteristic of an age when religious faith had come to be seen by many as just a repository of legend. Macleod compares Rossetti's libretto to poems by Tennyson ('Ulysses') and Swinburne ('Hymn to Proserpine').

Rossetti frequently incorporated musical instruments into his works, finding them a decorative and exotic adjunct to his figures. Here, however, the musical theme of the drawing is more than a mere motif, for the subject indicates the artist's view that music transcends all other means of communication, and that its power is magical and capable of enchantment. This was a fundamental precept of aestheticism, in the course of which movement the way in which different forms of expression and media might be drawn together to synaesthetic effect was explored. Other art forms were judged according to the degree that they satisfied the musical faculty.

This powerful drawing, modelled from 'a singular housemaid of advanced ideas ... come hither as a model, not as a housemaid' (quoted in Surtees 1971, I, p.134) proved too much for either of the two patrons whom Rossetti had hoped would buy it. Frederick Leyland and William Graham both passed it up on the grounds of the nudity of the figure, and before it was finished Rossetti adapted the figure's headwear to provide some concealment, as he explained to C.A. Howell: 'the unpopular central detail will eventually be masked by a fillet of flying drapery coming from a veil twisted in the hair so as to render it saleable' (quoted in Macleod, p.90, n.2).

CSN

Dante Gabriel Rossetti 1828–1882

73 **Veronica Veronese** *c.*1870–2

Oil on canvas 105.4 × 86.4 (41½ × 34)
Inscribed with monogram and dated '1872' lower right

Prov: F.R. Leyland 1872; his sale, Christie's 28 May 1892 (50); bt Agnew's; Joseph Ruston (see no.76); his sale 21 May 1898 (48), bt Agnew's; Reginald Vaile in 1899; his sale, Christie's 23 May 1903 (15); bt Agnew's; W. Imrie; his sale, Christie's 28 June 1907, bt Agnew's and from them by Fairfax Murray; by descent sold by his son via Agnew's to the Bancroft Estate 1923

Exh: RA Winter 1883 (295); Wilmington 1976 (4–9); New Haven 1976 (57); (see Elzea 1984 for further exhibitions)

Lit: Sharp 1882, pp.227–8, list no.219; Rossetti 1884, pp.205–8; Robinson 1892, pp.134–8; Stephens 1894, p.82; Marillier 1899, pp.159, 170, 194, 252 (no.252); Doughty and Wahl 1965–8, III, pp.1045–6; Surtees 1971, I, no.228; II, pl.325; Bayard 1976, pp.97–8; Fennell 1978, esp. letter nos.37, 38, 40, 41, 42, 46, 89; Elzea 1984, pp.120–1; Faxon 1989, p.169, pls.152, 182

Delaware Art Museum. Samuel & Mary R. Bancroft Memorial

Veronica Veronese is one of Rossetti's most gorgeous paintings, epitomising his mature style in oils. He painted it, as he had *Lady Lilith* (no.6), on commission from his patron Frederick Leyland. Although only mentioned by the artist in early 1872, the year it was completed, it is hard to believe, knowing his slow progress, that he had not begun it earlier. Even so, it apparently proceeded fairly quickly and easily. Discussions were certainly afoot for the next work for Leyland in late 1871 when plans for large paintings fell through. Leyland visited Rossetti's studio in early January 1872, and shortly after told him that

> working very hard at an entirely new picture from the Palmifera model ... The figure is mainly done except for last glazing &c, and I am going on with the thing like a house on fire ... Its price will be 800 guineas—and you will see that it is not dear. Shall I consider it yours? In that case I trust to have it ready for you by the time you come to settle in town ...
> (25 Jan. 1872, quoted in Fennell 1978, no.37)

The painting shows Alexa Wilding, discovered by Rossetti around 1866 and portrayed as *Sibylla Palmifera* (Lady Lever Art Gallery, Port Sunlight), the companion piece to *Lady Lilith*. Alexa superseded Fanny Cornforth, whose hearty sensuality inspired a different class of female image. Alexa's elegant beauty pervades *Veronica Veronese*, as it had in *Sibylla Palmifera*, lending it a new quality of removal and mystery. Later, at Leyland's suggestion, Rossetti repainted the head in *Lady Lilith* as Alexa Wilding so the two works appear more harmonious together. In 1877, the artist produced a true companion of comparable size and subject, *A Sea Spell* (fig.39 on p.68).

Initially Rossetti called *Veronica Veronese*, 'the Day Dream', enclosing this description in his letter of 25 January to Leyland:

> The girl is in a sort of passionate reverie & is drawing her hand listlessly along the strings of a violin which hangs against the wall, while she holds the bow with the other hand, as if arrested by thought at the moment when she was about to play. In colour I shall make the picture chiefly a study of varied Greens. I have not yet quite settled the background but am going ahead at it
> (Ibid.)

Also known as 'Lady with Violin' during the working process, the painting acquired the title *Veronica Veronese* by March 1872 when Rossetti wrote to Leyland that it 'sounds like the name of a musical genius'. *Veronica Veronese* plays upon the associations of colour and musical sound so much a part of Aesthetic taste. The canary's fluent singing is a natural contrast to the listless and entirely impractical pose adopted by the model as she fingers the violin. Musical composition is suggested by the inclusion of old sheet music (specifically requested by Rossetti from his friend, Boyce; see Surtees 1971). As a portrayal of a beautiful woman making music, *Veronica Veronese* belongs to a distinct genre earlier essayed by Rossetti in several Pre-Raphaelite watercolours, and continued by various artists in the 1860s, but in this work, the mood becomes one of withdrawn reverie enhanced by the heavily draped background of velvet which lends a sense of enclosure and introversion to the scene. The title of the picture, which might be translated simply as 'Veronica of Verona', calls up associations with the great sixteenth-century master Veronese. Rossetti's interest in Veronese as a colourist (Doughty and Wahl 1965–8, III, p.1009) seems to have influenced the use of saturated green worked up with shiny highlights.

Rossetti designed a frame for the picture to which he affixed a label (following the precedent of Whistler and Swinburne with *The Little White Girl* 1864; fig.22 on p.39) inscribed with a fragment of text written in French:

> Se penchant vivement, la Veronica jeta les premières notes sur la feuille vierge. Ensuite elle prit l'archet du violon pour réaliser son rêve; mais avant de décrocher l'instrument suspendu, elle resta quelques instants immobile en écoutant l'oiseau inspirateur, pendant que sa main gauche errait sur les cordes cherchant le motif suprême encore éloigné. C'était le marriage des voix de la nature et de l'âme – l'aube d'une création mystique.

Although credited to the *Lettres de Girolamo Ridolfi*, this text is usually ascribed to Swinburne, or perhaps Rossetti himself (see Rossetti 1884, pp.205–6). Swinburne, with his taste for French literature, seems the most likely author. While the lines sound very much like Swinburne, the reference to the author Girolamo Ridolfi was not merely an invention. Ridolfi, the real name of the so-called Conte Girolamo Lucchini – 'deliquente famoso' according to his biography – may well have been an Italian counterpart of the notorious Marquis de Sade who so intrigued Swinburne. His readings in the risqué literature of the eighteenth century may have unearthed Ridolfi, and the reference to a real individual gave hidden meanings to his invented lines about Veronica. By choosing to quote the text in French, Rossetti also paid homage to the French roots of the Aesthetic movement.

The text dwells on the momentary interruption of the creative process, as Veronica hears the canary's song, and ceases her own composing, which in itself aimed to replicate the bird's music. This 'musical picture', as Rossetti dubbed it, went beyond the interests of the Aesthetic movement to set up more intriguing meanings. References to her dream and the union of the sounds of nature and the soul enhance the spell of quiet reverie that pervades the painting. In particular, the final line – 'the dawn of a mystic creation' – foreshadows a range of Symbolist interests in the intangible and the inexplicable. Although well known in the collection of Leyland, *Veronica Veronese* had a fresh impact in 1883 when it appeared in the retrospective selection at the Royal Academy, fully catalogued with its tantalisingly untranslated text appearing in full.

73

In translation, it reads: 'Suddenly leaning forward, the Lady Veronica rapidly wrote the first notes on the virgin page. Then she took the bow of the violin to make her dream reality; but before commencing to play the instrument hanging from her hand, she remained quiet a few moments, listening to the inspiring bird, while her left hand strayed over the strings searching for the supreme melody, still elusive. It was the marriage of the voices of nature and the soul – the dawn of a mystic creation' (trans. in Elzea 1962, p.13).

BB

74

HENRY JOHN STOCK 1853–1930

74 The Poet in the Flames of First Love 1883

Pen and ink 26 × 35 (10¼ × 13¾)
Inscribed 'HJS 1888' lower right
Prov: …; Sotheby's 27 March 1996 (40, repr.), bt by present owner

Private Collection

Stock is a lesser-known artist of the later Symbolist period, whose highly personal work reveals a richly varied range of artistic and literary sources. This is an early drawing which sets out an inner emotion in visual terms. The subject apparently derives from Dante, the source of great inspiration to Rossetti, and whose pen-and-ink technique is imitated in this drawing. Compositionally it has connections too with the work of Watts, an artist who was of particular interest to Stock. The sheet provides early evidence too of Stock's expression in art of his emotional responses to other creative forms. Poetry and literature were recurrent concerns, but he also treated musical themes, including *Listening to Brahms* 1901 and three pictures entitled *In the Night – Schumann* 1908–27, recalling similarly titled works by James Ensor and Fernand Khnopff.

Stock went blind in childhood, but miraculously recovered his sight after being sent to live at Beaulieu in Hampshire. This experience may have stimulated his interest in the interior world of the imagination, for although he supported himself through portraiture, imaginative subject-matter was the true focus of his art. Stock drew inspiration from a wide variety of artistic and literary sources. He produced pictures based on Shakespeare, Dante, Coleridge, Wordsworth, Browning, William Morris and Walt Whitman. Several works employed Wattsian imagery and subject-matter, although it was the writings and pictures of Blake that most influenced him. It seems likely that Stock felt some connection with Blake, having like him been born in Soho, and in 1909 he decided to move to Felpham in Sussex where Blake had once lived (see John Christian, Christie's sale catalogue, 4 Nov. 1994, p.42). Stock made illustrations to Dante's *Inferno* and the Book of Revelations, as Blake had done before him. Notable from this last group is *The Four and Twenty Elders* 1911 which casts various Victorian luminaries in the roles of the Elders, including Tennyson, Carlyle, Dickens and Leighton (repr. in col. Christie's, ibid., no.64).

RU

GEORGE FREDERIC WATTS 1817–1904

75 The Dweller in the Innermost
c.1885–6

Oil on canvas 106 × 69.8 (41¾ × 27½)

Prov: As no.49

Exh: Grosvenor Gallery 1886 (10, as *The Souls' Prism*); Royal Birmingham Society of Artists, 1887; St Jude's, Whitechapel 1890 (168, as *The Dweller in the Infinite*); Munich 1893 (1639); St Jude's, Whitechapel 1894 (156); New Gallery 1896 (131); Whitechapel 1974 (40)

Lit: F.G. Stephens, *Athenaeum*, 1 May 1886, pp.591–2; 'Royal Birmingham Society of Artists', *Art Journal*, 1887, p.350; Macmillan 1903, p.263; Barrington 1905, p.162; Crane 1907, pp.252–3; MS. Cat., I, p.40; Watts 1912, II, pp.57, 180

Tate Gallery. Presented by the artist 1897

The Dweller in the Innermost, with its strangely spectral colouring and obscure meaning, is one of Watts's most obvious forays into Symbolist imagery. First entitled *The Souls' Prism*, it appeared at the annual Grosvenor Gallery exhibition of 1886 along with *Hope* (no.76). A winged female figure stares out of the picture. She wears a greenish dress with a square neckline trimmed with feathers which as they go round the back create the shape of a bizarre Van Dyck collar. At the centre of this collar, a heart-shaped brooch appears. Her headdress, akin to that associated with Mercury, consists of two small red wings, one on each side; a delicate fillet encircles her head, at its centre a shining star of white. Massive wings rise behind her, lending a sense of importance to the figure, as she sits within a large oval mandorla of palpitating orange light. But who is this strange figure? Upon her lap is a row of arrows, but without a bow, so she cannot be a cupid; also one sees a silver trumpet, yet with her contemplative, rather than celebratory, demeanour she can hardly be the allegorical figure of Fame.

This painting is one of Watt's new designs of the 1880s, created in the wake of the artist's retrospective at the Grosvenor Gallery, when he gained renewed confidence in his abilities to reach out to the public with his art. An experiment in new imagery, it presents a far-from-clear message. While the design came about within a short space of time in the winter of 1885–6, Watts wrestled with its title over the seven years following its first exhibition in 1886, indicating some uncertainty over its intended meaning.

Watts, true to his usual habit, invited friends to the studio few months before the summer exhibition, seeking their opinion on his new work. Walter Crane (see no.61), whose judgement Watts valued highly (he also owned Crane's *Renaissance of Venus*, Tate Gallery), was so struck with the then untitled image that he composed a sonnet, perhaps having in mind Rossetti's pairings of picture and poem. In his letter thanking Crane Watts hinted at the meaning he sought:

> If you would like to print the sonnet I shall be very pleased for the picture will admit of no explanation or name in the Grosvenor catalogue. Indeed it is but a stuttering that I should never have expected even you to follow or make any sense of. I myself can hardly give a

> mental form to the confused ideas which it endeavours in some slight way to focus, vague murmurings, rather than fancies which constantly beat me and rather prevent any kind of work than aid.
>
> (Crane 1907, p.252)

The sonnet had a wide circulation in tandem with the painting, first at the instigation of F.G. Stephens who included it in the *Athenaeum* (wrongly calling the painting *The Souls' Prison*) and later when it was printed in *Grosvenor Notes*.

> Star-steadfast eyes that pierce the smouldering haze
> Of Life and Thought, whose fires prismatic fuse
> The palpitating mists with magic hues
> That stain the glass of Being, as we gaze,
> And mark in transit every mood and phase,
> Which, sensitive, doth take or doth refuse
> The lights and shadows Time and Love confuse,
> When, lost in dreams, we thread their wandering maze.
>
> Fledged, too, art thou with plumes on brow and breast
> To bear thee, brooding o'er the depths unknown
> Of human strife, and wonder, and desire;
> And silence, wakened by thy horn alone,
> Behind thy veil behold a heart on fire,
> Wrapped in the secret of its own unrest.

If, as Watts indicated, the painting was untitled at this time, some months before the exhibition, then it seems that Crane's sonnet with its reference to 'prismatic fire' inspired the first title, *The Souls' Prism*. Allusions to Watts's earlier paintings occur with Time and Love, but it is the reference to the 'veil' (see pp.72–3) which opens out the context to other-worldly matters so much a part of Symbolist thinking.

Crane sent Watts a copy of his ambitious illustrated poem, *The Sirens Three*, published by Macmillan in December 1885 (shortly after publication in *The English Illustrated Magazine*). On the back of Crane's letter (Ashmolean Museum, Oxford) proffering this gift, Watts sketched out details for the headdress of *The Dweller in the Innermost*. He may well have been particularly receptive to some of the ideas and images contained in *The Sirens Three*, which is itself a fascinating example of Symbolist tendencies in British art. This book, integrating text and illustrations belongs to the tradition of William Blake (and indeed some of the imagery is notably Blakean), but *The Sirens Three* is more directly allied to the recent 'symbolical' works of Watts. The visual imagery of Crane's illustrations, with youthful allegorical types, the direct descendants of Watts's figures in *Love and Death*, heralds a distinctly Symbolist mode. The enigmatic figures populate a strange land filled with symbols, resulting in an atmosphere replete with mystery. The fully worked out programme of *The Sirens Three* provides a cast of allegorical characters as the drama unfolds in Time's House, with Hope surviving as the poem draws to a close. As a decorative artist, Crane was attuned to details as a way of enriching his invented Symbolist style with, for example, hovering spheres and loose, cascading hair merging into waves. His reference to the 'man's winged brain' relates to Watts's conception of the head of *The Dweller in the Innermost*.

As Crane fulfilled the role of painter-poet in the spirit of Blake and Rossetti, he also forged some distinctly odd images within the format of this illustrated book. Crane's desire to illuminate Watts's untitled picture can be seen in the context of his own efforts at uniting word and image in *The Sirens Three*. Both artists were attuned to a new kind of non-naturalistic imagery, taking a mystical view, as can be detected in Crane's sonnet, where the images of light and colour, 'palpitating mists', 'magic hues', as reflected light, provide a verbal parallel to Watts's painting.

Watts found the title *The Souls' Prism* an unsatisfactory elucidation of the 'vague murmurings' he sought to convey. A geometrical prism is nowhere to be seen in the work, and the title was regularly misread as *The Soul's Prison*. In the autumn after the exhibition, Watts carried out a large red chalk drawing of the subject (Watts Gallery, Compton) and to Mrs Barrington he wrote 'what can she be called? "The Daughter of Duty and Introspection"'. Mrs Watts indicated that the artist also considered the possibility of the title *Spirit of the Ages*; when Watts exhibited the painting in Birmingham in 1887 without a title, one writer supposed that the 'weird mysterious figure, with gleaming eyes' bore the title *Spirit of the Ages* the previous year. By 1890, Watts arrived at *The Dweller in the Infinite*, and by the time it went to Munich in 1893, its title took final form.

In 1896, when the painting was included in the massive exhibition of Watts's work at the New Gallery, to which the artist himself contributed, it appeared in the catalogue with the following note: 'Conscience, winged, dusk-faced, and pensive, seated facing, within a glow of light; on her forehead she bears a shining star, and on her lap lie the arrows that pierce through all disguise, and the trumpet which proclaims truth to the world'. In the introduction to the catalogue, as if realising that the esoteric meaning of this work (among others) required further explanation, he added 'the vague figure may be vaguely called conscience'. Macmillan (whose book

Watts read through before publication) added a further gloss on the meaning of the work in 1903 seeing the figure 'who sits enthroned as judge in the heart of each man, and from whose eyes, which are as a flame of fire, no sin can be hidden'. The notions of truth and conscience seem joined together in a figure who is more mystical than judgemental. Watts's technique enhanced such qualities, as a network of feathery brushstrokes allowed atmospheric effects of light, almost an iridescence, to ceate a convincing sense of an ethereal creature hovering in space.

BB

George Frederic Watts 1817–1904

76 **Hope** *c.*1885–6

Oil on canvas 150 × 109 (60 × 43)

Prov: Sold by the artist in 1887 to Joseph Ruston of Monk's Manor, Lincoln; Ruston Trustees sale, Christie's 4 July 1913 (113); Sir Jeremiah Colman Bt, of Gatton Park, Surrey; his sale, Christie's 18 Sept. 1942 (113); bt Mitchell; ...; Ben Welch; sold to Ronald Staples and remaining with his family until *c.*1960 when bt back by Ben Welch; ...; private collection; Sotheby's 26 Nov. 1986 (55), bt by present owner

Exh: Grosvenor Gallery 1886 (61); RA 1905 (201); Newcastle 1905 (160); Brussels 1929 (191); Washington 1997 (33)

Lit: Spielmann 1886, cat. p.30 (as unfinished); Phillips 1893, pp.40–2, repr. p.40; Chesterton 1904, pp.94–108, 135; Barrington 1905, pp.37, 93, 162; MS. Cat., I, p.71; Watts 1912, II, pp.57, 106, 150, 163; Tate Gallery 1954, on the subject, see no.65 (the oil sketch); Blunt 1975, pl.126; Staley 1978 (see no.31, the Tate Gallery version); Bryant 1987, pp.62–5; Morris 1996, p.487

Private Collection

EXHIBITED IN LONDON AND MUNICH ONLY

As a design conceived and executed over a short time in the 1880s, *Hope* represents the new directions in Watts's art in this decade (see pp.71 et seq.). It uses the traditional allegorical figure of Hope, but is designed to be read as an unencumbered visual statement accessible to all. Watts sensed that *Hope* 'promised to be popular' while it was in his studio, before exhibition. Indeed it has proved to be one of his most enduring images.

Two major versions of *Hope* exist: this one is the first, which re-emerged in 1986 after decades in private collections. The Tate Gallery's *Hope* (fig.35 on p.65) is the second, presented by the artist in 1897 as part of the Watts Gift. The artist had an offer of £1,500 for his original version even before its exhibition at the Grosvenor Gallery in 1886. He realised that a replica painted for a favoured private client, far from detracting from his original plan to present the work to the nation, would spread its consolatory message even wider. Following studio practice of the time, his assistant, Cecil Schott, probably began this work and Watts himself carried on with painting, completing it fairly quickly. According to Mrs Barrington, who was at Little Holland House nearly every day in these years, 'Signor has painted a second "Hope", far more beautiful than the one in the Grosvenor Gallery, and one of these he intends to give to the Nation'. By 1887, he decided to sell the first *Hope* and, believing the second to be better, reserved it for his planned bequest; it was also this second version which he exhibited at the South Kensington Museum and then sent to Paris for the Exposition Universelle in 1889.

The differences between the two principal versions amount mainly to changes in handling, colour and detail. In the first (the present work), the drapery is greyish-white rather than tinged with green as it is in the Tate's version. The background is more noticeably brushy, while the second is softer overall, perhaps a deliberate choice by Watts to create a more diffused atmospheric space, further enhanced by the softer more varied mists that envelop the lower area of the globe-like sphere. In the second version, as well, the figure fills slightly less of the picture space, accentuating her isolation. Details in the first version are, as one would expect, more precise, with the hint of a smile playing over the lips of Hope, where in the second version her expression is more enigmatic. The detail of the star set high in the sky injects a note of optimism which the artist virtually edited out of the more serious and sombre second version.

The details of the star and lyre with all strings broken but one, as well as the overall blue tonality, suggest a mood of sadness at variance with the title, leading at least one commentator, G.K. Chesterton, to read the subject as 'Despair'. Thanks to this ambiguity *Hope* has proved endlessly fascinating to observers. The gloomy note may reflect a family tragedy, the death of Watts's grown-up adopted daughter Blanche's one-year-old infant.

The traditional figure of Hope had a long lineage in art as one of the three theological virtues, but Watts rejected the standard accessory of an anchor as a means of identification, and instead animated an allegorical cliché by taking a fresh perspective. Even so, a range of near-contemporary works of art can be related to *Hope*. The figure seated on a globe appeared as a motif in Watts's own work just before *Hope* in *The Idle Child of Fancy* (formerly Watts Gallery, Compton) in which a sportive cupid displays a bow and arrow. But the idea of a figure on a globe had other associations. It had appeared in Elihu Vedder's *Rubáiyát of Omar Khayyám*, published in London by Quaritch in 1884. This work was discussed along with the rest of Vedder's œuvre in an article of 1885 in the *Magazine of Art*. Several plates from the *Rubáiyát* were reproduced, including *The Throne of Saturn* (no.87) showing an adolescent winged figure sitting on a planet, spinning in outer space. The swirling rings around the sphere lend a sense of sweeping movement to the small design. The lines associated with the design dwell on the 'master-knot of human fate', and Vedder's attempt to unravel the knot is akin to Watts's thinking, in both works of 1886, *Hope* and *The Dweller in the Innermost*. Vedder's publication coincided with the inception of *Hope* in 1885, but there was more than just the compositional similarity of the plate for *The Throne of Saturn* and *Hope*, since Vedder was well known for the 'psychical quality' of his work. His concern with 'the visionary' and with 'a symbolic sense of mind' (A. Mary F. Robinson, *Magazine of Art*, 1885, p.122) was held in common with Watts and others (for example, Walter Crane and Evelyn de Morgan) in the 1880s who sought visual expression of cosmic ideas.

Other echoes can be seen, particularly in the pose of the figure. Watts arrived at this through a series of sketches, yet there are some recollections of the siren in Rossetti's *A Sea Spell* 1877 (fig.30 on p.68) who also plays and listens to her instrument with rapt concentration. The pose also recalls Albert Moore's passively sleeping women as in *Dreamers* exh. 1882 (City Museum and Art Gallery, Birmingham). Her bandaged head alluding to blindness has links with the bent
figure of blind Fortune in the small gouache by Burne-Jones for *The Wheel of Fortune* (no.28), once in Watts's own collection. All these associations indicate a level of awareness among artists who shared similar concerns in the 1870s and 1880s.

The public exhibition of *Hope* exceeded Watts's expectations, confounding his worries that the work would be 'destroyed' by the critics. While there was criticism of the angularity of the arm of Hope (perhaps one of the aspects of the painting he planned to improve in the second version), the quality of colour, light and atmosphere prompted Cosmo Monkhouse to comment on its 'tender opalescence' (*Academy*, 15 May 1886, p.350), singling out Watts's increasing attention to colour, a new feature of his work at this time. F.G. Stephens called *Hope* a 'piece of tone harmony' (*Athenaeum*, 24 April 1888, p.561), drawing attention to its qualities as a 'tone poem' – to use the language of contemporary European music. The point links the picture once again to Vedder's *Throne of Saturn* and its evocation of the music of the spheres.

BB

GEORGE FREDERIC WATTS 1817–1904

77 The Happy Warrior *c.*1884

Oil on canvas 76 × 64 (29⅞ × 25¼)

Prov: Collection of the artist (on view at the Little Holland House Gallery); bt by the Bavarian state from the Munich Jahresausstellung 1893

Exh: Grosvenor Gallery 1884 (135); New York 1884 (87); Birmingham 1885 (115); Nottingham 1885 (40); Rugby School 1886*; St Jude's, Whitechapel 1889 (158); Cambrian Academy 1889*; Southwark 1890*; Tottenham 1891*; Sheffield 1891*; Munich 1893 (1654a)
*exh. listed in MS. Cat. but untraced

Lit: Spielmann 1886, cat. p.30; Macmillan 1903, pp.185–7; von Schleinitz 1904, pp.67–8; Barrington 1905, p.125; MS. Cat., I, p.69; Watts 1912, II, p.244; Girouard 1981, pp.150–4, 267, 288, illus.101; Neue Pinakothek, Munich 1990, no.7926, pp.313–15

Bayerische Staatsgemäldesammlungen, Munich, Neue Pinakothek

EXHIBITED IN LONDON AND MUNICH ONLY

The Happy Warrior is the last and most visionary of a series of depictions of knights in armour, a preoccupation for Watts from the outset of his career and one with which the artist himself personally identified. He painted his self-portrait as a young knight in armour in Italy in 1843; and two decades later, his own features appear as the face of the older knight in *Eve of Peace* (Dunedin Art Gallery, New Zealand). By the early 1880s, in *The Happy Warrior*, Watts no longer projected his actual appearance onto the knight, but the experience of the moment of death and the vision of a beautiful woman summed up a potent ideal for Watts. In his hands, by the 1880s, the ideal is transformed into a Symbolist vision of the moment of death.

Very little is recorded about the inspiration and progress of *The Happy Warrior*, presumably carried out fairly rapidly in the year or so before its exhibition at the Grosvenor Gallery in 1884. The depiction of an actual vision reflects the artist's interest in the other-worldly, and just at this time he was elected to the Society for Psychical Research (see p.72). Indeed the image of the female face appearing out of a swirl of mist and colour seems like one of the 'apparitions' described in the psychic literature with which Watts was familiar. The imagery of this much-exhibited painting provided a model for an art moving into new, non-naturalist territory and as such one might consider it a variation on the theme of Rossetti's *Beata Beatrix* (no.44).

In the catalogue of the exhibition in New York, Mrs Barrington linked a poetic fragment with the painting (which, however, went unidentified):

> Not conquered he who sinks upon the field,
> Consents to die, consenting not to yield
> Whose steadfast heart death perils cannot
> move,
> True to his faith, his duty, and his love.

The title of the painting, however, derives from Wordsworth's famous poem the 'Character of the Happy Warrior' (1807) included in *Poems of Sentiment and Reflection*:

> Who is the happy warrior: Who is he
> Whom every man in arms should wish to be …
> Whose high endeavours are an inward light
> That makes the path before him always bright …

The poem's conclusion suggests imminent death:

> And, while the mortal mist is gathering, draws
> His breath in confidence of Heaven's
> applause …

At least one image from the poem relates to the painting, the gathering 'mortal mist', although Watts's mist seems to speak more of other-worldly

78

realms. The imagery in the painting goes further than what is evoked in the poem, for the protagonist in the painting, swooning backward, is submerged in the moment of death. The beautiful woman, representing the ideal which the warrior sought in life, emerges from darkness to place a kiss of death upon him. She is a vision, disembodied but identifiable as a woman with her long hair turning into an enveloping mist. In breaking up the surface into a mass of small, scattered brushstrokes, Watts arrived at a way of painting a vision, but this technique also relates to a whole range of Post-Impressionist methods in the mid to late 1880s.

Appropriately, given the northern European taste for the mystical and magical, this painting, one of Watts's most deeply Symbolist works, found its true audience in Germany, where it has remained since 1893, having (as far as we know) never been seen in England since it left his studio for exhibition in Munich.

BB

GEORGE FREDERIC WATTS 1817–1904

78 **The Genius of Greek Poetry** late 1850s–*c.*1878

Oil on canvas 66 × 53.3 (26 × 21)

Prov: Collection of the artist; ?probably sold after the exhibitions of 1885–6 to Sir Horace Davey, QC, MP (later Baron Davey of Fenhurst); his sale, 20 April 1907 (85) to Hamilton; Agnew's, bt by the Preston Corporation Art Gallery 1907

Exh: Probably Grosvenor Gallery 1881 (55); New York 1884 (121); Birmingham 1885 (171); Nottingham 1886; New Gallery 1896 (74); Cardiff 1913 (14, cat. not traced)

Lit: Spielmann 1886, p.10 and p.30 lists only the Davey version (1878); Macmillan 1903, pp.124–5; Barrington 1905, pp.109, 135; Preston Corporation Art Gallery, *Illustrated Catalogue*, Harris Museum ..., London, etc., 1907, no.228; MS. Cat., I, p.60; Watts 1912, I, p.235 and II, p.74; Staley 1978, no.25 for discussion of Watts Gallery version

Harris Museum and Art Gallery, Preston

The inspiration for *The Genius of Greek Poetry* dates from Watts's travels around the Greek islands in 1856, with Sir Charles Newton's expedition to excavate the remains of the ancient city of Halicarnassus. The vivid experience of Greek lands with Mediterranean light reflecting off blue seas, creating an atmosphere steeped in colour, resulted in a range of works including the versions of *The Island of Cos* (see no.59). *The Genius of Greek Poetry* is unusual in being predominantly a figure composition. The pose of the 'genius' derives from *Achilles and Briseis*, a much larger work on mural scale carried out by Watts for Lord Lansdowne at Bowood in 1858.

As a separate composition, with an entirely new meaning, *The Genius of Greek Poetry* advanced during the late 1860s, reaching completion in 1878 (Spielmann 1886), though it did not appear at exhibition until 1881. According to Mrs. Barrington, the painting derived from Wordsworth's lines beginning 'the world is too much with us', but there is no direct correlation with Watts's work (see Staley 1978, p.83). The exact meaning of the painting has eluded many commentators, despite the artist's short explanation in the catalogue of the Grosvenor retrospective: 'symbolical figure representing the genius of Greek art inspired by the forces and phenomena of nature as they pass in vision before his eyes'. Even Spielmann in 1886 found that the painting was 'not sufficiently or immediately intelligible'. Certainly it presents a bewildering range of ideas and images centred on the ancient world which had preoccupied Watts for much of his career. His actual experiences in Greek lands had a real impact on his work, as he later wrote:

> Those who have visited Asia Minor, or sailed among the Islands of the Greek Seas, have seen ... assembled in nature, a concurrence of conditions that may well account for the birth and development of the divine faculties. The graceful mythology of the Greeks... was the outcome of a constant communion with such rich loveliness.
>
> (from Watts's own writings 'On Style', Watts 1912, III, p.51)

The catalogue entry on the painting for the exhibition in New York in 1884, written by Mrs Barrington in consultation with Watts, refers to

> The prominence humanity held in the Greek mind, the association of the effects in nature, and the entire conditions in the world with humanity being so strong that all effects and moods of nature weave themselves in his imagination into semi-human existences; the winds and the currents, the hours of the day, the earth, sea, and air, all natural phenomena he invests with human forms, attributes and moods. The figure seated on a rock is intended to be an emblem of this Greek Genius, not a Greek man.

For a moderately sized work, *The Genius of Greek Poetry* displays a breadth of composition and sense of movement that suggests its ultimate derivation from one of Watts's mural projects. The nude genius adopts the pose of Phidias's Theseus from the Parthenon pediment which was one of the artist's greatest sources of inspiration. The sculptural origin of the figure is underlined by Watts's own wax model of the genius figure, presumably made to study the pose (perhaps as early as the 1850s); this model was later cast in bronze (Watts Gallery, Compton). The sculptor Sir Joseph Edgar Boehm thought *The Genius of Greek Poetry* one of Watts's finest works, and other sculptors, such as Alfred Gilbert, often saw in Watts's works potential subjects for their own medium.

The upper portion of *The Genius of Greek Poetry* shows a series of uninhibited flying figures, dipping, swooning and twisting through the air. This chain of nymphs repeats a motif seen in the small version of *The Island of Cos* and in *Chaos* (no.49), in both of which Watts designated them as symbolic of the passage of time.

Mrs Barrington also indicated that the meaning of *The Genius of Greek Poetry* 'would be more easily explained were the pendant picture beside it, "The Genius of Northern Poetry," darker, more mysterious, less human in attributes than the Greek Genius' (Barrington 1905, p.136). Watts may never have executed the pendant (or if he did it has been lost) but a depiction of a genius inhabiting a cold, northern realm would certainly be an appropriately Symbolist study of darkness, night and a 'less human' vision (cf. no.121).

There are several versions of *The Genius of Greek Poetry* but it seems clear that as the most highly finished version, the painting at Preston is probably the much-exhibited version of the 1880s. It seems almost certain, given the sale of Lord Davey's collection in 1907 and the acquisition of *The Genius of Greek Poetry* by Preston in the same year that these are one and the same; that is, the prime version sold by Watts around 1886. The painting in the Fogg Art Museum is closely related to the Preston version but less finished. The version at the Watts Gallery varies the composition, but is not highly finished; and the version in the Clarendon collection is even more sketchy.

BB

James Abbott McNeill Whistler 1834–1903

79 Nocturne: Blue and Silver – Chelsea 1871

Oil on panel 50.2 × 60.8 (19¾ × 23⅞)
Signed with butterfly and dated '71'

Prov: W.C. Alexander 1871; by descent to the Misses R. and J. Alexander, by whom given to the National Gallery by Deed of Gift 1959; transferred to the Tate Gallery 1972

Exh: Dudley Gallery 1871 (265, as *Harmony in Blue-Green*); ?Durand-Ruel, Paris 1873; Grosvenor Gallery 1879 (192, as *Nocturne in Blue-Green*); ?Paris 1883 (5, as *Nocturne en bleu et argent*); ?Brussels 1884 (2, as *Nocturne en bleu et argent, No.1*); Goupil 1892 (18, as *Nocturne, Blue and Silver – Chelsea*); London 1905 (31, as *Nocturne in Blue and Green*); Paris 1905 (72); Tate Gallery 1994 (46)

Lit: Sutton 1966, pl.65; Young et al. 1980, no.103

Tate Gallery. Bequeathed by Miss Rachel and Miss Jean Alexander

This is chronologically the first of Whistler's Nocturnes. It was painted in August 1871 as pair to a daylight scene (*Variations in Violet and Green*, private collection; Young et al. 1980, no.104) which continued the mood of the 'Six Projects' (see no.16) while increasing the importance of the landscape in relation to the figures. Here the single figure is reduced to a mere suggestion and the picture is explicitly and almost exclusively concerned with the effect of twilight on water. The artist's mother recorded that she and her son had just seen together 'the river in a glow of rare transparency an hour before sunset'; Whistler 'was inspired to begin a picture & rushed upstairs to his Studio'.

There are vestigial topographical details: the tower of Chelsea Old Church on the horizon to the right indicates that this is a view across the Thames from Battersea, but there is clearly no intention to convey geographical or social information. The influence of Japanese prints is very evident, as much in the artist's butterfly signature as in the simplification of the image, but it is worth noting that while Japanese prints were nearly always very specific in their reference either to recognisable places or to social events and characters, Whistler borrowed only their clarity of design, never their documentary function. The French critic Théodore Duret, in the course of a long appreciation of what was almost certainly this Nocturne in 1881, pointed out that Whistler had 'chosen as his subject a river and its banks, for after all he needed a motif to carry (*porter*)

79

the colour' which is the true subject of the picture (quoted in Young et al. 1980).

As with the 'Six Projects' the apparent absence of subject-matter is compensated by the deliberate naming of a musical form in the title. The name 'Nocturne' was not Whistler's own invention; it had been suggested to him by F.R. Leyland who, as a pianist (see no.16) would naturally have been thinking of Chopin, and was evidently prompted by Whistler's own use of the term 'Symphony' in some of his recent titles. It was enthusiastically adopted by the artist, even if a somewhat perverse choice in so far as this and some others in the series are not strictly night scenes but scenes of dusk or twilight.

The incorporation of both natural and artificial light into the design can be related to a long tradition of night scenes in Western art going back at least to Elsheimer; here the delicacy of the contrast in the context of exquisitely tender tonal variations refers once again to music rather than to any painted precedents. The implied contrast between this tranquil idyll and the busy Thames of the daylight hours, with its steam barges and pollution, makes for a particularly poignant sense of the tension between the achievements of civilisation and the poet's need for quiet and calm. In a well-known passage of his 'Ten O'Clock Lecture' Whistler spoke of the moment 'when the evening mist clothes the riverside with poetry as with a veil and the poor buildings lose themselves in the dim sky, and the tall chimneys become campanili, and the warehouses are palaces in the night'. He professed to be an artist of the world, of an artificial society in which raw nature had no place. It is in the Nocturnes that that claim becomes transparent. Despite their generalisation, they are nevertheless true to a vividly experienced reality. They are pictures that crystallise the intensely personal, existential relationship between the painter and nature.

There is in any case an inherent ambiguity in the fading light of late evening. Denys Sutton has argued that the choice of twilight as a subject 'accorded with certain definite contemporary preoccupations', and speaks of 'the consolations afforded by night, as when Dante Gabriel Rossetti, tortured by recriminations and a prey to melancholy, wandered through the London streets on his nocturnal excursions'. He adds that 'the moment of nightfall, *l'heure bleue*, which appealed so deeply to Whistler, is one when dreams and regrets are engendered: reveries envelop the mind; and passions, too, as Baudelaire had disclosed in *Les Fleurs du mal*' (1966, pp.27–8). The Nocturnes, then, are central statements of the Symbolist position. See also no.80.

AW

James Abbott McNeill Whistler 1834–1903

80 **Nocturne: Blue and Silver – Cremorne Lights** 1872

Oil on canvas 50.2 × 74.9 (19½ × 29¼)
Signed lower right with butterfly and dated '72'

Prov: Gerald Potter, after 1882; Goupil Gallery; A.H. Studd 1894, by whom bequeathed to the National Gallery 1919; transferred to the Tate Gallery 1949

Exh: Dudley Gallery 1872 (237); ?Brighton 1875 (98, as *Nocturne in Blue and Gold*); ?Durand-Ruel, Paris 1873; Grosvenor Gallery 1882 (2, as *Nocturne in Blue and Silver*); Goupil 1892 (34); Boussod, Valadon & Cie, Glasgow 1893; ?Goupil 1898 (25, as *Nocturne – Blue and Gold*); Boston 1904 (56); Paris 1905 (69); London and New York 1960 (27); Berlin 1969 (17); Tate Gallery 1994 (47)

Lit: Cary 1907, no.6; Sickert 1908, no.103; Sutton 1966, pl.64; Young et al. 1980, no.115, pl.110

Tate Gallery. Bequeathed by Arthur Studd 1919

80

It was noticed in connection with no.79 that the series of night or twilight scenes on the Thames that Whistler painted in the early 1870s were a continuation of the thought behind the 'Six Projects' of the years immediately preceding (see no.16). The point is underlined by the fact that there are traces of a figure subject akin to those of the 'Six Projects' beneath the paint of this Nocturne, a change of purpose that embodied for the authors of the 1994 catalogue 'the transition from the decorative figure subjects of the 1870s to the Nocturnes and portraits which dominated the 1870s'. As with Watts, Whistler's work as a portraitist belongs to some extent in a category apart; but the continuity between figure subjects and landscapes is real and significant in the case of both artists. Whereas Watts tended to incorporate literal or implied symbolic content in both his allegories and his landscapes, Whistler was content in both his arrangements of figures and his river views simply to suggest states of mind by means of subtly deployed colour harmonies and restrained compositional devices.

The composition of this Nocturne is a development out of the *Nocturne in Blue and Silver* of the previous year: although rather wider in format, its layout is almost identical, with empty foreground and high horizon; yet its scale is much more expansive and its colour register higher, more luminous. The sluggish, sleeping river enclosed by the great capital city has given way to a silvery highway, seen from Battersea Bridge, leading to an enchanted fairground, the Cremorne pleasure gardens just beyond Chelsea: the opposition of man and nature seems here to be reconciled in a dreamlike idyll.

AW

Charles Ricketts 1866–1931

81 **The Sphinx** 1894

Written by Oscar Wilde (1854–1900); designed and illustrated by Charles Ricketts; published by Elkin Mathews and John Lane 1894
Book bound in vellum-covered boards with stamped gilt design by Charles Ricketts
Page size 25.5 × 19 (10 × 7½)
47 unnumbered pages, 10 plates printed on handmade paper with unbleached Arnold and Vale Press watermarks
Open at pages 29–30: 'Still from his chair of porphyry gaunt Memnon strains his lidless eyes ...'

Prov: Copyright edition presented 28 Sept. 1894 to British Museum Library
Exh: Barbican 1989 (323)
Lit: Calloway 1979, p.16, repr. pl.37; Delaney 1990, pp.82–3; Kooistra 1995, pp.94–107

The British Library Board

EXHIBITED IN LONDON ONLY

In 1892 Oscar Wilde commissioned Ricketts to illustrate *The Sphinx*, the poem he was currently working on. Ricketts also took complete charge of the design, typography and binding of the book, and started work in June that year. The poem itself, however, was not completed until 1893, and there were further delays before its eventual publication in 1894. In the intervening period Wilde's *Salome* was published, illustrated by Beardsley (see no.89), which was received with public outrage. Ricketts felt that by the time *The Sphinx* appeared, its reception was eclipsed (see Delaney 1990, p.82–3). However, Wilde's slow-

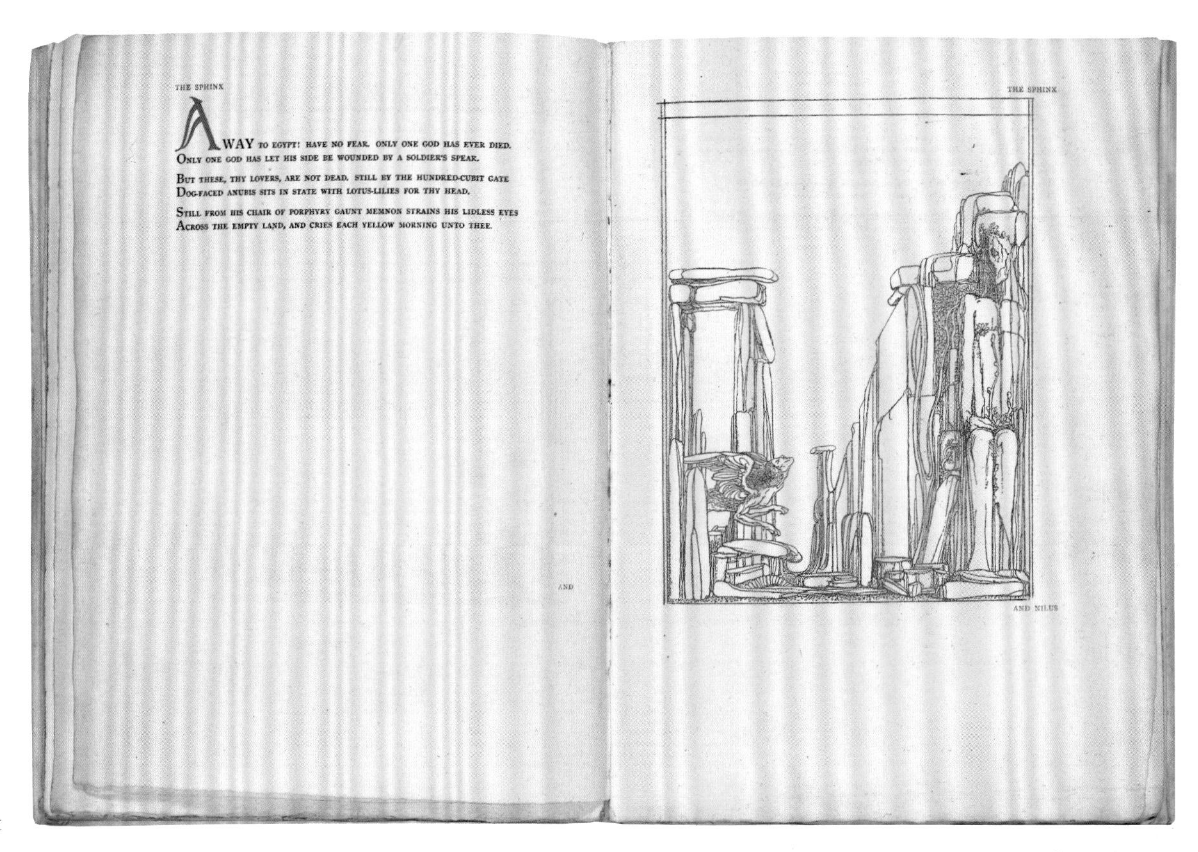
THE SPHINX

AWAY TO EGYPT! HAVE NO FEAR. ONLY ONE GOD HAS EVER DIED.
ONLY ONE GOD HAS LET HIS SIDE BE WOUNDED BY A SOLDIER'S SPEAR.

BUT THESE, THY LOVERS, ARE NOT DEAD. STILL BY THE HUNDRED-CUBIT GATE
DOG-FACED ANUBIS SITS IN STATE WITH LOTUS-LILIES FOR THY HEAD.

STILL FROM HIS CHAIR OF PORPHYRY GAUNT MEMNON STRAINS HIS LIDLESS EYES
ACROSS THE EMPTY LAND, AND CRIES EACH YELLOW MORNING UNTO THEE.

AND

THE SPHINX

AND NILUS

81

ness in publication was partly deliberate. Despite the furore over *Salome*, *The Sphinx* was the most overtly decadent of his writings so far. It was fairly clearly an account of homoerotic yearning, and it was the last thing published before Wilde's conviction for homosexuality. He himself said publication was delayed because 'it would destroy domesticity in England' (Hyde 1982, p.31). Curiously, however, its publication aroused little general notice.

Wilde's poem characterised the Sphinx as a creature of supreme sexual attraction, ruled by its passions and eliciting the same powerful responses in others. It also possesses arcane knowledge of the ancient world, a metaphor for revelation through sensual experience. The Sphinx combines feminine softness with a bestial passion, and there are strong elements of both sexual violence and violent sexual passion in the poem:

> Couch by his side upon the grass and set your
> white teeth in his throat
> And when you hear his dying note lash your
> long flanks of polished brass
> And take a tiger for your mate, whose amber
> sides are flecked with black,
> And ride upon his gilded back in triumph
> through the Theban gate
> And toy with him in amorous jests, and when
> he turns, and snarls, and gnaws,
> O smite him with your jasper claws! And bruise
> him with your agate breasts!

The narrator tries in vain to banish the Sphinx from his consciousness:

> Get hence, you loathsome mystery! Hideous
> animal, get hence!
> You wake in me each bestial sense, you make
> me what I would not be.
> You make my creed a barren sham, you wake
> foul dreams of sensual life,
> And Atys with his blood-stained knife were
> better than the thing I am.

The Sphinx for Wilde, therefore, personifies unwelcome yet compelling deviant fantasies, and is in fact an allegory of his homosexuality. When it was published Wilde was accused of imitating the metre of Tennyson's 'In Memoriam' (1850), to which he replied 'No, it is printed quite differently' (Hyde 1982, p.31). The rhythms do actually differ, but the subject-matter underlying the two poems might be seen as the same. Tennyson's feelings for his dead friend Arthur Hallam may have been wholly chaste and pure, but repressed homosexual attraction has since been seen as an underlying theme. It would certainly have amused and suited Wilde to promote this, for 'In Memoriam' had become a pure icon of Victorian culture and sensitivity, its author a literary colossus.

Wilde's description of the Sphinx at the beginning of the poem interestingly anticipates Fernand Khnopff's subsequent pictorial representation in *Les Caresses* (*The Sphinx*) (fig.2 on p.17) quite closely. It is tempting to suppose that Wilde's poem had some influence on Khnopff, who was keenly aware of cultural developments in England:

> Half woman and half animal!
> Come forth my lovely languorous sphinx!
> And put your head upon my knee!
> And let me stroke your throat and see your body spotted like the lynx!
> And let me touch those curving claws of yellow and ivory and grasp
> The tail that like a monstrous asp coils round your heavy velvet paws!

By the early 1890s Carlyle's *Sartor Resartus* had become widely known in Europe and its reference to the Colossus of Memnon (see p.29–30) found echoes in many Symbolist pictures. Wilde may well have been thinking of the same passage when he wrote the lines on this page.

Wilde's poem was printed in an edition of two hundred, plus twenty-five large paper copies. It sold poorly, and a large proportion of the unsold copies perished in a fire. It is therefore an exceptionally rare item. The book contained ten plates by Ricketts, printed in brownish-red. They illustrate lines from the poem but also add to them by often taking the range of symbolism and meaning further than the poem itself. Ricketts also designed the initial letters and the supremely aesthetic binding in white vellum, stamped with a gilt design. This combines delicately drawn rectangular panels with further Sphinx illustrations, including an attenuated figure holding a lantern before which the Sphinx recoils. This figure is indebted to both Burne-Jones and Beardsley, but also apparently to Holman Hunt's famous painting *The Light of the World* 1853 (Keble College, Oxford). The illustrations inside display a rich variety of visual sources and references, too numerous to analyse fully here. The frontispiece, for instance, which opposes the Sphinx with an allegorical figure of Melancholy, features a twisting vine that recalls both the decorated pages of Kelmscott Press books and Burne-Jones's tangled thicket in *The Briar Rose* series, as does the decorated initial letter of the text. The '*Diver of the Colchian Caves*' derives from soaring figures in numerous illustrations by Blake. Several plates display Moreau's influence in their composition and use of pictorial space, and in the scale of figures in landscapes. The swirling lines of '*Moon Horned Io*' appear to have partly influenced Klimt's illustration *Fischblut* for *Ver Sacrum*, III, 1900 (see no.109).

Ricketts considered *The Sphinx* his best work as an illustrator (see Ricketts 1932, p.38), and described in detail his approach to the project:

> This is the first book of the modern revival of printing in red, black and green; the small bulk of the text and unusual length of the lines necessitated quite a peculiar arrangement; here I made an effort away from the Renaissance towards a book marked by surviving classical traits, printing it in Capitals. In the pictures I have striven to combine … those affinities in line work broadcast in all epochs. My attempt there as elsewhere was to evolve what one might imagine as possible in one charmed moment or place.
>
> (Ricketts 1899, p.25)

Wilde was peculiarly indifferent to Ricketts's efforts, and told him 'No, my dear Ricketts, your drawings are not of your best. You have seen them through your intellect, not through your temperament' (Ricketts 1932, p.38). Sturge Moore recalled further friction when Ricketts, 'his face crimson … tore out the fly-leaf Wilde had inscribed from the copy of *The Sphinx* sent to him. "Vulgar beast!" he cried, for the signature … scrawled right across the leaf, an outrage to the exquisite niceties of the artist's book building' (Sturge Moore 1933, p.3).

Nevertheless, Ricketts greatly admired Wilde, although he only fully appreciated him in retrospect, and eventually recorded his recollections of him, published posthumously in 1933. He noted in his diary entry for 23 September 1905: 'It is astonishing that I viewed him as the most genial, kindly and civilised of men, but it never entered my head that his personality was the most remarkable one that I should ever meet, that in intellect & humanity he is the largest type I have come across' (quoted Delaney 1990, p.143). When Wilde was released from Reading Gaol in 1897, and many of his circle avoided contact with him, Ricketts sent him £100. Robert Ross, however, ensured this was returned, 'as he knew the sender to be in dire need' (Sturge Moore 1933, p.4).

In 1904 Ricketts gave his original page layouts for *The Sphinx* to Ross, Wilde's literary executor (see Delaney 1990, p.230), by whom they were subsequently presented to the British Museum.

RU

MAURICE DENIS 1870–1943

82 La Damoiselle élue 1893

Lithograph in three colours 30 × 11 (11¾ × 4⅜) on a page 42 × 30 (16⅝ × 11⅞)
Signed vertically 'MAUD' lower right
Handwritten dedication 'à Monsieur Roger Marx, affectueusement Maurice Denis' in the margin lower right

Prov: Roger Marx; Emile Laffron; E. Béjot, by whom presented to Bibliothèque Nationale 1931
Exh: Hayward Gallery 1972 (47, repr.)
Lit: See Hayward 1972

Bibliothèque Nationale de France

EXHIBITED IN LONDON ONLY

This three-colour lithograph represents Dante Gabriel Rossetti's Blessed Damozel at the golden bar of heaven. It was executed as the cover for the first edition of Claude Debussy's setting of Rossetti's poem, *La Damoiselle élue* [The Blessed Damozel], *poème lyrique d'après D.G. Rossetti*, which was published by Edmond Bailly in Paris in 1893 (La Librairie de l'Art Indépendant).

Rossetti's poetry had been introduced into France as early as 1871 by Edmond Blémont, a close friend of Fantin-Latour. However, the English poet's work received far wider dissemination in France through the publication in 1885 of Gabriel Sarrazin's series, *Les Poètes Modernes de l'Angleterre*. This provided Debussy with the text for his 'poème lyrique' for choir and orchestra which he composed shortly after his return to Paris from Rome in 1887.

By 1887, Debussy had already questioned the dominant influence of Wagner on contemporary French music. When *La Damoiselle élue* was given its first performance by students of César Franck at the Société Nationale on 8 April 1893, it was received with shock and a realisation that his sound world contained affinities with the Symbolist movement. Indeed, the innovative character of Debussy's work, of which this was an example, led to the inclusion of *La Damoiselle élue* in the first concert devoted solely to Debussy's music, presented on 1 March 1894 by La Libre Esthétique, the successor avant-garde exhibition organisation to Les XX in Brussels.

The commission to create a cover for a musical composition whose text dealt with the unobtainable woman, and whose music denoted an affiliation with Symbolism, lay wholly within the aesthetic concerns of Maurice Denis. Introduced to the pictorial symbolism of Paul Gauguin in late 1888 by his fellow student Paul Sérusier, Denis had quickly adopted the non-naturalist principles of bold outline and flattened colour which he has applied in this lithograph. In addition, as a limited edition print, the lithograph proclaims the Symbolists' commitment to the revival of the original print as a valid expression of the artist's discrete right to give visual expression to the subject of art, the Idea. The engagement with the image of an unobtainable woman, the damozel at the golden bar, reflects Denis's own perception of women. More so than his fellow Nabis, notably Vuillard, Bonnard and Serusier, Denis cast women in his art as sacred beings, made manifest either as holy women of Christianity, medieval damosels or antique goddesses.

Although this lithograph represents Denis's sole reference to an English poetic source, he demonstrated from early in his career an awareness of the synesthesia of the arts which marked so many manifestations of Symbolism. He undertook illustrations for texts by two major figures in the Symbolist literary movement: Paul Verlaine's *Sagesse*, worked on between 1889 and 1890 and subsequently published in 1911, and André Gide's *Le Voyage d'Urien*, written in 1892 and published the following year. He provided designs for other music covers, notably for André Rossignol's *Douce Vision* (1896) and *Concerts du petit frère et de la petite soeur* (1903). And he drew inspiration from music for his own work, notably for the decorations for his bedroom made in 1895 entitled, after Schumann's *Frauenliebe und Leben, L'Amour et la vie d'une femme*, and provided decorative schemes for the composer Ernest Chausson (*Avril*, 1890). In addition, critics found in his work specific affinities or references to music. When Paul Jamot reviewed the album of ten colour lithographs, *Amour*, commissioned by Ambroise Vollard in 1897 and published two years later, he referred to them as 'a suite of music where honesty and depth of emotion makes me think of Schumann while its subtleties of sound remind me of Debussy' (Jamot 1945, p.17). Finally, Denis shared with his fellow Nabis an engagement with the avant-garde Symbolist theatre of Paul Fort (Théâtre d'Art) and of its successor, Lugné-Poë's Théâtre de l'Oeuvre, where Symbolist plays were performed on semi-abstract sets designed by the Nabis, accompanied by appropriate music: a bold attempt at the realisation of Wagner's *Gesamtkunstwerk*.

MAS

84

HENRI FANTIN-LATOUR 1836–1904

83 *Siegfried*, Act III: The Invocation of Erde 1886

Lithograph 22.9 × 14.9 (9 × 5⅞)
Lit: Hediard 1906, no.71

Private Collection

84 *Parsifal*, Act II: The Invocation of Kundry 1886

Lithograph 22.9 × 14.9 (9 × 5⅞)
Lit: Hediard 1906, no.73

Private Collection

83

These two lithographs were included in the fourteen commissioned as *hors texte* illustrations to Adolphe Jullien's biography and critical appraisal of the composer, *Richard Wagner, sa vie et son œuvre*, published in

Paris and London in 1886. Their publication, accompanied by the exhibition of several of the *hors texte* plates at the Paris Salons of 1886 and 1887, caused a major sensation. Although somewhat smaller in format than Fantin's earlier exhibited lithographs of Wagnerian subjects created from 1877, these fourteen prints formed a complete suite or series which caused critics to greet their publication as the most important event in the history of lithography since the appearance of Delacroix's *Faust* and *Hamlet* series.

Fantin had been introduced to Jullien by a mutual friend, Edmond Maître, in 1871. A music critic and musicologist who played a major role in shaping French musical taste after 1870, Jullien shared Fantin's enthusiasm for contemporary music, notably that of Berlioz, Schumann and Wagner.

These lithographs represent a further stage in Fantin's long-term enthusiasm for Wagner and the steady evolution of a taste for his music which had grown in France from the 1850s. Not only had Fantin demonstrated in oil, pastel and lithograph from 1862 onwards the wealth of inspiration which he could draw from the composer's works, but his commission came from one year after Fantin had become closely involved in the recently created *Revue Wagnérienne*. As well as offering examples of his Wagnerian lithographs for sale for the benefit of the review, Fantin, in keeping with two other Wagnerites, Jacques-Emile Blanche and Odilon Redon, was commissioned to create a lithograph to be published *hors texte* in the fourth number of the review and offered free to the review's subscribers (8 May 1885).

Unlike the somewhat etiolated linear style of Aubrey Beardsley's Wagnerian renderings which seem to dwell more specifically upon the narrow, sinister aspect of the *Ring Cycle* (see nos.66, 67), Fantin's more fully modelled forms capture the vast dimension of the human drama which Wagner lays out in his tetralogy, while their strong formal structure establishes their concern with the world of the supernatural, the domain of the gods.

MAS

Henri Fantin-Latour 1836–1904

85 The First Scene from *Das Rheingold* 1888

Oil on canvas 115 × 77 (45¼ × 30⅜)
Signed 'Fantin' lower left

Prov: Mme Robert Esnault-Pelterie, Paris; Mme Gaston Popelin; M. Raymond Popelin; on deposit with the Philadelphia Museum of Art before 1978; Peter Nathan, Zurich 1979; bt by the Kunsthalle, Hamburg

Exh: Salon, Paris 1888 (962); Exposition Triennale, Antwerp 1888 (338); RA 1890 (1109); Glasgow 1892 (553); Lyon 1893 (872)

Lit: 'Le Salon de 1888 par un exposant', *La Revue Indepéndante*, June 1888, p.424; Alexandre 1888; 'The Triennial Exhibition at Antwerp – II', *Architect*, 21 Sept. 1888, p.158; Geffroy 1888, p.2; Guigou 1888, p. 578; Leroi 1888, p.174; Michel 1888, p.146; Paulet 1888, p.2; 1888, t.11, p.250; *Athenaeum*, 24 May 1890, p.678; *Observer*, 11, May 1890, p.5; Bouyer 1895, p.93; Proust 1902, p.232; Jullien 1909, pp.120–1; Heesemann-Wilson 1980, pp.103–16, fig.9; Lippien 1980, p.175

Hamburger Kunsthalle

The subject depicts the opening passages of *Das Rheingold*, the first of the four music dramas which constitute Richard Wagner's *Ring Cycle (Der Ring des Nibelungen)*. It shows the three Rhinemaidens, guardians of the Rheingold, ecstatically singing of their precious charge which lies upon the rocks to the top right of the composition. Its luminescence travels down through the waters of the River Rhine failing only to penetrate the protruding rocks on the lower left. Here, in deep shadow, lurks the evil Alberich who, taunted by the Rhinemaidens beyond endurance, will shortly plunder the magic gold and unleash the sequence of dramatic events which brings death to giants and heroes, evil-doers and a dragon, and eventually seals the destruction of the gods and the ultimate return of the gold to the River Rhine.

Fantin's interest in Wagnerian subject-matter combined his own specific admiration for the composer's œuvre, his more general love of music, notably German nineteenth-century music, and his search for 'un art de l'avenir' (an art of the future) which forsook the accurate transcription of the external world and sought instead to convey the 'féérique' (imaginary-fantastical).

Fantin was probably introduced into the musical circles of Paris where contemporary German music, notably that of Schumann, Wagner and Brahms, was performed and discussed, by the German artist, admirer of Courbet and gifted amateur violinist Otto Scholderer in 1857. Three years later he almost certainly attended one of three concerts given in Paris at the Théâtre des Italiens of selections from *Tannhäuser, Lohengrin, Tristan und Isolde* and *The Flying Dutchman*, and participated in the discussions of Wagner's music which were pursued at the Café Andler and which were frequented by two of the most ardent of the composer's supporters in France, Baudelaire and Champfleury. In addition, Fantin attended the musical soirées held by the father of Antoine Lascaux who himself, after the Franco-Prussian War, instituted similar musical evenings where the music of Schumann, Brahms and Wagner would be enjoyed by Gabriel Fauré, Camille Saint-Saëns, André Messager, the pianist Edmond Maître and Fantin. Indeed, it was through the good offices of Lascaux that Fantin was able to attend in August 1876 the third presentation of the *Ring Cycle* given in the opening season of Bayreuth.

Fantin, in keeping with many of his Wagnerite contemporaries, had been profoundly moved by the opening scene of *Das Rheingold* in its visually magical production at Bayreuth:

> Oh, it is unique. Nothing else is like it. It represents a feeling as yet only partially understood ... There is nothing more beautiful, more realised among my 'féérique' memories. These movements of the Maidens who swim while singing are perfect, Alberich who desires the gold, the lighting, the beam of light which the gold throws down into the water, is ravishing. It is feeling, it is not music, nor theatre decor, nor subject, but the enthralment of the spectator – yet 'spectator' is not the right word, nor is auditor correct. All is contained [within the production].

Fantin's understanding of the ability of music, poetry and stage picture to instil in the spectator/auditor a profound emotion was proof of the efficacy of Wagner's belief in the concept of the total work of art, the *Gesamtkunstwerk*, and confirmed Baudelaire's affirmation of the interdependence of art forms (poetry ends where music begins) spelled out in his essay, 'l'Art Romantique' (1863). It was on the basis of this concept of equivalence that Baudelaire had sought the formulation of a new art, a modern art – a search upon which Fantin was also engaged. Increasingly exercised by his realisation that the objective depiction of the external world was unable to express the truth of man's interior world, he was drawn to evolve a pictorial vocabulary which would profoundly move the spectator. In so far as he found his most intense emotional experiences within the world of music, it was to the making of paintings inspired by music that he turned in his search to create 'an art of the future'. In an œuvre dominated by realist portraits, group subjects and still lifes, Fantin increasingly from the 1870s exhibited paintings, and lithographs, whose subjects were inspired by music. In 1888, the year that the painting shown here was exhibited at the Salon, all six works presented by Fantin represented his commitment to imaginary subjects rather than to those drawn from reality.

This picture was first exhibited at the Salon of 1888. It was subsequently shown at the Royal Academy in London in 1890, and in Glasgow two years later. Its critical reception in each country is indicative of the relative significance of Wagner and his music and its role in the evolution of Symbolism in each country. In France, the enthusiasm for Wagner which had emerged in the 1850s was given specific focus in launching *La Revue Wagnérienne* in 1885. Devoted to the interpretation of all artistic manifestations through Wagnerian principles, this review became one of the leading apologists for the innovative artistic programme of Symbolism. Hence, when Fantin exhibited paintings and lithographs derived from Wagnerian subjects, he was hailed as the only 'pure symbolist' in the Salon (Alfred Paulet) and as an artist who had given unity on canvas to music, poetry and the visual arts. In Britain, there was neither a coherently organised promotion of the music of Wagner nor a systematisation of Wagner's aesthetic as enshrined in *La Revue Wagnérienne*. Thus, the critic of the *Athenaeum*, when reviewing *The First Scene from Das Rheingold* in 1890 remained unmoved by the emotive qualities of Fantin's attempt to represent the principle of the *Gesamtkunstwerk*, dismissing the painting as being no more than a depiction of a theatrical scene.

The Hamburg painting was based upon a lithograph of the same subject made in 1876, which in turn provided the basis for a pastel which was exhibited, together with a pastel of the final scene from *The Valkyrie* (*Die Walküre*) at the Salon of 1877. The texture of the painting seems to approximate to that of pastel, an effect common in many Symbolist works by British and continental artists such as Watts (no.76) and Previati (no.127).

MAS

85

86

FERNAND KHNOPFF 1858–1921

86 Who Shall Deliver Me? (Christina Georgina Rossetti) 1891

Coloured chalksr 22.2 × 13 (8¾ × 5⅛)
Inscribed 'Fernand Khnopff' upper right

Prov: M. Penton; The Piccadilly Gallery and Ewan Philipps

Exh: Brussels 1891 (112); ?Autumn Exhibition, New Gallery 1892; Paris 1970 (72); Paris 1972 (36); Paris 1973 (35)

Lit: Delevoy et al. 1987; Draguet 1995, pp.304–6, repr. p.307

Private Collection, Belgium. Courtesy Patrick Derom

EXHIBITED IN LONDON ONLY

The chalk drawing takes its title from that of a poem by Christina Rossetti dated 1 March 1864 (*The Poetical Works of Christina Georgina Rossetti*, 1904, p.238). Khnopff had also had recourse to the same poem for the title of another work created in the same year, *I Lock my Door upon Myself* (fig.8 on p.22), which was subsequently revised in 1900 under the title *A Recluse*. Both works were exhibited in London in 1892, the one shown here probably that included in the Autumn Exhibition of the New Gallery.

As with his references to other literary sources such as Georges Rodenbach's *Bruges la morte* and Stéphane Mallarmé's poetry, Khnopff does not provide a literal illustration to Christina Rossetti's text. Rather, he uses its essence as a springboard for the articulation of his own private symbolic language. The idealised head of a woman whose flaming hair and wide-staring eyes certainly convey a haunted look is comparable to the poem's subject, who identifies herself as her own worst enemy: 'I lock my door upon myself, / And bar them out; but who shall wall / Self from myself, most loathed of all? ... Myself, arch-traitor to myself; / My hollowest friend, my deadliest foe, / My clog whatever road I go.' However, whereas in the poem the possibility of salvation is suggested in the opening line, 'God strengthen me to bear myself' and returned to in the final stanza, 'Yet one there is can curb myself, / Can roll the strangling load from me, / Break off the yoke and set me free.' Khnopff's visual equivalent contains no reference to salvation. Rather, the claustrophobic verticality of the composition, closed in by the glimpse of medieval doorway and cobbled courtyard, appears in one sense to tie the figure to the temporal world. Yet her elusive gaze also interrogates the viewer, inviting him/her to enter into a seemingly enigmatic reading of the figure, her identity, her relationship with the past and her apparent confinement therein. In this respect, Khnopff has indeed sought to provide a pictorial parallel to the almost desperate tone of the question which stands as the title of the poem.

The idealisation of the female figure in *Who Shall Deliver Me?* presents direct parallels with those of the poetess's brother, Dante Gabriel Rossetti and, even more so, of Burne-Jones. Indeed, Khnopff and Burne-Jones were well acquainted to the extent that they exchanged drawings (see nos.96, 108), characteristically each of an idealised female head. However, unlike Burne-Jones's dependence upon medieval reference in his presentations of idealised women, Khnopff determinedly sought to carry his subjects outside time. In the case of *Who Shall Deliver Me?*, as in so many of Khnopff's studies of single idealised women gazing into the distance, a finger resting against their closed lips, the process has created a closed and silent world which symbolises meditation, the turning in on oneself, the suspension of all possible action.

MAS

ELIHU VEDDER 1836–1923

87 The Rubáiyát of Omar Khayyám by Edward FitzGerald 1884

Title page reads: 'Rubaiyat | of | Omar Khayyam | The Astronomer-Poet of Persia | Rendered into English verse by | Edward FitzGerald | with | an accompaniment of Drawings | by | Elihu Vedder. | Boston. Houghton Mifflin and Company | London. | Bernard Quaritch.'
56 pages and 8 pages end-matter, bound in gilt-stamped boards
Page size: 39.6 × 30.5 (15⅝ × 12), image size: left 26.8 × 20.5 (10⁹⁄₁₆ × 8¹⁄₁₆), right 27.8 × 21 (10½ × 8¼)

Lit: Vedder 1910, pp.231, 403–8; Soria 1970, nos.365–70 (16, 17); Soria et al. 1979, pp.127–49

Private Collection

The book is shown open at stanzas 37–9:

Up from Earth's Centre through the Seventh Gate
I rose, and on the Throne of Saturn sate,
And many a Knot unravel'd by the Road;
But not the Master-Knot of Human Fate.

There was the Door to which I found no Key;
There was the Veil through which I could not see:
Some little talk awhile of Me and Thee
There was – and then no more of Thee and Me.

Earth could not answer; nor the stars that mourn
In flowing Purple, of the Lord Forlorn;
Nor rolling Heav'n, with all his Sighs reveal'd
And hidden by the sleeve of Night and Morn.

Vedder's two illustrations are titled 'Vain Questioning' and 'The Throne of Saturn'. His notes provide this gloss: 'Omar's horoscope, presented symbolically. The vine permeates the two influences of Jupiter and the Pleiades, under which Omar was born. Accepting this tendency of mind in the Poet, one can see how *he* would compare favourably the absolute freedom and sincerity of the search for truth within the Tavern with the stagnation and ultimate putrefaction of thought within the Temple.'

87

Vedder had been introduced to FitzGerald's *Rubáiyát* by his friend the artist E.J. Ellis. 'This was the seed of Omar planted in a soil peculiarly adapted to its growth, and it grew and took to itself all of sorrow and of mirth that it could assimilate, and blossomed out in the drawings' (Vedder 1910, p.404; and see pp.407–8). Vedder's version of FitzGerald's *Rubaiyat* was first published in Boston in 1884. It contains fifty-two plates including frontispiece, title page and publisher's mark; at the end there are in addition the artist's signature and three plates with decorative borders for Vedder's notes, which explain the imagery of some of the illustrations. In pursuing his fascination with FitzGerald's poem, Vedder conceived the book as a development of his own interpretation of the philosophy underlying it. 'I do not intend the drawings to be clear illustrations of the text,' he wrote, '– except when they naturally happen to be so – they are an accompaniment to the verses, parallel, but not identical in thought' (letter to Joseph B. Millet, 1883). Thus FitzGerald's verses on existence as a game of chess or tennis are illustrated with a design showing the Fates of Greek mythology, while the Cup of Death (no.88) is an image derived from Christian iconography.

Vedder made a selection of stanzas and arranged them partially in his own order, to create a coherent narrative expressive of his interpretation of the poem, placing one or more on each page in a panel surrounded by an elaborate drawing. The designs are reproduced in the published book by a photomechanical process. The *mise en page* is based on that of Blake's Prophetic Books, to which this work is perhaps the most significant homage of the nineteenth century. Many of the drawings are strongly reminiscent of the work of Vedder's friend Simeon Solomon, through whom he may have had access to the Blake material in Rossetti's possession.

The Blakean reference is brought out more conspicuously in a book for which Vedder's *Rubáiyát* was the immediate inspiration: Walter Crane's *The Sirens Three* appeared shortly after it, in 1885, its page layout and lettering closely modelled on those of Blake's books. It was, in the words of Isobel Spencer, Crane's 'first poetic manifesto of Socialism', and might seem to spring naturally enough out of Crane's earlier work as a book illustrator. His dependence on Vedder's book is however apparent in the fact that Crane's own poem is couched in the distinctive stanza-form of FitzGerald's *Rubáiyát*. See Spencer 1975, p.90.

The inspiration that Vedder found in the *Rubaiyat* fuelled much of his other work. A number of the designs were worked up into oil paintings, sometimes more or less exactly reproducing an image in the book, as in *The Cup of Death* (no.88), sometimes considerably modifying it, as in *The Sphinx of the Seashore* (no.65). The Pleiades, mentioned in his note, are illustrated in another plate, and the design was used for a painting of the same subject (Metropolitan Museum of Art, New York).

AW

Elihu Vedder 1836–1923

88 **The Cup of Death** 1885

Oil on canvas 112.7 × 52.7 (44⅜ × 20¾)

Prov: Miss Susan Minns of Boston 1900; Mrs John Griffith Booton, Boston

Lit: Downes 1887, pp.842–6; De Bosis 1895, Pt II, Bk VII, July 1885–March 1896; Soria 1970, pp.226, 333–4, no.49; Reich 1974, p.47; Soria et al. 1979, pp.142, 143, repr. p.144

Virginia Museum of Fine Arts, The Williams Fund

This is the second of two versions of the picture; the first (National Collection of Fine Arts, Smithsonian Institution, Washington; repr. Soria et al. 1979, p.114, fig.137) was begun by Vedder at about the same time, but not finished; it was reworked and completed between 1909 and 1911. This canvas was executed on commission for a Miss Susan Minns of Boston, 'whose fad is to have the greatest collection of dances of death going' (Letter from Vedder to his wife, Vedder Papers, Washington, Smithsonian Institution, Archives of American Art). The subject was developed from one of Vedder's plates for the *Rubáiyát* (see no.87), an illustration to stanza XLIII in the poem (stanza 49 in Vedder's order), for which the drawing is in the National Collection of Fine Arts, Washington:

> So when the Angel of the darker Drink
> At last shall find you by the river-brink,
> And, offering his Cup, invite your Soul
> Forth to your Lips to quaff – you shall not shrink.

In the illustration the figures are cut off at the knee; otherwise the design is substantially the same. A second drawing for it (J.B. Speed Art Museum, Louisville) has the sinking sun to the right of the Angel's wings, and the letter Omega on his breast. The Washington version of the painting has minor differences, notably a taller bank of reeds in the background, and flowers dropping from the hand of the fainting soul.

The picture exemplifies Vedder's indebtedness to the British Symbolists, with its suggestions of Burne-Jones, Solomon and Watts. It has been suggested that the conception of the Angel of Death here is influenced by Watts's consolatory personifications of Death (see Reich 1974, p.47). This connection is perhaps more apparent in the Washington drawing, where the Angel's eyes are not closed but open, cast down and obscured by shadow, giving them the vacant aspect often found in Watts's Death-figures.

AW

Private Thoughts II

Despite a tendency to paint ever larger pictures depicting visions of the Ideal and the Decadent, much of the most interesting work of the high Symbolist period of the closing decades of the century took the form of small-scale objects – prints, bronzes, drawings and especially illustrated books – which suggest the intimate atmosphere in which their often suggestive, erotic or devotional content required to be appreciated. It was not until the late 1880s that Symbolism came into its own as a full-blown 'movement' consciously recognised throughout Europe. By then the principal works of Rossetti, Burne-Jones and Watts had become universally familiar, both in originals at Salons and International Exhibitions, and in widespread reproductions. Oscar Wilde's Decadent play *Salomé* of 1891 was admired in Paris and made into an opera by Richard Strauss; it was illustrated by Beardsley, who gained great notoriety when his drawings for it were published (nos.89, 92). In Glasgow there emerged a further development of the Rossetti tradition, springing from William Morris's Arts and Crafts movement, led by the architect-designer Charles Rennie Mackintosh. The Glasgow school derived its visual language from the linear style of Burne-Jones and its development in the work of Beardsley. Its rarefied, abstracted pattern-making was to have a considerable impact on Viennese art and design in the great days of the Secession. Illustrations by Gustav Klimt for the Secession's magazine *Ver Sacrum* show Klimt very much indebted to Beardsley and his followers. Another channel for this influence was the work of Khnopff, who was much attached to England and familiar with English literature, notably with the writings of Thomas Carlyle, Alfred Tennyson and Christina Rossetti. He was closely associated with several British artists, including Millais, Watts, Richmond and Leighton. He particularly admired Burne-Jones, of whose *King Cophetua and the Beggar Maid* (no.40) he said that in it 'the artist's dream, deliciously bewildering, had become the real'. His one-man show at the Hanover Gallery in 1890 was acclaimed and in 1892 he became a member of the London-based Society of Portrait Painters. He wrote regularly for the *Studio* from 1894. Later in the decade his work was to be featured in an issue of *Ver Sacrum* (no.109), and in the same year, 1898, he showed a work at the Secession's exhibition. His eerie pastels appeared often at the Salon de la Rose+Croix in that decade, and so acted as a vital link between Paris and the artistic centres of London, Brussels, Munich and Vienna at a critical time (see Howe 1982, pp.8, 9, 13). The concern for the surface of the work, as the membrane through which a world parallel to reality is glimpsed, preoccupied artists in all media. Significantly pastel, with its special qualities of softness and fragmentation, enjoyed greater favour than it had done since the late eighteenth century. It is no coincidence that the Society of British Pastellists was founded at the zenith of Symbolism.

fig.56 Edward Burne-Jones, *Study for the 'Briar Rose' series: The Sleeping Knights* c.1870, oil on canvas 61 × 82.5 cm. Board of Trustees of the National Museums and Galleries on Merseyside (Walker Art Gallery, Liverpool)

Aubrey Beardsley 1872–1898

89 **The Toilette of Salome** 1893

Pen and black ink and wash
22.7 × 16.2 (9 × 6³⁄₈)
Inscribed with the artist's device, lower right

Prov: Robert Ross, by whom bequeathed to the British Museum 1918

Exh: Carfax & Co. 1904 (31); Art Institute of Chicago 1911 (41); V&A 1966 (361); New York 1967 (154)

Lit: Reade 1967, no.281, repr.; Easton 1972, p.120; Weintraub 1976, p.72; Wilson 1983, no.14, repr.; Heyd 1986, pp.39–41; Fletcher 1987, p.76; Snodgrass 1995, pp.213–16, repr.

Trustees of the British Museum

EXHIBITED IN LONDON AND MUNICH ONLY

This is one of sixteen illustrations and a cover design that Beardsley made between July and November 1893 for the English edition of Oscar Wilde's play *Salome*, published in London in February 1894. Beardsley was at his most provocative in these drawings and John Lane, the book's publisher, demanded alterations to or refused to use, five of them. It seems that after altering one, Beardsley adopted the policy of providing fresh drawings rather than tampering with his work. This is the replacement for a first version in which both Salome and one of her attendants appear to be masturbating. On the face of it this second version is radically cleaned up, certainly formally, and it has been widely admired as exemplifying Beardsley's powers of abstract design which give his particular contribution to Symbolism its place in the history of modernism. Beardsley's modernism is also apparent in his furniture, dependent upon but, in its minimalist refinement, going beyond the Japanese influenced designs of E.W. Godwin (who built a house for Whistler and created a celebrated interior for Wilde). However, for Reade 'a phallic interpretation must be given to … the chair'. Also, on the dressing table shelf, Salome's current reading is seen to include a volume of de Sade, and Zola's *Nana*, the scandal of whose publication in 1879 and 1880 had only been exceeded by that surrounding, in 1887, *La Terre*, with a copy of which Beardsley had provided Salome in the first version. The first English translation of *La Terre* was prosecuted for obscenity in London in 1888 and Henry James remarked that the very name of Zola was 'a stench' in English nostrils.

Easton has pointed out that Salome's dress relates to contemporary models by Worth. For Snodgrass the intense artifice and formality of the drawing make it an outstanding example of the *fin de siècle* attack on 'bourgeois conceptions of "natural order"', in which the artist responds to 'Victorian objections' to the first version by 'denaturalising the picture utterly while in a sense retaining its original onanistic fetishism'. In her extensive discussion of the Pierrot in Beardsley's work Heyd characterises the one here as a threatening 'anti-Pierrot' having 'demonic associations symbolised by the use of a black eye mask'. The scissors, also a clear phallic symbol, become a particular threat in the context of the play's theme of decollation.

SW

Aubrey Beardsley 1872–1898

90 How King Arthur Saw the Questing Beast and thereof Had Great Marvel 1893

Pen and black ink and wash 40 × 28 (15¾ × 11)
Inscribed 'Aubrey Beardsley' on base of left-hand plant stem lower left; 'March 8 1893' on base of right-hand plant stem lower left; and with the artist's device lower right

Prov: ...; Dr A.E. Tebb 1903; Baron Garvens von Garvensburg; Catherine Boelcke; Sotheby's 17 April 1957, bt R.A. Harari, by whom bequeathed to Victoria and Albert Museum 1972

Exh: V&A 1966 (169); New York 1967 (48); Munich 1984 (32)

Lit: Reade 1967, no.56, repr.; Wilson 1983, no.3, repr.; Heyd 1986, pp.126–7, 147–8, 170; Kooistra 1990, pp.59–66; Snodgrass 1995, p.251

The Board of Trustees of the Victoria and Albert Museum

According to R.A. Walker, this is one of a grand total of 351 separate designs by Beardsley, consisting of 240 chapter headings, forty-three large and small borders, twenty-five initial letters, twenty full and double-page illustrations, nineteen small ornaments and four head-pieces, used in the first issue of the illustrated edition of Malory's *Le Morte Darthur*. This was published by J.M. Dent in London, in parts, between June 1893 and November 1894 and then bound into two-volume sets with a cover by Beardsley which is a masterpiece of art nouveau design. There was also a three-volume deluxe edition. The commission launched Beardsley as a professional artist and this drawing was used as the frontispiece for the first volume. It is one of the few drawings by Beardsley that are so precisely dated and only a handful of others are dated at all. It is also signed both with his name and his emblem. All this does suggest that it had a special significance for him, and it is among the most striking and complex of all his productions, marking the climax of the early style that appeared first in drawings such as *La Femme incomprise* (no.91). The dating and double signature perhaps lend weight to Heyd's view that it is 'Beardsley's own features which are the model for Arthur's'.

Beardsley's signature device or emblem, or in his words, 'trade-mark', inspired by Persian calligraphy and signatures on Japanese prints (Zatlin) first appeared in *The Achieving of the Sangreal*, a drawing of summer 1892 which gained him the *Morte Darthur* commission and became the frontispiece of volume two. It has been widely seen as a complex sexual image, representing at once vulva and penetrating phallus, ejaculation, and the tripartite male genitalia (Reade 1967, Brophy 1968, Beckson 1989). A stylised but quite explicit phallus, complete with ejaculation, appears, somewhat hidden, on the extreme lower left of the river bank.

In her ground-breaking commentary on the *Morte Darthur* illustrations Kooistra points out that in them Beardsley 'gives the lie to' traditional views that Malory's text is 'a nostalgic hearkening back to the golden age of chivalry', by responding to 'the black underside of the fellowship of the Round Table ... whose sexuality is its driving destructive force'. If Arthur here is really a self-portrait, Beardsley could hardly have chosen a better model, a consumptive, aesthetically and erotically obsessed youth, for this devastating subversion of the heroic king of tradition. Semi-recumbent, Arthur hardly looks capable of rising, let alone of wielding Excalibur, nowhere in sight, anyway. From bruised eyes that perfectly exemplify Octave Mirbeau's comment on those of Burne-Jones's androgynous figures that 'one cannot tell whether they are the result of onanism, sapphism, natural love or tuberculosis', Arthur shoots, not surely at the beast, but at the passing and ithyphallic figure of Pan, what can only be characterised as a coy glance. Heyd points out that the beast's heavily clawed left paw appears to hover menacingly above Arthur's lap, and Snodgrass suggests that the snapped-off tree trunk against which Arthur leans represents castration.

Kooistra also argues that the episode of the Questing Beast is far from an inconsequential choice for illustration (as has been suggested): Malory, she notes, describes it as 'a full wonderful beast and a great signification', it appears in a number of episodes and 'acts as a metaphoric representation of the internal divisions caused by sex and violence within the Round Table'. In short the drawing sets the tone for the whole of Beardsley's *Morte Darthur*, one of the most remarkable of English illustrated books.

SW

90

Aubrey Beardsley 1872–1898

91 La Femme incomprise 1892

Pen and ink and wash 45 × 18.5 (17¾ × 7¼)
Inscribed with the title upper centre-right

Prov: …; Charles Alan, New York 1974; ?…; Sotheby's 12 Nov. 1992 (189)

Lit: Reade 1967, no.252, repr.; Maas, Duncan and Goode 1970, p.46

Private Collection

La Femme incomprise (The Misunderstood Woman) is one of a group of drawings made in the spring and early summer of 1892 in which Beardsley added the influence of Whistler and Japanese art to that of Burne-Jones, Rossetti and the early Italians to produce what he legitimately described in a letter of autumn 1892 as 'a new style and method of work … founded on Japanese art but quite original in the main … they were extremely fantastic in conception but perfectly severe in execution. I took them to Paris with me in June … and received the very greatest encouragement from the President of the Salon des Beaux-Arts [Puvis de Chavannes] who introduced me to one of his brother painters as "un jeune anglais qui fait des choses étonnantes" [a young Englishman who makes astonishing things]'.

The Japanese influence on Beardsley has been noted by all his commentators but has only recently been made the subject of a full-length study, Linda Zatlin's forthcoming *Aubrey Beardsley's Japanese Connection*. She points out, inter alia, that the long, narrow format of this and related drawings is that of the Japanese *kakemono* – a narrow painted scroll used as a wall hanging – and that the particular dimensions of some of the group, including this one, correspond closely to the type called a *tanzaku*. Beardsley's creation of images by reserving them in the white paper ground in a field of black, a technique used extensively in this drawing and central to Beardsley's art from this time on, she identifies as inspired by the Japanese effect, in stone prints and woodcuts, known as *ishizuri-e*.

Reade has suggested that the cyclopean spider clinging to the curtain may have been inspired by the lithograph *The Spider* by the French Symbolist, Odilon Redon (see no.110). An important difference is that Redon's spider has two eyes, and it is very tempting to read Beardsley's version as an emblem of the female *pudenda*; it is certainly a voyeur.

The subject of the drawing remains unknown; the 'misunderstood woman' may be an invention of Beardsley's own as is, or appears to be, the case with a number of these early drawings with enigmatic titles. However, there may be a literary source so far unidentified. Whichever, her mood is realised with

91

an intensity and empathy which seems extraordinary for a twenty-year-old male of Beardsley's time, and is indicative of the unusually sympathetic portrayal of women which is such a notable characteristic of Beardsley's art (Zatlin 1990). The image itself is clearly Japanese in general inspiration – there are many seated courtesans with cats in Japanese art. An example is Joran's *Beauty with a Cat* c.1800–10 (British Museum). In Western art the image is reminiscent of northern European bare-breasted madonnas such as *Madonna of the Iris* in the style of Dürer (National Gallery, London) or Fouquet's *Virgin and Child Surrounded by Angels* (Musée Royal des Beaux-Arts, Antwerp) either feeding, or contemplating on their lap, the Christ child. The cat takes its place in a whole line of cats on or about women's laps from the Rococo onwards. However, its size, exoticism, savagery and central place in the composition seem quite without precedent, even taking account of Manet's cat angrily arching its back in *Olympia* (Musée d'Orsay, Paris). Here the cat seems to have become the embodiment of the woman's bitter and vengeful thoughts, and bodes ill for the man who, it may be speculated, inspired them. The suggestion that this drawing might be (among other things) a subversion of the Christian tradition of the Madonna and Child is supported by the group of passion flower blossoms in the lower part, or predella, of the drawing, identifiable by their prominent triple styles, seen as representing the three nails of the Cross, and by the continuation of the passion flower motif on the woman's robe. The viciously thorned thistle growing up the entire right side of the drawing adds both to the expression of angst and to the iconography of the Passion. The blossom in the upper panel has been identified as a variety of *prunus* (the cherry, plum and almond family). It seems likely that Beardsley intended it to represent cherry blossom, an important symbol of spring in Japan, when the ancient ceremony of *hanami* – flower watching – still takes place. Significantly here, cherry blossom is also a common metaphor for the courtesans of the Yoshiwara, the brothel district of old Edo. 'Spring Pictures' – *shunga* – are the Japanese erotic prints of which Beardsley was reported by Julius Meier-Graefe to own 'the finest and most explicitly erotic in London ... the wildest phantasies of Utamaro'.

SW

Aubrey Beardsley 1872–1898

92 **The Climax** 1893

Line block reproduction
34.3 × 27.2 (13½ × 10¾)
Inscribed in the block with the artist's device, lower right

Lit: Reade 1967, no.286, repr.; Brophy 1968, p.60; Wilson 1983, no.16; Fletcher 1987, pp.90–3; Zatlin 1989, p.192; Beckson 1989, p.215, repr.; Zatlin 1990, pp.94–5, repr.; Snodgrass 1995, pp.145–6, repr.

Alessandra and Simon Wilson

This is one of Beardsley's illustrations to Wilde's *Salome* (see no.89). The original is lost and the drawing is now best known from this roughly same-size line block reproduction published in 1906 by John Lane (who owned the drawings) as part of a loose-leaf portfolio of all seventeen of Beardsley's designs for *Salome*. In his play, Wilde gave a distinctively *fin de siècle* and compelling twist to the Biblical legend by imagining that Salome lusted after the Baptist and brought about his death in revenge for his spurning of her advances. When brought his head she seizes it, harangues it in a great prose poem of passion, triumph and despair (she has killed the thing she loved) and finally embraces it in death as she could not in life, crying 'Ah! J'ai baisé ta bouche, Iokanaan, j'ai baisé ta bouche ('I've kissed your lips ...'). These words, of Wilde's original French text, were inscribed by Beardsley on his earlier drawing of this scene, presumably made shortly after he first read the play in, again presumably, late February or March 1893 and which secured him the commission to illustrate the English edition. (The first, French, edition of the play was published simultaneously in Paris and London on 22 February 1893. A copy was inscribed by Wilde to Beardsley with the date 'March '93'.) The moment depicted in both drawings is thus that immediately following Salome's necrophiliac act, as she gazes with grim, heavy satisfaction at her prey.

Commentators from Freudians to feminists have, entirely justifiably, had a field day with this image. For Brophy it is one of 'castration-orgasm-death'. The blood from the head both falls and rises forming a spike whose upper part Snodgrass sees as a *glans penis*. It also suggests an ejaculation and a candle flame. Snodgrass notes too the 'sexualised lilies' (while Reade sees them as symbolic of the Baptist's chastity) and the 'petals approximating female labia' on the most rigidly phallic of these which, for Beckson, is 'subverted by the adjacent lily, more obviously phallic, impotently drooping ... the entire design suggesting sexual aggression and relief from tension'. The title's pun on the sexual meaning of climax has also not been overlooked. For Zatlin, Salome's face bears 'marks of hardness and cynicism' as a result of her 'evanescent success in reversing the rules of power when she bargains with Herod for the Baptist's head as if she were a man'; to the Victorians she represented 'a distortion of femininity ... caused by her desire for vengeance and her acceptance of a masculine role to achieve it.'

Fletcher crucially points out that 'Salome has assumed ... the appearance of that central emblem of Romantic beauty and horror, the Medusa [whose] face and hair can kill at a glance, and it is this power that Beardsley most dramatically portrays in Salome's hungry peering at Iokanaan's severed head and in the head's blind reciprocating gaze'. But he stresses too that the Baptist also is represented as a Medusa: 'hermaphroditism, self-reflectiveness and the fatality of unmediated nature are unforgettably focused here'. It remains only to add that in the play, Salome herself, following her triumphant, quasi-orgasmic cry, is at once killed.

SW

92

93

94

EDWARD BURNE-JONES 1833–1898

Designs for 'The Story of Perseus'

93 The Call of Perseus; Perseus and the Graiae; Perseus and the Nereids 1875–6

Bodycolour, gold paint and pen and ink on buff paper 36.7 × 102.7 (14½ × 40⅜)

Prov: By descent to the artist's son, Sir Philip Burne-Jones, from whom bt by the Trustees of the Chantrey Bequest 1919

Exh: Burlington Fine Arts Club 1899 (116); Chantrey Exhibition 1949 (73); Tate Gallery 1993 (54); Rome 1996 (41, repr. in col.)

Lit: Löcher 1973, pp.98–100, pl.19

Tate Gallery. Presented by the Trustees of the Chantrey Bequest 1919

94 The Finding of Medusa; The Death of Medusa (The Birth of Pegasus and Chrysaor); Perseus Pursued by the Gorgons 1875–6

Bodycolour, gold paint and pen and ink on buff paper 36.8 × 128.4 (14½ × 50½)

Prov: As no.93

Exh: Burlington Fine Arts Club 1899 (117); Chantrey Exhibition 1949 (64); Hayward Gallery 1975 (158); Montreal 1995 (39, col. pl.19); Tate Gallery 1993 (55); Rome 1996 (42, repr. in col.)

Lit: Löcher 1973, pp.100–3, p.20; Harrison and Waters 1973, p.174 repr.

Tate Gallery. Presented by the Trustees of the Chantrey Bequest 1919

95

95 **Atlas Turned to Stone; The Rock of Doom and the Doom Fulfilled; The Court of Phineas; The Baleful Head** 1875–6

Bodycolour, gold paint, pencil and chalk on buff paper 36.7 × 148.7 (14½ × 58½)
Inscribed 'fireplace' b.r., 'doo'[r] b.c. and '4.10 ½' b.r.

Prov: As no.93
Exh: Burlington Fine Arts Club 1899 (118); Chantrey Exhibition 1949 (55); Tate Gallery 1993 (56); Rome 1996 (43, repr. col.)
Lit: Löcher 1973, pp.104–7, pl.21

Tate Gallery. Presented by the Trustees of the Chantrey Bequest 1919

These sheets are early studies for the 'Perseus Series', a large-scale decorative scheme commissioned in 1875 by the Conservative politician Arthur Balfour for the music room of his London house, 4 Carlton Gardens. Burne-Jones took considerable care over the initial research for the project, writing to his son Philip at Whitsun 1875 'I have worked at the British Museum lately looking up all the most ancient ways of pourtraying Medusa, and they are very few but very interesting, and I know much more about it than I did' (quoted G.B.-J. 1904, II, p.58). Lady Burne-Jones recalled that the subject of this major project seems to have come about spontaneously when

> Mr Arthur Balfour had come with Lady Airlie one day to the Grange, and the result of his then making the acquaintance of Edward and his art had been an important commission. He wished for a set of pictures to ornament a music room in his house: the subject of the Perseus story was soon agreed upon, and much of the year went in arranging a scheme and making studies for the different pictures. There were to be eight of them, for special spaces, and at first Edward intended them to have a setting of ornamental raised plaster, the design for which is seen in a small watercolour that he made of the whole series: but finally this idea was given up. The Medusa part of the legend, which attracted him most, he studied deeply; the Andromeda scenes, though they came later in the story, were finished first.
>
> (G.B.-J. 1904, II, p.60)

The extent and scale of the ornamental foliate plasterwork surrounding Burne-Jones's pictures is most clearly appreciated in no.94. The panels over the doors were originally also intended to be executed in gesso relief shown clearly in all three sheets, although Burne-Jones later decided to execute these subjects in oils along with the other panels. Work proceeded slowly; he made full-sized gouache cartoons of each of the subjects, now in Southampton Art Gallery, and the oils were never fully completed (see no.113). There are a number of differences between the final designs and the initial studies shown here.

RU

EDWARD BURNE-JONES 1833–1898

96 **Head of a Woman** 1890

Red, black and white chalks on buff paper
31.4 × 23.5 (12⅜ × 9¼)
Inscribed 'EBJ | 1890' b.r. and 'TO FERNAND KHNOPFF from EDWARD BURNE-JONES 1894' along bottom edge

Prov: Fernand Khnopff; …; present owner
Lit: Delevoy et al. 1987, no.278, repr. in col. p.59

Private Collection

Burne-Jones presented this drawing to Khnopff in 1894, a gesture to which the Belgian artist responded two years later (see no.108). Khnopff believed Burne-Jones to be the most interesting artist working in Britain at the time, and on his first visits to London sought out his work, eventually coming to be on friendly terms with him. There are affinities between the two painters, and it is interesting to note the similarities of approach demonstrated by the two drawings they exchanged. Both were known for their intense, ambiguous pictures of introspective, androgynous women, as demonstrated by this pair of sheets. There are also technical parallels between the drawings which illustrate the closeness of their draughtsmanship.

Khnopff first saw Burne-Jones's work in 1878 when the British artist exhibited abroad for the first time, sending three works to the Universal Exhibition in Paris. These included *The Beguiling of Merlin* 1874 (fig.32 on p.57), which was greeted with critical but not popular acclaim. However, in 1889 when Burne-Jones sent *King Cophetua and the Beggar Maid* (no.40) to that year's Paris Exposition Universelle it caused a sensation among critics and public alike. Joséphin Péladan, the exotic occultist, author of *Le Vice Suprême* and founder of the Salons de la Rose+Croix, was also impressed. In his manifesto founding the Rose+Croix Péladan wrote 'we will go to London to invite Burne-Jones, Watts and five other Pre-Raphaelites' to participate in the exhibitions. Instead of meeting them in England, Péladan wrote to at least Burne-Jones and Watts, but received a rather cool response. In a letter to Watts, Burne-Jones wrote:

> I dont know about the Salon of the Rose-Cross – a funny high falutin sort of pamphlet has reached me – a letter asking me to exhibit there, but I feel suspicious of it – it was so silly a piece of mouthing that I was ashamed of it … at any rate I shall not [exhibit] at once … but will make further enquiries … the pamphlet was disgracefully silly, but I was in the mood you are in, at first, to help in anything that upholds the ideals I care for … Do you know Puvis de Chavannes? Who has lifted the same banner.
> (quoted in Harrison and Waters 1973, pp.175–7)

None of Burne-Jones's works was shown at the Rose+Croix Salons, which included a wide variety of French and Belgian Symbolist art, but photographs of his and Rossetti's pictures were apparently exhibited.

RU

Evelyn Pickering De Morgan
1855–1919

97 **The Worship of Mammon** *c.*1909

Oil on canvas 60.3 × 50.2 (23¾ × 19¾)
Inscribed 'EDeM 1909' lower right

Prov: Collection of the artist; probably sold from her studio after her death in 1919, for the benefit of St Dunstan's (a charity for blind soldiers); bt by her sister, Mrs Anna Maria Wilhelmina Stirling (née Pickering); bequeathed, with some 80 other works by De Morgan, to form the De Morgan Foundation

Exh: Bournemouth 1996 (76, repr. in col.)

Lit: Stirling 1922, pp.311–12; *The De Morgan Collection of Pictures and Pottery* [?*c.*1953], p.15, no.41; *The De Morgan Foundation at Old Battersea House*, 1992, p.14, no.4; Gordon et al., 1996, no.76, pl.54

De Morgan Foundation

As an artist beginning to exhibit in the 1870s, Evelyn De Morgan belonged to a generation who matured as painters in the post-Pre-Raphaelite era, under the combined influence of Rossetti, Burne-Jones and Watts. De Morgan's close personal link with Watts inspired a range of allegorical subject-matter and Symbolist imagery which can be seen in much of her early work from the 1870s and 1880s and in the later *Worship of Mammon*.

Evelyn Pickering's early life, as the daughter of wealthy and well-connected parents and as the niece of the painter John Roddam Spencer Stanhope, who was later her own teacher, allowed her free access to artistic circles. Watts, who knew her family well as the teacher of Spencer Stanhope in the 1850s, commented that Evelyn and her brother were 'the most beautiful children he had ever seen' (Stirling 1922, p.146). He followed her career with interest. From 1873–5, Evelyn attended the Slade School of Art, where her accurate draughtsmanship (see Bournemouth 1996, pp.4–7) developed during the era of Edward Poynter, an academic artist *par excellence*. Travel in Italy during the next two years confirmed her love of Renaissance art and enhanced her first-hand familiarity with this period which inspired her own early efforts in oils. Regular travel in Italy thereafter, especially to Florence, provided continued exposure to Botticelli whose hard-edged style she adapted to her own art. In 1887, when in her thirties, well after establishing her own career, she married the designer and ceramicist William De Morgan and they lived part of each year in Florence where Spencer Stanhope, her artistic mentor, had also settled. Much of De Morgan's art remained in her own collection and many of those that did sell to private owners were bought back by her sister.

De Morgan's debut at the first Grosvenor Gallery exhibition of 1877 with *Ariadne in Naxos* (De Morgan Foundation) and her work of the following year, *Venus and Cupid* (De Morgan Foundation) reveal the technical skill of her tight, linear style ultimately derived from Botticelli and the Quattrocento but also akin to the tempera paintings of Spencer Stanhope. Critics linked her with Burne-Jones, the presiding genius of the Grosvenor, but over the next decade she came under the sway of the new trends of the 1880s. Her interest in spiritualism, combined with that of her husband, filtered into her work (see Oberhausen 1994, pp.1–11; expanded in Gordon 1996, pp.33–52). Equally important for De Morgan was the example and friendship of Watts. During the 1880s, Watts's allegories and his imagery of the other-worldly had become more public (see p.75). De Morgan's *Angel of Death* 1881 (De Morgan Foundation) is a variation on the theme of *Love and Death* (no.51); *Hope in the Prison of Despair* 1887–8 (whereabouts unknown; Gordon 1996, no.28) reworks *Hope*

98

(no.75) as a fully fledged allegorical scene laden with hidden meanings but without the correspondingly Symbolist style of Watts's painting. The closeness between the two artists can be gauged by Watts's admiration for De Morgan's mature style: 'She is a long way ahead of all the women and considerably ahead of most of the men. I look upon her as the first woman-artist of the day – if not of all time' (Stirling 1922, p.193).

De Morgan first essayed one of Watts's favourite themes on the futility of seeking riches for their own sake in *Earthbound* 1897 (De Morgan Foundation) in which a king counts his gold while the figure of Oblivion comes to cloak him in eternal night. The *Worship of Mammon* of 1909 is a smaller, more intimate work, closer in spirit to Watts's cruel *Mammon* (no.52). In De Morgan's painting Mammon clutches a bag of gold, holding it beyond reach of the supplicating woman who grasps his knees. The partial view of Mammon, with only his lower body and half his face revealed, conveys the sheer terror of his presence. Like Watts's enthroned Mammon, this bizarrely bronzed creature is like a sculptural monument come to life in a nightmarish setting. De Morgan's late work belongs to the twentieth century, but the theme, imagery and stylistic language of *The Worship of Mammon* reveal it as a direct descendant of the art of the 1880s and 1890s.

BB

Frances Macdonald 1873–1921

98 The Sleeping Princess *c.*1895–6

Pastel 19 × 46.4 (7½ × 18¼)
Inscribed 'FRANCES E. MACDONALD.' t.l. and 'LOVE IF THY TRESSES BE SO DARK | HOW DARK THOSE HIDDEN EYES MUST BE' on frame

Prov: Talwin Morris, by whose widow presented to Glasgow Art Gallery
Exh: Edinburgh 1968 (75)
Lit: *Yellow Book*, vol.10, July 1896, repr. p.177; White 1897, p.89; Bilcliffe 1978, no.ix, repr. p.70; Burkhauser 1990, pp.128–9, fig.163; Neat 1994, pp.138–40, repr. in col. p.139

Glasgow Museums: Art Gallery and Museum, Kelvingrove

EXHIBITED IN LONDON ONLY

Macdonald evidently took this subject and composition from Burne-Jones's picture of the same title in the *Briar Rose* series. Burne-Jones had first treated Perrault's story *Sleeping Beauty in the Wood* (1692) in a series of tiles, but he translated the designs into paintings firstly in the 'small Briar Rose series' 1870–3 (Museo de Arte, Ponce, Puerto Rico), and subsequently in the much larger canvases finished in 1890. These were bought the same year by Alexander Henderson for the saloon of Buscot Park, where they remain. They were exhibited to great popular acclaim at Agnew's in 1890 and again the following year at Toynbee Hall. It is possible that Frances Macdonald saw *The Sleeping Princess* at one of these showings.

Although her composition is similar, her treatment is radically different. The most notable difference is the Princess's boldly patterned dress, featuring stylised, art-nouveau floral motifs, and forms that resemble both tulip heads and spermatozoa. However, this aspect too has a link with Burne-Jones, for in its patterned effect it has similarities with his watercolour *Sidonia von Bork* (no.20). Macdonald's pastel is suffused with a mood of sensual and erotic tension, heightened by the Princess's ecstatic expression and her hands pressed together as if in prayer but pointing towards her pudenda. The viewer is perhaps intentionally put in the role of the Prince who, gazing down on her, will release her from her enchantment. Her flowing raven hair contributes to the erotic mood, a characteristic clearly derived from Rossetti, an artist whom Frances Macdonald, her sister Margaret and Charles Rennie Mackintosh all revered. Another Rossettian device is the decorated frame, an integral part of the work which provides interpretation of the subject. The verse is a quotation from Tennyson's treatment of the story 'The Day Dream: The Arrival' (IV, 7–8), published in *English Idylls and other Poems* (1842). Macdonald's use of it forces the viewer to speculate on the beauty of the Princess's eyes, making us imagine their opening, just as the Prince has done before kissing her and breaking the spell. On the frame the cobwebs testify to the passing of time, while on the top member are four pod-like features that reintroduce again the theme of fertility, although they additionally resemble closed eyes. The combination of these frame elements with the sperm-like decorations on the Princess's dress suggest that the underlying subject of the picture is the passage from chastity, symbolised by the metaphor of sleep, to fertility and the pleasures of physical love.

In July 1896 this picture was published in the *Yellow Book* by John Lane, who was a collector of Frances Macdonald's work. Neat has speculated that Klimt may have been influenced by this plate, and notes that he had not used stylised, geometric fabric motifs in his work before this date, but did afterwards. Klimt and other members of the Vienna Secession such as Moser greatly admired the Glasgow artists' work, which they are known to have seen in the *Studio* in 1897. They were invited to contribute to the Secession exhibitions and as a result similarities to the style and subjects of Frances and Margaret Macdonald, Charles Rennie Mackintosh and Herbert MacNair were felt in the work of Viennese artists such as Klimt and Moser. See also *Ver Sacrum* (no.109).

RU

FRANCES MACDONALD 1873–1921

99 **Autumn** 1898

Pencil and watercolour on vellum
45.4 × 14.7 (17⅞ × 5¾)
Inscribed 'FRANCES MACDONALD, 1898' b.l.

Prov: As no.98
Lit: Bilcliffe 1978, no.vi, repr. p.67

Glasgow Museums: Art Gallery and Museum, Kelvingrove

EXHIBITED IN LONDON ONLY

This is one of a series of four designs now in Glasgow Art Gallery illustrating the seasons, which Frances Macdonald undertook in collaboration with her sister Margaret. Frances painted *Spring*, 1897, and *Autumn*, 1898; while Margaret executed *Summer*, 1897, and *Winter*, 1898. Their subject-matter is an allegory of fertility and the cycle of life, which is articulated in terms of human reproduction. A young garlanded maid is depicted in *Spring*, standing above two babies, apparently buried, who press upwards towards life. In *Summer* she has ripened to ample-breasted motherhood; babies surround her head and her flowing dress is decorated with spermatozoa. Macdonald's *Autumn* shown here deals with the subject of death and decay. The now naked maiden soars upwards towards Heaven, accompanied by a figure who is apparently the Angel of Death. There are close affinities of format and composition with *'She Shall Be Called Woman'* by Watts (no.124), and the figure is also apparently influenced by his *Psyche* 1880 (Tate Gallery). However, *Autumn* is closer still to the principal figure group in Harry Bates's sculpture *Mors Janua Vitae* ('Death the Gateway to Life'; fig.53 on p.92) which deals with the same subject-matter and was itself influenced by Watts (see p.92). In an arrestingly macabre touch, perhaps influenced by Toorop (see no.111), Macdonald's figure floats towards Heaven accompanied by sperm with skull heads. The final panel of the sequence, *Winter*, shows a scene presumably set in Heaven. Bright child-angels float above a woman who scatters the seeds of new life in an act of renewal.

The format, delicate tracery and attenuated figures of Frances Macdonald's two designs for the series show the impact on her of works by Beardsley such as *The Climax* (no.92). They also appear to share a similar approach to composition to that found in Klimt's designs, such as those for *Ver Sacrum* (no.109). The atmosphere of mystery and use of a closely graduated tonality are, however, undoubtedly Wattsian.

RU

99

Symbolism. In the drawing exhibited here he utilised the subject-matter of Burne-Jones's introspective maidens, and his floral imagery, but transformed it into something completely new. The rose bush entwining the figure is likely to have been inspired by Burne-Jones's *Briar Rose* series (see no.98). The drawing makes an interesting comparison with Alfred Gilbert's later figure *The Virgin* 1899 (no.118) which also features a rose bush, entwining the Madonna and surmounting her with a crown of roses. The two are extremely close, and it is not impossible that Gilbert was influenced by the Buchanan Street murals. The shallow pictorial space, stylised forms, tracery and decoration also echo Beardsley's designs, especially the Salome Series (see nos.89, 92), which influenced several of the Glasgow Group.

Mackintosh's drawing is in fact a portrait of his future wife, Margaret Macdonald. The hearts on the frame symbolise his love for her, as do the roses in the picture. The twining vegetation, as in other drawings by Mackintosh, is a reference to fertility and the central place of woman in the cycle of renewal.

RU

Charles Rennie Mackintosh 1868–1928

100 **Part Seen, Imagined Part** 1896

Pencil and watercolour on tracing paper
39 × 19.5 (15⅜ × 7⅝)
Inscribed 'PART | SEEN | IMAGI | NED: | PART.' t.r. and 'CHAR | L | ES | RENNIE | MACKINT | OSH. | APRIL | 1896' b.r

Prov: As no.98
Exh: Arts and Crafts Exhibition Society 1896 (589); Glasgow 1933 (82)
Lit: Howarth 1977, p.38; Bilcliffe 1978, no.51, repr. p.71; Burkhauser 1990, p.121, fig.149; Neat 1994 pp.113–17, repr. p.116

Glasgow Museums: Art Gallery and Museum, Kelvingrove

EXHIBITED IN LONDON ONLY

Mackintosh used this design for the series of repeated figures in his mural for the Ladies Room of the Buchanan Street Tea Rooms in Glasgow, completed in 1897 (repr. Neat 1994, p.116). Mackintosh, and others among the Glasgow group of artists and designers, evolved a wholly personal treatment of

Henry Pegram 1862–1937

101 **Ignis Fatuus** 1889

Bronze 52.1 × 52.1 × 10.2 (20½ × 20½ × 4)
Inscribed 'Henry Pegram 1889' b.r.

Prov: Bt from the artist by the Trustees of the Chantrey Bequest 1889
Exh: RA 1889 (2156); Chantrey exhibition 1949 (377)
Lit: Read 1982, p.321

Tate Gallery. Presented by the Trustees of the Chantrey Bequest 1889

The title translates as 'foolish fire', and is generally used to describe the phenomenon of marsh gas combustion, whose flame-like phosphorescence can sometimes be seen flitting over marshy ground. It is traditionally considered foolhardy to try to follow it into the marshes, and therefore 'Ignis Fatuus' became a description applied to foolish or deluded ventures. Pegram's relief shows a woman sitting on a throne, her head supported by her arm in an attitude that mixes boredom, despair and resignation. Like his broken bow, she has been forsaken by the man in warrior's garb who reaches up towards a group of extraordinary, Redon-like creatures with human heads and the bodies of birds, bats and insects. These are chimeras of his fantasies, imaginations and desires, and represent their ultimate folly.

Pegram was greatly inspired by Alfred Gilbert, and *Ignis Fatuus* is evidently partly indebted to his relief roundel *Post Equitem Sedet Atra Cura* (Behind the Horseman Sits Gloomy Care) *c.*1883–7 (Dorment 1986, no.88), which was exhibited at the Royal Academy in 1887. Similar in technique, format and modelling, this also warns of the danger and vanity of human aspiration.

There is another cast of *Ignis Fatuus* in the National Museum of Wales, presented by the sculptor William Goscombe John (1860–1952).

RU

101

Charles Ricketts 1866–1931

102 **Oedipus and the Sphinx** 1891

Pen and ink 23 × 15.2 (9 × 6)
Inscribed 'R91' upper right side

Prov: Frederic, Lord Leighton; his sale 1896, bt Robert Dunthorne; Charles Ricketts; …; William Rothenstein by 1933; bt Gordon Bottomley 1936, by whom bequeathed to Carlisle Museum and Art Gallery 1949

Exh: RA 1933 (403); International Society 1913 (84); Carlisle 1971 (70); British Council, 1973 (51C); Durham 1975; Cambridge 1979 (A6); Sheffield 1971 (208); Twickenham 1979 (32); Barbican 1989 (291, repr.)

Lit: *The Pageant*, 1896, repr. p.65; Holmes 1936, p.164; Lewis 1939, p.19; Ormond 1975, pp.117–18; Calloway 1979, p.11, pl.14; Daracott 1980, p.72, repr.; Barclay 1985, no.1, repr.; Delaney 1990, pp.46–8, 84, fig.7

Tullie House Museum and Art Gallery, Carlisle

Although he later reviled them, and even destroyed a number, in 1890 Ricketts started making illustrations for the first time for the *Magazine of Art*, and the following year for the new journal *Black and White* (see Delaney 1990, p.46). Whatever Ricketts thought of them, these designs were evidently much admired by Leighton. Wanting to encourage him, he wrote to Ricketts commissioning a drawing 'of the same imaginative and fanciful character of those I have seen', leaving the choice of subject 'absolutely in your hands so that you may be wholly untrammelled and able to give me an entirely personal and characteristic specimen of your charming gift' (letter dated 16 Feb. 1891, quoted Delaney 1990, p.46). Ricketts clearly took great care over the commission, which after magazine illustration he viewed as a liberation; it was not until 22 December 1891 that Leighton wrote again to thank him for the drawing, which he had received the previous day:

> the design is full of imagination and a weird charm – it is also, in such passages, for instance, as the wings of the Sphinx and the hair of Oedipus, a marvellous piece of penmanship. It is a great pleasure for me to possess it. Pray let me know at the earliest convenience what my debt is to you that I may acquit myself of it. – I shall be very happy, if occasion presents itself, to serve you in your profession.
>
> (Lewis 1939, p.19)

Ricketts charged him £5 for it. He always considered it his best drawing, and after the sale following Leighton's death in 1896 bought it back, reproducing it the same year in *The Pageant*.

From 1890 to 1891 Ricketts was immersed in his interest in Rossetti, and indeed the draughtsmanship of *Oedipus and the Sphinx* is indebted to Rossetti's early, highly worked pen-and-ink drawings. There are strong similarities, in particular, with Rossetti's *Mary Magdalene at the Door of Simon the Pharisee* 1858 (Fitzwilliam Museum, Cambridge) which Ricketts had acquired by 1890 (see Cambridge 1979, no.174). Ricketts and Shannon owned several drawings by Rossetti, as well as works by Burne-Jones, Holman Hunt and Millais, demonstrating their admiration for that older generation (see Cambridge 1979). Ricketts was, however, dismissive of Leighton's work despite his patronage of him. Rossetti's poetry was a further source of fascination for Ricketts, particularly 'Hand and Soul', which he republished himself in 1899 (see Delaney 1990, p.26).

Oedipus and the Sphinx is, however, also closely indebted to French art. Gustave Moreau, who along with Puvis was Ricketts's great idol, had treated the story in both *Oedipe et le Sphinx* (Metropolitan Museum of Art, New York) and *Oedipe Voyageur* (*Egalité devant la mort*) (no.54). While there are similarities between these and Ricketts's drawing, both ultimately derive from Ingres, whose figure of Oedipus in *Oedipus Explains the Riddle of the Sphinx* 1808 (Musée du Louvre, Paris) served as the model for Ricketts's treatment.

The Theban Sphinx was a recurrent Symbolist subject, often used, clearly, to articulate conscious or unconscious feelings about women, notably fear and attraction. Representations of the Sphinx are usually a mixture of terrifying harpy and voluptuous temptress. The consumption or tearing apart of her victims serves as a further cipher for male fears of powerlessness, subjection and compulsion. Ricketts's lithe and sensual Sphinx pushes Oedipus away as he grips her arm and answers her riddle. The erotic charge of the drawing is accentuated further by the ecstatic expression of the figure crouching at the base of the right-hand, vine-clad column, which in this context must be read as a phallic symbol. The severed heads littering the foreground recall contemporary depictions of the story of Salome (see no.92).

Delaney has noted that throughout his life Ricketts was fascinated by key historical or mythical moments, when man struggles with his destiny (1990, p.48). This drawing captures a moment of double-edged fate, where Oedipus triumphs over the threat of death, and rids Thebes of the Sphinx, but in so doing, is rewarded by marriage to his mother.

Maxwell Armfield (1881–1972) made a coloured copy in tempera around 1900, probably from the plate published in *The Pageant* (Sotheby's, 5 March 1997, lot 120, repr.).

RU

102

SIMEON SOLOMON 1840–1905

103 **The Head of Medusa** 1884

Coloured chalks 40 × 31.4 (15¾ × 12⅜)
Inscribed 'SS | 1884' b.r.

Prov: ...; private collection, USA; Christie's 14 March 1997 (44, repr.); bt by present owner

Lit: Reynolds 1985, p.94

Private Collection

Solomon was closely associated with many of the central figures of Symbolism in Britain: he had a mutually influential relationship with Burne-Jones, and importantly, became close to Swinburne and Walter Pater. Through Rossetti, whom he met for the first time in 1858, he was introduced to many of the members of the Aesthetic and Pre-Raphaelite circle, who rated his abilities highly. Solomon visited Paris in 1859 where he saw the work of Gustave Moreau, whose example he quickly assimilated. Swinburne, however, appears to have been a destructive influence on his character. With Burne-Jones, Solomon made a series of illustrations to the poet's de Sade-influenced *Lesbia Brandon*, and he exchanged

103

letters with Swinburne in which they related their sexual fantasies (see Reynolds 1985, pp.13–14). Solomon grew increasingly reckless and open in his decadence and homosexuality, culminating in 1873 with his arrest and conviction for gross indecency with another man in a public lavatory. His friends immediately distanced themselves from him, not least Swinburne, who wrote to their mutual confidant George Powell encouraging him not to let kindness persuade him to have any contact, advice repeated to Theodore Watts-Dunton (Reynolds 1985, pp.83–4). Abandoned by his friends and family, Solomon became a destitute alcoholic, ending his days in the Seven Dials workhouse. To a certain degree he appears to have relished his role as a sensualist vagabond outsider, but evidence of his inner turmoil and pain is perhaps revealed in the series of drawings he made of agonised heads, of which this is an unusually finished example.

In this sheet Solomon lends what is a Classical subject an original and Symbolist dimension by revealing the anguish underlying the Medusa's terrifying persona, and equating her torment with a personal psychological state. Two pencil drawings of the same subject bear inscriptions which further reveal Solomon's identification with the Medusa's character: *'The Tormented Soul'* 1894 (Reynolds 1985, pl.77) and *'Let not thine eyes see Evil itself, but be its shadow upon life enough for thee'* 1890 (ibid., pl.72). Like the first of these, *The Head of Medusa* has a pair of staring eyes superimposed on the closed eyelids. Reynolds has suggested that *'Let not thine eyes ...'* offers the key to this Symbolic device – that while evil weighs down on us, we should not invite its entry into the soul open-eyed (p.94). This could suggest a rueful consideration by Solomon of his fall from respectability.

The disembodied head in itself had become a leitmotif of Symbolist art by this period, occurring in treatments of the Salome story as well as that of Perseus and Medusa, and having resonances from Moreau and Redon (no.110) to Wilde and Beardsley (no.92).

RU

William Strang 1859–1921

104 **Grotesque** 1897

Two impressions, etched mezzotint, each 20.3 × 17.5 (8 × 6⅞)
Inscribed (i) 'To Lady Dilke from Wm Strang' and 'Final state (of 3) DS' below (ii) 'Wm Strang fec DS', 'Final state (of 3) DS' and 'Illustration to written description of a dream by WS. Probably etched soon after visit to "The Villa of Monsters", near Rome' below

Prov: (i) given by the artist to Lady Dilke; Campbell Dodgson, by whom presented to the British Museum 1922
Exh: Barbican 1989 (221)
Lit: Binyon 1912, no.311 (repr.); Strang 1962, no.405; Strang 1980, no.71, repr. p.16

Trustees of the British Museum

EXHIBITED IN LONDON AND MUNICH ONLY

As the inscription by the artist's son records, this design was inspired by a dream Strang had after visiting the Villa of Monsters near Rome. Issued in an edition of fifty proofs, it illustrates Strang's dark taste for the sensuous and macabre that runs through much of his etched work of this period. It displays a range of influences, the principal one in both technique and subject being Goya, who enjoyed renewed admiration in Britain in the 1890s. The diabolical, horned skull, and perhaps also the corseted woman, are evidently a response to Felicien Rops – whose prints were officially banned in Britain, although they circulated surreptitiously among artists and connoisseurs. Strang's etchings were much admired in Germany, and it was in the same year that Strang made *Grotesque* that he won a gold medal at the Dresden International Exhibition. Here he was exposed to a wide range of Symbolist material, and in 1898 he was one of the small number of British artists invited to contribute to the First Vienna Secession, where he showed five works. A friend of Ricketts and Shannon, who also introduced Strang to continental Symbolist work, he shared their admiration for the Venetian Old Masters, Puvis and Watts.

Strang's developing Symbolist tendency was most fully expressed in the remarkable cycle of ten paintings he made on the theme of Adam and Eve commissioned for Compton Hall near Wolverhampton (1899–1901). These were generally recognised as landmarks of British imaginative painting of the period. As Philip Atthill has noted, they reflect Strang's interest in Puvis and the German Symbolist painter Hans Thoma (see Barbican 1989, no.218), and also reveal an awareness of Hodler (see nos.135, 136).

RU

104

WILLIAM STRANG 1859–1921

105 **Mother Earth** 1897

Etched mezzotint 20.1 × 15 (7⅞ × 6)
Inscribed 'Wm Strang –' b.r., 'David Strang: imp.' and 'Final state (probably of 2 only).' b.l.

Prov: Presented to the British Museum by the National Art Collections Fund 1953

Lit: Binyon 1912, no.312 (repr.)

Trustees of the British Museum

EXHIBITED IN LONDON AND MUNICH ONLY

Issued in an edition of thirty-five proofs, this print dates from the same year as no.104, but shows Strang in less morbid vein. He treated a related theme the following year in his humorous *A Book of Giants* (1898), but the print shown here is altogether more serious and lyrical. The subject and design are very much akin to Watts, and to a lesser extent German artists such as Arnold Böcklin (see no.62). In particular it recalls the subjects of Watts's creation pictures *The Titans* 1873–5 (Watts Gallery, Compton) and *Chaos* (no.49), featuring oversized allegorical figures.

RU

105

George Frederic Watts 1817–1904

106 **The Recording Angel** *c.*1890

Red chalk on buff paper 64 × 44 (25¼ × 17⅜)

Prov: …; Cecil French; bequeathed by his executors to the Fulham Public Libraries 1954; on deposit at Leighton House

Lit: MS. Cat., I, p.2 (under the entry for *'The All-Pervading'*); *Catalogue of the Cecil French Bequest*, Central Library, Fulham 1954, no.54

London Borough of Hammersmith and Fulham

This drawing belongs to a distinct, and essentially Symbolist, category in Watts's œuvre in which he translated his major compositions into the medium of soft red chalk studies of great subtlety (see p.73). This one follows the composition of *'The All-Pervading'* (no.125), with the addition of a scroll, unfurling across the top of the globe. The angel writes on her scroll, transcribing a message which the artist preferred to leave as an open question.

The Recording Angel had a surprisingly wide currency in the 1890s in its engraved form. It is interesting that Watts considered it as an independent work suitable for reproduction. The wood engraving by Walter Biscombe Gardner appeared at the Royal Academy in 1891 (no.1715); reproduced in large format, this print provided a lavish illustration to an article on Watts in the periodical *Black and White* in 1896.

The image of the angel played a major role in Watts's work. The most notable examples are the Angel of Death in *Love and Death* (no.51), *The Court of Death* (fig.45 on p.74), *The Messenger* (fig.44 on p.74). The angel is a benign though powerful presence, with massive folded wings, often heavy drapery drawn up over the head so that it obscures the face without actually concealing it, lending a mystery to the image. Here Watts places the angel in a mandorla shape which seems to hover upon the sheet like a vision. The use of red chalk suggests a fascinating connection with the work of Khnopff (see no.107) in the years around 1890. As in Watts's other red chalk drawings, the soft focus heightens the mood of silence and mystery. Although a modest work, *The Recording Angel* encapsulates Watts's Symbolist approach in both theme and technique.

As in *'The All-Pervading'*, the sphere can be taken to represent 'The Globe of Systems', thus providing a thematic link with another late work, *The Sower of the Systems* (no.134). All these works share a residual link with the artist's early scheme for the 'history of cosmos' (see no.49). Watts's own self-confessed belief was that the

> aim [of art] should be to give the impression of some great truth of nature, something so far too great for expression that finally it must remain indefinite. The infinite looming large behind the finite – that is the impression which great art alone can convey.

BB

FERNAND KHNOPFF 1858–1921

107 **Silence** 1890

Pastel 85 × 41.5 (33½ × 16⅜)
Inscribed with Knopff's monogram 'FK |
Fernand Khnopff' lower left

Prov: Paul Errera, Brussels; Isabelle Errera, Brussels, by whom bequeathed to the Musées Royaux de Beaux-Arts de Belgique

Exh: Gosvenor Gallery 1890 (180); and see Delevoy et al. 1987, no.151

Lit: See Delevoy et al. 1987, no.151; Draguet 1995, pp.296–7

Musées Royaux des Beaux-Arts de Belgique

EXHIBITED IN LONDON ONLY

The source for this pastel was a posed photograph of Khnopff's sister, Marguerite. As in the pastel, the photograph was deliberately taken from below in order to emphasise the monumental, inaccessible nature of his model. In keeping with so many of his representations of women, the subject is treated as a hieratic, immobile image, distanced from the world through timeless costume and abstracted gaze.

The subject of silence had been a persistent element in Khnopff's work. In his portraits of the 1880s, his few 'genre' scenes such as *Listening to Schumann* 1882 (Musées Royaux des Beaux-Arts de Belgique, Brussels) and his landscapes made at the family estate of Le Fosset in the Ardennes, the communication of a world without sound was achieved primarily through the depiction of motionless subjects. Sitters are in arrested poses, contained within carefully manipulated, harmoniously formalised spaces; views of buildings, a bridge, the open moor are devoid of human presence and seemingly frozen in time; the making of music becomes divorced from the action of playing and is internalised within the listener as a purely private, silent experience. The primacy of silence, and the need to convey it through a disregard for detail which would detract from the fact that silence is conveyed through the relationship between the component parts of a composition, relates Khnopff's work both to the literary worlds of the Belgian Symbolist writers Georges Rodenbach and Maurice Maeterlinck, but also to the pictorial world of Odilon Redon (see no.110). In the same year as *Silence* was created, Redon produced the first of several versions of *Closed Eyes* 1890 (Musée d'Orsay, Paris), in which the interior gaze of the head portrayed in the painting signifies the seat of ultimate truth.

Silence was first publicly exhibited in London at the Society of British Pastellists, recently inaugerated.

MAS

FERNAND KHNOPFF 1858–1921

108 **Study of a Woman** 1896

Pencil on grey paper heightened with white chalk 20 × 13 (7⅞ × 5⅛)
Inscribed with Khnopff's monogram and 'TO SIR EDWARD BURNE-JONES from FERNAND KHNOPFF.' below

Prov: Sir Edward Burne-Jones; ...; Piccadilly Gallery by 1967; Galleria Galatea, Turin

Exh: Piccadilly Gallery 1967 (55); Turin 1970 (no no., repr); Paris 1979 (92, repr. in col. p.50)

Lit: Dumont-Wilden 1907, p.72; Biermé 1911, p.3; Delville 1925, p.25; Hamacher 1981, p.191; McDonnell 1985, pp.90, 93 n.12; Delevoy et al. 1987, no.278, repr.

Private Collection, Belgium

Khnopff was greatly interested in developments in contemporary British art, and in particular was an admirer of Burne-Jones, with whom he exchanged letters, and whose obituary he wrote for the *Magazine of Art* in 1898. Dedicated to Burne-Jones, this sheet is a tangible record of the friendship between the two artists.

Khnopff was a frequent visitor to Britain, and also often exhibited his work here, the first time being at the Liverpool Art Club in 1886. In 1889 English dealers showed a number of his pictures, and that year saw the beginnings of his friendship with Burne-Jones, Watts and Holman Hunt. The following year the Hanover Gallery held the first British exhibition of Khnopff's work. In March 1892 Khnopff held a conference in Brussels at which he proposed an exhibition of Hollyer's photographs of the paintings of Watts, Ford Madox Brown, Rossetti and Burne-Jones, and spoke of the importance of their work. He also recalled a visit to Watts and spoke of Rossetti's career (see Delevoy et al. 1987, pp.499–500). Khnopff wrote extensively on British and Belgian art, notably for the *Studio*. He published his first article there in 1894, on the English exhibits at the first Libre Esthétique exhibition, and until the outbreak of the First World War he was a contributor to almost every issue, acting as Brussels correspondent.

Khnopff wrote passionately of Burne-Jones in his obituary of him:

> The works remain – the man is no more – the man whom those who loved him were so glad and proud to call on in his home ... But he did not leave us till he had produced a vast amount of work, all stamped with the seal of brilliant individuality – not till the world had given him not merely the most universal celebrity, but even, alas! had granted him popularity ... The name of Burne-Jones became a watch-word, a standard hailed with the enthusiasm of younger men in the new effort for idealism, the most vigorous artistic movement of later days.
>
> I am proud to have been chosen to write ... these few lines of intense and reverent admiration and of deep gratitude for the great artist who was led by his high ideal to produce such noble and beautiful work – work which will always be a supreme joy to those who liberate their sensations and ideas from the hampering weight of material hindrances and bonds, and to uplift them to those higher spheres where a subtle intelligence can find and purify the very essence of those sensations and ideas.
>
> (*Magazine of Art*, 1898, pp.525–6)

RU

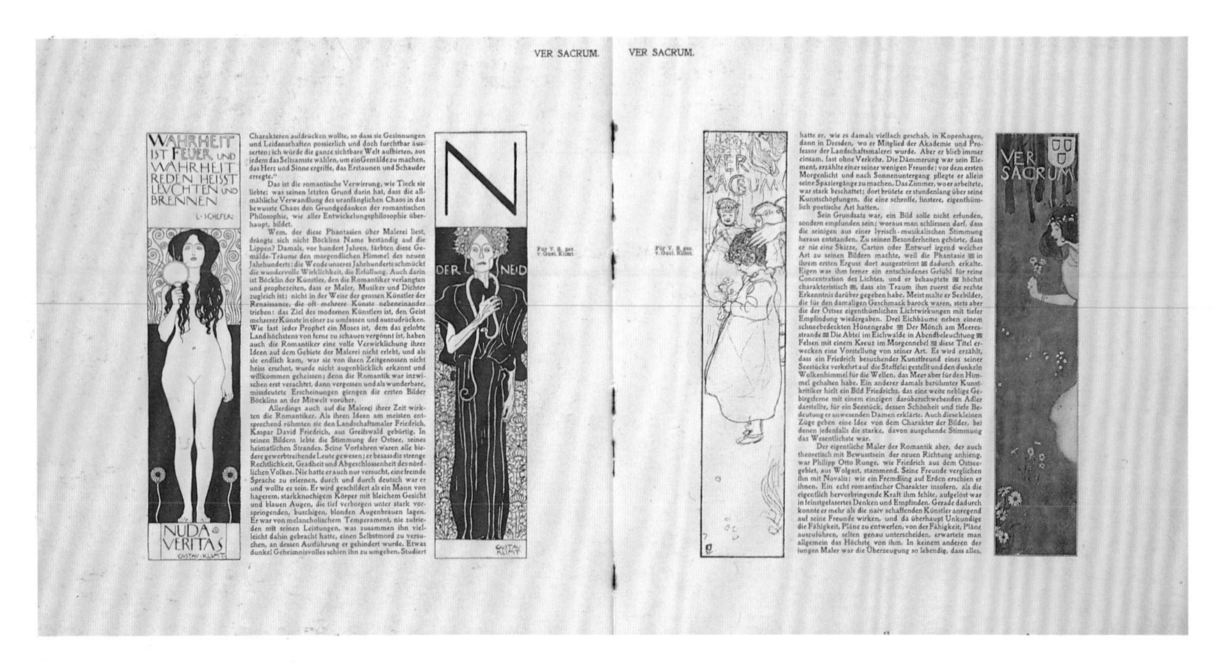

Gustav Klimt 1862–1918

109 **Four Illustrations for *Ver Sacrum*** 1898

Bound set of 12 issues for 1898. Cloth boards
Page size 29 × 28 (11⅜ × 11)

Lit: Neberhay 1977, pp.112–13; Whitford 1990, pp.45–7, pls.52–3

Sims Reed Limited

Ver Sacrum was the official publication of the Secession, which set itself up in opposition to the art establishment of Vienna in 1897. Its title, taken from a poem by Uhland, is Latin for 'Sacred Spring', referring to the artistic renewal the journal sought to promote. It began as a monthly magazine, later coming out every two weeks, and set itself the highest standards of design and production. The first issue appeared in 1898, a Viennese answer to the flood of art publishing that had overtaken the capitals of Europe in the course of the decade. It contained the declaration that 'For years the cheerful war has been raging along the whole of the front from London to Munich, from Paris to St Petersburg. It was only in Vienna that scarcely a breath of its spirit could be felt' (quoted in Neberhay 1977, p.24). The magazine had a successful life until it ceased publication in 1903.

One obvious precursor from London was the *Studio*, well established since 1893 and widely read in Europe. *Ver Sacrum* frequently referred to the British art world. When Burne-Jones died in June 1898 it published a tribute to him, 'One of the noblest artists of our time', from the Union of Austrian Painters. It was an 1897 issue of the *Studio* that brought Mackintosh and the Glasgow artists (see nos.98–100) to the attention of the Viennese, and when in 1900 they took Vienna by storm at the Secession exhibition, their work was featured in an issue of *Ver Sacrum*.

From its inception, Klimt was a major protagonist of the Secession, and he was at one time on the editorial board of *Ver Sacrum*. His work appeared often in its pages. This opening from the issue for March 1898 shows four of his drawings, reproduced as usual in greenish-grey ink. By this date Klimt had evolved a distinctive style considerably removed from the academic idiom of his decorative *Idyll* of 1884 (no.52). It is highly personal but, as these examples show, displays the influence of Beardsley in various ways. The left-hand design on the first page is a black-and-white drawing showing a nude woman holding a mirror. It is inscribed, in a panel above, 'WAHRHEIT IST FEUER UND WAHRHEIT REDEN HEISST LEUCHTEN UND BRENNEN' ('Truth is fire and to speak truth is to illumine and to burn'), a quotation from L. Schefer; and below 'NUDA VERITAS' ('Naked Truth') with Klimt's signature. The linear idiom is stiffer, less orotund than Beardsley's, but the deployment of bold contrasts of black and white and the insistence on the value of sinuous line is similar. Opposite on the same page is 'Der Neid', ('Jealousy'), showing a clothed female figure with a snake coiled round her neck. A large capital letter N occupies the panel above, the title is inscribed on either side of the woman's neck, and Klimt has signed in a panel below. Both these drawings make use of a stylised linear ornamental motif as background and are hieratic, simplified and solemn in Klimt's best Secession manner. Both make use of a tall upright format that echoes one used by Beardsley in, for instance, his 1894 design for a poster advertising the *Yellow Book* (Reade 1967, no.341). Klimt was to make an oil painting of the *Nuda Veritas* subject, incorporating a different quotation, in 1899 (Theatre Collection, Nationalbibliothek, Vienna).

The facing page has two drawings by Klimt in a quite different mode. Instead of crisp contrasts of pen line and blocks of black and white, one appears to have been executed in pencil, the other in washes of tone. Both are inscribed 'VER SACRUM'. In the left-hand design, small children holding posies have wreaths of flowers adjusted on their heads by a woman. In the right-hand illustration, a dark-haired young woman gathers flowers in a field with trees beyond. This last has uncanny similarities with Beardsley's Singer sewing-machine advertisement, of 1894 (Reade 1967, no.321), which however was not reproduced until 1898 and not widely used.

AW

Odilon Redon 1840–1916

110 **The Beheaded** *c.*1885

Charcoal and black chalk with incising, stumping, rubbing out and brush work on cream paper prepared with a buff ground
48.5 × 34.5 (19 × 13⅝)
Inscribed 'ODILON REDON' down left side

Prov: Bt from the artist by Edmond Picard 1888; ...; Ian Woodner, New York

Exh: Les XX 1890 (7); Les XX 1892 (1, as *Tête de décapité*); Libre Esthétique 1894 (35); Tokyo 1989a (64, as *Destin*); Memphis 1990 (20); Chicago 1994 (89, repr. in col. p.144)

Lit: Demolder 1890, p.100; *Le Mercure Français*, March 1890; Bacou 1960, p.161, no.12; Wildenstein 1992, no.383

The Woodner Collections, New York

EXHIBITED IN LONDON AND MUNICH ONLY

In the 1880s and 1890s Redon was hailed in Paris as the quintessential Symbolist artist. He was a friend of Mallarmé, and Huysmans admired his work greatly, writing enthusiastically about Redon in his art criticism as well as in his best-selling novel of diabolic excess *A Rebours* (1884). Dredged from the world of dreams and the unconscious, Redon's imagery is frequently dark and disturbing, operating on a deeply psychological level. Until the late 1880s he worked solely in monochrome, which serves to accentuate the anti-realist, fantastic quality of his art.

The severed head was a recurrent motif throughout Redon's career. One of the first drawings he made of the subject was after Andrea Solario's *Head of St John the Baptist* (1507) which he copied in the Louvre (*c.*1868, Woodner Collections, New York, repr. Chicago 1994, fig.73). The image of the cut-off or disembodied head came to have deeply personal associations for him, along with the story of Salome. He identified strongly with John the Baptist, and in *Salome* 1877 (Nelson-Atkins Museum of Art, Kansas City) the features of the head on the platter resemble his own. Moreover, as Druick and Zegers have noted (Chicago 1994, p.86), Redon appears to have associated his mother with Salome because of her harsh treatment of him in childhood. The Salome story has been widely understood as a parable about male fear of women, sex and castration. The recurrent reference to it by Redon and other Symbolists anticipates the investigations by psychologists of the role of archetypal myth. Redon's casting of his mother in the role of Salome lends his treatments of the subject an extra dimension of disturbed and disturbing oedipal anxiety.

The most arresting quality about the sheet exhibited here is the head's continuing alertness and expressive eyes. This feature derives in part from the myth of Orpheus, whose head continued singing even after his body was torn to pieces. Redon seems to have also identified himself with Orpheus, partly because of the 'castration complex' element of the story, in which the Thracian women rip him apart and decapitate him in their Bacchanalian passion. Orpheus was able to move even inanimate objects with the beauty of his music, and this element of the myth held resonance for Redon, who believed in the transforming potential of artistic creation. The severance of the head from the body also represents the separation and victory of the mind over the body. The head symbolised the world of thought and creativity, the spiritual and eternal, while the body represented all that was corporeal in life. Redon described *The Beheaded* as 'a hand presenting its own head' (quoted ibid., p.145) suggesting perhaps that he saw the image as an act of self-liberation.

Druick and Zegers (ibid., p.101) have noted that such subjects should also be viewed against a long-running debate in France about how long perception continued in criminals executed by the guillotine. Anecdotal and quasi-scientific evidence, the subject of great argument, suggested that awareness might indeed continue for some time. The common contemporary belief that at the moment of execution victims experienced orgasm adds a further disturbing dimension to the psycho-sexual elements of Redon's subject-matter.

An additional point of reference was the 'talking head' entertainment (see ibid.). After its premiere in London in 1865 this transferred to the wax museum in the boulevard de la Madeléine in Paris. Here visitors were led into a room where a severed head lay on a platter, which would then miraculously open its eyes and relate the grisly story of its execution. Eventually it was exposed as a clever hoax, but not before the attraction of its horror was lauded at the 1867 Universal Exhibition and the Larousse Dictionary had given it a lengthy entry in 1870. This phenomenon and its exposure is apparently referred to directly in Redon's *After the Execution* 1877 (private collection, repr. Chicago 1994, fig.58), which features a head which is similarly alert.

By the 1880s the severed head had become a decadent leitmotif of Symbolism. In England, Simeon Solomon made a series of intense drawings of the Medusa's head (see no.103), a myth which held personal significance for him, as Salome did for Redon. Flaubert and Mallarmé were similarly fascinated by the story of Salome, and Moreau made it the subject of some of his most important pictures, notably *The Apparition* 1876 (fig.34 on p.61), which Redon particularly admired, and which was exhibited in London at the Grosvenor Gallery in 1877. It was against this enthusiasm for the story and imagery of Salome that in 1891 Wilde wrote his play devoted to it in Paris. Beardsley later produced illustrations for Wilde, and it was the alarming image of Salome kissing the Baptist's head (no.92) which quickly became the most notorious of these designs. Wilde's version of the story accentuated the contrast between Salome's sexual physicality and John the Baptist's transcendent spirituality, a duality which Redon articulated in the symbolic severance of the head from the body.

RU

Jan Toorop 1858–1928

111 **Fatalism** 1893

Pencil and black and coloured chalks heightened with white
60 × 75 (23⅝ × 29½)
Inscribed 'J. Th. Toorop 1893' b.l.

Exh: Amsterdam 1970; The Hague 1989 (42, repr. in col.)

Lit: Plasschaert 1925 pl.16 (as *Symbolische Teekening*)

Kröller-Müller Museum, Otterlo, The Netherlands

EXHIBITED IN LONDON AND AMSTERDAM

Born in Java in the Dutch East Indies, Toorop trained first in the Netherlands and then in Brussels. Here he shared a studio with the Symbolist artist William Degouve de Nunques, was a member of Les XX and through this became friendly with Maurice Maeterlinck and Emile Verhaeren, two of the outstanding Symbolist writers in Belgium. In 1884 Toorop came to London accompanied by Verhaeren and Paul Destrée, where he made paintings of the city, and admired the Turners which he saw in the National Gallery. He came again to England in 1886 to marry Annie Hall, an English woman he had met in Brussels, and on this trip Alma-Tadema introduced him to Leighton. Toorop stayed for a longer period in England in 1889, during which time he met Whistler and William Morris. It is from this period that his interest in British art appears to have grown, and it marked too an abandonment of his Impressionist and Pointilliste style in favour of Symbolist subjects. Toorop met Péladan in Brussels in 1892, and consequently exhibited at the first Salon of the Rose+Croix. He was represented regularly at the Libre Esthétique and later at the Vienna Secession, where in 1902 a room was devoted solely to his work.

The theme of the drawing shown here is the endurance of good and evil, and the unavoidability of fate and death. The central figure, Toorop explained, 'is squeezed between rectangular pits as if frozen, with her arms rigid by her sides and strangely staring eyes, as if she is embittered by life and full of despair. She tries to repulse fate; three fate figures are rising up on the left … They want to surprise their prey and destroy it' (quoted The Hague 1989, no.42). The principal figure of fate – whom Toorop does not mention – has succeeded in encircling her victim with her hair and train of fabric. The 'rectangular pits' are graves, and the clear message is that death is unavoidable. The women in the background, Toorop added, are 'a procession of virgins … as a symbol of those who want to make life into something beautiful and serene, which is continually perfecting itself' (quoted ibid., p.23). They appear to represent the purity and

111

perfection of artistic creation, which Toorop associates with the forces of good. They are clothed in dresses as exotically decorated as that of Burne-Jones's *Sidonia von Bork* (no.20) and fulfil a similar thematic function to the line of maidens in his *Golden Stairs* (no.68). Toorop's central figure enwrapped by fate has the same features and pose as the principal right hand bride in *The Three Brides* (Rijksmuseum Kröller-Müller, Otterlo), also made in 1893. There she is dressed in white, and was intended by Toorop to represent 'the pernicious bride of evil with her necklace of skulls and the dish which is constantly filled with human blood' (quoted ibid.). In *Fatalism* she wears a black dress, traditional widow's mourning, as well as the colour associated with evil. Toorop seems to be suggesting that even evil cannot escape fate, and cannot escape punishment at the moment of death. The figures personifying fate first appeared in Toorop's drawing *O Grave, Where is Thy Victory* 1892 (Rijksmuseum, Amsterdam), although he described these as 'sylphs', spirits of the air (ibid., no.38), perhaps indicating that they are creatures associated specifically with neither good nor evil. They were clearly inspired by the wayang puppets of Toorop's Javanese childhood. The closely regulated lines with which their hair is drawn are reminiscent of the style of Beardsley's illustrations to the *Morte Darthur*, started the same year as *Fatalism*. They are likely to have been aware of each other's work, for several of Beardsley's designs and drawings were reproduced in the first issue of the *Studio* in 1893, and Toorop's *Three Brides* was illustrated later that year along with an article by W. Shaw Sparrow (vol.1, pp.247–8). They were co-exhibitors the following year at the inaugural exhibition of the Libre Esthétique.

Toorop demonstrated an awareness of Burne-Jones's work in his drawing *Aurore* 1892 (Museum Boymans-van Beuningen, Rotterdam): the subject-matter and imagery of thornbushes, roses and armour-clad knight come straight from the *Briar Rose* series, while its delicate, stylised draughtsmanship make further connections with Beardsley and the Glasgow group of artists. Charles Rennie Mackintosh and the Macdonald sisters greatly admired the reproductions of Beardsley's and Toorop's work when they appeared in the *Studio*. Toorop's influence is perhaps discernible in Frances Macdonald's *Autumn* (no.99), where the skull-headed sperm may be inspired by the evil bride's skull necklace.

RU

The Climax

The 1890s were the high period of a international Symbolism when the strands of Decadence and Idealism attained explicit definition, and at the same time came together to create some of the most ambitious works of the nineteenth century. London became a forum in which this new 'ism' could be studied in depth. The Grafton Gallery which opened in 1893 was one of several new exhibiting houses in which painters and sculptors from all over Europe could regularly show their work. Watts, Rossetti and Burne-Jones enjoyed the status, along with Moreau and Puvis de Chavannes, of unofficial founding fathers of the movement.

fig.57 Walter Crane, *The Mower* 1901, tempera on canvas 80 × 117 cm. Staatliche Kunsthalle Karlsruhe

The Paris Exposition Universelle of 1889 reinforced this perception, especially of course in France. Leighton, Watts and Burne-Jones were all represented, the latter's *King Cophetua* having an extraordinary impact (see Laurent 1996, section 4, pp.49–50). Fashionable Parisians like the actress Georgette Lemaire affected costumes and poses inspired by Burne-Jones, Watts and Rossetti (ibid., p.52). Joséphin Péladan opened his annual exhibition the Salon de la Rose+Croix in 1892 and invited Burne-Jones and Watts to send work; pictures by both were acquired for the new Luxembourg Gallery. In Brussels Jean Delville's Salon de l'Art Idéaliste, inspired by the Rose+ Croix, established a distinctively Belgian version of Idealism from 1896; Watts and Burne-Jones were both formative influences. La Libre Esthétique, another Brussels exhibiting group, followed Les XX in welcoming British artists, showing work by, among others, Watts, Beardsley and George Frampton. Both Beardsley and Walter Crane were in different ways influential through their book designs. Crane was especially appreciated in Germany, where his strange allegorical paintings found widespread admirers. The Berlin dealer Ernst Seeger acquired several canvases by Crane in the 1890s (see Spencer 1975, p.127) (fig.57). Watts's work was seen at the Munich Jahresaustellung von Kunstwerken aller Nationen in 1893, from which his *Happy Warrior* (no.77) was acquired by the Bavarian state; and in 1897 the Stockholm International Exhibition sealed his reputation in Scandinavia. Dresden too held an International Exhibition in 1897 at which British artists were shown, and Watts sent work to the Venice International Exhibition of 1895. This was the first of what were to become the Venice Biennales, which often included British work. In Rome the In Arte Libertas group, founded by Nino Costa in 1885 under the inspiration of the poet Gabriele d'Annunzio, held exhibitions in the Palazzo delle Esposizioni. In 1890 this group brought 'Pre-Raphaelitism', i.e. the art of Rossetti and Burne-Jones, to a Roman audience.

By the beginning of the decade the New Sculpture had established itself as a significant and innovatory school. There is throughout the movement a sense of the interpenetration of the two arts. The subject of Pygmalion (see no.38) offers a paradigm of the created image becoming real, of stone metamorphosing into flesh. This is the primary effect of the flowing, elusive surfaces of Gilbert's work, and that of other sculptors of the school. The trait is also conspicuous in the work of Auguste Rodin, who pioneered many of the new techniques and admired Gilbert's work. His famous *Kiss* (fig.58) takes up a theme from Dante that had been treated by Rossetti and Burne-Jones (and before them by Ingres) – the illicit love of Paolo and Francesca – transforming it into one of the most powerful of all Symbolist sculptures.

In the output of all these artists, physical ambiguity is achieved in the least ambiguous of media – a particularly potent example of Symbolist thinking remoulding an art form to suit its purposes.

fig.58 Auguste Rodin, *The Kiss* 1901–4, Pentelican marble 182.2 × 121.9 × 153 cm. Tate Gallery

Harry Bates 1850–1899

112 **Pandora** *c.*1890

Inscribed 'Harry Bates. Sc.' on back
Marble, ivory, bronze and gilt 94 × 50.8 × 73.7 (37 × 20 × 29)

Prov: Purchased from the artist by the Trustees of the Chantrey Bequest 1891

Exh: RA 1891 (2117); Chantrey exhibition 1949 (80); Stoke on Trent 1992 (4, repr.)

Lit: Winter Johnson 1897, p.586, repr. opp. p.589; Beattie 1983, p.167, pl.163; Warner 1985, p.237

Tate Gallery. Presented by the Trustees of the Chantrey Bequest 1891

EXHIBITED IN LONDON ONLY

Bates took many of his subjects from Classical mythology. In Greek myth Pandora was the first mortal woman, whom Zeus decreed should be beautiful but also foolhardy. In a story that parallels that of Eve and the apple, against instructions to the contrary Pandora opened a box which contained all the troubles and ills of life. These flew free to plague human existence ever after, and the only thing left in the box was Hope.

Bates shows the moment of hesitation before Pandora opens the box. He suggests Pandora's mood of consideration and temptation – the moment of choice as her finger touches the clasp – while also recognising the inevitable fulfilment of the myth, and so acknowledging the compulsion of character, and frailty of the human spirit.

Bates's treatment of the marble creates a surface that is both perfectly smooth and deeply sensuous, attributes that are accentuated by both the naturalism of the figure's pose, and its contrast to the ivory and bronze casket. Bates has repeated, but adapted, the pose that he used for the relief figure of Cupid in his earlier triptych *The Story of Psyche* 1887, silvered bronze (fig.52 on p.91). This was itself derived and adapted from Burne-Jones's gouache *Cupid Finding Psyche* 1865–87 (Manchester City Art Gallery), in which the figure of Cupid bends rather than crouches. Bates's first use of this source is in the relief *Dido and Aeneas: Then indeed Aeneas Weeps* 1885, although the connection here to Burne-Jones is fainter. Eugène Delaplanche's slightly later marble *Eve before Committing the Sin* 1891 (Musée d'Orsay, Paris) is close in both subject and arrangement to Bates's *Pandora*. It is, however, a much more vapid treatment, demonstrating succinctly the frequent superiority at this time of British sculpture over French (see Beattie 1983, p.167, pl.164).

The ivory box is carved with figures relating to the creation of Pandora, the gods imbuing her with different attributes, as the eighth century BC poet Hesiod related in his poem 'Works and Days'. This sequential approach to the events of the story derives from Italian Renaissance art. Pandora was escorted to earth by Zeus's messenger Hermes, who is represented here in bronze on each corner of the box. He holds a golden caduceus, a wand entwined with serpents, with which he could cast a spell of sleep, and his winged helmet and sandals are also gilded. On the lid of the box Pandora is carved in the round, reclining asleep in Hermes's arms, held between creation and life, in a chariot that conducts her to earth. The pose is again repeated from *The Story of Cupid and Psyche*, in which Psyche's pose is virtually identical with that in Burne-Jones's *Cupid Finding Psyche*, although Bates portrays her naked. It was a figure arrangement Bates used repeatedly, in his reliefs *Dido and Aeneas: Whither Does he Fly?* 1885, *Homer* 1886, *Endymion and Selene* 1892 and elsewhere.

Bates's detailed summary of Pandora's origin in

combination with the dramatic conclusion of her story, suggests that he wanted to draw parallels between her creation – divinely modelled from clay – and the role of the sculptor, and his construction of a life-like form. The Pandora story has strong similarities with that of Pygmalion in Ovid's *Metamorphoses*, which was also treated by several painters and sculptors in this period, notably Burne-Jones (see no.38). The desire by a male to create life alone, in a rejection of woman and nature, is present in both myths, and this, as Bates realised, has its counterpart in the role of the artist. Pandora, the original temptress, was used in nineteenth-century art and literature as a recurrent vehicle for contemporary ambivalent feelings about women. The Pre-Raphaelite sculptor Thomas Woolner even wrote an epic poem in twelve volumes about Pandora. Her powers of attraction demonstrated male helplessness against the compulsion of desire, and this dimension of the myth served as a paradigm for Victorian male feelings of fear and attraction towards women. Pandora, like Eve, additionally represented to them the reckless susceptibility to temptation of the female character (see Warner 1985, chap.10).

RU

Edward Burne-Jones 1833–1898

113 **The Rock of Doom** 1885–6

Oil on canvas 155 × 130 (61 × 51⅛)

Prov: Arthur Balfour; Huntingdon Hartford; Agnew's and Marlborough Fine Art; Staatsgalerie, Stuttgart

Exh: New Gallery 1888 (53); New Gallery 1898 (118); Indianapolis 1964 (18); Baden-Baden 1973 (172); Hayward Gallery 1975 (169)

Lit: *Times*, 9 May 1888; Bell 1892, p.64; de Lisle 1904, pp.132–3, 185; Lucie-Smith 1972, p.101; Löcher 1973, no.8, pl.12; Harrison and Waters 1973, p.120; Stuttgart 1982, pp.38–46; Rome 1986, pp.175–9; Benedetti 1992, pp.341–66

Staatsgalerie Stuttgart

EXHIBITED IN LONDON ONLY

This is the sixth of eight canvases in the cycle of paintings known as the Perseus Series that Arthur Balfour commissioned from Burne-Jones in 1875 to decorate the music-room of his London house, 4 Carlton Gardens. The scheme as first devised (see nos.93–5) was to consist of six main panels and four gesso reliefs, all to be set within a surround to be decorated with acanthus leaves by William Morris. The room was to have no windows and to be lit entirely by candles. The present subject, as originally conceived, was to be combined with the next – *The Doom Fulfilled* – in one wide composition, but these were later made into two separate panels so as to avoid the confusion of having two figures of Andromeda side by side. Full-scale cartoons in gouache (Southampton Art Gallery) were made in the years up to 1885, when Burne-Jones embarked on the oil versions, first painting the final episodes in the story – Perseus's arrival at the Rock of Doom (the present subject), his battle with the sea monster (*The Doom Fulfilled*), and the scene where Perseus shows Andromeda the Medusa's head by reflecting its image in the surface of a well (*The Baleful Head*). These three were shown together at the first exhibition of the New Gallery in 1888. The cycle was never completed as intended, but as it is now seen in the Staatsgalerie, Stuttgart, it remains one of the most enduring and powerful of all nineteenth-century artistic schemes and a testament to the vast inventiveness and originality of Burne-Jones.

Morris had treated the Perseus legend as 'The Doom of King Acrisius' in *The Earthly Paradise*, and Burne-Jones chose to follow the story as given there. Perseus is commanded to fetch the Medusa's head, the magic power of which causes all who see it to be turned to stone. Armed with magic weapons by the goddess Athena, and with winged sandals, a pouch into which to put the head, and the means of becoming invisible, by the sea-nymphs, he is able to find and kill the Medusa, and to cut off its head with impunity. On his way back Perseus comes across Andromeda, daughter of Cepheus, King of Joppa in Ethiopia, chained to a rock as sacrifice to appease the gods, who have been displeased by insulting remarks made by Andromeda's mother, Queen Cassiopeia. Perseus's finding of Andromeda is described by Morris:

> Now hovering there, he seemed to hear a sound
> Unlike the sea-bird's cry, and, looking round,
> He saw a figure standing motionless
> Beneath the cliff, midway 'twixt ness and ness,
> And as the wind lulled, heard that cry again,
> That sounded like the wail of one in pain;
> Wondering thereat, and seeking marvels new
> He lighted down, and toward the place he drew,
> And made invisible by Pallas' aid,
> He came within the scarped cliff's purple shade,
> And found a woman standing lonely there,
> Naked, except for tresses of her hair
> That o'er her white limbs by the breeze were
> wound,
> And brazen chains her weary arms that bound
> Unto the sea-beat overhanging rock,
> As though her golden crownéd head to mock.

113

As Perseus sets sight on Andromeda he falls in love with her, and determines to save her. He removes the chains that bind her, and when the monster sent by Poseidon arrives to devour her, Perseus engages the fearsome creature in a battle to the death. As victor, he receives Andromeda as his bride.

In the later 1870s, when the Perseus Series was devised, Burne-Jones found himself in an unstable and volatile condition of mind, suffering a sense of isolation and moods of spiritual desolation. He was increasingly out of touch with his old friends Rossetti and Ruskin, and even found that a distance had grown up between himself and Morris. His love affair with Maria Zambaco had ended unhappily in 1871, but was not forgotten. Two Italian journeys, in 1871 and 1873, had radically altered his style of painting, causing him to lose interest in the aesthetic classicism that he had explored in the 1860s in favour of a more dramatic and psychologically charged type of art dependent on Michelangelo and Mantegna.

Burne-Jones had previously treated the story of St George, in a series of paintings made for the artist Birket Foster in the 1860s (now dispersed). Each of these two heroes – one from Greek mythology, the other a Christian warrior and patron saint of England – had a strong hold on the contemporary imagination. Brave and morally upstanding figures, who risked their lives to defend others (but who looked for sexual rewards for their heroic interventions), they were seen as representing an age of chivalry of which a certain type of Victorian believed himself to be the inheritor. Quite different to the escapism and other-worldliness of *The Golden Stairs* (no.68), the symbolism of *The Rock of Doom*, which is treated with utter simplicity and clarity, is intended to inflame and excite.

CSN

Edward Burne-Jones 1833–1898

114 The Dream of Sir Lancelot at the Chapel of the Holy Grail 1896

Oil on canvas 138.5 × 169.8 (54½ × 66⅞)
Inscribed 'EBJ 1896', b.l.

Prov: Graham Robertson
Exh: New Gallery 1896 (165); New Gallery 1898 (122); Paris Exhibition (Fine Arts Section) 1900 (34); Sheffield 1971 (11); Hayward Gallery 1975 (192); Tokyo 1987 (29)
Lit: Bell 1898, p.69; de Lisle 1904, p.148; G.B.-J. 1904, II, pp.258, 277, 282–3

Southampton City Art Gallery

EXHIBITED IN LONDON ONLY

Burne-Jones shows the moment in Lancelot's quest for the Holy Grail when he reaches the Chapel where it is held. In his sleep he is visited by the Angel that guards the Grail, who tells him that he will never be able to find it. This is because of his adultery with Queen Guinevere, and its destructive consequences.

In the 1890s, perhaps consciously reviewing his life and achievements, Burne-Jones returned to his early sources and ideas. Arthurian legend was foremost among these, and it took its place once again as the central inspiration for his work, as it had been in his youth in the 1850s. Partly nostalgic and partly a rediscovery of a fertile creative stimulus, it was also encouraged by Burne-Jones's warm friendship with Dr Sebastian Evans (1830–1909). They discussed such material together at length, and Burne-Jones illustrated Evans's translation of *Perceval le Gallois* which appeared in 1898 as *The High History of the Holy Graal.*

The major Arthurian works Burne-Jones worked on in the 1890s were the enormous *Sleep of King Arthur in Avalon* 1881–98 (Museo de Arte, Ponce, Puerto Rico) and the set of six tapestries illustrating the quest for the Holy Grail (1891–4) made by Morris and Co for Stanmore Hall near Uxbridge. It was from one of these that Burne-Jones derived *The Dream of Sir Lancelot* exhibited here, although he has painted the subject in a radically different style, one that in common with other works of the 1890s was boldly experimental, as John Christian has noted (Hayward Gallery 1975, p.64).

If in the 1890s Burne-Jones was reviewing his artistic life, he seems to have been considering his personal life too. His adulterous love affair with the beautiful Greek sculptress Maria Zambaco in the late 1860s and early 1870s, and his eventual loss of her, seemed to be paralleled in the story of Lancelot's inability to attain the Grail, which thus came to hold very personal connotations. Burne-Jones allegorised

114

his affair in many of his works of the period in which it took place, such as *Love among the Ruins* (see no.41), and *The Dream of Sir Lancelot* apparently presents a retrospective view of the significance of the affair and its destructive effects on his life and career. In less personal terms, Lancelot represents the hard moral reality of mankind; moral lapses or imperfections caused by compulsions of character or nature mean that few will achieve spiritual purity.

In a further act of retrospection and self-reference, Burne-Jones took the figure of Lancelot from Rossetti's Oxford Union mural of the same subject, for which Burne-Jones had himself been the model. Lady Burne-Jones concluded 'indeed, I think the whole composition was commemorative' (G.B.-J. 1904, II, p.258).

RU

GEORGE FRAMPTON 1860–1928

115 **Mysteriarch** 1892

Polychrome plaster 91.4 × 63 (36 × 24¾)
Inscribed 'Geo. Frampton, 1892' on left and 'MYSTERIARCH' bottom centre

Prov: Bt from the artist 1902 by the Walker Art Gallery

Exh: RA 1893 (1787); Libre Esthétique, Brussels 1894; International Exhibition, Paris 1900; Autumn Exhibition, Liverpool 1902; FAS 1968 (44, repr.); RA Bicentenary 1968 (248); Stoke on Trent 1992 (13, repr.)

Lit: Beattie 1983, pp.88–9, 158, repr. pl.152; Stevens 1989, p.76, repr. pl.5

Board of Trustees of the National Museums and Galleries on Merseyside (Walker Art Gallery, Liverpool)

EXHIBITED IN LONDON AND MUNICH ONLY

This is one of a revealing series of head-and-shoulder sculptures of women that Frampton made between 1889 and 1900 (see pp.89–91). Here woman is presented as both an object of mystery in herself, and presiding as a priestess over life's enigma. Frampton has made her specific identity, however, deliberately obscure. The flaming or swirling disc behind her head is a pagan version of a halo, and may therefore allude to sun worship. If so, it might identify her with the fertility goddess Isis, who in Egyptian iconography sports a solar disc on her crown. The Mysteriarch could also be intended to be one of the priestesses who presided over the 'Mysteries' of the secret cults of ancient Greece, and the unfocused eyes might well support this, for these women were known to go into a trance-like state while discharging their rites. Other symbols suggest further links. The clasp on the Mysteriarch's bodice bears a bat, a symbol of the night, and a terrifying Medusa-like head with entwined snakes. This device may be intended to represent Zeus's Aegis, but this is deliberately left unresolved. The winged headdress is usually associated with Hermes, messenger of the gods, but in this context it may merely relate to the free flight of the imagination. Frampton, therefore, presents a range of symbolic references which are deliberately inexplicit, but which contribute to the mystifying and compelling presence of the bust.

The mystic, all-seeing, inward-looking gaze and androgynous features find their counterpart in Khnopff's pictures of women (nos.86, 107), and indeed, the Belgian Symbolist took particular interest in Frampton's *Mysteriarch*. After he saw it at the Royal Academy in 1893, it seems to have inspired his own sculpture *Sibyl* (fig.51 on p.89). This repeated the ambiguous title, colouring, format and background disc. The principal differences in Khnopff's version are the lowered eyes and hands framing the face.

Frampton sent his *Mysteriarch* to the inaugural exhibition of the Libre Esthétique, to which he had been invited to contribute. Having evolved from Les XX, this was a forum for European Symbolist art, and in this first exhibition Frampton's sculpture was seen alongside work by Puvis, Toorop, Redon, Gauguin, Maurice Denis, Carrière, Ensor and Beardsley. Reviewing the exhibition, the French critic Roger Marx singled out Frampton, writing: 'Beyond our frontiers the movement against materialism accelerates ... The fight for spiritual expression was taken up by Watts ... and is now continued by another artist from across the Channel, Mr George Frampton, a sculptor-decorator obsessed with dream and mysticism' (Marx 1894, pp.475–8, quoted Beattie 1983, p.158).

Frampton's polychrome finish illustrated his commitment to the emotive potential of coloured sculpture. Shortly after completing his *Mysteriarch* he published an article in which he detailed the technique and effect of colouring plaster ('On Colouring Sculpture', *Studio*, vol.3, 1894, pp.78–80).

RU

116

George Frampton 1860–1928

116 My Thoughts Are my Children
1894, cast *c*.1900

Bronze relief, partly gilded 255.5 × 62 (100½ × 24½) in oak frame
Inscribed 'George Frampton 1894' b.l. and 'MY THOUGHTS ARE | MY CHILDREN' below

Prov: By descent to Meredith Frampton (1894–1984), the artist's son, by whom presented to the Walker Art Gallery 1984
Exh: Paris 1900; Rome 1911 (1121)
Lit: Phillips 1894, p.69; Beattie 1983 pp.158, 160; Stevens 1989, pp.76–7, repr. pl.6

Board of Trustees of the National Museums and Galleries on Merseyside (Walker Art Gallery, Liverpool)

Frampton exhibited the original polychrome plaster of *My Thoughts Are my Children* at the RA in 1894 (repr. Beattie 1983, pl.153). It is now untraced, but around 1900 Frampton had this bronze cast from it, and the plaster may have been destroyed in the process. The bronze apparently took pride of place in Frampton's studio, and a photograph in the *Tatler* (16 April, 1902) shows it surrounded by reproductions of his favourite pictures. These include Burne-Jones's *Mirror of Venus*, Botticelli's *Portrait of a Lady* and *Primavera*, Ambrogio de Predis's *Portrait of a Lady*, and van Eyck's *Portrait of Margaretha Van Eyck* (see Stevens 1989, p.77). When shown in Paris in 1900 it was awarded the Grand Medal of Honour.

Stevens notes that the format, composition and large size are reminiscent of Burne-Jones's *King Cophetua and the Beggar Maid* (no.41) which Frampton had seen in Paris at the Exposition Universelle in 1889 and greatly admired. Glaves-Smith has noted the similarities of the sculpture's composition to contemporary photographs – genuine or otherwise – of spirit manifestations during seances (see Glaves-Smith 1992, pp.17–18).

When *My Thoughts Are my Children* was first shown it provoked a vehement attack from the critic Claude Phillips, who in addition to disliking its composition and modelling, objected particularly to its Symbolist content:

> The strange upright bas relief … is a more definite expression of that pseudo-mysticism which coloured the 'Mysteriarch' which he sent to the Academy last year. Its attempt to give back what, if anything, is a dream-vision – one, however, which I shall not attempt to unravel – in all too human shapes of a studied naturalism, recalls the fantastic, half-realistic, half-idealistic French art of to-day, which has for

the moment taken the place of realism pure and simple.

(*Magazine of Art*, 1894, p.69)

There are in fact indications of its subject-matter both in the relief and in its title. The principal full-length female figure, staring out of the composition, holds a lily, the traditional emblem of chastity, innocence and purity. Its iconographic use is most common in pictures of the Annunciation, but here the woman is not apparently intended to be the Virgin Mary. Her hair is plaited so that it resembles ears of corn, a pagan symbol of fertility which crowned Greek and Roman representations of Isis. James Frazer's *Golden Bough*, which had appeared in successive parts from 1890, spent considerable space examining different corn fertility myths and rites, and it is possible Frampton, like so many of his contemporaries, absorbed the content and imagery of these researches. The angle of the woman's feet suggests that she is rising, moving upwards towards the muscular-faced, but androgynous, figure whose arms encircle two younger women, one of whom plants a kiss on the head of the baby she holds. Behind this group, at the top of the composition, burst the rays of the sun. The whole design is apparently devoted to fertility, and the aspiration from chastity to motherhood. It seems likely that in employing the lily, a central icon of Marian imagery, and references to ancient pagan belief, Frampton intended to allude to common ground between the two. The idea that Christian belief had its roots in pagan myth was one of the central elements that underlay Frazer's *Golden Bough*.

The 'strange, pseudo-mystical title and subject' of *My Thoughts are my Children* 'puzzled many' when it was shown at the Royal Academy in 1894 according to Marion Spielmann (1901, p.90). There appears to be some connection between Frampton's title and the birth of his son (George) Meredith on 17 March 1894. He must have worked on the relief while his wife Christabel was in the last months of pregnancy, and the title implies some consideration by Frampton of contrasts between the relationship of the artist to his works and ideas, and his creation of a new life, and role as father. Frampton named his son after the poet George Meredith, who had treated the Persephone fertility myth in his poem 'The Day of the Daughter of Hades' (see p.21). This contains material which is closely parallel to *My Thoughts Are my Children*, indicating that it provided Frampton with an additional source:

> ... lo, the Great Mother, She! ...
> The embrace of the Twain, of whom
> To men are their day, their night,
> Mellow fruits and the shearing tomb:
> Our Lady of the Sheaves
> And the Lily of Hades, the Sweet
> Of Enna: he saw through leaves
> The Mother and Daughter meet.

Frampton appears to have copied the principal figure from Jan Toroop's *O Thou, My Spirit's Mate* 1891 (Rijksmuseum, Kröller-Müller, Otterlo), which he may have seen at the first Libre Esthétique exhibition in Brussels in 1892.

RU

ALFRED GILBERT 1854–1934

117 **Icarus** 1884

Bronze 106.7 (42) high
Inscribed on rock below right heel 'ALFRED GILBERT ROME 1884'

Prov: Commissioned by Frederic Leighton; his sale, Christie's, 8 July 1896 (104) bt Robert Dunthorne; sold to Somerset Beaumont; bt back by Dunthorne; sold to William Vivian 1899; Lt Col Valentine Vivian; bt back by Dunthorne; Sir William Goscombe John, by whom presented to the National Museum of Wales 1938

Exh: RA 1884 (1855); Manchester 1887 (555); Paris 1889 (311); White City 1908 (1434); Manchester 1978 (94); RA 1986 (15, repr.; repr. in col. p.54)

Lit: Michel 1889, p.404, repr. p.395; Spielmann 1901, p.76, repr. p.78; Dorment 1985, pp.45–50, pl.20–2, col. pl.1; see RA 1986, no.15 for full bibliography

National Museum & Gallery, Cardiff

This is the second in a series of bronzes of male nudes in which Gilbert stated he was 'writing my own history by symbol' (Hatton 1903, p.10). The first of these was *Perseus Arming* 1882 (private collection), in which Gilbert compared himself to the hero from Greek myth, preparing himself to do battle before his major triumph. This was a great success when it was exhibited at the Grosvenor Gallery, and was particularly admired by Leighton. Leighton did much to raise the quality and importance of sculpture in Britain, not just by the often-cited example of his own essays in the discipline – particularly *An Athlete Struggling with a Python* 1877 and *The Sluggard* 1885 (both Tate Gallery) – but through practical measures such as the improvement of the teaching of sculpture at the Royal Academy, and his increase of the numbers of sculptors given recognition by the institution. He sought to give Gilbert encouragement by

117

commissioning from him a bronze of a subject to be entirely decided by Gilbert himself. Since 1878 Gilbert had been based in Italy, and Leighton called unannounced on him there to deliver this commission. It was an important moment for Gilbert's career, which he fully realised; Leighton was, after all, President of the Royal Academy, and his endorsement of the young sculptor would undoubtedly boost his prospects. Gilbert therefore took great care over the commission, striving to produce something worthy of Leighton's faith in him.

Contemplating the subject for this work, Gilbert recalled that 'It flashed across me that I was very ambitious: why not "Icarus" with his desire for flight?' (McAllister 1929, p.62). This was to be a continuation of his autobiography in sculpture, and Gilbert's portrayal of himself as Icarus indicates that he was already aware of the dangerously reckless streak in his character, which eventually was to bring about his disgrace and ruin. His choice of subject, as Dorment has noted (1985, pp.46–9), was undoubtedly a conscious tribute to Leighton's painting *Daedalus and Icarus* c.1869 (Faringdon Collection, Buscot Park). Gilbert may also have wished, unconsciously, to invite comparison between their relative positions in the Victorian art world, and sought to portray his admiration for Leighton. Daedalus was the greatest artist of ancient Greece, and Gilbert perhaps mentally cast Leighton as this wise father-figure, and himself as Icarus, the rash son.

Gilbert finished the figure in 1884, casting it himself in Naples using the lost wax method. Both the pose and exquisite casting show that Gilbert had studied and sought to match Donatello's fifteenth-century bronze masterpiece *David* (Bargello, Florence). So too does the integration of the base into the composition, and the accentuation of the figure's sensuality by contrasting nude flesh with elaborate headgear and wings. The base features a bird being devoured by a snake, signifying the futility of Icarus's ambition for flight, and that temptation, as symbolised by the snake, will be his undoing.

The bandeau and downcast, sombre features of Icarus recall Gilbert's slightly earlier *Study of a Head* 1883 (fig.48 on p.85). This facial expression and combination of nudity with headgear are also found in the contemporary French sculptural source of Mercié's *David with the Head of Goliath* 1878 (Musée d'Orsay, Paris), which Gilbert had seen at the 1878 Exposition Universelle in Paris. The overall mood of *Icarus* – sombre anticipation and introspection, the inevitability of doom dictated by character – is also reminiscent of a number of paintings from the preceding years by Watts, depicting characters from Classical myth whom he considered relevant to contemporary life. Gilbert greatly admired Watts, and discovered a mutual sympathy with him when in 1888 he was commissioned to make a bust of the older artist.

Icarus was one of the group of works that also included *Perseus Arming, Study of a Head, Capri Fisherman* and *An Offering to Hymen* which Gilbert exhibited at the 1889 Univeral Exhibition in Paris, where he won a Medal of Honour. Both Leighton and the sculptor Homo Thornycroft, a member of the selection panel, were instrumental in persuading Gilbert to exhibit there (see Dorment 1985, p.99).

RU

118

Alfred Gilbert 1854–1934

118 **The Virgin** 1899

Painted bronze 49.5 (19½) high on a wooden base 7.6 (3) high, bronze pedestal 127 (49½) high and wooden floor base 8.9 (3½) high

Prov: Bt from the artist by Robert Dunthorne; bt William Vivian; Valentine Vivian, by whom sold 1930s; London art market 1936 when bt by Sir David Young Cameron, by whom presented to present owner

Exh: FAS 1968 (75G); Manchester 1979 (108, repr.); Whitechapel 1981 (20); RA 1986 (75, repr.; repr. in col. pp.66–7 and back cover); Amsterdam 1996 (36, repr. in col.)

Lit: Beattie 1983, p.165, pl.158; Dorment 1985, pp.198–9, 228, col. pl.v; see RA 1986, no.75 for full bibliography

A Scottish Parish Church

EXHIBITED IN LONDON AND MUNICH ONLY

This was one of the dozen figures of saints that Gilbert made to surround his memorial to the Duke of Clarence in the Albert Memorial Chapel, Windsor Castle. Prince Albert Victor, Duke of Clarence, eldest son of the Prince and Princess of Wales, died on 14 January 1892. Soon after, Gilbert was asked by them to design his tomb. It was Gilbert's most prestigious commission, and he went to great lengths to create something that was startlingly original, eventually producing a complex ensemble that is a remarkable tour de force. The life-size, recumbent figure of the Duke is portrayed in military uniform, and is sumptuously executed in an adventurous combination of white marble, bronze, brass and aluminium. An angel crouches weeping at his feet, while another holds over his head a crown constructed in the form of a miniature city, which appears to have been in part based on Pieter Breughel the Elder's *Tower of Babel* (Kunsthistorisches Museum, Vienna). Surrounding the Duke's casket and effigy is an intricate grille of painted bronze uprights, linked by twelve pairs of graceful bronze angels. Above them stand the polychrome figures of the saints.

Gilbert took infinite pains over the commission, adapting the design of the grille a number of times. By the time of his bankruptcy in 1901 he had largely finished the tomb, but still had five of the saints to complete. Edward VII's patience had already been taxed, but when in 1903 he discovered Gilbert had sold versions of four of the existing figures (one of which was no.118) he severed all contact with the sculptor. The King considered the sale of these items not just a breach of protocol and trust, but sacrilegious. An equally upset Queen Alexandra nonetheless tried to persuade Gilbert to complete the remaining figures, but it was not until 1928 that the tomb was finished. The definitive account of this remarkable commission is given by Richard Dorment (1985, chap.5).

Gilbert chose the subject of *The Virgin* for one of the Clarence Tomb figures because the chapel in which it stands had once been a Lady Chapel, dedicated to the Madonna. He explained that this statuette was also

> the outcome of reflection upon the nature and character of the divine personage. I have represented her as standing in the midst of a wild rose bush. Circling her feet, it forms a natural Crown of Thorns, which, sprouting, send their shoots upwards around the figure, in their turn giving off roses to within reach of her clasped hands, when a white lily rises to her touch. Thence the fronds ascend and twine around her head and form a natural crown of full-blown roses. The Virgin is simply draped, with a head-covering overshadowing her half-sad expression of features; and she is meant to be in an attitude of resignation rather than prayer.
>
> (Hatton 1903, pp.30–1)

The Madonna's downturned eyes evoke a mood of sad introspection, as do those of the other Clarence figures, recalling facial expressions used by Gilbert many times previously in his work, starting with early pieces such as *Study of a Head* 1883 (fig.48 on p.85) and *Icarus* 1884 (no.117). Dorment has suggested that the *Virgin* was intended to be a personification of Prince Albert Victor's grieving mother, Princess Alexandra (1985, p.170).

As with other figures for the tomb, for the *Virgin* Gilbert dispensed with traditional representations and attributes to create an iconography that was wholly original to himself. Made entirely of bronze, the figure is painted with soft colours. The red roses symbolise Christ's blood, while their thorns refer to his crown. The enmeshment of the Madonna in the rose bush recalls Burne-Jones's *Briar Rose* pictures, which Gilbert had seen in progress on a visit to his studio many years before, and much admired (McAllister 1929, p.147). Only two casts were made of *The Virgin*, both in 1899, and while the figures are identical there are distinct differences in the rose bushes and haloes. Dorment has noted that the halo of the version exhibited here may be made from a curtain ring (1986, no.75).

Certain similarities between *The Virgin* and Mackintosh's *Part Seen, Imagined Part* (no.100) suggest that Gilbert may have seen the murals at the Buchanan Street Tea Rooms in Glasgow.

RU

Frederic, Lord Leighton 1830–1896

119 **Solitude** *c.*1889–90

Oil on canvas 167.7 × 78.7 (66 × 31)

Prov: F.W. Armytage; his sale, Christie's 22 May 1897 (121); …; Sotheby's 20 Jan. 1965 (90), bt Old Hall Gallery, Iden, Rye; given by Dr W.M. Fitzhugh to the Maryhill Museum of Fine Arts, Goldendale, Washington

Exh: RA 1890 (166); Manchester 1978 (56); Tokyo 1989 (22)

Lit: Rhys 1898, pp.37, 90, 92; Corkran 1904, pp.101, 211; Barrington 1906, II, pp.260–1, 309–10, 390; Ormond 1975, no.348, pp.124–5, 170, 177; Manchester 1978, p.119

Maryhill Museum of Art, Washington, USA

Solitude shows a woman draped in white, her head wrapped, eyes downcast, deep in thought. She appears precariously vulnerable, almost hovering in space as she sits upon a rocky outcrop over a still pool of water. The cavern-like setting reinforces the mood established by the pensive figure who personifies solitude.

Mrs Barrington quotes a letter in which the artist described the area around the Linn of Dee in north-east Scotland: 'It is the veriest note of solitude! a wonderful spot, full of poetic inspiration'. He travelled there both before and after painting the picture. Several landscape studies in oil of rocks near the Findhorn river appeared in his studio sale where they were identified as serving as the background of *Solitude* (see Rhys 1898, App., and Ormond 1975, p.177, no.483; see RA 1996, nos.102–4). He rhapsodised about the waters of the Findhorn saying that he had 'nothing short of a craze for your dark brown Scotch (and Irish) rivers, as dark as treacle, as clear as cairngorm. This particular stream contrives to rush part of the way through fantastic rocks of pink granite' (Barrington 1906, p.262). However, it should be noted that the Linn of Dee is in Braemar, some forty miles away from the portion of the lengthy Findhorn river with which Leighton was familiar near Forres, with the whole Cairngorm mountain range dividing the two sites. The landscape background can be seen as a conflation of the two sites. Leighton's discovery of the natural gloom of Scotland followed upon that of Millais who painted a series of moody landscapes in the Perth area from 1870 onward, culminating in *Dew-drenched Furze* of 1890 (no.57).

Solitude appeared as one of three major contributions by Leighton to the Royal Academy of 1890, along with *The Bath of Psyche* (Tate Gallery) and *The Tragic Poetess* (private collection, Japan), all presumably worked on over a few years. In the later 1880s, after his great *Captive Andromache* (Manchester City

Art Galleries) was completed, Leighton produced a series of monumental studies of women, without narrative context, some alluding to the Antique as in *The Sibyl* (art market 1987) and *The Tragic Poetess*, but each one essentially presenting the personification of an idea. The artist's favoured model, Dorothy Dene, an aspiring actress, brought a theatrical dimension to these powerful studies. She may well have posed for *Solitude*, but that is not as important as the nature of the pose itself, with the strongly sculptural figure seeming to have been hewn out of marble, contorting herself into an immediately readable attitude of gloomy contemplation. Studies for the painting indicate that the artist conceived the figure first (see chalk drawing, Rhys 1898, repr. opp. p.90) allowing the natural language of the human body to convey the idea before inventing the setting of a dark, rocky landscape, bereft of vegetation.

The theme of the isolated figure in a landscape whose character fuels the mood of the work is best known in the icy mountainous scenes of Caspar David Friedrich or in a work like *Disappointed Love* 1821 (Victoria and Albert Museum, London) by Francis Danby in England. Leighton's painting updated this tradition dramatically, belonging as it does fully to the Symbolist era. The notion of solitude is presented as an almost cosmic comment on human life and futility, a theme he returned to in a related work, *The Spirit of the Summit* (no.121).

Solitude, with its contorted figure conveying a disturbing message, emerged from the same kind of thinking that inspired Watts's *Hope* (no.76), exhibited in 1886; in its second version *Hope* was selected by Watts and Leighton (see fig.35 on p.65) as an entry for the Exposition Universelle of 1889 in Paris, at just the time Leighton was working on *Solitude*. Leighton certainly admired *Hope*, having received from Watts the gift of the oil study (Walker Art Gallery, Liverpool), which he positioned prominently in a display on the first floor of his house adjacent to his studio. There is also a parallel with Watts's *'The All-Pervading'* (no.125), where the draped contemplative figure gazing into the 'globe of the systems' can be compared with that of *Solitude* who gazes into the reflections in the dark waters below her. The mutual respect that existed between Watts and Leighton led to a cross-fertilisation of ideas that is also borne out by Watts's reciprocal admiration for *Solitude*, a print of which Leighton presented to him soon after the painting appeared at the Royal Academy (letter in Kensington and Chelsea Library). He may well have recognised in it echoes of *Hope* and *'The All-Pervading'*, and perhaps even his own projected *Genius of Northern Poetry* (see no.78) with its symbolic figure set in a bleak, unfriendly, distinctly northern landscape.

119

Solitude, even though based on an actual place, possesses a darkness of mood and a brooding spirit new to Leighton's art in the last years of the 1880s and early 1890s. These qualities are found in the work of a wide range of artists, reflecting the pervasive spirit of Symbolism at that moment.

BB

120

FREDERIC, LORD LEIGHTON 1830–1896

120 'And the Sea Gave Up the Dead which Were in it' *c.*1891–2

Oil on canvas 228.5 (90) diameter

Prov: Commissioned by Sir Henry Tate, by whom presented to the Tate Gallery 1894

Exh: RA 1892 (115); Autumn Exhibition, Liverpool 1892 (1099); RA Winter 1897 (108); RA 1996 (116)

Lit: *Art Journal*, 1892, p.188; *Magazine of Art*, 1892, pp.220–1; Barrington 1906, II, p.193; Staley 1906, pp.146–8; Ormond 1975, pp.107, 123–4, 170, no.353, pl.154; Newall 1990, p.129

Tate Gallery. Presented by Sir Henry Tate 1894

EXHIBITED IN LONDON ONLY

Leighton's stupendous tondo showing the resurrection of the dead as described in the Book of Revelation (20:13) is one of the most powerful and profound works of the artist's late career, and reflects his long and intense meditations on the state of death. Edgcumbe Staley, in his description of the painting, looked for the way in which Leighton had differentiated between the figures in their return to life, and his symbolical use of colour:

> The colour-scheme is very remarkable, defining separate regions of life and illumination. The man is alive, his pulses are beating again, his flesh is reddening. His wife wears the greenish ghastly hue of death: his boy is breathing, but still pale and only half alive. The colours of the drapery extend the truth and sincerity of this gradual glow of life. The green sea, leaping up – jealous of losing its prey – and the grey rocks around, with newly opened graves, whence the dead are rising, are painted with a masterly brush.

The present composition was conceived as one of eight mosaic roundels on the theme of the Apocalypse to decorate the spandrels of the dome of St Paul's Cathedral. The scheme had been devised by Alfred Stevens and had been taken up by Edward John Poynter and Hugh Stannus in the early 1880s; Leighton's full-scale (22 feet in diameter) oil cartoon of the subject (now untraced) was made in *c.*1882–4. In the event a vociferous campaign against the scheme led to its being abandoned in 1885. Leighton kept back his sketch and, when Henry Tate announced his intention of founding a national collection of British art, he offered to work up the composition on the present reduced scale, stating in a letter to Tate: 'Now this is the work which I should like to be remembered by in our Natl Gallery' (quoted in RA 1996, p.231).

By the time *'And the Sea Gave Up the Dead which Were in It'* was painted Leighton had abandoned the Hellenism of his middle period in favour of a style that was darker and more ominous (although always highly crafted). The new solemnity of Leighton's art from the late 1880s onwards owed much to his study of the painting of Michelangelo, for whom he felt 'a profound reverence [and] who satisfies those modern sides of our nature that the Greeks leave untouched' (quoted in RA 1996, p.194).

S.P. Cockerell thought the subject 'worthy to rank with the finest work in the Sixtine Chapel' (quoted in Staley 1906, p.147), and indeed the influence of Michelangelo is very evident. No doubt his huge *Last Judgement* was in Leighton's mind; and Stephen Jones has pointed out the relevance of the National Gallery's *Entombment*, which Leighton much admired. Its central group of linked vertical figures is one possible source for the main group in this picture. That motif also seems to suggest an acquaintance with Blake's scene of the *Resurrection*, an alternative design for Robert Blair's poem 'The Grave' (fig.10 on p.25), which had been in the collection of the British Museum since 1856. The Blake derivation is entirely appropriate, confirming the sense that this is a work at the heart of British Symbolism, embodying all too vividly a preoccupation with death – in Leighton's own case imminent; he was to live only another four years – and Idealist aspirations to higher things.

Although Leighton seems not to have been a man of conventional religious faith he was clearly absorbed by the idea of the return from death to life, and conversely the transition from life to the eternity of death, themes which occur in a series of metaphysical paintings of biblical and mythological subjects from the mid-1860s onwards. *Ariadne Abandoned by Theseus: Ariadne Watches for his Return: Artemis Releases her by Death* (Salar Jung Museum, Hyderabad) and *Hercules Wrestling with Death for the Body of Alcestis* (Wadsworth Atheneum, Hartford, Connecticut) represent two essays on the theme of death, while a later mythological subject, *The Return of Persephone* (Leeds City Art Gallery), shows the release of Persephone from her annual period of imprisonment in Hades as a supernatural rebirth, her body symbolically raised as if by the osmotic power of spring.

The long-recognised parallels between the yearly return of Persephone to earth from the Underworld and the spiritual renewal of Christian resurrection, were dwelt on by Meredith and Frazer among other writers, and Leighton signals his own awareness of the connection very clearly in his use of the motif of linked, rising upright figures in both subjects. With its unambiguous movement upwards from darkness to light *The Return of Persephone* conveys a clear and positive meaning; the much darker tonality and less certain ascent of the half-living, half-dead figures in *And the Sea Gave up the Dead* make for a disturbingly ambiguous expression of both the morbid and the optimistic aspects of the Symbolist world view. Not surprisingly, the picture baffled some of Leighton's most enthusiastic critics. The Chapter of St Paul's had objected to the original design as 'unsuitable for a Christian church', and in its achieved form it was no easier to digest. The *Magazine of Art* thought his new version possessed 'a cold – almost oppressive – dignity'. Leighton's application of his famous principles of Classical Idealism to the depiction of the dead was itself worrying; the way the subject hovers between hope and annihilation, the subtle balance of promised life and actual death, were both unexpected and hard to understand. Leighton was rarely so shocking.

CSN and AW

Frederic, Lord Leighton 1830–1896

121 **The Spirit of the Summit** 1894

Oil on canvas 197 × 99.7 (77½ × 39½)

Prov: Robert English; Moss Davis, by whom presented to the Auckland Art Gallery 1926

Exh: RA 1894 (190)

Lit: Rhys 1900, pp.51, 60, 113; Barrington 1906, I, p.10; Corkran 1904, p.101; Staley 1906, pp.152, 153; Newall 1990, p.133

Auckland Art Gallery Collection. Presented by Mrs Moss Davis 1926

This was one of five pictures that Leighton submitted to the Academy in 1894; the others included one other Symbolist work, *Fatidica* (Lady Lever Art Gallery, Port Sunlight), and three fancy subjects. The group illustrates well the way in which Leighton used the language of Symbolism for a certain category of works, while not consistently subscribing to Symbolist values and concepts. Staley comments on the 'superlative finish' of the group and on 'a diminishing of the strictness and distinction of outline' (p.152). He relates that Leighton traced the genesis of the picture to 'one night when he sat gazing at the drop-scene of a theatre on which were many spots' (p.153). His description of *The Spirit of the Summit* is as

121

follows: 'The superb figure of a fair-haired girl, with blonde carnations and features and head eclectic in their beauty, sits like a queen upon a snowy peak gazing with upturned face to the starlit sky. She is in thick, pure white draperies which reflect the silvery illumination of the night.' He concludes: 'She is, in short, the genius of Leighton personified' (pp.152–3).

From an early date this picture was seen as central to the meaning of Leighton's art. In Rhys's words it is 'the symbol, not so much of things attained, and Art Victorious, as of things that are always to be attained, and of Art striving and undeterred.' Rhys adds that 'it may serve, too, as in some sort the emblem of Leighton's own ideals, and of his whole career ... always seeking out new embodiments, under all difficulties, of Man's pursuit, in a difficult, and often an unbeautiful world, of Truth and Beauty.' Corkran (pp.101–2) speaks of the 'white-clad figure gazing upwards into a starlit sky, solitary on the heights in a rarefied atmosphere, an allegory of genius high above ordinary mortals in the cold world of contemplation.'

The Spirit of the Summit is then an example of Idealism at its most exalted, dealing at once in terms of the general aspirations of mankind and of the creative individual struggling against, and surmounting, obstacles. Mrs Barrington cites the picture as one of Leighton's 'expressions of the home-sickness that yearned for an abiding resting-place not found in the conditions of this world.' Not only in England was its significance appreciated. Robert de la Sizeranne, who saw the picture at the Academy when it was first shown there, wrote in connection with it shortly afterwards:

122

> Subjects that elevate the mind to the high points of life or of history, so that one cannot think of a nose or a leg without being reminded of some grand moral lesson or at least some noble human need – these are what Mr Leighton deals with… The grandeur of the community of man, the nobility of peace, that is the theme that has most often inspired him. And he has not found it in France, or anywhere else: it is a truly English idea.
>
> (*La Peinture Anglaise Contemporaine*, 1895, quoted by Rhys 1900, pp.113–14)

AW

HENRY PEGRAM 1862–1937

122 **Sibylla Fatidica** 1904

Bianco duro marble 155 × 124 × 98 (61 × 49 × 38½) on a shallow verde mare plinth and with a detachable crystal ball
Inscribed 'Henry Pegram Sc.t 1904' lower right

Prov: Bt from the artist by the Trustees of the Chantrey Bequest 1904
Exh: RA 1904 (1694); Chantrey exhibition 1949 (319)
Lit: *Royal Academy Pictures*, 1904, p.7, repr.; Spielmann 1901, p.97

Tate Gallery. Presented by the Trustees of the Chantrey Bequest 1904

The title simply means 'the Sibyl who foresees the future'. The Sibyl's enigmatic prophecies in Classical mythology were realised as moments of fate that highlighted the futility of human endeavour. Perhaps the perfect Symbolist subject, they actually occur rarely. Pegram portrays the Sibyl as a terrifying, almost aggressive figure, whose wizened features contrast markedly with the sensual treatment of the nude young woman draped over her lap. She has apparently fallen across the Sibyl's knees in despair at the decree of the Fates. However, the sculpture also suggests an implicit warning of the dangers the voluptuous temptress potentially presents. This familiar characterisation of woman as threatening siren can be traced throughout British and continental Symbolism, but Pegram presents it here in a highly original context. The crystal ball and astrological symbols around the base of the sculpture are familiar means of prophecy, although their connection with Sibylline predictions is invented.

Sibylla Fatidica was widely viewed as Pegram's masterpiece when the subject was first exhibited, and it marks the fullest expression of his Symbolist style. Like no.101, it displays the influence on him of Alfred Gilbert. The concept of the nude figure draped over the Sibyl's lap undoubtedly derives in part from Gilbert's *The Enchanted Chair* 1886 (destroyed). Pegram revered Gilbert, and was one of the few sculptors among the small number of people who attended his funeral (see Dorment 1985, p.333). However, the ultimate source for Pegram's composition is, of course, Michelangelo's *Pietà* 1498–9 (St Peter's Basilica, Rome).

This marble version of *Sibylla Fatidica* was shown at the Royal Academy in 1904, the same year Pegram was elected an Associate, although he had exhibited the plaster of the group there several years before, in 1891. The plaster was shown at the 1891 Salon, and it won a silver medal at the 1900 Paris International Exhibition. The first French showing evidently partly inspired Julien Dillens's *Silence of the Tomb* 1896 (Musées Royaux des Beaux-Arts, Brussels), although an even closer source for this is Watts's *'The All Pervading'* (no.125).

RU

GEORGE FREDERIC WATTS 1817–1904

123 **Time, Death and Judgement** 1870s–1886

Oil on canvas 245.5 × 169.8 (96⅝ × 66⅞)

Prov: Presented by Watts to the National Gallery of Canada, Dec. 1886
Exh: ?Grosvenor Gallery 1878 (62); ?Walker Art Gallery, Liverpool 1878 (77); ?St Jude's, Whitechapel 1884 (9); ?New York 1884 (103); ?Birmingham 1885 (174); ?St Jude's, Whitechapel 1886 (64); Ottawa 1965 (159); Manchester 1978 (29b); Montreal 1995 (465, repr. in col. no.60)
Lit: *Athenaeum*, 13 March 1886, pp.366–7; Spielmann 1886, p.24 with line engraving, cat. p.32; Macmillan 1903, pp.236–42; Barrington 1905, pp.92, 94, 112, 116, 118, 127–8; MS. Cat., I, pp.145–6; Watts 1912, I, pp.228, 235, 307, 319, 327–8; II, pp.86, 215; Staley 1978, nos. 29a, 29b

Gift of the artist, London, England 1887, on the occasion of Queen Victoria's Jubilee. National Gallery of Canada, Ottawa

Watts exhibited the first large version of the subject at the Grosvenor Gallery in 1878 with the title *Time and Death*; later that year it appeared at the Walker

123

Art Gallery, on both occasions with a title to link it with *Love and Death*. Soon after, the artist added the word *Nemesis*, then *Judgement* to reflect the presence of the third figure. In 1884, Watts authorised a large-scale mosaic to be executed on the side of the church of St Jude's in Whitechapel. Spielmann listed the 'great picture' as exhibited in New York in 1884–5 (even though it was unfinished) and Birmingham in 1885. By 1886, the year he presented *Time, Death and Judgement* to Canada, Watts had already carried out two large versions, one the 'great picture' and one a replica, both listed by Spielmann as unfinished. It is not entirely clear which was the much exhibited 'great picture' and which the replica; according to a notice in the *Athenaeum* in March 1886, the artist intended to give the duplicate to Canada, but in the same year, Spielmann wrote that the original was destined for Canada. Watts gave the other large *Time, Death and Judgement* to St Paul's Cathedral (now on loan to the Watts Gallery, Compton) in 1893. These two versions, nearly identical in composition, varying only slightly in details, do, however, reveal differences in handling. No.123 displays Watts's rich yet restrained handling of the 1880s while the other is somewhat overworked, since the artist continued to paint it until 1893.

Time, Death and Judgement shows three monumental figures: Time, a young man, 'the type of unfailing youth and vigour'; Death, a passive and pale female figure much like that in *Love and Death* (see no.51); and Judgement, flying above the two main figures, her own face hidden as she extends her arm with the scales, 'the attribute of Eternal Law' (exh. cat., Grosvenor Gallery 1881) and (less easily visible) a fiery sword, extended backward, seen as a rich glow of orange. Time carries a scythe, a traditional attribute, and Death 'in a fold of her drapery, bears plucked flowers and buds and withered leaves' (Spielmann). All the figures are 'poised in the clouds', with Time and Death clasping hands as they wade 'through the waves of the stream of life' (as Mrs Barrington described it in 1884). Behind the figures one sees a massive orb, the setting sun, and just visible on the right side, the rising crescent moon.

Apparently the idea for *Time, Death and Judgement* came to Watts suddenly, appearing before his 'inner sight' in a vision, according to Mrs Barrington. Yet the subject derives from Watts's early allegory, *Time and Oblivion* 1848, exh. RA 1864 (Eastnor Castle). It is a logical continuation of the thinking behind *Love and Death*; indeed Watts considered these two works along with the subject of *The Court of Death* as three of his most important 'suggestive pictures'. He explained: 'I have a strong idea that they should appeal purely to human sympathies, without reference to creed or dogma of any kind. In one sense they are lowered by this view, but in another they are more universal in their appeal' (letter to Charles Rickards 1876, Watts 1912, I, p.307). The colossal scale of the work cannot cancel out the deeply pessimistic message; yet there are passages of great beauty in the painting which enhance the sense of imminent loss and the pervasive spirit of death, as in the carefully executed still life of dying flowers and withered leaves or the curious winged gold crown of Time (similar to, though not as grotesque as Mammon's crown, see no.52) and the detail of the clasped hands of Time and Death, a small touch that humanises these stony presences.

Although *Time, Death and Judgement* was not as widely exposed on the Continent as some of the artist's other compositions, it was well known to visitors to London through exhibitions and other displays and known to those further afield through publications on the artist's work. His characters from a 'Titanic race belonging to larger spheres than those of our earth' (Barrington 1905, p.128, from the catalogue of 1884), are presented on massive scale, in the artist's own bold 'symbolical' language.

BB

George Frederic Watts 1817–1904

124 'She Shall Be Called Woman' *c.*1888–1892, reworked later

Oil on canvas 257.8 × 116.8 (101½ × 46)
Inscribed 'G.F. Watts 1892' b.l. and 'G.F. Watts' b.r.

Prov: As no.49
Exh: RA 1892 (164); St Jude's, Whitechapel 1894 (35); New Gallery 1896 (153)
Lit: Spielmann 1886, p.30; Barrington 1905, pp.33–4, 136–7; MS. Cat., I, p.46; Watts 1912, I, pp.261–2; II, pp.45, 138–40; 200–3

Tate Gallery. Presented by the artist 1897

'She Shall Be Called Woman' is the first part of a trilogy of large paintings showing the single figure of Eve, all of which in their final versions are in the Tate Gallery. This painting shows Eve after her creation, 'in the glory of her innocence', rising upward in an explosion of light and colour. The subject first bore the title *The Newly Created Eve*, and is probably also the subject called *Eve*, seen at Watts's Grosvenor Gallery retrospective in 1881–2. It is not to be confused with *The Creation of Eve*, a multi-figure composition,

paired with *The Denunciation of Cain* (the prime versions are both in the Fogg Art Museum, Harvard). While Watts carried on with the large version of *'She Shall Be Called Woman'*, he had the design in hand, a work which can be identified as the painting in the Lady Lever Art Gallery (Morris 1994, pp.124–6). Another small version is in the Watts Gallery, Compton.

Watts conceived the series depicting Eve in the later 1860s; the full-length nude figure formed a new feature in paintings by young artists in the late 1860s, such as Sandys's *Gentle Spring* (no.13) but Watts himself had a long-established interest in this figural type and indeed his own works, such as *Thetis c.*1866–9 (Watts Gallery) probably encouraged the revival. From an early stage, Watts considered the series of Eves as destined for a public space. As a 'perfectly naked figure', he considered it 'more fit for a gallery than a dwelling house'; he then offered his own view of its importance as part of a group in a letter of 1873:

> these designs – Eve in the glory of her innocence, Eve yielding to temptation, and Eve restored to beauty and nobility by remorse – form part of one design and can hardly be separated, any more than one would think of separating the parts of an epic poem. My intention was to make them part of an epic, and they belong to a series of six pictures illustrating the story in Genesis, viz. the three Eves – 'The Creation of Eve,' 'After the Transgression,' and 'Cain' – three single figures, and three full compositions. These I always destined to be public property …
>
> (Watts 1912, I, p.262)

He showed his paintings throughout the 1880s, usually in exhibitions devoted to his work. The Eves appeared at the retrospective at the Grosvenor Gallery in 1881–2, including probably the Lady Lever version of *'She Shall Be Called Woman'*, where they were described as 'a series of compositions treating of the Creation of Man'. The artist's ideas evolved by the time of the exhibition in New York in 1884, when Mrs Barrington recorded his intention to include the Eves in his grand scheme for the 'story of mankind' (later dubbed the 'House of Life'). The paintings themselves were not sent, but photographs of all three of the single-figure Eve compositions were exhibited and catalogued with the explanation that the woman represented a 'type which may suggest the mother of all the human race'.

Watts sent this painting to the Royal Academy exhibition in 1892 without the other two in the series. These may not have been as finished as he wished, or he may have regarded *'She Shall Be Called Woman'* as a work that could stand on its own. But officials of

124

the Academy wrote to Watts explaining that they were not going to hang it on the line. Frederic Leighton, the President, intervened in order to soften the blow, though he too found the painting not highly finished enough, writing to Watts of the 'inequality in the execution and lack in places of completeness'. The painting was certainly not carried to a degree of finish one finds in Leighton's exhibited works. This was always a question about which the two artists differed, with Watts urging Leighton not to rush the completion of works begun in the autumn just for the Royal Academy exhibition in May. Nonetheless, the affair bothered him and he wrote in his own defence to Leighton that 'he hoped the picture had not been painted for a season's exhibition'. Leighton arranged to have the picture rehung in a more advantageous position. The Eve we see now was probably considerably reworked after 1892.

Whether it was just the question of finish that preoccupied the Academy or the actual imagery is also an open question. Another rather negative opinion of the large versions of this trio was Burne-Jones's comment about the '3 whacking Eves which I can't abide' at the time of Watts's retrospective in 1896 (see Lago 1982, p.130).

In this work, largely a product of the 1890s, the artist developed the notion of the female figure as a potent force of nature. Falling from above, sunlight illuminates her torso, while her golden hair streams outward merging with an enveloping cloud, which seems to bear Eve upward in gravity-defying fashion. New to this version is an elaboration of the clouds, flowers, and birds with flapping wings, all swirling in a circular motion which engulfs the figure. Her face, more readable in this version than in any of the others, tilts upward toward the sun almost as if she were in a trance, under the spell of the sun. The colour, characterised for this subject as 'glowing and golden', enhances the life-giving spirit of Eve. She is also a representative of the eternal feminine, a key theme in Symbolist art. Watts also saw the figure in an even wider context, as the 'incarnation of the spirit of our own time'. The biblical origins of the Eve subjects were left far behind, as the artist developed the idea of a life force, igniting a new set of meanings for the 1890s.

BB

George Frederic Watts 1817–1904

125 **'The All-Pervading'** 1887–*c.*1893

Oil on canvas 162.6 × 109.2 (64 × 43)

Prov: Collection of the artist; bequeathed by him to the Tate Gallery as one of the additions to the original Watts Gift 1899

Exh: New Gallery 1896 (129); Munich 1897 (according to MS. Cat.; exh. cat. not traced)

Lit: Macmillan 1906, pp.67–8 (on the small oil version), 189–193; MS. Cat., I, p.2; Watts 1912, II, pp.104–5, 173, 230 (on the small oil version)

Tate Gallery. Presented by the artist 1897

According to the artist's wife, Watts conceived *'The All-Pervading'* during his stay at Sliema on Malta in late 1887, a visit which also inspired the Symbolist seascape *Neptune's Horses* (no.61). The initial impulse for *'The All-Pervading'* lay not in the natural environment but in Watts's observation of the play of light created by the glass beads and drops of an elaborate chandelier in the drawing room he used as a studio.

One must deduce that these reflections suggested the motif, described by Mrs Watts as 'the solemn and mystic figure holding the universe in hands that encircle the sphere'. The subject developed logically from the recent *Dweller in the Innermost* (no.75), Watts's visualisation of man's conscience as a higher force.

Back in London, Watts worked on *'The All-Pervading'* over the next few years. It was 'especially worked on' (Watts 1912, II, p.173) in the studio whilst he painted the portrait of Lady Katherine Thynne, carried out in 1890 and completed for the Royal Academy exhibition in the spring of 1891. At the same time, he used a variation of the design for the *The Recording Angel* (no.106). Probably the oil was more or less completed by 1893 (but with some additional painting *c.*1896; fig.43 on p.73) when Watts drew the composition in red chalk (now unlocated). Clearly, all these angel subjects comprised an informal group in his mind as he strove to articulate and express his thoughts on the universe. Yet the meaning of *'The All-Pervading'* has remained elusive. At least one writer found it a picture 'from which we are at first inclined to turn away with impatience and even dislike' (Macmillan 1903, p.189). Indeed, Watts may well have kept it for some years because it looked more comfortable in his own gallery than it ever would have in a mixed public exhibition.

Watts finally considered it ready for public viewing at the time of his retrospective show at the New Gallery in 1896. His own contributions to the catalogue provide the first direct clues as to his intentions. Two related explanations appeared: in the preface (p.8) he wrote: 'The figure with the Globe of the Systems may be called the Spirit that pervades the immeasurable expanse'; while the catalogue entry speaks of 'The all-pervading Spirit of the Universe represented as a winged figure, seated, holding in her lap the "Globe of Systems"'.

The spirit appears seated and suspended in a misty expanse of space. Her weightlessness defies gravity, announcing her removal from normal earthly constraints. Heavy draperies swathe the figure, preventing any individualised reading of her body and distancing her from the observer. Her huge scale commands attention. The antecedents for such monumental seated female figures are Michelangelo's Sibyls on the Sistine Ceiling about which Watts wrote in 1889 (while working on *'The All-Pervading'*): 'the Prophets and Sibyls ... are on a level with the noblest poetry' (Watts 1912, III, pp.230–1). There was also a thematic link between the sibyls who gazed into the future and Watts's spirit, whose 'globe of systems' seems to hover between her hands, its edges dissolved in a green haze.

The suggestion of a crystal-ball reader is perhaps one way that Watts's interest in spiritualism, established by his election to the Society for Psychical Research in 1884 (see p.72), seeped into his art. From the association with the later *Sower of the Systems* (no.134) and from some reliable commentators, we know that for Watts the 'systems' referred to stars and galaxies spread throughout the universe. Upon the sphere one can detect dots and trails of light like shooting stars. It is possible to imagine how the star-like configurations of the scattered reflections from the crystal chandelier may have set the artist thinking. Scientific matters and men of science had long interested Watts. Particularly relevant in this context was his friendship with Sir John Herschel, the astronomer, who frequented Mrs Prinsep's salon at Little Holland House, in the gardens of which he spotted what was known as 'the great comet' (probably Donati's comet of 1858 rather than 1857 as Mrs Watts noted). When Watts drew a portrait of Herschel (Watts 1912, I, p.203) he left the eyes as compelling voids as if to convey the impossibility of truly seeing all the secrets of the universe. Watts also befriended another astronomer, Sir James South, whose home in Campden Hill he visited to peer through a telescope strong enough to view Saturn and its rings. These personal links with real 'star-gazers' seem to have had an impact on the artist's visual vocabulary as he sought to convey the immensity of the universe.

The figure with the 'all-pervading' vision gazes into her globe of systems, looking into the future and into infinite space. Her contained pose and calm demeanour seem somewhat undermined by the blank expression upon her face and the unreality of the green tones. Although the notion of a pervading spirit might connote benevolence and reassurance, Watts's picture, with the blackish depths of its background, spectral lighting effects, and shadowy forms, instead suggests the uncertainty and even the disturbing qualities of the unknown, qualities which render it quintessentially Symbolist.

Watts always considered *'The All-Pervading'* as part of his group for the nation and in 1899, apparently after exhibiting it in Munich where a taste for Watts's 'Symbolical' paintings was already established (see no.77), he finally sent it to the Tate Gallery to join the Watts Gift.

Watts completed a smaller version in 1904, which was set within an arched compartment, to serve as a secular altarpiece for the Watts Chapel at Compton where it remains.

BB

GEORGE FREDERIC WATTS 1817–1904

126 **'Sic Transit'** 1890–2

Oil on canvas 102.9 × 204.5 (40½ × 80½)
Inscribed 'WHAT I SPENT, | I HAD, | WHAT I SAVED, | I LOST, | WHAT I GAVE, | I HAVE,' on the curtain in the background along the top edge; 'G.F. Watts 1892' lower left

Prov: As no.49

Exh: Munich 1893 (1648); St Jude's, Whitechapel 1894 (31); Rugby School 1894*; New Gallery 1896 (139); Glasgow 1896*; Edinburgh 1896*; Whitechapel 1974 (45). *Exh. refs. in MS. Cat.

Lit: Macmillan 1903, pp.254–7; Barrington 1905, pp.38, 40, 164–5, 177; MS. Cat., I, p.133; Watts 1912, II, pp.189–90, 197–9; Richard Dorment, in Manchester 1978, pp.48–9, fig.24

Tate Gallery. Presented by the artist 1897

Watts began work on *'Sic Transit'* in 1891 after an illness, and the imagery may well reflect an even greater involvement with his long-standing preoccupation with death. Death is not personified (see nos.51, 123), rather the idea is presented in a recumbent, shrouded figure with all the accessories of worldly success lying uselessly beside the bier. The stark contrast between the simplicity of the dead figure in its grey-white shroud and the accumulation of beautiful, glittering objects points up the meaning of the picture.

Watts's title comes from the well-known Latin tag 'sic transit gloria mundi', meaning 'so passes the glory of the world'. The painting comments 'not so much on the passing of the glory of the world but rather the end of all human existence' (Watts 1912, II, p.199). When a preacher focused on *'Sic Transit'* for a sermon, commenting on the man in the shroud, Watts considered this a misreading for he saw 'the shrouded figure as the symbol of human life ended, and with all its possibilities laid away' (Watts 1912, II, p.200).

The unusual device of inscribing words along the upper edge of the picture, on a curtain behind the shroud, attracts attention. The artist turned to a favourite saying, according to Mrs Barrington (1905, p.177), which was said to be an old German proverb (Macmillan 1903, p.254), alluding to the futility of accumulating wealth and possessions, a theme that Watts took up in *Mammon* (no.52). But it seems the actual phrase also had a distinctly English connotation as the epitaph of Edward Courtney, Earl of Devonshire (d.1419) and his wife, at Tiverton: 'What wee gave, wee have | What wee spent, wee had | What wee kept, wee lost' (*The Oxford Dictionary of Quotations*, 4th ed., Oxford and New York 1993, p.19). A variant found its way into *The Shepherd's Calendar* by Edmund Spenser, a writer whose work was familiar to the artist. In the preface to the catalogue of his retrospective at the New Gallery, Watts singled out *'Sic Transit'* as 'an illustration of the noble medieval inscription'. In also referring to it as the 'epitaph picture', he directly alluded to the connotations of his chosen text.

Watts carried out this painting as a fully formed idea, new to his thinking around 1890, with few preparatory or related works. The unusually textured canvas received special preparation with plaster of Paris, and was then soaked in water to 'remove all lime'. For the figure, he made 'a little study in gesso', presumably to study the effects of the drapery (see no.50 for the use of sculptural maquettes). He also drew several studies of a medieval helmet, beautiful for its patina and curving lines. This helmet belonged to the famous collection of armour owned by Baron de Cosson, lent (and eventually bequeathed) to the Victoria and Albert Museum.

The silvery grey tonality of the picture demonstrates Mrs Barrington's assertion (1905, pp.163–4) that it showed Watts's interest in colours and textures with the softness of pastel.

While planning *'Sic Transit'* in 1890, Watts received a visit from Queen Elizabeth of Roumania (1843–1916) whose writings, under the *nom-de-plume* Carmen Sylva, he admired. She enjoyed fame throughout Europe as a woman of letters, specialising in philosophical aphorisms best known through her *Pensées d'une reine* (1882) which went through many editions and translations (including an English one in 1890, the year she met Watts). Her biography records that meeting, when Watts 'could not make enough of her' (Burgoyne 1941, p.159). One only has to read *Pensées* to see why they got on so well: one of these aphorisms is 'Man is a violin. It is not until his last string has snapped that he becomes a piece of work' which has obvious parallels with *Hope*.

In *'Sic Transit'*, the visual imagery derives from two relevant areas: funerary sculpture with its focus on death and the *vanitas* still-life with its focus on the fragility of man and the transience of life and beauty. Watts made overt reference, as Richard Dorment has shown, to the idea of the *transi*, a sculpted version of a shrouded body common in late Gothic art and carried into the nineteenth century in the famous memorial to General Cavaignac (1847) by François Rude in the Cimetière Montmartre. Watts's *transi*, painted on canvas, has an undeniable evocative power as an uncompromising symbol of death.

The *vanitas* theme also had a particular application in *'Sic Transit'* as a way of harnessing an array of associations with each object revealing some aspect of life that has come to an abrupt end: ermine fur with connotations of royalty and wealth; armour, spear and gauntlet for success in war; the lute and books for the contemplative pursuits of music and learning; the goblet for high living; the laurel crown for fame; cut flowers soon to wither and die; and a scallop shell, emblematic of the pilgrim on his travels. A bunch of peacock feathers assume prominence in the foreground, not as Aesthetic accessories, but as the traditional Christian symbol for immortality and resurrection. The strangely hovering letters of the inscription lend it a distinctly Symbolist mood.

BB

Gaetano Previati 1852–1920

127 **Paolo and Francesca** *c.*1901

Oil on canvas 230 × 262 (90½ × 103⅛)
Inscribed 'Previati' lower right
Exh: Venice 1909; Ferrara 1969 (34)
Lit: Barbantini 1919, p.193, pl.73

Ferrara, Civiche Gallerie d'Arte Moderna e Contemporanea, Museo dell'Ottocento

In *Paolo and Francesca*, Previati painted a well-known scene from Dante's *Inferno* on a large scale, adapting his divisionist technique of the 1890s to create a sense of movement through flowing strokes of colour. Several writers have suggested that he looked to Watts and Walter Crane for such handling (Rosci 1970; Tosini 1995, p.277; Macmillan's *Dictionary of Art*, 1996, vol.25, p.568).

Previati, after academic training in Milan, shifted toward a distinctly Symbolist art in the 1890s, primarily under the influence of the artist and dealer Vittore Grubicy, who promoted Divisionism. Previati's handling with its long threads and dots of colour lent great luminosity to his paintings and a shimmering surface quality first evident in *Motherhood* 1890–1 (Banca Populare, Novara). This painting, with its new technique and mystical evocation of a Madonna and child, appeared in the first Rose+Croix salon in 1892 in Paris.

Like Watts and Rossetti (no.30), Previati found in Dante's work continual inspiration; he painted an earlier version of *Paolo and Francesca* 1887 (Galleria Academia Carrara, Bergamo) in which the lovers embrace, and planned an unrealised panorama with scenes from Dante's *Inferno* for an exhibition in Milan in 1894. In 1901 at the Venice Biennale, Previati sent a drawing in charcoal for *Paolo and Francesca* (Civico Cabinetto dei Disegni, Castella Sforzesco, Milan); this work established the composition as a series of long undulating lines which transform into anguished bodies. The oil finally appeared at exhibition in Venice in 1909.

The immediately identifiable scene from Dante's *Divine Comedy* presents the second circle where amid 'the warring winds', carnal lovers suffer 'the stormy blast of hell' which 'with restless fury drives the spirits on'. These condemned spirits, especially Paolo and Francesca da Rimini, whose adultery precipitated their murder and eternal punishment, provided much rich material for the Romantics earlier in the century. Foremost among these artists is William Blake whose *Circle of the Lustful ('The Whirlwind of Lovers')* 1827 (Birmingham City Museums and Art Gallery), best known in its engraved form as one of an unfinished group (published in 1838 and 1892),

127

relied on an emphatically circular movement of the stream of lovers which may well have inspired Previati.

Although as an Italian Previati commemorated his own identification with the literature of Dante, the subject of Paolo and Francesca had considerable resonance in recent European art in the work of Ary Scheffer, Gustave Doré and especially Watts (no.48). In comparing Previati's version with that of Watts, certain parallels emerge – the sweeping upward motion of the linked figures, and the use of swirling drapery to emphasise this movement, as well as the exploitation of the empty spaces in the compositions which serve to enhance the misery of the doomed lovers, lost in an infinite void. However, the differences in colour between the two paintings could not be greater, with Watts relying on a deep crimson amid essentially dark tones and with Previati revealing his intense commitment to the depiction of light as a transforming force, here bathing the figure in an orange glow to contrast with the nocturnal blues, in a colour combination reminiscent of Watts's *Neptune's Horses* (no.61).

Previati's familiarity with Watts's *Paolo and Francesca*, certainly one of his best-known and most-exhibited works since its completion in 1879, probably came through the medium of photography or engraving. Given the interest among artists in Milan for Symbolist events in Paris and elsewhere, it seems likely that Previati had access to Hollyer's photograph or saw the engraving after the painting that appeared regularly after its first publication in Blackburn's *Grosvenor Notes* of 1879 (as, for example, the frontispiece to the European edition of *Harper's Monthly Magazine*, vol.10, 1885). Articles on Watts's work appeared in Italian periodicals and he sent paintings to exhibitions in Italy in the 1890s, including the *Esposizione Internazionale* in Venice where Previati himself exhibited. This direct access to actual works by Watts seem to have fuelled even more compelling parallels into the next century. Previati's *Day Awakens Night* 1905 (Civico Museo Revoltella, Trieste) has much in common with the colour, broken handling of paint, light imagery and the cosmic themes of *The Sower of the Systems* (fig.46 on p.76 and no.134).

BB

Epilogue: A New Century

By the time of the Paris Exposition Universelle of 1900 the heyday of the Victorian painters was effectively over, though some important canvases were shown there, including work by Watts, Leighton and Burne-Jones, who had died in 1898. His *Dream of Sir Launcelot at the Chapel of the Holy Grail* (no.114) was an exhibit. But even as the European world moved on and began to relegate the older generation to the past, younger artists with very different aims were imbibing their work and recasting their ideas. In Switzerland, Hodler made pencil copies of Burne-Jones's designs for the *Saint George* series, which was shown in the Munich International Exposition of 1897, and his *Heilige Stunde* of 1907 (Kunstmuseum Solothurn) is a paraphrase of Burne-Jones's *The Hours* 1882 (City Art Gallery, Sheffield). Hodler's *The Dream* (no.135) also reflects his interest in Burne-Jones and is, in addition, specifically a paraphrase of Rossetti's *Blessed Damozel* (fig.55 on p.186). In the work of Klimt there is a possible link between his well-known, embryo-like *Danaë* 1907–8 (Kunstmuseum, Vienna) and Leighton's languorous *Flaming June c.*1895 (Ponce Museo de Arte, Puerto Rico). Munch's famous *Madonna* (no.137), for all its Expressionist language, is an ambivalent goddess-temptress of a type that derives directly from Rossetti.

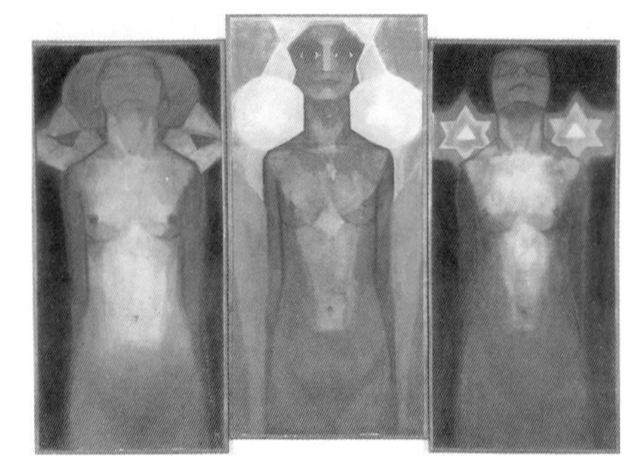

fig.59 Piet Mondrian, *Evolution* 1910–11, oil on canvas in three sections 181.8 × 87.8, 187.1 × 90.6, 181.8 × 87.8 cm. Haags Gemeentemuseum

Picasso's interest, for a short period, in the work of Burne-Jones has been noted but not generally seen as reflected in his own output; in fact there are several Blue Period figures of women seen in pale profile who have their undoubted origin in Burne-Jones (see p.32, figs.15, 16). It has been suggested that there may be echoes of Beardsley in some of Picasso's early work (Washington 1997, p.265), and Beardsley's work was certainly well known in the Barcelona of Picasso's youth (see Blunt and Pool 1962). There seems to be a reminiscence of the archetypal pouting Beardsley vamp in Picasso's 1901 oil painting *Lady in Blue* (Museo Nacional Centro de Arte Reina Sofia, Madrid). Memories of Watts too percolated into early Modernist painting: the dependence of Picasso's *Old Guitarist* of 1905 on *Hope* has already been noted (see p.00); and in 1910 the 'Signor' was accorded the homage of the young Mondrian in his triptych *Evolution* (fig.59), which quotes directly from *'She Shall Be Called Woman'* (no.124). This was a picture that evoked echoes in many parts of Europe. Even so extreme a work of Modernism as Marcel Duchamp's *Nude Descending a Staircase* 1912 (fig.60) may, as has been pointed out above (p.68), have had its origin in a recent memory of Burne-Jones's *Golden Stairs*.

fig.60 Marcel Duchamp, *Nude Descending a Staircase no.2* 1912, oil on canvas 147.3 × 88.9 cm. Philadelphia Museum of Art: The Louise and Walter Arensberg Collection

On the whole the British younger generation did not adopt the adventurous painting techniques of their continental contemporaries. Ricketts translated his evocative line-drawings into richly coloured romantic designs which have something in common with Expressionism, but these cannot really be said to break the new ground that the French and Germans were tackling. Nevertheless artists in this country continued to explore the linear vocabulary of Beardsley and the Glasgow School, and in Cayley Robinson produced a designer of great originality, who combined the influence of Beardsley with that of Puvis and even Rodin in a remarkable, personal version of the new international style. Watts for his part continued to develop his themes in surprisingly original ways. His study for the painting of 1903 *The Sower of the Systems* (no.134) is a remarkable feat of the octogenarian imagination, as powerfully expressive as any work of its time, and unexpectedly prophetic of the new age.

Louis Welden Hawkins 1849–1910

128 Girls Singing Music by Gabriel Fabre *c.*1903

Oil on canvas 54.9 × 46 (21⅝ × 18⅛)
Prov: ...; Julian Hartnoll, London; present owner

Robin de Beaumont

This strange and beautiful painting shows three girls singing from a page of music by Gabriel Fabre. The signature of the composer may be read in a mirror-image through the transparent sheet. The piece seems to come from Fabre's *Sonatines Sentimentales* (1894–1902), which include a *Ronde: Les Trois Filles*.

No.128 – and other works by Louis Welden Hawkins like it – such as *Innocence* (Van Gogh Museum, Amsterdam), *Autumn* (Victor Arwas collection) and *Les Auréoles* (ex Christie's, 1 Dec. 1989, no.1074) – were made in the late mid-1890s and at around the turn of the century. All have the similar ranges of muted colour, and they share the characteristic device of crowding the figures together into overlapping patterns cropped at the edges.

Hawkins was invited to exhibit with the Salon de la Rose+Croix in 1894–5, and seems to have made this series of visionary and idealised figure paintings to satisfy the Salon's determined rejection of all that was mundane or prosaic. Works of a similar type by Hawkins were shown at La Libre Esthétique in Brussels, but it seems that the present picture was not among the artist's exhibited works.

Hawkins was the son of an Austrian aristocrat, Louise Sopransi, Baroness von Welden, and a British naval officer. He was born at Esslingen in Germany, brought up in England, and sent to sea at fifteen. He settled in France in about 1870, embarking on a career as a painter and joining the Anglo-American circle of young artists that gathered at the Académie Julian. His first success was a painting entitled *The Orphans* 1881 (Hôtel de Ville, Pouyastruc) which reveals his early debt to Bastien-Lepage. In 1887 Hawkins applied to Puvis de Chavannes to work as an assistant, but was rejected; nonetheless, the influence of Puvis is seen in the silent and monumental subjects to which Hawkins turned, such as *The Procession of Spirits* (private collection). In the 1890s he came into contact with various advanced writers, including (from 1893) Paul Adam, who in the *Manifeste Littéraire* (1886) had first applied the word 'Symbolism' to the literary movement of which he was a leading figure. Hawkins was also a close friend of Stéphane Mallarmé, attending his weekly receptions and dedicating his painting *The Closed Door* (Musée Départmental Stéphane Mallarmé, Vulaines-sur-Seine) to him.

Hawkins and his fellow painters in the Parisian Symbolist circle who were members of the Salon de la Rose+Croix were known to admire the work of English Aesthetic painters, notably that of Rossetti. Clearly the influence of Rossetti on Hawkins was generic rather than based on known examples. Nonetheless, comparison may be drawn between the present work and Rossetti's drawing *Rosa Triplex* (Hearn Family Trust) of 1874, where three portraits of the same model are given, and in which the subtle nuances of expression and the variety of hand gestures make the subject intriguing and complex. Even before this in the tradition of figurative threesomes stands Simeon Solomon's *The Sleepers, and the One that Watcheth* of 1870 (no.36).

CSN

Glyn Warren Philpot 1884–1937

129 **Melampus and the Centaur** 1919

Oil on canvas 121.9 × 204.3 (48 × 80⅜)
Inscribed 'Glyn Philpot 1919' b.r.

Prov: Bt at Grosvenor Galleries by Glasgow Art Gallery 1923
Exh: Grosvenor Galleries, 1919; Philpot 1923 (17); Philpot 1984–5 (22, repr. in col.)
Lit: *Studio*, vol.78, 1919, repr. p.161; Sewter 1951, p.5, pl.33

Glasgow Museums: Art Gallery and Museum, Kelvingrove

Born into the generation that produced authentically modern British art in the early decades of this century, Philpot nevertheless continued using Symbolist and Classical themes and subjects, albeit in a new and wholly original manner. This picture is easily the finest among such works and was greeted with great critical and popular acclaim when it was first exhibited. In Greek mythology Melampus was the first physician, and Philpot shows him being taught his art by Chiron the centaur. Philpot's choice of a Classical subject was no doubt influenced in part by Ricketts, with whom he had formed a mutually admiring friendship. There are echoes too of pictures of centaurs by Arnold Böcklin, such as *Centaur by the Water's Edge* (Andree 1977, no.323), and *Pan and Dryads* (ibid., nos.462.1, 463–4). There is also a perhaps coincidental parallel to Hodler, who used figures in expansive landscapes in a similar way, and whose youth in *Spring* (no.136) is posed similarly to Philpot's Melampus. The figures in Philpot's picture also testify to his growing interest in sculpture at this time. The mysterious background landscape anticipates Dalí to a certain degree, and may have been inspired by Philpot's knowledge of Spain (see Philpot 1984–5, no.22).

This is one of a series of allegorical nude groups that Philpot made around this time, which includes *The Coast of Britain* c.1919–20 (private collection), *The Journey of the Spirit* 1921 (untraced, repr. Sewter 1951, pl.39), and *Himalaya* c.1921 (untraced, repr. Philpot 1984–5, fig.37). Depicting nude figures among mountain-top boulders, this last work is clearly derived from the massive figures of Titans in Watts's painting *Chaos* (no.49). There are further references to the generation of older British artists in Philpot's work of this type. Gibson has noted the connection between the rocky outcrops of *Himalaya* and *The Creation of Man* 1930 with Leighton's *Spirit of the Summit* (no.121, see Philpot 1984–5, p.27). There are further connections too between *The Creation of Man* and Watts's *Love and Life* c.1884–5 (fig.49 on p.86). Rossetti was an early influence on Philpot's artistic development, whose draughtsmanship he imitated in early drawings (see, for example, Philpot 1984–5, nos.72–3, 75), although this was abandoned in his mature work. A recurrent Symbolist theme in Philpot's pictures was his treatment of the Sphinx myth. Gibson has attributed his fascination with it to Ricketts, and it was a subject to which he returned on numerous occasions ranging in date from 1905 to the early 1930s (see Philpot 1984–5, no.49).

There are a group of thirteen preliminary drawings for *Melampus and the Centaur* in the Courtauld Institute, some of which trace Philpot's transformation of the face of a young model into that of the older Chiron (see ibid., no.22).

RU

130

Charles Ricketts 1866–1931

130 **Bacchus in India** *c.*1913

Oil on canvas 117 × 95 (46 × 37½)

Prov: ...; bt from their 1935 Spring Exhibition by the Atkinson Art Gallery

Exh: International Society 1913 (84); Southport 1935; Cambridge 1979 (A6); Barbican 1989 (288, repr. in col. p.38)

Sefton MBC Leisure Services Department, Arts and Cultural Services Section, The Atkinson Art Gallery, Southport

In one of his most dramatic pictures, Ricketts shows the young Bacchus, god of wine and revelry, on his arrival in India, mounted on an elephant. His drunken, half-naked followers precede him in a state of orgiastic abandon. This testament to the pleasures of alcoholic revelry also serves as a metaphor for sexual abandon, activities which were inextricably linked in so many Old Master representations of Bacchanals. In Ricketts's picture the face of Bacchus bears a passing resemblance to Charles Shannon, his partner. The general composition is similar to that of an earlier picture by Ricketts, *Don Juan in Hell c.*1908 (untraced, repr. Delaney 1990, fig.28).

Ricketts's admiration for Titian was centred particularly on the *Bacchus and Ariadne c.*1523 (National Gallery, London; see no.133). Although Ricketts's treatment is altogether more decadent, he clearly had this picture in mind and makes references to it. The red sash and blue and white gown of the woman in the right foreground correspond to those worn by Ariadne in Titian's picture. Ricketts's left foreground figure draped in gold, white and aquamarine repeats the colours worn by Titian's bacchante with cymbals, while the pink cape of Bacchus in the Titian can be equated with the similarly coloured billowing canopy that dominates the left side of Ricketts's picture.

Another major influence here, however, is Delacroix, whom Ricketts greatly revered. Visiting Leighton, it was his Delacroix studies he admired, not Leighton's own work. He later acquired these at Leighton's sale. The sprawling figures in *Bacchus in India* are reminiscent of those found in *Chaos* (no.49), by Watts, an artist of the older generation of whom Ricketts thought highly. Having been shown some naturalistic work by the now virtually forgotten sculptor Reginald Fairfax Wells, Ricketts correctly predicted in his diary entry for 21 August 1901 the decline of critical interest in the Symbolist Victorian artists:

> This corroborates an impression of mine that the future English School will turn its back completely on Watts and Burne-Jones and

> show a strong realistic tendency. Rothenstein, then Nicholson, were the first two signs of it, now we have this youngster [Wells] and John. This tendency will probably strengthen Strang, who should be the head of that school, if he were rather more self-respecting. I suppose the output of Watts and Burne-Jones was too definite.
>
> (quoted Lewis 1939, pp.66–7)

Rothenstein himself observed a similar phenomenon, when he had to explain to an uncomprehending Harold Nicolson:

> how we, as youngsters, revered Browning, Tennyson, Swinburne, Matthew Arnold, Whistler, Watts, Burne-Jones, Holman Hunt and others who were still alive. 'Are there no elders about whom you to-day feel as we did?' I asked him. 'No', said Nicolson, he didn't think so; and then he added – 'Well, perhaps Max Beerbohm.'
>
> (Rothenstein 1932, p.209)

RU

131

FREDERICK CAYLEY ROBINSON 1862–1927

131 **Cain and Abel** *c.*1913

Pencil, watercolour, crayon and pastel on board 52.8 × 40.7 (20¾ × 16)
Inscribed 'CAYLEY | ROBINSON' b.r. and 'ML' in oval b.l., the collection stamp of the Louvre

Prov: Sir Edmund Davis, by whom presented 1915 to the Luxembourg Gallery, Paris; transferred to Musée d'Orsay

Lit: Reynolds 1980, p.463, fig.10

Musée du Louvre Département des Arts Graphiques, Fonds du Musée d'Orsay

EXHIBITED IN LONDON ONLY

Cayley Robinson was born in Brentford and studied at the St John's Wood School of Art, and later at the Royal Academy Schools. In the 1890s he spent a number of years in Paris, where he lived again from 1902 to 1906. The years 1898 to 1902 were passed in Florence studying Renaissance art. Cayley Robinson evolved a distinct and personal style, albeit one whose colouring, draughtsmanship and texture were influenced by Puvis de Chavannes (see no.132). As well as making easel paintings, he illustrated books, designed costumes and sets for the stage, and was commissioned to make murals for Dublin Art Gallery and Middlesex Hospital.

This is one of Cayley Robinson's most dramatic and disturbing pictures. It shows the killing of Abel by his jealous brother Cain, a subject taken from Genesis 4:1–15. According to the biblical account the murder took place in the fields, but Cayley Robinson has transferred the action to a more psychologically intense setting, at the foot of a flight of stairs leading up to an altar. In the top left corner an eagle, perhaps symbolising the word of God, spreads its wings ominously, while smoke from incense on the altar drifts across the centre of the composition. Above the figures Abel's sacrifice to God of a sheep still smoulders. Cain stands back from Abel's body, his figure contorted with horror and remorse. Blood from his fingers is smeared on the wall, and a bloody footprint is on one of the steps. Cain's anguish illustrates the moment when he is told by God that he is 'cursed from the earth', and he replies 'My punishment is greater than I can bear' (verses 11, 13).

The relief design on the wall behind Cain is evidently derived from medieval Kabbalah-influenced depictions of the Tree of Life. This reference is significant, for the Kabbalah's philosophy of correspondence, interconnection and hidden meaning is analogous with the continental Symbolists' theories about the 'correspondence' and equivalence of poetry, music and art, which it no doubt partly inspired, theories which Cayley Robinson would have encountered while he was in Paris. The story of Cain and Abel has wide-ranging connections with hermetic and esoteric tradition. Abel's murder is often characterised as the first blood sacrifice, and his death a precursor of Christ's. Cain's sin banished him to the Land of Nod, 'on the east of Eden', where 'he builded a city, and called the name of the city, after the name of his son, Enoch' (4:17). This role as an architect means that he holds significance for Masonic tradition. Cayley Robinson is likely to have known of such connotations, for the revival of interest in esoteric study in London, Paris and elsewhere from the 1880s onwards had certainly penetrated the artistic and literary communities.

Abel's body fills the left foreground, a compositional device perhaps inspired by the dead troops in the epic Napoleonic battle scenes of Baron Gros, which Cayley Robinson is likely to have seen in the years he was in Paris. Like the principal figure in no.132, Cain's pose derives from Michelangelo's *Dying Slave* c.1513 (Musée du Louvre, Paris), and it also shares similarities with Rodin's *Age of Bronze* 1875–7 (Victoria and Albert Museum, London). The figures and setting are particularly reminiscent in their treatment of Charles Ricketts's *The Death of Montezuma* c.1905 (private collection; repr. Calloway 1979, col. pl.1), which, like the present picture, was once owned by Edmund Davis. Also featuring a figure near a stone altar, it has a similar theme of human sacrifice, and the outstretched arm of a body in the foreground closely resembles that of Cayley Robinson's Abel.

The picture exhibited here appeared as an illustration in *The First Book of Moses, Called Genesis* (repr. opp. p.14), published in 1914 by the Medici Society for the Riccardi Press. This was an edition of the Book of Genesis 'printed in the Authorised version' for which Cayley Robinson provided ten plates.

RU

Frederick Cayley Robinson 1862–1927

132 **Youth** 1923

Charcoal, watercolour, gouache, pastel, oil and pencil on panel prepared with a gesso ground 46.3 × 62.2 (18¼ × 24½)
Inscribed 'Cayley-Robinson 1923' b.l.

Prov: The artist's widow, Winifred Robinson; FAS
Exh: RA 1923 (34); RA Winter 1928 (589); FAS 1976 (126); Cayley Robinson 1977 (60, repr.); Barbican 1989 (231)
Lit: Stevens 1977, p.26, repr. fig.8

Private Collection

Cayley Robinson's work characteristically incorporates a rich variety of symbolic allusion, but meaning is often reserved, or implicit, creating an aura of mystery and ambiguity. In this picture the principal nude figure represents Youth, stretching as he wakes into life. He apparently also serves as a metaphor for Spring, for tiny leaves have appeared on the trees in this barren landscape. The new moon above similarly represents renewal of life, and in combination with the male figure refers also to the story in Classical myth of Selene, the moon goddess. She loved the beautiful Endymion, to whom Zeus had given eternal life and youth, but condemned to sleep for ever. The ravens in the tree, traditional symbols of death, strike a still darker note. Below them, figures in the background lever away a boulder from the mouth of a cave, which immediately recalls Christ's tomb. This picture therefore serves as an allegory of the cycle of life and death, and ultimate rebirth. It proposes an equality between pagan and Christian myth. Cayley Robinson alludes also to the passing of once great civilisations, represented here by the columns sunk into the hillside, below which men with shovels appear to be excavating. This was a theme found in a number of his works, and was derived from Claude, a debt which he specifically acknowledged in *Souvenir of Claude Lorraine* (private collection, Stevens 1977, fig.5).

There are a wide diversity of references in this picture, which is a later version of a work of 1907 (repr. Greig 1928). The figure of Youth partly derives from *The Dying Slave* c.1513 (Musée du Louvre, Paris) by Michelangelo, whom Cayley Robinson revered. It is similar also to Leighton's life-size bronze *The Sluggard* 1885 (Tate Gallery), originally entitled *An Athlete Awakening from Sleep*. In modified form, Cayley Robinson had reused this figure to serve as Adam in his frontispiece design *The Expulsion* for his illustrated edition of *The First Book of Moses called Genesis* published by the Medici Society and Riccardi Press in 1914 (see no.131).

132

The expansive, populated landscape punctuated by a gently curving pool has a source in works by Puvis de Chavannes. His *Poor Fisherman* 1881 (Musée d'Orsay, Paris) had particularly influenced Cayley Robinson, who saw it on display in the Luxembourg during his years in Paris. He imitated it most closely in *To Pastures New (Dawn)* c.1904 (untraced, repr. Stevens 1977, fig.6), and to a lesser extent in works such as *Pastoral* 1923–4 (Tate Gallery). The draughtsmanship and soft colouring of such works, including *Youth*, also comes from Puvis. Augustus John's *Childhood of Pyramus* 1908 (Johannesburg Art Gallery) and *Lyric Fantasy* c.1911–14 (Tate Gallery) were similar responses to Puvis, and although modulated differently, there is some similarity between the figures and landscapes of these pictures and those by Cayley Robinson such as *Youth*. The smooth tree stems evidently descend from Beardsley, as in for instance no.90 here; and the twisting tree roots are contemporary manifestations of the same idea articulated by Arthur Rackham.

From 1891 to 1894 Cayley Robinson was a student at the Académie Julian in Paris, studying under Bouguereau and Ferrier. As Stevens has noted, here he was able to absorb the prevalent admiration for Puvis, Gauguin and Japanese art (p.23). However, following the Exposition Universelle of 1889, Paris was gripped with enthusiasm for the late Pre-Raphaelites, notably Burne-Jones. He rejected his initial tendency towards Newlyn naturalism, and from now on it was this influence that became dominant in Cayley Robinson's work (Stevens, ibid.). The Arthurian *Beautiful Castle* 1894 (untraced, Stevens 1977, fig.4) paid direct homage to Burne-Jones's *Danaë and the Brazen Tower* 1887–8 (Glasgow Art Gallery) and *King Cophetua and the Beggar Maid* (no.40). *A Souvenir of a Past Age* 1894 (Art Gallery of South Australia, Adelaide) and *The Close of Day* c.1898 (untraced, Stevens 1977, fig.10) add in elements of Rossetti, Stanhope and John Melhuish Strudwick; the last of these also directly quotes the figure in Whistler's *Little White Girl* (no.15). Interestingly, as Stevens has noted, it was from *A Souvenir ...* that Cayley Robinson's distinct mature style evolved, in his series of ambiguous, disquieting pictures of figures in domestic interiors such as *A Winter Evening* 1898 (untraced, Stevens 1977, fig.12) and *The Depth of Winter* 1901 (private collection, Stevens 1977, fig.11).

From 1898 to 1902 Cayley Robinson lived in Florence, and here he studied the work of Giotto, Mantegna and Michelangelo, and developed a great interest in the possibilities of working in tempera. Much of his work after 1901 was in tempera, or more precisely, in different materials with which he experimented to mimic its limpid effect. *Youth* is a good instance of his wide-ranging technical experimentation, using combinations of charcoal, watercolour, gouache, pastel, oil and pencil on a gesso ground (see Stevens 1977, p.28).

Cayley Robinson's position as one of the leading British Symbolists working in the early years of the twentieth century was enhanced in 1909 when he was asked to design the sets and costumes at the Haymarket Theatre for the first English production of *The Blue Bird* by Maurice Maeterlinck (1862–1949). Described since as a 'transcendental pantomime' and 'a philosophical Peter Pan', it was an instant success. Methuen's ecition of the play, also hugely successful, was reissued in 1911 with illustrations by Cayley Robinson. To a certain extent these were based on his work for the stage production, but they also introduced new material. He borrowed from diverse sources that included Blake, Michelangelo, Raphael, Poussin, Guido Reni and Böcklin. Maeterlinck was delighted with the book, and wrote to Cayley Robinson:

> when one slowly turns over the leaves, when one lingers long, a charm, powerful, unexpected, and much more fairylike than the most spontaneous fantasies of the most extravagant imagination, escapes, little by little, from your pictures, purposely restrained and subdued. You have interpreted the story from within, instead of translated it from without ... I thank you with all my heart for the honour you have done to my little fairy tale.
>
> (letter dated 1911, quoted *Watercolour Drawings Illustrating Maeterlinck's The Blue Bird by F. Cayley Robinson ARWS*, exh. cat. Leicester Galleries, Nov.–Dec. 1911)

RU

CHARLES SHANNON 1863–1937

133 **The Golden Age** 1921–2

Oil on canvas 142 × 109.2 (56 × 43)
Prov: Lord Northcliffe; N. Mitchell; Leicester Galleries; Sotheby's 8 March 1978 (9, repr.); ...; Forbes Collection
Exh: RA 1922 (137)
Lit: George 1924, pl.27

Simon Reynolds

This is one of Shannon's most sumptuously beautiful pictures, an idyllic, languorous scene which represents the mythic origin of mankind when all men lived as gods. Its colouring, technique and composition are strongly influenced by Titian, who Shannon, like his companion Ricketts, believed was the principal genius in the history of art. It is a later version of the picture of the same title exhibited in 1907 at the International Society's Exhibition. One review noted that:

> It is as a subject-painter that Mr C H Shannon is to us most interesting. Like Watts and Burne-Jones, in each canvas he extends the boundaries of a new country which he has made his own ... [In *The Golden Age*] the curse of the world is removed, the supreme virtue is indolence ... A great command of colour, and imagination that finds its rest in dreams, these are the qualities that give to his art an extraordinary and personal character.
>
> (anon., *Studio*, vol.40, 1907, p.144)

The Golden Age is closely related to a slightly earlier picture by Shannon, *The Childhood of Bacchus* 1919–20 (private collection). This was inspired by *Bacchus and Ariadne* 1523 (National Gallery, London), which Shannon and Ricketts considered Titian's greatest picture, and to which the latter devoted an entire chapter in his 1910 monograph on the Venetian painter. Shannon sought to emulate the iridescent glow that such painters gave their pictures by combining bright underpainting with translucent glazes, as opposed to using opaque colour. In the 1880s Ricketts had supported him while he researched this method of painting, apparently consulting Reynolds's *Discourses* and Eastlake's *Materials for a History of Oil Painting*. In addition to Titian, Shannon revered Van Dyck for his similar use of rich glazes, and sought to follow his example in his own portraits, one of Kate Hargood being specifically entitled *Souvenir of Van Dyck* 1897 (National Gallery, Melbourne).

This admiration for the Old Masters was combined, however, with equal regard for a number of more recent painters. Like Ricketts, he considered Puvis the greatest French artist of the nineteenth century, and together they had travelled to France to visit him in 1887. Watts was also held in high esteem, and Shannon visited him on numerous occasions. There are some similarities to Watts in Shannon's treatment of the figures in *The Golden Age*, a phenomenon which was noted by E.B. George in one of the first books devoted to Shannon. George detected 'a marked temperamental affinity ... it shows itself chiefly in a similar response, felt by each, to a certain aspect of the beauty of women, expressed in a droop of the head, sidelong and forwards carrying with it in each case a similar emotion' (1924, pp.13–14). In addition to the imaginative and emotional conception of his pictures, Shannon was absorbed by Watts's own emulation of Titian's method of working, which the older artist had studied in Italy. Burne-Jones had also travelled to Italy and made similar investigations, and it is interesting to note that his example was felt in Shannon's *The Bath of Venus* 1898–1904 (Tate Gallery), started in the year of Burne-Jones's death. This adopted the title and composition of a picture painted by Burne-Jones between 1873 and 1889, now lost. While Shannon's *Venus* was received with critical acclaim, his later *Wise and Foolish Virgins* 1919–20 (Walker Art Gallery, Liverpool) was universally dismissed, specifically by one critic for the similarity of its figures to Burne-Jones, perhaps demonstrating the change in critical taste in the intervening period. Many of Shannon's pictures have technical similarities with Rossetti, and frequently also share their allusive content. A wealth of anecdotal material about him was supplied through Shannon's friendship with Charles Fairfax Murray, and in his youth he also met Ford Madox Brown on several occasions. In his 1926 guide *Hours in the Tate Gallery*, James Bolivar Manson judged that 'Rossetti's influence as a painter was not a good one, save, perhaps, in one or two isolated cases, but it is now practically worn out, and C.H. Shannon has the distinction of being, probably, the only painter of any repute, who is still influenced by him' (p.144).

Shannon's pictures enjoyed popularity on the Continent, particularly in Germany, where a number found their way into public collections. He was awarded a gold medal for his *Portrait of Sturge Moore* at the Munich International Exhibition in 1897.

RU

George Frederic Watts 1817–1904

134 The Sower of the Systems *c.*1902

Oil on canvas 65 × 53 (25⅝ × 20⅞)

Prov: Collection of the artist and remaining as part of the Watts Gallery

Exh: Tate Gallery 1954 (84); Paris 1972 (323); Manchester 1978 (34a); Munich 1979 (382); Washington 1997 (34)

Lit: Macmillan 1903, p.288; MS. Cat., I, p.134; Watts 1912, II, pp.105, 245, 302

Trustees of the Watts Gallery

134

The painting is the smaller preliminary version of a larger picture (122.6 × 91.4 cm; fig.46 on p.76) seen at the New Gallery in 1903. It is one of Watts's very latest works, conceived and executed in the new century. It is also one of his better-known subjects, often cited for its proto-abstract qualities. In fact, this seemingly abstract whirl of light and movement is yet another attempt by the artist to visualise his thoughts on the universe. Both pictures are much the same in composition but in the later, slightly more upright version, the forms take on greater definition, as befits a work destined for exhibition.

According to Mrs Watts the subject was 'a vision of a figure impelled rapidly forward, while stars, suns and planets fly from hands that scatter as seeds'. Another writer described the figure as having his head in the clouds, and indeed the absence of a readable face lends the work a real sense of enigma. Like *'The All-Pervading'* and *Chaos* (nos.125, 49), *The Sower of the Systems*, had a seemingly random inspiration in effects of light – 'the curiously refracted rays of light thrown up by a night-light upon the ceiling of his bedroom', presumably contemplated while he lay in bed drifting between the world of consciousness and the unconsciousness of sleep. One also feels, however, that these accounts of moments of pure inspiration belong to the mythology on Watts, allowing him to seem in touch with the forces of the universe in an unpremeditated way for his cosmic themes.

The figure itself embodies a generalised creator at work. On this matter Watts believed 'There is only one great mystery – the Creator. We can never return to the early ideas of Him as a kind white-bearded old man. If I were ever to make a symbol of the Deity, it would be as a great vesture into which everything that exists is woven' (Watts 1912, II, p.245).

One might perhaps consider this great cosmic robe as the garment enveloping Watts's Sower. It is certain that the picture does not depict a deity, but is a statement on the nature of the act of creation. The most significant art-historical precedent is Michelangelo's Sistine Ceiling with its depiction of God in *The Creation of Sun and Moon* and *The Creation of the Planets*, as well as the vague presence of God amid swirling drapery in *Dividing Light from Darkness* (Staley 1978, nos.34a–b). But Watts also claimed that in attempting to give form to his ideas he was like a child who had been asked to draw God and 'made a great number of circular scribbles' then 'stuck his pencil through the centre, making a great void'. In all these approaches and explanations Watts, like other Victorians, was trying to come to terms with a post-Darwinian world. In this he shared the concern of Elihu Vedder, whose image of *The Pleiades* from the *Rubáiyát of Omar Khayyám* (see no.87) shows a group of figures casting stars through the firmament in a similar swirl of light. Veddor's oil painting of this subject (1885; Metropolitan Museum of Art, New York) was exhibited in London in 1899.

In both versions of *The Sower of the Systems*, the figure takes on the role of a creative artist painting the void with light and filling it with energy. As the conception of an eighty-five year old artist, it is a remarkable achievement. In sending the larger version to exhibition in 1903, Watts reinforced his unique position in the art world – by this time, the twentieth-century art world. The concerns expressed in *The Sower of the Systems* fed into the new century, as did some of Watts's other late canvases such as *Progress* (Watts Gallery), grappling visually with issues which became even more immediate at the dawn of a new age.

BB

FERDINAND HODLER 1853–1918

135 **The Dream** 1897/1903

Pencil, ink, chalk, watercolour, bodycolour and oil on brown paper laid down on board
98.5 × 69.5 (38¾ × 27⅜)
Inscribed 'F. Hodler' b.r.

Prov: …; private collection, Switzerland; …; present owner

Exh: Vienna Secession 1904 (31); Munich 1911; Berkeley 1972–3 (81); Tokyo 1975 (28); Rotterdam 1975–6 (63); Zurich 1983 (66, repr. in col.); Cincinatti 1994 (20, repr. in col.); Montreal 1995 (160, pl.209)

Lit: Loosli, IV, 1919, no.2109; Hirsch 1982, no.20 (repr. in col.)

Private Collection

EXHIBITED IN LONDON ONLY

Hodler was born in Bern and trained in Thun under the landscape painter Ferdinand Sommer. He travelled and exhibited widely throughout Europe, and contributed to the Symbolist movement at its apogee in France and Germany. After early success in his homeland, his famous picture *Night* 1889–90 (Kunstmuseum, Bern) was banned by the mayor of Geneva. It was subsequently exhibited in Paris where it attracted the admiration of Puvis de Chavannes. Hodler showed at the inaugural Salon of the Rose+Croix and became a member. In 1903 he became friendly with Klimt and joined the Vienna Secession. He exhibited frequently in Germany, where until the First World War he enjoyed enormous admiration.

The design exhibited here appears to borrow elements from Rossetti's *Blessed Damozel* (fig.55 on p.186). The most striking similarity is the use of a recumbent youth in a plaque or predella. As in Rossetti's picture, he is dreaming of his beloved, who appears above him. As Rossetti had done, Hodler referred to his own life by using as his model Berthe Jacques, whom he was to marry the following year. However, *The Blessed Damozel* is primarily about death and separation, a theme absent from Hodler's *Dream*, although the dreaming man was copied from his picture *The Dead Youth* 1885 (Kunstmuseum, Bern). Hirsch has noted a similarity with both Rodin's *The Sculptor's Dream* 1900 (Kunsthalle, Bremen) and Munch's *Vision* 1892 (Munch Museum, Oslo). The main figure in *The Dream*, with her streaming red hair and introspective, contemplative mood, seems to have been influenced by Rossetti's female portraits, and as in so many of these works, flowers are used symbolically. She holds a rose, the emblem of love, although the flowers surrounding her appear to be poppies. These symbolise dreams, which fits the title, but they can also represent death. The thin, angular treatment of the figure is reminiscent of Burne-Jones, who seems to have interested Hodler (see no.136), although there is also a broad correspondence with Watts's *Hope* (no.76), which by 1897 was well known through its publication as a print. Hodler appears to have had a wide-ranging knowledge of contemporary European art. He was able to see examples of the work of Burne-Jones, Watts and other British artists at the 1889 Paris Universal Exhibition, where he himself was an exhibitor, and at subsequent international exhibitions throughout the Continent. He contributed to the first two Rose+Croix Salons and cannot have been unaware of Péladan's enthusiasm for the British 'Ideal' artists.

The woman in *The Dream* represents the perfection of the ideal, although she is also the muse of art, for in some preliminary studies she holds a paintbrush in her right hand (Zurich 1983, nos.67–8). Hodler intended the picture to be a companion to *Art*, also known as *Poetry* 1897 (Godfried Keller Foundation). This shows a woman in a white shift

135

seated on a mountain top, and apparently shares affinities of subject-matter with British pictures such as Leighton's *Spirit of the Summit* (no.121). Hirsch has noted the connection between the subject of *The Dream* and the Symbolist poetry of Hodler's close friend Louis Duchosal, who in *Livre de Thule* (1891) wrote in praise of the world of dreams. This connection is strengthened by the similarity of the main figure's pose to that found in Hodler's portrait of Duchosal's daughter Louise-Delphine 1885 (Kunsthaus, Zurich), who also holds a flower.

Hodler originally made *The Dream* as a design for a Zurich Kunstgesellschaft poster (see Zurich 1983, no.65, repr.). Here the plaque was occupied by text, but when the project fell through he adapted the design by adding the figure of the dreaming man. This was used on its own in Hodler's poster design for the 1904 Vienna Secession (see ibid., no.111, repr. in col.).

RU

FERDINAND HODLER 1853–1918

136 **Spring** 1901

Oil on canvas 99 × 129 (39 × 50¾)
Inscribed 'F. Hodler | 1901' b.r.

Exh: Vienna Secession 1901
Lit: Hirsch 1982, no.15, repr. in col.

Museum Folkwang Essen

EXHIBITED IN LONDON ONLY

Hodler's theme here is fertility, puberty and communion with nature. The young girl has a rhapsodic expression, indicating the ecstasy she feels at the awakening of spring and her own adolescent sexuality. She is placed in the fertile area of the picture, amid lush grass and blooming flowers, while her companion, modelled by Hodler's fourteen year old son Hector, sits on barren rock. His contrasting ambiguous facial expression – partly querulous, partly sad – combined with the curiously contorted pose of his

136

arm, bent back towards himself, create a mood of insecurity and tension. Hirsch (ibid.) has noted his spatial separation from the girl – only her toe touches him. Hodler may therefore be alluding to feelings in him of powerlessness in the face of fertility, and related to this by implication, the by now traditional Symbolist subject of fear of women and sex. The picture's subject might possibly have been suggested to Hodler by the play *Spring Awakening* by the German dramatist Frank Wedekind. Written in 1890, this dealt frankly with the awakening of youthful sexual desire, and its potentially disastrous consequences. In a celebrated act of censorship it was banned, and remained unperformed until 1906.

The use of a pose or expression to communicate raw emotion or more subtle psychological states had become a leitmotif of Symbolism, and Holder was a highly adept exponent. It was this aspect of Burne-Jones's pictures that many on the Continent found so stimulating, and Hodler was no exception. He was able to see his work in depth for the first time at the Exposition Universelle in Paris in 1889, and in 1897 he made sketches of Burne-Jones's *St George* series when it was exhibited at the Munich International Exhibition. Hodler's statuesque women clothed in pale-coloured drapery, and his use of flower imagery, owe a great deal to Burne-Jones, as do his friezes of hieratic figures. The floating angels in Hodler's *The Consecrated One* 1893–4 (Kunstmuseum, Bern, lent by Gottfried Keller Foundation) closely resemble those found in Burne-Jones's mosaic decorations for the American Episcopal Church of St Paul's in Rome. Bätschmann (Cincinatti 1994, pp.40–2) has noted the similarity of Hodler's *Eurhythmy* 1894–5 (Kunstmuseum, Bern) to the recently rediscovered canvas from Burne-Jones's *St George* series, *Moritura: Princess Sabra Draws the Lot* 1865–6 (Hanover College, Hanover, Indiana). The Swiss artist's *Sacred Hour II* is even more heavily indebted to Burne-Jones, in this case to *The Hours* 1882 (Sheffield Art Gallery). In *Eurhythmy* Bätschmann has also demonstrated the similarity to *The Body of Christ Borne to the Tomb* c.1799–1800 by William Blake (Tate Gallery).

RU

EDVARD MUNCH 1863–1944

137 **Madonna** 1895–1902

Coloured lithograph 60.5 × 44 (23¾ × 17⅜)
Inscribed 'Edv Munch' b.l.

Lit: Schiefler 1974, no.33; National Gallery 1992–3, no.26; Toronto 1997, no.17

Munch-Museet, Oslo

From early in his career Munch sought consciously to create 'an art that arrests and engages. An art created of one's innermost heart' (quoted National Gallery 1993–4, p.15). His subjects are the eternal traumas and fears of human existence, much influenced by his own experience and troubled subconscious. After initial training at the Royal School of Art and Design in Christiania, Munch visited Paris in 1885, and again for a longer period in 1889. In November 1892 a large group of his pictures was shown at the Berlin Artists' Association, but the exhibition was quickly closed down by its conservative members. This made Munch an instant celebrity, and particularly admired in Germany by those of advanced taste, and his exhibition toured to Copenhagen, Breslau, Dresden and Munich the following year. The Berlin closure was one of the key events leading to the founding of the Secession there in 1898.

Munch's *Madonna* is one of the subjects from his *Frieze of Life*, the cycle of works devoted to love, death and anxiety. 'No longer shall I paint interiors, and people reading, and women knitting', Munch stated, 'I shall paint living people, who breathe and feel and suffer and love – I shall paint a number of pictures of this kind. People will understand the sacredness of it' (quoted Lucie-Smith 1972, pp.186–7). Other works in the series include *The Scream* 1893 (National Gallery, Oslo), *Vampire* 1893 (Museum of Art, Gothenburg) and *The Sphinx* 1894 (Rasmus Meyer Collection, Bergen). Munch made three oil versions of the *Madonna* before embarking on his lithographic treatments of the subject.

It is a remarkable and troubling image, the provocative opposite of calm and chaste traditional religious pictures of the Blessed Virgin. This Madonna is a siren who oozes sexual allure but combines it with fatal menace. Crowned with a red halo, the colour of passion, she writhes in ecstasy. Munch's accentuation of the shadows around her closed eyes, cheek bones and nose, turn her face into a terrifying death's head that warns of the danger of sex. As so many Symbolists had done before him through stories such as that of Salome and John the Baptist or Oedipus and the Sphinx, Munch was making connections between sex and death, between orgasm and extinction. In this respect it is an interesting comparison with Rossetti's *Beata Beatrix* (no.44) which also treats some of these themes. Indeed, Munch's Madonna, with her wild and flowing hair, is the supreme *femme fatale*, the ultimate incarnation of the Rossetti temptress (see nos.2–6). However, the composition, tonality and subject matter appear to have also been influenced by Franz von Stuck's *Sin* 1893 (Neue Pinakothek, Munich) which Munch is likely to have seen in Germany. The border of spermatozoa derives from Munch's frame for the first oil version of the subject. It recalls the decorative dialogue between frame and subject which Rossetti established and which can also be seen in work by such artists as Frances Macdonald (no.98). Faxon has also noted connections between the two artists, comparing Munch's *The Kiss* 1897 (Munch Museum, Oslo) with Rossetti's *Paolo and Francesca da Rimini* 1855 (Tate Gallery), although the embracing couples in *The Blessed Damozel* (fig.22 on p.186) are perhaps a closer point of reference. Another work even closer in idiom and composition to Rossetti is Munch's lithograph *The Brooch* 1903 (repr. Toronto 1997, no.51), a portrait of the English violinist Eva Mudocci, whose long hair and far-away look directly imitate Rossetti's subjectless female portraits of the 1860s.

Munch described the *Madonna* as 'A pause when the world stops revolving. Your face encompasses the beauty of the whole earth. Your lips, as red as ripening fruit, gently part as if in pain. It is the smile of a corpse. Now the hand of death touches life. The chain is forged that links the thousand families that are dead to the thousand generations to come' (quoted in Toronto 1997, p.99). The image has often been thought to illustrate the perception of a woman by her lover at the moment of conception, when a new life is begun, but an event that Munch saw only as another link in a chain that ultimately led to death. The circle of sperm represents this cycle of creation, death and renewal. Their encircling of the Madonna is interrupted by the foetus huddling in the corner. It crosses its arms as if to protect itself, and has an expression of worry or fear. Its features are very similar to the central figure of *The Scream*, and like this it may be a personification of Munch himself, who did once question having to be born. The foetus may also owe something to Redon's bizarre creations in his series of prints of 1883, *Les Origines*, concerning the seeds of life. An almost contemporary preoccupation with the foetus is found in Beardsley's work, e.g. *Incipit Vita Nova* 1893 (Reade 1967, no.269).

RU

GUSTAV VIGELAND 1869–1943

138 **Horse of Hell** 1893

Bronze 19.5 × 43.5 (7⅝ × 17¼)
Prov: The artist; bequeathed by him to the City of Oslo
Exh: Paris 1981 (2, repr.)

Nasjonalgalleriet, Oslo

Vigeland, little known outside his native Norway, is one of the most impressive European sculptors of the generation following Rodin. He began to show work at the Norwegian Salon in 1889, initially under the influence of Thorwaldsen but quickly developing a forceful, often highly realistic style in which he tackled ambitious and dramatic subjects. In 1893 he won a bursary to study in Paris, where he absorbed a wide range of current influences. Among these Rodin was pre-eminent, and throughout his life Vigeland was much preoccupied with the assessment of Rodin's genius, though he never acknowledged any direct inspiration from his work. During his Parisian stay Vigeland probably attended the exhibitions of the Order of the Rose+Croix as well as the Salon.

His long career was extraordinarily productive, and he became a celebrity in Oslo where at the beginning of this century the extensive Frogner Park was given to him, with municipal and private funding, to design and fill with sculptures. His plans for this were ambitious, and constitute a vast survey of human life in all its variety (see no.139). He was also

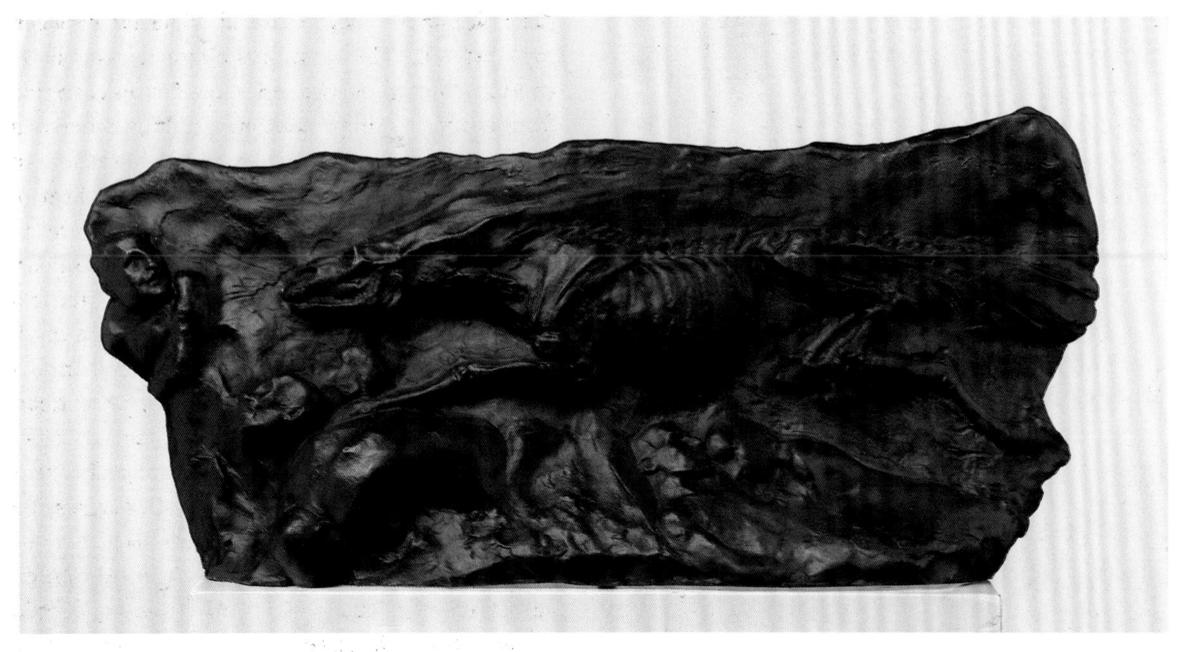

138

a portrait sculptor, completing powerful heads and full-length statues of Norwegian celebrities, including Grieg and Ibsen. Many of these are sited in public places in Oslo and other Norwegian cities. When he visited London in 1901 he showed a particular interest in Watts, 'the most vibrant artist in England – and further afield', Burne-Jones and Beardsley (see Stang 1955).

This small relief of the *Horse of Hell* is an early work but its imagery, dominated by a vision of Death, even perhaps of the Apocalypse, is in the spirit of the frieze that surrounds the Frogner Park fountain, begun more than a decade later. The subject-matter is derived from Nordic mythology, with perhaps a reminiscence of the death-ride in Gottfried August Bürger's famous poem 'Lenore'. Its allusive and dynamic handling is characteristic of the youthful Vigeland's energetic individuality. However, Tone Wikborg has pointed out that there are similarities between this subject and works shown at the Salon de la Rose+Croix in 1893 under titles such as *Le Vice Suprême* (see Paris 1981, p.9). The skeletal horse, half embedded in its parent metal, seems to allude to the contemporary interest in fossil evidence of evolution theory, which British palaeontologists had pioneered earlier in the century. The sculpture can be related to two much larger reliefs by Vigeland, with many figures, of *Hell* (National Gallery, Oslo) and *Resurrection* (Vigeland Museum, Oslo).

AW

Gustav Vigeland 1869–1943

139 Young Girl and Boy under a Tree
1905

Bronze 48 × 14 × 13 (18⅞ × 5½ × 5⅛)
Prov: The artist; bequeathed by him to the City of Oslo
Exh: Paris 1981 (55, repr.)

Vigeland-Museet, Oslo

The first project connected with the Vigeland park (see no.138), begun in 1906, was a colossal fountain consisting of a huge basin supported by six titanic figures and surrounded by a low wall bearing a frieze containing sixty reliefs on the subject of death. These occupied him for about a decade. The frieze is surmounted by a sequence of twenty life-size sculptures showing different human types entangled in the stems of umbrella-like trees, symbolic of Life. Other projects followed: in the 1920s he worked on a circular flight of steps, dotted with large groups of figures, culminating in a granite obelisk made up of writhing figures; he worked at the third main component of the park, a bridge with bronze figures, into the mid-1930s. Vigeland's style changed considerably over the decades, though his imagery remains consistent. The great fountain is the most striking of his Symbolist works. He was influenced in his grand conception by Rodin and by Michelangelo, who 'could not be further from the French', and in his view 'exploded the idea of the accepted human shape as he had no way of fitting into it himself' (see Stang 1955, pp.184, 186)

This is a small version of one of the twenty 'tree-groups' placed on the balustrade surrounding the

139

great fountain. They occupied Vigeland between 1906 and 1914. The form of the tree remains fairly constant throughout the series, the figures changing from group to group: some are children, others old men and women; infants play in the branches, an adolescent plunges downwards. The symbolism of the figure in the tree is complex, with resonances in Norse, Greek and many other mythologies. In particular a virginal woman is identified with a tree in a number of paradigmatic stories. The Ovidian myth of Phyllis and Demophoön, in which a young bride is deserted at the altar and turned into a tree, was treated by a number of British artists of the late nineteenth century, notably Burne-Jones; and an incident during Breuer's examination of Anna O. may also be borne in mind (see p.11), as may Paul Klee's famous etching of a *Virgin in a Tree* 1903. Vigeland himself later made woodcuts showing a woman standing in a delicately ramified tree looking out to sea (see Wikborg 1995).

In the 'tree-groups' for the great fountain, the tracery of the tree stems and the surreal interlacing of plant and human forms recalls medieval carving on capitals, misericords and elsewhere. Vigeland had made a study of gothic carving when he was commissioned to make sculptures for the interior and exterior of Trondheim cathedral, on which he worked between 1897 and 1902. In connection with this project he visited French and English cathedrals during a tour in 1900–1: starting in Paris he saw Chartres, Reims, Laon, Amiens, and, in England, Westminster, Salisbury, Wells, Gloucester, Ely, Lincoln, York and Beverley (Stang 1955). Because of this interest he was alive to the continuity in British art between gothic carving and stained glass and the medieval imagery of Rossetti and his followers, a subject he comments on in his letters (Stang 1955).

AW

Notes

Symbolism in Britain

1 Peter Gay, ed., *The Freud Reader*, 1995, pp.64–75.
2 See Richard Webster, *Why Freud Was Wrong*, 1995, chap.4.
3 Webster 1995 points out that Freud's hypothesis was in any case mistaken; in so far as it had validity the notion of an 'unknown' aspect of the mind has been familiar since ancient times. For a discussion of the relationship between certain aspects of Symbolism and late nineteenth-century views of hysteria see Rodolphe Rapetti, 'From Anguish to Ecstasy: Symbolism and the Study of Hysteria' in Montreal 1995, pp.224–34.
4 Sir James Frazer, *The Golden Bough*, abridged version (1922), paperback ed., 1993, p.712.
5 Michael Gibson, *Les Symbolistes*, 1984 (trans. as *The Symbolists* 1988).
6 Montreal 1995, p.18.
7 Jean Moréas was the *nom de plume* of Iannis Papadiamantopoulos.
8 Clair, in Montreal 1995, p.18 refers to the question whether Symbolism was 'a decadent movement or a modern one'; as he says, this is a gratuitous problem.
9 Ibid.
10 Though dated a year earlier. See Sturgis 1995, pp.277–8, and for Symons's connections with France, chap.4.
11 Arthur Symons, *The Symbolist Movement in Literature*, 1899 [sic]. See Sturgis 1995, pp.277–8.
12 G.M. Trevelyan, *The Poetry and Philosophy of George Meredith*, 1906, p.2; on p.65 Trevelyan speaks of Meredith as 'the poet of common sense, the inspired prophet of sanity'.
13 Trevelyan 1906, p.163.
14 J.C. Heywood, *Salome: A Dramatic Poem*, New York 1867; new ed., London 1887. Another play by Heywood, *Herodias*, is listed in the British Library catalogue with the same publication dates. Compare O.J. Rejlander's photographs illustrating the Salome story of the late 1850s.
15 The novel was condemned for its obscenity and several passages were purged from the second edition. Lewis was nineteen when he wrote it.
16 Charles Baudelaire, *The Painter of Modern Life and Other Essays*, trans. and ed. Jonathan Mayne, 1964, p.78.
17 Alison Smith, *The Victorian Nude: Sexuality, Morality and Art*, 1996, esp. chap.4.
18 George Du Maurier, *Trilby*, 1895, p.95. The novel later reveals, consciously or unconsciously, the social hypocrisy which complicated these views.
19 *Alice's Adventures in Wonderland* appeared in 1865, *Through the Looking-glass* in 1871. Both books might be assimilated into the Symbolist canon on the basis of William Empson's Freudian interpretation of *Alice in Wonderland*. See Empson, 'Alice: the Child as Swain' in *Some Versions of Pastoral: a Study of the Pastoral Form in Literature*, 1966. The looking-glass is an obviously Symbolist image.
20 See Lionel Lambourne, *The Aesthetic Movement*, 1996, chap.6.
21 The phrase had an earlier history; Cousin gave it currency in France. See Sturgis 1995, pp.15–16.
22 Walter Pater, 'The School of Giorgione' in *The Renaissance*, 1877, Everyman ed., 1912, p.140.
23 Formally, the Pre-Raphaelite Brotherhood had ceased to exist as early as 1853. Ruskin, its greatest champion, was appalled by Millais's desertion of the principles of the movement in his *A Dream of the Past; Sir Isumbras at the Ford*, which was shown at the Royal Academy in 1857. See Mary Bennett, *Millais*, RA 1967, pp.42–3.
24 A relevant example is to hand in the Paragon Book Service 1997 Calendar, entitled *Pre-Raphaelites*, which includes reproductions of works by Watts (1886), Poynter (1890), Moore (1892), Waterhouse (1900) and Godward (1918). None of these artists was ever an exponent of Pre-Raphaelite style, subject-matter or technique.
25 It has been argued that despite the very evident differences between Pre-Raphaelitism and French Realism the movements were parallel in important respects. See Andrea Rose, Preface to *The Germ: The Literary Magazine of the Pre-Raphaelites*, Oxford 1979, p.xv. Rose points out that Louis-Emile Duranty's magazine *Le Réalisme*, which appeared in 1856–7, 'closely echoes the concerns of the Pre-Raphaelite Brotherhood' (p.xvii). See also Annie Dubernard Laurent, 'Le Pré-Raphaélisme en Angleterre; Les Arts et les Lettres en France; Essai d'Etude Comparative', doctoral thesis submitted at the University of Paris-Sorbonne, 1996.
26 Sir E.T. Cook and A. Wedderburn, eds., *The Works of John Ruskin*, 39 vols., 1903–1912, III, p.624.
27 Rossetti Angeli 1949, p.76. The precise definition of Pre-Raphaelitism and the relationship between each of the founding artists and the movement were, and perhaps remain, subject to debate; but the essential distinction between Rossetti's vision and that of his colleagues is evident from their respective work. Preoccupied as they were with the unflinching depiction of modern life, Hunt and Millais inevitably defined their aims differently from Rossetti, who, according to Angeli (p.72), in Hunt's eyes produced only one 'genuine Pre-Raphaelite expression' – *Found* – and that 'remained for ever in limbo', i.e. unfinished. Curiously, Jullian (1973, p.12) considers Hunt the 'strangest Pre-Raphaelite, the most Symbolist down to the minutest detail'. This judgement illustrates the difficulty of arriving at agreement as to what Symbolism is, and how it manifests itself in painting.
28 One that is frequently cited as an example is *Autumn Leaves* of 1855–6; see Christopher Newall's essay below, p.36, fig.18.
29 Surtees 1971, I, p.69, no.114.
30 For Rossetti's interest in German art see William Vaughan, *German Romanticism and English Art*, 1979, pp.150–1.
31 Rossetti also painted two pictures on the same theme; see no.71.
32 Frazer 1993, chap.XLIV.
33 Rossetti Angeli 1949, p.125.
34 In the mid-1850s Edward Moxon commissioned illustrations from Rossetti, Millais and others for a new edition of Tennyson's poem, published 1857, a book that was to have a profound effect on, among others, Maeterlinck.
35 See Delevoy et al. 1987, p.447, no.281.
36 Du Maurier 1895, p.24. Two particularly famous examples are *Elaine* by the American artist Toby Edward Rosenthal (1874; Art Institute of Chicago), painted in Munich and inspired by Tennyson's 'Idylls of the King', and *The Lady of Shalott* by John William Waterhouse (1888, Tate Gallery).
37 See Reynolds 1995, pp.111, 119, and pl.XIII. Although the details of Richmond's picture are different from those of the poem – the dead person is 'an artist', male rather than female, and the watchers' wings are red rather than white – the central idea of three figures guarding a recently dead person is the same in both.
38 See Rossetti 1895, I, p.102: 'Confronted with Browning, all else seemed pale and in neutral tint.' Rossetti considered Browning's 'knowledge of early Italian art beyond that of anyone I ever met – encyclopaedically beyond that of Ruskin himself'. See Roy E. Gridley, *The Brownings and France*, 1982, p.170.
39 See Gridley 1982, p.25 and chap.5.
40 Algernon Charles Swinburne, 'Erotion', lines 1–4.
41 Swinburne, 'Notes on Designs of the Old Masters at Florence', *Fortnightly Review*, July 1868 (repr. *Essays and Studies*, 1875). Quoted in Clyde K. Hyder, ed., *Swinburne as Critic*, 1972, p.129.
42 Pater 1912, p.130 'Leonardo da Vinci'.
43 Swinburne, 'Notes on Some Pictures of 1868' in *Essays and Studies*, 1875; quoted in Hyder 1972, p.132.
44 For examples of Degas's use of this subject see *Degas: After Impressionism*, exh. cat., National Gallery 1996.
45 Hyder 1972, p.133.
46 Rossetti was one of a small group of people of the mid-century who appreciated Blake; he owned one of Blake's books, and assisted William Gilchrist in the compilation of his *Life of Blake*. His enthusiasm fired Swinburne's. In 1910 Yeats produced an edition of the *Poetical Works of William Blake*, for which he wrote a long Introduction.
47 Hyder 1972, p.133.
48 William Blake, *Songs of Experience*, 1794; Geoffrey Keynes, ed., *Blake Complete Writings*, paperback ed., 1971, p.175.
49 Though des Esseintes was, as is well known, based on another real-life personality, the Count Robert de Montesquiou, later also the model for the Baron de Charlus in Proust's *A la Recherche du Temps Perdu*.
50 Among Péladan's numerous other writings are *Comment on devient Mage* and a tragedy entitled *Oedipe et le Sphinxe*.
51 Francine-Claire Legrand, *Symbolism in Belgium*, trans. Alastair Kennedy, 1972, p.42.

52 It is usefully abridged in Lucie-Smith 1972, pp.111–12.
53 Ontario 1975, pp.3, 4.
54 Quoted in Lucie-Smith 1972, p.82.
55 Ibid., p.84.
56 See Dubernard Laurent 1996.
57 See Watts 1912, II, p.49.
58 Of Watts and Rhodes it has been said 'there existed between them a wonderful kinship of the spirit' (J.G. McDonald, *Rhodes: A Life*, 1927, p.341).
59 Letter from Lady Brownlow, 1880. See Watts 1912, III, p.192.
60 Watts 1912, I, p.219.
61 Watts 1912, II, p.101.
62 See David Stewart, 'Theosophy and Abstraction in the Victorian era: The Paintings of G.F. Watts', *Apollo*, vol.139, Nov. 1993, p.300.
63 Trevelyan 1906, p.85.
64 Watts 1912, II, pp.89–90.
65 Watts 1912, III, p.236.
66 A particularly interesting example is Thayer's *Stevenson Memorial* 1903 (National Museum of American Art, Washington). This is a homage to R.L. Stevenson, whose writings exerted a wide influence at the end of the century and who has been called a Symbolist if only on account of his imaginative exploration of psychosis in *The Strange Case of Dr Jekyll and Mr Hyde* (1886). I am grateful to Richard N. Murray of the National Museum of American Art for an illuminating discussion of Thayer's processes and other Symbolist questions. Compare also the 'unfocused' technique of the Symbolist photographer F. Holland Day.
67 See RA 1986, p.127.
68 Watts 1912, II, p.134. See Robert Upstone's essay below.
69 Watts 1912, II, p.196.
70 Watts 1912, II, p.180.
71 Watts 1912, II, p.257.
72 See D. Stewart 1993, pp.298–302. Watts's comment refers to the subject-matter of *Love and Death*; see New York 1884. The entries were compiled by Mrs Russell Barrington in close collaboration with Watts; see also Barrington 1905, p.130. I am grateful to Barbara Bryant for drawing my attention to this reference.
73 Jean Delville, *The New Mission of Art: A Study of Idealism in Art*, trans. Francis Colmer, 1910, 'The Prayer of a Magician', trans. Clifford Bax. Delville stresses Idea as Burne-Jones does: 'It is from Idea, by way of Sentiment and Sensation, that a work of art arises in the artist's spirit' (Introductory Note by Edouard Schuré, p.xxix).
74 Delville 1910, p.46.
75 Emile Zola, *L'Oeuvre*, trans. Thomas Walton as *The Masterpiece*, paperback ed., 1993, p.229.
76 See Wilfred Blunt, *England's Michelangelo*, 1975, p.230. The specific parallel was between Cosima Wagner and Mary Watts as widows devoted to preserving the memory of their husbands and their work, but the fact that such a comparison could be made in Germany is an indication of Watts's standing in Europe.
77 Watts 1912, II, p.55; see also the *Journals* of Mary Watts, 17 Feb. 1892.
78 For instance, according to Mary Watts, Carlyle 'had not the vaguest sense of the proportionate value of great art in the history of civilisation'. Watts 1912, I, p.105. The portrait (1868) is in the Victoria and Albert Museum, Forster Bequest.
79 See Carlyle, *Past and Present*, 1843, Bk III, chap.vi: 'As if, in truth, there were no God of Labour; as if godlike Labour and brutal Mammonism were convertible terms. A serious, most earnest Mammonism grown Midas-eared; an unserious Dilettantism, earnest about nothing, grinning with inarticulate incredulous incredible jargon about all things, as the *enchanted* Dilettanti do by the Dead Sea!' (Everyman edition, 1912, p.163).
80 Carlyle 1843, Pt I, ii, p.7. Compare a much later use of the image, in Nietzsche's *Also Sprach Zarathustra* (1883–5), where the Wanderer describes himself as 'ensphinxed' (*umsphinxt*) by 'little winged bugs – / Also by still smaller, / More foolish, more sinful / Wishes and notions' (Pt IV, 'Among Daughters of the Wilderness', trans. Walter Kaufmann).
81 Trevelyan 1906, p.84.
82 *Sartor Resartus*, Temple Classics ed., 1908, p.132.
83 Ibid., p.150.
84 Ibid., p.224.
85 See David Sweetman, *Paul Gauguin: A Complete Life*, 1995, p.221. The books are accompanied by a still life with lamp and apples: 'The lamp and the Carlyle represent enlightenment or wise knowledge, while the apples and the Milton convey the idea of temptation and the Fall, and thus bad or foolish knowledge.' Sweetman also discusses Carlyle's popularity with the Symbolists, p.220; and see p.432.
86 *Sartor Resartus*, 1908, p.54. Compare Gauguin's famous canvas *D'Où venons-nous? Que sommes-nous? Où allons-nous?* (fig.14).
87 Howe 1982, p.14. Khnopff's many and strong connections with British artists are thoroughly explored in this book.
88 *Sartor Resartus*, 1908, pp.225–6.
89 Watts 1912, II, p.265.
90 Ibid., p.74. Howe 1982 cites many other relevant passages.
91 G.B.-J. 1904, II, p.34.
92 G.B.-J. 1904, II, p.135.
93 *Laus Veneris* 1873–8 (Laing Art Gallery, Newcastle). See Tate Gallery 1984, pp.229–31, no.150. The watercolour is in a private collection.
94 Soria et al. 1979, p.128.
95 The British artists in the Stockholm exhibition were: Brangwyn, Rivière, Clausen, Crane, H.W.B. Davis, Stanhope Forbes, Lavery, Leighton, J.D. Linton, Orchardson, James Paterson, J.J. Shannon, Stott of Oldham, J.M. Swan and J.W. Waterhouse. Burne-Jones was represented by his *Fall of Lucifer* and Watts by eight works: *Paolo and Francesca*, *The Repentance of Eve*, *'She Shall Be Called Woman'*, *Time, Death and Judgement*, and four portraits including a self-portrait and one of Burne-Jones. The *Fall of Lucifer* was priced at £2,000; none of Watts's pictures was for sale.
96 See Stang 1955, p.165.
97 As an architect, Mackintosh was heavily indebted to the ideas of functional design promulgated by William Morris and the Arts and Crafts movement, a further strand in late nineteenth-century aesthetics which also goes back to Rossetti, but which, unfortunately, there is no room to discuss here. For recent assessments of both see *William Morris*, exh. cat., Victoria and Albert Museum 1996, and Glasgow 1996.
98 See Oskar Bätschmann, 'Ferdinand Hodler the Painter' in *Views and Visions: Ferdinand Hodler*, 1984, esp. pp.38–43. Bätschmann also notices the influence of Blake on Hodler.
99 Roland Penrose, *Picasso: His Life and Work*, 1958, 3rd ed. 1981, p.37.
100 Shaw, who was born in 1856, could not entirely escape the atmosphere of the Symbolist period in which his career had begun. In the late 1880s he was a music critic with a particular interest in Wagner. His *Caesar and Cleopatra* of 1898 (one of the 'Three Plays for Puritans') has many Symbolist features, with much use of the Sphinx and the 'Harp of Memnon', as well as focusing on a Symbolist icon, Cleopatra. Its Prologue can be read as a Shavian (and 'Puritan') derivation from Wilde's *Salomé*. As late as 1922, in his long 'metabiological pentateuch' *Back to Methuselah*, and especially in its first part, set in the Garden of Eden, he continued to rework Symbolist themes.

Themes of Love and Death in Aesthetic Painting of the 1860s

The author is very grateful to Elizabeth Prettejohn and Andrew Wilton, both of whom have read this essay and have made most useful suggestions.

1 William Butler Yeats, 'Symbolism in Painting', from *Ideas of Good and Evil*, 1903, republished as *Essays*, 1924, pp.180–7, p.183.
2 Virginia Surtees (ed.), *Sublime and Instructive: Letters from John Ruskin to Louisa, Marchioness of Waterford, Anna Blunden and Ellen Heaton*, 1972, p.173.
3 By Effie Millais, who modelled for the painting, in her MS journal (private collection); quoted Malcolm Warner, in Tate Gallery 1984, p.141.
4 Quoted Tate Gallery 1984, p.139.
5 Quoted John Dixon Hunt, *The Pre-Raphaelite Imagination 1848–1900*, 1968, p.119. The original text comes in an account of Sydney Dobell's poem 'England in Time of War' in a review 'Recent Poems and Plays', *Oxford and Cambridge Magazine*, Dec. 1856, p.724.
6 See Warner and Hough 1983, p.163.
7 Ibid., p.196.
8 See Paul Goldman, *Victorian Illustration*, Aldershot 1996, p.2.
9 Doughty and Wahl 1965–8, I, p.252.
10 *Athenaeum*, 1859, p.618.
11 Cecil Y. Lang (ed.), *The Swinburne Letters*, 6 vols., New Haven 1959, I, p.27.
12 This quotation comes from a letter to Thomas Combe of May 1860. The original is in the Bodleian Library, and is quoted in Cherry 1980, pp.237–44.
13 Rossetti's letter, addressed to William Graham and dated 11 March 1873, is given in full in Frances Horner, *Time Remembered*, 1933, p.25.
14 Rossetti and Swinburne 1868, p.46.
15 Ibid.
16 Ibid., p.47.
17 *Athenaeum*, 1862, p.859.
18 Quoted Young et al. 1980, Text, p.18.
19 Quoted Denys Sutton, *Nocturne: The Art of James McNeill Whistler*, 1963, p.37.
20 Ibid. The original letter, dated May 1863, is in the collection of the University of Glasgow.
21 Tate Gallery 1994, p.78.
22 The original frame with its attached verses is lost, but is recorded in a plate in the revised fifth edi-

tion of Pennell and Pennell 1908, revised ed. 1911, opp. p.124. The photograph (fig.22) from which this plate was made, possibly a unique print and with an inscription from Whistler to Swinburne, was included in Sotheby's sale 'English Literature and History', 11 July 1996, lot 236.

23 Lang 1959, I, p.120.
24 A.C. Swinburne, 'Simeon Solomon: Notes on his "Vision of Love" and Other Studies', *The Dark Blue*, 1871, p.572.
25 Surtees 1980, p.35
26 G.B.-J. 1904, I, p.207.
27 A.C. Swinburne, *Notes on Poems and Reviews*, 1866, p.23.
28 Philippe Burty, 'Exposition de la Royal Academy', *Gazette des Beaux-Arts*, Paris 1869, pp.45–61, p.54: 'une peinture de la plus haute valeur: pour l'impression, qui est aussi troublante et plus saine que celle de certaines pièces des *Fleurs du Mal*, de Baudelaire; pour le rendu, qui est magistral. C'est là qu'il faut juger cet artiste si bien doué.'
29 *Art Journal*, 1869, p.173.
30 See Tate Gallery 1984, pp.303–4.
31 The quotation comes from Ruskin's *Munera Pulveris, Essays on Political Economy*, pub. 1862–3. See E.T. Cook and Alexander Wedderburn (eds.), *The Works of John Ruskin*, 39 vols., 1903–12, XVII, p.213.
32 Crane 1907, p.84.
33 It seems that this description of the Dudley clique which formed around Robert Bateman was originated by Emily Pattison in her notice of the 1869 Dudley Gallery watercolour exhibition, *Westminster Review*, vol.91, April 1869, p.594. It has been much repeated (for example in Crane 1907, p.98).
34 *Art Journal*, 1870, p.87.
35 *Art Journal*, 1869, p.81.
36 Ibid.
37 *Art Journal*, 1872, p.309.
38 Swinburne's article (cited in n.24), appeared in the periodical *Dark Blue*, July 1871, pp.568–77, but was never reprinted, probably because Swinburne sought to distance himself from the disgraced painter, but perhaps also because he had made so obvious his own pleasure in the sado-masochistic themes of Solomon's art. The pattern of Solomon's life after his conviction has been described by Gayle Seymour, 'The Trial and its Aftermath', in Geffrye Museum 1985.
39 Swinburne 1871, p.572.
40 Ibid., p.575.
41 Ibid.
42 Lang 1959, II, pp.158–9.
43 Rossetti and Swinburne 1868, pp.31–2.
44 Ibid., p.32.
45 Ibid., p.44.
46 Burty 1869, pp.45–61, 52: 'le même style bizarrement archaïque, la même accumulation singulière de détails.'
47 *Art Journal*, 1869, p.164.
48 *Spectator*, 12 June 1869, p.706.
49 See Alison Smith, *The Victorian Nude: Sexuality, Morality and Art*, Manchester 1996, pp.129–31.
50 Burty 1869, pp.45–61, p.56: 'le paysagiste qui m'émeut le plus. Il met dans ses sites ce quelque chose de vibrant et de passionné … Il a le sens des colorations romantiques, des lumières inondant les vallées et s'éteignant sous les feuillées comme les ondes sonores d'une chanson de pâtre.'
51 *Art Journal*, 1869, p.199.
52 *Saturday Review*, 1869, p.743.
53 See Warner and Hough 1983, II, p.30.
53 Ibid., p.276, n.32.
55 *Contemporary Review*, Oct. 1871, pp.234–50.
56 See Reynolds 1985, pp.87–8; the painting *Bowl Players* is illustrated p.87.
57 T. Early Welby, *The Victorian Romantics 1850–70: The Early Work of Dante Gabriel Rossetti, William Morris, Burne-Jones, Swinburne, Simeon Solomon and their Associates*, 1929, p.96.

Symbolism – A French Monopoly?

1 Edmond Wilson, *Axel's Castle*, New York 1931, p.32.
2 Published 1900.
3 Arthur Symons, *The Symbolist Movement in Literature*, 2nd ed. 1906, p.5.
4 Symons 1906, p.3.
5 For Arthur Symons and his youthful engagement with French literature, see Roger Lhombreaud, *Arthur Symons: A Critical Biography*, 1963. Sturgis 1995 also covers the subject, notably in Pts I and II.
6 See for example, Jean Clair, 'Lost Paradise', in Montreal 1995, pp.17–22.
7 Jean Moréas, 'Un manifeste littéraire: Le Symbolisme', *Figaro Littéraire*, 18 Sept. 1886.
8 'Une nouvelle manifestation d'art était donc attendue, nécessaire, inévitable.' ('A new manifestation of art was, then, awaited, necessary, inevitable.')
9 For the full text of Jean Moréas's article, see Guy Michaud, *Message Poétique du Symbolisme*, Paris 1947, pp.723–6.
10 *Le Temps*, 26 Sept. 1886, quoted Michaud 1947, p.341.
11 Founded by three ardent Wagnerites, Houston Stewart Chamberlain, Téodor de Wyzéwa and Edouard Dujardin during the 1884 Bayreuth Festival, *La Revue Wagnérienne* was issued on 8 Feb. 1885. It lasted, ultimately somewhat intermittently, until 1888. It had as its programme the consideration of all aspects of Richard Wagner's musical and literary work, as well as relating all manifestations of the arts to the composer's programme: 'The purpose [of *La Revue Wagnérienne*] was not, as most people thought, merely to propagate the works of Wagner, but to go more deeply into them and to publicise their more profound significance. Subtleties apart, what we wanted, Chamberlain and I was to spread abroad a discovery: Wagner a great musician? That seemed to be self-evident; but Wagner a great poet, Wagner a great thinker; and above all Wagner the creator of a new form of art.' Edouard Dujardin, *La Revue Musicale*, Oct. 1923, p.144. The review attracted a number of distinguished contemporary writers, including Catulle Mendès, Villiers de l'Isle Adam, J.-K. Huysmans, Emile Hennequin, Stéphane Mallarmé, Paul Verlaine, Stuart Merrill and Gustave Kahn. It also published an article entitled 'La Mort de Richard Wagner' by Charles Swinburne (April 1886). Although not committed to an extensive programme of support for the visual arts, it did commission lithographs on Wagnerian subjects from Jacques-Emile Blanche and Odilon Redon, and advertised the publication of the latter's albums of lithographs, as also those of Fantin-Latour.
12 'd'impollues vocables, la période qui s'arcboute alternant avec la période aux défaillances ondulées, les pléonasmes significatifs, les mystérieuses ellipses, l'anacoluthe en suspens, tout trop hardi et multiforme' (discourteous words, the cycle coming up alternating with the cycle collapsing in a gentle flow, the magnificent pleonasms, the mysterious ellipses, the suspended anacoluthon, everything too bold and multiform), quoted Michaud 1947, p.725.
13 For more information about Edouard Dujardin's associaton with Emile Bernard, Louis Anquetin, etc., see MaryAnne Stevens, 'Introduction: Emile Bernard and his Artistic and Literary Context', p.17, in *Emile Bernard 1868–1941: A Pioneer of Modern Art*, Mannheim and Amsterdam 1990. For elaboration of Emile Bernard's espousal of Symbolism, see Stevens 1990, pp.13–17, and Stevens, 'Bernard as Critic', ibid., pp.70–2. For the fullest exposition of Bernard's views on Symbolism see 'Le Symbolisme picturale: 1886–1936', *Mercure de France*, 15 June 1936, pp.43–65.
14 *La Revue Indépendante*, 1888.
15 A true Wagnerian, de Wyzéwa, in his article, 'La Peinture Wagnérienne et le Salon de 1886', published in May 1886, called for painting to adopt the attributes of music; it should allow form to dominate content, since this would free it from the expression of sentiment engendered through description and permit it to convey depth of emotion commensurate to the revelation of the Idea. He therefore argued for a separation of colour and line from subject-matter: 'colours and lines, through habit, have acquired an emotional value for souls which is independent of the object which line and colour actually describe … Today, these colours and these lines can serve two different ends; one appeals to the senses and is descriptive since it recreates the exact image of the object; the other appeals to the emotions and is musical, since it neglects the service of the objects which these colours and lines represent, using them only as signs of emotions, uniting them in such a way that they produce in us a total impression, comparable to that of a symphony, through their total independence from the object.'
16 Paul Gauguin, *Letters*, p.20.
17 Gustave Kahn, 'Réponse des Symbolistes', *L'Evénement*, 28 Sept. 1886.
18 See for example Emile Bernard's avoidance of a precise definition of Beauty in 'Les Primitifs et la Renaissance', *Gazette des Beaux-Arts*, Nov. 1894.
19 Stuart Merrill, 'Chroniques', *L'Ermitage*, Aug. 1893, p.107.
20 Stéphane Mallarmé, in J. Huret, *Enquête sur l'Evolution Littéraire*, Paris 1981, p.60.
21 For detailed information on these central aspects of Redon's work, see Chicago 1994.
22 Albert Aurier, 'Les Peintres symbolistes', *La Revue Encyclopédique*, April 1892, reprinted in Albert Aurier, *Oeuvres posthumes*, Paris 1893, pp.293–309.
23 J.-K. Huysmans, *Certains*, Paris 1889.
24 Paul Claudel, *Mémoires Improvisées*, Paris 1954, p.57.
25 Various editions of French translations of Schopenhauer appeared from 1876; four were published during the 1880s. In his 'Promenades littéraires – 4ème série', published by the *Mercure de France* in 1912, Rémy de Gourmont summarised the impact that Schopenhauer had had on the entire generation of the 1880s: 'To be sure, our philosophical education, for many, had already been undertaken by the Schopenhauer of M. Bourdeau and that of M. Ribot. We had dis-

covered, and with what delirium, all at once that the world was bad and that it only existed as a relative rather than as an absolute object. "The universe is my representation", that formulation had penetrated all our minds.'

26 J.-K. Huysmans, *A Rebours*.
27 Ibid.
28 Charles Morice, *La Littérature de toute à l'heure*, Paris 1889.
29 Emile Verhaeren, *Impressions III*, ed. Mercure de France, Paris, pp.113–15, quoted in Michaud 1947, pp.753–4.
30 Téodor de Wyzéwa, 'Le Salon de 1886', *La Revue Wagnérienne*, 1886.
31 Quoted in Maurice Pottecher, *Le Théâtre du Peuple*, Paris 1899, p.152.
32 John Conlon, *Walter Pater and the French Tradition*, London and Toronto 1982, p.136.
33 Walter Pater, *The Renaissance*, 1873, p.236.
34 Lee McKay Johnson, *The Metaphor of Painting: Essays on Baudelaire, Ruskin, Proust and Pater*, Ann Arbor, 1980, p.200.
35 Ibid.
36 Arthur Symons, *Studies in Seven Arts*, 1910, p.43.
37 Symons 1910, pp.43–4.
38 Ibid., p.61.
39 Emile Verhaeren, 'Exposition des XX', *La Jeune Belgique*, 15 Feb. 1884, p.195.
40 Letter from Burne-Jones to Octave Maus, dated 'West Kensington, 13 November 1888', Archives de l'Art Contemporain en Belgique, Musées Royaux des Beaux-Arts de Belgique, Brussels.
41 Watts was considered together with Meunier and Mellery, to be a 'true and pure' artist, still 'preoccupied with a great ideal in art'. See Kalophile, 'Chronique artistique, Exposition de la Libre Esthetique', *La Jeune Belgique*, vol.14, April 1895.
42 F.K. [Fernand Khnopff], 'Studio-Talk', *Studio*, no.13, 15 April 1896, p.183.
43 Chesneau 1891.
44 Ibid., p.237.
45 'Beaux-Arts: L'Art à l'étranger en 1892–1893: l'Angleterre', p.436.
46 'Beaux-Arts: Salon du Champ de Mars', *Supplément des Essais d'Art Libre*, June–July 1893, p.44.
47 pp.1138–9.
48 'M', '7ème Exposition annuelle des XX', *Le Journal de Charleroi*, 30 Jan. 1890.
49 Khnopff showed *Un Modèle* 1883 (now lost) in the exhibition entitled *Belgian Artists*, no.72.
50 Khnopff exhibited in London in 1890 twice at the Hanover Gallery (*Summer Exhibition; Fernand Khnopff*) and at the Grosvenor Gallery (*Society of British Pastellists*); in 1891 at the New Gallery (*Summer Exhibition*); in 1892 at the Royal Institution (*Society of Portrait Painters*) and twice at the New Gallery (*Summer Exhibition, Autumn Exhibition*); in 1893 at the New Gallery (*Summer Exhibition*) and twice at the Grafton Galleries (*British and Foreign Artists of the Present Day; Society of Portrait Painters*); in 1894 twice at the New Gallery (*Summer Exhibition; 4th Exhibition of the Society of Portrait Painters*); in 1895 twice at the New Gallery (*Summer Exhibition; Society of Portrait Painters*); in 1896–8 and 1900 at the New Gallery (*Summer Exhibition*); in 1901 at the *Society of Sculptors, Painters and Gravers*; in 1902 at the New Gallery (*Summer Exhibition*); and in 1906 at the New Gallery (*Society of Sculptors, Painters and Gravers*) and the Art Gallery of the Corporation of London (*Flemish and Modern Belgian Painters*). He exhibited again in Liverpool in 1892, 1896 and 1897 at the *Autumn Exhibition*, Walker Art Gallery.
51 For fuller detail of the artists invited to exhibit with La Libre Esthétique from 1896 to its final exhibition held in 1913, see *Les XX – La Libre Esthetique: Cent ans après*, exh. cat., Musées Royaux des Beaux-Arts de Belgique, Brussels 1993.
52 A. Fosset (ed.), *Fernand Knopff*, exh. cat., Hanover Gallery 1890, no.15 (*d'Après Joséphin Péladan: Le Vice suprême* 1885); no.21 (*Avec Joséphin Péladan, Istar* 1888 (frontispiece for the book of the same title, Paris 1888)).
53 Exh. cat., no.375. This work had already been reproduced in the Berlin avant-garde review, *Pan*, in 1895.
54 Conlon argues that Pater's interpretation of 'art for art's sake' was individual. Rather than providing the rationale for art to abdicate all social and moral responsibilies, which found expression in the daring, effete forms of decadence, Pater used Gautier's programme to formulate a salvific role for art. See Conlon 1982, p.137.
55 Symons 1906, p.8.
56 Quoted in Sturgis 1995, p.8.
57 This appreciation of the Symbolist literature as 'decadent' may have been informed by Havelock Ellis's familiarity with Paul Bourget's theory of decadence, outlined in his *Essais de Psychologie Contemporaine*, published in 1881 (new ed. 1885). Ellis published 'A Note on Paul Bourget' in *The Pioneer*, in the autumn of 1889, shortly before the departure of Symons and Ellis to Paris. See Sturgis 1995, p.72.
58 For a detailed study of Decadence in French literature, see A.E. Carter, *The Idea of Decadence in French Literature, 1830–1900*, Toronto 1958. For a useful attempt to distinguish between Symbolism and Decadence, see also John Milner, *Symbolists and Decadents*, 1971.
59 George Moore, *Confessions of a Young Man*, 1928, p.54.
60 Ibid., p.66.
61 Ibid., p.62.
62 Equally, it is arguable that Huysmans's next novel, *Là-Bas*, published in 1891, was not primarily a final fling for Decadence through its exploration of satanism and the occult, but rather a programmatic search for a new form of Symbolism which could embrace both the spiritual and the physical realities of human existence. The solution, according to the novel's hero, Durtal, lay in 'spiritual naturalism'. For an English translation of the relevant passage, see *Down There*, 1974, pp.9–10. This critical assessment of *Là-Bas* was also put forward by Arthur Symons in *The Symbolist Movement in Literature*, 1906, p.137. Symons develops the implications of such an assessment by declaring that it was 'only with *En Route* (1892) that Huysmans can be said to have discovered the direction in which he had really been travelling from the beginning' (ibid., p.136).
63 Alphonse Germain succinctly summarised the role of decoration as a means of escaping from the contemporary world: see *L'Ermitage*, 1893.
64 Schopenhauer, French trans., 1880, p.41. The first full edition of Schopenhauer's philosophy had appeared in French in 1876.
65 J.-K. Huysmans, *Against Nature*, 1959, p.219.
66 'This is like the great peel of Easter Bells which repressed the moans of grief, the terrible Whitsuntide of torn-out tongues and of charred outpourings of Justice, the lugubrious All Saints' Day of witches and scorpions. And all this depicted in a holocaust of crushed colours emerging for eternity ... [The artist] selects the most appropriate mode of extermination by torture for all the passive Christians, for all the satisfied people, for all the sowers of bitterness and the growers of ignominy.'
67 Paul Bourde, 'Les Poètes décadents', *Le Temps*, 6 Aug. 1885.
68 Jean Moréas, 'Les Décadents', *Le XIXe Siècle*, 11 Aug. 1885.
69 Symons 1906, p.7. This statement summarised Symons's position at the end of the decade of the 1890s. At its opening, he was not only less clear about the position of decadence vis-à-vis Symbolism, but his early literary works, such as *Silhouettes*, published 1892, show a strong indebtedness to decadent subject-matter.
70 Hanover Gallery 1890, no.18, *De la bruine* 1884; no.6, *Le jardin de la ferme* c.1887.
71 Ibid., no.22, *La Garde qui attend* 1882.
72 Ibid., no.11.
73 Ibid., See no.52.
74 Ibid., no.1, *Une Sphinge* 1884; nos.3, 19, *Deux Etudes pour 'Une Sphinge'* 1889.
75 Ibid., nos.17, 5 and 7.
76 Walter Shaw Sparrow, 'Fernand Khnopff', *Magazine of Art*, Dec. 1890, pp.42–3.
77 See Andrew Wilton's essay, above.
78 Maurice Denis, in an entry to his diary made towards the end of his life, came to the same conclusion as he reflected upon the relationship between Symbolism, its rejection of naturalism and subsequent developments in the visual arts: 'We [Gauguin and the second generation of Symbolist painters including the Nabis] undertook a reaction against Impressionism: no sensations, no windows on to nature. Our generation had been responsible for the creation of the Idea ['la notion'] of a painting, something which others have pushed all the way to abstraction', 3 Nov. 1943, in M. Denis, *Journal*, III, Paris 1957.

G.F. Watts and the Symbolist Vision

1 The term appears in Watts's catalogue for his retrospective at the Grosvenor Gallery, *Collection of Works by G.F. Watts, R.A.*, 1881–2 to which the artist himself contributed. Just how this term relates to French 'Symbolism' has yet to be examined, but it affirms that Watts's way of thinking was akin to later developments in France. See also Barbara Bryant, 'The Origins of G.F. Watts's "Symbolical" Paintings: A Lost Study Identified', *Porticus: Journal of the Memorial Art Gallery of the University of Rochester*, vol.10–11, 1987–8, pp.53–9.
2 It should also be noted that at this time the French State awarded Burne-Jones the Cross of the Legion of Honour. 'Fine Art Gossip', *Athenaeum*, 13 July 1878, p.56. See also Henry Blackburn, 'Pictures at the Paris Exhibition: The British school', *Magazine of Art*, vol.1, 1878–9, pp.126–8. There were 283 British works shown in total.
3 Bryant 1996, pp.109–128. The classic article by Jacques Lethève, 'La Connaissance des Peintures Préraphaélites Anglais en France (1855–1900)', *Gazette des Beaux Arts*, 1959, does not actually discuss the importance of the Exposition of 1878.
4 Edmond Duranty, 'Les écoles étrangères de peinture ... Angleterre', Gazette des Beaux-Arts,

vol.18, 1878, p.319; reprinted in *L'Art Moderne à l'Exposition de 1878*, Paris 1879, pp.172.

5 Bryant 1996, pp.117–20.

6 'La Grosvenor Gallery', *L'Art*, vol.10, 1877, p.265; trans. in Carr 1878, pp.13–14. See Bryant 1996, pp.116–18 for a further discussion of *Love and Death*.

7 Carr 1878, p.14.

8 Carr 1878, p.16.

9 Carr 1880, p.172. For a further discussion see Bryant 1996, pp.124, 126.

10 For the version shown in Paris, and the correct translation of the title, see Manchester 1978, no.24 and p.83, n.1. Lethève 1959, p.320 first mentioned that Watts's works appeared in the Petit exhibition.

11 Joris-Karl Huysmans, *À Rebours (Against Nature)*, trans. Robert Baldick, Penguin Classics, first published 1959, p.136. How well known this work was in England is open to question since the first translation did not appear until 1922; its fame came through here largely via Oscar Wilde's descriptions in *The Portrait of Dorian Gray* (1891) (see Brian Stableford (ed.), *The Second Daedalus Book of Decadence: The Black Feast*, Sawtree, Cambridgeshire, 1992, p.1). On Huysmans as an art critic, see Elizabeth Gilmore Holt (ed.), *The Expanding World of Art, 1874–1902*, I, Universal Expositions and State-Sponsored Fine Arts Exhibitions, New Haven and London 1988, pp.208 et seq., 226 et seq.

12 Watts 1912, I, pp.267–70.

13 Surtees 1971, I, no.236 (II, pl.337) for the painting and no.236B (II, pl.338) for the drawing.

14 Surtees 1971, I, no.248 (II, pl.367); illustrated in colour in Craig Faxon 1989, p.16.

15 Barrington 1905, p.196.

16 Allen Staley, '"Art is upon the Town!": The Grosvenor Gallery Winter Exhibitions' in Casteras and Denney 1996, pp.64–5 on the high quality of the exhibitions produced by the Burlington Fine Arts Club.

17 H. Virtue Tebbs [signed January 1883], 'Dante Gabriel Rossetti', [introduction to] Burlington Fine Arts Club 1883, p.5.

18 Ibid., no.88. This striking drawing (100.7 × 75.3 cm) shows a woman seen in three-quarter length holding a flame in her right hand with, according to the catalogue entry, a 'spirit therein'. Surtees 1971, I, no.216; II, pl.308.

19 Ormond 1975, p.104.

20 Watts 1912, I, p.270.

21 Theodore Duret, as a friend of Whistler already knew Rossetti's work; he wrote in the *Gazette des Beaux-Arts* as early as 1881, as quoted in Holt 1988, p.264.

22 J. Comyns Carr, 'Rossetti's Influence in Art', *Papers on Art*, 1885, p.206.

23 Ibid., p.226.

24 Frederic Myers, 'Rossetti and the Religion of Beauty', *Cornhill Magazine*, Feb. 1883; repr. in *Essays: Modern*, II, 1883, pp.312–34.

25 See below note 58.

26 Myers 1883, p.320.

27 Ibid., pp.321–2.

28 Ibid., pp.325–6.

29 Ibid., pp.331–2.

30 J. Beavington Atkinson, 'Contemporary Art – Poetic and Positive: Rossetti and Tadema … ', *Blackwood's Magazine*, March 1883, p.398.

31 On the widespread interest in other-wordly matters in his circle, chiefly spearheaded by Rossetti himself, see Boyce's account of 'mesmeric phenomenon' at Rossetti's on 27 July 1870 attended by Whistler and Leyland among others (Surtees 1980, p.51); Pedrick 1964, pp.98–101, 106 on how 'everything that appertained to the mystic had a strnge fascination for him' according to his studio assistant Henry Treffy Dunn; Fennell 1978, letter no.107 (28 March 1877) regarding Rosetti's 'late clairvoyant experience'.

32 Originally published in *The Nineteenth Century*, June 1883, pp.956 et seq.; reprinted in Mrs Russell Barrington, *A Retrospect and other Articles*, 1896, pp.159–94.

33 Barrington 1896, p.191.

34 Ibid.

35 Chesneau 1887, p.267. Chesneau was critical of other aspects of Watts's œuvre, but he praised *The Three Goddesses* (no.14) and *Orpheus and Eurydice*, apart from its 'decidedly too sombre colouring'.

36 Barrington 1905, p.203.

37 Ibid.

38 *Olympus on Ida* has been on the art market several times, most recently Sotheby's, 19 June 1991, lot 239 (repr.); for *Iris*, formerly Black Sun Books, see Manchester 1978, no.33.

39 See *Journal for the Society for Psychical Research*, vol.1, April 1884, pp.33–4; this is the single most compelling reference to his great interest in other-worldly matters.

40 That Watts was interested in a wide range of phenomena is completely missed by David Stewart in 'Theosophy and Abstraction in the Victorian Era: The Paintings of G.F. Watts', *Apollo*, 1993, pp.298–302, who insists on presenting the artist a follower of Theosophy. His sole evidence is Mary Watts's comments in her own Diaries. Her unreliability is notorious; and it seems clear that these Diaries may well tell us much about her own manifold religious interests, but hardly anything about Watts's. Watts had a far more searching approach to such matters, dating from well before his marriage in 1886.

41 The comments of Julia Cartwright, an eminently sensible and careful writer on art in the 1890s, reveal much about how Mary Watts was perceived by those who knew her. On 25 June 1896, Cartwright wrote of a popular Hindu Yogi giving Swami lectures in London: 'who lectures on the Vedantas after dear Mrs. Watts's own heart I am sure it must be. He proclaims universal religion', as quoted in Emanuel 1989, p.205.

42 Barrington 1905, p.152.

43 'The Present Conditions of Art', *The Nineteenth Century*, Feb. 1880, pp.235–51; repr. Watts 1912, III, pp.148–90.

44 Ibid., p.179.

45 Ibid., p.180.

46 Ibid., pp.181–2.

47 Ibid., p.166.

48 Ibid., p.190.

49 For a recent discussion and colour illustration, see Nottingham 1994, no.72, repr. p.123.

50 This group of drawings considered as Symbolist works of art, dating from 1890 and after, will form the subject of a forthcoming article by the author.

51 Reference to 'the enigma of being' suggests that Watts knew one particular study, albeit more of a religious than mystical nature, W.R. Greg's *Enigmas of Life* (1872; this would be very likely since Greg was Mrs Barrington's brother-in-law; Barrington 1905, pp.73–4). Mrs Barrington herself had an interest in mysticism and the other-worldly, as one can deduce from her remarks about Watts offering 'glimpses, through the veil, and behind what we call reality, into the primeval and permanent facts of the universe' (Barrington 1905, p.144). It can be seen that such matters were a pervasive concern of the 1880s.

52 Rossetti's interests have already been discussed; both Evelyn De Morgan, through her husband William (whose mother was an authority on the subject of automatic writing) and Walter Crane had an active interest in mystical matters. De Morgan's interests have been the subject of an excellent recent study (Oberhausen 1994).

53 In 1882, John Hanson Walker, the young artist and protégé of Frederic Leighton, had his daughter baptised at the Swedenborgian Church of the New Jerusalem, in Palace Gardens Terrace, Kensington (as noted in the entry on a portrait of a girl, Christie's sale cat., 8 Nov. 1996, no.177). There were other Swedenborgians in the art world, as for example, the bookseller and photographer Frederick Evans, who was a friend of Beardsley (see Ulrich Pohlmann, 'The Dream of Beauty', in Montreal 1995, p.431).

54 In 1874, this periodical became affiliated with the British National Association of Spiritualists (see Alan Gauld, *The Founders of Psychical Research*, 1968, p.119).

55 The Sidgwick group, named after Henry Sidgwick, included Frederic Myers, Edmund Gurney, Arthur and Eleanor Balfour (see Gauld 1968, pp.88–136). Watts was friendly with other members of the Gurney family; and Arthur Balfour was a major patron of Burne-Jones.

56 Watts was one of the early Honorary Members of this group (as was Alfred Lord Tennyson), elected in March 1884. An Honorary Member was defined as someone invited by the Council because that individual was 'distinguished for knowledge and experience of Psychical Research … or has rendered services to the Society', see *Journal of the Society for Psychical Research*, vol.1, 1884–5, p.17.

57 Janet Oppenheim, *The Other World: Spiritualism and Psychical Research in England 1850–1914*, Cambridge, London, etc., 1985, p.135. Leighton was elected in 1890, at just the time his painting reflected more mystical content (see no.119).

58 Watts 1912 does refer to Myers as a friend of Watts in several places in the Annals, but without considering their shared interest in psychical matters.

59 On their father see J. Dugdale, 'Sir Charles Tennant: The Story of a Victorian Collector', *Connoisseur*, vol.178, 1971, pp.3–15; and on Watts's friendship with the family, see Watts 1912, I, p.313.

60 *Edwardian Women Photographers: Eveleen Myers, Alice Hughes, Christina Broom and Olive Edis*, National Portrait Gallery 1994.

61 Dorothy trained at the Slade School and in Paris in the studio of Henner; she was a great friend of Bastien-Lepage, apparently introduced by Watts at the summer exhibition of the Grosvenor Gallery. She married Henry Morton Stanley, the great explorer, in 1890.

62 Watts 1912, I, pp.313–16.

63 Watts painted Dorothy in a portrait exhibited at the Royal Academy in 1877 (Tate Gallery) and Eveleen, in a more informal study in the Bancroft collection, called *Jessamine*, and exhibited at the Grosvenor Gallery in 1885.

64 As quoted in Gauld 1968, p.103.

65 Ibid., p.137, n.3.

66 Oppenheim 1985, pp.254–5. She also notes that Myers through his work in this area invented the term 'stream of consciousness', p.258.
67 Some of this poem is printed in Watts 1912, II, pp.20–1. The entire work appears in F. Myers, *The Renewal of Youth and Other Poems*, 1882, pp.190–4 (repr. in *Collected Poems with Autobiographical and Critical Fragments*, 1921).
68 Myers 1882, p.191.
69 It was first reprinted in Frederic W.H. Myers, *Fragments of Prose and Poetry*, ed. Eveleen Myers, London, etc., 1904, pp.115–16.
70 G.F. Watts, 'The Aims of Art', *Magazine of Art*, 1888, p.254; repr. in Watts 1912, III, p.233.
71 Watts 1888, p.254.
72 See *Catalogue of the British Fine Art Section, Universal Exposition of 1889*, 1889 for a complete list, showing that Edward John Gregory had one more work than Watts on view but about half of his exhibits were watercolours; see also Henry Blackburn, *Pictures at the Paris Exhibition*, 'British Section', 1889 for some illustrations.
73 As quoted in Lethève 1959, p.323 from the *Rapport du Jury ... Exposition ... 1889*.
74 Elizabeth Pennell, 'Pictures of the Year, No.II: The French Salons', *Fortnightly Review*, 1895; quoted in Holt 1988, p.366.
75 Henry Havard, 'L'Exposition des Beaux Arts: Les Ecoles Etrangères', in F.G. Dumas, ed., *Revue de l'Exposition Universelle de 1889*, Paris, p.182.
76 Sizeranne 1898.
77 Ibid., pp.101–2.
78 Ibid., xiii–xiv.
79 Ibid., xv.
80 'In Memoriam: Sir Edward Burne-Jones, Bart.: A Tribute from France', *Magazine of Art*, vol.22, 1897–8, p.515.
81 Sizeranne 1898, p.116.
82 Léonce Benedite, *The Luxembourg Museum: Its Paintings*, Paris and London 1913, p.598.
83 For a recent consideration of *Love and Life* and other cross currents in European art, see *1893: L'Europe des peintres*, Musées d'Orsay, Paris 1993, pp.184–5.
84 Barrington 1905, pp.163–4.
85 William Rothenstein's portrait of Jan Toorop in the Tate Gallery dates from 1894.
86 'Grosvenor Gallery: Society of British Pastellists', *Athenaeum*, 25 Oct. 1890, p.553.
87 By 1894, aged only thirty-five, Khnopff was fully integrated into the London art world, and his œuvre very familiar, especially through his one-man exhibition at the Hanover Gallery in 1890 (see Howe 1982, p.7). See W. Shaw Sparrow, 'English Art and M. Fernand Khnopff', *Studio*, vol.2, 1894, pp.203–7. Sparrow considered him ready to 'forsake the phantasms of the Rose Croix, for the more substantial glories of Burlington House, the New Gallery and the Grafton'.
88 Crane and Khnopff carried out one chalk drawing, *Lily*, together as a gesture of friendship, sold at Christie's, 24 Nov. 1983, no.10.
89 See for example A.L. Baldry, 'The Grafton Galleries', *Art Journal*, 1893, p.145.
90 For comparison see Manchester 1978, no.15 for the large version of *Thetis* now in the Watts Gallery.
91 See Theofore Reff, 'Le Papillon et le Vieux Boeuf', pp.23–29 and the entire catalogue of the seminal exhibition, Philadelphia 1971.
92 As quoted in Holt 1988, p.333.
93 Ibid., p.331.
94 See Robert Pincus-Witten, in Piccadilly Gallery 1968 and *Occult Symbolism in France: Joséphin Péladan and the Salons of the Rose+Croix*, New York and London 1979, Appx I for a full translation of the Manifesto of the Rose+Croix.
95 Cambridge 1946, no.100 and *The Souls*, an exhibition compiled and catalogued by Jane Abdy and Charlotte Gere, Bury Street Gallery, March 1982, no.5 for a study of Violet and no.6 for the full-face portrait without the background.
96 Ibid., no.7 and passim.
97 Such a setting evokes Walter Pater's study on Leonardo, first published as an essay in the *Fortnightly Review*, Nov. 1869, later appearing in *The Renaissance*, 1873. Watts had however resorted to such evocative backgrounds in portraits of the late 1850s.
98 Watts did not feature in Les XX, the predecessor of La Libre Esthétique, and Khnopff's first major venue, see Bruce Laughton, 'The British and American contribution to Les XX, 1884–93', *Apollo*, vol.86, 1967, p.376.
99 Fernand Khnopff, 'Some English Art Works at the "Libre Esthetique" at Brussels', *Studio*, vol.3, 1894, p.32.

Symbolism in Three Dimensions

Any writer on these sculptors is greatly indebted to the pioneering work of Richard Dorment, Benedict Read, Timothy Stevens and the late Susan Beattie.

1 Gosse 1894, p.138. See Beattie 1983.
2 Spielmann 1901, p.1.
3 *Magazine of Art*, vol.7, 1884, p.396.
4 Quoted Grunfeld 1987, p.208.
5 Quoted Grunfeld 1987, p.456.
6 Hatton 1903, p.10.
7 Ibid.
8 Gilbert's choice of subject undoubtedly paid tribute to Leighton's *Daedalus and Icarus* c.1869 (Buscot Park); see Dorment 1985, pp.46–9. Daedalus was the greatest artist of ancient Greece, and Gilbert perhaps mentally cast Leighton as this father-figure, and himself as Icarus, the rash son.
9 McAllister 1929, p.62.
10 Watts 1912, II, p.134.
11 Ibid.
12 Untraced, repr. McAllister 1929, opp. p.89.
13 Watts 1912, II, p.135.
14 Quoted RA 1905, p.ix.
15 See Dorment 1985, p.63.
16 G.B.-J. 1904, II, p.147.
17 McAllister 1929, p.145.
18 Ibid.
19 G.B.-J. 1904, II, pp.146–7.
20 McAllister 1929, p.147.
21 Hatton 1903, p.32.
22 E.B.S., 'Afternoons in Studios: A Chat with Mr George Frampton, A.R.A.', *Studio*, vol.6, 1896, pp.206–9.
23 Spielmann 1901, p.95.
24 Repr. *Art Journal* 1897, p.321.
25 Repr. *Studio*, vol.6, 1896, p.207.
26 See Beattie 1983, p.258, n.30.
27 Repr. *Studio*, vol.6, 1896, p.209.
28 Roger Marx, 'La Libre Esthétique', *La Revue Encyclopédique*, 1 Nov. 1894, pp.475–8, quoted Beattie 1983, p.158.
29 Fernand Khnopff, 'Some English Art Works at the "Libre Esthétique" at Brussels', *Studio*, vol.3, 1894, p.32. Frampton also showed *The Vision*, *St Christina* and 'a very interesting terra-cotta study for a portrait, and a fragment of a coloured frieze'. Some of these items were purchased by the Belgian Museum of Decorative Arts.
30 Fernand Khnopff, 'The Revival of Ivory Carving in Belgium', *Studio*, vol.4, 1894, p.150.
31 Ibid.
32 Keats's 'Lamia', II, 276.
33 Beattie 1983, p.231.
34 See Guy Gogeval, 'The Cycles of Life: The Femme Fatale' in Montreal 1995, pp.305–8.
35 Armstrong 1888, p.171.
36 She is also similar to the right-hand attendant in *The Sleeping Princess* in Burne-Jones's *Briar Rose* series 1870–90 (Buscot Park).
37 See John Christian, 'Burne-Jones and Sculpture', in Read and Barnes 1991, pp.77–91.
38 See Read and Barnes 1991, nos.6a–b, figs.54–5. The figure of Christ in *The Entombment* has similarities with Bates's Psyche in the central panel of *The Story of Psyche*.
39 See Girouard 1981, chap.18.

Bibliography

Exhibitions: Abbreviations

Exhibitions in London are referred to by Gallery.

Alpine Club 1894: *A Collection of Mountain Paintings and Photographs*, The Alpine Club Exhibition at the XIXth Century Art Gallery

Amsterdam 1970: *Jan Toorop*, Wisselingh & Co.

Amsterdam 1996: *The Colour of Sculpture 1840–1910*, Van Gogh Museum, Amsterdam; Henry Moore Foundation, Leeds

Antwerp 1894: *Exposition Universelle des Beaux-Arts*

Arts Council 1983: *Landscape in Britain 1850–1950*, The Arts Council of Great Britain

Ashmolean 1991: *Rossetti's Portraits of Elizabeth Siddall: A Catalogue of the Drawings and Watercolours*, Ashmolean Museum, Oxford; Birmingham City Museum and Art Gallery

Auckland 1962: *British Taste*, City Art Gallery

Baden-Baden 1973: *Präraffeliten*, Staatliche Kunsthalle, Baden-Baden; Städelsches Kunstinstitutem Fraabkfurt am Main

Barbican 1989: *The Last Romantics: The Romantic Tradition in British Art: Burne-Jones to Stanley Spencer*, Barbican Art Gallery

Barbican 1991: see Barbican and Tokyo 1991

Barbican and Tokyo 1991: *Japan & Britain: An Aesthetic Dialogue*, Barbican Art Gallery; Setagaya Art Museum, Tokyo

Berkeley 1972: *Ferdinand Hodler*, University Art Museum and touring

Berlin 1969: *James McNeill Whistler (1834–1903)*, Nationalgalerie

Birmingham 1947: *The Pre-Raphaelite Brotherhood*, Birmingham City Museums and Art Gallery

Birmingham 1885: *Collection of Paintings by G.F. Watts, R.A and Edward Burne-Jones*, Birmingham City Museums and Art Gallery

Boston 1904: *Memorial Exhibition of Works by Mr J. McNeill Whistler*, Copley Hall

Bournemouth 1951: *Paintings and Drawings by the Pre-Raphaelites and their Followers*, Russell-Cotes Art Gallery and Museum

Bournemouth 1996: *Drawings and Paintings: Evelyn De Morgan*, Russell-Cotes Art Gallery and Museum

Bradford 1904: *Catalogue of the Works of Art in the Cartwright Memorial Hall*

Brighton 1875: *Second Annual Exhibition of Modern Pictures*, Royal Pavilion Gallery

Brighton 1884: *Art Loan Exhibition*

Brighton and Sheffield 1974: *Frederick Sandys*, Brighton Museum and Art Gallery; Mappin Art Gallery, Sheffield

Brussels 1884; *Société des Vingts*

Brussels 1891: *Exposition d'Oeuvres d'Art*

Brussels 1929: *Exposition étrospective de Peinture Anglaise (XVIIIe et XIXe Siècle)*, Musée Moderne

Burlington Fine Arts Club 1883: *Pictures, Drawings, Designs and Studies by the Late Dante Gabriel Rossetti*

Cambridge 1946: *Paintings and Drawings of the Pre-Raphaelites and their Circle*, Fogg Art Museum

Cambridge 1979: *All for Art: The Ricketts and Shannon Collection*, Fitzwilliam Museum

Carfax & Co. 1904: *Aubrey Beardsley*

Carlisle 1971: *Gordon Bottomley: Poet and Collector*, Carlisle Museum and Art Gallery

Chantrey exhibition 1949: see RA 1949

Chicago 1893: *The World's Columbian Exposition*

Chicago 1911: *Aubrey Beardsley*, Art Institute of Chicago

Chicago 1994: *Odilon Redon 1840–1916* Art Institute of Chicago and touring

Cincinatti 1994: *Ferdinand Hodler: Views and Visions*, Cincinatti Art Museum

Commonwealth Institute 1978: *D.G. Rossetti*

Deschamps Gallery 1876: *Winter Exhibition of Oil Paintings by British Artists*

Dublin 1906: *Watts Memorial Exhibition*, Royal Hibernian Academy

Dublin 1907: *Irish International Exhibition*

Dudley Gallery 1870: *Sixth General Exhibition of Drawings*

Dudley Gallery 1872: *Sixth Winter Exhibition of Cabinet Pictures in Oils*

Durham 1975: *British Art to 1930*, DLI Museum

Edinburgh 1902: *76th Exhibition of the Royal Scottish Academy of Painting, Sculpture and Architecture*, Royal Scottish Academy

Edinburgh 1905: *Memorial Exhibitionof the Works of George Frederick Watts, R.A., O.M.*, Royal Scottish Academy

Edinburgh 1968: *Charles Rennie Mackintosh: Architecture, Design, Painting*, Royal Scottish Museum

FAS 1968: *British Sculpture 1850–1914*, Fine Art Society

FAS 1976: *Centenary Exhibition*, Fine Art Society

FAS 1977: *Frederick Cayley Robinson, ARA*, Fine Art Society

Ferrara 1969: *Gaetano Previati (1852–1920): Mostra antologica*, Palazzo dei diamanti, galleria Civica d'Arte Moderna, Ferrara 1969

French Gallery 1865: *13th Annual Winter Exhibition of Pictures by British Artists*

Geffrye Museum 1985: *Solomon: A Family of Painters*, Geffrye Museum; City Art Gallery, Birmingham

Glasgow 1888: *Works of Modern Artists*, Institute of Fine Arts

Glasgow 1892: *Exhibition of Works of Modern Artists*, Institute of Fine Arts

Glasgow 1893: Boussard, Valard & Cie of the Goupil Gallery at Wellington Studios

Glasgow 1933: *Charles Rennie Mackintosh, Margaret Macdonald Mackintosh, Memorial Exhibition*, McLellan Galleries

Glasgow 1996: *Charles Rennie Mackintosh*, Glasgow Art Gallery

Goupil Gallery 1892: *Nocturnes, Marines and Chevalet Pieces*, Boussard, Valadon & Cie.

Goupil Gallery 1896: *Sale Exhibition of the Leathart Collection*

Goupil Gallery 1898: *A Collection of Selected Works by the Painters of the English, French and Dutch Schools*

Grafton Gallery 1894: *Fair Women*

Grosvenor Gallery 1877: *Summer Exhibition*

Grosvenor Gallery 1881: *Winter Exhibition: Collection of the Works of G.F. Watts, R.A.*

Grosvenor Galleries 1919: *International Society of Painters, Sculptors and Gravers*

Grosvenor Galleries 1923: *Paintings and Sculpture by Glyn Philpot R.A.*

The Hague 1892: *Tentoonstelling van Schilderijen en Teekeningen van eenigen uit de 'XX' en uit de Association pour l'Art in den Haagschen Kunstkring*

The Hague 1894: *Odilon Redon*, Haagsche Kunstkring

The Hague 1989: *Jan Toorop*, Haags Gemeentemuseum

Hamburg 1978: *Courbet und Deutschland*, Hamburger Kunsthalle

Hayward 1972: *French Symbolist Painters: Moreau, Puvis de Chavannes and their Followers*, Hayward Gallery; Walker Art Gallery, Liverpool

Hayward 1975: *Burne-Jones: The Paintings, Graphic and Decorative Work of Sir Edward Burne-Jones 1833–1898*, Hayward Gallery and touring

Hayward 1994: *The Romantic Spirit in German Art 1790–1990*, Hayward Gallery

Indianapolis 1964: *The Pre-Raphaelites: A Loan Exhibition*, Herron Museum of Art, Indianapolis; Gallery of Modern Art, New York

International Exhibition 1872: Fine Art Department, South Kensington Museum

Las Palmas 1990: *Symbolism in Europe*, Centro Atlantico de Arte Moderna, Las Palmas de Gran Canaria

Leger Galleries 1968: *Truth to Nature*

Leicester 1968: *The Victorian Vision of Italy*, Leicester Museum and Art Gallery

Liverpool 1885: *Annual Autumn Exhibition*, Walker Art Gallery

Liverpool 1886: *Grand Loan Exhibition*, Walker Art Gallery

Liverpool 1902: *Annual Autumn Exhibition*, Walker Art Gallery

Liverpool and RA 1967: *Millais*, Walker Art Gallery, Liverpool; RA

London 1905: *Memorial Exhibition of the Works of the Late James McNeill Whistler*, New Gallery

London and New York 1960: *James McNeill Whistler*, Arts Council Gallery, London; Knoedler Galleries, New York

Lyon 1893: *Exposition de la Société lyonnaise des Beaux-Arts*

Lyon 1966: Musée de Lyon

Maas Gallery 1974: *Stunners*, Maas Gallery 1974

Madrid 1993: see Munich and Madrid 1993

Manchester 1878: *Exhibition of Art Treasures in Aid of the Fund for Erecting a School of Art*, Royal Manchester Institution

Manchester 1880: *Pictures and Sculpture: G.F. Watts, Esq., R.A.* [the collection of Charles Rickards], Royal Manchester Institution

Manchester 1887: *Manchester Royal Jubilee Exhibition*, Manchester Institution

Manchester 1892: Manchester City Art Gallery 1892

Manchester 1905: *G.F. Watts Memorial Exhibition*, Manchester City Art Gallery

Manchester 1911: *Loan Exhibition of Works by Ford Madox Brown and the Pre-Raphaelites*, Manchester City Art Gallery

Manchester 1977: *A Pre-Raphaelite Passion: The Private Collection of L.S. Lowry*, Manchester City Art Gallery

Manchester 1978: *Victorian High Renaissance*, Manchester City Art Gallery and touring

Manchester 1984: *William Morris and the Middle Ages*, Whitworth Art Gallery

Melbourne 1888: *Centennial Exhibition*

Memphis 1990: *Odilon Redon: The Ian Woodner Family Collection*, The Dixon Gallery and Gardens

Montreal 1995: *Lost Paradise: Symbolist Europe*, Montreal Museum of Fine Arts

Munich 1892: *VI International Kunst-Austellung*

Munich 1893: *Munchener Jahresausstellung von Kunstwerken aller Nationen*, Glaspalast

Munich 1979: *Zwei Jahrhanderte Englische Malerei: Britische Kunst und Europe 1680 bis 1880*, Haus der Kunst

Munich 1984: *Aubrey Beardsley*, Museum Villa Stuck

Munich 1993: see Munich and Madrid 1993

Munich and Madrid 1993: *Victorianische Malerei*, Neue Pinakothek, Munich; *Pintura Victoriana*, The Prado, Madrid 1993

National Gallery 1992: *Edvard Munch: The Frieze of Life*

National Gallery, Millbank 1923: *Loan Exhibition of Drawings by Aubrey Beardsley, 1872–1898*

National Portrait Gallery 1984: *Glyn Philpot*

New Gallery 1896: *Winter Exhibition of the Work of G.F. Watts*

New Gallery 1897: *Pictures Ancient and Modern by Artists of the British and Continental Schools, including a Special Selection from the Works of Dante Gabriel Rossetti*

New Gallery 1892: *Exhibition of the Works of Edward Burne-Jones*

New Gallery 1898: *Exhibition of the Works of Sir Edward Burne-Jones, Bart*

New Gallery 1900: *William Blake Richmond*

New Gallery 1905: *Watts Memorial Exhibitions*

New Gallery 1896: *Winter Exhibition: The Works of G.F. Watts*

New Haven 1976: *Dante Gabriel Rossetti and the Double Work of Art*, Yale University Art Gallery

New York 1884: *Paintings by G.F. Watts, R.A.*, Metropolitan Museum of Art

New York 1894: *Paintings, Pastels, Decorations by Puvis de Chavannes*, Durand-Ruel Gallery

New York 1923: *Nineteenth-Century French Painters*, Knoedler Gallery

New York 1967: *Aubrey Beardsley*, Gallery of Modern Art, Huntington Hartford Collection

New York 1995: *The Post-Pre-Raphaelite Print*, Miriam & Ira D. Wallach Art Gallery

New York and Philedelphia 1971: *From Realism to Symbolism: Whistler and his World*, Wildenstein, New York; Philadelphia Museum of Art

Newcastle 1905: *Special Loan Collection of Works by G.F. Watts, R.A., O.M.*, Laing Art Gallery

Newcastle-upon-Tyne 1968: *Paintings and Drawings from the Leathart Collection*, Laing Art Gallery

Newcastle-upon-Tyne 1971: *Dante Gabriel Rossetti 1828–1882*, Laing Art Gallery

Newcastle-upon-Tyne 1972: *Albert Moore and his Contemporaries*, Laing Art Gallery

Nottingham 1886: *Collection of Pictures by G.F. Watts, R.A.*, Nottingham Castle

Nottingham 1994: *Heaven on Earth: The Religion of Beauty in Late Victorian Art*, Djanogly Art Gallery, University of Nottingham Arts Centre

Ottawa 1965: *Victorian Artists in England*, National Gallery of Canada

Otterlo 1978: *J. Th. Toorop: De Jaren 1885 tot 1910*, Rijksmuseum Kröller-Müller

Paris 1878: Exposition Universelle

Paris 1883: Paris Salon 101st exhibition

Paris 1883: *Exposition Internationale de Peinture*, Galerie Georges Petit

Paris 1889: Exposition Universelle

Paris 1900: Exposition Universelle

Paris 1905: *Oeuvres de James McNeill Whistler*, Ecole des Beaux-Arts

Paris 1970: *Esthetes et Magiciens*, Palais Galliere

Paris 1972: *La Peinture Romantique Anglaise et Les Préraphaélites*, Petit Palais

Paris 1972: *Peintres de l'Imaginaire*, Grand Palais

Paris 1973: *Idealistes et Symbolistes*, Galerie J.C. Gaubert, Paris 1973

Paris 1979: *Fernand Khnopff*, Musée des Arts Decoratif and touring

Paris and Ottawa 1976: *Puvis de Chavannes 1824–1898*, Grand Palais, Paris; National Gallery of Canada, Ottawa

Paris 1981: *Gustave Vigeland (1869–1943)*, Musée Rodin

Philadelphia 1892: *Examples of the English Pre-Raphaelite School of Painters*, The Pennsylvania Academy of the Fine Arts

Philadelphia 1971: *From Realism to Symbolism: Whistler and his World*, Phildelphia Museum of Art

Philpot 1923: see Grosvenor Galleries 1923

Philpot 1984: see National Portrait Gallery 1984

Piccadilly Gallery 1967: *Les Salons de la Rose+Croix*

RA 1883: See RA Winter 1883

RA 1905: See RA Winter 1905

RA 1949: *Exhibition of the Chantrey Collection*, Royal Academy

RA 1973: *Dante Gabriel Rossetti: Painter and Poet*, Royal Academy

RA 1979: *John Flaxman, RA*, Royal Academy

RA 1986: *Alfred Gilbert: Sculptor and Goldsmith*, Royal Academy

RA 1996: *Frederic Leighton 1830–1896*, Royal Academy

RA Bicentenary 1968: *Royal Academy of Arts Bicentenary Exhibition 1768–1968*, Royal Academy

RA Winter 1883: *Works by the Old Masters and by Deceased Masters of the British School, Including a Special Selection from the Works of John Linnell and Dante Gabriel Rossetti: Winter Exhibition*, Royal Academy

RA Winter 1897: *Exhibition of Works by the Late Lord Leighton of Stretton: Winter Exhibition* Royal Academy

RA Winter 1898: *Works of the Late Sir John Everett Millais, Bart., President of the Royal Academy: Winter Exhibition*, Royal Academy

RA Winter 1905: *Works by the Late George Frederic Watts, R.A., O.M. and the Late Frederick Sandys: Winter Exhibition*, Royal Academy

RA Winter 1906: *Works by Old Masters and by Deceased Masters of the British School ... also a Selection of Drawings and Sketches by George Frederic Watts and Dante Gabriel Rossetti: Winter Exhibition*, Royal Academy

RA Winter 1922: *Works by Deceased Members: Winter Exhibition*, Royal Academy

RA Winter 1928: *Works by Late Members: Winter Exhibition*, Royal Academy

RA Winter 1933: *Commemorative Exhibition of Works by Late Members: Winter Exhibition*, Royal Academy

RA and Birmingham 1973: *Dante Gabriel Rossetti: Painter and Poet*, Royal Academy; City Museum and Art Gallery, Birmingham

Rhode Island 1985: *Ladies of Shalott*, Museum of Art, Rhode Island School of Design

Riverside Studios 1981: *Victorian Paintings at Riverside*, Riverside Studios, Hammersmith 1981

Robinson 1977: see FAS 1977

Rome 1911: *International Fine Arts Exhibition*

Rome 1986: *Burne-Jones*, Galleria Nazionale d'Arte Moderna

Rome 1996: *Dei ed Eroi: Classicità e mito fra '800 e '900*, Palazzo delle Esposizioni

Rotterdam 1975: *Symbolism in Europe*, Museum Boymans-van Beuningen and touring

Seattle 1995: *Visions of Love and Life*, Seattle Art Museum and touring

Sheffield 1971: *Burne-Jones*, Mappin Art Gallery

Southampton 1996: *John Everett Millais 1829–1896: A Centenary Exhibition*, Southampton City Art Gallery

Southport 1935: *Spring Exhibition*, Atkinson Art Gallery

Stockholm 1897: *L'Exposition Générale des Arts et de l'Industrie*

Stoke on Trent 1992: *Reverie, Myth, Sensuality: Sculpture in Britain 1880–1910*, Stoke on Trent City Museum and Art Gallery; Cartwright Hall, Bradford

Stuttgart 1982: *Malerei und Plastik des 19.Jahrhunderts*, Staatsgalerie

Sydney 1975: *Victorian Olympians*, Art Gallery of New South Wales and touring

Takamatsu 1996: *Symbolism in Europe*, Takamatsu City Museum and touring

Tate Gallery 1911: *Works by the English Pre-Raphaelite Painters Lent by the Art Gallery Committee of the Birmingham Corporation*

Tate Gallery 1923: *Loan Exhibition of Paintings and Drawings of the 1860 Period*

Tate Gallery 1933: *Centenary Exhibition of Paintings and Drawings by Sir Edward Burne-Jones, Bart.*

Tate Gallery 1948: *The Pre-Raphaelite Brotherhood, 1848–1948: A Centenary Celebration*

Tate Gallery 1954: *George Frederic Watts, O.M., R.A., 1817–1904*

Tate Gallery 1984: *The Pre-Raphaelites*

Tate Gallery 1993: *Burne-Jones: Watercolours and Drawings*

Tate Gallery 1994: *Whistler*, Tate Gallery and touring

Tate Gallery 1995: *Picturing Blackness in British Art 1700s–1900s*

Tokyo 1975: *Ferdinand Hodler*, National Museum of Western Art, Tokyo; City Museum, Kyoto

Tokyo 1985: *The Pre-Raphaelites and their Times*, Isetan Museum of Art

Tokyo 1987: *Burne-Jones and his Followers*, Isetan Museum of Art and touring

Tokyo 1989: *Victorian Dreamers: Masterpieces of the Neoclassical and Aesthetic Movements*, Tokyo Shimbun 1989

Tokyo 1989a: *Odilon Redon*, National Museum of Modern Art and touring

Tokyo 1990: *Dante Gabriel Rossetti*, Bunkamara Museum of Art and touring

Toronto 1975: *Puvis de Chavannes and the Modern Tradition*, Ontario Museum of Art

Toronto 1997: *The Symbolist Prints of Edvard Munch: The Vivian and David Campbell Collection*, Art Gallery of Ontario

Turin 1970: *Del Simbolismo*, Galleria Galatea

Twickenham 1979: *Charles Ricketts and Charles Shannon*, Orleans House

V&A 1966: *Aubrey Beardsley*, Victoria and Albert Museum

Venice 1895: *I Esposizione Internazionale d'Arte della Città di Venezia*

Venice 1909: *VIII Esposizione Internazionnale d'Arte*

Vienna 1896: *Ausstellung sämtlicher Originalzeichnungen, Olskizzen und Aquarelle zu dem Prachtwerke 'Allegorien und Embleme'*, Künstlerhaus

Washington 1977: *English Pre-Raphaelite Painting*, Federal Reserve System

Washington 1997: *The Victorians: British Painting in the Reign of Queen Victoria, 1837–1901*, National Gallery of Art

White City 1908: *Franco–British Exhibition*, White City 1908

Whitechapel 1948: *The Pre-Raphaelites: A Loan Exhibition of their Paintings and Drawings Held in the Centenary Year of the Foundation of the Brotherhood, 1848–1948*, Whitechapel Art Gallery

Whitechapel 1974: *G.F. Watts: A Nineteenth-Century Phenomenon*, Whitechapel Art Gallery

Whitechapel 1981: *British Sculpture in the Twentieth Century Part I: Image and Form 1901–1950*, Whitechapel Art Gallery

Williamstown 1955: *Exhibit 4, The First Two Rooms*, Sterling and Francine Clark Art Institute

Wilmington 1899: *Exhibition of Paintings, Statuary, and Valuable Curios: Loaned by the Artists and Residents of Wilmington*, New Century Club

Wilmington 1917: *Sixth Annual Exhibition of the Wilmington Society of the Fine Arts*

Wilmington 1934: *Samuel Bancroft, Jr. Collection. English Pre-Raphaelite Paintings*, Wilmington Society of the Fine Arts

Wilmington 1976: *The Pre-Raphaelite Era: 1848–1914*, Delaware Art Museum

Wolverhampton 1902: *Art and Industrial Exhibition*, Fine Art Section

York 1989: *The Etruscans: Painters of the Italian Landscape, 1850–1900*, York City Art Gallery and touring

Zurich 1986: *Gustave Moreau Symboliste*, Kunsthaus

Zurich 1992: *Klimt*, Kunsthaus

Zurich 1983: *Ferdinand Hodler und das Schweizer Künstlerplaket 1890–1920*, Kunstgewerbermuseum der Stadt and touring

Literature: Abbreviations

Place of publication is London unless otherwise stated. Where two dates are given, these refer to different editions.

Agresti 1904: Olivia Rossetti Agresti, *Giovanni Costa: His Life, Work and Times*, 1904

Ainsworth 1976: M.W. Ainsworth, '"The Prince's Progress": Works from 1863 to 1871', in New Haven 1976

Alexandre 1888: Arsène Alexandre, 'Les Os du titan (à Fantin-Latour)', *Journal de Paris*, 1888

Alexandre 1905: Arsène Alexandre, *Puvis de Chavannes*, London and New York 1905

Allingham 1907: Helen Allingham and D. Radford (eds.), *William Allingham: A Diary*, 1907

Alston 1929: Roland Alston, *The Mind and Work of G.F. Watts*, 1929

Anderson and Koval 1994: Ronald Anderson and Anne Koval, *James McNeill Whistler*, 1994

Andree 1977: Rolf Andree, *Arnold Böcklin: Die Gemälde*, Zurich 1977

Bacou 1960: Roseline Bacou, *Lettres de Gauguin, Gide, Huysmans, Jammes, Mallarmé, Verhaeren ... à Odilon Redon*, Paris 1960

Baldry 1894: Alfred Lys Baldry, *Albert Moore: His Life and Works*, 1894

Barbantini 1919: Nino Barbantini, *Gaetano Previati*, Rome 1919

Barclay 1985: Michael Richard Barclay, *Catalogue of the Works of Charles Ricketts RA from the Collection of Gordon Bottomley*, Carlisle 1985

Barrington 1905: Mrs Russell Barrington, *G.F. Watts: Reminiscences*, 1905

Barrington 1906: Mrs Russell Barrington, *The Life, Letters and Work of Frederic Leighton*, 2 vols., 1906

Bate 1899: Percy Bate, *The English Pre-Raphaelite Painters*, 1899

Bate 1905: Percy Bate, 'The Late Frederick Sandys: A Retrospect', *Studio*, vol.33, 1905

Battersea 1922: Lady Battersea, *Reminiscences*, 1922

Baum 1940: Paul Franklin Baum (ed.), *Dante Gabriel Rossetti's Letters to Fanny Cornforth*, Baltimore 1940

Bayard 1976: J. Bayard, '"Lustral Rites and Dire Portents": Works from 1872 to 1882', in New Haven 1976

Bayes 1906: Walter Bayes, *The Landscapes of George Frederic Watts*, London and New York [1906]

Beattie 1983: Susan Beattie, *The New Sculpture*, New Haven and London 1983

Beckson 1989: Karl Beckson, 'The Artist as Transcendent Phallus', in Langenfeld 1989

Bell 1892, 1898: Malcolm Bell, *Edward Burne-Jones: A Record and Review*, 1892, 4th ed., 1898

Bell 1927: Clive Bell, *Landmarks in Nineteenth-Century Painting*, 1927

Bell Scott 1892: William Bell Scott, *Autobiographical Notes of the Life of William Bell Scott*, 2 vols., 1892

Benedetti 1980: Maria-Teresa Benedetti, 'Disegni classici di Burne-Jones nella cultura della Victorian renaissance', *Paragone*, 1980

Benedetti 1984: Maria-Teresa Benedetti, *D.G. Rossetti*, Florence 1984

Benedetti 1985: Maria-Teresa Benedetti, 'Primo e secondo preraffaellismo, in margine alla mostra londinese', *Paragone*, 1985

Benedetti 1992: Maria-Teresa Benedetti, 'Il ciclo di Perseo di Burne-Jones', in Sinisi 1992

Biermé 1911: Maria Biermé, *Les Artistes de la pensée et du sentiment*, Brussels 1911

Bilcliffe 1978: R. Bilcliffe, *Mackintosh Watercolours*, 1978

Binyon 1912: Laurence Binyon, *William Strang: Catalogue of his Etched Work 1882–1912*, Glasgow 1912

Bittler and Mathieu 1983: Paul Bittler and Pierre-Louis Mathieu, *Catalogue des dessin de Gustave Moreau: Musée Gustave Moreau*, Paris 1983

Bolger Burke 1977: D. Bolger Burke, 'Astarte: Sargent's Study for *The Pagan Gods*', *Fenway Court*, 1977

Borel 1951: *Lettres de Gustave Courbet à Alfred Bruyas*, pub. Pierre Borel, Geneva 1951

Bouyer 1895: Raymond Bouyer, 'Un peintre melomane: Henri Fantin-Latour', *L'Artiste*, 1895

Brophy 1968: Brigid Brophy, *Black and White: A Portrait of Aubrey Beardsley*, 1968

Brown Price 1972: Aimee Brown Price, 'Puvis de Chavannes: A Study of the Easel Paintings and a Catalogue of the Painted Works', unpublished Ph.D thesis, Yale University, New Haven, Conn., 1972

Bryant 1987: Barbara Bryant, 'G.F. Watts's First *Hope*', *Sotheby's Art at Auction 1986–87*, 1987

Bryant 1990: Barbara Bryant. 'The Origins of G.F. Watts's "Symbolical Paintings: A Lost Study Identified', *Porticus: Journal of the Memorial Art Gallery University of Rocheseter*, vol.10/11, 1987–8 [sic]

Bryant 1996: Barbara Bryant, 'G.F. Watts at the Grosvenor Gallery: "Poems Painted on Canvas" and the New Internationalism' in Casteras and Denney 1996

Bryson and Troxwel 1976: John Bryson and Janet Camp Broxwel, *Dante Gabriel Rossetti and Jane Morris: Their Correspondence*, Oxford 1976

Burgoyne 1941: Elizabeth Burgoyne, *Carmen Sylva: Queen and Woman*, 1941

Burkhauser 1990: J. Burkhauser (ed.), *Glasgow Girls: Women in Art and Design 1880–1920*, Edinburgh 1990

Caine 1928: T. Hall Caine, *Recollections of Rossetti*, 1928

Calloway 1979: Stephen Calloway, *Charles Ricketts: Subtle and Fantastic Decorator*, 1979

Carr 1877: Joseph Comyns Carr, 'La Grosvenor Gallery', *L'Art*, vol.10, 1877

Carr 1878: Joseph Comyns Carr, *Examples of Contemporary Art*, 1878

Carr 1880: Joseph Comyns Carr, 'La Royal Academy and la Grosvenor Gallery', *L'Art*, vol.12, 1880

Cartwright 1896: Julia Cartwright, 'George Frederic Watts, R.A.', *Art Journal, Easter Annual*, 1896

Cary 1907: Elisabeth L. Cary, *The Works of James McNeill Whistler*, New York 1907

Casteras and Denney 1996: S. Casteras and C. Denney (eds.), *The Grosvenor Gallery: A Palace of Art In Victorian England*, exh. cat., New Haven and London 1996

Chamberlain 1925: Arthur B. Chamberlain, 'Works by Frederick Sandys in the Birmingham Art Gallery', *Apollo*, 1925

Chan 1983: Victor Chan, 'Aubrey Beardsley's Frontispiece to *The Comedy of The Rheingold*', *Arts Magazine*, vol.57, Jan. 1983

Cheney 1995: Liana de Girolami Cheney, 'Burne-Jones: Mannerist in an Age of Modernism' in Susan Casteras and Alicia Craig Faxon (eds.), *Pre-Raphaelite Art in its European Context*, Madison 1995

Cherry 1980: Deborah Cherry, 'The Hogarth Club: 1858–1861', *Burlington Magazine*, vol.122, 1980

Chesneau 1887, 1891: E. Chesnau, *The English School of Painting*, trans. Lucy N. Etherington 1887, 1891

Chesterton 1904: G.K. Chesterton, *G.F. Watts*, 1904

Christian 1973a: John Christian, 'Burne-Jones Studies', *Burlington Magazine*, vol.115, 1973

Christian 1973b: John Christian, 'Sources for Burne-Jones's von Bork Designs', *Burlington Magazine*, vol.115, 1973

Christian 1973c: John Christian, 'Early German Sources for Pre-Raphaelite Designs', *Art Quarterly*, vol.36, 1973

Cline 1978: C.R. Cline (ed.), *The Owl and the Rossettis*, Pennsylvania 1978

Coll. Cat. Munich 1990: see Neue Pinakothek, Munich 1990

Colvin 1870: S. Colvin, 'English Painters of the Present Day. iv. – Simeon Solomon', *Portfolio*, vol.1, 1870

Colvin 1870: S. Colvin, 'Albert Moore', *Portfolio*, vol.1, 1870

Colvin 1877: S. Colvin, *Fortnightly Review*, June 1877

Comyns Carr 1880: see Carr 1880

Corkran 1904: Alice Corkran, *Frederic Leighton*, 1904

Craig Faxon 1989: Alicia Craig Faxon, *Dante Gabriel Rossetti*, Oxford 1989

Crane 1907: W. Crane, *An Artist's Reminiscences*, 1907

Daracott 1980: J. Daracott, *The World of Charles Ricketts*, 1980

d'Argencourt and Foucart 1976: Louise d'Argencourt and Jacques Foucart, *Puvis de Chavannes*, Paris 1976

De Bosis 1895–6: Arturo De Bosis, 'Note su Omar Khayyam e su Elihu Vedder', *Il Convito Roma*, Pt i, Bk vi, June 1895, Pt ii, Bk vii, July 1885–March 1896

Delaney 1990: J.G.P. Delaney, *Charles Ricketts: A Biography*, Oxford 1990

Delevoy et al. 1987: Robert L. Delevoy, Catherine de Croës, Giselle Ollinger-Zinque, *Fernand Khnopff*, Brussels 1979, 2nd ed 1987

de Lisle 1904: Fortunée de Lisle, *Burne-Jones*, 1904

Delville 1925: Jean Delville, 'Notice sur Fernand Khnopff', *Annuaire de l'Académie Royale des Sciences, des Lettres et des Beaux-Arts de Belgique*, Brussels 1925

Dorment 1977: Richard Dorment, 'A Roman Lady by Frederic Leighton', *Bulletin of the Philadelphia Museum of Art*, vol.73, no.317, 1977

Dorment 1978: Richard Dorment, 'The Loved One: Alfred Gilbert's *Mors Janua Vitae*', in Manchester 1978

Dorment 1985: Richard Dorment, *Alfred Gilbert*, New Haven and London 1985

Dorment and MacDonald 1994: see Tate Gallery 1994

Doughty and Wahl 1965–8: Oswald Doughty and J.R. Wahl (eds.), *The Letters of Dante Gabriel Rossetti*, Oxford, 4 vols., 1965–8

Downes 1887: W.C. Downes, 'Elihu Vedder's Pictures', *Atlantic Monthly*, vol.59, no.356, June 1887

Draguet 1995: Michel Draguet, *Khnopff ou l'ambigu poetique*, Brussels 1995

Dumont-Wilden 1907: Louis Dumont-Wilden, *Fernand Khnopff*, Brussels 1907

Duval 1986: M. Susan Duval, 'F.R. Leyland: A Maecenas from Liverpool', *Apollo*, 1986

Easton 1972: Malcolm Easton, *Aubrey and the Dying Lady*, 1972

Elzea 1962: Rowland Elzea, *The Samuel and Mary R. Bancroft English Pre-Raphaelite Collection*, Wilmington, 1962

Elzea 1980: Rowland Elzea, ed., *The Correspondence between Samuel Bancroft, Jr. and Charles Fairfax Murray 1892–1916*, Delaware Art Museum Occasional Paper no.2, 1980

Elzea 1984: Rowland Elzea, *The Samuel and Mary R. Bancroft, Jr. and Related Pre-Raphaelite Collections*, Wilmington 1984

Emanuel 1989: A. Emanuel (ed.), *A Bright Remembrance: The Diaries of Julia Cartwright 1851–1924*, 1989

Faxon 1989: see Craig Faxon 1989

Fennell 1978: *The Rossetti–Leyland Letters: The Correspondence of an Artist and his Patron*, ed. Francis L. Fennell, Jr., Athens, Ohio 1978

Fernier 1977: Robert Fernier, *La Vie et l'oeuvre de Gustave Courbat: catalogue raisonné*, 2 vols., Lausanne and Paris 1977

Fitzgerald 1975: P. Fitzgerald, *Edward Burne-Jones*, 1975

Fletcher 1987: Ian Fletcher, *Aubrey Beardsley*, Boston 1987

G.B.-J. 1904: G.B.-J., [Lady Georgiana Burne-Jones], *Memorials of Edward Burne-Jones*, 2 vols., 1904

Geffroy 1888: Gustave Geffroy, 'Salon de 1888: IX. Avant-dernière promenade', *La Justice*, 22 June 1888

George 1924: E.B. George, *Charles Shannon*, 1924

Gibson 1975: Robin Gibson, *Catalogue of Portraits in the Collection of the Earl of Clarendon*, 1975

Girouard 1981: Mark Girouard, *The Return to Camelot: Chivalry and the English Gentleman*, New Haven and London 1981

Glaves-Smith 1992: John Glaves-Smith, 'Frampton's Mysteries' in Stoke on Trent 1992

Gordon et al. 1996: see Bournemouth 1996

Gose and Wise 1918: *The Letters of Algernon Charles Swinburne*, ed. Edmund Gosse and Thomas J. Wise, 2 vols., 1918

Gosse 1894: Edmund Gosse, 'The New Sculpture', *Art Journal*, 1889

Greig 1928: J. Grieg, 'Frederick Cayley Robinson', *Old Water-Colour Society's Club*, Fifth Annual Vol., 1928

Guigou 1888: Paul Guigou, 'l'Art en 1888: 2e article', *Le Revue Moderne*, 25 June 1888

Gutch 1968: R.E. Gutch, 'G.F. Watts's Sculpture', *Burlington Magazine*, vol.110, 1968

Hamacher 1981: A.M. Hamacher, *Phantoms of the Imagination*, New York 1981

Harris Museum 1907: Preston Corporation Art Gallery, *Illustrated Catalogue*, Harris Museum ..., London, etc., 1907

Harrison and Waters 1973: Martin Harrison and Bill Waters, *Burne-Jones*, 1973

Hartnoll 1988: *The Reproductive Engravings after Sir Edward Coley Burne-Jones*, ed. Julian Hartnoll, 1988

Hediard 1906: G. Hediard, *Fantin-Latour: Catalogue de l'oeuvre lithiographique du maitre*, Paris 1906

Heesemann-Wilson 1980: A. Heesemann-Wilson, 'Henri Fantin-Latours "Rheingold"', *Jahrbuch der Hamburger Kunstsammlungen*, vol.25, Hamburg 1980

Heyd 1986: M. Heyd, *Aubrey Beardsley*, New York 1986

Hirsch 1982: Sharon L. Hirsch, *Ferdinand Hodler*, 1982

Holmes 1936: C.J. Holmes, *Self and Partners*, 1936

Howarth 1977: T. Howarth, *Charles Rennie Mackintosh and the Modern Movement*, enlarged ed. 1977

Howe 1982: J. Howe, *The Symbolist Art of Fernand Khnopff*, Ann Arbor 1982

Hueffer 1896: Ford Madox Hueffer, *Ford Madox Brown*, 1896

Hyde 1982: *The Annotated Oscar Wilde*, ed. H. Montgomery Hyde, New York, 1982 ed.

Hyder 1972: C.K. Hyder (ed.), *Swinburne as Critic*, 1972

Ironside and Gere 1948: Robin Ironside and John Gere, *Pre-Raphaelite Painters*, 1948

Jamot 1945: Paul Jamot, *Maurice Denis*, 1945

Jenkyns 1980: Richard Jenkyns, *The Victorians and Ancient Greece*, Oxford 1980

Jouin 1897: H. Jouin, *Vus de profile*, Paris 1897

Jullian 1973: Philippe Jullian, *The Symbolists*, 1973

Jullian 1971: Philippe Jullian, *Dreams of Decadence: Symbolists Painters of the 1890s*, 1971

Jullien 1909: Adolphe Jullien, *Fantin-Latour: Sa Vie et ses amities*, 1909

Kavanagh 1989: Amanda Kavanagh, 'Robert Bateman: A True Victorian', *Apollo*, Sept. 1989

Khnopff 1898: Fernand Khnopff, 'In Memoriam: Sir Edward Burne-Jones, Bart.: A Tribute from Belgium', *Magazine of Art*, 1898

Kooistra 1990: L.J. Kooistra, 'Beardsley's Reading of Malory's *Morte Darthur*, Images of a Decadent World', in *Mosaic*, vol.23, no.1, 1990

Kooistra 1995: L.J. Kooistra, *The Artist as Critic: Bitextuality in Fin-de-Siècle Illustrated Books*, Aldershot 1995

Lago 1982: *Burne-Jones Talking*, ed. Mary Lago, 1982

Langenfeld 1989: Robert Langenfeld (ed.), *Reconsidering Aubrey Beardsley*, Ann Arbor 1989

Lascelles 1984: Helen Lascelles, *The Life and Work of Sir William B. Richmond*, 1902

Leger 1929: Charles Leger, *Courbet*, Paris 1929

Leroi 1888: P. Leroi, 'Salon de 1888', *L'Art*, vol.4, 1888

Lewis 1939: Cecil Lewis (ed.), *Self-Portrait: Letters and Journals of Charles Ricketts*, 1939

Lippien 1980: H.R. Lippien, 'Hamburger Kunsthalle: Erwerbunger fur die Gemaldegalerie im Jahre 1979', *Jahrnbuch der hamburger Kunstsammlungen* 25, 1980

Löcher 1973: Kurt Löcher, *Der Perseus-Zyklus von Edward Burne-Jones*, Stuttgart 1973

Lochnan, Shoenherr and Silver 1993: *The Earthly Paradise*, exh. cat., eds. K.A. Lochnan, D.E. Shoenherr and C. Silver, Art Gallery of Ontario, Toronto 1993

Loshak 1963: David Loshak, 'G.F. Watts and Ellen Terry', *Burlington Magazine*, vol.105, 1963

Loosli 1919: Carl-Albert Loosli, *Ferdinand Hodler*, 4 vols., Zurich 1919

Lucie-Smith 1972: E. Lucie-Smith, *Symbolist Art* 1972

Maas 1969: Jeremy Maas, *Victorian Painters*, 1969

Maas, Duncan and Good 1970: *The Letters of Aubrey Beardsley*, eds. H. Maas, J.L. Duncan and W.G. Good, 1970

McDonnell 1985: P. McDonnell, 'Pre-Raphaelitism, Art Nouveau and Symbolism' in Rhode Island 1985

Macleod 1982: Dianne Macleod, 'Rossetti's Two *Ligeias*: Their Relationship to Visual Art, Music and Poetry', *Victorian Poetry*, vol.20, nos.3–4, 1982

Macleod 1996: Dianne Macleod, *Art and the Victorian Middle Classes*, Cambridge 1996

Macmillan 1903: Hugh Macmillan, *The Life-Work of George Frederic Watts, RA*, 1903

Marillier 1899: H.C. Marillier, *Dante Gabriel Rossetti: An Illustrated Memorial of his Art and Life*, 1899

Marsh 1985: Jan Marsh, *The Pre-Raphaelite Sisterhood*, New York, etc., 1985

Marsh 1994: Jan Marsh, *Christina Rossetti*, 1994

Marx 1894: 'La Libre Esthétique', *La Revue Encyclopédique*, 1 Nov. 1894

Maryon 1933: Herbert Maryon, *Modern Sculpture: Its Methods and Ideals*, 1933

Mathieu 1976: Pierre-Louis Mathieu, *Gustave Moreau, sa vie, son oeuvre: catalogue raisonné de l'oeuvre achevé*, Fribourg 1976

Mauclair 1928: C. Mauclair, *Puvis de Chavannes*, Paris 1928

Michel 1888: André Michel, 'Salon de 1888 (3e et dernier article)', *Gazette des Beaux-Arts*, 1 Aug. 1888

Michel 1889: André Michel, 'Exposition Universelle de 1889: La Sculpture', *Gazette des Beaux-Arts*, 1889

Michel and Laran 1911: A. Michel and J. Laran, *Puvis de Chavannes* [n.d., 1911–12]

Millais 1899: J.G. Millais, *The Life & Letters of Sir John Everett Millais*, 2 vols., 1899

Monkhouse II 1889: W. Cosmo Monkhouse, 'Alfred Gilbert, ARA – II', *Magazine of Art*, 1889, pp.37–40

Mourey 1895: Gabriel Mourey, 'Puvis de Chavannes', *Studio*, vol.4, March 1895

MS. Cat.: 'Catalogue of the Works of G.F. Watts, Compiled by his Widow' (3 MS vols by M.S. Watts), Watts Gallery, Compton

Neat 1994: Timothy Neat, *Part Seen, Part Imagined: Meaning and Symbolism in the Work of Charles Rennie Mackintosh and Margaret Macdonald*, Edinburgh 1994

Neberhay 1977: Christian Neberhay, *Ver Sacrum 1898–1903*, 1977

Neue Pinakothek, Munich 1990: *Impressionism, Post-Impressionism und Symbolisten Auslandische Kunstler*: Catalogue of the Paintings, vii, Bayerischen Staatsgemalde-sammlungen, Neue Pinakothek, Munich 1990

Newall 1987: Christopher Newall, *Victorian Watercolours*, 1987

Newall 1990: Christopher Newall, *The Art of Lord Leighton*, 1990

Nicoll 1975: John Nicoll, *Dante Gabriel Rossetti*, New York and London 1975

Novotny and Dobai 1967: Fritz Novotny and Johannes Dobai, *Gustav Klimt*, 1967

Oberhausen 1994: Judy Oberhausen, 'Evelyn Pickering De Morgan and Spiritualism: An Interpretative Link', *Journal of Pre-Raphaelite Studies*, vol.3, Spring 1994, pp.1–11 and expanded in Bournemouth 1996

Ormond 1975: Leonée and Richard Ormond, *Lord Leighton*, New Haven and London 1975

Paulet 1888: Alfred Paulet, 'Le Salon de 1888: II', *Le National*, 4 May 1888

Pearsall Jacks 1917: Lawrence Pearsall Jacks, *Life and Letters of Stopford Brooke*, 2 vols., 1917

Pedrick 1964: Gale Pedrick, *Life with Rossetti*, 1964

Péladan 1888: Josephin Péladan, *BN ACT*, 1888

Pennell and Pennell 1908: E.R. and J. Pennell, *The Life of James McNeill Whistler*, 2 vols. 1908; revised ed., Philadelphia 1911

Phillips 1893: Claude Phillips, 'The Ruston Collection: The Modern Pictures – 1', *Magazine of Art*, vol.17, 1893

Phillips 1894: Claude Phillips, 'Sculpture of the Year', *Magazine of Art*, 1894

Phythian 1908: J.E. Phythian, *Fifty Years of Modern Painting: Corot to Sargent*, New York 1908

Plasschaert 1925: A. Plasschaert, *Jan Toorop*, Amsterdam 1925

Proust 1902: Antonin Proust, 'The Art of Fantin-Latour', *Studio*, Jan. 1902

Read 1981: Benedict Read, 'Classical and Decorative Sculpture' in Whitechapel 1981

Read 1982: Benedict Read, *Victorian Sculpture*, New Haven and London 1982

Read and Barnes 1991–2: Benedict Read and Joanna Barnes (eds.), *Pre-Raphaelite Sculpture: Nature and Imagination in British Sculpture 1848–1914*, exh. cat., Joanna Barnes Fine Art and Birmingham City Museums and Art Gallery 1991–2

Reade 1967: Brian Reade, *Beardsley*, 1967

Redon and Bacou 1960: *Lettres de Gauguin, Gide, Huysmans, Jammes, Mallarme, Verhaeren ... a Odilon Redon*, ed. Ary Redon and R. Bacou, Paris 1960

Reich 1974: Marjorie Reich, 'The Imagination of Elihu Vedder as Revealed in his Book Illustrations', *American Art Journal*, vol.6, May 1974

Reynolds 1980: S. Reynolds, 'Sir Edmund Davis, Collector and Patron of the Arts', *Apollo*, June 1980

Reynolds 1984, 1985: Simon Reynolds, *The Vision of Simeon Solomon*, Stroud [1984 or 1985]

Reynolds 1995: Simon Reynolds, *William Blake Richmond: An Artist's Life* , Norwich 1995

Rhys 1898, 1900: Ernest Rhys, *Frederic Lord Leighton Late President of the Royal Academy of Arts, An Illustrated Record of his Life and Work*, 1898, 1900

Riat 1906: G. Riat, *Gustave Courbet, peintre*, Paris 1906

Ricketts 1899: Charles Ricketts, *A Defence of the Revival of Printing*, 1899

Ricketts 1932: Charles Ricketts, *Recollections of Oscar Wilde*, 1932

Riordan 1891: R. Riordan, *Art Amateur*, Jan. 1891

Robinson 1892: Lionel Robinson, 'The Leyland Collection', *Art Journal*, 1892

Rosci 1970: M. Rosci, 'Symbolism e divisionismo', in *Mostra del divisionismo*, 1970

[?Rossetti] 1876: [probably W.M. Rossetti], 'Fine Art: Mr. Deschamps Gallery', *Academy*, 11 Nov. 1876

Rossetti 1884: William Michael Rossetti, 'Notes on Rossetti and his Works', *Art Journal*, 1884

Rossetti 1889, 1894: William Michael Rossetti, *D.G. Rossetti as a Designer and Writer*, 1889 , 2nd ed., 1894

Rossetti 1895: William Michael Rossetti, *Dante Gabriel Rossetti: His Family Letters, with a Memoir*, 2 vols., 1895

Rossetti 1899: William Michael Rossetti, *Ruskin: Rossetti; Pre-Raphaelitism*, 1899

Rossetti 1900: William Michael Rossetti, *Pre-Raphaelite Diaries and Letters*, 1900

Rossetti 1903: William Michael Rossetti (ed.), *Rossetti Papers 1862–1870*, 1903

Rossetti 1911: William Michael Rossetti (ed.), *The Works of Dante Gabriel Rossetti*, 1911

Rossetti and Swinburne 1868: William Michael Rossetti and Algernon Swinburne, *Notes on the Royal Academy Exhibition, 1868*, 1868

Rossetti Angeli 1949: Helen Rossetti Angeli, *Dante Gabriel Rossetti: His Friends and Enemies*, 1949

Rossetti Angeli 1954: Helen Rossetti Angeli, *The Pre-Raphaelite Twilight*, 1954

Rothenstein 1932: William Rothenstein, *Men and Memories: Recollections 1900–22*, vol.2, 1932

Schmid 1903: H.A. Schmid, *Arnold Böcklin-Verzeichnis*, 1903

Sewter 1951: A.C. Sewter, *Glyn Philpot 1884–1937*, 1951

Sharp 1882: William Sharp, *Dante Gabriel Rossetti, A Record and Study*, 1882

Shone 1882: W. Shone, *D.G. Rossetti*, 1882

Sickert 1908: Bernhard Sickert, *Whistler*, London and New York 1908

Silvestre 1873: A. Silvestre, *Galerie Durand-Ruel; recueil d'estampes gravees a l'eau-forte*, Paris 1873

Silvestre 1887: A. Silvestre, *La Grande Revue de St Petersbourg*, 1887

Sinisi 1992: S. Sinisi (ed.), *Miti e Figure dell'immaginario simbolista*, Salerno 1992

Sizéranne 1898: Robert de la Sizéranne, *English Contemporary Art*, trans. H.M. Poynter, 1898

Smith 1996: Alison Smith, *The Victorian Nude*, Manchester 1996

Snodgrass 1995: Chris Snodgrass, *Aubrey Beardsley: Dandy of the Grotesque*, Oxford 1995

Soria 1970: Regina Soria, *Elihu Vedder: American Visionary Artist in Rome (1836–1923)*, 1970

Soria et al. 1979: Regina Soria, Joshua C. Taylor, Jane Dillenberger, Richard Murray, *Perceptions and Evocations: The Art of Elihu Vedder*, 1979

Spencer 1975: Isobel Spencer, *Walter Crane*, 1975

Spencer 1978: Stephanie Spencer, '*La Bionda del Balcone* by D.G. Rossetti', *Porticus: Journal of the Memorial Art Gallery*, University of Rochester, NY, vol.1, 1978

Spielmann 1886: M.H. Spielmann, 'The Works of Mr George F. Watts, R.A., with a Complete Catalogue of his Pictures', *Pall Mall Gazette, Extra Number*, 1886

Spielmann 1887: see Spielmann 1886

Spielmann 1891: M.H. Spielmann, 'Current Art: The New Gallery', *Magazine of Art*, 1891

Spielmann 1898: M.H. Spielmann, *Millais and his Works*, 1898

Spielmann 1901: M.H. Spielmann, *British Sculpture and Sculptors of Today*, 1901

Staley 1906: Edgcumbe Staley, *Lord Leighton of Stretton, P.R.A.*, 1906

Staley 1967: Allen Staley, 'The Condition of Music', 'Arts News Annual', *Academy*, vol.33, 1967

Staley 1971: see Philadelphia 1971

Staley 1978: see Mancester 1978

Stang 1955: Ragna Stang, *Gustav Vigeland Om Kunst og Kunstnere*, 1955, trans. Erick Falck-Therkelsen

Stephens 1877: F.G. Stephens, 'Mr. Rossetti's New Pictures', *Athenaeum*, 14 April 1877

Stephens 1884: F.G. Stephens, 'The Private Collections of England ...', *Athenaeum*, 27 Sept. 1884

Stephens 1892: F.G. Stephens, 'Venus Astarte, otherwise Astarte Syriaca', *Portfolio*, 1892

Stephens 1894: F.G. Stephens, *The Portfolio Monographs: Dante Gabriel Rossetti*, no.5, May 1894

Stevens 1977: MaryAnne Stevens, 'Frederick Cayley Robinson', *Connoisseur*, Sept. 1977

Stevens 1989: Timothy Stevens, 'George Frampton' in Penelope Curtis (ed.), *Patronage and Practice: Sculpture on Merseyside*, Liverpool 1989

Stirling 1922: A.M.W. Stirling, *William De Morgan and his Wife*, 1922

Stirling 1926: A.M.W. Stirling, *The Richmond Papers*, 1926

Strang 1962: David Strang, *Catalogue of the Printed Work of William Strang*, Glasgow 1962

Sturge Moore 1933: T. Sturge Moore, *Charles Ricketts R.A.: Sixty Five Illustrations*, 1933

Sturgis 1995: Matthew Sturgis, *Passionate Attitudes: The English Decadence of the 1890s*, 1995

Surtees 1971: Virginia Surtees, *The Paintings and Drawings of Dante Gabriel Rossetti (1828–1882): A Catalogue Raisonné*, Oxford 1971

Surtees 1980: Virginia Surtees (ed.), *The Diaries of George Price Boyce*, Norwich 1980

Sutton 1966: Denys Sutton, *James McNeill Whistler: Paintings, Etchings, Pastels and Watercolours*, 1966

Taylor 1973: W.S. Taylor, 'King Cophetua and the Beggar Maid', *Apollo*, Feb. 1973

Tosini 1995: Aurora Scotti Tosini, 'Divisionist Painters in Italy between Modern Chromatics and New Symbols' in Montreal 1995

Vedder 1910: E. Vedder, *The Digressions of 'V'*, 1910

von Schleinitz 1904: Otto von Schleinitz, 'George Frederic Watts', *Kunstler-Monographien*, vol.73, 1904

Waissenberger 1984: Robert Waissenberger, ed., *Wien 1870–1930 Traum und Wirklichkeit*, 1984

Warner 1985: Marina Warner, *Monuments and Maidens: The Allegory of the Female Form*, 1985

Warner and Hough 1983: *Strangeness and Beauty: An Anthology of Aesthetic Criticism 1840–1910*, I, *Ruskin to Swinburne*, eds. Eric Warner and Graham Hough, Cambridge 1983

Waters 1993: Bill Waters, 'Burne-Jones: A Quest for Love' in *Burne-Jones: A Quest for Love*, exh. cat., Peter Nahum Galleries 1993

Watts 1912: M.S. Watts, *George Frederic Watts: Annals of an Artist's Life*, 3 vols., 1912

Watts-Dunton 1916: T. Watts-Dunton, *Old Familiar Faces*, 1916

Weintraub 1976: Stanley Weintraub, *Aubrey Beardsley: Imp of the Perverse*, Pennsylvania and London 1976

White 1897: Gleeson White, 'Some Glasgow Designers', *Studio*, 1897

White 1897, 1903: Gleeson White, *English Illustration, 'The Sixties': 1855–70*, 1897, 1903

Whitford 1990: Frank Whitford, *Klimt*, 1990

Wikborg 1995: Tone Wikborg, Gustave Vigeland Woodcuts, trans. Ruth Waaler

Wilcox 1986: Timothy Wilcox, 'High Victoriana in Hyderabal: The Paintings in the Salar Jung Museum', *Apollo*, vol.124, 1986

Wildenstein 1992: Alec Wildenstein, *Odilon Redon: Catalogue Raisonné de l'ouevre peint et dessiné*, vol.1, Paris 1992

Wildman 1990: S. Wildman, intro. to Tokyo 1990

Wildman 1995: Stephen Wildman, *Visions of Love and Life*, Alexandria, Virginia 1995

Wilson 1983: Simon Wilson, *Beardsley*, 1976, revised and enlarged 1983

Winter Johnson 1897: E.J. Winter Johnson, 'Mr Harry Bates, A.R.A.', *Artist*, vol.20, 1897

Wood 1896: E. Wood, *A Consideration of the Art of Frederick Sandys, The Artist*, Special Winter Number, 1896

Young et al. 1980: Andrew McLaren Young, Margaret MacDonald, Robin Spencer and Hamish Miles, *The Paintings of James McNeill Whistler*, New Haven and London 1980

Zatlin 1989: Linda Zatlin, 'Félicien Rops and Aubrey Beardsley', in Langenfeld 1989

Zatlin 1990: Linda Zatlin, *Aubrey Beardsley and Victorian Sexual Politics*, Oxford 1990

Index of Works

Lenders

Private Collections

Victor Arwas 34
Nicholas Bagshawe 71
Robin de Beaumont 19, 128
De Morgan Foundation 97
The Faringdon Collection Trust 14
The Forbes Magazine Collection, New York 35
Jacqueline Loewe Fowler 32
The Geoffroy Richard Everett Millais Collection 57
Pre-Raphaelite Inc. by courtesy of Julian Hartnoll 8
Sims Reed Limited 109
Alessandra and Simon Wilson 92
Simon Reynolds 133
A Scottish Parish Church 118
The Woodner Collections, New York 110
Private Collection, Belgium. Courtesy Patrick Derom 86
Private Collection 1, 12, 17, 22, 26, 27, 29, 33, 39, 46, 59, 63, 72, 74, 76, 83, 84, 87, 91, 96, 103, 108, 132, 135

Public Collections

Auckland Art Gallery Collection 121
Birmingham Museums and Art Gallery 38, 47
Boston, Museum of Fine Arts 2
Bournemouth, The Russell-Cotes Art Gallery and Museum 43
Brussels, Musées Royaux des Beaux Arts de Belgique 107
Cambridge, Fitzwilliam Museum 56
Cardiff, National Museum and Gallery 117
Carlisle, Tullie House Museum and Art Gallery 28, 102
Compton, Watts Gallery 37, 48, 50, 60, 62, 134
Delaware Art Museum. Samuel and Mary R. Bancroft Memorial 6, 7, 73
Dublin, The Hugh Lane Municipal Gallery of Modern Art 11
Essen, Museum Folkwang 136
Ferrara, Civiche Gallerie d'Arte Moderna e Contemporanea, Museo dell'Ottocento 127
Glasgow, Art Gallery and Museum, Kelvingrove 98–100, 129
Hamburger Kunsthalle 3, 85
Leamington Spa Art Gallery and Museum 36
Liverpool, Walker Art Gallery 115, 116
London, The British Library Board 81
London, Trustees of the British Museum 89, 104, 105
London, Fenton House, Hampstead, The Binning Collection (The National Trust) 61
London, Borough of Hammersmith and Fulham 106
London, Royal Academy of Arts 69
London, Tate Gallery 4, 5, 10, 15, 16, 20, 21, 30, 31, 40, 44, 49, 52, 68, 70, 75, 79, 80, 93–5, 101, 112, 120, 122, 124–6
London, Victoria and Albert Museum 23, 24, 67, 90
London, Wellcome Institute Library 18
London, William Morris Gallery 25
Los Angeles County Museum of Art 64
Manchester City Art Galleries 45, 58
Maryhill, Museum of Art, Washington 119
Metz, La Cour d'Or-Musées de Metz 54
Munich, Bayerische Staatsgemäldesammlungen. Neue Pinakothek 77
Oslo, Munch-Museet 137
Oslo, Nasjonalgalleriet 138
Oslo, Vigeland-Museet 139
Ottawa, National Gallery of Canada 123
Otterlo, Kröller-Müller Museum 111
Oxford, Ashmolean Museum 13
Paris, Bibliothèque Nationale de France 82
Paris, Musée du Louvre Département des Arts Graphiques, Fonds du Musée d'Orsay 131
Preston, Harris Museum and Art Gallery 78
Providence, Museum of Art, Rhode Island School of Design 66
San Francisco, Fine Arts Museum 65
Southampton City Art Gallery 114
Southport, The Atkinson Art Gallery 130
Stockholm, Nationalmuseum 9
Stuttgart, Staatsgalerie 113
Vancouver Museum 42
Vienna, Museen der Stadt Wien 53
Virginia Museum of Fine Arts, The Williams Fund 88
Williamstown, Sterling and Francine Clark Art Institute, Massachusetts 55
Wolverhampton, The Bearsted Collection (The National Trust) on indefinite loan to Wightwick Manor 41

Photographic Credits

Bayer and Mitko – Arthotek; Ashmolean Museum, Oxford; Atkinson Art Gallery; Auckland Art Gallery; Bibliothèque Nationale de France; Birmingham Museums and Art Gallery; Museum of Fine Arts, Boston; Bridgeman Art Library; British Library; British Museum; National Gallery of Canada (C. Cretney); National Museum and Gallery, Cardiff; Art Institute of Chigago; Clark Art Institute 1990; A.C. Cooper (Colour) Ltd.; Courtauld Institute of Art; Prudence Cuming Associates Ltd; Robin de Beaumont; The De Morgan Foundation, London / Bridgeman Art Library, London; Delaware Art Museum; Patrick Derom Gallery; Vincent Everarts; Faringdon Collection, Buscot Park; Ferrara, Civiche Gallerie d'Arte Moderna e Contemporana; The Fine Art Society, London / Bridgeman Art Library,London; Fitzwilliam Museum, University of Cambridge; Museum Folkwang Essen; Lynton Gardiner; Glasgow Museums; Haags Gemeentemuseum; Harris Museum; Julian Hartnoll; Harvard University Art Museums; Hugh Lane Municipal Gallery of Modern Art; Ann Hutchinson; Staatliche Kunsthalle Karlsruhe; Kröller-Müller Museum, Otterlo; David Lambert; J. Lathion, Nasjonalgalleriet 1997; Marcella Leith; Marcus Leith; Leamington Spa Museum and Art Gallery, Warwickshire / Bridgeman Art Library, London; 1996 Museum Associates, Los Angeles County Museum of Art; Mallett; Manchester City Art Galleries; Maryhill Museum of Art; Minneapolis Institute of Arts; National Art Collections Fund; National Museums & Galleries on Merseyside; Musée de Metz; Musée d'Ixelles, Brussels; Musées Royaux des Beaux Arts de Belgique; Neue Pinakothek, Munich; Peter Nahum Ltd.; National Trust Photographic Library / Derrick E. Witty; Art Gallery of Ontario; Oslo Kommunes Kunstsamlinger, Munch-Museet; Oslo Kommunes Kunstsamlinger, Vigelandmuseet / Bono 1997; Fotostudio Otto; Philadelphia Museum of Art; Matt Pia; Rhode Island School of Design; RMN; Photo RMN – Hervé Lewandowsi; Royal Academy; Royal Academy of Arts, London; Russell-Cotes Art Gallery and Museum / Bridgeman Art Library, London; Fine Arts Museum of San Francisco; National Gallery of Scotland; Sotheby's; Southampton City Art Gallery; Statens Konstmuseer, Stockholm; Staatsgalerie Stuttgart; Tate Photographic Department; Rodney Todd – White & Son; Tullie House Museum and Art Gallery; V&A Picture Library; Vancouver Museum; Virginia Museum of Fine Arts; Wadsworth Atheneum; National Museum of Wales; Elke Walford, Fotowerkstatt, Hamburger Kunsthalle; National Gallery of Art, Washington; Watts Gallery; John Webb; Wellcome Insitute Library; Museen der Stadt Wien; Whitworth Art Gallery; William Morris Gallery; The Woodner Collections

Ways of Giving to the Tate Gallery

The Tate Gallery attracts funds from the private sector to support its programme of activities in London, Liverpool and St Ives. Support is raised from the business community, individuals, trusts and foundations, and includes sponsorships, donations, bequests and gifts of works of art. The Tate Gallery is an exempt charity; the Museums & Galleries Act 1992 added the Tate Gallery to the list of exempt charities defined in the 1960 Charities Act.

Donations

There are a variety of ways through which you can make a donation to the Tate Gallery.

Donations All donations, however small, will be gratefully received and acknowledged by the Tate Gallery.

Covenants A Deed of Covenant, which must be taken out for a minimum of four years, will enable the Tate Gallery to claim back tax on your charitable donation. For example, a covenant for £100 per annum will allow the Gallery to claim a further £31 at present tax rates.

Gift-Aid For individuals and companies wishing to make donations of £250 and above, Gift-Aid allows the gallery to claim back tax on your charitable donation. In addition, if you are a higher rate taxpayer you will be able to claim tax relief on the donation. A Gift-Aid form and explanatory leaflet can be sent to you if you require further information.

Bequests You may wish to remember the Tate Gallery in your will or make a specific donation In Memoriam. A bequest may take the form of either a specific cash sum, a residual proportion of your estate or a specific item of property, such as a work of art. Certain tax advantages can be obtained by making a legacy in favour of the Tate Gallery. Please check with the Tate Gallery when you draw up your will that it is able to accept your bequest.

American Fund for the Tate Gallery The American Fund was formed in 1986 to facilitate gifts of works of art, donations and bequests to the Tate Gallery from the United States residents. It receives full tax exempt status from the IRS.

Individual Membership Programmes

Friends

Friends share in the life of the Gallery and contribute towards the purchase of important works of art for the Tate. Privileges include free unlimited entry with a guest to exhibitions; *tate: the art magazine*; private views and special events; 'Late at the Tate' evening openings; exclusive Friends Room. Annual rates range from £22 to £65. Tate Friends Liverpool and Tate Friends St Ives offer local events programmes and full membership of the Friends in London.

The Friends of the Tate Gallery are supported by Tate & Lyle PLC.

Further details on the Friends in London, Liverpool and St Ives may be obtained from:
Membership Office
Tate Gallery
Millbank
London SW1P 4RG
Tel: 0171-887 8752

Patrons and Fellows

Fellows support the acquisition of works of art for the British and Modern Collections of the Tate Gallery. Privileges include invitations to Tate Gallery receptions, curatorial talks and behind-the-scene tours, complimentary catalogues and Joint or Family membership of the Friends. Annual membership ranges from £100 to £500.

Patrons of British Art support British painting and sculpture from the Elizabethan period through to the early twentieth century in the Tate Gallery's collection. They encourage knowledge and awareness of British art by providing an opportunity to study Britain's cultural heritage.

Patrons of New Art support contemporary art in the Tate Gallery's collection. They promote a lively and informed interest in contemporary art and are associated with the Turner Prize, one of the most prestigious awards for the visual arts.

Privileges for both groups include invitations to Tate Gallery receptions, an opportunity to sit on the Patrons' executive and acquisitions committees, special events including visits to private and corporate collections and complimentary catalogues of Tate Gallery exhibitions.

Annual membership of the Patrons ranges from £350 to £750, and funds the purchase of works of art for the Tate Gallery's collection.

Further details on the Patrons may be obtained from:
Membership Office
Tate Gallery
Millbank
London SW1P 4RG
Tel: 0171-887 8743

Corporate Membership Programme

Membership of the Tate Gallery's Corporate Membership Programme offers companies outstanding value-for-money and provides opportunities for every employee to enjoy a closer knowledge of the Gallery, its collection and exhibitions.

Membership benefits are specifically geared to business needs and include private views for company employees, free and discount admission to exhibitions, discount in the Gallery shop, out-of-hours Gallery visits, behind-the-scenes tours, exclusive use of the Gallery for corporate entertainment, invitations to VIP events, copies of Gallery literature and acknowledgment in Gallery publications.

Tate Gallery Corporate Members

Partners
The British Petroleum Company plc
Ernst & Young
Freshfields
Glaxo Wellcome plc
Manpower PLC
Prudential
Unilever

Associates
Alliance & Leicester
American Express
Amersham International plc
BUPA
Channel 4
Digital Equipment Co. Limited
Drivers Jonas
The EMI Group
The Guardian
Global Asset Management
Goldman Sachs International
Lazard Brothers & Co Limited
Linklaters & Paines
Mercury Asset Management
Merrill Lynch
Morgan Stanley International
NatWest Group
Nomura International
Salomon Brothers
Schroder Investment Management
Simmons & Simmons
United Utilities PLC

Corporate Sponsorship

The Tate Gallery works closely with sponsors to ensure that their business interests are well served, and has a reputation for developing imaginative fund-raising initiatives. Sponsorships can range from a few thousand pounds to considerable investment in long-term programmes; small businesses as well as multi-national corporations have benefited from the high profile and prestige of Tate Gallery sponsorship.

Opportunities available at Tate Gallery London, Liverpool and St Ives include exhibitions (some also tour the UK), education, conservation and research programmes, audience development, visitor access to the Collection and special events. Sponsorship benefits include national and regional publicity, targeted marketing to niche audiences, exclusive corporate entertainment, employee benefits and acknowledgment in Tate Gallery publications.

Tate Gallery London: Principal Corporate Sponsors (alphabetical order)

The British Petroleum Company plc
1990–2000, *New Displays*
Channel Four Television
1991–9, *The Turner Prize*
Ernst & Young
1994, *Picasso: Sculptor/Painter**
1996, *Cézanne**
J.P. Morgan & Co. Incorporated
1995, *Willem de Kooning**
Magnox Electric plc
1993, *Turner: The Final Years*
1994, *The Essential Turner*
1995–8, *The Magnox Electric Turner Scholarships*
1997, *Turner's Watercolour Explorations*
Pearson plc
1992–5, Elizabethan Curator Post
1995, *Dynasties: Painting in Tudor and Jacobean England 1530–1630*
Prudential
1996, *Grand Tour*
1997, *The Age of Rossetti, Burne-Jones and Watts: Symbolism in Britain 1860–1910*
Reed Elsevier
1994, *Whistler*
Tate & Lyle PLC
1991–7, Friends Marketing Programme
1997, *Henry Tate's Gift*
Volkswagen
1991–6, The Volkswagen Turner Scholarships

Tate Gallery London: Corporate Sponsors (alphabetical order)

ABN AMRO Bank
1994, *Turner's Holland*
AT&T
1997, *Piet Mondrian*
Beck's
1992, *Otto Dix*
1994, *Rebecca Horn*
1995, *Rites of Passage*
Blackwall Green Ltd
1994, Frames Conservation
The British Printing Company Ltd
1994–5, sponsorship in kind
Calor Gas
1994, *Turner's Holland*
The Government of Canada and The Canadian High Commission, London
1995, *Rites of Passage*
1995, *Art Now – Genèvieve Cadieux*
CDT Design Ltd
1995–6, *Art Now*
Classic FM
1995–6, Regional tour of David Hockney's 'Mr and Mrs Clark and Percy' (in kind)
Clifton Nurseries
1991–5, Christmas Tree (in kind)

Coutts Contemporary Art Foundation
1997, *Luciano Fabro*
Deutsche Bank A.G.
1994, *Rebecca Horn*
The German Government
1992, *Otto Dix*
1994, *Rebecca Horn*
1997, *Lovis Corinth*
The Guardian
1995, *Rites of Passage* (in kind)
Glaxo Wellcome plc
1997, *Turner on the Loire*
Häagen-Dazs Fresh Cream Ice Cream
1995–6, *Art Now*
The Hiscox Group
1995–6, Friends Room
HUGO BOSS
1997, *Ellsworth Kelly*
J.R.F. Panels
1994, Christmas Tree (in kind)
Makro
1994, *Turner's Holland*
Pro Helvetia
1995, *Through Switzerland with Turner*
1997, Art Now – Beat Streuli
Romulus Construction Limited
1996, Bill Woodrow: *Fools' Gold*
Russell & Chapple Ltd
1994, Christmas Tree (in kind)
W.H. Smith Ltd
1994, Sponsorship-in-kind
Swiss National Tourist Office
1995, *Through Switzerland with Turner*
Tarmac Group plc*
1995–9, Paintings Conservation
The EMI Group
1993, *Turner's Painting Techniques*
1997, *Centre Stage* education project
TSB Group plc
1992, *Turner and Byron*
1992–5, *William Blake* display series
1995, Paintings Conservation

Tate Gallery of Modern Art: Corporate Sponsors (alphabetical order)

Ernst & Young
1995, *Tate Gallery of Modern Art: Selecting an Architect*
1997–2000, Tate Gallery of Modern Art Visitor Centre

Tate Gallery Liverpool: Corporate Sponsors (alphabetical order)

American Airlines
1993, *David Hockney*
Beck's
1993, *Robert Gober*
Canadian High Commission, London and Government of Canada
1993, *Elective Affinities*
Girobank plc
1995, *Primary Cooking* Education booklet
Ibstock Building Products Ltd
1993, *Antony Gormley*
Ian Short Partnership
1995, *Testing the Water*
Korean Air
1992, *Working with Nature* (in kind)
The Littlewoods Organisation plc
1992–5, *New Realities*
Merseyside Development Corporation
1992, *Myth-Making*
1992, *Stanley Spencer*
MOMART plc
1991–5, The Momart Fellowship
North West Water Group PLC
1994, Corporate Membership Brochure
David M Robinson Jewellery
1994, *Venus Re-Defined*
Royal Liver Assurance
1995, *Making It*
Samsung Electronics
1992, *Working With Nature*
Tate & Lyle PLC
1995, Tate Friends Liverpool membership leaflet

Tate Gallery St Ives: Corporate (alphabetical order)

Barclays Bank PLC*
1995, *Porthmeor Beach: 'A Century of Images'*
First Class Pullman, InterCity*
1993–4, *Annual Displays*
Northcliffe Newspapers in Education*
1995–7, Education Programme
South Western Electricity plc (sweb)*
1993–4, Education Programme

*denotes a sponsorship in the arts, recognised by an award under the Government's 'Pairing Scheme' administered by the Association for Business Sponsorship of the Arts.

Tate Gallery Founding Benefactors (date order)

Sir Henry Tate
Sir Joseph Duveen
Lord Duveen
The Clore Foundation

Tate Gallery Principal Benefactors (alphabetical order)

American Fund for the Tate Gallery
The Annenberg Foundation
Calouste Gulbenkian Foundation
Friends of the Tate Gallery
The Henry Moore Foundation
Heritage Lottery Fund
The Kreitman Foundation
National Art Collections Fund
National Heritage Memorial Fund
The Nomura Securities Co., Ltd
Patrons of New Art
Dr Mortimer and Theresa Sackler Foundation
St Ives Tate Action Group
The Wolfson Foundation and Family Charitable Trust

Tate Gallery Benefactors (alphabetical order)

The Baring Foundation
Bernard Sunley Charitable Foundation
Gilbert and Janet de Botton
Mr and Mrs James Brice
Mr Edwin C.Cohen
The Eleanor Rathbone Charitable Trust
Esmée Fairbairn Charitable Trust
Foundation for Sport and the Arts
GABO TRUST for Sculpture Conservation
GEC Plessey Telecommunications
The Getty Grant Program
Granada Group plc
The Paul Hamlyn Foundation
Horace W. Goldsmith Foundation
John Hughes
The John S.Cohen Foundation
The John Ellerman Foundation
John Lewis Partnership
The Leverhulme Trust
Museums and Galleries Improvement Fund
Ocean Group plc (P.H. Holt Trust)
Patrons of British Art
Peter Moores Foundation
The Pilgrim Trust
Mr John Ritblat
The Sainsbury Family Charitable Trusts
Save and Prosper Educational Trust
SRU Limited
Weinberg Foundation

Tate Gallery Donors
(alphabetical order)

London

Professor Abbott
The Andy Warhol Foundation for the Visual Arts, Inc
The Fagus Anstruther Memorial Trust
Lord Attenborough CBE
The Austin and Hope Pilkington Charitable Trust
BAA plc
Friends of Nancy Balfour OBE
Balmuir Holdings
The Hon. Robin Baring
B.A.T. Industries plc
Nancy Bateman Charitable Trust
Mr Tom Bendhem
Mr Alexander Bernstein
David and Janice Blackburn
Michael and Marcia Blakenham
Miss Mary Boone
Frances and John Bowes
The Britwell Trust
Mr and Mrs Donald L. Bryant, Jr
Mrs Melva Bucksbaum
Card Aid
Carlsberg Brewery
Mr Vincent Carrozza
Mrs Beryl Carpenter
Cazenove & Co Charitable Trust
Charlotte Bonham Carter Charitable Trust
Christie, Mason & Woods Ltd
The Claire Hunter Charitable Trust
The Clothworkers Foundation
Mrs Elisabeth Collins
Mr R.N.Collins
Mr Christopher Cone
Giles and Sonia Coode-Adams
Mrs Dagny Corcoran
C.T. Bowring (Charitable Trust) Ltd
Cognac Courvoisier
Mr Edwin Cox
Antony d'Offay Gallery
Mr and Mrs Kenneth Dayton
Mr Damon and The Hon. Mrs de Laszlo
Madame Gustava de Rothschild
Baroness Liliane de Rothschild
Deutsche Bank AG
Miss W.A. Donner
Mr Paul Dupee
Mrs Maurice Dwek
Elephant Trust
Eli Broad Family Foundation
Elizabeth Arden Ltd
The Essick Foundation
European Arts Festival
Evelyn, Lady Downshire's Trust Fund
Roberto Fainello Art Advisers Ltd
First Boston Corporation
Mr and Mrs Donald G. Fisher
The Flow Foundation
Foreign & Colonial Management Limited
Miss Kate Ganz
Mr Henry Geldzahler
Ms Laure Genillard
Mr and Mrs David Gilmour
The German Government
Goethe Institut
Jack Goldhill
Sir Nicholas and Lady Goodison Charitable Settlement
Mr William Govett
Mr and Mrs Richard Grogan
Gytha Trust
Mr and Mrs Rupert Hambro
Miriam and Peter Haas
Mrs Sue Hammerson
Harry Kweller Charitable Trust
The Hon. Lady Hastings
The Hedley Foundation
Hereford Salon
Mr and Mrs Michael Heseltine
Mr Rupert Heseltine
Mr Robert Hornton
Hurry Armour Trust
Idlewild Trust
The Italian Government
Sir Anthony and Lady Jacobs
Mrs Gabrielle Keiller
James and Clare Kirkman Trust
Knapping Fund
Mr and Mrs Richard Knight
Mr and Mrs Jan Krugier
The Lauder Foundation-Leonard and Evelyn Lauder Fund
The Leche Trust
Robert Lehman Foundation,Inc
The Helena and Kenneth Levy Bequest
Mr and Mrs Gilbert Lloyd
Mr and Mrs George Loudon
Mr and Mrs Lawrence Lowenthal
Mail on Sunday
Mr Alexander Marchessini
The Mayor Gallery
Midland Bank Artscard
Mr and Mrs Robert Mnuchin
Mr and Mrs Peter Nahum
Mr and Mrs Philip Niarchos
Dr Andreas Papadakis
The Paradina Trust
Mr William Pegrum
Philips Fine Art Auctioneers
The Earl of Plymouth
Old Possum's Practical Trust
The Hon. Mrs Olga Polizzi
Paul Nash Trust
Peter Samuel Charitable Trust
Mr Jean Pigozzi
Ptarmigan Trust
Sir Gordon Reece
Reed International P.L.C.
Richard Green Fine Paintings
Mrs Jill Ritblat
Rothschild Bank AG
Kathy and Keith Sachs
Mrs Jean Sainsbury
Salander-O'Reilly Galleries, LLC
The Hon. Simon Sainsbury
Sebastian de Ferranti Trust
Schroder Charity Trust
Ms Dasha Shenkman
South Square Trust
Mr A. Speelman
Standard Chartered Bank
The Swan Trust
Sir Adrian and Lady Judith Swire
Mrs Barbara Thomas
Time-Life International Ltd
The 29th May 1961 Charitable Trust
Lady Juliet Townsend
Laura and Barry Townsley
The Triangle Trust
U.K. Charity Lotteries Ltd
Mrs Anne Uribe-Mosquera
Visiting Arts
Mr and Mrs Leslie Waddington
Waley-Cohen Charitable Trust
Mr Mark Weiss
Weltkunst Foundation
Mrs Alexandra Williams
Graham and Nina Williams

Willis Faber plc
Mr Andrew Wilton
Thomas and Odette Worrell
The Worshipful Company of Goldsmiths
The Worshipful Company of Grocers
Mrs Jayne Wrightsman

and those donors who wish to remain anonymous

Friends Benfactors and Life Members 1958–1988

The André Bernheim Charitable Trust
Dr and Mrs David Cohen
Mrs Isobel Dalziel
Mr and Mrs Charles Dickinson
Lady Gosling
Miranda, Countess of Iveagh
Sir Anthony and Lady Jacobs
Mr and Mrs AGW Lang
Sir Sydney and Lady Lipworth
The Sir Jack Lyons Charitable Trust
Mr Michael Rose
Lieutenant Commander and Mrs Shilling
Mrs Jack Steinberg
Mr John B Sunley
Mr and Mrs Terry Willson

Tate Gallery of Modern Art

Arthur Andersen (pro-bono)
The Annenberg Foundation
Lord and Lady Attenborough
The Baring Foundation
David and Janice Blackburn
Mr and Mrs Anthony Bloom
Gilbert de Botton
Mr and Mrs John Botts
Mr and Mrs James Brice
Mrs Melva Bucksbaum
Monsieur Alain Camu
Mr Edwin C Cohen
The John S Cohen Foundation
Sir Harry and Lady Djanogly
English Heritage
English Partnerships
Ernst & Young
Esmée Fairbairn Charitable Trust
The Foundation for Sport and the Arts
Friends of the Tate Gallery
GJW Government Relations (pro-bono)
Hanover Acceptances Limited
André and Rosalie Hoffmann
Horace W Goldsmith Foundation
Sir Anthony and Lady Jacobs
Mr and Mrs George Loudon
McKinseys & Co (pro-bono)
The Millennium Commission
The Monument Trust
The Rayne Foundation
Simmons & Simmons
London Borough of Southwark
The Starr Foundation
Mr and Mrs Dennis Stevenson
Miss M F Stevenson
Mr and Mrs Ian Stoutzker
Mr John Studzinski
Laura and Barry Townsley
The 29th May 1961 Charitable Trust
Graham and Nina Williams
The Worshipful Company of Fishmongers
The Worshipful Company of Goldsmiths

and those donors who wish to remain anonymous

Tate Gallery of Modern Art: Collections Benefactor

Janet Wolfson de Botton

Tate Gallery of British Art

The Annenberg Foundation
Sir Harry and Lady Djanogly
Friends of the Tate Gallery
Heritage Lottery Fund
The P F Charitable Trust
Mrs Coral Samuel CBE
The Duke of Westminster OBE TD DL

and those donors who wish to remain anonymous

Liverpool (alphabetical order)

ABSA
Arrowcroft Group Limited
Arts Council of Great Britain
The Australian Bicentennial Authority
Barclays Bank plc
The Baring Foundation
BASF
Solomon and Isabel Blankstone Charitable Trust
Boddingtons plc
British Alcan Aluminium plc
The British Council
British Gas
British Telecom plc
Calouste Gulbenkian Foundation
Coopers & Lybrand
Mr and Mrs Henry Cotton
Cultural Relations Committee
David M Robinson Jewellery
Deloitte Haskins & Sells
D'Oyly Carte Charitable Trust
The John Ellerman Foundation
English Estates
The Esmée Fairbairn Charitable Trust
European Arts Festival
European Regional Development Fund
The Foundation for Sport and the Arts
GPT Ltd
The Granada Foundation
Granada Television
The Henry Moore Sculpture Trust
Heritage Lottery Fund
Mr John Heyman
Higsons Brewery plc
Ian Short Partnership
IBM United Kingdom Trust
Ibstock Building Products Ltd
ICI Chemicals & Polymers Limited
The John Lewis Partnership
The John S Cohen Foundation
The Laura Ashley Foundation
The Littlewoods Organisation
Liverpool Council for Voluntary Services
Liverpool John Moores University
Mr & Mrs Jack Lyons
Manchester Airport plc
Manor Charitable Trust
Merseyside Development Corporation
Mobil Oil Company Ltd
Momart plc
The Henry Moore Foundation
The Moores Family Charitable Foundation
The Nigel Moores Family Charitable Trust
New Moorgate Trust Fund
NSK Bearings Europe Ltd
Ocean Group plc (P.H. Holt Trust)
P & P Micro Distributors Ltd
Parkman Consulting Engineers
The Pilgrim Trust
Pilkington plc
Pioneer High Fidelity (GB) Ltd
Eleanor Rathbone Charitable Trust
Royal Insurance (UK) Ltd
Royal Liver Assurance
RTZ Chemicals Ltd
Sainsbury Family Charitable Trusts
Samsung Electronics
Save & Prosper Educational Trust
Scottish & Newcastle Breweries
Stanley Thomas Johnson Foundation
The Summerfield Charitable Trust
Bernard Sunley Charitable Foundation
Friends of the Tate Gallery
Tate Friends Liverpool
Trinity International
Trustee Savings Bank Foundation
Unilever
United Biscuits (UK) Limited
United Utilities plc
The University of Liverpool
Vernons Organisation Ltd
Visiting Arts
Volkswagen
Whitbread & Company plc
The Wolfson Foundation

and those donors who wish to remain anonymous

St Ives (alphabetical order)

Donors to the Appeal coordinated by the Steering Group for the Tate Gallery St Ives and the St Ives Action Group.

Viscount Amory Charitable Trust
Barbinder Trust
Barclays Bank PLC
The Baring Foundation
BICC Group
Patricia, Lady Boyd and Viscount Boyd
British Telecom plc
Cable and Wireless plc
Carlton Communications
Mr Francis Carnwath
Christie, Manson & Woods Ltd
Mr Peter Cocks
John S. Cohen Foundation
Miss Jean Cooper
D'Oyly Carte Charitable Trust
David Messum Fine Paintings
Dewhurst House
Dixons Group plc
Mr Alan Driscoll
The John Ellerman Foundation
English China Clays Group
Esmee Fairbairn Charitable Trust
Foundation for Sport and the Arts
J. Paul Getty Jr Charitable Trust
Gimpel Fils
Grand Metropolitan Trust
Ms Judith Hodgson
Sir Geoffrey and Lady Holland
Mr and Mrs Philip Hughes
Mr Bernard Jacobson
Mr John Kilby
Lloyds Bank plc
Lord Leverhulme's Trust
The Manifold Trust
The Mayor Gallery
Marlborough Fine Art
Mercury Asset Management plc
Meyer International plc
The Henry Moore Foundation
National Westminster Bank plc
New Art Centre
Pall European Limited
The Pilgrim Trust
The Joseph Rank (1942) Charitable Trust
Mr Roy Ray
The Rayne Foundation
Royal Bank of Scotland
The Sainsbury Family Charitable Trusts
Mr Nicholas Serota
Mr Roger Slack
Trustees of the Carew Pole Family Trust
Trustees of H.E.W. Spurr Deceased
South West British Gas
South West Water plc
South Western Electricity plc
Sun Alliance Group
Television South West
The TSB Foundation for England and Wales
Unilever
Mrs Angela Verren Taunt
Weinberg Foundation
Wembley plc
Western Morning News, West Briton, Cornish Guardian and The Cornishman
Westlake & Co
Mr and Mrs Derek White
Mr and Mrs Graham Williams
Wingate Charitable Trust
The Worshipful Company of Fishmongers
The Worshipful Company of Mercers
Mrs Monica Wynter

and those donors who wish to remain anonymous